JAVA BASICS AND ADVANCED A BEGINNERS GUIDE

BY ROBERT PETERSON

CONTENTS

1 JAVA BASICS

Portability

Java programs are portable across operating systems and hardware environments.
Portability is to your advantage because:

- You need only one version of your software to serve a broad market.
- The Internet, in effect, becomes one giant, dynamic library.
- You are no longer limited by your particular computer platform.

Three features make Java String programs portable:

- **The language.** The Java language is completely specified; all data-type sizes and formats are defined as part of the language. By contrast, C/C++ leaves these "details" up to the compiler implementor, and many C/C++ programs therefore

-1

are not portable.

- **The library**. The Java class library is available on any machine with a Java runtime system, because a portable program is of no use if you cannot use the same class library on every platform. Window-manager function calls in a Mac application written in C/C++, for example, do not port well to a PC.

- **The byte code**. The Java runtime system does not compile your source code directly into machine language, an inflexible and nonportable representation of your program. Instead, Java programs are translated into machine-independent byte code. The byte code is easily interpreted and therefore can be executed on any platform having a Java runtime system. (The latest versions of the Netscape Navigator browser, for example, can run applets on virtually any platform).

Security

The Java language is secure in that it is very difficult to write incorrect code or viruses that can corrupt/steal your data, or harm hardware such as hard disks. There are two main lines of defense:

- Interpreter level:
- No pointer arithmetic
- Garbage collection
- Array bounds checking
- No illegal data conversions
- Browser level (applies to applets only):
- No local file I/O
- Sockets back to host only
- No calls to native methods

Robustness

The Java language is robust. It has several features designed to avoid crashes during program execution, including:

- No pointer arithmetic

>>> Garbage collection–no bad addresses

>>> Array and string bounds checking

>>> No jumping to bad method addresses

>>> Interfaces and exceptions

Java Program Structure

A file containing Java source code is considered a compilation unit. Such a compilation unit contains a set of classes and, optionally, a package definition to group related classes together. Classes contain data and method members that specify the state and behavior of the objects in your program.

Java programs come in two flavors:

- Standalone applications that have no initial context such as a pre-existing main window
- Applets for WWW programming

The major differences between applications and applets are:

- Applets are not allowed to use file I/O and sockets (other than to the host platform). Applications do not have these restrictions.
- An applet must be a subclass of the Java Applet class. Aplications do not need to subclass any particular class.
- Unlike applets, applications can have menus.
- Unlike applications, applets need to respond to predefined lifecycle messages from the WWW browser in which they're running.

Java Program Execution

The Java byte-code compiler translates a Java source file into machine-independent byte code. The byte code for each publicly visible class is placed in a separate file, so that the Java runtime system can easily find it. If your program instantiates an object of class A, for example, the class loader searches the directories listed in your CLASSPATH environment variable for a file called A.class that contains the class definition and byte code for class A.

There is no link phase for Java programs; all linking is done dynamically at runtime.

The following diagram shows an example of the Java compilation and execution sequence for a source file named A.java containing public class A and non-public class B:

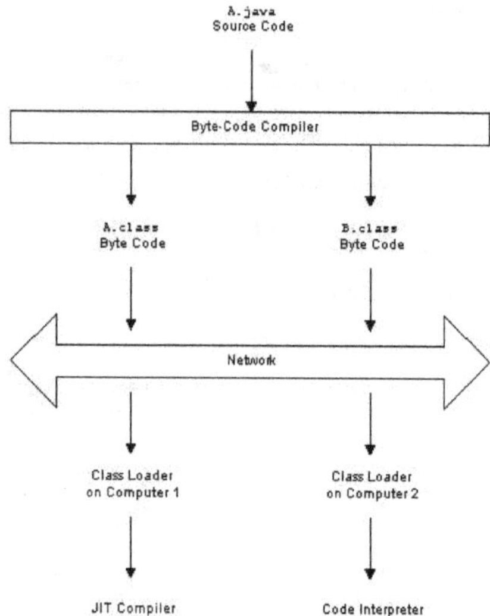

Java programs are, in effect, distributed applications. You may think of them as a collection of DLLs (dynamically loadable libraries) that are linked on demand at runtime. When you write your own Java applications, you will often integrate your program with already-existing portions of code that reside on other machines.

A Simple Application

Consider the following trivial application that prints "hi there" to standard output:

```
public class TrivialApplication {
•        args[0] is first argument
•        args[1] the second
   public static void main(String args[]) {
      System.out.println("hi there");
   }
}
```

The command java TrivialApplication tells the Java runtime system to begin with the class file TrivialApplication.class and to look in that file for a method with the signature:

```
public static void main(String args[]);
```

The main() method will always reside in one of your class files. The Java language does not allow methods outside of class definitions. The class, in effect, creates scoped symbol StartingClassName.main for your main() method.

Applet Execution

An applet is a Java program that runs within a Java-compatible WWW browser or in an appletviewer. To execute your applet, the browser:

- Creates an instance of your applet
- Sends messages to your applet to automatically invoke predefined lifecycle methods

The predefined methods automatically invoked by the runtime system are:

- init(). This method takes the place of the Applet constructor and is only called once during applet creation. Instance variables should be initialized in this method. GUI components such as buttons and scrollbars should be added to the GUI in this method.
- start(). This method is called once after init() and whenever your applet is revisited by your browser, or when you deiconify your browser. This method should be used to start animations and other threads.
- paint(Graphics g). This method is called when the applet drawing area needs to be redrawn. Anything not drawn by contained components must be drawn in this method. Bitmaps, for example, are drawn here, but buttons are not because they handle their own painting.
- stop(). This method is called when you leave an applet or when you iconify your browser. The method should be used to suspend animations and other

threads so they do not burden system resources unnecessarily. It is guaranteed to be called before destroy().

- destroy(). This method is called when an applet terminates, for example, when quitting the browser. Final clean-up operations such as freeing up system resources with dispose() should be done here. The dispose() method of Frame removes the menu bar. Therefore, do not forget to call super.dispose() if you override the default behavior.

The basic structure of an applet that uses each of these predefined methods is:

```
import java.applet.Applet;
•     include all AWT class definitions import
java.awt.*;

public class AppletTemplate extends Applet { public
   void init() {
      // create GUI, initialize applet
   }
   public void start() {
      // start threads, animations etc...
   }
   public void paint(Graphics g) {
      // draw things in g
   }
   public void stop() {
      // suspend threads, stop animations etc...
   }
   public void destroy() {
      // free up system resources, stop threads
   }
}
```

All you have to do is fill in the appropriate methods to bring your applet to life. If you don't need to use one or more of these predefined methods, simply leave them out of your applet. The applet will ignore messages from the browser attempting to invoke any of these methods that you don't use.

A Simple Applet

The following complete applet displays "Hello, World Wide Web!" in your browser window:

```
import java.applet.Applet;
import java.awt.Graphics;

public class TrivialApplet extends Applet { public
   void paint(Graphics g) {
      // display a string at 20,20
```

• where 0,0 is the upper-left corner g.drawString("Hello, World Wide Web!", 20, 20);

```
    }
}
```

An appletviewer may be used instead of a WWW browser to test applets. For example, the output of TrivialApplet on an appletviewer looks like:

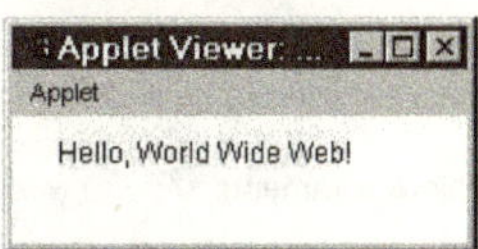

HTML/Applet Interface

The HTML applet tag is similar to the HTML img tag, and has the form:

```
<applet code=AppletName.class width=w height=h>
[parameters]
</applet>
```

where the optional parameters are a list of parameter definitions of the form:

```
<param name=n value=v>
```

An example tag with parameter definitions is:

```
<applet code=AppletName.class width=300 height=200>
<param name=p1 value=34>
<param name=p2 value="test">
</applet>
```

where p1 and p2 are user-defined parameters.

The code, width, and height parameters are mandatory. The parameters codebase, alt, archives, align, vspace, and hspace are optional within the <applet> tag itself. Your applet can access any of these parameters by calling:

```
Applet.getParameter("p")
```

which returns the String value of the parameter. For example, the applet:

```
import java.applet.Applet;

public class ParamTest extends Applet { public
  void init() {
    System.out.println("width is " + getParameter("width"));
    System.out.println("p1 is "            + getParameter("p1"));
```

```
        System.out.println("p2 is "                    + getParameter("p2"));
    }
}
```

prints the following to standard output:

```
width is 300
p1 is 34
p2 is test
```

Comments

Java comments are the same as C++ comments, i.e.,

```
/* C-style block comments */
```

where all text between the opening /* and closing */ is ignored, and

```
// C++ style single-line comments
```

where all text from the opening // to the end of the line is ignored.

Note that these two comments can make a very useful combination. C-style comments (/* ... */) cannot be nested, but *can* contain C++ style comments. This leads to the interesting observation that if you always use C++-style comments (// ...), you can easily comment out a section of code by surrounding it with C-style comments. So try to use C++ style comments for your "normal" code commentary, and reserve C-style comments for commenting out sections of code.

The Java language also has a document comment:

```
/** document comment */
```

These comments are processed by the javadoc program to generate documentation from your source code. For example,

```
/** This class does blah blah blah */
class Blah {
    /** This method does nothing
    /**
•        This is a multiple line comment.
•        The leading * is not placed in documentation.
     */
    public void nothing() {;}
}
```

Declarations

A Java variable may refer to an object, an array, or an item of primitive type. Variables are defined using the following simple syntax:

TypeName variableName;

For example,

```
int a;          // defines    an integer
int[] b;        // defines    a reference to array of ints
Vector   v;     // reference to a Vector object
```

Primitive Types

The Java language has the following primitive types:

Primitive Types

Primitive Type	*Description*
boolean	true/false
byte	8 bits
char	16 bits (UNICODE)
short	16 bits
int	32 bits
long	64 bits
float	32 bits IEEE 754-1985
double	64 bits IEEE 754-1985

Java int types may **not** be used as boolean types and are always signed.

Objects

A simple C++ object or C struct definition such as "Button b;" allocates memory on the stack for a Button object and makes b refer to it. By contrast, you must specifically instantiate Java objects with the new operator. For example,

```
// Java code

void foo() {
>>>         define a reference to a Button; init to null Button b;
>>>         allocate space for a Button, b points to it b = new
Button("OK");
    int i = 2;
}
```

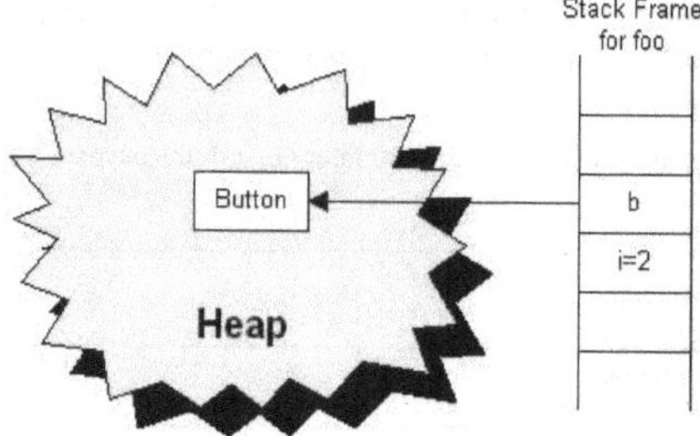

As the accompanying figure shows, this code places a reference b to the Button object on the stack and allocates memory for the new object on the heap.

The equivalent C++ and C statements that would allocate memory on the heap would be:

```
// C++ code
Button *b   = NULL;              // declare a new Button pointer
b = new Button("OK");          // point it to a new        Button

/* C code    */
Button *b   = NULL;                        /* declare a    new Button   pointer */
b = calloc(1, sizeof(Button)); /*             allocate space for a          Button */
init(b, "OK");                             /* something  like this to init b */
```

All Java objects reside on the heap; there are no objects stored on the stack. Storing objects on the heap does not cause potential memory leakage problems because of garbage collection.

Each Java primitive type has an equivalent object type, e.g., Integer, Byte, Float, Double. These primitive types are provided in addition to object types purely for efficiency. An int is much more efficient than an Integer.

Strings

Java string literals look the same as those in C/C++, but Java strings are real objects, not pointers to memory. Java strings may or may not be null-terminated. Every string literal such as

```
"a string literal"
```

is interpreted by the Java compiler as

```
new String("a string literal")
```

Java strings are constant in length and content. For variable-length strings, use StringBuffer objects.

Strings may be concatenated by using the plus operator:

```
String s = "one" + "two"; // s == "onetwo"
```

You may concatenate any object to a string. You use the toString() method to convert objects to a String, and primitive types are converted by the compiler. For example,

```
String s = "1+1=" + 2; // s == "1+1=2"
```

The length of a string may be obtained with String method length(); e.g., "abc".length() has the value 3.

To convert an int to a String, use:

```
String s = String.valueOf(4);
```

To convert a String to an int, use:

```
int a = Integer.parseInt("4");
```

Array Objects

In C and C++, arrays are pointers to data in memory. Java arrays are objects that know the number and type of their elements. The first element is index 0, as in C/C++.

Generic Array Object
elements

element type
element 0
element 1
...
element n-1

The syntax for creating an array object is:

TypeName[] variableName;

This declaration defines the array object–it does *not* allocate memory for the array object *nor* does it allocate the elements of the array In addition, you may not specify a size within the square brackets.

To allocate an array, use the new operator:

```
int[] a = new int[5];        // Java code: make array of 5 ints
```

new int[5]
5
int
0
0
0
0
0

In C or C++, by contrast, you would write either

```
/* C/C++ code: make array of 5 ints on the stack */ int a[5];
```

or

```
/* C/C++ code: make array of 5 ints on the heap */
```

int *a = new int[5];

An array of Java objects such as

>>> Java code: make array of 5 references to Buttons Button[] a = new Button[5];

creates the array object itself, but not the elements:

new Button[5]
5
Button
null pointer
null pointer
null pointer
null pointer
null pointer

You must use the new operator to create the elements:

```
a[0] = new Button("OK");
a[3] = new Button("QUIT");
```

In C++, to make an array of pointers to objects you would write:

>>> C++: make an array of 5 pointers to Buttons

```
Button **a = new Button *[5]; // Create the array
a[0]   = new Button("OK");              // create two new buttons
a[3]   = new Button("QUIT");
```

In C, code for the same task would look like:

```
/* C: make an array of 5 pointers to structs */ /*
Allocate the array */
Button **a = calloc(5, sizeof(Button *)); /*
Allocate one button */
a[0] = calloc(1, sizeof(Button));
/* Init the first button */
setTitle(a[0], "OK");
/* Allocate another button */
a[3] = calloc(1, sizeof(Button));
/* Init the second button */
```

```
setTitle(a[3], "QUIT");
```

Multi-dimensional Java arrays are created by making arrays of arrays, just as in C/C++. For example,

```
T[][] t = new T[10][5];
```

makes a five-element array of ten arrays of references to objects of type T. This statement does not allocate memory for any T objects.

Accessing an undefined array element causes a runtime exception called ArrayIndexOutOfBoundsException.

Accessing a defined array element that has not yet been assigned to an object results in a runtime NullPointerException.

Initializers

Variables may be initialized as follows:

- Primitive types

```
int i = 3;
boolean g = true;
```

- Objects

```
Button b = null;
Employee e = new Employee();
```

- Arrays

```
int[] i = {1, 2, 3, 4};
```

or in Java 1.1

```
int[] i;
i = new int[] {1, 2, 3, 4};
```

Constants

Variables modified by the static final keywords are constants (equivalent to the const keyword in C++; no equivalent in C). For example,

- same as "const int version=1;" in C++ static
final int version = 1;

```
static final String Owner = "Terence";
```

Expressions

Most Java expressions are similar to those in C/C++.

Constant Expressions

Item	Examples or Description
id	i, nameList
qualified-id	Integer.MAX_VALUE, obj.member, npackage.class, package.obj
id[e][f]...[g]	a[i], b[3][4]
String literal	"Jim", delimited by ""
char literal	'a', '\t', delimited by ''
Unicode character constant	\u00ae
boolean literal	true, false (*not* an int)
int constant	4
float constant	3.14f, 2.7e6F, f or F suffix
double constant	3.14, 2.7e6D, (default) / d or D suffix
hexadecimal constant	0x123
octal constant	077
null	the null object (note lowercase!)
this	the current object
super	the superclass view of this object

General Expressions

Item	Examples or Description
id	i, nameList
obj.method(args)	instance method call
class.method(args)	class method call
(*expr*)	(3+4)*7
new T(*constructor-args*)	instantiates a new object or class T
new T[e][f]...[g]	allocates an array object

Operators

The Java language has added the >>> zero-extend right-shift operator to the set of C++ operators. (C++ operators include instanceof and new, which are not present in C. Note that sizeof has been removed, as memory allocation is handled for you.) The operators, in order of highest to lowest priority, are:

- new
- .
- – ++ + - ~ ! (TypeName)
- * / %
- + -
- << >> >>>
- < > <= >= instanceof

- == !=
- &
- ^
- |
- &&
- ||
- ?:
- = *= /= %= += -= <<= >>= >>>= &= ^= |=

Note that the precedence of the new operator and the '.' operator bind

---

differently than in C++. A proper Java statement is:

```
// Java code
new T().method();
```

In C++, you would use:

```
// C++ code

(new T)->method();
```

Statements

Java statements are similar to those in C/C++ as the following table shows.

Forms of Common Statements

Statement	*Examples*

if	if (*boolean-expr*) *stat1*
	
	if (*boolean-expr*) *stat1* else *stat2*

switch	switch (*int-expr*) {
	case *int-const-expr* : *stat1*
	case *int-const-expr* : *stat2*
	default : *stat3*
	}

for	for (int i=0; i<10; i++) stat
while	while (*boolean-expr*) *stat*
do-while	do { *stats* } while (*boolean-expr*)
return	return *expr*;

The Java break and continue statements may have labels. These labels refer to the specific loop that the break or continue apply to. (Each loop can be preceded by a label.)

Part 1 - Getting Started

The Java Development Kit – JDK

In order to get started in Java programming, one needs to get a recent copy of the Java JDK. This can be obtained for free by downloading it from the Sun Microsystems website, http://java.sun.com/

Once you download and install this JDK you are ready to get started. You need a text editor as well and Microsoft's Notepad (standard with all Windows versions) suits fine.

My first Java program

Open your text editor and type the following lines of code:

```
/*

My first program

Version 1 */

public class Example1 {

        public static void main (String args []) { System.out.println ("My first

                Java program");

        }

}
```

This is known as a Block Comment. These lines are useful to the programmer and are ignored by the Compiler

Save the file as Example1.java[2]. The name of the program has to be similar to the filename. Programs are called classes. Please note that Java is ***case-sensitive.*** You cannot name a file "Example.java" and then in the program you write "public class example". It is good practice to insert comments at the start of a program to help you as a programmer understand quickly what the particular program is all about. This is done by typing "/*" at the start of the comment and "*/" when you finish. The predicted output of this program is:

My first Java program

In order to get the above output we have to first compile the program and then execute the compiled class. The applications required for this job are available as part of the JDK:

- javac.exe – compiles the program
- java.exe – the interpreter used to execute the compiled program

In order to compile and execute the program we need to switch to the command prompt. On windows systems this can be done by clicking Start>Run>cmd

---

[2] Ideally you should create a folder on the root disk (c:\) and save the file there

At this point one needs some basic DOS commands in order to get to the directory (folder), where the java class resides:

- cd\ (change directory)
- cd\[folder name] to get to the required folder/directory

When you get to the required destination you need to type the following:

c:\[folder name]\javac Example1.java

The above command will compile the java file and prompt the user with any errors. If the compilation is successful a new file containing the bytecode is generated: **Example1.class**

To execute the program, we invoke the interpreter by typing:

c:\[folder name]\java Example1

The result will be displayed in the DOS window.

Using an IDE

Some of you might already be frustrated by this point. However there is still hope as one can forget about the command prompt and use an IDE (integrated development environment) to work with Java programming. There are a number of IDE's present, all of them are fine but perhaps some are easier to work with than others. It depends on the user's level of programming and tastes! The following is a list of some of the IDE's available:

- BlueJ – www.bluej.org (freeware)
- NetBeans – www.netbeans.org (freeware/open-source)
- JCreator – www.jcreator.com (freeware version available, pro version purchase required)
- Eclipse – www.eclipse.org (freeware/open-source)
- IntelliJ IDEA – www.jetbrains.com (trial/purchase required)
- JBuilder – www.borland.com (trial/purchase required)

Beginners might enjoy BlueJ and then move onto other IDE's like JCreator, NetBeans, etc. Again it's just a matter of the user's tastes and software development area.

Variables and Data Types

Variables

A variable is a place where the program stores data temporarily. As the name implies the value stored in such a location can be changed while a program is executing (compare with constant).

```
class Example2 {

    public static void main(String args[]) { int var1; // this

        declares a variable

        int var2; // this declares another variable var1 = 1024; // this

        assigns 1024 to var1 System.out.println("var1 contains " +

        var1); var2 = var1 / 2;

        System.out.print("var2 contains var1 / 2: ");

        System.out.println(var2); }

}
```

Predicted Output:

var2 contains var1 / 2: 512

The above program uses two variables, var1 and var2. var1 is assigned a value directly while var2 is filled up with the result of dividing var1 by 2, i.e. var2 = var1/2. The words ***int*** refer to a particular data type, i.e. integer (whole numbers).

>>> Test your skills – Example3

As we saw above, we used the '/' to work out the quotient of var1 by 2. Given that '+' would perform addition, '-' subtraction and '*' multiplication, write out a program which performs all the named operations by using two integer values which are hard coded into the program.

Hints:

- You need only two variables of type integer
- Make one variable larger and divisible by the other
- You can perform the required calculations directly in the print statements, remember to enclose the operation within brackets, e.g. (var1-var2)

Mathematical Operators

As we saw in the preceding example there are particular symbols used to represent operators when performing calculations:

Operator	Description	Example - given a is 15 and b is 6
+	Addition	a + b, would return 21
-	Subtraction	a - b, would return 9
*	Multiplication	a * b, would return 90
/	Division	a / b, would return 2
%	Modulus	a % b, would return 3 (the remainder)

```
class Example4 {

    public static void main(String args[]) { int iresult, irem;

        double dresult, drem;

        iresult = 10 / 3;

        irem = 10 % 3;

        dresult = 10.0 / 3.0;

        drem = 10.0 % 3.0;

        System.out.println("Result and remainder of 10 / 3: " + iresult + " " + irem);

        System.out.println("Result and remainder of 10.0 / 3.0: "
• dresult + " " + drem);

        }

}
```

Predicted Output:

Result and Remainder of 10/3: 3 1
Result and Remainder of 10.0/3.0: 3.3333333333333335 1

The difference in range is due to the data type since 'double' is a double precision 64-bit floating point value.

Logical Operators

These operators are used to evaluate an expression and depending on the operator used, a particular output is obtained. In this case the operands must be Boolean data types and the result is also Boolean. The following table shows the available logical operators:

|

Operator	Description
•	AND gate behaviour (0,0,0,1)
	OR gate behaviour
|	(0,1,1,1)
•	XOR - exclusive OR (0,1,1,0)
•	Short-circuit AND
•	Short-circuit OR
!Not	

```
class Example5 {

    public static void main(String args[]) { int n, d;

        n = 10;

        d = 2;

        if(d != 0 && (n % d) == 0)

        System.out.println(d + " is a factor of " + n); d = 0; // now, set d to

        zero

        • Since d is zero, the second operand is not evaluated. if(d != 0 && (n % d) ==

        0)

        System.out.println(d + " is a factor of " + n);

        /* Now, try same thing without short-circuit operator. This will cause a divide-

        by-zero error.

        */

        if(d != 0 & (n % d) == 0)

        System.out.println(d + " is a factor of " + n);

        }

}
```

Predicted Output:

*Note if you try to execute the above program you will get an error (division by zero). To be able to execute it, first comment the last two statements, compile and then execute.

2 is a factor of 10

|

Trying to understand the above program is a bit difficult, however the program highlights the main difference in operation between a normal AND (&) and the short-circuit version (&&). In a normal AND operation, both sides of the expression are evaluated, e.g.

if(d != 0 & (n % d) == 0) – this returns an error as first d is compared to 0 to check inequality and then the operation (n%d) is computed yielding an error! (divide by zero error)

The short circuit version is smarter since if the left hand side of the expression is false, this mean that the output has to be false whatever there is on the right hand side of the expression, therefore:

if(d != 0 && (n % d) == 0) – this does not return an error as the (n%d) is not computed since d is equal to 0, and so the operation (d!=0) returns false, causing the output to be false. Same applies for the short circuit version of the OR.

Character Escape Codes

The following codes are used to represents codes or characters which cannot be directly accessible through a keyboard:

Code	Description
\n	New Line
\t	Tab
\b	Backspace
\r	Carriage Return
\\	Backslash
\'	Single Quotation Mark
\"	Double Quotation Mark
*	Octal - * represents a number or Hex digit
\x*	Hex
\u*	Unicode, e.g. \u2122 = ™ (trademark symbol)

```
class Example6 {

    public static void main(String args[]) {

        System.out.println("First line\nSecond line");

        System.out.println("A\tB\tC");

        System.out.println("D\tE\tF") ;

        }

}
```

Predicted Output:

```
First Line
Second Line
A    B    C
D    E    F
```

>>> **Test your skills – Example7**

Make a program which creates a sort of truth table to show the behaviour of all the logical operators mentioned. Hints:

- >>> You need two Boolean type variables which you will initially set both to false
- >>> Use character escape codes to tabulate the results

The following program can be used as a guide:

```
class LogicTable {

    public static void main(String args[]) {

        boolean p, q;

        System.out.println("P\tQ\tPANDQ\tPORQ\tPXORQ\tNOTP");

        p = true; q = true;

        System.out.print(p + "\t" + q +"\t");

        System.out.print((p&q) + "\t" + (p|q) + "\t");

        System.out.println((p^q) + "\t" + (!p));

        p = true; q = false;

        System.out.print(p + "\t" + q +"\t");

        System.out.print((p&q) + "\t" + (p|q) + "\t");

        System.out.println((p^q) + "\t" + (!p));

        p = false; q = true;

        System.out.print(p + "\t" + q +"\t");

        System.out.print((p&q) + "\t" + (p|q) + "\t");

        System.out.println((p^q) + "\t" + (!p));

        p = false; q = false;

        System.out.print(p + "\t" + q +"\t");

        System.out.print((p&q) + "\t" + (p|q) + "\t");

        System.out.println((p^q) + "\t" + (!p));

        }

}
```

|

Predicted Output:

P	Q	PANDQ	PORQ	PXORQ	NOTP
true	true	true	true	false	fals
true	false	false	true	true	fals
false	true	false	true	true	true
false	false	false	false	false	true

Data Types

The following is a list of Java's primitive data types:

Data Type	Description
int	Integer – 32bit ranging from -2,147,483,648 to 2,147,483,648
byte	8-bit integer ranging from -128 to 127
short	16-bit integer ranging from -32,768 to 32,768
long	64-bit integer from -9,223,372,036,854,775,808 to -9,223,372,036,854,775,808
float	Single-precision floating point, 32-bit
double	Double-precision floating point, 64-bit
char	Character , 16-bit unsigned ranging from 0 to 65,536 (Unicode)
boolean	Can be true or false only

The 'String' type has not been left out by mistake. It is not a primitive data type, but strings (a sequence of characters) in Java are treated as Objects.

```
class Example8 {

    public static void main(String args[]) {

        int var; // this declares an int variable

        double x; // this declares a floating-point variable var = 10; // assign var the

        value 10 x = 10.0; // assign x the value 10.0 System.out.println("Original

        value of var: " + var); System.out.println("Original value of x: " + x);

        System.out.println(); // print a blank line
```

```
>>> now, divide both by 4 var = var
/ 4;
x = x / 4;
System.out.println("var after division: " + var);
System.out.println("x after division: " + x);
  }
}
```

Predicted output:

Original value of var: 10

Original value of x: 10.0

var after division: 2

x after division: 2.5

One here has to note the difference in precision of the different data types. The following example uses the character data type. Characters in Java are encoded using Unicode giving a 16-bit range, or a total of 65,537 different codes.

```
class Example9 {
    public static void main(String args[]) {
      char ch;
      ch = 'X';
      System.out.println("ch contains " + ch); ch++; //
      increment ch System.out.println("ch is now " + ch); ch =
      90; // give ch the value Z System.out.println("ch is now " +
      ch); }
}
```

Predicted Output:

ch is now X
ch is now Y
ch is now Z

The character 'X' is encoded as the number 88, hence when we increment 'ch', we get character number 89, or 'Y'.

The Boolean data type can be either TRUE or FALSE. It can be useful when controlling flow of a program by assigning the Boolean data type to variables which function as flags. Thus program flow would depend on the condition of these variables at the particular instance. Remember that the output of a condition is always Boolean.

```
class Example10 {

    public static void main(String args[]) {

        boolean b;

        b = false;

        System.out.println("b is " + b);

        b = true;

        System.out.println("b is " + b);

        •   a boolean value can control the if statement if(b)

        System.out.println("This is executed."); b = false;

        if(b) System.out.println("This is not executed.");

        •   outcome of a relational operator is a boolean value System.out.println("10

        > 9 is " + (10 > 9));

        }

}
```

Predicted output:

b is false
b is true
This is executed
10 > 9 is true

Introducing Control Statements

These statements will be dealt with in more detail further on in this booklet. For now we will learn about the ***If*** and the ***for loop***.

```
class Example11 {

    public static void main(String args[]) { int a,b,c;

        a = 2;

        b = 3;

        c = a - b;

       if (c >= 0) System.out.println("c is a positive number"); if (c < 0)

       System.out.println("c is a negative number");

        System.out.println();

        c = b - a;

       if (c >= 0) System.out.println("c is a positive number"); if (c < 0)

       System.out.println("c is a negative number");

    }

}
```

Predicted output:

c is a negative number
c is a positive number

The 'if' statement evaluates a condition and if the result is true, then the following statement/s are executed, else they are just skipped (refer to program output). The line System.out.println() simply inserts a blank line. Conditions use the following comparison operators:

Operator	Description
<	Smaller than
>	Greater than
<=	Smaller or equal to, (a<=3) : if a is 2 or 3, then result of comparison is TRUE
>=	Greater or equal to, (a>=3) : if a is 3 or 4, then result of comparison is TRUE
==	Equal to
!=	Not equal

The for loop is an example of an iterative code, i.e. this statement will cause the program to repeat a particular set of code for a particular number of times. In the following example we will be using a counter which starts at 0 and ends when it is smaller than 5, i.e. 4. Therefore the code following the for loop will iterate for 5 times.

```
class Example12 {

    public static void main(String args[]) { int count;

        for(count = 0; count < 5; count = count+1) System.out.println("This

        is count: " + count); System.out.println("Done!"); }

}
```

Predicted Output:

This is count: 0

This is count: 1

This is count: 2

This is count: 3

This is count: 4

Done!

Instead of count = count+1, this increments the counter, we can use count++

The following table shows all the available shortcut operators:

Operator	Description	Example	Description
++	Increment	a++	a = a + 1 (adds one from a)
–	Decrement	a–	a = a - 1 (subtract one from a)
+=	Add and assign	a+=2	a = a + 2
-=	Subtract and assign	a-=2	a = a - 2
*=	Multiply and assign	a*=3	a = a * 3
/=	Divide and assign	a/=4	a = a / 4
%=	Modulus and assign	a%=5	a = a mod 5

Blocks of Code

Whenever we write an IF statement or a loop, if there is more than one statement of code which has to be executed, this has to be enclosed in braces, i.e. ', ... -'

```
class Example13 {

    public static void main(String args[]) { double i, j, d;

        i = 5;

        j = 10;

        if(i != 0) {

            System.out.println("i does not equal zero"); d = j / i;

            System.out.print("j / i is " + d);

        }

        System.out.println();

    }

}
```

Block of Code

Predicted Output:

```
i does not equal to zero

j/i is 2
```

- **Test your skills – Example14**

Write a program which can be used to display a conversion table, e.g. Euros to Malta Liri, or Metres to Kilometres.

Hints:

- **One variable is required**
- **You need a loop**

The Euro Converter has been provided for you for guidance. Note loop starts at 1 and finishes at 100 (<101). In this case since the conversion rate does not change we did not use a variable, but assigned it directly in the print statement.

```
class EuroConv {
```

```
|
public static void main (String args []){
        double eu;
        System.out.println("Euro conversion table:");
        System.out.println();
        for (eu=1;eu<101;eu++)
                System.out.println(eu+" Euro is euqivalent to Lm "+(eu*0.43));
    }
}
```

The Math Class

In order to perform certain mathematical operations like square root (sqrt), or power (pow); Java has a built in class containing a number of methods as well as static constants, e.g.

Pi = 3.141592653589793 and E = 2.718281828459045. All the methods involving angles use radians and return a double (excluding the Math.round()).

```
class Example15 {
    public static void main(String args[]) { double x, y, z;
        x = 3;
        y = 4;
        z = Math.sqrt(x*x + y*y); System.out.println("Hypotenuse
        is " +z);
    }
}
```

Predicted Output:

Hypotenuse is 5.0

Please note that whenever a method is called, a particular nomenclature is used where we first specify the class that the particular method belongs to, e.g. Math.round( ); where Math is the class name and round is the method name. If a particular method accepts parameters, these are placed in brackets, e.g. Math.max(2.8, 12.9) – in this case it would return 12.9 as being the larger number. A useful method is the Math.random( ) which would return a random number ranging between 0.0 and 1.0.

Scope and Lifetime of Variables

The following simple programs, illustrate how to avoid programming errors by taking care where to initialize variables depending on the scope.

```
class Example16 {

    public static void main(String args[]) { int x; // known to all

        code within main x = 10;

        if(x == 10) { // start new scope

                int y = 20; // known only to this block

                    x and y both known here. System.out.println("x and y: " + x + "

                " + y); x = y * 2;

                }

        •   y = 100; // Error! y not known here

        •   x is still known here.

        System.out.println("x is " + x);

        }

}
```

Predicted Output:

x and y: 10 20
x is 40

If we had to remove the comment marks from the line, y = 100; we would get an error during compilation as y is not known since it only exists within the block of code following the 'if' statement.

The next program shows that y is initialized each time the code belonging to the looping sequence is executed; therefore y is reset to -1 each time and then set to 100. This operation is repeated for three (3) times.

```
class Example17 {

    public static void main(String args[]) { int x;

        for(x = 0; x < 3; x++) {

                                        int y = -1; // y is initialized each time block is
entered

                System.out.println("y is: " + y); // this always
prints -1

                y = 100;

                System.out.println("y is now: " + y);

                }

        }

}
```

Predicted Output:

```
y is: -1
y is now: 100

y is: -1
y is now: 100

y is: -1
y is now: 100
```

Type Casting and Conversions

Casting is the term used when a value is converted from one data type to another, except for Boolean data types which cannot be converted to any other type. Usually conversion occurs to a data type which has a larger range or else there could be loss of precision.

```
class Example18 {                    //long to double automatic conversion

    public static void main(String args[]) {

        long L;

        double D;

        L =   100123285L;

        D =   L;     // L = D is impossible
```

```
System.out.println("L and D: " + L + " " + D);

}

}
```

Predicted Output:

L and D: 100123285 1.00123285E8

The general formula used in casting is as follows: (target type) expression, where target type could be int, float, or short, e.g. (int) (x/y)

```
class Example19 { //CastDemo

public static void main(String args[]) {

double x, y;

byte b;

int i;

char ch;

x = 10.0;

y = 3.0;

i = (int) (x / y); // cast double to int System.out.println("Integer outcome of x /

y: " + i); i = 100;

b = (byte) i;

System.out.println("Value of b: " + b); i = 257;

b = (byte) i;

System.out.println("Value of b: " + b); b = 88; // ASCII

code for X ch = (char) b;

System.out.println("ch: " + ch);

}

}
```

Predicted Output:

Integer outcome of x / y: 3

Value of b: 100

Value of b: 1

ch: X

In the above program, x and y are doubles and so we have loss of precision when converting to integer. We have no loss when converting the integer 100 to byte, but when trying to convert 257 to byte we have loss of precision as 257 exceeds the size which can hold byte. Finally we have casting from byte to char.

```
class Example20 {

    public static void main(String args[]) { byte b;

        int i;

        b = 10;

        i = b * b; // OK, no cast needed b = 10;

        b = (byte) (b * b); // cast needed!! as cannot assing int to byte

        System.out.println("i and b: " + i + " " + b);

        }

}
```

Predicted Output:

i and b: 100 100

The above program illustrates the difference between automatic conversion and casting. When we are assigning a byte to integer, i = b * b, the conversion is automatic. When performing an arithmetic operation the byte type are promoted to integer automatically, but if we want the result as byte, we have to cast it back to byte. This explains why there is the statement: b = (byte) (b * b). Casting has to be applied also if adding variables of type char, as result would else be integer.

Console Input

Most students at this point would be wondering how to enter data while a program is executing. This would definitely make programs more interesting as it adds an element of interactivity at run-time. This is not that straight forward in Java, since Java was not designed to handle console input. The following are the three most commonly used methods to cater for input:

Using the Keyboard Class

One can create a class, which would contain methods to cater for input of the various data types. Another option is to search the internet for the Keyboard Class. This class is easily found as it is used in beginners Java courses. This class is usually found in compiled version, i.e. keyboard.class. This file has to be put in the project folder or else placed directly in the Java JDK. The following is the source code for the Keyboard class just in case it is not available online!

```
import java.io.*;

import java.util.*;

public class Keyboard {

//*************        Error Handling Section

    private static boolean printErrors = true; private static int

    errorCount = 0;

    •    Returns the current error count. public static

    int getErrorCount(){

              return errorCount;
      }

    •    Resets the current error count to zero.

    public static void resetErrorCount (int count){ errorCount = 0;

    }

    •    Returns a boolean indicating whether input errors are

    •    currently printed to standard output.

    public static boolean getPrintErrors(){ return printErrors;

    }
```

- Sets a boolean indicating whether input errors are to be
- printed to standard output.

```
public static void setPrintErrors (boolean flag){ printErrors = flag;

}
```

- Increments the error count and prints the error message
- if appropriate.

```
private static void error (String str){ errorCount++;

    if (printErrors)

        System.out.println (str);

}

//*************     Tokenized Input Stream Section          ****

private static String current_token = null; private static

StringTokenizer reader;

private static BufferedReader in = new BufferedReader (new

    InputStreamReader(System.in));
```

- Gets the next input token assuming it may be on
- subsequent input lines.

```
private static String getNextToken() { return

    getNextToken (true);

}
```

- Gets the next input token, which may already have been //read.

```
private static String getNextToken (boolean skip) { String token;

    if (current_token == null)

        token = getNextInputToken (skip);
```

|

```
        else {
            token = current_token;
            current_token = null;
        }
        return token;
}
```

- Gets the next token from the input, which may come from
- the current input line or a subsequent one. The
- parameter determines if subsequent lines are used. private static String

```
getNextInputToken (boolean skip) {
    final String delimiters = " \t\n\r\f"; String token = null;
    try {
            if (reader == null)
            reader = new StringTokenizer (in.readLine(),
                delimiters, true);
        while (token == null ||
                ((delimiters.indexOf (token) >= 0) && skip)){ while
          (!reader.hasMoreTokens())
                reader = new StringTokenizer (in.readLine(),
                    delimiters,true);
            token = reader.nextToken();
        }
    }
    catch (Exception exception) {
                token = null;
    }
```

```
      |

    return token;

}

•   Returns true if there are no more tokens to read on the

•   current input line.

public static boolean endOfLine() { return

    !reader.hasMoreTokens();

}
//*************      Reading Section

•   Returns a string read from standard input. public static String

readString() {

    String str; try {

        str = getNextToken(false); while (!

        endOfLine()) {

            str = str + getNextToken(false);

        }

    }

    catch (Exception exception){

        error ("Error reading String data, null value returned.");

        str = null;

    }

    return str;

}

•   Returns a space-delimited substring (a word) read from

•   standard input.

public static String readWord() { String token;
```

```
try {
    token = getNextToken();
  }
catch (Exception exception) {
    error ("Error reading String data, null value returned.");
    token = null;
 }
return token;
}
```

- Returns a boolean read from standard input. public static

```
boolean readBoolean() {
    String token = getNextToken(); boolean
    bool;
    try {
        if (token.toLowerCase().equals("true")) bool = true;
        else if (token.toLowerCase().equals("false")) bool = false;
        else {
            error ("Error reading boolean data, false value
returned.");
            bool = false;
        }
    }
    catch (Exception exception) {
        error ("Error reading boolean data, false value returned.");
```

|

bool = false;

}

return bool;

}

- Returns a character read from standard input. public static char

readChar() {

String token = getNextToken(false); char value;

try {

if (token.length() > 1) {

current_token = token.substring (1, token.length());

} else current_token = null; value =

token.charAt (0);

}

catch (Exception exception) {

error ("Error reading char data, MIN_VALUE value returned.");

value = Character.MIN_VALUE;

}

return value;

}

>>> Returns an integer read from standard input. public static int

readInt() {

String token = getNextToken(); int value;

try {

value = Integer.parseInt (token);

```
    |
    }
    catch (Exception exception) {
      error ("Error reading int data, MIN_VALUE value returned.");
          value = Integer.MIN_VALUE;
    }
    return value;
}
```

- Returns a long integer read from standard input. public static long

```
readLong(){
    String token = getNextToken(); long value;
    try {
          value = Long.parseLong (token);
    }
    catch (Exception exception) {
          error ("Error reading long data, MIN_VALUE value returned.");
          value = Long.MIN_VALUE;
    }
    return value;
}
```

>>> Returns a float read from standard input. public static float

```
readFloat() {
    String token = getNextToken(); float value;
    try {
            value = (new Float(token)).floatValue();
```

```
            |
        }
        catch (Exception exception) {
          error ("Error reading float data, NaN value returned.");
              value = Float.NaN;
        }
        return value;
    }
    >>>  Returns a double read from standard input. public static
    double readDouble() {
        String token = getNextToken(); double
        value;
        try {
              value = (new Double(token)).doubleValue();
                 }
        catch (Exception exception) {
            error ("Error reading double data, NaN value returned.");
              value = Double.NaN;
        }
        return value;
    }
}
```

The above class contains the following methods:

- public static String readString ()
  Reads and returns a string, to the end of the line, from standard input.
- public static String readWord ()
  Reads and returns one space-delimited word from standard input.
- public static boolean readBoolean ()

Reads and returns a boolean value from standard input. Returns false if an exception occurs during the read.

- public static char readChar ()

  Reads and returns a character from standard input. Returns MIN_VALUE if an exception occurs during the read.
- public static int readInt ()

  Reads and returns an integer value from standard input. Returns MIN_VALUE if an exception occurs during the read.
- public static long readLong ()

  Reads and returns a long integer value from standard input. Returns MIN_VALUE if an exception occurs during the read.
- public static float readFloat ()

  Reads and returns a float value from standard input. Returns NaN if an exception occurs during the read.
- public static double readDouble ()

  Reads and returns a double value from standard input. Returns NaN if an exception occurs during the read.
- public static int getErrorCount()

  Returns the number of errors recorded since the Keyboard class was loaded or since the last error count reset.
- public static void resetErrorCount (int count)

  Resets the current error count to zero.
- public static boolean getPrintErrors ()

  Returns a boolean indicating whether input errors are currently printed to standard output.
- public static void setPrintErrors (boolean flag)

  Sets the boolean indicating whether input errors are to be printed to standard input.

Let's try it out by writing a program which accepts three integers and working the average:

```
public class KeyboardInput {

    public static void main (String args[]) { System.out.println("Enter a

    number:"); int a = Keyboard.readInt (); System.out.println("Enter a

    second number:"); int b = Keyboard.readInt ();

    System.out.println("Enter a third number:"); int c =

    Keyboard.readInt ();
```

|

```
        System.out.println("The average is " + (a+b+c)/3);

        }

}
```

After printing a statement, the program will wait for the use r to enter a number and store it in the particular variable. It utilizes the **readInt( )** method. Finally it will display the result of the average.

Using the Scanner Class

In Java 5 a particular class was added, the Scanner class. This class allows users to create an instance of this class and use its methods to perform input. Let us look at the following example which performs the same operation as the one above (works out the average of three numbers):

```
import java.util.Scanner;

    public class ScannerInput {

     public static void main(String[] args) {

            //... Initialize Scanner to read from console. Scanner input = new

            Scanner(System.in); System.out.print("Enter first number : "); int a

            = input.nextInt(); System.out.print("Enter second number: "); int b =

            input.nextInt(); System.out.print("Enter last number : "); int c =

            input.nextInt(); System.out.println("Average is " + (a+b+c)/3);


     }

}
```

By examining the code we see that first we have to import the java.util.Scanner as part of the java.util package. Next we create an instance of Scanner and name it as we like, in this case we named it "input". We have to specify also the type of input expected (System.in). The rest is similar to the program which uses the Keyboard class, the only difference is the name of the method used, in this case it is called **nextInt ( )** rather than readInt( ). This time the method is called as part of the instance created, i.e. **input.nextInt( )**

Using Swing Components

This is probably the most exciting version, since the Swing package offers a graphical user interface (GUI) which allows the user to perform input into a program via the mouse, keyboard and other input devices.

```
import javax.swing.*; // * means „all" public class

SwingInput {

    public static void main(String[] args) {

        String temp;          // Temporary storage for input.

        temp = JOptionPane.showInputDialog(null, "First number");

        int a = Integer.parseInt(temp); // String to int

        temp = JOptionPane.showInputDialog(null, "Second number");

        int b = Integer.parseInt(temp);

        temp = JOptionPane.showInputDialog(null, "Third number");

        int c = Integer.parseInt(temp);

        JOptionPane.showMessageDialog(null, "Average is " + (a+b+c)/3);

    }

}
```

One has to note that the input is stored as a string, **temp**, and then parsed to integer using the method **parseInt( )**. This time the method accepts a parameter, temp, and returns an integer. When the above program is executed, a dialog box will appear on screen with a field to accept input from user via keyboard (JOptionPane.showInputDialog). This is repeated three times and finally the result is again displayed in a dialog box (JOptionPane.showMessageDialog).

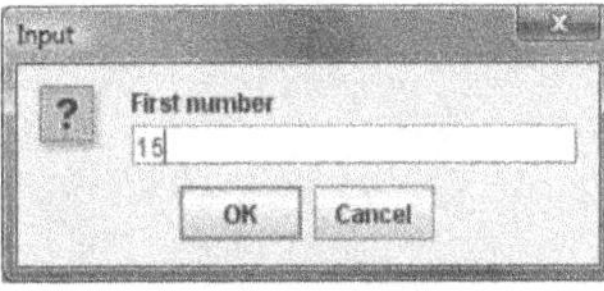

JOptionPane.showInputDialog

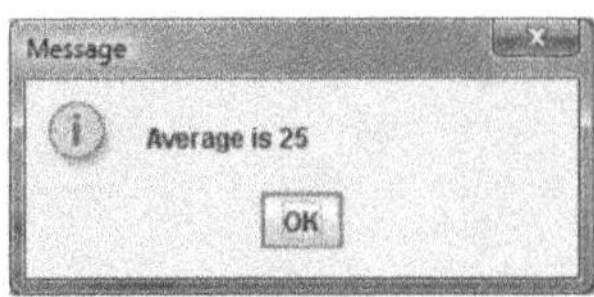

JOptionPane.showMessageDialog

Control Statements - The If Statement

if(**condition**) statement;

else statement;

Note:

- >>> **else** clause is optional
- >>> targets of both the **If** and **else** can be blocks of statements.

The general form of the **If**, using blocks of statements, is:

```
if(condition)
    {
    statement sequence
    }
else
    {
    statement sequence
    }
```

If the conditional expression is true, the target of the **If** will be executed; otherwise, if it exists,

the target of the **else** will be executed. At no time will both of them be executed. The conditional

expression controlling the **If** must produce a **boolean** result.

Guessing Game (Guess.java)

The program asks the player for a letter between A and Z. If the player presses the correct letter on the keyboard, the program responds by printing the message **Right **.

>>> Guess the letter game.

```
class Guess {
        public static void main(String args[]) throws
        java.io.IOException {
                char ch, answer = 'K';
                System.out.println("I'm thinking of a letter between A and Z.");
                System.out.print("Can you guess it: ");
                ch = (char) System.in.read(); // read a char from the keyboard
                if(ch == answer) System.out.println("** Right **");
        }
}
```

Extending the above program to use the else statement:

```
# Guess the letter game, 2nd version. class
Guess2 {
        public static void main(String args[]) throws
        java.io.IOException {
                char ch, answer = 'K';
                System.out.println("I'm thinking of a letter between A and Z.");
                System.out.print("Can you guess it: ");
                ch = (char) System.in.read(); // get a char
                if(ch == answer) System.out.println("** Right **"); else
                System.out.println("...Sorry, you're wrong.");
        }
}
```

Nested If

The main thing to remember about nested **Ifs** in Java is that an **else** statement always refers to the nearest **If** statement that is within the same block as the **else** and not already associated with an **else**. Here is an example:

```
if(i == 10) {

        if(j < 20) a = b;

        if(k > 100) c = d;

        else a = c; // this else refers to if(k > 100)

}

else a = d; // this else refers to if(i == 10)
```

Guessing Game v.3

- Guess the letter game, 3rd version. class

```
Guess3 {

        public static void main(String args[])

                throws java.io.IOException {

                        char ch, answer = 'K';

            System.out.println("I'm thinking of a letter between A and Z.");

            System.out.print("Can you guess it: ");

            ch = (char) System.in.read(); // get a char

            if(ch == answer) System.out.println("** Right **"); else {

                    System.out.print("...Sorry, you're "); // a nested if

            if(ch < answer) System.out.println("too low"); else

            System.out.println("too high"); }


        }

}
```

A sample run is shown here:

I'm thinking of a letter between A and Z.

Can you guess it: Z

...Sorry, you're too high

If-else-If Ladder

```
if(condition)
        statement;
else if(condition)
        statement;
else if(condition)
        statement;
        ...
else
        statement;
```

The conditional expressions are evaluated from the top downward. As soon as a true condition is found, the statement associated with it is executed, and the rest of the ladder is bypassed. If none of the conditions is true, the final **else** statement will be executed. The final **else** often acts as a default condition; that is, if all other conditional tests fail, the last **else** statement is performed. If there is no final **else** and all other conditions are false, no action will take place.

- Demonstrate an if-else-if ladder. class

```
Ladder {
public static void main(String args[]) { int x;
        for(x=0; x<6; x++) {
        if(x==1)
                System.out.println("x is one"); else
        if(x==2)
                System.out.println("x is two");
```

```
|
else if(x==3)
System.out.println("x is three"); else if(x==4)
System.out.println("x is four");
else
System.out.println("x is not between 1 and 4");
}
}
}
```

The program produces the following output:

x is not between 1 and 4

x is one

x is two

x is three

x is four

x is not between 1 and 4

Ternary (?) Operator

Declared as follows:

Exp1 ? Exp2 : Exp3;

Exp1 would be a **boolean** expression, and Exp2 and Exp3 are expressions of any type other than void. The type of Exp2 and Exp3 must be the same, though. Notice the use and placement of the colon. Consider this example, which assigns absval the absolute value of val:

absval = val < 0 ? -val : val; // get absolute value of val

Here, absval will be assigned the value of val if val is zero or greater. If val is negative, then absval will be assigned the negative of that value (which yields a positive value).

The same code written using the **If-else** structure would look like this:

```
if(val < 0) absval = -val;
else absval = val;
```

e.g. 2 This program divides two numbers, but will not allow a division by zero.

```
•   Prevent a division by zero using the ?. class
NoZeroDiv {
        public static void main(String args[]) {
                int result;
                for(int i = -5; i < 6; i++) { result = i != 0 ? 100 / i
                        : 0; if(i != 0)
                        System.out.println("100 / " + i + " is " + result); }
        }
}
```

The output from the program is shown here:

```
100 / -5 is -20
100 / -4 is -25
100 / -3 is -33
100 / -2 is -50
100 / -1 is -100
100 / 1 is 100
100 / 2 is 50
100 / 3 is 33
100 / 4 is 25
100 / 5 is 20
```

Please note:

```
result = i != 0 ? 100 / i : 0;
```

result is assigned the outcome of the division of 100 by I. However, this division takes place only if I is not zero. When I is zero, a placeholder value of zero is assigned to **result**. Here is the preceding program rewritten a bit more efficiently. It produces the same output as before.

```
>>>     Prevent a division by zero using the ?. class
NoZeroDiv2 {
        public static void main(String args[]) { for(int i = -5; i <
                6; i++)
                        if(i != 0 ? true : false)
                        System.out.println("100 / " + i +
                        " is " + 100 / i);
        }
}
```

Notice the **If** statement. If I is zero, then the outcome of the **If** is false, the division by zero is prevented, and no result is displayed. Otherwise the division takes place.

switch Statement (case of)

The **switch** provides for a multi-way branch. Thus, it enables a program to select among several alternatives. Although a series of nested **if** statements can perform multi-way tests, for many situations the **switch** is a more efficient approach.

```
switch(expression) {
    case constant1:
      statement sequence
      break;
  case constant2:
      statement sequence
      break;
  case constant3:
      statement sequence
      break;
      ...
  default:
      statement sequence
}
```

2. The **switch** expression can be of type **char**, **byte**, **short**, or **int**. (Floating-point expressions, for example, are not allowed.)
3. Frequently, the expression controlling the **switch** is simply a variable.
4. The **case** constants must be literals of a type compatible with the expression.
5. No two **case** constants in the same **switch** can have identical values.
6. The **default** statement sequence is executed if no **case** constant matches the expression. The **default** is optional; if it is not present, no action takes place if all matches fail. When a match is found, the statements associated with that **case** are executed until the **break** is encountered or, in the case of **default** or the last **case**, until the end of the **switch** is reached.

The following program demonstrates the **switch.**

2. Demonstrate the switch. class

```
SwitchDemo {

    public static void main(String args[]) { int i;

        for(i=0; i<10; i++)

        switch(i) {

        case 0:

        System.out.println("i is zero"); break;

        case 1:

        System.out.println("i is one"); break;

        case 2:

        System.out.println("i is two"); break;

        case 3:

        System.out.println("i is three"); break;

        case 4:

        System.out.println("i is four"); break;

        default:

        System.out.println("i is five or more");

        }

    }

}
```

|

The output produced by this program is shown here:

```
i is zero
i is one
i is two
i is three
i is four
i is five or more
i is five or more
i is five or more
i is five or more
i is five or more
```

The **break** statement is optional, although most applications of the **switch** will use it. When encountered within the statement sequence of a **case**, the **break** statement causes program flow to exit from the entire **switch** statement and resume at the next statement outside the **switch**. However, if a **break** statement does not end the statement sequence associated with a **case**, then all the statements *at and following* the matching **case** will be executed until a **break** (or the end of the **switch**) is encountered. For example,

2. Demonstrate the switch without break statements. class

```
NoBreak {

    public static void main(String args[]) { int i;

        for(i=0; i<=5; i++) { switch(i)

        {

        case 0:

        System.out.println("i is less than one"); case 1:

        System.out.println("i is less than two"); case 2:

        System.out.println("i is less than three"); case 3:

        System.out.println("i is less than four"); case 4:

        System.out.println("i is less than five");

        }
```

```
            |
            System.out.println();
            }
      }
}
```

Output:

```
i is less than one
i is less than two
i is less than three
i is less than four
i is less than five
i is less than two
i is less than three
i is less than four
i is less than five
i is less than three
i is less than four
i is less than five
i is less than four
i is less than five
i is less than five
```

Execution will continue into the next **case** if no **break** statement is present.

You can have empty **cases**, as shown in this example:

```
switch(i) {
      case 1:
      case 2:
      case 3: System.out.println("i is 1, 2 or 3");
      break;
      case 4: System.out.println("i is 4");
      break;
      }
```

|

Nested switch

```
switch(ch1) {
        case 'A': System.out.println("This A is part of outer switch.");
                switch(ch2) {
                case 'A':
                System.out.println("This A is part of inner switch");
                break;
                case 'B': // ...
                }// end of inner switch break;
        case 'B': // ...
```

- **Mini-Project – Java Help System (Help.java)**

Your program should display the following options on screen:

Help on:

>>> if
>>> switch

Choose one:

To accomplish this, you will use the statement

```
System.out.println("Help on:");
System.out.println(" 1. if");
System.out.println(" 2. switch");
System.out.print("Choose one:
```

Next, the program obtains the user's selection

```
choice = (char) System.in.read();
```

Once the selection has been obtained, the display the syntax for the selected statement.

```
switch(choice) {
case '1':
System.out.println("The if:\
System.out.println("if(condition)
System.out.println("else statement;");
break;
case '2':
System.out.println("The switch:\
System.out.println("switch(
System.out.println(" case
System.out.println(" statement
System.out.println(" break;");
System.out.println(" // ...");
System.out.println("}");
break;
default:
System.out.print("Selection not found.");
}
```

default *clause catches invalid choices. For example, if the user enters 3, no* ***case*** *constants will match, causing the* ***default*** *sequence to execute.*

Complete Listing

```
/*
Project 3-1
A simple help system.
*/
class Help {
    public static void main(String args[])
    throws java.io.IOException {
```

```
char choice;
System.out.println("Help on:");
System.out.println(" 1. if");
System.out.println(" 2. switch");
System.out.print("Choose one: ");
choice = (char) System.in.read();
System.out.println("\n");
switch(choice) {
case '1':
        System.out.println("The if:\n");
        System.out.println("if(condition) statement;");
        System.out.println("else statement;");
        break;
case '2':
        System.out.println("The switch:\n");
        System.out.println("switch(expression) {");
        System.out.println(" case constant:"); System.out.println("
        statement sequence"); System.out.println(" break;");
        System.out.println(" // ..."); System.out.println("}"); break;

default:
        System.out.print("Selection not found.");
}
    }
}
```

Sample run:

Help on:

- if
- switch Choose one: 1 The if:

if(condition) statement; else

statement;

The for Loop

Loops are structures used to make the program repeat one or many instructions for 'n' times as specified in the declaration of the loop.

The for Loop can be used for just one statement:

for(initialization; condition; iteration) statement;

or to repeat a block of code:

for(initialization; condition; iteration)

{

statement sequence

}

Initialization = assignment statement that sets the initial value of the *loop control variable*, (counter)
Condition = Boolean expression that determines whether or not the loop will repeat
Iteration = amount by which the loop control variable will change each time the loop is repeated.

>>> The **for** loop executes only/till the condition is true.

Example: using a 'for' loop to print the square roots of the numbers between 1 and 99. (It also displays the rounding error present for each square root).

- Show square roots of 1 to 99 and the rounding error. class SqrRoot {

```
        public static void main(String args[]) { double num,

                sroot, rerr;

                for(num = 1.0; num < 100.0; num++) {

                        sroot = Math.sqrt(num);

                        System.out.println("Square root of " + num +

                        " is " + sroot);

                        >>>     compute rounding error rerr = num - (sroot * sroot);

                        System.out.println("Rounding error is " + rerr);

                        System.out.println();


                }

        }

}
```

'For' loop counters (loop control variables) can either increment or decrement,

- A negatively running for loop. class

```
DecrFor {

        public static void main(String args[]) { int x;

                for(x = 100; x > -100; x -= 5)

                System.out.println(x);

        }

}
```

Counter

decrements by 5 (x = x - 5)

Multiple Loop Control Variable

Using more than one variable in the same loop is possible:

```
// Use commas in a for statement.

class Comma {

        public static void main(String args[]) { in the same loop int i, j;

                for(i=0, j=10; i < j; i++, j–) System.out.println("i and j: " + i + " " + j);

        }

}
```

'i' and 'j' are the two variables used in the same loop

Expected output:

i and j: 0 10

i and j: 1 9

i and j: 2 8

i and j: 3 7

i and j: 4 6

Terminating a loop via user intervention

Let us write a program which involves a loop and this is stopped when the user types 's' on the keyboard:

```
>>>     Loop until an S is typed. class

ForTest {

        public static void main(String args[]) throws

                java.io.IOException { int i;

                System.out.println("Press S to stop.");

                for(i = 0; (char) System.in.read() != 'S'; i++)

                        System.out.println("Pass #" + i);

        }

}
```

Interesting For Loop Variations

It is possible to leave out parts of the loop declaration:

- Example 1 - Parts of the for can be empty. class Empty {

```
public static void main(String args[]) { int i;

    for(i = 0; i < 10; ) {

        System.out.println("Pass #" + i);

        i++; // increment loop control var

    }

}

}
```

>>> Example 2 - Parts of the for can be empty. class

```
Empty2 {

public static void main(String args[]) { int i;

     = 0; // move initialization out of loop for(; i < 10; ) {

        System.out.println("Pass #" + i); i++; //

        increment loop control var

    }

}

}
```

Initialising the loop out of the 'for' statement is only required when the value needs to be a result of another complex process which cannot be written inside the declaration.

Infinite Loops

Sometimes one needs to create an infinite loop, i.e. a loop which never ends! (However it can be stopped using the break statement). An example of an infinite loop declaration is as follows:

```
for(;;)

{

        // ... statements

}
```

*N.B. Using **break** to terminate an infinite loop will be discussed later on in the course.*

No 'Body' Loops

Loops can be declared without a body. This can be useful in particular situations, consider the following example:

- Loop without body.

```
class Empty3 {

        public static void main(String args[]) { int i;

                int sum = 0;

                >>>     sum the numbers through 5 for(i = 1; i

                <= 5; sum += i++) ; System.out.println("Sum is "

                + sum);

        }

}
```

Two operations are carried on, sum = sum + i and

i = i + 1

Predicted Output:

Sum is 15

Declaring variables inside the loop

Variables can be declared inside the loop itself but one must remember that in such case the variable exists only inside the loop!

|

- Declare loop variable inside the for. class ForVar {

```
public static void main(String args[]) { int sum = 0;
        int fact = 1;
            compute the factorial of the numbers through 5 for(int i = 1; i
        <= 5; i++) {
                sum += i; // i is known throughout the loop fact *= i;
        }
            but, i is not known here. System.out.println("Sum is "
        + sum); System.out.println("Factorial is " + fact);
    }
}
```

Enhanced For loop

This type of loop will be discussed later on in the course as it involves arrays.

The While Loop

while (condition) statement; //or more than one statement

The condition could be any valid Boolean expression. The loop will function only if the condition is true. If false it will move on to the next line of code.

- Demonstrate the while loop. class

```
WhileDemo {

        public static void main(String args[]) { char ch;

                print the alphabet using a while loop

            ch = 'a';

            while(ch <= 'z') {

            System.out.print(ch);

            ch++;

            }

        }

}
```

The above program will output the alphabet. As can be seen in the code the while loop will result false when the character is greater than 'z'. The condition is tested at the beginning of the program.

>>> Compute integer powers of 2.

```
class Power {

        public static void main(String args[]) { int e;

            int result;

            for(int i=0; i < 10; i++) {

                result = 1;

                e = i;

                while(e > 0) {

                    result *= 2;

                    e–;

                }
```

```
|
                    System.out.println("2 to the power of " + i + " is "
        >>>     result);
        }
    }
}
```

Predicted Output:

2 to the power of 0 is 1

2 to the power of 1 is 2

2 to the power of 2 is 4

2 to the power of 3 is 8

2 to the power ... (up to „of 9 is 512")

The do-while Loop

This conditional statement checks the Boolean expression after going at least one time through the loop. The do-while is declared as follows:

```
do {
statements;
} while(condition);
```

Braces are used if there is more than one statements and to improve program readability.

```
#   Demonstrate the do-while loop. class
DWDemo {
    public static void main(String args[]) throws
        java.io.IOException {
        char ch;
        do {
            System.out.print("Press a key followed by ENTER: "); ch = (char)
            System.in.read(); // get a char } while(ch != 'q');
        }
    }
```

- Guess the letter game, 4th version. class

Guess4 {

public static void main(String args[]) throws

java.io.IOException { char ch, answer = 'K';

do {

System.out.println("I'm thinking of a letter between A and Z.");

System.out.print("Can you guess it: ");

- read a letter, but skip cr/lf do {

ch = (char) System.in.read(); // get a char } while(ch ==

'\n' | ch == '\r');

The function of this statement is to skip carriage return and line feed characters

if(ch == answer) System.out.println("** Right **"); else {

System.out.print("...Sorry, you're ");

if(ch < answer) System.out.println("too low"); else

System.out.println("too high"); System.out.println("Try

again!\n");

}

} while(answer != ch);

}

}

Predicted Output:

I'm thinking of a letter between A and Z.

Can you guess it: A

...Sorry, you're too low

Try again!

I'm thinking of a letter between A and Z.

Can you guess it: Z

...Sorry, you're too high

Try again!

I'm thinking of a letter between A and Z.

Can you guess it: K

** Right **

|

- **Mini-Project 2– Java Help System (Help2.java)**

We are going to work on our previous project. Copy all the code and add the following code:

```
do {
        System.out.println("Help on:");
        System.out.println(" 1. if"); System.out.println(" 2.
        switch"); System.out.println(" 3. for");
        System.out.println(" 4. while");
        System.out.println(" 5. do-while\n");
        System.out.print("Choose one: "); do {
                choice = (char) System.in.read();
        } while(choice == '\n' | choice == '\r'); } while( choice <
'1' | choice > '5');
```

Now extend the switch as follows:

```
switch(choice) {
        case '1':
                System.out.println("The if:\n");
                System.out.println("if(condition) statement;");
                System.out.println("else statement;");
                break;
        case '2':
                System.out.println("The switch:\n");
                System.out.println("switch(expression) {");
                System.out.println(" case constant:"); System.out.println("
                statement sequence"); System.out.println(" break;");
                System.out.println(" // ..."); System.out.println("}");
```

```
|
        break;
    case '3':
        System.out.println("The for:\n");
        System.out.print("for(init; condition; iteration)");
        System.out.println(" statement;");
        break;
    case '4':
        System.out.println("The while:\n");
        System.out.println("while(condition) statement;"); break;
    case '5':
        System.out.println("The do-while:\n");
        System.out.println("do {");
        System.out.println(" statement;");
        System.out.println("} while (condition);");
        break;
        }
```

The default statement has been removed as the loop ensures that a proper response is entered or else the program will continue to execute.

Complete listing

```
/*
    Project 3-2
    An improved Help system that uses a do-while to
    process a menu selection.
*/
class Help2 {
    public static void main(String args[]) throws
        java.io.IOException { char choice;
```

```
do {
        System.out.println("Help on:");
        System.out.println(" 1. if"); System.out.println(" 2.
        switch"); System.out.println(" 3. for");
        System.out.println(" 4. while");
        System.out.println(" 5. do-while\n");
        System.out.print("Choose one: "); do {
                choice = (char) System.in.read();
        } while(choice == '\n' | choice == '\r'); } while( choice <
'1' | choice > '5'); System.out.println("\n");
switch(choice) { case
        '1':
                System.out.println("The if:\n");
                System.out.println("if(condition)
                statement;");
                System.out.println("else statement;");
                break;
        case '2':
                System.out.println("The switch:\n");
                System.out.println("switch(expression) {");
                System.out.println(" case constant:");
                System.out.println(" statement sequence");
                System.out.println(" break;");
                System.out.println(" // ...");
                System.out.println("}");
                break;
        case '3':
                System.out.println("The for:\n");
```

```
            System.out.print("for(init; condition; iteration)");
            System.out.println(" statement;");
            break;
        case '4':
            System.out.println("The while:\n");
            System.out.println("while(condition)
            statement;");
            break;
        case '5':
            System.out.println("The do-while:\n");
            System.out.println("do {"); System.out.println("
            statement;"); System.out.println("} while (condition);");
            break;
        }
    }
}
```

Using Break to Terminate a Loop

One can use the 'break' command to terminate voluntarily a loop. Execution will continue from the next line following the loop statements,

e.g. 1 Automatic termination (hard-coded)

```
class BreakDemo {
  public static void main(String args[]) { int num;
     num = 100;
     for(int i=0; i < num; i++) {
          if(i*i >= num) break; // terminate loop if i*i >= 100 System.out.print(i
          + " ");
     }
     System.out.println("Loop complete.");
  }
}
```

*When i = 10, i*i = 100. Therefore the 'if' condition is satisfied and the loop terminates before i = 100*

Expected Output:

0 1 2 3 4 5 6 7 8 9 Loop complete.

e.g. 2 Termination via user intervention

```
class Break2 {
   public static void main(String args[])
      throws java.io.IOException {
      char ch;
      for( ; ; ) {
           ch = (char) System.in.read(); // get a char if(ch == 'q')
           break;
      }
      System.out.println("You pressed q!");
   }
}
```

In the above program there is an infinite loop, for(; ;) . This means that the program will never terminate unless the user presses a particular letter on the keyboard, in this case 'q'.

If we have nested loops, i.e. a loop within a loop, the 'break' will terminate the inner loop. It is not recommended to use many 'break' statement in nested loops as it could lead to bad programs. However there could be more than one 'break' statement in a loop. If there is a switch statement in a loop, the 'break' statement will affect the switch statement **only**. The following code shows an example of nested loops using the 'break' to terminate the inner loop;

```
// Using break with nested loops

class Break3 {
   public static void main(String args[]) { for(int i=0; i<3; i++) {
     System.out.println("Outer loop count: " + i); System.out.print("
     Inner loop count: "); int t = 0;
       while(t < 100) {
          if(t == 10) break; // terminate loop if t is 10 System.out.print(t
          + " "); t++;

       }
       System.out.println();
     }
   System.out.println("Loops complete.");
  }
}
```

Predicted Output:

```
Outer loop count: 0
Inner loop count: 0 1 2 3 4 5 6 7 8 9
Outer loop count: 1
Inner loop count: 0 1 2 3 4 5 6 7 8 9
Outer loop count: 2
Inner loop count: 0 1 2 3 4 5 6 7 8 9
Loops complete.
```

Terminating a loop with break and use labels to carry on execution

Programmers refer to this technique as the GOTO function where one instructs the program to jump to another location in the code and continue execution. However Java does not offer this feature but it can be implemented by using break and labels. Labels can be any valid Java identifier and a colon should follow. Labels have to be declared before a block of code, e.g.

```
// Using break with labels.

class Break4 {

   public static void main(String args[]) {
     int i;
     for(i=1; i<4; i++) {
         one: {
         two:     {
         three:       {
                        System.out.println("\ni is " + i);
                        if(i==1) break one;
                        if(i==2) break two;
                        if(i==3) break three;
                        •   the following statement is never executed
                        System.out.println("won't print");
                      }
```

One, two and three are labels

```
            System.out.println("After block three."); □ three }
          System.out.println("After block two."); □ two
        }
        System.out.println("After block one."); □ one
      }

      //the following statement executes on termination of the
      for loop
      System.out.println("After for.");
    }
}
```

Predicted Output:

```
i is 1
After block one.
i is 2
After block two.
After block one.
i is 3
After block three.
After block two.
After block one.
After for.
```

Interpreting the above code can prove to be quite tricky. When 'i' is 1, execution will break after the first 'if' statement and resume where there is the label 'one'. This will execute the statement labelled 'one' above. When 'i' is 2, this time execution will resume at the point labelled 'two' and hence will also execute the following statements including the one labelled 'one'.

The following code is another example using labels but this time the label marks a point outside the loop:

```
class Break5 {
  public static void main(String args[]) { done:
   for(int i=0; i<10; i++) {
     for(int j=0; j<10; j++) {
       for(int k=0; k<10; k++) {
         System.out.println(k);
         if(k == 5) break done; // jump to done
       }
       System.out.println("After k loop"); // skipped
     }
     System.out.println("After j loop"); // skipped
   }
   System.out.println("After i loop");
  }
}
```

Predicted Output:

0
1
2
3
4
5
After i loop

The 'k' loop is terminated when 'k' = 5. However the 'j' loop is skipped since the break operation cause execution to resume at a point outside the loops. Hence only the 'i' loop terminates and thus the relevant statement is printed.

The next example shows the difference in execution taking care to where one puts the label:

```
class Break6 {
   public static void main(String args[]) { int x=0, y=0;
      stop1: for(x=0; x < 5; x++) {
                  for(y = 0; y < 5; y++) {
                      if(y == 2) break stop1;
                      System.out.println("x and y: " + x + " " + y);
                  }
               }
      System.out.println();
               for(x=0; x < 5; x++)
               stop2: {
                  for(y = 0; y < 5; y++) {
                      if(y == 2) break stop2;
                      System.out.println("x and y: " + x + " " + y);
                  }
               }
      }
}
```

Predicted Output:

x and y: 0 0
x and y: 0 1

x and y: 0 0
x and y: 0 1
x and y: 1 0
x and y: 1 1
x and y: 2 0
x and y: 2 1
x and y: 3 0
x and y: 3 1
x and y: 4 0
x and y: 4 1

In the first part the inner loop stops when 'y' = 2. The break operation forces the program to skip the outer 'for' loop, print a blank line and start the next set of loops. This time the label is placed after the 'for' loop declaration. Hence the break operation is only operating on the inner loop this time. In fact 'x' goes all the way from 0 to 4, with 'y' always stopping when it reaches a value of 2.

|

The break – label feature can only be used within the same block of code. The following code is an
example of misuse of the break – label operation:

```
class BreakErr {
   public static void main(String args[]) { one: for(int i=0;
      i<3; i++) {
                              System.out.print("Pass " + i + ": ");
            }
            for(int j=0; j<100; j++) {
               if(j == 10) break one;
                  System.out.print(j + " ");
               }
            }
}
```

This break cannot continue from the assigned label since it is not part of the same block

Use of Continue (complement of Break)

The 'continue' feature can force a loop to iterate out of its normal control behaviour. It is regarded as the complement of the break operation. Let us consider the following example,

```
class ContDemo {
    public static void main(String args[]) { int i;
        for(i = 0; i<=100; i++) {
            if((i%2) != 0) continue;
            System.out.println(i);
        }
    }
}
```

Predicted Output:

0

2

4

6

...

100

The program prints on screen the even numbers. This happens since whenever the modulus results of 'i' by 2 are not equal to '0', the 'continue' statement forces loop to iterate bypassing the following statement (modulus refers to the remainder of dividing 'i' by 2).

In 'while' and 'do-while' loops, a 'continue' statement will cause control to go directly to the conditional expression and then continue the looping process. In the case of the 'for' loop, the iteration expression of the loop is evaluated, then the conditional expression is executed, and then the loop continues.

Continue + Label

It is possible to use labels with the continue feature. It works the same as when we used it before in the break operation.

```
class ContToLabel {
        public static void main(String args[]) { outerloop:
                for(int i=1; i < 10; i++) { System.out.print("\nOuter loop pass " + i
                        + ", Inner loop: ");
                        for(int j = 1; j < 10; j++) {
                            if(j == 5) continue outerloop;
                            System.out.print(j);
                        }
                }
        }
}
```

Predicted Output:

Outer loop pass 1, Inner loop: 1234
Outer loop pass 2, Inner loop: 1234
Outer loop pass 3, Inner loop: 1234
Outer loop pass 4, Inner loop: 1234
Outer loop pass 5, Inner loop: 1234
Outer loop pass 6, Inner loop: 1234
Outer loop pass 7, Inner loop: 1234
Outer loop pass 8, Inner loop: 1234
Outer loop pass 9, Inner loop: 1234

Note that the inner loop is allowed to execute until 'j' is equal to 5. Then loop is forced to outer loop.

>>> Mini-Project 3– Java Help System (Help3.java)

This project puts the finishing touches on the Java help system that was created in the previous projects. This version adds the syntax for 'break' and 'continue'. It also allows the user to request the syntax for more than one statement. It does this by adding an outer loop that runs until the user enters 'q' as a menu selection.

- Copy all the code from Help2.java into a new file, Help3.java
- Create an outer loop which covers the whole code. This loop should be declared as infinite but terminate when the user presses 'q' (use the break)
- Your menu should look like this:

```
do {
        System.out.println("Help on:"); System.out.println(" 1. if");
        System.out.println(" 2. switch"); System.out.println(" 3. for");
        System.out.println(" 4. while"); System.out.println(" 5. do-
        while"); System.out.println(" 6. break"); System.out.println("
        7. continue\n"); System.out.print("Choose one (q to quit): ");
        do {
                choice = (char) System.in.read();
                } while(choice == '\n' | choice == '\r');
    } while( choice < '1' | choice > '7' & choice != 'q');
```

>>> Adjust the switch statement to include the 'break' and 'continue' features.

Complete Listing

```
class Help3 {

    public static void main(String args[])

        throws java.io.IOException {

        char choice;


        for(;;) {

            do {

                System.out.println("Help on:");

                System.out.println("          1. if");

                System.out.println("          2. switch");

                System.out.println("          3. for");

                System.out.println("          4. while");
```

```
|

    System.out.println(" 5. do-while"); System.out.println(" 6.
    break"); System.out.println(" 7. continue\n");
    System.out.print("Choose one (q to quit): "); do {
        choice = (char) System.in.read();
    } while(choice == '\n' | choice == '\r');
} while( choice < '1' | choice > '7' & choice != 'q');

if(choice == 'q') break;

System.out.println("\n");

switch(choice) {
    case '1':
        System.out.println("The if:\n");
        System.out.println("if(condition) statement;");
        System.out.println("else statement;");
        break;
    case '2':
        System.out.println("The switch:\n");
        System.out.println("switch(expression) {");
        System.out.println("            case constant:");
        System.out.println("                statement sequence");
        System.out.println("                break;");
        System.out.println("            // ...");
        System.out.println("}");
        break;
    case '3':
```

```
            |
            System.out.println("The for:\n");
            System.out.print("for(init; condition; iteration)");
            System.out.println(" statement;");
            break;
          case '4':
            System.out.println("The while:\n");
            System.out.println("while(condition) statement;"); break;
          case '5':
            System.out.println("The do-while:\n");
            System.out.println("do {"); System.out.println("
            statement;"); System.out.println("} while (condition);");
            break;
          case '6':
            System.out.println("The break:\n");
            System.out.println("break; or break label;"); break;
          case '7':
            System.out.println("The continue:\n"); System.out.println("continue;
            or continue label;"); break;
        }
        System.out.println();
      }
    }
}
```

Nested Loops

A nested loop is a loop within a loop. The previous examples already included such loops. Another example to consider is the following:

```
class FindFac {
        public static void main(String args[]) {
                for(int i=2; i <= 100; i++) { System.out.print("Factors of " + i + ":
                        "); for(int j = 2; j < i; j++)
                                if((i%j) == 0) System.out.print(j + " ");
                                System.out.println();
                }
        }
}
```

The above code prints the factors of each number starting from 2 up to 100. Part of the output is as follows:

```
Factors of 2:
Factors of 3:
Factors of 4: 2
Factors of 5:
Factors of 6: 2 3
Factors of 7:
Factors of 8: 2 4
Factors of 9: 3
Factors of 10: 2 5
...
```

Can you think of a way to make the above code more efficient? (Reduce the number of iterations in the inner loop).

Class Fundamentals

Definition

A class is a sort of template which has attributes and methods. An object is an instance of a class, e.g. Riccardo is an object of type Person. A class is defined as follows:

```
class classname {
    >>> declare instance variables type var1;
    type var2;
    >>>...
    type varN;
    // declare methods
    type method1(parameters) {
        // body of method
    }
    type method2(parameters) {
        // body of method
    }
        // ...
    type methodN(parameters) {
      // body of method
    }
}
```

The classes we have used so far had only one method, **main()**, however not all classes specify a main method. The main method is found in the main class of a program (starting point of program).

The Vehicle Class

The following is a class named 'Vehicle' having three attributes, 'passengers' – the number of passengers the vehicle can carry, 'fuelcap' – the fuel capacity of the vehicle and 'mpg' – the fuel consumption of the vehicle (miles per gallon).

```
class Vehicle {
        int passengers; //number of passengers int fuelcap;
        //fuel capacity in gallons int mpg; //fuel consumption
}
```

Please note that up to this point there is no OBJECT. By typing the above code a new data type is created which takes three parameters. To create an instance of the Vehicle class we use the following statement:

```
Vehicle minivan = new Vehicle ();
```

To set the values of the parameters we use the following syntax:

```
minivan.fuelcap = 16; //sets value of fuel capacity to 16
```

Note the general form of the previous statement: *object.member*

Using the *Vehicle* class

Having created the Vehicle class, let us create an instance of that class:

```
class VehicleDemo {

    public static void main(String args[]) { Vehicle minivan =

        new Vehicle(); int range;

        >>>assign values to fields in minivan

        minivan.passengers = 7; minivan.fuelcap = 16;

        minivan.mpg = 21;
```

Till now we have created an instance of Vehicle called 'minivan' and assigned values to passengers, fuel capacity and fuel consumption. Let us add some statements to work out the distance that this vehicle can travel with a tank full of fuel:

```
        #   compute the range assuming a full tank of gas range =

        minivan.fuelcap * minivan.mpg;

      System.out.println("Minivan can carry " + minivan.passengers + " with a
      range of " + range); }
}
```

Creating more than one instance

It is possible to create more than one instance in the same program, and each instance would have its own parameters. The following program creates another instance, *sportscar*, which has different instance variables and finally display the range each vehicle can travel having a full tank.

```
class TwoVehicles {
      public static void main(String args[]) { Vehicle minivan =
            new Vehicle(); Vehicle sportscar = new Vehicle();

            int range1, range2;
            >>>assign values to fields in minivan
            minivan.passengers = 7; minivan.fuelcap = 16;
            minivan.mpg = 21;
```

|

- assign values to fields in sportscar
sportscar.passengers = 2; sportscar.fuelcap = 14;
sportscar.mpg = 12;

- compute the ranges assuming a full tank of gas range1 =
minivan.fuelcap * minivan.mpg;
range2 = sportscar.fuelcap * sportscar.mpg;
System.out.println("Minivan can carry " + minivan.passengers
+
" with a range of " + range1); System.out.println("Sportscar can
carry " + sportscar.passengers +
" with a range of " + range2);

}

}

Creating Objects

In the previous code, an object was created from a class. Hence 'minivan' was an object which was created at run time from the 'Vehicle' class – vehicle minivan = **new** Vehicle( ) ; This statement allocates a space in memory for the object and it also creates a reference. We can create a reference first and then create an object:

Vehicle minivan; // reference to object only minivan = new Vehicle ( ); //
an object is created

Reference Variables and Assignment

Consider the following statements:

Vehicle car1 = new Vehicle ( );

Vehicle car2 = car 1;

We have created a new instance of type Vehicle named car1. However note that car2 is **NOT** another instance of type Vehicle. car2 is the same object as car1 and has been assigned the same properties,

car1.mpg = 26; // sets value of mpg to 26

If we had to enter the following statements:

System.out.println(car1.mpg);

System.out.println(car2.mpg);

The expected output would be 26 twice, each on a separate line.

car1 and car2 are not linked. car2 can be re-assigned to another data type:

```
Vehicle car1 = new Vehicle();

Vehicle car2 = car1;

Vehicle car3 = new Vehicle();

car2 = car3; // now car2 and car3 refer to the same object.
```

Methods

Methods are the functions which a particular class possesses. These functions usually use the data defined by the class itself.

```
>>> adding a range() method class

Vehicle {

        int passengers; // number of passengers int fuelcap; //

        fuel capacity in gallons

        int mpg; // fuel consumption in miles per gallon

        >>> Display the range. void

        range() {

                System.out.println("Range is " + fuelcap * mpg);

        }

}
```

Note that 'fuelcap' and 'mpg' are called directly without the dot (.) operator. Methods take the following general form:

```
ret-type name( parameter-list ) {

• body of method

}
```

'ret-type' specifies the type of data returned by the method. If it does not return any value we write **void**. 'name' is the method name while the 'parameter-list' would be the values assigned to the variables of a particular method (empty if no arguments are passed).

```
class AddMeth {

        public static void main(String args[]) {
```

```
|
        Vehicle minivan = new Vehicle(); Vehicle

        sportscar = new Vehicle(); int range1, range2;

        >>> assign values to fields in minivan

        minivan.passengers = 7; minivan.fuelcap = 16;

        minivan.mpg = 21;

        >>> assign values to fields in sportscar

        sportscar.passengers = 2; sportscar.fuelcap = 14;

        sportscar.mpg = 12;

        System.out.print("Minivan can carry " +
        minivan.passengers + ". ");

        minivan.range(); // display range of minivan

        System.out.print("Sportscar can carry " +
        sportscar.passengers + ". ");

        sportscar.range(); // display range of sportscar.

    }
}
```

Returning from a Method

When a method is called, it will execute the statements which it encloses in its curly brackets, this is referred to what the method *returns*. However a method can be stopped from executing completely by using the **return** statement.

```
void myMeth() {

    int i;

    for(i=0; i<10; i++) {

        if(i == 5) return; // loop will stop when i = 5

        System.out.println();

    }
}
```

|

Hence the method will exit when it encounters the **return** statement or the **closing curly bracket ' } '**

There can be more than one exit point in a method depending on particular conditions, but one must pay attention as too many exit points could render the code unstructured and the program will not function as desired (plan well your work).

```
void myMeth() {

        // ...

        if(done) return;

        // ...

        if(error) return;

}
```

Returning a Value

Most methods return a value. You should be familiar with the **sqrt( )** method which returns the square root of a number. Let us modify our range method to make it return a value:

- Use a return value. class

```
Vehicle {

        int passengers; // number of passengers int fuelcap; //

        fuel capacity in gallons

        int mpg; // fuel consumption in miles per gallon

        >>> Return the range. int

        range() {

                return mpg * fuelcap; //returns range for a particular vehicle

        }

}
```

Please note that now our method is no longer **void** but has **int** since it returns a value of type integer. It is important to know what type of variable a method is expected to return in order to set the parameter type correctly.

Main program:

class RetMeth {

public static void main(String args[]) { Vehicle minivan =

new Vehicle(); Vehicle sportscar = new Vehicle(); int

range1, range2;

- assign values to fields in minivan

minivan.passengers = 7; minivan.fuelcap = 16;

minivan.mpg = 21;

- assign values to fields in sportscar

sportscar.passengers = 2; sportscar.fuelcap = 14;

sportscar.mpg = 12;

- get the ranges

range1 = minivan.range();

range2 = sportscar.range();

System.out.println("Minivan can carry " + minivan.passengers + " with range of " + range1 + " Miles");

System.out.println("Sportscar can carry " + sportscar.passengers + " with range of " + range2 + " miles");

}

}

Study the last two statements, can you think of a way to make them more efficient, eliminating the use of the two statements located just above them?

Methods which accept Parameters:

We can design methods which when called can accept a value/s. When a value is passed to a method it is called an **Argument**, while the variable that receives the argument is the **Parameter**.

>>> Using Parameters. class

ChkNum {

return true if x is even

boolean isEven(int x) { ← if((x%2) ==

0) return true;

else return false;

}

}

The method accepts a value of type integer, the parameter is x, while the argument would be any value passed to it

class ParmDemo {

public static void main(String args[]) { ChkNum e = new

ChkNum();

if(e.isEven(10)) System.out.println("10 is even."); if(e.isEven(9))

System.out.println("9 is even."); if(e.isEven(8)) System.out.println("8 is

even.");

}

}

Predicted Output:

10 is even.

8 is even.

A method can accept more than one parameter. The method would be declared as follows:

int myMeth(int a, double b, float c) {

>>> ...

}

The following examples illustrates this:

```
class Factor {

    boolean isFactor(int a, int b) { if( (b % a) == 0)

        return true; else return false;

    }

}

class IsFact {

    public static void main(String args[]) { Factor x = new

        Factor();

        if(x.isFactor(2, 20)) System.out.println("2 is a factor.");

        if(x.isFactor(3, 20)) System.out.println("this won't be displayed");

    }

}
```

Note that these statements are validating 'x', and print the correct statement.

Predicted Output:

2 is a factor.

If we refer back to our 'vehicle' example, we can now add a method which works out the fuel needed by a particular vehicle to cover a particular distance. One has to note here that the result of this method, even if it takes integers as parameters, might not be a whole number.

Therefore one has to specify that the value that the method returns, in this case we can use 'double':

```
double fuelneeded(int miles) {

    return (double) miles / mpg;
}
```

Updated vehicle class:

```
class Vehicle {

      int passengers; // number of passengers int fuelcap; //

      fuel capacity in gallons

      int mpg; // fuel consumption in miles per gallon


      >>> Return the range. int

      range() {

            return mpg * fuelcap;

      }


      >>> Compute fuel needed for a given distance. double

      fuelneeded(int miles) {

            return (double) miles / mpg;

      }

}
```

Main Program:

```
class CompFuel {

      public static void main(String args[]) { Vehicle minivan =

            new Vehicle(); Vehicle sportscar = new Vehicle();

            double gallons;

            int dist = 252;


            >>>assign values to fields in minivan

            minivan.passengers = 7;
```

```
minivan.fuelcap = 16;

minivan.mpg = 21;
```

- assign values to fields in sportscar

```
sportscar.passengers = 2; sportscar.fuelcap = 14;

sportscar.mpg = 12;

gallons = minivan.fuelneeded(dist);

System.out.println("To go " + dist + " miles minivan needs " +

gallons + " gallons of fuel.");

gallons = sportscar.fuelneeded(dist); //overwriting same variable

System.out.println("To go " + dist + " miles sportscar needs " +

gallons + " gallons of fuel.");

    }

}
```

Predicted Output:

To go 252 miles minivan needs 12.0 gallons of fuel.

To go 252 miles sportscar needs 21.0 gallons of fuel.

☐ **Project: Creating a Help class from the Help3.java**

In order to carry out this task we must examine the Help3.java and identifies ways how we can break down the code into classes and methods. The code can be broken down as follows:

A method which displays the 'help' text - helpon( )
A method which displays the menu - showmenu( )
A method which checks (validates) the entry by the user - isvalid( )

Method helpon( )

```
void helpon(int what) {

    switch(what) {

      case '1':

            System.out.println("The if:\n");

            System.out.println("if(condition) statement;");

            System.out.println("else statement;");

            break;

      case '2':

            System.out.println("The switch:\n");

            System.out.println("switch(expression) {"); System.out.println("

            case constant:"); System.out.println(" statement sequence");

            System.out.println(" break;"); System.out.println(" // ...");

            System.out.println("}"); break;


      case '3':

            System.out.println("The for:\n");

            System.out.print("for(init; condition; iteration)");

            System.out.println(" statement;");

            break;
```

```
        case '4':
                System.out.println("The while:\n"); System.out.println("while(condition)
                statement;"); break;
        case '5':
                System.out.println("The do-while:\n"); System.out.println("do
                {"); System.out.println(" statement;"); System.out.println("}
                while (condition);"); break;
        case '6':
                System.out.println("The break:\n"); System.out.println("break; or
                break label;"); break;
        case '7':
                System.out.println("The continue:\n"); System.out.println("continue; or
                continue label;"); break;
        }
        System.out.println();
}
```

Method showmenu( )

```
void showmenu() {
        System.out.println("Help on:");
        System.out.println(" 1. if");
        System.out.println(" 2. switch");
        System.out.println(" 3. for");
```

```
        System.out.println(" 4. while");
        System.out.println(" 5. do-while");
        System.out.println(" 6. break");
        System.out.println(" 7. continue\n");
        System.out.print("Choose one (q to quit): ");
}
```

Method isvalid( )

```
boolean isvalid(int ch) {
        if(ch < '1' | ch > '7' & ch != 'q') return false; else return true;
}
```

Class Help

```
class Help {
        void helpon(int what) {
                switch(what) {
                case '1':
                        System.out.println("The if:\n");
                        System.out.println("if(condition) statement;");
                        System.out.println("else statement;");
                        break;
                case '2':
                        System.out.println("The switch:\n");
                        System.out.println("switch(expression) {");
                        System.out.println(" case constant:");
                        System.out.println(" statement sequence");
```

```
System.out.println(" break;");

System.out.println(" // ...");

System.out.println("}");

break;

case '3':

System.out.println("The for:\n");

System.out.print("for(init; condition; iteration)");

System.out.println(" statement;"); break;

case '4':

System.out.println("The while:\n");

System.out.println("while(condition)
statement;");

break;

case '5':

System.out.println("The do-while:\n"); System.out.println("do

{"); System.out.println(" statement;"); System.out.println("}

while (condition);"); break;

case '6':

System.out.println("The break:\n"); System.out.println("break; or

break label;"); break;

case '7':

System.out.println("The continue:\n");
```

```
System.out.println("continue; or continue label;");
break;
}
System.out.println();
}
void showmenu() {
System.out.println("Help on:");
System.out.println(" 1. if");
System.out.println(" 2. switch");
System.out.println(" 3. for");
System.out.println(" 4. while");
System.out.println(" 5. do-while");
System.out.println(" 6. break");
System.out.println(" 7. continue\n");
System.out.print("Choose one (q to quit): ");
}
boolean isvalid(int ch) {
if(ch < '1' | ch > '7' & ch != 'q') return false;
else return true;
}
}
```

Main Program:

```
class HelpClassDemo {
public static void main(String args[])
throws java.io.IOException {
char choice;
```

```
        Help hlpobj = new Help();

        for(;;) {

                do {

                        hlpobj.showmenu();

                        do {

                                choice = (char) System.in.read();

                        } while(choice == '\n' | choice == '\r'); } while(

                !hlpobj.isvalid(choice) );

                if(choice == 'q') break;

                System.out.println("\n");

                hlpobj.helpon(choice);

                }

        }

}
```

Constructors

In previous examples when working with the vehicle class we did assign values to the class variables by using statements like: minivan.passengers = 7;

To accomplish this task Java programmers use constructors. A constructor is created by default and initializes all member variables to zero. However we can create our constructors and set the values the way we want, e.g.

```
class MyClass {

        int x;

        MyClass() {

                x = 10;

        }

}
```

This is the constructor

```
class ConsDemo {

        public static void main(String args[]) { MyClass t1 = new

                MyClass(); MyClass t2 = new MyClass();

        System.out.println(t1.x + " " + t2.x);

        }

}
```

Predicted Output:

10 10

Constructor having parameters

We can edit our previous constructor to create a parameter:

```
MyClass(int i) {

x = i;

}
```

If we edit the main program, by changing the statements which initiate the two objects:

```
MyClass t1 = new MyClass(10);

MyClass t2 = new MyClass(88);
```

The output would now be:

10 88

The values 10 and 88 are first passed on to 'i' and then are assigned to 'x'.

Now we can modify our vehicle class and add a constructor:

```
>>> Constructor for Vehicle class Vehicle(int p,

int f, int m) {

        passengers = p;

        fuelcap = f; mpg = m;

}
```

|

The main program would be as follows:

```
class VehConsDemo {

        public static void main(String args[]) {

        // construct complete vehicles

        Vehicle minivan = new Vehicle(7, 16, 21);

        Vehicle sportscar = new Vehicle(2, 14, 12);

        double gallons;

        int dist = 252;

        gallons = minivan.fuelneeded(dist);

        System.out.println("To go " + dist + " miles minivan needs " + gallons + "
        gallons of fuel.");

        gallons = sportscar.fuelneeded(dist);

        System.out.println("To go " + dist + " miles sportscar needs " + gallons + "
        gallons of fuel.");

        }

}
```

Overloading Methods and Constructors

The term overloading refers to the act of using the same method/constructor name in a class but different parameter declarations. Method overloading is an example of Polymorphism.

Method Overloading

```
>>> Demonstrate method overloading. class

        Overload {

                void ovlDemo() { System.out.println("No

                parameters");

                }

            Overload ovlDemo for one integer parameter. void ovlDemo(int

                a) {
```

```
System.out.println("One parameter: " + a);
}
// Overload ovlDemo for two integer parameters.
int ovlDemo(int a, int b) {
System.out.println("Two parameters: " + a + " " + b);
return a + b;
}
>>> Overload ovlDemo for two double parameters. double
ovlDemo(double a, double b) { System.out.println("Two double
parameters: " + a + " "+ b);
return a + b;
}
}
```

Main Program:

```
class OverloadDemo {
public static void main(String args[]) { Overload ob = new
Overload(); int resI;
double resD;
>>> call all versions of ovlDemo() ob.ovlDemo();
System.out.println(); ob.ovlDemo(2);
System.out.println();
resI = ob.ovlDemo(4, 6); System.out.println("Result of ob.ovlDemo(4, 6): "
+
```

```
|

        resI);

        System.out.println();

        resD = ob.ovlDemo(1.1, 2.32);

        System.out.println("Result of ob.ovlDemo(1.1, 2.32):
        " + resD);

    }

}
```

Predicted Output:

```
No parameters

One parameter: 2

Two parameters: 4 6

Result of ob.ovlDemo(4, 6): 10

Two double parameters: 1.1 2.32

Result of ob.ovlDemo(1.1, 2.32): 3.42
```

Automatic Type Conversion for Parameters of overloaded Methods

```
class Overload2 {

    void f(int x) {

                System.out.println("Inside f(int): " + x);

    }

    void f(double x) {

        System.out.println("Inside f(double): " + x);

    }

}
```

Main Program:

```
class TypeConv {

        public static void main(String args[]) { Overload2 ob = new

                Overload2(); int i = 10;

                double d = 10.1;

                byte b = 99;

                short s = 10;

                float f = 11.5F;


                ob.f(i); // calls ob.f(int)

                ob.f(d); // calls ob.f(double)

                ob.f(b); // calls ob.f(int) – type conversion ob.f(s); // calls ob.f(int) –

                type conversion ob.f(f); // calls ob.f(double) – type conversion

        }

}
```

Predicted Output:

Inside f(int): 10

Inside f(double): 10.1

Inside f(int): 99

Inside f(int): 10

Inside f(double): 11.5

Even though "f" had been defined with two parameters, 'int' and 'double', it is possible to pass a different data type and automatic conversion occurs. 'byte' and 'short' are converted to 'int' while 'float' is converted to 'double' and the respective methods are called.

Overloading Constructors

>>> Overloading constructors. class

```
MyClass {
        int x;
    MyClass() {
        System.out.println("Inside MyClass()."); x = 0;
    }
    MyClass(int i) {
        System.out.println("Inside MyClass(int).");
        x = i;
    }
    MyClass(double d) {
        System.out.println("Inside MyClass(double).");
        x = (int) d;
    }
    MyClass(int i, int j) {
        System.out.println("Inside MyClass(int, int)."); x = i * j;
    }
}
```

Main Program:

```
class OverloadConsDemo {
    public static void main(String args[]) {
        MyClass t1 = new MyClass();
        MyClass t2 = new MyClass(88);
        MyClass t3 = new MyClass(17.23);
```

```
            MyClass t4 = new MyClass(2, 4);

            System.out.println("t1.x: " + t1.x);

            System.out.println("t2.x: " + t2.x);

            System.out.println("t3.x: " + t3.x);

            System.out.println("t4.x: " + t4.x);

        }

}
```

Predicted Output:

Inside MyClass().

Inside MyClass(int).

Inside MyClass(double).

Inside MyClass(int, int).

t1.x: 0

t2.x: 88

t3.x: 17

t4.x: 8

In Java programming, overloading constructors is a technique used to allow an object to initialize another. This makes coding more efficient.

```
class Summation {

        int sum;

        #    Construct from an integer

        Summation(int num) {

                sum = 0;

                for(int i=1; i <= num; i++) sum += i;

        }

        #    Construct from another object (ob)
```

|

```
        Summation(Summation ob) {

                sum = ob.sum;

        }

}
```

Main Program:

```
class SumDemo {

        public static void main(String args[]) { Summation s1 = new

                Summation(5); Summation s2 = new Summation(s1);

                System.out.println("s1.sum: " + s1.sum);

                System.out.println("s2.sum: " + s2.sum);

        }

}
```

Predicted Output:

s1.sum: 15

s2.sum: 15

In the above example, when s2 is constructed, it takes the value of the summation of s1. Hence there is no need to recompute the value.

Access Specifiers: public and private

Whenever we started a class, we always wrote 'public'. If one writes 'class' only, by default it is taken to be public.

- Public and private access. class

```
MyClass {

        private int alpha; // private access public int beta;

        // public access

        int gamma; // default access (essentially public)
```

|

/* Methods to access alpha. Members of a class can access a private member of the same class.

*/

```
        void setAlpha(int a) {
                alpha = a;
        }
        int getAlpha() {
                return alpha;
        }
}
```

Main Program:

```
class AccessDemo {
        public static void main(String args[]) {
                MyClass ob = new MyClass();
                ob.setAlpha(-99);
                System.out.println("ob.alpha is " + ob.getAlpha());
```

- You cannot access alpha like this:
- ob.alpha = 10; // Wrong! alpha is private!
- These are OK because beta and gamma are public.

```
                ob.beta = 88;
                ob.gamma = 99;
        }
}
```

Another example using arrays:

class FailSoftArray {

private int a[]; // reference to array

private int errval; // value to return if get() fails public int length; // length is

public

/* Construct array given its size and the value to return if get() fails. */

public FailSoftArray(int size, int errv) { a = new int[size];

errval = errv;

length = size;

}

- Return value at given index. public int

get(int index) {

if(ok(index)) return a[index]; return errval;

}

- Put a value at an index. Return false on failure. public boolean put(int

index, int val) {

if(ok(index)) { a[index] = val;

return true;

}

return false;

}

- Return true if index is within bounds.

private boolean ok(int index) {

```
|
        if(index >= 0 & index < length) return true; return false;
        }
}
```

Main Program:

```
class FSDemo {
    public static void main(String args[]) { FailSoftArray fs = new
        FailSoftArray(5, -1); int x;
        >>>show quiet failures System.out.println("Fail
        quietly."); for(int i=0; i < (fs.length * 2); i++)
            fs.put(i, i*10);
        for(int i=0; i < (fs.length * 2); i++) {
              = fs.get(i);
            if(x != -1) System.out.print(x + " ");
        }
        System.out.println("");
        >>>now, handle failures System.out.println("\nFail with error reports.");
        for(int i=0; i < (fs.length * 2); i++) if(!fs.put(i, i*10))
        System.out.println("Index " + i + " out-of-bounds"); for(int i=0; i < (fs.length *
        2); i++) {
              = fs.get(i);
            if(x != -1) System.out.print(x + " ");
        else
```

```
|
            System.out.println("Index " + i + " out-of-bounds");
            }
      }
}
```

Predicted Output:

Fail with error reports.

Index 5 out-of-bounds

Index 6 out-of-bounds

Index 7 out-of-bounds

Index 8 out-of-bounds

Index 9 out-of-bounds

0 10 20 30 40 Index 5 out-of-bounds Index 6 out-of-bounds Index 7 out-of-bounds

Index 8 out-of-bounds

Index 9 out-of-bounds

Arrays and Strings

Arrays

An array can be defined as a collection of variables of the **same** type defined by a common name, e.g. an array called *Names* which stores the names of your class mates:

Names *name1, name2, name3, ... nameX+

Arrays in Java are different from arrays in other programming languages because they are implemented as objects.

One-dimensional Arrays

Declaration: ***type*** array-name[ ] = new ***type***[***size***];

e.g. int sample[] = new int[10];

The following code creates an array of ten integers, fills it up with numbers using a loop and then prints the content of each location (index) of the array:

```
class ArrayDemo {

        public static void main(String args[]) { int sample[] = new

                int[10];

                int i;

                for(i = 0; i < 10; i = i+1)

                sample[i] = i;

                for(i = 0; i < 10; i = i+1) System.out.println("This is sample[" + i + "]: " +

                sample[i]);

        }

}
```

Predicted Output:

This is sample[0]: 0

This is sample[1]: 1

This is sample[2]: 2

This is sample[3]: 3

This is sample[4]: 4

This is sample[5]: 5

This is sample[6]: 6

This is sample[7]: 7

This is sample[8]: 8

This is sample[9]: 9

The following program contains two loops used to identify the smallest and the largest value stored in the array:

```
class MinMax {

        public static void main(String args[]) {

                int nums[] = new int[10];

                int min, max;

                nums[0] = 99;

                nums[1] = -10;

                nums[2] = 100123;

                nums[3] = 18;

                nums[4] = -978;

                nums[5] = 5623;

                nums[6] = 463;

                nums[7] = -9;

                nums[8] = 287;

                nums[9] = 49;

                min = max = nums[0];

                for(int i=1; i < 10; i++) {

                                        if(nums[i] < min) min = nums[i];
```

```
                    if(nums[i] > max) max = nums[i];
          }
          System.out.println("min and max: " + min + " " + max);
     }
}
```

Predicted Output:

min and max: -978 100123

Sorting an Array – The Bubble Sort

The Bubble sort is one type, the simplest, of sorting algorithms. It can be used to sort data stored in arrays but it is not ideal when the size of the array to sort is large.

```
class Bubble {
     public static void main(String args[]) {
          int nums[] = { 99, -10, 100123, 18, -978, 5623, 463, -9,
          287, 49 }; int a, b, t;
          int size;
          size = 10; // number of elements to sort
          >>> display original array System.out.print("Original
          array is:"); for(int i=0; i < size; i++) System.out.print(" " +
          nums[i]); System.out.println();
          >>> This is the Bubble sort.
          for(a=1; a < size; a++) for(b=size-1; b >= a; b--) {
```

103

```
            if(nums[b-1] > nums[b]) { // if out of order

            >>> exchange elements t =

                nums[b-1];

                nums[b-1] = nums[b];

                nums[b] = t;

                }

            }
```

- display sorted array System.out.print("Sorted array is:"); for(int

```
        i=0; i < size; i++)

            System.out.print(" " + nums[i]);

            System.out.println();

        }

}
```

Predicted Output:

Original array is: 99 -10 100123 18 -978 5623 463 -9 287 49

Sorted array is: -978 -10 -9 18 49 99 287 463 5623 100123

Two-Dimensional Arrays:

A two dimensional array is like a list of one-dimensional arrays. Declaration is as follows:

int table[][] = new int[10][20];

This would create a table made up of 10 rows (index: 0 to 9) and 20 columns (index: 0 to 19). The following code creates a table, 3 rows by 4 columns, and fills it up woth numbers from 1 to 12. Note that at index [0][0] = 1, [0][1] = 2, [0][2] = 3, [0][3] = 4, [1][0] = 5, etc.

```
class TwoD {

    public static void main(String args[]) {
```

```
            int t, i;
            int table[][] = new int[3][4];
            for(t=0; t < 3; ++t) {
                for(i=0; i < 4; ++i) { table[t][i] = (t*4)+i+1;
                    System.out.print(table[t][i] + " ");
                    }
                System.out.println();
            }
        }
}
```

Different syntax used to declare arrays:

Consider the following: type[ ] var-name;

The square brackets follow the type specifier, not the name of the array variable. For example, the following two declarations are equivalent:

```
int counter[] = new int[3];

int[] counter = new int[3];
```

The following declarations are also equivalent:

```
char table[][] = new char[3][4];

char[][] table = new char[3][4];
```

This alternative declaration form offers convenience when declaring several arrays at the same time.

```
int[] nums, nums2, nums3; // create three arrays
```

This creates three array variables of type **int**. It is the same as writing:

```
int nums[], nums2[], nums3[]; // also, create three arrays
```

The alternative declaration form is also useful when specifying an array as a return type for a method:

```
int[] someMeth( ) { ...
```

This declares that someMeth( ) returns an array of type **int**.

Array References:

Consider a particular array, nums1, and another array, nums2 and at one point in the code we assign one array reference to the other, i.e. nums2 = nums1. Then every action on nums2 will be as if it were on nums1 (nums2 reference is lost).

```
class AssignARef {

        public static void main(String args[]) {

                int i;

                int nums1[] = new int[10];

                int nums2[] = new int[10];

                for(i=0; i < 10; i++)

                        nums1[i] = i;

                for(i=0; i < 10; i++)

                        nums2[i] = -i;

                System.out.print("Here is nums1: ");

                        for(i=0; i < 10; i++)

                                System.out.print(nums1[i] + " ");

                System.out.println();

                System.out.print("Here is nums2: ");

                        for(i=0; i < 10; i++)

                                System.out.print(nums2[i] + " ");

                System.out.println();

                nums2 = nums1; // nums2 is now nums1

                System.out.print("Here is nums2 after assignment:
                ");

                for(i=0; i < 10; i++)

                        System.out.print(nums2[i] + " ");

                System.out.println();
```

```
// now operate on nums1 array through nums2 nums2[3] =
                99;
                System.out.print("Here is nums1 after change through nums2: ");
                for(i=0; i < 10; i++) System.out.print(nums1[i] + " ");
                        System.out.println();
                }
}
```

Predicted Output:

Here is nums1: 0 1 2 3 4 5 6 7 8 9

Here is nums2: 0 -1 -2 -3 -4 -5 -6 -7 -8 -9

Here is nums2 after assignment: 0 1 2 3 4 5 6 7 8 9

Here is nums1 after change through nums2: 0 1 2 99 4 5 6 7 8 9

The Length Variable:

This variable automatically keeps track of the number of items an array can hold and ***NOT*** the actual items. When an array is declared to have ten items, even if one does not put actual data, the length of the array is 10. Something to keep in mind is also when dealing with two dimensional arrays. As already explained in the theory lessons, two dimensional arrays are considered to be an array of arrays. Hence calling up the length of such array would return the number of sub-arrays. To access the length of the particular sub-array, one has to write the 'row' index, e.g. ***arrayname* [0].length**

```
!   length of array demo class
LengthDemo {
        public static void main(String args[]) { int list[] = new
                int[10];
                int nums[] = { 1, 2, 3 };
```

```
int table[][] = { // a variable-length table

        {1, 2, 3},

        {4, 5},

        {6, 7, 8, 9}

};
```

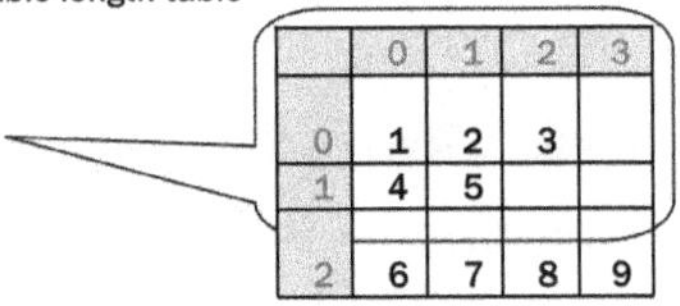

	0	1	2	3
0	1	2	3	
1	4	5		
2	6	7	8	9

```
System.out.println("length of list is " + list.length);

System.out.println("length of nums is " + nums.length);

System.out.println("length of table is " + table.length); //
returns number of rows

System.out.println("length of table[0] is " + table[0].length);

System.out.println("length of table[1] is " + table[1].length);

System.out.println("length of table[2] is " + table[2].length);

System.out.println();

•   using length to initialize list for(int i=0; i <

list.length; i++)

        list[i] = i * i; System.out.print("Here is list:

");

•   using length to display list

for(int i=0; i < list.length; i++) System.out.print(list[i] +

        " ");

System.out.println();

    }

}
```

Predicted Output:

length of list is 10

length of nums is 3

length of table is 3

length of table[0] is 3

length of table[1] is 2

length of table[2] is 4

Here is list: 0 1 4 9 16 25 36 49 64 81

Using the Length to copy elements from one array to another while previously checking for size to prevent errors:

```
//copying an array

class ACopy {

        public static void main(String args[]) { int i;

                int nums1[] = new int[10];

                int nums2[] = new int[10];

                for(i=0; i < nums1.length; i++)

                        nums1[i] = i;

                if(nums2.length >= nums1.length)//size check for(i = 0; i <

                        nums2.length; i++)//limit set

                                nums2[i] = nums1[i];

                for(i=0; i < nums2.length; i++)

                                System.out.print(nums2[i] + " ");

        }

}
```

Using Arrays to create a Queue data structure **

Data structures are used to organize data. Arrays can be used to create ***Stacks*** and ***Queues***. Imagine a stack to be a pile of plates. Stacks implement a Last In First Out system (LIFO). Queues use a First In First Out order (FIFO). We can implement this as a class and also two methods to PUT and GET data to and from a queue. Therefore we put items at the end of the queue and get items from the front. Once a data item is retrieved, it cannot be retrieved again (consumptive). A queue can also be full or empty. The following code creates a noncircular queue (does not reuse locations once they are emptied).

```
class Queue {

    char q[]; // array of type char

    int putloc, getloc; // the put and get indices Queue(int size) {

    q = new char[size+1]; // allocate memory for queue

    putloc = getloc = 0;

    }

    !    method put - places a character into the queue void put(char ch) {

    if(putloc==q.length-1) { System.out.println(" - Queue is full.");

        return;

        }

    putloc++; q[putloc] =

    ch;

    }

    !    method get - get a character from the queue char get() {

        if(getloc == putloc) { System.out.println(" - Queue is

        empty.");

        return (char) 0;
```

```
|
        }
        getloc++;
        return q[getloc];
        }
    }
    #   MAIN PROGRAM
class QDemo {
    public static void main(String args[]) { Queue bigQ = new
        Queue(100); Queue smallQ = new Queue(4);
        char ch;
        int i;
        System.out.println("Using bigQ to store the alphabet.");
        •   put some numbers into bigQ for(i=0; i
        < 26; i++)
            bigQ.put((char) ('A' + i));
        •   retrieve and display elements from bigQ
        System.out.print("Contents of bigQ: "); for(i=0; i < 26; i++) {
            ch = bigQ.get();
            if(ch != (char) 0) System.out.print(ch);
        }

    System.out.println("Using smallQ to generate errors.");
    !   Now, use smallQ to generate some errors for(i=0; i < 5;
    i++) {
```

```
System.out.print("Attempting to store " +
(char) ('Z' - i));
smallQ.put((char) ('Z' - i));
System.out.println();
}
System.out.println();
>>> more errors on smallQ System.out.print("Contents of
smallQ: "); for(i=0; i < 5; i++) {
ch = smallQ.get();
if(ch != (char) 0) System.out.print(ch);
}
}
}
```

Predicted Output:

Using bigQ to store the alphabet.

Contents of bigQ: ABCDEFGHIJKLMNOPQRSTUVWXYZ

Using smallQ to generate errors.

Attempting to store Z

Attempting to store Y

Attempting to store X

Attempting to store W

Attempting to store V – Queue is full.

Contents of smallQ: ZYXW – Queue is empty.

The Enhanced 'for' Loop:

While studying loops we had mentioned the 'enhanced for loop'. This special loop was designed to cater for situations where one would need to manipulate each data item of an array. Declaration of this for loop includes an *iteration variable (itr-var)*, which is a variable that will be used to store temporarily each item from a particular collection (e.g. array, vectors, lists, sets, maps):

```
for(type itr-var : collection) statement-block
```

The type of itr-var should be similar or compatible to the type of the data items held in the array.

Traditional vs. enhanced version:

Traditional:

```
int nums[] = { 1, 2, 3, 4, 5, 6, 7, 8, 9, 10 }; int sum = 0;

for(int i=0; i < 10; i++) sum += nums[i];
```

Enhanced:

```
int nums[] = { 1, 2, 3, 4, 5, 6, 7, 8, 9, 10 };

int sum = 0;

for(int x: nums) sum += x;
```

x will automatically increment

Sample program:

```
class ForEach {

        public static void main(String args[]) {

                int nums[] = { 1, 2, 3, 4, 5, 6, 7, 8, 9, 10 }; int sum = 0;
```

- Use for-each style for to display and sum the values. for(int x : nums) {

```
                System.out.println("Value is: " + x);

                sum += x;

                }

                System.out.println("Summation: " + sum);

        }

}
```

Predicted Output:

Value is: 1

Value is: 2

Value is: 3

Value is: 4

Value is: 5

Value is: 6

Value is: 7

Value is: 8

Value is: 9

Value is: 10

Summation: 55

Strings

The string data type defines is used in Java to handle character strings. It is important to note that in Java, strings are Objects. Every time we write an output statement, the characters we enclose within the quotes are automatically turned into a String object,

System.out.println("Hello World");

Strings are constructed just like other objects, e.g.

String str = new String ("Hello");

String str2 = new String (str); //str2 = "Hello" String str = "I love Java.";

Basic String example:

- Introduce String. class

```
StringDemo {
    public static void main(String args[]) {
        // declare strings in various ways
```

```
String str1 = new String("Java strings are objects.");

String str2 = "They are constructed various ways.";

String str3 = new String(str2);

System.out.println(str1);

System.out.println(str2);

System.out.println(str3);

}

}
```

Predicted Output:

Java strings are objects.

They are constructed various ways.

They are constructed various ways.

Using String Methods

- Some String operations. class

```
StrOps {

    public static void main(String args[]) { String str1 =

        "When it comes to Web programming, Java is #1."; String str2 = new

        String(str1);

        String str3 = "Java strings are powerful."; int result, idx;

        char ch;

        System.out.println("Length of str1: " + str1.length());

        // display str1, one char at a time. for(int i=0; i <

        str1.length(); i++)
```

```
System.out.print(str1.charAt(i));

System.out.println();

if(str1.equals(str2))

        System.out.println("str1 equals str2");

else

System.out.println("str1 does not equal str2"); if(str1.equals(str3))

System.out.println("str1 equals str3"); else

        System.out.println("str1 does not equal str3");

        result = str1.compareTo(str3);

if(result == 0)

System.out.println("str1 and str3 are equal"); else if(result < 0)

System.out.println("str1 is less than str3"); else

        System.out.println("str1 is greater than str3");

// assign a new string to str2

str2 = "One Two Three One";

idx = str2.indexOf("One");

System.out.println("Index of first occurrence
of One: " + idx);

idx = str2.lastIndexOf("One");

System.out.println("Index of last occurrence of
One: " + idx);

}

}
```

Predicted Output:

Length of str1: 45

When it comes to Web programming, Java is #1.

str1 equals str2

str1 does not equal str3

str1 is greater than str3

Index of first occurrence of One: 0

Index of last occurrence of One: 14

String Arrays

- Demonstrate String arrays. class

```
StringArrays {
        public static void main(String args[]) {
        String strs[] = { "This", "is", "a", "test." }; System.out.println("Original
        array: "); for(String s : strs)

        • change a string strs[1] = "was"; strs[3] = "test, too!";
        System.out.println("Modified array: "); for(String s : strs)

                System.out.print(s + " ");
        }
}
```

Predicted Output:

Original array:

This is a test.

Modified array:

This was a test, too!

Strings are said to be 'immutable', i.e. they cannot be changed once they are created. However we can use the method substring() to capture part of a string. The method is declared as follows:

String substring(int *startIndex*, int *endIndex*)

Example:

- Use substring(). class

```
SubStr {
        public static void main(String args[]) {
                String orig = "Java makes the Web move."; // construct a
                substring
                String subst = orig.substring(5, 18);
                System.out.println("Original String: " + orig);
                System.out.println("Sub String: " + subst);
                }
}
```

Note:

0	1	2	3	4	5	6	7	8	9	10	11	12	13	14	15	16	17	18	19	20	21	22	23
J	a	v	a		m	a	k	e	s		t	h	e		W	e	b		m	o	v	e	.

Predicted Output:

Original String: Java makes the Web move.

Sub String: makes the Web

|

- Understanding the "public static void main(String args[])" line of code – FYI only

This line really represents a method call, main, having 'args' (a string array) as parameter. This array stores *command-line arguments* (CLI arguments), which is any information which follows the program name. Consider the following examples:

Example 1:

```
! Display all command-line information. class CLDemo {

    public static void main(String args[]) { System.out.println("There are "

    + args.length +

        command-line arguments.");

    System.out.println("They are: "); for(int i=0;

    i<args.length; i++)

            System.out.println("arg[" + i + "]: " + args[i]);

    }

}
```

If we execute this program in a DOS shell[3] (not via IDE), we use the following syntax:

C:\ java CLDemo one two three **(press enter)**

[!] Put your file (*.class, after compilation) in root drive. Then Start > Run > cmd

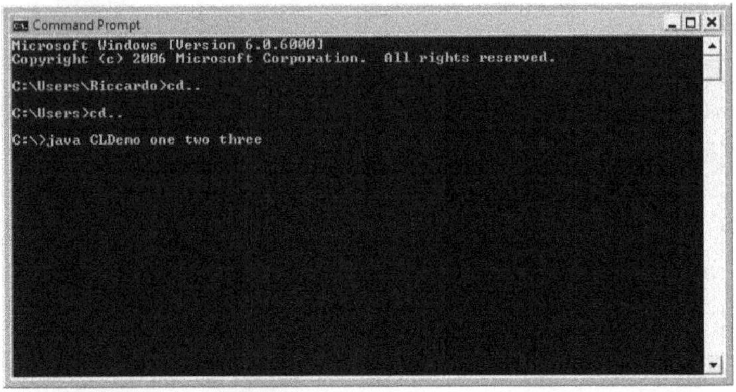

```
Command Prompt
Microsoft Windows [Version 6.0.6000]
Copyright (c) 2006 Microsoft Corporation.  All rights reserved.

C:\Users\Riccardo>cd..

C:\Users>cd..

C:\>java CLDemo one two three
```

The following output will be generated:

There are 3 command-line arguments.

They are:

arg[0]: one

arg[1]: two

arg[2]: three

Example 2:

```
!   A simple automated telephone directory. class Phone {
        public static void main(String args[]) { String numbers[][] =
                {
                { "Tom", "555-3322" }, { "Mary",
                "555-8976" }, { "Jon", "555-1037"
                }, { "Rachel", "555-1400" }
                };
                int i;
                if(args.length != 1)
```

```
System.out.println("Usage: java Phone <name>"); else {
for(i=0; i<numbers.length; i++) { if(numbers[i][0].equals(args[0])) {
        System.out.println(numbers[i][0] + ": " + numbers[i][1]);
        break;
        }
}
if(i == numbers.length) System.out.println("Name not
found."); }
    }
}
```

Execute the code as follows (after compilation):

C>java Phone Mary

Mary: 555-8976

|

Vector and ArrayList

A vector can be defined simply as an Array which can 'grow'. Nowadays it has been replaced by
ArrayList. The following code snippets are examples of implementing Vectors:

>>> beware Vector's List-compatible set method with the parameters reversed:

vector.set(i, object);

>>> yet in the old form: vector.setElementAt(

object, i);

>>> get has two forms, the new List-compatible: Object o =

vector.get(i);

>>> or the old form:

- there is no such thing as: Object o =

vector.getElementAt(i);

- similarly add has two forms: the new list-compatible: vector.add (o);
- or the old form:

vector.addElement(o);

[Further details can be obtained by referring to text book]

As already stated in the previous page ArrayList have replaced Vector in versions of Java following 1.1. ArrayList are much faster than Vector. You can add items to an ArrayList either at a particular index, 'i', or simply at the end of the list. The methods used are as follows:

! adding an element to the middle of a list arrayList.add(i,

object); //i = index

! adding an element to the end of a list arrayList.add(

object);

If one tries to add an element to a list, and this operation results in an error one would get an
ArrayIndexOutOfBoundsException. Possible sources of error include:

! Using a negative index.
! Indexing past the current end of the ArrayList with get or set.

|

>>> Doing a lastIndexOf starting out past the end.

Code snippets used to remove items from an ArrayList:

- Removing item at particular index

```
arrayList.remove( i, object );
```

To remove an item at an unknown index, one must first search for it (better if list is sorted). To remove elements from the entire list one must work backwards since the list shrinks as we go.

```
// removing empty Strings.

for ( int i=arrayList.size(); i>=0; i– )                                    {

    String element = (String)arrayList.get(i);

    if ( element == null || element.length() == 0 )

        {

        arrayList.remove(i);

        }

else

        {

        break;

        }

    }
```

To remove undesirable elements from the head end of a list one has to work forwards without incrementing, always working on element 0. The list shrinks as we go.

- removing empty Strings. while (

```
arrayList.size() > 0 )

    {

    String element = (String)arrayList.get(0);

    if ( element == null || element.length() == 0 )

        {

        arrayList.remove(0);
```

```
        }
    else
        {
        break;
        }
    }
```

To delete the last 'n' elements from the list one can use the following:

```
arrayList.setSize( arrayList.size() - n );
```

Or to delete a portion of it:

```
arrayList.subList( from, to ).clear();
```

Once all the unwanted items have been removed, unless the list will grow again, it is best to use the method ArrayList.trimToSize(). One has to note that some programmers prefer to convert ArrayLists into arrays to perform certain functions as it is much faster. Once done the arrays can be converted back to ArrayLists.

Sample code:

```
import java.util.ArrayList;
public class AraryListDemo {
   public static void main(String[] args) { ArrayList al = new ArrayList();
      System.out.print("Initial size of al : " + al.size()); System.out.print("\n");

      //add.elements to the array list
      al.add("C");
      al.add("A");
      al.add("E");
      al.add("B");
      al.add("D");
      al.add("F");
      al.add(1,"A2");//inserts "A2" into array at index 1
```

```
System.out.print("size of al after " + al.size()); System.out.print("\n");

//display the array list System.out.print("contents of al: " + al );
System.out.print("\n");

//Remove elements from the array list
al.remove("F");
al.remove(2);
System.out.print("size after deletions : " + al.size());
System.out.print("\n");
System.out.print("contents of al:" + al);
    }
}
```

Predicted Output:

Initial size of al: 0

size of al after 7

contents of al: [C, A2, A, E, B, D, F]

size after deletions : 5

contents of al:[C, A2, E, B, D]

Sorting Collections using Comparable Interface (collection of methods):

Employee.java

```
public class Employee implements Comparable {

        int EmpID;
        String Ename;
        double Sal;
        static int i;

        public Employee() {
                EmpID = i++;
                Ename = "dont know";
                Sal = 0.0;
        }

        public Employee(String ename, double sal) {
```

```
        |
            EmpID = i++;
            Ename = ename;
            Sal = sal;
        }

        public String toString() {
            return "EmpID " + EmpID + "\n" + "Ename " + Ename + "\ n" + "Sal" + Sal;
        }

        public int compareTo(Object o1) {
            if (this.Sal == ((Employee) o1).Sal)
                return 0;
            else if ((this.Sal) > ((Employee) o1).Sal)
                return 1;
            else
                return -1;
        }
}
```

ComparableDemo.java

```
import java.util.*;

public class ComparableDemo{

        public static void main(String[] args) {

List ts1 = new ArrayList();
            ts1.add(new Employee ("Tom",40000.00)); ts1.add(new
            Employee ("Harry",20000.00)); ts1.add(new Employee
            ("Maggie",50000.00)); ts1.add(new Employee
            ("Chris",70000.00)); Collections.sort(ts1); Iterator itr =
            ts1.iterator();

            while(itr.hasNext()){
                Object element = itr.next();
                System.out.println(element + "\n");

            }

        }
}
```

Predicted Output:

EmpID 1

Ename Harry

Sal20000.0

EmpID 0

Ename Tom

Sal40000.0

EmpID 2

Ename Maggie

Sal50000.0

EmpID 3

Ename Chris

Sal70000.0

The following is another example of sorting. Please note that this code is being presented for reference. The term package is used to group related pieces of a program together. All the related classes will be stored in a sort of folder:

```
package test;

import java.util.*;

public class Farmer implements Comparable { String name;

        int age;

        long income;


        public Farmer(String name, int age) {
```

```
this.name = name;

this.age = age;

}

public Farmer(String name, int age,long income)

{

this.name = name;

this.age = age;

this.income=income;

}

public String getName()

{

return name;

}

public int getAge()

{

return age;

}

public String toString()

{

return name + " : " + age;

}
```

- natural order for this class public int

compareTo(Object o)

```
{
                return getName().compareTo(((Farmer)o).getName());
}

static class AgeComparator implements Comparator
{
    public int compare(Object o1, Object o2)
    {
        Farmer p1 = (Farmer)o1;
        Farmer p2 = (Farmer)o2; if(p1.getIncome()==0 &&
        p2.getIncome()==0 )
            return p1.getAge() - p2.getAge();
        else
            return (int)(p1.getIncome() -
p2.getIncome());
    }
}

public static void main(String[] args)
{
    List farmer = new ArrayList(); farmer.add( new
    Farmer("Joe", 34) ); farmer.add( new Farmer("Ali", 13)
    ); farmer.add( new Farmer("Mark", 25) ); farmer.add(
    new Farmer("Dana", 66) );

    Collections.sort(farmer);
```

```
System.out.println("Sort in Natural order");

System.out.println("t" + farmer);


Collections.sort(farmer,
Collections.reverseOrder());

System.out.println("Sort by reverse natural order"); System.out.println("t" +

farmer);


List farmerIncome = new ArrayList(); farmerIncome.add( new

Farmer("Joe", 34,33)); farmerIncome.add( new Farmer("Ali",

13,3)); farmerIncome.add( new Farmer("Mark", 25,666));

farmerIncome.add( new Farmer("Dana", 66,2));


Collections.sort(farmer, new AgeComparator());

System.out.println("Sort using Age Comparator");

System.out.println("t" + farmer);


Collections.sort(farmerIncome, new AgeComparator());

System.out.println("Sort using Age Comparator But Income Wise");

System.out.println("t" + farmerIncome);


}


public long getIncome() {

return income;

}
```

```
    public void setIncome(long income) { this.income =
            income;
    }

    public void setAge(int age) {
            this.age = age;
    }

    public void setName(String name) { this.name =
            name;
    }
}
```

Predicted Output:

Sort in Natural order

[Ali : 13, Dana : 66, Joe : 34, Mark : 25] Sort by reverse natural order

[Mark : 25, Joe : 34, Dana : 66, Ali : 13] Sort using Age Comparator

[Ali : 13, Mark : 25, Joe : 34, Dana : 66]

Sort using Age Comparator But Income Wise

[Joe : 34, Ali : 13, Mark : 25, Dana : 66]

The following simple example utilizes the Scanner[4] for input:

```
//import package containing scanner
import java.util.*;
```

[4] Scanner is part of the java.util package and can be used for input (keyboard/file)

```
//read an integer and return it to user public class Scan {

        public static void main (String args[]){ //creating instance

                Scanner kb = new Scanner(System.in);

                System.out.println("Enter a number: "); //read integer

                int x = kb.nextInt(); System.out.println("Number: " +

                x);

        }

}
```

Using the scanner to capture text (string variable) from keyboard:

```
import java.util.*;

public class Alphabetize {

        public static void main(String[] args) { //... Declare

            variables.

            Scanner in = new Scanner(System.in); ArrayList<String> words = new

            ArrayList<String>();

            //... Read input one word at a time.

            System.out.println("Enter words. End with EOF (CTRL-Z then Enter)");

            //... Read input one word at a time, adding it to an array list, hasNext to
read more than one word
```

```
while (in.hasNext()) {
                words.add(in.next());
        }

        //... Sort the words.
        Collections.sort(words);

        //... Print the sorted list. System.out.println("\n\nSorted
        words\n"); for (String word : words) {
                System.out.println(word);
        }
    }
}
```

Using the Scanner is the most suggested method compared to the Keyboard Class or the System.in.read . Remember that the Keyboard class was created by you (or given) and is not a standard in Java.

Through file handling, we can read data from and write data to files besides doing all sorts of other operations. Java provides a number of methods for file handling through different classes which are a part of the "java.io" package. The question can arise in the mind of a new programmer as to why file-handling is required. The answer of this question would be in two parts, why do we need to read data from the files and why do we need to save it (write it) to a file.

To answer the first part, Let us suppose that we have a very large amount of data which needs to be input into a program, Something like a 1000 records, If we start inputting the data manually and while we are in half-way through the process, there is a power-failure, then once power is restored, the entire data has to be input again. This would mean a lot of extra work, an easier approach would be to write all the records in a file and save the file after writing 10 or so records, in this case even if there is a power-failure, only some records would be lost and once power is restored, there would be only a few records that would need to be input again. Once all the records are saved in that file, the file-name can be passed to the program, which can then read all the records from the file.

For the second part, consider a system which needs to record the time and name of any error that occurs in the system, this can be achieved through saving the data into a file and the administrator can view the file any time he/she wishes to view it.

Note that if you use a "/" in a path definition in Java in Windows, the path would still resolve correctly and if you use the Windows conventional "\", then you have to place two forward slashes "\\" as a single "\" would be taken as an escape-sequence.

```
import java.io.*;


public class streams

{

        public static void main(String []args)

        {

                File f1=new File("Folder/FILE");

                File f2=new File("Folder/FILE1");


                String s;


                if(f1.exists())
```

```
{
    if(f1.isFile())
    {
        System.out.println("File Name is
"+f1.getName());
        s=f1.getParent();

        File f3=new File(s);

        f1.renameTo(new File("Folder/abc"));

        f2.delete();

        if (f3.isDirectory())
        {
            System.out.println(f2.getPath());
        }
    }
    else
    {
        System.out.println("Not a File");
    }
}
}
}
```

The output of the program is:

File Name is FILE

Folder

If successfully run , the " FILE " file inside the folder " Folder " will be renamed to " abc " and the " FILE1 " file will be deleted.

Here is an example of a program that reads its own first six bytes, we have:

```
//0123

import java.io.*;

public class read

{

        public static void main(String []args)

        {

                int s=6;

                int b[]=new int[6];

                char c[]=new char[6];

                try

                {

                        FileInputStream f = new
FileInputStream("read.java");

                        for (int i=0; i&lt;6; i++)

                        {

                                b[i] = f.read();

                                c[i] = (char) b[i];

                        }

                        System.out.println("First 6 bytes of the file
are :");

                        for (int i=0;i&lt;6;i++)
```

```
                        System.out.print(b[i]+" ");


                System.out.println("nnFirst 6 Bytes as characters :");

                for (int i=0;i&lt;6;i++)

                        System.out.print(c[i]);

        }

        catch (Exception e)

        {

                System.out.println("Error");

        }

    }

}
```

Predicted Ouptut:

First 6 bytes of the file are :

47 47 48 49 50 51

First 6 Bytes as characters are :

//0123

Notice that the FileInputStream object is created inside a try-catch block since if the specified-file does not exist, an exception is raised. In the same way to write data to a file byte-by-byte, we have:

```
import java.io.*;


public class writer

{
```

```
public static void main(String []args) throws IOException

{

        String s="Hello";

        byte b[]=s.getBytes();

        FileOutputStream f=new FileOutputStream("file.txt");

        int i=0;

        while(i < b.length)

        {

                f.write(b[i]);

                i++;

        }

}

}
```

If the file called file.txt does not exist, it is automatically created. If we place a true in the constructor for the FileOutputStream, then the file would be opened in append mode.

Template to read data from disk

```
import java.util.Scanner;

import java.io.File;

import java.io.FileNotFoundException; class

_______________{

    public static void main(String args[])

        throws FileNotFoundException { Scanner diskScanner

        = new Scanner(new

    File("__________"));
```

```
            ________ = diskScanner.nextInt();
            ________ = diskScanner.nextDouble();
            ________ = diskScanner.nextLine();
            ________ = diskScanner.findInLine(".").charAt(0);
            // etc
    }
}
```

The following program reads item from a file on disk. You have to create the file using a text editor (MS Notepad), and save the file in the same location as your classes. You can use the following examples for the riddles file (save the file as riddles.txt):

What is black and white and red all over?

An embarrassed zebra

What is black and white and read all over?

A newspaper

What other word can be made with the letters of ALGORITHM?

LOGARITHM

Program Code:

```
public class Riddle{
    private String question;
    private String answer;
    public Riddle(String q, String a) { question = q;
        answer = a;
    }

    public String getQuestion() {
```

```
            |

            return question;

        }

        public String getAnswer(){

            return answer;

        }

}
```

Main Program:

```
import java.io.*;

import java.util.Scanner;

public class RiddleFileReader

{  private Scanner fileScan; // For file input

      private Scanner kbScan;                    // For keyboard input


      public RiddleFileReader(String fName)

      { kbScan = new Scanner(System.in); try

            { File theFile = new File(fName); fileScan = new Scanner(theFile);

                  fileScan = fileScan.useDelimiter("\r\n");

            } catch (IOException e)

            { e.printStackTrace(); } // catch()

      } // RiddleFileReader() constructor public Riddle

      readRiddle()

      { String ques = null; String ans = null;

            Riddle theRiddle = null;
```

```
|
        if (fileScan.hasNext())
            ques = fileScan.next();
        if (fileScan.hasNext())
        { ans = fileScan.next(); theRiddle = new Riddle(ques,
            ans);
        } // if
        return theRiddle;
    } // readRiddle()
    public void displayRiddle(Riddle aRiddle)
    { System.out.println(aRiddle.getQuestion()); System.out.print("Input any letter to
        see answer:"); String str = kbScan .next(); // Ignore KB input
        System.out.println(aRiddle.getAnswer());

    } // displayRiddle()
    public static void main(String[] args)
    {   RiddleFileReader rfr =
            new RiddleFileReader("riddles.txt"); Riddle riddle =
        rfr.readRiddle(); while (riddle != null)
        {   rfr.displayRiddle(riddle);
            riddle = rfr.readRiddle();
        }
    }
}
```

Template to write (save) data to disk

```
import java.io.File;

import java.io.FileNotFoundException; import

java.io.PrintStream;

class ________________ {

        public static void main(String args[]) throws

                FileNotFoundException { PrintStream diskWriter

                =

                new PrintStream("____________");

                diskWriter.print(_____);

                diskWriter.println(_____);

                // Etc.

        }

}
```

Introduction to GUI using AWT/Swing

Java GUIs were built with components from the Abstract Window Toolkit (AWT) in package **java.awt**. When a Java application with an AWT GUI executes on different Java platforms, the application's GUI components display differently on each platform. Consider an application that displays an object of type Button (package java.awt). On a computer running the Microsoft Windows operating system, the Button will have the same appearance as the buttons in other Windows applications. Similarly, on a computer running the Apple Mac OS X operating system, the Button will have the same look and feel as the buttons in other Macintosh applications.

Swing GUI components allow you to specify a uniform look-and-feel for your application across all platforms or to use each platform's custom look-and-feel. An application can even change the look-and-feel during execution to enable users to choose their own preferred look-and-feel. Swing components are implemented in Java, so they are more portable and flexible than the original Java GUI components from package java.awt, which were based on the GUI components of the underlying platform. For this reason, Swing GUI components are generally preferred.

Swing advantages:

- ☐ Swing is faster.
- ☐ Swing is more complete.
- ☐ Swing is being actively improved.

AWT advantages:

- ☐ AWT is supported on older, as well as newer, browsers so Applets written in AWT will run on more browsers.
- ☐ The Java Micro-Edition, which is used for phones, TV set top boxes, PDAs, etc, uses AWT, not Swing.

Using Swing to create a small Window

[Refer to the code on the next page]

1. First we have to import all classes in the javax.swing package, although we use only the JFrame class in the following example. "Windows" are implemented by the JFrame class.
2. Make the application quit when the close box is clicked.
3. After the window has been constructed in memory, display it on the screen. The setVisible call also starts a separate thread to monitor user interaction with the interface.
4. When we are finished setting up and displaying the window, don't call System.exit(0). We don't want to stop the program. Although main returns, execution continues because the call to setVisible(true) created another execution thread, A GUI program builds the user interface, then just "goes to sleep" until the user does something.

```
import javax.swing.*;

class FirstWindow {

        public static void main(String[] args) { JFrame window =

          new JFrame();

          window.setDefaultCloseOperation(JFrame.EXIT_ON_CLOSE);
          window.setVisible(true);

        }

}
```

The window created can be resized and dragged around. One can also minimize, maximize or close the window. Now that we created a window we can set the text which appears in the title bar:

```
import javax.swing.*;

class MyWindow2 extends JFrame {

          public static void main(String[] args) {

                    MyWindow2 window = new MyWindow2();

                    window.setVisible(true);

                    }

                    public MyWindow2() {                    //constructor

                    setTitle("My Window Title using JFrame Subclass");

                    setDefaultCloseOperation(JFrame.EXIT_ON_CLOSE); }

}
```

Inserting Text Inside Window

```
import java.awt.*;                                   // required for FlowLayout.
import javax.swing.*;

class MyWindow3 extends JFrame {

        public static void main(String[] args) {
```

```
            MyWindow3 window = new MyWindow3();
            window.setVisible(true);
        }
        public MyWindow3 () {
            //Create content panel and set layout
            JPanel content = new JPanel();
            content.setLayout(new FlowLayout());
            //... Add one label to the content pane.
            JLabel greeting = new JLabel("Hello World.");
            content.add(greeting);

            //... Set window (JFrame) characteristics
            setContentPane(content); pack();
            setTitle("MyWindow using JFrame Subclass");
            setDefaultCloseOperation(JFrame.EXIT_ON_CLOSE);
            setLocationRelativeTo(null); // Centre window.
        }
}
```

Creating a simple application implementing JButton, JTextfield and JLabel

```
import java.awt.*;
import javax.swing.*;
class DogYears extends JFrame {
        private JTextField _humanYearsTF = new JTextField(3);
        private JTextField _dogYearsTF              = new JTextField(3);
```

```
public DogYears() {

        JButton convertBtn = new JButton("Convert");

        JPanel content = new JPanel();
        content.setLayout(new FlowLayout());

        content.add(new JLabel("Dog Years")); content.add(_dogYearsTF);

        content.add(convertBtn); content.add(new JLabel("Human

        Years")); content.add(_humanYearsTF); setContentPane(content);

        //window attributes pack();

        setTitle("Dog Year Converter");
        setDefaultCloseOperation(JFrame.EXIT_ON_CLOSE);

        setLocationRelativeTo(null);

        }

    public static void main(String[] args) { //main DogYears window =

    new DogYears(); window.setVisible(true);

  }

}
```

The final touch to our application is to set the action to perform while the user interacts with the application:

```
import java.awt.*;

import javax.swing.*;

import java.awt.event.*;                    // Needed for ActionListener

class DogYears2 extends JFrame {

    private static final int DOG_YEARS_PER_HUMAN_YEAR = 7;

    private JTextField _humanYearsTF = new                  JTextField(3);
    private JTextField _dogYearsTF                  = new   JTextField(3);
```

```
public DogYears2() {

JButton convertBtn = new JButton("Convert"); convertBtn.addActionListener(new

ConvertBtnListener()); _dogYearsTF.addActionListener(new ConvertBtnListener());

_humanYearsTF.setEditable(false);


JPanel content = new JPanel();

content.setLayout(new FlowLayout());


    content.add(new JLabel("Dog Years"));

    content.add(_dogYearsTF); content.add(convertBtn);

    content.add(new JLabel("Human Years"));

    content.add(_humanYearsTF);

      setContentPane(content);

      pack();

      setTitle("Dog Year Converter");

      setDefaultCloseOperation(JFrame.EXIT_ON_CLOSE);

      setLocationRelativeTo(null); // Center window.

}

        class ConvertBtnListener implements ActionListener {

    public void actionPerformed(ActionEvent e) { String dyStr =

      _dogYearsTF.getText();

      int dogYears = Integer.parseInt(dyStr);

      int humanYears = dogYears *
      DOG_YEARS_PER_HUMAN_YEAR;
```

```
                    _humanYearsTF.setText("" + humanYears);
            }
        }

        public static void main(String[] args) { DogYears2 window
            = new DogYears2(); window.setVisible(true);
        }
}
```

Predicted Final Output:

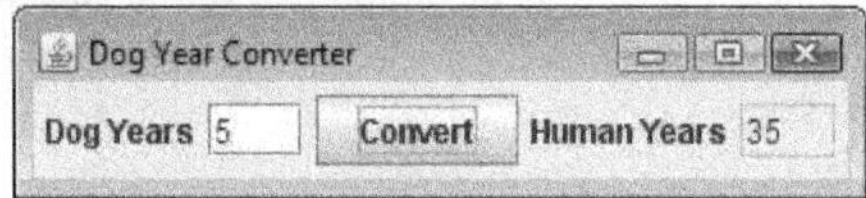

Chapter 4

Basic use of Java

4.1 Data types, constants and operations

The first section of these notes introduced a few small but com plete Java programs, but when you type them into the computer you still have to take a great deal on trust. But with those examples to use as a framework I can now start a more systematic introduction of the Java language and its associated libraries. Actually in the lectures I expect to skim over this material very rapidly: you will in reality learn about the Java data types and syntax as you write programs. However I view it as important that you have reference material in your handout that shows what everything is so that if you have trouble in your coding you have somewhere reasonably close at hand where you can check some details. However if you need a gentle path to settle into Java programming I do suggest that you try various of the example programs and exercises here so that you get used to and comfortable with a good range of Java syntax.

4.1.1 Reserved Words

The first thing to do is to catalogue the words that are reserve d: if you accidentally try to use one of these names as the name of one of your variables or functions you can expect most curious error messages from Java! So even though I do not want to explain what all of these mean yet it may help you if I provide a list of words to be avoided. In some cases of course the presence of a word here will alert you to the availability of some operation, and you can then look up the details in the manual. A clever editor might display words from this list in some alternative colour to help you notice any unintentional uses. An even more clever one might use different colours for the one (such as int) that name basic types, the ones such as for that introduce syntax and ones like true that are just the names of

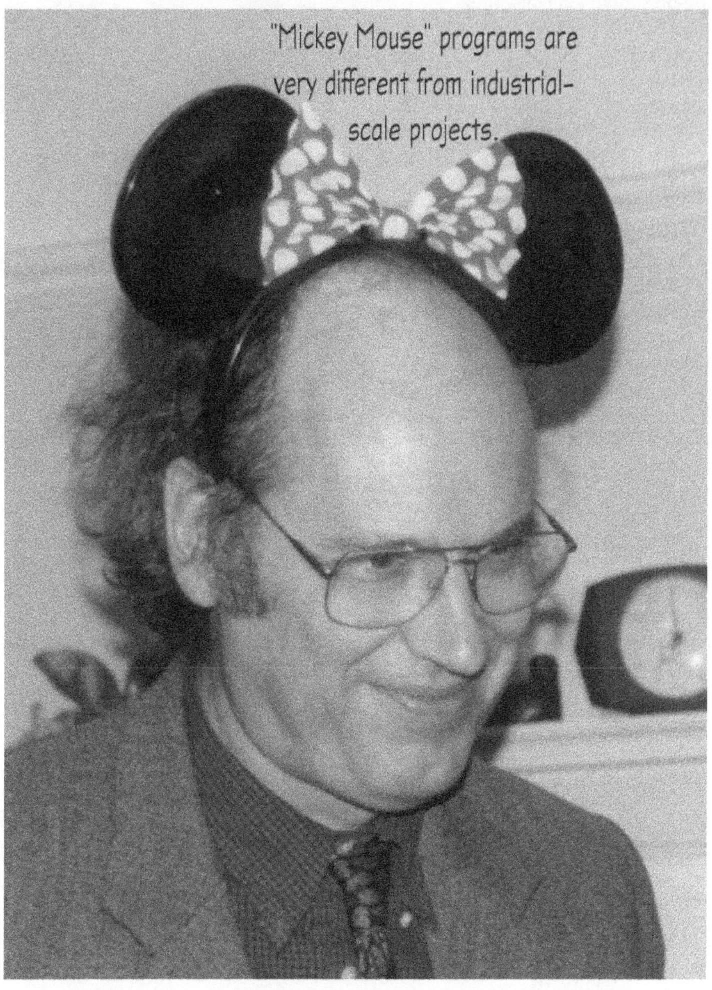

Figure 4.1: Start with some small examples. . .

important built-in constants.

abstract	assert	boolean	break	byte
case	catch	char	class	const
continue	default	do	double	else
enum	extends	false	final	finally
float	for	goto	if	implements
import	instanceof	int	interface	long
native	new	null	package	private
protected	public	return	short	static
strictfp	super	switch	synchronizedthis	
throw	throws	transient	true	try
void	volatile	while		

A joke about the above table of reserved words is that at present Java does not actually use them all — specifically const and goto do not represent any oper-ation supported by Java. By prohibiting people from using these words as names for variables the Java designers have left themselves a little flexibility to extend the language in the future if they want to or are forced to, and they can perhaps give better error messages when people who are used to some other language that does include these keywords first tries out Java.

There are some other words which are used for names that perform important system functions. If you unintentionally define a function w ith one of these names you might find that you have introduced side-effects of amazi ng magnitude when the system calls your function instead of the one it was expecting! Beware here, because although incorrect use of a genuine reserved word will result in a syntax error it could be that defining a function with one of the follo wing names would have subtle or delayed bad consequences rather than a nice clean instant crash.

clone	equals	finalize	getClass	hashCode
notify	notifyAll	toString	wait	

OK so the above information is more negative then positive, but I hope it will rescue a few of you from otherwise most mysterious behaviour when you might otherwise have tried to use one of the reserved words for your own purposes.

4.1.2 Basic Types

Earlier examples used the word int to declare integer variables, and the range of values that can be represented goes from around −2 billion to around +2 billion. To be more precise the smallest valid int is $-2^{31} = -2147483648$ and the largest one is $2^{31} - 1 = 2147483647$. You are not expected to remember the decimal form of the numbers, but you should be aware of roughly how big they are. Integer overflow is ignored: the result of an addition, subtraction o r multiplication will always be just what you would get by representing the true result as a binary number and just keeping the lowest 32 bits. A way to see the consequences of this is to change the Powers program so it goes up to higher powers, say 20. The final section of the output I get is

```
...
8^8 =  16777216
9^9 =  387420489
10^10  = 1410065408
11^11  = 1843829075
12^12  = -251658240
13^13  = -1692154371
14^14  = -1282129920
15^15  = 1500973039
16^16  = 0
17^17  = 1681328401
18^18  = 457441280
19^19  = -306639989
```

where the value shown for 10^{10} is clearly wrong and where we subsequently get values that probably count as rubbish. Note both the fact that overflow can turn positive values into negative ones (and vice versa) and the special case (obvious in retrospect) where 16^{16} shows up as zero. Since 16 is 2^4 the binary representation of 16^{16} is clearly a 1 followed by a string of 64 zeros, and in particular the least significant 32 bits are all zero. This lack of detection of int eger overflow is some-times convenient but it is also a potential major source for getting wrong answers without even knowing it.

Java provides several alternative integer-style primitive data-types which rep-resent different trade-offs between expected speed, space and accuracy. They are:

byte: 8-bit integers in the range −128 to +127;

short: 16-bit integer, range $-2^{15} = -32768$ to $2^{15} - 1 = 32767$;

int: 32-bit integers as discussed already;

long: 64-bit integers, is range is from -2^{63} to $2^{63} - 1$ which means that almost all numbers with up to 19 decimal digits can be represented.

It may be helpful to those who are not already used to the binary representation of signed values if I tabulate the representation used for the byte datatype. The wider integral types use just the natural generalisation:

Number	*Representation in binary*							
	-2^7	2^6	2^5	2^4	2^3	2^2	2^1	2^0
127	0	1	1	1	1	1	1	1
126	0	1	1	1	1	1	1	0
...								
3	0	0	0	0	0	0	1	1
2	0	0	0	0	0	0	1	0
1	0	0	0	0	0	0	0	1
0	0	0	0	0	0	0	0	0
−1	1	1	1	1	1	1	1	1
−2	1	1	1	1	1	1	1	0
−3	1	1	1	1	1	1	0	1
−4	1	1	1	1	1	1	0	0
...								
−126	1	0	0	0	0	0	1	0
−127	1	0	0	0	0	0	0	1
−128	1	0	0	0	0	0	0	0

One way to understand how the negative numbers arose is to see that −1 is the bit-pattern that has the property that if you add 1 to it and ignore the final carry you get the representation that means 0. It can also help to suppose that negative number "really' have an infinite string of 1 bits glued onto th eir left hand end. The representation used is known as "two's complement".

When you write an integer literal in your Java code you can write it in decimal, octal or hexadecimal (base-16). You can also make your written integer either of type int or type long; there is no direct way to write either a byte or short. Decimal numbers are written in the utterly ordinary way you would expect. You add a suffix " L" if you want to make the value a long and you should always do this if the value is outside the range of ordinary available to an int, but you might sometimes like to do it for even small values when using them in a context where arithmetic on them should be done in long precision. Examples are:

12345	an ordinary int
1234567890123L	a long value
10L	a long but with a smallish value
1000000L*1000000L	an expression where the L suffix matters
1000000*1000000	without the L this would overflow.

My belief is that hardly anybody ever wants to write a number in octal these days[1], but Java allows it, taking any number that starts with 0 as being in octal.

[1]But this may be just a matter of fashion, and perhaps elsewhere in the world octal is still appreciated.

Thus 037 is the octal way of writing the number 31. The L suffix can be used to specify long octal values. Observe a slight jollity. If you write the number 0 it is interpreted as being in octal. Fortunately zero is zero whatever radix is used to write it!

Hexadecimal is much more useful. Each hexadecimal digit stands for four bits in the number. Letters from A to F are used to stand for the digits with weight 10 . . .15. Hexadecimal numbers are written with the prefix 0X. Note that the suffix L for long, the X in hexadecimal numbers and the extended digits from A to F can all be written in either upper or lower case. I strongly recommend use of upper case for L since otherwise it is painfully easy for a casual reader to muddle 10l (long ten) and 101 (one hundred and one).

Here are some numbers written in hexadecimal

0X0	this is zero, not gravy powder
0xe	otherwise 14
0xffffffff	-1 as an int
0xBadFace	what other words can you spell?
0x7fffffff	largest int
0x80000000	most negative int
0x00010000	2 to the power 16
0x7fffffffffffffffL	largest long

I rather suspect that the main importance of byte and short is for when you have huge blocks of them[2] where the fact that they take up less space can be of practical value.

Floating point values also come in two flavours, one with a lar ger range and precision than the other. The more restricted one is called float. A float uses 32-bits of memory and can represent values up to about 3.4e38[3] with a precision of six to seven significant figures. Until you have sat through the course on numer-ical analysis please avoid use of it[4]. The more sensible floating point type is called double and uses 64 bits to store numbers with magnitude up to about 1.7e308, with an accuracy of sixteen or seventeen significant figures. The internal repre-sentation of floating point values and the exact behaviour in all circumstances was originally taken from an International Standard referred to as IEEE 754. Some bit-patterns are reserved to represent " +¥" and " −¥" while others are values that are explicitly not representations of valid floating point v alues — these are known as NaNs (Not A Number). A few possibly unexpected effects arise from this. For

---

• See the description later on of arrays.

• ie 3.4×10^{38}.

• In fact a number of the Java library functions require arguments of type float, so it is not possible to avoid this type. Its use is satisfactory in circumstances where the precision it supports is all that is justifiable, for instance when specifying the b rightness of a colour.

instance floating point division never fails: 0.0/0.0 yield s a NaN, while any other value divided by 0.0 results in an infinity. Also if u is a floating point value then it is possible for the expression u == u to evaluate to false (!) because the rules for all numeric comparison operators is that they return false when at least one of their arguments is a NaN. Another oddity is that one can have two floating point values u and v such that both u == v and (1.0/u) != (1.0/v)! This oddity is achieved by having u = -0.0 and v = +0.0. These delicacies are al-most certainly exhibited by most other languages you will come across, but Java documents them carefully since it is very keen indeed to make sure that Java pro-gram will give exactly the same results whatever computer it is run on. Even if it does very delicate things with the marginal and curious cases of floating point arithmetic. Recent versions of the Java language use a keyword strictfp to indicate places where *all* the consequences of IEEE floating point must be hon-oured: specifically its use means that the results computed s hould be identical whatever machine run on, and will have rounding errors exactly as expected. Without strictfp and on some computers Java will deliver results that are both more accurate and are computed faster!

Here are some floating point constants:

0.0	this is	double (by default)	
0.0F	if you REALLY want a float		
1.3e-11	specify	an exponent (double)	
22.9e11F	float not double		
22.9e11D	be explicit that		a double is required
1e1	no "." needed if		there is an "e"
2.	"." can	come at end	
.2	"." can	come at start	
2D	must be	a double	because of the D

I would suggest that you always make your floating point const ants start with a digit and contain a decimal point with at least one digit after it since I think that makes things more readable.

In Java the result of a comparison is of type boolean, and the boolean constants are true and false. As in ML (and unlike the situation in C, in case you know about that), boolean is a quite separate type from int.

Despite the fact that this section is about the Java primitive types and not about the operations that can be performed on data, it will make some of my examples easier if I next mention the ways in which Java can convert from one type to another. In some cases where no information will be lost (eg converting from a byte or short to an int) the conversion will often happen without you having to worry much about it and without anything special having to be written. However the general construction for making a type conversion is called a *cast*, and it is written by using a type name in parentheses as an operator. We have already

already seen a couple of examples in the Draw program where (int)x was used to convert the floating point value x into an integer. The opposite conversion can then of course be written as in

```
for (int i=1; i<10; i++)
        System.out.printf("%22.8g%n", 1.0/(double)i);
```

where the (double) is a cast to convert i to floating point [5]. The format spec-ifier [6] %22.8g is for printing a floating point value in a General format usin g a precision of 8 significant figures and padding with blanks to m ake 22 characters printed in all. Until you understand exactly when automatic conversions apply it may be safest to be explicit. Java allows you to write casts for those conversions that it thinks are sufficiently reasonable. You can cast betw een any of the flavours of integer. When you promote from a narrower integer to a wider one the value is always preserved. When you cast from a wider integer to a narrower one the result is what you get from considering the binary representation of the values concerned, and the cast just throws away unwanted high-order bits. Casts from integers to float and double preserve value as best they can[7]. Casts from float-ing point values to integers turn NaNs into 0, and infinities i nto either the most positive or most negative integer. Floating point values that are too large to be an int or long also turn into the largest available integer. The exact rules for casts from floating point values to byte and short are something to look up in the reference manual in the improbable case it matters to you. There are no casts between boolean and other types. You need to use explicit expressions such as (i != 0) to map from an integer to a truth-value[8].

The type char can be used to declare a variable that holds a single character. To write a constant suitable for putting into such a variable you just write the relevant character within single quote marks, as in

```
char mychar = 'A';
if (myChar == 'q') ...
```

It is frequently necessary to use characters that do not fit so neatly or clearly between quotes. For instance the single quote character itself, or a "character" to represent the end of a line. A set of escape codes are used for these, where instead of a single character one writes a short sequence starting with the escape character " \". The supported escape sequences are:

· In this case the cast is not needed: Java will do the required conversion so that it can perform the division.

· You will see a bunch of common format specifiers just in exampl es here. You can look up full details in the on-line documentation, or find a medium-sized synopsis later in these notes.

· Casts from int or long to float or from long to double can not always preserve an exact result because the floating point format may not have enough precision available. The closest floating point value to the true result will be delive red.

· Unlike the position in C where there is not much distinction between integers and booleans.

\n	newline, linefeed (very commonly used)
\"	double quote mark
\'	single quote mark
\\	use when a single \ is wanted
\b	backspace
\t	tab
\f	newpage, formfeed (unusual)
\r	carriage-return

Carriage returns are used in Windows text files and as line sep aration in some Internet protocols, but when creating simple text files you d o not generally see or need to mention it: Java does any necessary conversions to you so that on Windows, Macintosh and Unix an end of line in a file is talked ab out in your programs as just `\n'.

In addition it is possible to write *nnn* where *nnn* stands for 1, 2 or 3 octal digits: this indicates the character with the specified char acter-code in a standard encoding. Use of octal escapes is not at all common. Furthermore Java allows inclusion of characters from an astonishingly large character set by use of a nota-tion \u followed by four hexadecimal digits. The 16-bit number represented by the hexadecimal digits is taken as being in a set of character encodings known as Unicode. Casts between int and char give direct access to this encoding. For example \u2297 and (char)0x2297 both give the character " ⊗". In fact the Unicode escapes do not just apply within Java character literals but can be used **anywhere** in a Java program where you want an unusual symbol — and this means that in some sense you can have variables names with Greek, Rus-sian and Eastern glyphs in them. Unicode gradually becoming more widely used, but most computers still do not have full Unicode fonts installed, and so exotic characters will not always be displayed properly even though within Java they are handled carefully. The following applet displays the characters that are available using the viewer it is run under. It uses a cast (char) to convert an integer to a character and some fresh library calls (eg setFont(new Font(...)) and drawString). It also illustrate something that you will probably want to retrofit to most of the little examples in these notes. It allocates a BufferedImage that it draws into, and then the paint method just displays whatever is in the bitmap. This does wonders for arranging that when you obscure bits of your window the content gets re-painted nicely!

It also makes a crude modification of the earlier Draw program so that mouse clicks at various places in the window adjust the range of characters displayed.

```
/*
 *  Unicode.java                                    A C Norman
 *
```

```
 .   Display the Unicode characters as supported
 .  by the current browser.
 */
import java.awt.*;
import java.awt.event.*;
import javax.swing.*;
import java.awt.image.*;

public class Unicode extends JApplet implements
                                MouseListener

{
        private boolean isFilled = false;
        private int fontSize = 20; // or whatever!
        private int page = 0;
        private BufferedImage p =
          new BufferedImage(
               32*fontSize,
               35*fontSize,
               BufferedImage.TYPE_BYTE_BINARY);

     public void init()
     {
          addMouseListener(this);
     }

     public void mousePressed(MouseEvent e)
     {
          if (e.getX() < 200) page++;
          else page–;
          if (page > 63) page = 0;
          if (page < 0) page = 63;
          isFilled = false;
          repaint(); // force screen to re-draw
     }

     public void paint(Graphics g)
     {
          if (!isFilled) fillImage();
// Note drawImage may need repeating!!! while
          (!g.drawImage(p, 0, 0, this));
     }
```

```
void fillImage()
{
        Graphics g = p.getGraphics(); g.setColor(Color.WHITE); //
        background g.fillRect(0, 0, 32*fontSize, 35*fontSize);
        g.setFont(new Font("Serif",
                                          Font.PLAIN, fontSize));
        g.setColor(Color.BLACK); // text
        g.drawString("page = " +
                              Integer.toHexString(32*32*page),
                              0, fontSize);
        for (int y=0; y<32; y++)
        {  for (int x=0; x<32; x++)
             { char c = (char)((32*page+y)*32+x);
                  g.drawString(String.valueOf(c),
                                       fontSize*x,
                                       fontSize*(y+2));
             }
        }
        isFilled = true;
}

public void mouseReleased(MouseEvent e) {} public
void mouseClicked(MouseEvent e) {} public void
mouseEntered(MouseEvent e) {} public void
mouseExited(MouseEvent e) {}
}
/* end of Unicode.java */
```

The output from this program will depend on the range of fonts installed on the computer you run it on. PWF Linux has a range of European characters, math-ematical symbols and oddments available. While preparing these notes I ran the code on my home Windows XP system where all sorts of fonts have accumulated over the years, and the image included here (figure 4.2.) is fr om there. I also use a program called Vmware which lets me install many "virtu al" computers on my single home one: using that I installed essentially the version of Linux used on the PWF but told the Linux installer to include support for all available lan-guages: by moving some files into a directory " jre/lib/fonts/fallback" I could get results very similar to those that I get from Windows. A message I hope you will absorb here is that Java itself provides portable support for international and special-purpose character sets you may need to configure its runtime before you can take *full* advantage of it. Also before you distribute applications relying

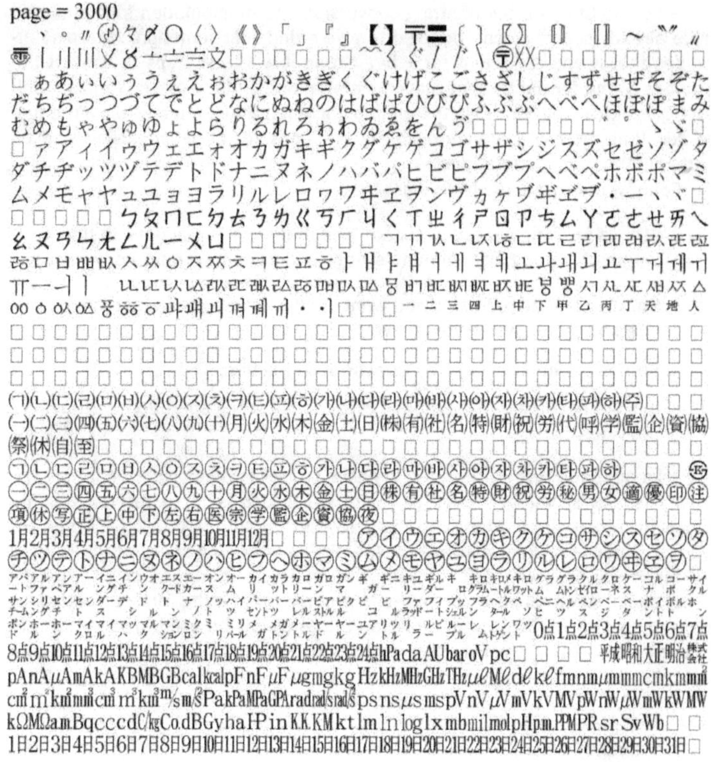

Figure 4.2: Unicode characters in the range 0x3000 to 0x33ff

on that you have to concern yourself with how well your customers' operating systems will deal with the fonts!

We have already seen string literals in our code, just written within double quote-marks. The associated type is String. Although the use of capitals and lower case is just a convention in Java the fact that the type is String rather than string is a hint that this does not have exactly the same status as the types int, char and so on. In fact String is the name of a quite complicated data-type (in Java we will find that this is known as a class) and this class provides access to a number of string conversion and manipulation functions. We have already seen " +" can be used to give string concatenation. Java also arranges that if one argument for + is a String it will take steps to convert the other to String format so that this concatenation can take place. You can look up " Class java.lang.String" in the on-line documentation or a reference manual to see that there are standard library functions for case-conversion and all sorts of other string operations.

For now the points to observe are that

- Strings are represented by a data-type that exports functions to find the length of a string, concatenate strings and perform various conversions;
- Strings are read-only, so if you want to change one you in fact make a new string containing the adjusted text;
- Strings are not the same as arrays[9] of characters;
- It is not necessary to memorise every single string operation that Java pro-vides.

Java supports arrays. An array is just a block of values where one has the ability to use an integer *index* to select which one is to be referenced. The types for arrays are written with the array size in square brackets. An empty pair of square brackets means that the size is not being specified at that poi nt, but it will be made definite somewhere else in the program. We saw an array declar ation as early as the Hello program where the function main was passed an array of Strings. In this case the array will be used to pass down to the Java application any words given on the command line after the parts that actually launch the application:

```
>>> File "Args.java"
>>>     Display arguments from command line

public class Args
{
    public static void main(String[] args)
    {
        for (String s : args)
            System.out.println(s)
    }
}
```

This introduces a new version of the for statement. It can be compiled and then run by saying

[9]Which will be covered in the next section of these notes!

```
javac Args.java
java Args one two three
```

it prints out

```
one
two
three
```

The points to notice here are that the type of argument that main was an array of strings, and the for loop will obey its body once for each string in that array. An alternative and older-fashioned way of achieving the same effect would be to find the length of the array and count, indexing into the array to extract values explicitly:

```
for (int i=0; i<args.length; i++)
      System.out.println(args[i])
```

In this case the array held Strings, but Java arrays can be declared in forms to hold any sort of Java data. This includes having arrays of arrays, which is the Java way of modelling multi-dimensional structures.

In Java a distinction is made between declaring a variable that can hold an array and actually creating the array that will live there. Declaring the variable happens just as for declaring integer or floating point varia bles, and you do not at that stage specify how big the array will be:

```
{ int[] a;
      ...
```

has declared[10] a to be ready to store an integer array (of unspecified size and currently unknown contents), much as

```
{ double d;
      ...
```

says that d will subsequently be able to store double-precision floatin g point val-ues. There are two ways that the actual concrete array can come into existence. The first is to combine the declaration with an initializer th at makes the array and fills in its elements:

· The syntax that I will try to use throughout these notes has all declarations written as a type followed by the name of the variable that is to be declared. Thus int[] is the type of an array able to hold integers. When you declare a variable of an array type Java allows you to put the brackets either next to the base type (as I will generally do) or after the name of the variable that is being declared, as in int myArray[];. This latter case is perhaps useful when you want to declare a bunch of variables at once, some scalars and some arrays, as in int simple,row[],grid[][];.

```
{ int[] p = {2,3,5,7,11,13,17};
     ...
```

where the values within the braces can in fact be arbitrary (integer-valued) expressions. The second way of creating an array uses a keyword new which is Java's general mechanism for allocating space for things. The word new is followed by a type that describes the structure of the item to be allocated.

```
{ int[] fairly_big = new int[1000];
     ...
```

In this case the array contents will be left in a default state. In fact Java is very keen to avoid leaving anything undefined or uncertain, since it wants all programs to execute in exactly the same way every time and on every machine, so it demands that a fresh integer array starts off holding 0 in every element. It has analogous rules to specify the initial value of any other field or array e lement that has not had a value given more explicitly.

Note that all Java arrays use subscripts that start at 0, so an array of length 1000 will accept subscripts 0, . . . , 999. Attempts to go outside the bounds will be trapped by the Java run-time system. Subscripts must be of type int. You may not use long values as subscripts. If you write a char, byte or short expression as a subscript Java will convert it to an int for you as if there had been a suitable cast visible.

When an array is passed as an argument to a function the called function can update the members of the array, but if it creates a whole new array by something such as

```
args = new String [5];
```

this will replace the array wholesale within the current function but have no effect on the calling routine. The terminology that Java uses for all this is that it will pass a "reference" to the array as the actual argument.

The following example shows the creation of an array, code that fills in entries in it, a slightly dodgy illustration of the fact that two-dimensional arrays can be viewed as arrays of one-dimensional arrays and a crude demonstration of how you might print multiple values of a single line by building up a string that maps the entire contents of the line.

```
>>>         Array1.java
>>> Create a 3 by 3 array, swap rows in it (!)
>>> and print tolerably neatly.

public class Array1
{
        public static void main(String[] args)
        {
                int [][]        a = new int[3][3];              // 3 by 3 array
                int     []  b;                                  // array of length 3
                for   (int    i=0; i<3; i++)                    //      fill in all of a
                        for      (int j=0;          j<3; j++) a[i][j] = i+10*j;
#    The next line recognises that a[i] are 1-dimensional
#    arrays of length 3. It swaps two of them around!
                b = a[0]; a[0] = a[2]; a[2] = b;
                for (int i=0; i<3; i++)                         // Print each row
                {       String s = "";                          // Build row up here
                        for (int j=0; j<3; j++)
                                s = s + "       " + a[i][j];
                        System.out.println(s);                  // Then print it
                }
        }
}
```

which prints

```
        2  12  22
        1  11  21
        0  10  20
```

The things to notice in the above example are firstly that vari ables a and b are declared with array types, but these types neither specify sizes nor imply that a genuine array actually exists, and secondly the way in which the two-dimensional array is dismembered. Observe also the syntax associated with new for allocating space for the array, and the fact that nothing special had to be done at the end to discard the space so allocated. Java will recycle memory previously used by arrays (and indeed any other structures) once it knows that they are no longer needed. This is of course just like the situation in ML.

We have seen a number of other types in the sample programs. As well as String there was Graphics, Font and MouseEvent. Java 1.2 defines over 500 such non-simple types! Thus one thing you can be certain of is that I will not discuss all of them, and neither will the follow-on Java course next year. Each of these has (in some sense) the same status and possibilities as the programs you have written where you start off by declaring a new class. Each of String,

Graphics and so on represents a class and its implementation might well be in Java stored in a file that starts off

```
public class Whatever ...
```

You have seen with the classes that you define for yourself tha t a class is a context within which you can define a collection of functions , and so it should be no surprise that each of the 500+ Java library classes provides a whole bunch of associated functions (eg for String we have mentioned the valueOf operation, and for Graphics we have used drawLine and drawString). There are thus literally thousands of library functions available. Their organisation into classes provides some structure to the collection, but in the end you probably have to find out about the ones you need to use by searching through the documentation. These notes will introduce a sampling of library classes and the functions they support with a view to directing you towards interesting areas of Java functionality. Very often I find that the best way to start to understand the use of a new part of the class library is to study and then try to modify some existing code that uses it.

The Java designers suggest use of a convention where the names of ordinary variables and functions start with a lower case letter while class-names start with a capital. They further recommend use of words spelt in all capitals for things that should be thought of as constants (such as PI that we used earlier). The syntax associated with declaring something immutable will be covered later on once we have got through the use of other important words such as public and static which are of course still unexplained.

4.1.3 Exercises

Tickable Exercise 3

The function System.currentTimeMillis() returns a long value that is the count of the number of milliseconds from midnight on 1st January 1970 to the moment at which it is executed. Thus something like

```
long start = System.currentTimeMillis(); for (int i=0;
i<13; i++)
{  System.out.println(binom(2*i, i));
}
long timeSpent = System.currentTimeMillis()-start;
System.out.println("Done in " + timeSpent +
                                   milliseconds");
```

in the middle of a program can be used to record how long it takes to run. Note that this is the time as measured by a stop-watch (or hour glass), and will depend quite strongly on how many other people are using the computer at the same time. On a single-user computer it can give a tolerably reliable indication of the cost of a computation and even on a shared machine it is better than no information at all.

- Adapt the Binomial Coefficients program suggested in the p revious set of examples so that it reports the time it takes to get as far as displaying ${}^{24}C_{12}$, which (I think) has the value 2704156. Your submission to the assessors should include a table of the values of ${}^{2n}C_n$ for n from 1 to 12, and the number of milliseconds that your program took to run.

- Remove the definition of the sub-function that you used to c ompute the bi-nomial coefficients, and add to your program a line that decla res and create an array called c of size 25 by 25. Set the c[0][0] to 1. Now the first row of the matrix holds values of ${}^{0}C_r$.
  Now fill in subsequent rows one at a time using the rules

  $$\begin{aligned} c[n][0] &= c[n][n] = 1 \\ c[n][r] &= c[n-1][r-1] + c[n-1][r] \end{aligned}$$

  so that the matrix gradually gets filled up with binomial coef ficients. Keep going until the 24th row has been filled in. Then print out the v alues of c[2*i][i] for i from 0 to 12, and again measure how long this takes.

- *[From here on is optional]* The above calculation can be done using a one-dimensional array, so that at each stage in the calculation it holds just one row of binomial coefficients, ie values of ${}^{n}C_r$ for a single value of n. At each stage by filling its values in in reverse order something like

  ```
  c[i] = 1;
  for (int j=i-1; j>0; j=j-1) c[j] = ...
  ```

  the new values can replace the old ones in such a way that nothing is over-written too early. The for loop shown here sets j first to the value i-1, then to i-2, and so on all the way down to 3, 2 and finally 1. I could of course have written j-- or --j where here I put j=j-1!

  Write this version of the program using an array of length 80, and make the array contain long values rather than just int. First arrange that on every even row it prints the middle element from the part of the array that is in use, so it duplicates the output printed by the previous two examples. Then make the loop continue further and thus find (by inspection) the la rgest value of i such that ${}^{2i}C_i$ can be represented exactly as a Java long. The value is less than 40.

(End of tickable exercise)

A Numerical Monster

A very fine paper called “Numeri-cal Monsters” by Essex et al[12] ex-plains how many calculations that you might think were straight-forward have extra depth when done using finite precision computer arith-metic. One example is the function

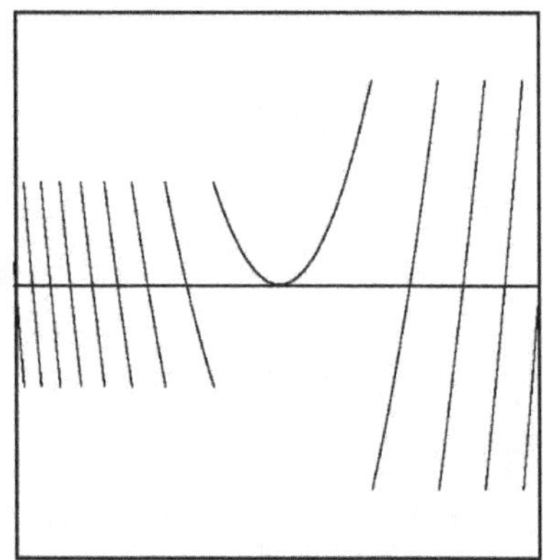

>>> $= (x^2 - 2x + 1) - (x - 1)^2$

In ideal arithmetic *y* would always be zero. If however the function is com-puted using floating point arithmetic as shown (and provided an over-clever compiler does not do alge-braic re-arrangement of the formula: the Java compiler is well-behaved in this respect) an interesting graph can emerge. For instance the graph shown here was produced using a very simple Java program and plotting for x in the range 1-3.0e-8<*x*<1.0+3.0e-8 and *y* from -1.5e-16 to +1.5e-16. Write your own version of a program to re-create this graph, and investigate the what it shows near other values of *x*. Two cases I will suggest investigating are 1.0e8<*x*<2.0e8, |*y*|<10 and 14999.99999999253<*X* <14999.99999999257, |*y*|<3.2e-8. Your challenge is to understand exactly how the finite nature of computer ari thmetic leads to the precise patterns generated, and how these patterns would vary if details of the arithmetic model were altered.

The Dutch National Flag

Provided that at the start of your program you have written

```
import java.util.*;
```

The code

```
int [] a = new int [1000];
Random r = new Random();
for (int i=0; i<1000; i++) a[i] = (byte) r.nextInt();
```

first makes an array of length 1000. It then creates a new rando m-number genera-tor (called r), and finally calls the random number generator 1000 times to fill in entries in the array. The cast to type byte ensures that each entry in the array will end up in the range from −128 to +127. There will of course be duplicate values in the array.

The task you have to achieve is to rearrange the numbers in the array so that they fall into three bands. The first band, say all the element s from 0 to m, should contain all the numbers x with $x < -40$. The second band ($m + 1$ to n) will be for $-40 \leq x < 40$, while the final band ($n + 1$ to 999) is for $x \geq 40$. This is known as the Dutch National Flag problem because its originator (E J Dijkstra) presented it in terms of values that had one of the three colours that his country's flag [11] used, rather than the numeric ranges I have suggested here.

The problem would probably be easy if you could allocate three fresh arrays and copy each item from the original into one or the other of these, based on its "colour". At the end you could then copy the three chunks back into the original array at the positions they needed to go. But this challenge involves the idea of efficiency too, and your final solution must not use any extra a rrays, and it should ideally inspect or move each value as few times as it can. Note that just sorting the values in the array into ascending order would satisfy the objectives that concern where values must end up, but since the problem does not state anything at all about any desired order of the items that fall within any of the three bands a solution based on sorting is over-elaborate and too expensive.

It may well be useful to try your hand at the Polish Flag problem — my ency-clopaedia shows the Polish flag as having just two stripes [12]. Thus the Polish Flag problem is to rearrange the values in the original chaotic array so that all negative ones (say) come before all positive ones, but without any further constraint on the re-ordering apart that it should be achieved reasonably effi ciently.

The Mauritian Flag seems to go Red, Blue, Yellow and then Green. . .

Matrix Operations

Set up two 5 by 5 arrays of type double[][]. Fill in the first so that [13] the element at position (i, j) has value $1/(i + j + 1.0)$. Fill in the other so that the the elements on the diagonal have the value 1.0 while all other elements hold 0.0.

The program wanted now will be one that gradually turns the fir st matrix into one that has just 1.0 elements down its diagonal and zeros elsewhere. The permit-ted operations are

7. Multiply all the elements in a row by the same non-zero value;

8. Subtract a multiple of one row from another.

---

3. Red, White and Blue in that order

4. Red and White

5. This form of matrix is known as a Hilbert Matrix.

and whenever one of these operations is performed on the first matrix it must also be performed on the second.

The first matrix can be made diagonal by tidying up first the firs t column, then the second, then the third and so on. To tidy up column *i* you first multiply row *i* by $1/a_{i,i}$, since this will leave[14] the element on the diagonal as 1.0. Then for every row apart from row *i* you subtract a suitable multiple of row *i* so as to make the element in column *i* vanish.

Do this and display the elements of the second matrix, which should in fact have ended up as the inverse of the original Hilbert matrix!

Encryption

The following code fragment starts with a string called key and fills out an array k with repeated copies of the character codes from the key until k has 256 entries in it:

```
String key = "My Secret Key";
int keyLength = key.length();
int [] k = new int [256];
for (int i=0; i<256; i++)
        k[i] = (int)key.charAt(i % keyLength) % 256;
```

All the values stored in k have been reduced so as to be in the range 0 to 255. Observe the use of functions length() and charAt() from the String class. I have used a fixed string as the keyword here.

The repeated use of the fixed numeric constant "256" in this co de is a stylistic oddity. In some ways once the array k has been declared it might be nicer to use k.length to talk about the number of elements it has. I took the view when writing this that the exact size of the array is part of the core specification of the algorithm I am implementing. . . When you write this program whatever else you do *please* do not use your password as text in the program you write!

The program you have to write here may be related to an encryption method known as RC4 that was once a trade secret of RSA[15] but which was published anonymously and presumably improperly a couple of years ago. RC4 is used as the encryption technology in a large number of generally used packages and although its security may not have been proved it is widely believed to be re-spectable. It is also fast.

---

3. For now assume please that the diagonal element was non-zero so that the division behaved properly and did not end up yielding and IEEE infinity.

4. The major American encryption and security company. You may like the

view consideration of the proper uses of such code as an exercise relating to

the Professional Practise and Ethics course.

The first part of the procedure is to create an array s of 256 integers, and ini-tialise it. It is first set so that the value at position *i* is just *i* (*i* runs from 0 to 255). Now your code should scramble this up using they key *k* using the following pro-cess:

For i from 0 to 255 do

Let j be (s[i] + k[i]) reduced to 8 bits

Swap the items at positions i and j in the array s

The term "reduced to 8 bits" can be implemented by just taking the remain-der[16] when the value concerned is divided by 256.

At the end of this the array s holds a working collection of scrambled data. This is used to generate a sequence of 8-bit numbers which can be combined with a message to encrypt it. Starting with variables *i* and *j* both zero the next encryption-number is obtained as follows:

Increment i modulo[17] *256*
Set j to j + s[i], again modulo 256
Swap s[i] with s[j]
Let t be s[i] + s[j] modulo 256
The result is s[t]

The algorithm is clearly short enough to be utterly memorable! The sequence of numbers it generates can be added to the (8-bit) character codes of a message to give the encoded version, and if the recipient knows the key that was used then decryption is just generating and subtracting the same sequence of values. It is vital that a key used with this method should *never* be re-used, and competent security tends to involve really careful attention to many details that do not belong in this course[18].

Code the scheme described above. Print the first dozen output values from it for your chosen key. You may like to check with a friend to see if their im-plementation generates the same sequence as yours when given the same key — by the nature of this code there is not obviously going to be any other way of characterising the correct output!

· In the next section we will also see that it can be achieved by writing something like
(s[i] + k[i]) & 0xff.

· "modulo" means just the remaindering operation.

· But which will be covered later in the CST.

4.2 Operators and expressions

The examples shown already have included uses of the usual arithmetic operators, both as used on integers and on floating point values. Now is th e time to present a systematic list of the operators that Java provides and the way they are used in expressions. One of the critical things in any programming language is the syntactic priority of operators. For instance in normal usage the expression $a + b \times c$ must be read as if it had been $a + (b \times c)$ rather than as $(a + b) \times c$. To stress the importance of knowing which operators group most tightly I will list things ordered by their syntactic precedence rather than by what they do. The simple arithmetic cases will be listed but not discussed at any great length.

++, –: We have already see use of ++ as a postfix operator that increments a variable. The full story is that the expression ++a has the side-effect of increasing the value of the variable a by 1 and its overall value is that incremented value while a++ increments a but the value of the expression is the *original* value of a. The use of – is similar except that it subtracts one rather than adds one to the variable mentioned. These operations can apply to either integer or floating point variables;

+, - *(unary)*: Unary + does not do anything but is there for completeness. Unary >>> negates its (numeric) argument;

˜: The ˜ operator treats its integer operand as a binary number and negates each bit in the representation. If you look back at the earlier table that illustrated binary numbers you can check that ˜0 will have the same value as -1;

!: The ! operator may only be applied to a boolean operand, and it complements the logical value concerned, so that !true is false;

(*type*): Casts are included here to show their precedence and to point out that as far as syntax is concerned a cast acts just as a unary operator;

*, /, %: Multiplication, division and remaindering on any arithmetic values. The odd case is the % operation when applied to floating point arguments. If

• % y is computed then Java finds an *integer* value q that is the quotient x/y truncated towards zero, and then defines the remainder r by $x = qy + r$. If integer and floating point values both appear in the same ex pression the integers are promoted to the floating type before the arithme tic is performed. Similarly if integers of different lengths are mixed or if flo ats and doubles come together the arithmetic is performed in the wider of the two types;

+, -: Both integers and floating point can be added and subtracted much as one might expect;

>>> *(string)*: If the + operator is used in a context where at least one argument is a string then the other argument will be converted to a string (if necessary) and the operation then denotes string concatenation. We have seen this used as a way of forcing a conversion from a numeric type to a string ready for printing. Note that the concatenation step will generally involve allocating extra memory and copying data from each of the two original strings, so it will tend to be much more expensive that the arithmetic uses of the + operator.

<<, >>, >>>: Consider an integer as represented in binary. Then the << operator shifts every bit left by a given number of places, filling in at the right hand end with zeros. Thus the program fragment:

```
for (int i=0; i<32; i++)
    System.out.printf("%d : %d%n", i, (1 << i));
```

will print out numbers each of which have representations that have a single 1 bit, with this bit in successive places. The result is a table of powers of 2, except that the penultimate line of output will display as a negative integer and the final one will be zero! There are two right-shift opera tors. The usual one, >>, treats numbers as signed values. A signed value is treated as if they were first converted to binary numbers with an unlim ited number of bits. For positive values this amounts to sticking an infin ite run of 0 digits to the left while for negative ones it involved preceding the number with lots more 1 digits. Next the value is shifted right, and fi nally the value is truncated to its proper width. The effect is that positive integers get 0 bits moved into the vacated high order positions while negative ones get 1s. When shifting an int the shift amount will be forced to lie in the range 0 to 31, while for type long it can only be from 0 to 63. The special right shift written as >>> shifts right but always fills vacated bits with 0. It is very useful when an integer is being thought of not as a numeric value but as a collection of individual bits;

<, <=, >, >=: The usual arithmetic comparisons are available, and I have already remarked that there are a few delicacies with regard to floating point comparisons and NaNs, infinities and signed zeros;

instanceof: This will be discussed later;

==, !=: Equality and inequality tests. For the primitive types they test to see if things have the same value. For other types (arrays and the object-types that are introduced later on) the test determines if the things compared are “the same object”;

&: On integer operands the & operator forms a number whose binary value has a 1-bit only where both of the inputs have a 1. For positive values, for instance

- & 0xf and a % 16 will always yield the same result. Long tradition of languages where the "and" operator is significantly faster t hen division and remainder means that many old-fashioned programmers will make what is now maybe excessive use of this idiom. The & operator can also be applied to boolean operand, in which case is means just "and";

^: Exclusive or. See below to compare inclusive and exclusive or;

|: Inclusive or. Note that for integer values a&~b | b&~a == a^b and the same identity holds for boolean values except that ! has to be used for the complement/negation operation rather than ~. Here are the truth tables for inclusive and exclusive or:

"|"	0	1
0	0	1
1	1	1

"^"	0	1
0	0	1
1	1	0

&&: In a boolean expression such as A & B if the value of A was false there is perhaps no need to evaluate B. The simple "and" notation does not take ad-vantage of this, but the alternate form A && B does. Apart from efficiency this can only make a difference if evaluating the sub-expression B would have side-effects. In general I think it is probably good style to use && rather than just & whenever a boolean expression is being used to control an if or similar statement, while & is probably nicer to use when calculations are being performed on boolean variables;

||: This is the version of the "or" operator that avoids process ing its right hand operand in cases where the left hand one shows that the final va lue should be true. Its use is entirely analogous to that of &&;

?: It is sometimes nice to embed a conditional value within an expression, and Java lets you do that using the slightly odd-looking syntax *a* ? *b* : *c*. This expects *a* to be of type boolean, while the other operands can have any type provided that they are compatible. If *a* is true the result is the first of these expressions, otherwise it is the second. For instance the messy-looking expression

```
(a==0 ? "zero" : "non-zero")
```

has the value "zero" if a is zero and "non-zero" otherwise. The phrase (a || b) could be replaced by the equivalent form (a ? true : b), while (a && b) has the same meaning as (a ? b : false);

=: Assignment in Java is just an operator. Thus you can assign to a variable anywhere within an expression. The value of a sub-expression that is an assignment is just the value assigned. Thus silly things like ((a=a+a) + (b=b-1)) are good syntax if not good sense. A more benign use of the fact that assignments are just expressions arises in the idiom (a = b = c

>>> d = 0). The assignment operator associates to the right so the example means (a = (b = (c = (d = 0)))) and thus assigns zero to all of the four variables named;

*=, /=, %=, +=, -=, <<=, >>=, >>>=, &=, ^=, |=: These operators combine assignment with one of the other operators that have been listed earlier. They provide a short-hand notation when the same thing would otherwise appear to the left and immediately to the right in an assignment. For instance

• = a+3 can be shortened to a += 3 The abbreviation has slightly more real value when the assignment concerned is to some variable with a name much longer than just a, or especially if it is into an array element, since the short form only has to evaluate the array subscript expression once. This can lead to a difference in meaning in cases where evaluating the subscript has a side-effect, as in the artificial fragment

```
int [] a = ...;
int [] b = ...;
int p = 0, q = 1;
for (int i=0; i<10; i++)
        a[p++] += b[q++];
```

where index variables p and q step along through the arrays a and b and it is important that they are each incremented just once each time around the loop.

4.2.1 Exercises

Bitwise operations on integers

Investigate, either on paper or by writing test programs, each of the following operations. Explain what they all mean, supposing that the variables used are all of type int:

```
>>>     ~a + 1;

>>>     a++ + ++b;

>>>     a & (-a);
```

- a & ((1<<b)-1);
- (a>>>i) | (a<<(32-i));
- a + (a<<2);
- (int)(byte)a;
- (a & 0x80000000) != 0;
- (a++ != b++) && (a++ == b++);
- (–a != –b) | (–a == –b);
- (a < 0 ? -a : a).

Counting bits in a word

Write a function that counts the number of non-zero bits in the binary representation of an integer. You can first do this using a test for each bit in the style >>> & (1<<n) != 0. Next see if any of the examples in the previous exercise give you a way to identify a single bit to subtract off and count. Consider also the expression

```
(c[a & 0xff] + c[(a>>8) & 0xff] + c[(a>>16) & 0xff] +
  c[(a>>24) & 0xff])
```

for some suitable array c.

What does this do?

This exercise and the few following it introduce a few fragments of amazingly twisted and "tricky" code. Please do not view the inclusion o f these programming techniques here as an indication that you will be examined on them or that you are being encouraged to use such obscure constructions in your own programs. It is more that puzzling through these examples can refine you r understanding of the interactions between the Java arithmetic operations such as + and % and the ones that work on the binary representations of numbers, ie & and >>. In a few circumstances the ultra-cunning bit-bashing might save time in a really critical part of some program and so could be really important, but almost always clarity of exposition is even more important than speed. Certainly use of these tricks will not make your programs any shorter, in that the bulk of the comments needed to justify and explain them will greatly exceed the length of more straight-forward code that has the same effect!

Start off with a any positive value. Execute the following[19] and discuss what value gets left in a at the end. Hint: look at the binary representation of a to start with.

```
a -= (a>>>1) & 03333333333;
a -= (a>>>1) & 03333333333;
a = ((a>>>3) + a) & 0707070707;
a = a % 63;
```

And this. . .

```
a &= 0x3f;
a = ((a * 02020202) & 0104422010) % 255;
```

And this. . .

```
c = a & -a;
r = a + c;
a = (((r ^ a) >>> 2) / c) | r;
```

[In each case it will help if you look at the numbers in binary.]

Integers used to represent fractions

Consider a as a value expressed in binary but now as a positive fractional value in the range 0 to 1. This means that there will be an implicit binary point just to its left. Then 0xffffffff will be just a tiny bit less than 1, 0x80000000 will stand for 1/2 and 0x40000000 for 1/4. In terms of this representation interpret the effect of executing the following four statements one after the other.

```
a += a >>> 2;
a += a >>> 4;
a += a >>> 8;
a += a >>> 16;
```

Division and Shifts

If a is a positive integer than a/2 and a>>1 give the same result. What is the relationship between their values if a is negative. Carry on the analysis for division by 4, 8, 16,. . . and the corresponding right shifts.

· Discussions with Alan Mycroft caused this and some of the other curious examples here to re-surface. For a collection of real programming oddities including some of these try searching
for "Hakmem" on the World Wide Web or find "The Hacker's Deligh t"[15] in a library

Some Exclusive-Or operations

What is the final effect on a and b of the sequence

```
a ^= b;
b ^= a;
a ^= b;
```

Sieve for primes

Create an array of type boolean and length 1000. Set all elements to true to start with. Then set items 0 and 1 to false

Repeat the following two steps

>>> Find the first true item in the array. If there are none left then exit. Print out the index of the value you have found, and call it p.

>>> Set each item in the array that is at a position that is a multiple of p to be false, for instance as in

```
for (i=p; i<1000; i+=p) map[i] = false;
```

The numbers you have printed should be the primes up to 1000.

If you wanted to find the primes up to several million (for inst ance to count them rather than to tabulate them) it would make sense to make the array represent just the odd numbers not all numbers. It might also save significant amounts of space to represent the array as an array on int rather than boolean and pack information about 32 odd-numbers into each int. You might note that some programming languages can implement boolean arrays in that way without much user intervention — Java does not.

4.3 Control structures

4.3.1 Exercises

Ambiguous If

Consider the sample code fragment

```
if (a == 0)
    if (b == 0) System.out.println("Both 0"); else
  System.out.println("Some other case");
```

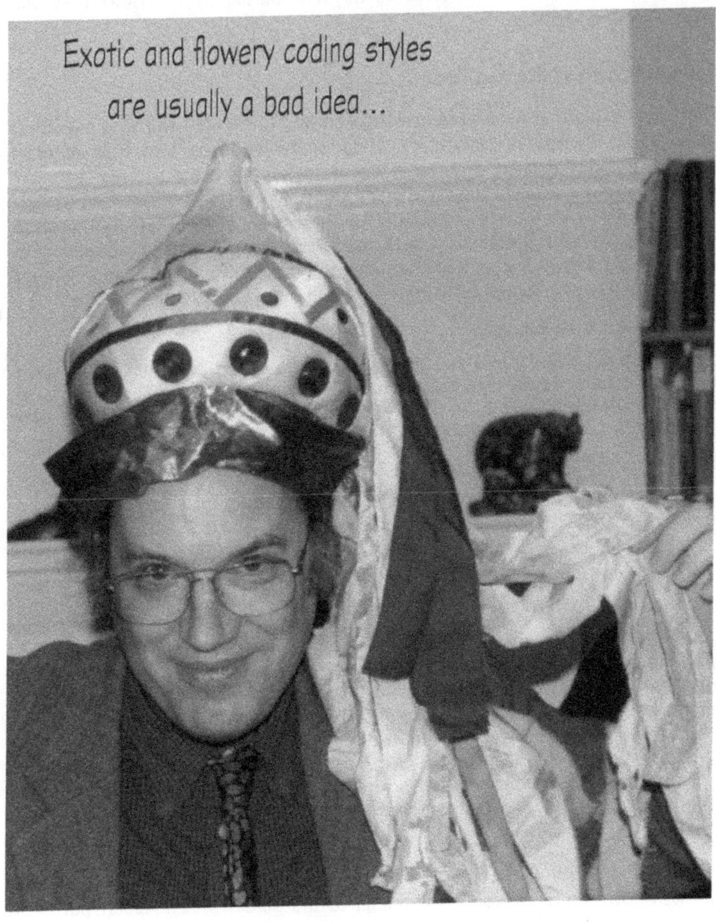

Figure 4.3: Keep control structures simple!

and wonder exactly what happens if one or other of a or b is non-zero. Write sample programs that test the actual behaviour of the real Java compiler either to discover how Java resolves the near-ambiguity in syntax that this example repre-sents.

Periodic Forests of Stunted Trees

The forms explained here were investigated by J C P Miller who was a lecturer here in the Computer Laboratory. Their study leads on into that of error correcting codes and so is perhaps less detached from the serious technical side of computer science than one might think.

A root-line for a forest is a periodic binary sequence. Since it is hard to draw things that repeat indefinitely it is useful to display such s equences by showing one or two cycles and than agreeing that the ends of display should be treated as being joined up to make a circle. Here is a sample root-line:

```
.X..XXX..X..XXX..X..XXX.
```

A forest grows from a root-line by the simple rule that a branch grows when and only when exactly one cell in the row beneath it is present (this is an exclusive OR operation). I am drawing lines upwards[20] following this rule from the root-line I showed above yields

```
?................?
?XXXXXXXXXXXXXXXXXXX?
?X.X.X.X.X.X.X.X.X.X?
?X..XX..XX..XX..XX..X?
?.XXX.XXX.XXX.XXX.XXX.?
?XX.X..X.XX.X..X.XX.X..?
?.X..XXX..X..XXX..X..XXX?
```

and the pattern seems to have died. In many cases after a number of rows the orig-inal row will re-appear[21]. Triangular clearings appear on the way. The challenge is to understand when a pattern will die and when it will repeat, how the vertical repetition period relates to the original horizontal one, and how large the largest clearings will be. Write a Java application or Applet that takes a command-line argument or otherwise accepts information from the user in the form of a string of X and . characters. It should then display the generated forest.

· If you print things to System.out it would probably be easier to print with growth down-wards. If you draw things to the screen in an Applet putting it either way up is easy. Observe that I have drawn question marks to show where the pattern depends on data beyond the initial segment of pattern. If you can allow for the (infinite) repetition of t he base-line you do not need these.

· You will see that I have only drawn a finite section of the infini te repeating base-line, and so the forest is drawn as getting narrower as you grow it upwards. However it should be understood to be of infinite width and so patters can re-occur exactly.

Life

The world consists of an infinite sheet of graph paper. Each square may at any one time be either black or white. Ev-ery square has eight neighbours Every so often all squares simultaneously follow the following rules:

3	4	5
2	⊙	6
1	8	7

- A square that is black at present remains black if it has two or three black neighbours. Otherwise it turns white;
- A white square becomes black if it has exactly three black neighbours.

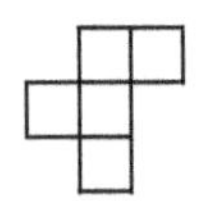

These rules define a behaviour which was invented by John Conw ay (who at the time was in the Mathematics department here) and which is known as Life. One starts off with a board that has a small number of black seed points and display the position as the generations go by. There are many astonishingly complicated things that can happen and people have designed starting positions that illustrate them. The challenge here is to make the computer run the rules and display the world-state. A useful starting configuration to try has just five black cell s arranged as at the head of this paragraph. It explodes and seethes for quite a long while before the situation stabilises. One thing to note is that all decisions about the next generation are expected to be taken simultaneously, so any program that updates the world incrementally is liable to get wrong answers. A further problem is that the the ideal playing surface for Life is infinite, while computers t end not to be. Two resolutions to this are usually considered. One places an immutable wall of white cells as a border around the world so that all activity is contained within them. The other scheme often used is to use a finite playing area but c onsiders its left hand column to be adjacent to its right most one and its top to be adjacent to its bottom row. This amounts (depending on how you think of it) to playing Life on a torus or to ensuring that all initial positions are replicated in a periodic manner across an infinite plane.

The easiest program for this will set up *two* boolean arrays. The first holds the current generation, while the second will be filled in with th e next. My version of a program that does this, complete with code to set up the initial pattern that I have suggested and to draw the board positions in an applet window is around 75 lines long. I used a 200 by 200 board and kept the outermost rows and columns permanently blank. That means that when accessing neighbours I can read from them without going outside my array. Clearly the first exerci se here is to reproduce something like that.

There are then three follow-up challenges. The first looks ba ck to the optional part of the binomial coefficient tickable exercise: can you g et away with just one boolean array rather than two, possibly keeping a boolean vector to store just one row of backup information but mostly updating the world in place. To do so would save around half of the memory that the simple program uses.

The second challenge observes that representing the playing area as arrays of type boolean is probably wasteful. This would be a typical application where packing 32 cells into an int and using lots of bitwise and, or and shift operations to deal with them would be common practice. It would of course be possible to achieve this by having nice abstract procedures to reference the bit at position (x, y) in an array even though the array was being represented in a packed way. But it would perhaps give big speed savings to look for ways to exploit the fact that bitwise operations on integers can handle 32 bits all at once and to try to use this to compute new values for several cells at the same time.

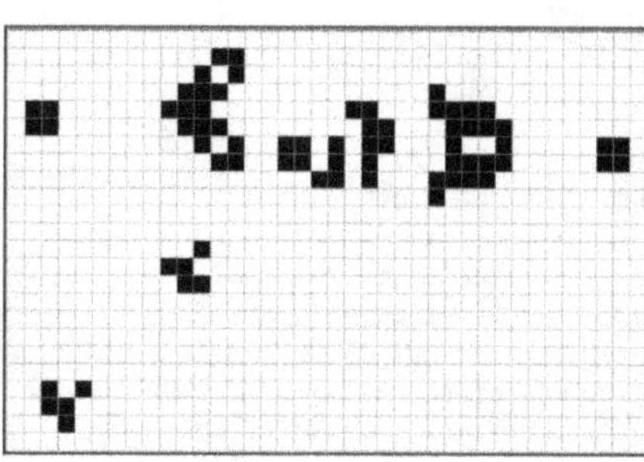

Figure 4.4: Gosper's Glider Gun.

Finally, and given that this program tends to run a little slowly, one looks at where the time goes. Much of it will be wastage on parts of the board that are totally white and hence where nothing is going to happen. Try to speed your code up by avoiding as much of such wasted as is reasonable.

Eight Queens

Count the number of ways of placing eight queens on a chess board so so that no pair are in the same row, column or diagonal as each other. This is a classical puzzle to go in an introduction to programming and there are lots of clever tricks that can be used. It is the sort of thing that most supervisors will have come across before so I will not provide a fully worked through solution here, but I might observe that the search might well be done by a recursive function that when called at depth n will try to place a queen on row n of the chess-board.

Permutations

In Java arrays can be passed as arguments and newly created arrays can be re-turned as results. Write a function that accepts an array of strings as its argument, and which hands back and array whose elements are themselves arrays of strings giving all possible permutations of the input. For instance if I use curly brackets to denote arrays here one might like {"a", "b", "c"} to turn into {{"a", "b", "c"}, {"a", "c", "b"} {"b", "a", "c"}, {"b", "c", "a"}, {"c", "a", "b"}, {"c", "b", "a"}}.

As with several of the other Java exercises I might suggest that you design and test an ML version first.

4.4 Control structures Part 2

There are two aspects of syntax that I will put off until a yet later section. One if the syntax associated with the word class that we have seen wrapped around every program we have written. The other is the matter of the " ." that ap-pears between or possibly within so many names, eg System.out.println and g.drawString. A few other bits of syntax will just not be covered in this firs t course, although you may find traces of them in the grammar and discussion of them in textbooks — and possibly also in next year's "Concurr ent Systems and Applications" course.

But I will talk through each of the important components of the syntax and give at least one illustration of each.

4.4.1 Expression Statements

Certain sorts of Java expression can be used as a statement — a ll that is necessary is to stick a semicolon on the end of it. The cases permitted are where evaluating the expression might have a side-effect. Thus an assignment expression, a function call or a pre- or post-increment expression can be used. As an example, consider the statement x++; which just increments x. An example such as 1+2+3; is not considered valid: it would calculates the value 6 and then throws it away!

4.4.2 Blocks

Several statements can be placed one after the other to make a single large state-ment. Braces { . . . } are used around the statements to group them. In various earlier languages the keywords begin and end were used instead of braces, but Java prefers the version where you type in fewer key-strokes. If you see a block with semicolons in the semicolons are just parts of expression statements and nothing special to do with the fact that there is a block there. Again some earlier languages differed by using semicolons between statements in a block rather than as termination of expression statements. Blocks can be nested any way you want. You may insert extra braces to stress the grouping of any collection of statements you feel deserves that, in much the same way that extra parentheses can always be used to emphasis the grouping within expressions. I think there are enough examples of blocks throughout these notes that I do not need to give a special one here.

4.4.3 Null statements

If you insert a stray semicolon into a Java program it (mostly) does not matter much, since a semicolon alone can be interpreted as an empty statement that does nothing. The most striking example of the use of a null statement is in something like

```
if (a > 7);
else System.out.println("Gotcha");
```

where the if needs a statement before its else part but no real action is needed. If you *really* need such a place-holder I would suggest that the following is clearer and flags your unusual intent more clearly.

```
if (a > 7) {/*NOTHING*/}
else System.out.println("Gotcha");
```

Better yet rearrange your code to make tests happen in a positive sense:

```
if (a <= 7) System.out.println("Gotcha");
```

4.4.4 if

It takes a little while to get used to the fact that the condition tested by if is written in parentheses. Some people prefer a style where the statement after an if is always written as a block, even if it is only a single statement, so that the range that the if controls is made very explicit. This point of view has some sense behind it, especially if the statement after the if is more than half a line long.

The control expression used by if must be of type boolean and so equality tests are written as in a==0 and not a=0[22]. Using a single rather than double equals sign is a common slip.

[22] Which would be an assignment and would have type inti.

4.4.5 while, continue and break

A while loop executes its command repeatedly for so long as the guarding expression remains true. Its syntax is very much like that of if. Within the iterated command you can embed a statement " break;", and execution of that will cause a premature exit from the loop. The command continue;[23] can be useful if the iterated command is a long block, and it causes the loop to proceed at once to its next cycle. Both break; and continue; are very convenient at times, but it is often good style to avoid them when reasonably convenient so that the boolean expression at the top of the while loop represents a total statement about the cir-cumstances in which it will loop and when it will terminate. The following sample shows a fairly typical while loop. Look back at your Discrete Mathematics notes for explanation of why it computes a highest common factor and to give clues to a reason for carrying out the extra computations. You may also like to code up an extended Euclidean algorithm as a function that calls itself (say in ML rather than Java) and observe that use of while loops does not always lead to the shortest or most transparent code.

```
int a = 72, b = 30;
int u = 1, v = 0;
while (b != 0)
{ int q = a / b; int r = a -
      q*b; a = b;
      b = r;
      int t = u - q*v; u = v;
      v = t;
}
// Here a is the HCF. What are u, v?
```

Note that break can be used to exit other loops, and it is also used with switch statements, which will be described soon.

4.4.6 do

Sometimes the most natural way to write a loop puts the test of a termination condition at the end of the loop rather than at the start. This circumstance is supported by the do statement, although I find it much less useful than while. In fact I will often express

```
do
```

>>> Observe that the syntax for each of these command includes a semicolon, The identifier men-tioned in the full grammar is something I will not discuss here.

```
{
    ...
} while (xxx);
```

by writing it instead as

```
while (true)
{
    ...
    if (!xxx) break;
}
```

since I think that do puts the details of what the loop is about rather too far down the page. Anyway that also gave me a chance to include an example of a break statement for you! The issues of programming style here could give rise to a variety of discussions. A good policy is to try rather hard to make it very clear and obvious just when each loop you write is going to terminate, and indeed to make it clear (in comments as necessary) why you know it will eventually terminate.

4.4.7 for

Iteration with for has been seen in several examples. What is shown in the Java syntax is that each of the three components within the parentheses and separated by semicolons is optional. The most extreme case is when none are present: for (;;) { ... } means just the same as while (true) { ... }.

In for (A;B;C) the expression A is an initializer evaluated just once at the start of the loop. B is a boolean expression and is used just as in a while statement to determine when to terminate. Finally C gets evaluated between each cycle of the loop, and it often increments some variable. The idiom for (i=0;i<N;i++) executes its command N times counting from 0 to N-1. The alternative way of writing things is for (i=1;i<=N;i++). It loops the same number of times but is maybe slightly less commonly used. Of course with the second version the variable i starts at 1 not 0: this typically makes it less suitable for use as an array subscript because in Java subscripts start at 0.

4.4.8 switch, case and default

There are occasions when one wants to dispatch to many different code fragments based on the value of some expression. This could be achieved by writing a chain of if .. else statements, but often switch provides a much neater way of expressing things.

The construction starts with switch (*Expression*). The expression given must be of type char, byte, short or int. Note that long is not allowed. The switch-header is followed by a block enclosed in braces, and within this block there can be special switch labels. The usual sort reads " case *Constant*:" and control arrives just after the colon if the integer value of the switch expression agrees with the constant after case. It is often useful to specify what action should be taken if none of the cases that have explicit coverage happen, and for this a label " default:" can be set. Case (and default) labels do not disturb the usual sequential execution of statements, and so unless something special is done after one case is processed control will proceed to the next one. This is usually not what is wanted. A break; can be used to exit from the entire switch block. Many programmers would count it is good style to put an explicit comment in whenever a break is not being used, to show that its omission was deliberate and not an accident.

If no explicit default label is given but a switch is executed in such a way that none of the cases match it just acts as if there had been a default label just before its final close brace.

It is generally a good thing to use switch whenever you have more than three or four options to select between, in that it tends to be much clearer and easier to understand than length strings of nested if statements. In the following rather silly example it is imagined that the user has provided the function show Observe that the case labels do not have to be in any special order, and that a single statement can be attached to several labels.

```
        switch ((int)n)
        {
    case 2: show("the only even ");
            #   drop through
    case 3:  case 5:  case 7:
    case 11: case 13: case 17:
            show("prime\n");
            break;
    case 4:  case 9:
    case 16: show("square\n"); break;
    case 8: show("cube\n");
            break;
    default:show("dull or too large\n");
            #   now just drop off the end
        }
```

4.4.9 return

When a function has done all it needs to it will want to return a result. This is achieved using the return statement. Function definitions (see later) always indicate what type of result is required. They may have used the keyword void to indicate that no result is needed. Such is the case with main. For void functions one just writes " return;", while in all other cases the syntax is " return *Expression*;".

4.4.10 try, catch and throw, finally

Real programming languages need to be able to implement code that can recover from errors and handle unusual cases tidily. The handling scheme in Java uses the throw statement to raise exceptions. Throw statements specify an object which should generally[24] be of type Exception[25] . The effect is that control exits from the current block or procedure and any enclosing ones, all the way until a suitable handler is found. If no such handler is present the computation is terminated. The system has a number of built-in exceptions it will generate. For instance an attempt to divide by the integer 0 raises an exception of type ArithmeticExpression. Various functions that read from files can raise ex-ceptions to indicate that the file did not exist, the current u ser did not have permis-sion to read it or an attempt was made to read data beyond its end.

Handling exceptions involves prefixing a block with the word try and adding on the end of it one or more clauses that describe what to do in unusual cases. A clause that starts catch (*Argument*) is followed by another block which gets obeyed if the system detects an exception whose type matches that declared for the *Argument*. A single try may be followed by catch handlers for several different types of exception.

```
try
{ z = 1/0; } // raises an exception! catch
(ArithmeticException e) { ... }
```

After all catch clauses you can put the keyword finally followed by another block. The intent here is that this block will get executed come whatever, and it will usually be used to tidy files or data-structures that the program might other-wise have left in a mess. A typical scheme to provide robust access to files would go something like

```
<open the file for reading>
try
```

· I do not want to give the full and precise rules here!

· To be more precise of some type derived from Exception.

```
{ while (true) <read-more-from-file>
}
catch (<end-of-file-exception>)
{ // whole file read here. Good! <success
      code>
}
finally
{ // must tidy up even if some failure // other than
      end-of-file intruded
      <close the file>
}
```

Later on I will give concrete examples that fill in the functio n calls and so on in this framework.

Some programmers view catch and throw as neat and convenient language features to be used wherever they fit. Certainly the file-hand ling example above makes very good use of them. Others, and I tend to fit into this c ategory, would like to see them used rather sparingly in code since they can result in all sorts of loops and functions terminating unexpectedly early and therefore undermine attempts to make absolute statements about their end results.

4.4.11 assert

A statement of the form assert*Expression*; will evaluate the expression (which really ought not to have any side-effects. If its value is *false* and if some magic flag was supplied when the Java launcher was run then an except ion is raised. Assertions can have a second expression that can be used to give more details of what you thought had gone wrong. It is proper style to include them at places in your code where there is some reasonably cheap consistency check that you could apply and when used well they are a huge aid to testing and debugging.

If you run your program normally the assertions will not be checked, and furthermore having them in your source file will not hurt perf ormance enough to notice. If however you run the java command with the extra flag -ea the extra checks will be done. Usage such as

```
java -ea:CheckThisClass SomeClass
```

will arrange to check just the assertions in the named class.

4.4.12 Variable declarations

Variable declarations can occur anywhere within a block. They are also allowed in the first component of a for statement. The scope of a variable that is declared within a block runs from the declaration onwards until the end of the block. A declaration made in a for statement has a scope that covers the remainder of the for statement, including the end-test and increment expressions as well as the iterated block. In fact the scope of a declaration appears to include the initialiser for that variable, but if you try to use the variable there you should expect at least a warning message. So things like

```
{  int x = x+5;
     ...
}
```

should not be attempted! A local consists of a type, then the name of the variable being declared, and optionally one or more pairs of square brackets (to denote the declaration of an array). Any initializer follows an " =" sign, and for arrays the initializers are written in braces so that many individual values can be given so as to fill in the whole array. A local variable declaration can be preceded by the word final, and this marks the variable that is being declared as one that will not subsequently change. A convention is that constants should be spelt entirely in upper case, as have the examples PI and PLAIN that have been seen so far. Here is an example:

```
final double E = 2.718281828459045235;
E = 1/E;        // NOT valid because of "final"
```

4.4.13 Method definitions

A function definition starts with some optional qualifier wor ds. The available words are

public	protected	private	static
abstract	final	native	synchronized

and if present these can be written in any order. I will explain what they mean later on. Next comes the type of result the function will return, which is either an type or the special word void to indicate "no result". Next is the name of the function that is being declared, followed by a list of formal arguments (in parentheses). A formal argument must be given a type, and may be preceded by final if the body of the function will never update it. The grammar shown earlier indicated that pairs of square brackets may be written after the formal parameter list, but this should not be used in any new code[26]. If the execution of the function can cause an exception to be raised and this exception is to be caught somewhere then the fact must be mentioned by following the list of formal parameters by the

* It is a concession to some earlier versions of Java where it could be used for functions that returned arrays.

keyword throws and then a list of exception types. Finally there is a block (ie some statements within braces) that forms the body of the function that is being defined.

For the moment you will *still* have to take the qualifiers public and static on trust. They relate to the construction of the class that the whole file defines.

4.4.14 Exercises

Concerning $3n + 1$

Take any number n. If it is even then halve it, while if it is odd replace it with $3n + 1$. Repeat this process to see what happens in the long run. For various very small integers you will find that you end up in a cycle $1 \to 4 \to 2 \to 1 \ldots$ but it is not at first clear whether this is the ultimate fate when you st art from an arbitrary integer.

Write a program that generates the sequence starting from each integer from 1 to 1000. If the sequence ends at 1 record the number of steps it took to get there. If you have taken over 10000 steps on some particular sequence then stop and report just that value: after all maybe the sequence starting from that seed goes on for ever, either by diverging to infinity or by finding a cycle different from the one that includes 1. If on the way you generate an odd number larger -than (Integer.MAX VALUE-1)/3 you should also stop the calculation there since otherwise you would suffer from integer overflow and subsequ ent work would be nonsense. The constant Integer.MAX VALUE is another Java built-in constant useful in cases such as this.

Arrange that you only print anything when a new record is broken for the length of a sequence or when you would reach integer overflow. For each record-breaker display the seed, the number of steps taken before 1 is reached (or the fact that an overflow occurs) and the largest value in the sequence concerned.

Tickable Exercise 4

As you start this exercise note that ticks 1, 2, 3 and 4 are probably fairly easy. Tick 5 is going to be a somewhat larger piece of work so as soon as you have finished this one you might like to look ahead and get started on it!

In ML a function called quicksort could be defined as

```
fun select ff [] = []
  | select ff (a :: b) =
        if (ff a) then a :: select ff b
        else select ff b;
```

```
fun quicksort [] = []
  | quicksort (a :: b) =
      quicksort (select (fn p => p < a) b) @ [a] @
      quicksort (select (fn p => p >= a) b);
```

The idea is to use the first element of the input list as a *pivot*. One then selects out first all the remaining values that are less than this pivot, a nd all the values that are at least as large. Recursive calls sort the two sub-lists thus generated, and a final and completely sorted list is obtained by concatenating the various parts that have been collected.

The ML version is very elegant and shows some of the important ideas behind the Quicksort algorithm. However it misses out several other things that are im-portant in the real Quicksort method, mostly issues concerning use of memory. In this exercise you are to implement a version of Quicksort in Java. You should write a procedure with signature[27]

```
void quickSortInner(int [] v, int i, int j)
```

which will sort that part of the array v that has subscripts from i to j. It will be up to you to decide if these limits are inclusive or exclusive. The procedure should work by first seeing if the sub-array it has to work on is empty. If so it can return without doing anything! Otherwise it should take the first (active) element of the array as a pivot and rearrange[28] the remaining items so that the array gets partitioned at a point k such that the pivot has been moved to position k, all items to the left are smaller than the pivot and all items to the right are at least as large as it. It should do this re-arrangement without using more than a few extra simple variables: ie it is not acceptable to create a whole fresh array and copy material via it. quickSortInner can then call itself recursively in a way suggested by the ML code to complete the sorting process.

You should also define a function called just quickSort that takes only one argument — the array to be sorted. Remember that the .length selector can tell you how large the array is.

To show that your code works you should demonstrate the following tests:

>>> Create an array of length 10 and show the effect of sorting it when its initial contents are (a) the numbers 1 to 10 starting of in the right order to begin with, (b) 1 to 10 in exactly the opposite order to begin with, (c) ten num-bers generated by nextInt() from the random number package (d) ten numbers all of which are zero;

• The signature of a function is just the specification of the ty pes of its arguments and result.

• Remember the National Flag exercise.

>>> Measure the time taken to sort various length vectors of random data where you should use lengths 16, 32, 64, . . . up until the sorting run takes several seconds. For each test compute the quotient of the time taken and the value $N \log(N)$ where N is the number of items being sorted.

Optional part for those who are keen: Read the Java documentation for the Array.sort(int []) method that Java 2 provides. Write code to time it and compare the results with the code you wrote yourself. When measuring times work with arrays long enough that each test takes several seconds. Observe that the fact that the Java libraries provide you with sorting methods (see also Collections.sort) means that most Java users will never need to implement their own Quicksort: you are doing it here as an exercise and because it is good for Computer Scientists to understand what goes on inside libraries, since next time around it may be their job to implement libraries for some new language.

As a further *optional* extension to this exercise consider the following and adjust your code accordingly, then repeat all your tests:

>>> The ML quicksort partitions items by comparing them with the value that happened to be first in the list. In the plausible cases where t he original data is already in ascending or descending order this leads to excessive cost.
Selecting as the "pivot" the median of the first, last and midd le element from the array being sorted[29] does better;

>>> It is probably best to stop quickSort from recursing once it gets down to sub-arrays of length 3 or 4. The end result is that it *almost* sorts the array, but a final pass of bubble-sort can finish off the job nice and fa st. Is this born out in your code?

>>> The partitioning code here can be delicate! Unless you are careful it can escape beyond the bounds of the array, or it can get muddled about whether the two final values in the middle of the array need exchanging or not. Sim-ple implementations can be made safe by making all the end-conditions in your loops composite ones rather like

```
while (k>=i && v[k] > pivot) ...
```

while if we could get away with it it should be faster to go something more like

```
while (v[k] > pivot) ...
```

[29] Always supposing there are at least 3 items in the list.

Investigate how well you can trim down your inner loops while retaining code that always works! The Part IB course on Data Structures and Algorithms and the textbook by Cormen et al[9] are where this level of detailed study really belongs!

(End of tickable exercise)

Highest Common Factors

Implement code to compute Highest Common Factors using the Euclidean Algo-rithm. Extend it to use the extended algorithms that at the end will allow you to solve equations of the form

$$Au + Bv = 1$$

Tickable Exercise 5

The work called for here will be done in sections, and it is expected that while working towards the tick you will be able to design, code and test each section before moving on to the next. The idea involves creating a package of routines that can compute with (univariate) polynomials. For the purposes of this exercise a polynomial

$$(a_0 + a_1x + a_2x^2 + \ldots + a_nx^n)/b$$

will be represented as an instance of a the class:

```
class Poly
{
        private String variableName;
        private long [] coeffs;
        private long denominator;
        ... constructors and methods as needed
}
```

where variableName holds " x", the array called coeffs stores the coefficients a_0 to a_n and the long denominator holds the value shown as b above. Because Java lets you enquire as to the length of an array it is not necessary to store the degree n explicitly. In this representation common factors should be cancelled out between numerator and denominator, and the highest degree coefficient a_n should never be zero. In this exercise all polynomials will be in terms of the same variable, x, so the variableName should always be set to "x" and it will not play much of a part in any of the calculations! Step by step carry out the following tasks, testing what you have done as best you can as you go:

Create simple polynomials: Write functions that can create the "polynomial" that represents just a given integer, a given fraction and the simple polynomial " x";

Debug-quality printing: Write code that takes a polynomial and displays its coefficients. For this part of the exercise it is not at all impor tant that the display format you design be tidy or that it respects line-lengths. So for instance you may generate output such as

(1*x^0 + 0*x^1 + -3*x^2)/2

with various unnecessary symbols in there. The object is to be able to see your polynomials clearly enough that you can test and demonstrate what comes next!

Special-case multiplication: Write code to multiply a polynomial by an integer, to divide it by an integer, and to multiply it by x. Note that in the first two cases you will need to do calculations (involving greatest common divisors[30]) to reduce the coefficients to lowest terms. In the latter cas e the result will be of one higher degree than the input and so will be represented with a coefficient vector one item longer. These routines sho uld not alter their input, but should create new polynomial data to represent the results;

Addition and Subtraction: Take two polynomials and create another that represents their sum (or difference). This involves more fun with ensuring that the result is over a common denominator, and subtracting two polynomials can lead to a result of lower degree if the leading terms cancel (as can adding if the leading terms start off as similar but with opposite signs);

Multiply: If you have one polynominal of degree m and one of degree n then their product is of degree $m + n$. Write code that computes it;

Differentiate: in fact differentiation of a polynomial by its variable is rather an easy operation (and so would be integration, which you would need in an optional extra to this exercise). If the polynomial contains an original terms $a_i x^i$ then the derivative contains just $(ia_i)x^{i-1}$;

Proof of pudding part 1: Let $P_0 = 1$, $P_1 = x$ and from there on define a sequence using the recurrence relationship

$$P_n = ((2n - 1)xP_{n-1} - (n - 1)P_{n-2})/n$$

>>> Otherwise known as highest common factor.

Using your polynomial manipulation program calculate and tabulate the val-ues up to (and including) P_{12};

Proof of pudding part 2: Now instead define

$$P_n = \frac{1}{2^n n!} \frac{d^n}{dx^n} (x^2 - 1)^n$$

(This is known as Rodrigues formula, in case you wondered, and the polynomials you are computing are Legendre Polynomials)

Using this recipe compute and display values up to P_{12}. The two sequences of polynomials you have computed ought to match!

Testing to destruction: extend your tables until the values computed by the two recipies for P_n are incorrect because of some internal integer overflow, and report where your program first displays a result that is cert ainly incorrect;

Optional extra (a): Write code that evaluates a polynomial at an integer value of its variable, ie at $x = n$. Write code that computes the (indefinite) integral of a polynomial with respect to its variable. Combine these two to allow you to evaluate definite integrals. Display a table showing valu es of

$$\int_{x=-1}^{1} P_i(x) P_j(x)$$

for i and j running from 0 to 5 (say);

Optional extra (b): Let y be one of the polymonials (P_n) that you have just computed. Evaluate

$$(1 - x^2)y'' - 2xy' + n(n + 1)y$$

Tabulate this for various small values of n.

Note: the examples worked with here are Legendre polynomials, and provide an example taken from Sturm-Liouville theory. Optional extra (a) shows that they are orthogonal over the range from −1 to +1 and this in fact makes them useful for producing certain sorts of good numerical approximations to functions. Optional extra (b) is showing you that these polynomials are solutions of a differential equation: many other interesting sequences of functions satisfy recurrence for-mulae, have orthogonality properties *and* are solutions to differential equations! Abramowitz and Stegun's book of tables[1] is probably the easiest place to sug-gest you look to find out more.

(End of tickable exercise)

Pollard Rho integer factorisation

In previous years this was Tickable exercise 5. There are in fact a few delicacies with regard to integer overflow (which do not greatly damage i t as an exercise but which could raise questions about it). You may still like to try it!

The explanation of this exercise is quite long, and it maybe looks messy, but I can assure you that the code that has to be written is tolerably short and managable once you have sorted out what needs doing.

Randomised factorisation: Implement the following algorithm that (possibly) finds a factor of an integer that it is given:

A single trial that looks for a factor of N is performed by selecting a random positive number R and computing $S = R$ % N. This is a number between 0 and $N - 1$. If the number is 0 deem this trial a failure. Next compute the highest common factor of S and N. If this is 1 then again the trial is deemed a failure. However if the HCF is not 1 then it is a factor of N and because it is also a factor of S it must be less than N. This counts as success!

The complete factorisation algorithm works by running a number of trials.

If for a number N the first $\sqrt{N}$ trials all fail then we will pretend that N is prime. Otherwise a factor of it has been found, and dividing this into N gives us its co-factor. Smaller factors of each of these can then be sought using the same technique.

Use this procedure to try to factorise the numbers $2^i - 1$ for i from 2 upwards, stopping when your program starts to take more than a second or so to run.

The Birthday problem: Suppose we have a sequence of numbers all of which are less than N, and these values are generated in some way such that each number x_n is some fixed function of x_{n-1}. A concrete example would be if $x_n = (x_{n-1}^2 - 1)$ % N. For most N and for $x_0 = 2$ this sequence[31] is in fact pretty unpredictable.

Any such sequence must eventually repeat a value, and once it has it nec-essarily continues in a loop. If consecutive values behave well enough as if they are random up to this point then the expected length of the sequence

[31] There is a significant delicacy here: when you compute $x_{n-1}^2 -$ its value can be almost as large as N^2 even though the remaindering will rapidly bring it down to a smaller range. This can lead to integer overflow and a particularly un-wanted effect is th at a value you generate may end up unexpectedly negative (when N^2 is outside the valid range of integers). I suggest you mostly ignore this here (!) and at most take an absolute value to ensure that the sequences you generate consist of positive numbers. Also there is not much special about starting with $x_0 = 2$ and other randomish starting values might work just as well.

before a repeat is related to the problem of how many people you have to have in a room before you should expect to find that two of them s hare a birthday. In this case the room is on a planet in a galaxy far far away, where
the length of the year is N, and the statistics suggest that we need around $\sqrt{}$
>>> of our aliens.

For this exercise you are to imagine one algorithm that detects a cycle and implement a second and much better one.

The algorithm you just have to imagine guarantees to find a cyc le as soon as it arises. It allocates a big array and stores values in this array as they are generated. As each one is generated it also checks through the ones already seen to see if the new value has occurred before, and if so declare the loop detected. This method is easy to visualise but it needs an array as long as the longest potential loop, and the search means that before finding a loop at step n it has done about $n^2/2$ comparisons with old values. This is slow.
The second method, which you should implement, records the value of x_i each time i reaches the next power of 2 and compares newly generated val-ues against this one stored value. It argues that if there is a loop then even-tually the loop will be totally traversed between consecutive powers of 2, and thus will be detected. Furthermore this will be at worst a factor of two beyond the place where the first repeat happened.

Having coded the second loop-detection algorithms try it on sequences generated by $x_n =$ x_n^2 1 − 1 mod N for various N and verify that for a reasonable proportion of values of N and x_0 a loop is found after very roughly $\sqrt{N}$ steps.

Pollard Rho: This builds on the previous two parts, so please do not start it until you have completed them. But then re-work the loop detection code so that instead of comparing each new x_n with a saved value x_2k using an equality test compute the HCF of N and $x_n - x_2k$. Stop if this is not 1, ie if a factor of N has been found. In the case when $x_n = x_2k$ the method has failed: you may either give up in that case or try starting again with a different value for x_0.

Implement this using the Java long type. If the number N is composite it is probable (although not guaranteed) that this will find a factor of N within around $\sqrt[4]{N}$ trials, and will thus be able to find a factor any Java long value quite rapidly. Of course if N starts off as a prime this scheme will never manage to find a factor of it! To test this you should probably create numbers that are known to be composite by multiplying together two int-sized values.

Optional: The scheme above does not of itself find a complete decomposi tion of an integer into prime factors — it just splits composite nu mbers into two. A complete fatorisation method needs to extend it with fi rst a filter so that numbers that are prime are not attacked, and secondly with recursive calls that try to factor the two numbers that Pollard Rho split our num-ber into. Investigate the Java BigInteger class that provides arithmetic on long integers and which also provides a test for (probable) primality. Re-implement your code to use BigInteger rather than long and to use isProbablyPrime to avoid trying to factor when it is futile. Thus produce code that can produce complete factorisations of reasonably large numbers. How many digits long a number can you factorise in say 20 seconds?

Some of you no doubt consider yourselves to be Java experts! You may like to arrange that the calculation $x_{n-1}^2 - 1 \bmod N$ is computed exactly even when N is almost as large as a Java long can be, and that overflow does not interfere. An easy way to do this is to use the Java library big integer support, but what I would prefer here would be code expressed entirely in terms of use of long arithmetic.

4.5 Java classes and packages

What has been described thus far should provide a foundation for understanding the small-scale structure of Java programs. If you have understood it you are equipped to write programs that have up to (say) half a dozen sub-functions and that are limited to living in a single source file. So far the da ta that Java can work with has been limited to the primitive types int and so on, together with arrays of them. The time has now come to discuss the Java idea of a *class*. This is used both to support the construction of user-defined data-struc tures and to impose an order on programs that are large enough that they should properly be spread across several source files. A discussion of Java classes will inclu de an explanation of what all the " ." characters are doing in the sample programs seen so far. All of this counts as "Object Oriented Programming".

One of the aspects of programming language design that has proved to be especially important is that control of the visibility of names. This whole issue tends to look rather frivolous — a distraction — while your pr ograms are only a page or two long but it makes a critical difference to big (and perhaps especially collaborative) projects. There are several interlocking reasons to want to keep name-spaces under control. One as so that a large chunk of code can be given a cleanly defined interface consisting of the functionality that it makes visible to the outside world. Everything not so exported is then deemed private to the group who maintain that body of code, and they may change internal parts of their design

... old-fashioned approaches
to software construction ...

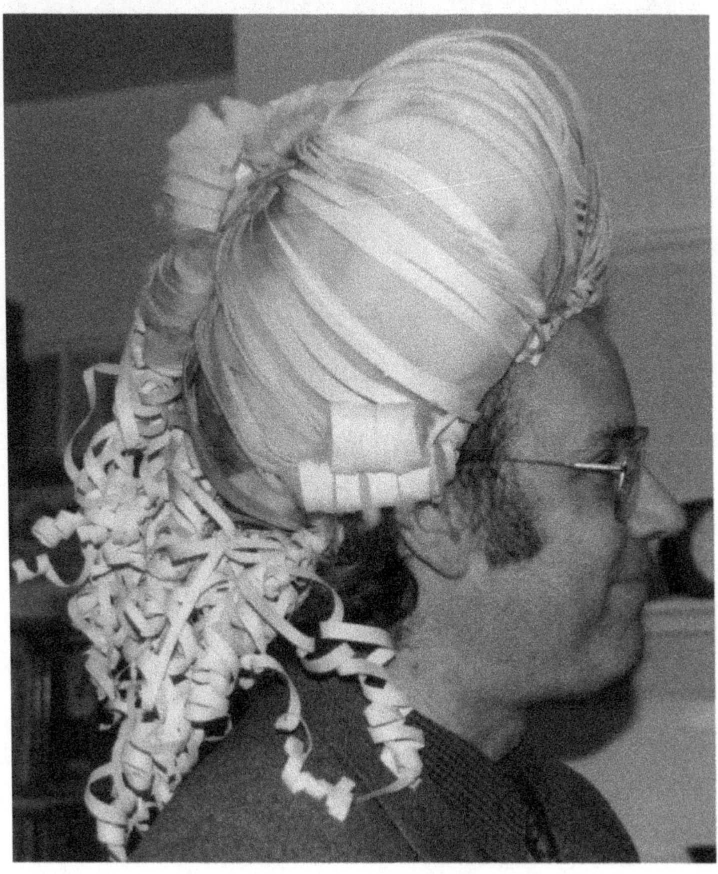

Figure 4.5: Classes and Packages make Java "modern".

with complete confidence that this can not hurt anybody else.

A second reason for keeping name-spaces well controlled is so that different parts of a large program are free to re-use the most obvious names for their func-tions and variables, secure that this can not introduce unexpected clashes.

Related to both of these is the fact that when trying to understand code limits on the visibility of names can allow you to concentrate on just the range in the code where something is relevant.

Java controls access to names at three levels. At the finest gr ain it has scope rules that are much like those of most other programming languages. If a local variable is declared within a block that variable can only be referenced using code textually within that block. Java understands the idea that a re-declaration of a variable in an inner block would create a different variable with the same name, and that within the inner block the new variable would shadow the old one, as in

```
int func(int a)
{
    {   int a = 4, b = 5; // ???? for (int a=0; a<10; a++)
        b++; // ???? System.out.printf("%d %d%n", a, b);
    }
    return a;
}
```

and it views this as something that could be codified and that t o a computer has a totally logical interpretation. But that it is a potential cause of real confusion to human programmers so it should be prohibited! Thus the above example will be rejected by the Java compiler and all the interesting computer-science discussion of exact rules about scope can be set aside. You may like to note, however, the variables do not clash in any way if their scopes do not overlap, so the following is valid:

```
int func(int a)
{
    { int i = 4;
        for (int j=0; j<a; j++) i++;
        System.out.println(a + " " + i);
    }
    for (int i=0; i<10; i++) a *= 2;
    for (int i=0; i<a; i++) a–;
    return a;
}
```

The scopes associated with each declaration of i are disjoint.

The other two aspects of Java name-space control are more interesting. The important words used here are *class* and *package*.

All names of Java variables and procedures[32] live in some class. In general you have to gain access to the class before you can use its members[33]. A member of the current class can be referred to just by giving its unqualified name, but in other cases you need to have access to an object of the required class and refer to the member using a dot " ." as a selector on it. This is what was happening in cases such as g.drawLine where g was a variable of type Graphics and drawLine was a member of that class. When a class is defined the user can a rrange which of its members can be referenced by other classes in this manner, so that internal details of the class can not even be accessed using this sort of explicit naming. The word public flags a component of a class that should be universally visibl e while private marks one that should not.

Classes thus contribute in two ways to the avoidance of confusion over names. Firstly they mean that most references to things outside the current class will include a dot selector that indicates fairly explicitly what context the name is to be taken from, and secondly they can arrange that some names are kept totally local to the class within which they are used and can *never* be accessed from anywhere else. It is perhaps worth reminding you at this stage of the qualifier final that can turn a variable declaration into the definition of a const ant. There are further refinements in the control of name visibility and use that Jav a provides, and the keywords protected, abstract and static relate to some of them: these will be discussed later on.

Classes themselves have names, and so a scheme is needed to structure the name-space that they live in. A collection of classes can be placed in a "package". When classes are declared only those that have been given the public attribute[34] are visible outside the package. Furthermore since the idea is that any other Java code[35] can access the public classes of a package there is a somewhat curious linkage between package names and the filing system on your co mputer. This linkage is mediated by a thing called the "class path" which c an list the places that Java should search to find the compiled code if you refer t o a class defined in some package. You can expect that any reasonable default Java setup will have your class path set up for you already so that you can access all of the standard Java libraries and so that code in the current directory can be used. The full names of classes generally contain dots. Various names starting with the component java are reserved for the system, and ones starting with sun are for use by Sun

>>> From now on I will increasingly move towards the Java notation and call these "methods".

[33] We will see later that in some cases, when the name has been declared as static, one can refer to the item via the name of its containing class. But in the more general case it will be necessary to have an instance of the class and access the item via that.

>>> Making a class public is a similar idea to making a member of that class public, but of course we are talking now about a different level in the structure of a program.

>>> Ideally anywhere in the world!

Computers, who designed Java. The various further parts to package names are intended to group packages into hierarchies. For instance every package whose name starts with java.awt is to do with the Java Abstract Window Toolkit, which is the part of Java that provides facilities to pop up windows on your display. The package java.awt.event is the sub-part of this that contains classes relating to events — we have seen an example where these could be caused by the user clicking with the mouse but there are others. The Java documentation contains a list of all the predefined packages that are part of the Java co re, and then lets you browse the complete set of classes defined in each. Each class of course provides a number of variables and methods: the number of standard library methods is huge!

Specifying full names in the package hierarchy could become very tedious, so Java provides a user-configurable way of setting up shorthan d forms of reference. Recall that various sample programs we have seen began with a collection of import statements

```
import javax.swing.*;
import java.awt.*;
import java.awt.event.*;
```

This adjusted Java's name resolution scheme so that the class MouseEvent (say) could be referred to by that short name. Without the import it would still have been possible to write the same program but it would have been necessary to use a fully spelt-out " java.awt.event.MouseEvent" to name the class, and that would involve knowing exactly which of the standard parts of the Java library MouseEvent belongs in. The " *" in the import statements show tells Java to support short names for all the classes in the packages named. It is also possible to put a single class name in an import statement. This could be useful if only one member of a package was to be used and you did not want to risk confusion with other names from that package. Some Java programmers take the view that import with a " *" introduces risk of giving them access to classes other than ones the know about, and so always spell their imports out fully, despite that being a little more verbose. Note that the syntax of Java only allows the wild-card " *" to be placed right at the end of an import where it means "all the classes in this package".

If you issue import statements that attach to two or more packages that define identically named classes then Java will refuse to get muddled: it just insists that you use fully spelt-out names for the classes that could otherwise be ambiguously resolved. This is probably safer than a scheme where the first (or possibly the last?) import statement took precedence.

Java comes with around 200 and huge numbers of pre-defined cla sses, and so getting to know them all is a big job. You are not expected to do so especially as future Java releases will add yet more, and it is probable that when you work on any big Java project you may find yourself using substantia l third-party class libraries. But it does make a lot of sense for you to have a good overview of what is available to you so that when relevant you can use existing well-tested library code rather than starting to write something of your won.

As well as being a way of organising the name-space all Java classes count as data-types. When something's type is a class it is usual to refer to the thing as an "object". Thought of in terms of objects, a class defines a data structure that contains fields that are the variables defined in it and ha ppens also to be able to contain definitions of functions that will access these fie lds. If the variables were declared public then any code anywhere can access them and so there do not really have to be any (explicit) methods defined within the cl ass. There will in fact always be a few implicitly defined ones that are to do with the creation and deletion of objects.

Taking a minimal approach[36] to class definition I can now set up a definition that would let me represent binary trees where each node in the tree contains an integer:

- Compare the ML version, which would be
- datatype Tree =
- nullTree |
- makeTree of int*Tree*Tree;
- or some such.

```
class BinaryTreeOfIntegers
{
    public int value;
    public BinaryTreeOfIntegers left;
    public BinaryTreeOfIntegers right;
}
```

Comparison with the ML version reminds us that it is important to be able to have some way of telling when the left and right children of such a tree do not really exist. In ML that was achieved with an explicit alternative constructor, which I called nullTree. In Java *any* variable which has a class[37] as its type can either hold a proper instance of that class (ie an object) or it can hold the special value null. This value is provided as a keyword in Java. Ie the word null is hard-wired into the Java language and not just some curious pre-defined variable. It also has the odd property that the same value may be used with any sort of class

>>> The class I define here would work, but it misses out on exploit ing a lot of structuring and
security features that classes can provide, and so is *just* a minimal start.

· Or array.

or array variable to set the variable to a state where it "does not hold an any object at all".

Once a class has been defined it will be useful to declare varia bles using it and create objects to go in them. Here I will create a rather small tree using the above class definition:

```
...
BinaryTreeOfIntegers a1, a2, a3;
>>> a1, a2, a3 are all un-initialised here, and
>>> Java complains if you try to compile a program
>>> that relies on the values of variables that
>>> might not have been given a value.
a1 = new BinaryTreeOfIntegers();
a2 = new BinaryTreeOfIntegers();
a3 = new BinaryTreeOfIntegers();
a1.value = 1;
a2.value = 2;
a3.value = 3;
a1.left     = a2;
a1.right = a3;
• the next 2 lines are not needed in that
• null is the default value given to a field
• that would hold an object.
a2.left = a2.right = null;
a3.left = a3.right = null;
...
```

Note (but do not worry about, for now) the parentheses after the class name fol-lowing new. And also observe how dreadfully clumsy all this is.

Note that Java provides default initialisers for instance variable in classes and elements in arrays, but not for local variables within methods. The default values used are zero for numeric fields, false for booleans, `\0' for characters and null for all references.

Anybody who is a C or C++ programmer is liable to have a question to ask at this stage, but those who have mostly seen ML should see all this as reasonable. You can also see " ." being used as a selector to access the components of a class object. The C programmers can read my footnote[38]! Java objects are created in much the same way as Java arrays are, using new, and there is no need to take

---

>>> In C or C++ one would distinguish rather carefully between a structure and a pointer to the structure. And in C terms all Java class variables hold pointers. However in Java it is not really useful to think this way since all Java operations have been designed to prevent any explicit tricks involving pointers. Please try to think of Java objects as more in the style of ML data. In C you the explicit visibility of the difference between a structure that is directly at hand and one that is referred to via a pointer leads to a distinction between the use of " ." and " ->" to access

any special action when you have finished with one. The Java ru n-time system is expected to tidy up memory for you. However grossly excessive object creation can either consume time or utterly run you out of memory. The fi rst loop in the following code does not do anything very useful with the objects it creates, and it discards them all rather rapidly. It may be a bit inefficient. The second loop creates a million objects and chains them all together so that none of space concerned can be recycled. At one million you may get away with this, but if you tried to do this a few hundred times more your computer's memory would not be able to keep up with the demands of the program and an exception would be raised to report this fact.

```
for (int i=0; i<1000000; i++)
{  BinaryTreeOfIntegers x =
               new BinaryTreeOfIntegers();
           x.value = i;
           // x is implicitly discarded here
}
BinaryTreeOfIntegers w;
for (int i=0; i<1000000; i++)
{  BinaryTreeOfIntegers x =
              new BinaryTreeOfIntegers();
      x.right = w;          // chain on to w
      w = x;
}
```

There are very few cases in Java where it would be considered good style to define a class that only had variables defined within it [39]. Mostly an attempt will be made to collect almost all of the methods that work with the class as part of it. Very frequently the variables in the class can then be made private, and the public methods provide a clean and abstract interface to everything. There is something of a convention about providing and naming methods to access the data stored in an instance of a class: methods that update variables have names starting with set, ones that retrieve boolean values start is while others that retrieve information start with get. Here is the previous example expanded to follow these conventions, and adjusted so that the case of boolean variables can be illustrated:

---

components. Again Java does not need this and so only has one notation, even though in some sense it uses dot where a C programmer would naturally reach for an arrow.

* The most plausible good case I can think of is when all the variables are marked as final so they are constants and the class is just used to encapsulate the name-space within which these constants are defined.

- Compare the previous Java version where
- the variables were public but there were
- no methods.

```
class BinaryTreeOfBools
{
        private boolean value;
        private BinaryTreeOfBools left;
        private BinaryTreeOfBools right;

        public void setValue(boolean n) { value = n; } public void
        setLeft(BinaryTreeOfBools t) { left = t; }
        public void setRight(BinaryTreeOfBools t)
        { right = t; }

        public boolean isValueTrue()
        { return (value==true); }
        public BinaryTreeOfBools getLeft()
        { return left; }
        public BinaryTreeOfBools getRight()
        { return right; }
}
```

For small classes this just adds way too much extra verbiage and feels silly. How-ever for a large and compilicated class with many other methods having a regular and predictable naming can be a real help. It also provides a way that you can give read-only access to some variables or you can check the sanity of values to be assigned to others, ending up with much finer-grained co ntrol over access than even use of the public and private qualifiers give you. The term "bean" is sometimes used for Java classes that follow this set of conventions, and some programming tools exploit it. Because it makes small programs so much bulkier I will not use this style in every example in these notes, but you can notice that many of the Java library classes clearly have and you might think about it again when you move on to writing large classes for yourself.

Here is a sample Java class that might be useful within other programs and that illustrate methods that actually do something useful. It is a start at code that will enable Java code to work with complex numbers. An odd-looking programming style that it illustrates is one where to combine two complex numbers, say a and b, one will call a method associated with one of them, passing the other as argument. Thus the sum of the two values will be requested as a.plus(b). It is not possible (in Java) to redefine or extend the basic " +" operator to make it "add" objects from some new user-defined class, hence use of a method name su ch as add is necessary here[40].

```
public class Complex
{  private double x, y;
      // define setX, setY, getX, getY here if you want.

      public Complex(double realPart, double imagPart)
      {  x = realPart;
           y = imagPart;
      }
      public double modulus()
      {  return Math.sqrt(x*x+y*y);
      }
      public Complex plus(Complex a)
      {  return new Complex(x + a.x, y + a.y);
      }
      public Complex times(Complex a)
      {  return new Complex(x*a.x - y*a.y,
                                          x*a.y + y*a.x);
      }
}
```

This would be placed in a file Complex.java and compiled using javac in the usual way to make a file Complex.class. Because I have not put in a package statement this class will live in a default package, and when other Java programs run and they want a class called Complex they might manage to find this one if its class file is still in the current directory.

The Complex class illustrates one new concept. Observe the method defini - tion that uses the name of the class as its own name and which does not specify a separate return type:

```
public Complex(double realPart, double imagPart)
     {  x = realPart; y =
              imagPart;
}
```

It has no return statement in it. A method whose name matches that of the class is a *constructor* and you will typically use it with new to create fresh instances of the class thing concerned. If you do not specify an explicit constructor function then a default one is supplied — it has no arguments and does not lea ves all variables in their default state. It is valid to have several constructors provided that the types

---

• In contrast the language C++ does allow you to extend the meaning of all the operators that are denoted by punctuation marks. Many people believe the conciseness and elegance that can be achieved that way is more then balanced out by the potential for severe confusion.

of their arguments are different. Observe here how the methods that are members of the class all have access to the private variables, but no code outside the class will have.

Sometimes when referencing a variable it is useful to stress that you are talking about one in the current instance. The keyword this always refers to the object from which you invoked a method, and so the constructor and the plus methods above could have been written out in a way that some would consider clearer:

```
public Complex(double x, double y)
{  this.x = x;
      this.y = y;
}

public Complex plus(Complex a)
{  return new Complex(this.x + a.x, this.y + a.y);
}
```

Explicit use of this can be used to avoid mixups if the name of a formal parameter for a method matches the name of a variable in the class. Consider the following and the muddle that would arise without the use of this, but also note how much nicer it is to select names that avoid any hint of a clash.

```
public Complex plus(Complex x)
{  return new Complex(this.x + x.x, this.y + x.y);
}
```

4.5.1 Exercises

Complete the Complex class

The class as shown here does not support division, and does not have an equal-ity test. If you define a method called toString() in it then will be called to "print" the number when you use " +" to concatenate it with a string. Finish off the Complex class adding in these and whatever other facilities you feel will be generally useful.

Polar Complex Numbers

The Complex represents complex numbers in Cartesian form, ie as $x + iy$. But the internal variables x and y that it uses are both private so nobody outside the class can tell this! An alternative representation of complex numbers would store a number as a pair (r, q) where the complex value concerned had modulus r and argument q. In other words one would have $z = re^{iq}$. At the cost of comput-ing a few arc-tangents and the like it is possible to create a re-worked complex class that has exactly the same external behaviour as the original one but which stores internal values in polar form. The constructor function and addition become messier, multiplication becomes easier and the modulus function becomes utterly trivial. Implement and test the polar version of the class.

Wolves and Caribou

On a certain island there live some wolves and some caribou. In year *n* there are obviously w_n wolves and c_n caribou. What happens the next year depends. . .

- Wolves hunt, and the total number of dinners they get is proportional to $w_n k_n$. The number of baby wolves is automatically proportional to the num-ber of dinners their (potential) parents are able to eat over and above the amount needed to keep the parents active. The wolf minimum feed intake and reproductive capability may be modelled as

$$w_{n+1} = w_n + k_1 w_n (c_n - k_2)$$

- In each year the stock of caribou would increase by a factor k_3 were it not for the depredations of the wolves, since each dinner for a wolf is one less member of the herd. Thus

$$c_{n+1} = k_3 c_n - k_1 w_n c_n$$

- Baby wolves eat, hunt and reproduce as from year $n + 1$, and there are no losses of caribou other than as described above. In particular we do not have to worry about over-grazing etc.

At the beginning of time the island is stocked with a herd of 100000 caribou, and a medium-sized pack of ravening wolves. Over a number of years various things could happen. Either wolves or caribou or both could die out, or the pop-ulations could stabilise. For some values of the constants and initial wolf popula-tion various of these do indeed occur. For instance if at the start there are twice as many wolves as caribou the next year there will only be wolves left (one should adjust the equations given so that negative populations get turned into zero ones), and the year after that the wolves all expire of hunger.

In fact for many configurations the populations do not stabil ise, but they do of-ten get locked into stable cycles that last several years. This improbable situation has been observed by real naturalists not only in the situation described here but with regard to disease spread (mumps and children say) and other natural systems. Write java code to investigate.

Packages and jar files

Make a sub-directory called (say) ex251 and put some Java source files there. Put package ex251 at the top of the files. Now compile the code, eg saying javac ex251/*.java. By unless you explicitly set a *classpath* Java looks for classes that are in a given package by using the package name as if it described a chain of sub-directories down from the current directory. So now set up several different packages and create files that illustrate the use of protected and others that fail to compile because you have not made allowance for suitable cross-package visibility. Now look up about *jar* files and prove to yourself that you can take a complete Java program (consisting of many classes) and consolidate it into a single (jar) file that can then let anybody else run it in a simp le and convenient way.

These activities are not essential for any of the example programs that you have to write for this year's Java course, but starting to investigate and practise now will put you in a good position for some of next year's work, and particularly the Group Project. I am also aware that this exercise is asking you to read ahead in these notes. . .

Tickable Exercise 6

The following definition of a paint method uses the rudimentary Complex class as shown earlier in this section. The Mandelbrot set can be drawn by considering the sequence defined by $z_0 = 0$ and $z_{n+1} = z_n^2 + c$ where both z and c are complex numbers. For most values of c eventually values of z_n become large. If one counts and finds the smallest n such that $|z_n| > K$ for some suitable K then that n will depend on the value of c that was used. The well-known pictures arise by using different colours to display the values of n associated with values of $c = x + iy$ as x and y vary. Because drawing this in-volves a significant calculation for every single point within the ap-plet's window it can be painfully time-consuming. To arrange that the screen looks more interesting this

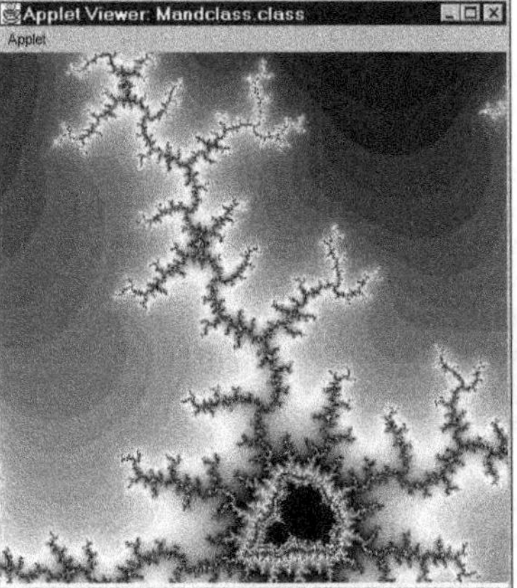

code arranges to draw a crude blocky version first and then gra dually refine it into the correct high-resolution image. You may have seen some web browsers do similar things to give better apparent responsiveness when loading and displaying pictures from web sites! The code draws a part of the Mandelbrot set centred around (midX, midY) and with width range, these referring to the values of the constant c in the iteration. If the value of *z* has not grown large within LIMIT steps it is supposed that it never will. The code illustrates use of the Color class. Colours are sometimes specified in terms of the amounts of Red , Blue and Green that go to make them up. Printers will tend to think in terms of Cyan, Magenta and Yellow[41] while in yet other circumstances one uses Hue (running through the colours of the rainbow), Saturation (eg white through pinks up to a full-blooded rich red) and Brightness (all colours fading to black at zero brightness, just as all wash out to white (or grey) at zero saturation).

Insert this program in a suitable framework and investigate other areas of the display by altering the relevant variables. You should be aware that if you increase the screen size or LIMIT the code can become very time-consuming. Indeed it might very well be sensible while testing to decrease the fine st resolution used to say 8 rather than 1. And because the paint method computes the whole picture each time it is called any disturbance of the screen is liable to provoke a complete re-calculation (at great cost). I find that the appletviewer does not exit until the end of a call to paint() and so even quitting from it can involve an amazingly long delay!

```
public void paint(Graphics g)
{ // I Paint first in crude 16*16 blocks and then
        in finer and finer tiles. This is so that
        SOMETHING appears on the screen rather rapidly.
    for (int resolution=16; resolution>=1; resolution/=2)
    { double midX = -0.25, midY = 0.85; // Adjust these
        double range = 0.004;                    // Adjust this
        int screenSize = 400;                    // Match .html
        int s2 = screenSize/2;
        for (int y=0; y<screenSize; y+=resolution)
        for (int x=0; x<screenSize; x+=resolution)
        { int n = 0;
            int LIMIT = 250;              // Maybe adjust this?
            Complex z = new Complex(0.0, 0.0);
            Complex c =
                new Complex((range*(x-s2))/s2 + midX,
                            (range*(y-s2))/s2 + midY);
            // Important loop follows.
```

[41] Printing inks favour analysis in terms of subtractive colours rather than additive ones.

```
while (n++ < LIMIT && z.modulus() < 4.0)
{  z = z.times(z); // z = z * z;
     z = z.plus(c);              // z = z + c;
}
// Draw in black if count overflowed
if (n >= LIMIT) g.setColor(Color.black);
•   ... otherwise select a colo(u)r based on
•   the Hue/Saturation/Brightness colour model.
•   This gives me a nice rainbow effect. If
•   your display only supports 256 (or fewer)
•   colours it will not be so good.
else g.setColor(Color.getHSBColor(
•   cycle HUE as n goes from 0 to 64
          (float)(n % 64)/64.0f,
•   vary saturation from 0.2 to 1.0 as n varies
          (float)(0.6+0.4*
                  Math.cos((double)n/40.0)),
•   leave brightness at 1.0
          1.0f));
•   screen coords point y downwards, so flip to
•   agree with norman human conventions.

          g.fillRect(x, screenSize-y,       // posn resolution,
                                            resolution); // size
        }
    }
}
```

Complete the program based on the above and test it.

Next check Graphics.getClipBounds and Rectangle.contains in the Java documentation. Adjust the program so that when paint is called it first finds the clip rectangle associated with the re-paint operation. This is a rectangle on the screen such that only points within this area need to be re-displayed. Arrange that the loop on x and y that at present re-computes the colour for every point on the whole screen just loops round doing nothing for points outside the clipping rectangle and so only does the expensive operations for points inside it. Try the new version, and in particular move other windows to obscure small parts of it and then move them away so you can see the effect of the partial re-draw operations.

Note that the above program will display best if your screen is set up to support lots of colours. On a display with either 16-bit colour (65536 colours) or true-colour (24 or 32 bit) and at high resolution the effect is fairly stunning. If only 256 colours are supported the shapes will remain nice and wiggly but the delicate shading will be lost. While preparing these notes I have adjusted the program to display a 1200 by 1200 image at best-possible resolution in 16-bit colour, and although it takes utterly ages for the screen to refresh I think it is almost worth it!

The program that I give has a bug that you can see if you watch carefully when it re-paints at the various different resolutions. It relates to the fact that in Java the x-co-ordinate increases from left to right (as expected) but the y-co-ordinate is zero at the top of the screen and largest at the bottom. Identify and correct the behaviour that I count as a defect.

Optional: Add a BufferedImage to make the re-painting of the screen cleaner. I might like to be able to reset the view to some standard one at the click of a mouse, and to be able to drag with the mouse to select a sub-part of the current picture for zooming in on. Those who are feeling keen can investigate these possibilities.

There is also quite some incentive to find ways of speeding up d rawing of the images here!

(End of tickable exercise)

Fractions

Create a class similar to the Complex one but that implements rational numbers, is fractions. You will probably want to make the internal representation a pair of long values rather than just int, and keep everything reduced to lowest terms by cancelling out highest common factors.

Series for tan(x)

It may be well known that

$$\tan(x) = x + \frac{1}{3}x^3 + \frac{2}{15}x^5 + \frac{17}{315}x^7 + \frac{62}{2835}x^9 + \ldots$$

but fewer people are happy about being able to predict what the next few coefficients in the expansion are. However if we have a computer pr ogram able to compute with rational numbers it is in fact easy to generate as many more coeffi-cients as are desired. The coefficients satisfy a recurrence formula

$$\begin{aligned} t_0 &= 0 \\ t_1 &= 1 \\ t_n &= \frac{1}{n}\sum_{i=0}^{n-1} t_i t_{n-i-1} \end{aligned}$$

Use this to confirm the series as I have tabulated it and displa y the next few terms. The result here may be derived from the fact that the derivative of tan(x) is 1 + tan^2(x), and is also related to (but rather harder than!) the discussion of “generating functions” in the probability course.

Complex elementary functions

Perhaps you already did this when making your complete version of the complex numbers class. . .

It might be useful to be able to construct complex numbers either by specifying real and imaginary parts or by giving argument and modulus[42]. Failing any better scheme you could distinguish between the two constructors by adding declarations

```
public static final int CARTESIAN = 0;
public static final int POLAR        = 1;
```

in the Complex class and then having the constructor take an extra argument that specifes which option is being used. It would then also make sense to provide data access methods that make it equally easy to access the number in polar or cartesian interpretation.

If that is done it becomes reasonably easy to support complex versions of several of the elementary functions. Observe the identities:

$$\begin{aligned}
\sqrt{re^{iq}} &= \sqrt{r}e^{iq/2} \\
\log(re^{iq}) &= \log(r) + iq \\
\exp(x + iy) &= \exp(x)e^{iy} \\
\sin(z) &= (\exp(iz) - \exp(-iz))/2i \\
\cos(z) &= (\exp(iz) + \exp(-iz))/2 \\
p^q &= \exp(q \log(p))
\end{aligned}$$

The expressions for sin and cos can be inverted to find ways of w riting the inverse trigonometric functions as messy complex logarithms. And it may be seen that the neatest way of using these formulae to implement complex-values versions of the elementary functions really does benefit from being able to s lip very comfortably between the cartesian and polar views of the values. Implement it all.

I should observe carefully that the code you have just written is liable to be a very long way from the last word in elementary function libraries, for the follow-ing reasons, which are given in descending order of importance:

- Several of the complex-valued elementary functions have branch-cuts. For instance the square root function has a principal value which is discontinu-ous as you cross the negative real axis, and the various inverse trig functions will also have cuts. Your code can not automatically be assumed to imple-ment these cuts in the way that will be considered proper by experts in the field. Probably the most readily accessible description of w hich cuts are desirable is in *Common Lisp, the Language* by Guy Steele[21];

• le by giving the polar version.

- Your implementation will probably suffer from arithmetic overflow (and hence give back answers that are infinities or NaNs) substant ially before the desired result would overflow. For instance the identity given for cos computes an intermediate result that is twice as big as the fin al answer, and hence can suffer in this way thereby returning incorrect answers;

- In many cases the naive use of the formula given can lead to serious loss of numerical accuracy when values of similar magnitude are subtracted one from the other. For instance this problem would arise in the calculation of sin(z) for z near zero;

- Direct use of these formulae will not even give an efficient set of recipes for the desired functions!

however the numerical analysis to address these problems is certainly beyond the scope of this course.

Binary Trees

Start from the BinaryTreeOfIntegers class sketched above and extend it so that as well as defining variables in the class it provides a se t of methods to work with them. The methods you introduce should arrange that any binary tree built is always structured so that all integers stored in the left sub-tree that hangs off a node are smaller than the integer in the node itself, while all integers in the right tree are greater (or equal). You should provide a constructor that creates such a tree out of all the integers in an integer array, and another function that first counts the size of a tree, then allocates an array that big and finally copies all the integers back into the array so that they end up in ascending order. I would fairly strongly suggest that you design and implement the key parts of this in ML before you move on to the Java version. Your code is an implementation of tree-sort: you should compare it with quicksort for clarity, amount of code that has to be written, robustness (ie are there any truly bad sorts of input it can be given) and performance.

4.6 Inheritance

There is one more major feature of the Java class mechanism. It provides yet further refined control over name visibility and it can often be a huge help when organising the structure of large projects. It is called *inheritance* and the idea of it is to allow the user to define new classes as variants on existi ng ones. When this happens the new class starts off with all the components and methods of the one upon which it is based, and it counts as having defined a sub-ty pe. It can however define extra variables and/or methods and implement more spe cialised versions of some of the methods already present in its parent class. This is what has been happening every time we have used the word extends, and so for instance every applet we have written has defined a new class extending the li brary class Applet. This library class implements all the major functionality for getting a window to appear, and to get the visual effects we wanted all that was needed was to provide our sub-class with its own version of a paint method.

There seem to be three interlocking reasons why inheritance is important when large programs are to be written:

- Class libraries can be provided in forms that implement all the generic be-haviour of really quite complicated programs, but by making a new program that inherits from such a class and that overrides some of its methods lots of flexibility is left for the programmer to create a system th at does exactly what they want. Prior to languages that supported inheritance there was a severe conflict between having libraries that contained lar ge enough com-ponents to give large time-savings and those that were adaptable enough to be realistically useful;
- Class inheritance serves a linguistic purpose in Java. If you start from a sin-gle base class it is possible to derive several other classes from it. All these count as specialisations of the original one, and a variable capable of hold-ing a member of the base class can therefore automatically refer to instances of any of the derived ones. This is how Java can support data-structures that can have several variants. Furthermore the name-visibility rules in Java can use the way in which inheritance groups classes into families to further re-fine access to class members.
- It often becomes possible to implement a set of basic classes first, and test them, and then leave those alone (and hence stable) while deriving new classes that add extra functionality. This both provides a respectable strat-egy for organising system development, and means that there is a significant chance that the basic classes that are developed will be useful in the next project;

I will try to illustrate these three points in turn.

4.6.1 Inheritance and the standard libraries

The richest and most valuable place where this happens in the libraries relate to applications that pop up windows. Examples given before show user code being derived from a class called Applet. One of the things that has been seen about Applet and hence any class derived from it is that the method paint has a special status, in that it is invoked whenever the screen needs to be refreshed. The fact that by deriving a new class you get an opportunity to write your own paint method and that in your new class your own definition takes the place o f a standard one (which probably does nothing much!) is obviously critical. If you could not alter the re-painting behaviour of an applet the whole structure would lose its point. If you look at the documentation for the Applet class you will find that it is listed as having around a couple of dozen associated methods. Each of these will define a default behaviour for an Applet and each can be replaced[43] in a derived class if some special behaviour is needed. However these two-dozen methods are very far from being the whole story. For instance paint is not listed among them. This is because Applet is descended from java.awt.Panel which in turn is derived from java.awt.Container which itself inherits from java.awt.Component and java.lang.Object. Each of these super-classes define (often many) meth-ods of their own. The lower-down ones sometimes replace a few of the higher level methods with more specialised versions, but they also tend to provide lots of new methods of their own. Thus in this case the paint method is defined as an aspect of a Container, and is only part of Applet via inheritance. The end effect is that something that is as easy to get started with as an Applet in fact comes complete with perhaps hundreds of bits of pre-defined b ehaviour almost any of which can be adjusted by the simple expedient of overriding some method.

Sometimes of course this arrangement whereby library facilities are structured into hierarchies of classes means that the very simplest thing one might want to do involves explicit construction of objects from various classes in a way that looks less smooth. To print simple text as the output from a simple Java stand-alone application one can invoke System.out.println. The long name is because System is a class (its full name is java.lang.System), and out is then a vari-able in that class. The field out has as its type PrintStream and the class PrintStream provides a method called println. It is possible to reference the variable out just by giving its class (without having to have a variable whose type is that class) because it was defined as being static. The recipe as typed in by the programmer is not too bulky but the full explanation of why it works is a bit clumsy. "Simple" input is if anything worse. There is a stati c variable System.in which is of type InputStream, and for an application to accept input from the keyboard one needs to use it. However the class InputStream only provides the most basic reading functions, and various derived classes are needed if flexible, efficient and convenient reading is to occur. A suggested pro tocol for a single

---

• The fuller story is that any member of a class that has been marked as final can not be redefined in a derived class. The use of final thus provides the designer of a class with a way to guarantee some aspects of class behaviour even in derived classes.

integer from the standard input ends up something like

```
BufferedReader in =
        new BufferedReader(
                new InputStreamReader(System.in),
                1);
int n;
try
{  n = Integer.parseInt(in.readLine());
}
catch (IOException e) { n = -
1; }
catch (NumberFormatException e)
{ n = 0; }
System.out.println("I got: " + n + "....");
```

This creates an InputStreamReader out of System.in, and then builds from that a BufferedReader where here I have indicated that a buffer size of 1 should be used. For reading directly from the keyboard a ridiculously small buffer size means that the program gets characters as soon as they are available. If the " , 1" was omitted the BufferedReader would use some default buffer size and you would have to have keyed in that many characters before anything ever happened! The BufferedReader class then provides a readLine method, and the string that it returns can be interpreted as an integer by the static method parseInt in the Integer class. Both readLine and parseInt may raise exceptions if any-thing goes wrong, and so a proper program should be prepared to handle these. The above tends to look very heavy-handed because "real" pro grams will gen-erally want to decode much more complicated input than just the single number shown above, and will really need to put in the catch clauses so that they can respond cleanly to erroneous input. Even the buffering control is really quite im-portant — direct keyboard input may need to be unbuffered so t hat interaction works well while input of large amounts of input from a file may be *much* faster if buffering is used.

Java in fact provides another rather larger class than BufferedReader which may be useful in many applications that want to accept free-format input. This is the class java.io.StreamTokenizer[44] which can help you read in a mixture of numbers and words. Here is a demonstration:

```
import java.io.*;
```

• Actually I think that StreamTokenizer is very useful while you are getting started, but although it can be customised quite substantially it is not fl exible enough for most really serious uses. In the Compiler Construction course in Part IB you may learn about a package called JLex that is harder to set up but which provides enormously more power and flexibility.

...

```
StreamTokenizer in =
      new StreamTokenizer(
            new BufferedReader(
                  new InputStreamReader(System.in),
                  1));
in.eolIsSignificant(true);           // see    newlines
in.ordinaryChar('/');                // '/'    is   not   special
in.slashSlashComments(true); // '//'            for   comment
try
{     int type;
• The next line loops reading tokens until end of file. while ((type =
      in.nextToken()) !=
                  StreamTokenizer.TT_EOF) {
      switch (type)
            {
• There are a number of predefined "token types" in
• StreamTokenizer, so I process each of them.
      case StreamTokenizer.TT_WORD:
                  System.out.println("word " + in.sval);
• If the user says "quit" then do so. NB "break" only
• exits the switch statement here.
                  if (in.sval.equalsIgnoreCase("quit"))
                        break;
                  continue;
• in.sval and in.nval get set when string or numeric
• tokens are parsed and contain the value.
      case StreamTokenizer.TT_NUMBER:
                  System.out.println("number " + in.nval); continue;
• the method lineno() tells us which line we are on. case
      StreamTokenizer.TT_EOL:
                  System.out.println("start of line " +
                                          in.lineno());
                  continue;
• quotes and doublequotes contain strings. case '\'': //
      drop through
      case '\"':
                  System.out.println("string " + in.sval); continue;
• Other characters end up here. Eg +, - etc. default:
```

```
                System.out.println("sym " + (char)type); continue;
            }
            break;      // here if "quit" typed in
        }
}
catch (IOException e)
{  System.out.println("IO exception");
}
```

The level of complexity here seems much more reasonable! The initial code that sets up a StreamTokenizer is not very different from that which set up the simpler buffered stream before, and is clearly a small overhead to pay to be able to have Java split your input up into words and numbers. The StreamTokenizer provides methods that allow you to customise its behaviour so that it can recognise one of several possible styles of comments and accept various string delimiters. The calls

```
in.eolIsSignificant(true);              // see newlines
in.ordinaryChar('/');                   // '/' is not special
     in.slashSlashComments(true); // '//' for comment
```

illustrate a little of this. The first call tells the tokenize r that newlines should be returned to the caller. By default they are counted as whitespace and so not passed back. The second call makes a single / into an ordinary character, where by default it introduces a comment if followed by a second / or a *. The final line enables recognition of comments that are started by //. As always you need to browse the full documentation to discover what all the other options are!

Two lessons emerge. The first is that the bigger and more power ful classes in the Java libraries may really save you time if you find out ho w to use them, while direct use of very low level facilities may end up feeling pretty clumsy. The other is that these high level facilities are often very fl exible, but if you need some feature that they do not support you may have to drop down a level. For instance StreamTokenizer does not know how to handle numbers expressed in hexadecimal or octal, and it always reads numbers in type double which is not good enough if what you needed was a long value.

4.6.2 Name-spaces and classes

When you derive one class from another it is sometimes desirable if the methods and fields of the base class are visible in the derived one, but in other cases it may not be. This aspect of name visibility needs to be considered in conjunction with the consequences of classes falling into different packages. Java confronts all this by defining four levels of name visibility within classes:

Figure 4.6: Classes and inheritance are a sort of magic.

private: is the most restrictive one. A method or variable that has been declared as private can be referenced from within the class in which it is defined, but not from anywhere else. In particular code that i s in another class can not see it regardless of whether the other class is in the same pack-age as or was derived from the original one;

package: relaxes things so that code in any class that is in the same package can reference a value. This is the default arrangement, and is indicated by *not* using any of the other visibility qualifiers. Note that the ke yword package is used at the head of a file to specify which package that class will reside in, and it is not valid in method or variable declarations;

protected: When a name is declared as protected it becomes visible in derived classes even if they are in other packages. Because during this first course you will probably not be creating new packages yourself this case will mostly be relevant where a library class has some protected members and you derive a few class from it. Your class will probably be in the default package but despite that you will be able to access the members involved;

public: is the final case, and it makes names generally available rega rdless of packages and inheritance.

It seems tidy to document the other possible qualifiers for de clarations here, even though they are not concerned with name visibility. Indeed their conse-quences are rather mixed, and since this is a first Java course it is not essential to be fully comfortable with them all.

final: When a variable is declared final nobody will be allowed to assign a new value to it. When a method is final then it can not be overridden in any derived class. In both cases the effect is to make the definition in its visible form the one that can be relied upon everywhere else;

static: The default situation for items defined within classes is tha t the items only come into existence when an object of the class-type is created. This makes obvious sense for data fields. For instance after the de claration

```
class IntList
{ public int head; public IntList
      tail;
}
```

it is clear that the only context in which the head and tail fiel ds can be used is in association with an object of type IntList as in

```
int sum(IntList x)
{ int r = 0; while (x != null) {
        r += x.head;
                x = x.tail;
        }
}
```

For consistency the same access rule is then applied to member functions (ie methods) in a class. If however an item in a class has been declared static it is as if a single globally allocated instance of the class gets cre-ated automatically, and the field can then be referred to rela tive to just the class name. For instance (a nonsense code fragment!)

```
class MyConsts
{ static final double ZETA2 =
                1.6449340668482264365;
        static final double CATALAN =
                0.9159655941772190150 5;
        static int square(int x)
        {       return x*x; }
}
...
double a = MyConsts.CATALAN -
                Myconsts.ZETA2 +
                (double)MyConsts.square(1729);
...
```

abstract: Sometimes it is useful to define a base class not because it is u seful as such, but because the various other classes that get derived from it might be. Consider the ML declaration

```
datatype option = A of int | B of double;
```

One way of producing a Java equivalent would be to start by defi ning a rather vacuous class called Option and then deriving from it two new classes one to correspond to each of the two cases in the ML version:

```
abstract class Option
{}
class OptionA extends Option
{ int a;
}
```

```
class OptionB extends Option
{  double d;
}
```

The base class here only exists to be extended, and it would be silly to create an object that was of that type[45]. The qualifier abstract prevents anybody from creating objects of the base class. It marks things that must be inherited from before meaningful use can be made of them. In cases such as this it is often useful to discriminate as to which derived class a particular instance belongs to. The instanceof operator can be used to do this. Again my illustrative code is artificial:

```
Option x = new OptionA(); // or maybe OptionB?
...
if (x instanceof OptionB) ...
else ...
```

It is very often neater and easier to define different overrid ings of a common (abstract) method in the two derived classes so that the correct behaviour is achieved for each. If that is done[46] the if statement and use of instanceof could be replaced by a simple call to the method concerned. It is of course not essential to make a base class in such examples abstract, but doing so prevents any possible embarrassment if some code created an instance of it in its raw and useless form, so it is generally considered to be good style.

native: If a method is defined as native then Java somehow expects there to be an implementation of it that was coded in some language other than Java. This can be used by system builders to interface Java code down to lower level and perhaps machine-specific system calls, but will no t be discussed further in these notes.

synchronized: related to Java code where several threads of computation may be active at once. Although the very basic aspects of this will be covered in this course a proper treatment needs to wait until you have had a Part IB course on concurrent systems.

interface: The keyword interface is not a modifier for use in class defini-tions but a keyword whose use is very much like that of class. An interface

---

· Of course objects of type OptionA and OptionB are also of type Option, so what I mean is it would be silly to go new Option().

46 A similar stylistic issue arises in ML where user of pattern-matching in function definitions can often reduce the number of explicit if statements that have to be written.

can be declared much as an abstract class is. Classes can be defined to ex-tend other classes, but a restriction that Java applies is that a new class can only be an extension of a single parent class. Interfaces provide an approx-imation to being able to extend several parent classes — a new class can specify that it implements one or more interfaces. When a class indicates that it will implement an interface it has to contain (concrete) definitions of all the (abstract) methods that the interface specifies.

At (very) long last we have covered all the magic that arose in the initial Hello.java program and can see what each keyword present there was indi-cating.

4.6.3 Program development with classes

In Java, as in other Object Oriented languages, the whole shape of a large pro-gram needs to be designed in terms of terms of the packages and classes that will be built. It is worth putting particularly careful thought into the way in which hierarchies of classes will be derived from one another via inheritance.

There are two application areas that were pioneers in illustrating the benefits and strengths of object oriented programming (which is what this is). It can thus be worthwhile considering examples of these as some of the earliest ones you work with when getting used to the idiom. The first applicatio n area was that of simulation[47], while the other was graphics and especially the display of geo-metric figures in windows. The following example, which is ta ken from *Java in a Nutshell* and shows how use of several classes rather than just one may allow the programmer to keep distinct aspects of their task separate. But doing this the size of unit that has to be debugged is reduced, and the possibility of re-using parts of the code later on in another project is increased. The example supposes that a graphical design and modelling package is being written. Within it it will keep data-structures that represent circles, squares and other shapes. For much of its time it will work on these busily computing their areas, their circumferences, whether they intersect and similar properties. It may also adjust their sizes and positions. As well as performing all these calculations the complete package will also have a user interface that can draw the objects. There will be options to con-trol the colour of each individual circle (and so on) as well as to determine whether the items are drawn just as outline figures or as filled-in shap es.

Without use of inheritance and thus without serious use of the Java class mech-anism the code would probably have to consist of a single class, say called Shape, which would contain a master variable indicating what sort of shape was involved,

---

· Indeed the way that object-oriented C++ developed from the simpler language C was initially specifically for use in this area.

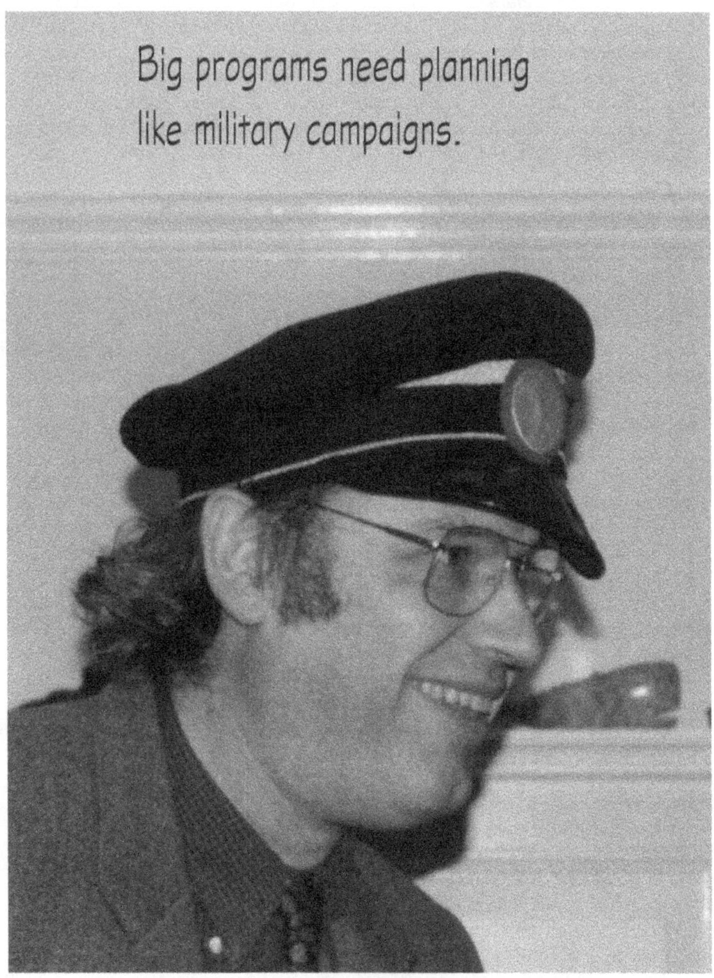

Figure 4.7: See also the “Software Engineering” courses.

then other variables that could be used to specify the exact parameters of that shape (eg its radius if it was a circle). The method functions such as area would need to dispatch on the type of the figure and do different calc ulations in each case. Further code would arrange to be able to draw pictures to represent the data. All the geometric and graphical parts of the code would be in the same class and thus the same source file — something which would not cause tro uble in tiny cases but would become clumsy for a fully elaborated version.

With inheritance it would be natural to start with a basic class (again I will call it Shape) which will probably be abstract. Its purpose is to allow the program to declare variable of type Shape and then store circles, squares, stars and all other possible sorts of shape in that single sort of variable. The methods declared for Shape can be given as just declarations, rather than as full definit ions:

```
public abstract class Shape
{
        public abstract double area();
        public abstract double circumference();
}
```

which makes these methods available in any object of class Shape but expects that concrete variants on the class will provide the real implementations.

For each sub-class of Shape a new class could then be derived:

```
class Circle extends Shape
{
        protected double radius;
        public Circle() { radius = 1.0; }
        public area() { return Math.PI*radius*radius; } public
        circumference()
        {  return 2.0*Maths.PI*radius; }
        public double getRadius() { return radius; }
}
```

Note that this can introduce new public members that are not relevant for general Shape quantities, but which do make sense when you know you have a Circle.

Next an interface would be set up, defining the methods relevant for drawing[48] things on the screen:

• Java is an American language, and so the character of being Red, White or Blue is Color rather than Colour. Given that the library uses this spelling it seems best to swallow nationalistic pride and adopt it elsewhere in the code. . .

```
public interface Drawable
{
        public void setColor(Color c);
        public void draw(Graphics g);
        // etc etc.
}
```

Now it is reasonable to derive a new class for a version of each sort of shape but in a form that supports the drawing operations:

```
class DrawableCircle extends Circle
          implements Drawable
{
        Color c;
        public void setColor(Color c)
        {  this.c = c; }
        public void draw(Graphics g)
        {  ... // whatever, maybe
              g.drawOval(...);
        }
        // etc etc.
}
```

It is now possible to use the drawing methods as well as the data manipulation methods in one of these ultimate data-structures.

Often when producing a derived class and overriding a method the newly ex-tended method needs to use the corresponding operation from its parent class. For instance if a class defines a method that is used to initialise its variables then a derived class may add extra variables that need initial values too, but it would be clumsy to insist that it also had to repeat all the code to setup the variables in the base class. And indeed if some of those were private or protected it might not be able to. The solution is hidden in the keyword super. This is a bit like this in that it always refers to the current object, but it views it as a member of the immediate parent class. Thus code like

```
class SubClass extends MyClass
{ private int variable; public void
        init()
        {  super.init(); // init as a MyClass
              variable = -1; // finish off as SubClass
        }
}
```

and the word super is only of relevance when extending a class and overriding methods. In the case of some library classes and methods the documentation will explain to you that you must use it, see for instance the method paint in the class Container.

4.7 Generics

The material here is now for Java 1.5 and I expect my coverage of it to grow over the next year or so. This year I will do hardly more than just mention it and let Part IbB coverage consider filling in the gaps. This seems especially reasonable since textbooks that catch up with this are still somewhat rare.

In ML you got used to having types that were polymorphic. For instance a sort function that took a predicate and a list might have had type

$$(a * a \rightarrow \text{bool}) * \text{alist} \rightarrow \text{alist}$$

to indicate that the elements of the input and output lists had the same type and the ordering predicate was compatible with that. A particular feature of ML to recall is the availability of parameterised types such as alist. In Java instead of saying "type" we will say "class", and instead of saying "pol ymorphic" we say "generic". A generic class is established by putting type va riables within angle brackets. You can then use the type variable within the class as if it were a regular type name: small

```
class MyClass<E>
{
        E myMethod(E arg1, int arg2)
        { MyClass<String> newvar = ...
             ...
        }
}
```

With your ML experience of polymorphism you can now probable see at once how to use this capability to write implementations of various generic data struc-tures (trees, lists and the like) and provide useful functions that traverse, search or sort them. In fact that Java libraries have done a great deal of that in their so-called Collection classes.

In ML polymorphism is all-or-nothing. If you have a type-variable a it can stand for absolutely any ML type. To improve security you may sometimes like to have a way of expressing more limited flexibility (eg gener ic over all sorts of numbers, but not over non-numeric data). Java provides a capability using a type wildcard written as question mark, and can limit the range of the wildcard using notation like

```
public void sum(List<? extends Number> arg)
{ for (n:arg)
    {...}
}
```

Here the sum method takes an argument that is some sort of List[49] but it insists that the polymorphism that List provides has been used in a way that means you know that all the objects in the list are some subclass on Number.

You will use generics every time you use the Java Collection Classes. You can use it in your own code too. There is a fair amount more that I could say about exactly how it interacts with the type-hierarchy that class inheritance provides and when a generic class is a sub-class of another, but I believe that the details there do not belong in a *first* Java course!

4.7.1 Exercises

Objects everywhere

The Java libraries make extensive use of classes in hierarchies (and also a more modest number of interfaces). The arrangement in the basic set of classes is that *everything* is ultimately descended from a base class called Object. The most immediate consequence is that an object of *any* class from the basic libraries may be stored in a variable of type Object. It is exactly as if whenever you define a new class and do not give an explicit extends clause as part of its definition Java just sticks in " extends Object" for you. Of course when you extend some other class it in turn will somehow have Object as an ancestor-class so this way as previously stated *every* instance of *any* class is an Object.

A few basic methods are defined for Object, of which perhaps the most inter-esting at present is getClass which returns an thing from the class Class. If x is any Object then x.getClass().getName() is a string that is the name of the class of x! The general parts of the Java libraries that allow you to investigate the classes that Objects belong to and then retrieve lists of the variables and methods that they provide are referred to as *Reflection* : as it were a Java program can look at itself as if in a mirror.

Check the documentation and write Java code that accepts an Object and prints out as detailed and as readable description of it as you reasonably can.

Note that Object underpins the polymorphism of Java generics, but now that generics are available programmers will use Object directly much less than they used to.

---

[49] A Collection class that does just what you expect!

Primitive is second class?

The ability to treat things as “Objects” does not (directly) extend to the Java prim-itive types. To work around that the libraries contain classes with names that are rather like those of the primitive types except that they are capitalised. Ie Boolean, Character, Byte, Short, Integer, Long, Float and Double. As of the most recent revision of Java you will find that the compi ler arranges to con-vert between int and Integer (and the other primitive types and their associated wrapper classes) when it believes that that will help you. The conversion naturally involves some run-time cost so it is perhaps advisable to be aware when it hap-pens. The sort of circumstance where it is especially convenient that this happens is when you want to store a primitive object (eg an integer, flo ating point number or character) in a Hashmap or a Vector (or indeed any of the collection classes).

It was then natural for the Java designers to set methods associated with these to implement a wide range of basic conversions and tests on the values, as in Integer.doubleValue and Double.isNaN (and many more).

The numeric types the classes Integer etc do not inherit directly from Object but via a class called Number Eg

```
Number a, b;
a = 2;          // new Integer(2);
b = 11.7; // new Double(11.7);
```

can be written as shown, but behaves as if the constructors in the comments have been used. If the Number objects are used in a context where primitive num-bers are needed (eg you try to perform arithmetic using them) the values will be unpackaged for you.

Write a class that defines lists of Numbers, with suitable set of facilities for constructing such lists and a method sum that can add up the values in a list return-ing the result as a double. You may need to use “ x instanceof Integer” to sort out which flavour of number is present in some particular node.

Some text output using Objects

Since Object is an almost universal type it can be used to pass arbitrary data to a function. This is in fact what happens with printf, but one extra thing happens there. If a method is declared with three dots after the type at the end of its argument list, as in

```
PrintStream printf(String format, Object... args)
{ // whatever definition you need
}
```

indicates that the final argument to printf will actually be passed as an array of Object values. But the *calls* to it will just appear to permit a variable number of arguments, and each argument will be converted to (if a primitive type) or interpreted as (if a class type) Object.

While this scheme can be used in your own code to support variable numbers of arguments, and it can also be used with more restrictive types than Object it will almost always count as poor style since it can easily reduce type-safety and cause confusion if you mix it with method overloading. But where it is useful it really helps make code concise. Without it instead of writing

```
int i=1, j=2;
System.out.printf("%d, %d", i, j);
```

you would need to wrap i and j up in the type Integer explicitly, and create an array to pass the multiple arguments explicitly.

```
int i=1, j=2;
myOwnMethod("%d, %d",
    new Object [] {new Integer(i), new Integer(j)});
```

But note very well that within the code that implements things such as printf everything has to work understanding that the concise calls are in fact mapped by the java compiler onto the clumsy looking code that packaged up primitive types and makes an array.

Now seems a good time to provide a summary of more of the formatting op-tions available with printf, and also to note that the method String.format does exactly the same job of layout but returns a formatted string rather than doing any direct printing. We have already seen "%d" for laying out integers, and know that "%n" generates a newline.

Within a format string the character "%" introduces a format specifier. After the percent sign a number of optional elements can appear:

- An argument index followed by a dollar sign ($). Without one of these the values to be converted are taken one at a time from the arguments provided. An index such as (2$) tells the formatter to use the second argument now, even if that is out of order. Often you may want to display the same data several times, eg in different formats. In that case (<) is very useful: it tells the system to re-use the argument most recently dealt with;

- Some flag characters. Just what is valid here will depend on ju st what sort of layout is being performed, but various punctuation marks as flags can, for instance, force left-justification of text within a field (-), ensure that num-bers are always displayed with an explicit sign (+), include leading zeros (0) or be more fussy about the actual types of arguments (#). You need to check fine details in the documentation when you use flags!

- a field-width, written as an unsigned non-zero integer. You s hould expect that if this is specified that the output from the conversion w ill have exactly that number of characters;

- A dot followed by a integer precision. Eg (.4). For some conversions this sets an upper limit on the number of characters to be generated. For floating
point conversions it controls either significant figures of t he number of digits after the decimal point.

- (and finally!) a character (or in some cases a pair of characte rs) that indicated just what sort of conversion is to be performed. Perhaps the more important cases are the letters s, each of which is discussed briefly below!

The full set of format letters and options can be found in the online documen-tation, but key cases are

s, S: This takes any value at all and tried to convert it] to a string. If the argument implements the Formattable interface then its formatTo method is used to do the conversion, otherwise its smalltoString method is used. When you define a class of your own you may often wish to overrid e or define one or both of these methods so that you can easily print instances of your class. Many of the Java library classes implement these methods in ways that at least try to be helpful. If you write a capital S the material that is displayed is forced into upper case. Similar effects apple for other use of upper case format letters;

d: This is the case most often seen in these notes so far, and prints an integer. But you can also display BigInteger values with this (and the x) format;

x, X: Integers can be displayed in hexadecimal rather than normal decimal notation this way;

c: character

e, f, g, E, F, G: Floating point and their display involve lots of compli-cation! The "e" formats always use scientific notation with a n explicit ex-ponent. The "f" formats use the specified precision as the num ber of digits to display after the decimal point (eg it is a good thing to use for printing pounds and pence with "%.2f"), while "g" tries to select between those two formats to select one that will be natural and will take up as little space as possible.

%: If you want to print a percent sign you will need to write two in a row!

n: Unix and Windows have different ideas about what constitutes a "newline". The format code %n makes allowance for that for you.

tx: Java provides an amazingly rich range of ways of formatting times and dates. YOu can use these formats when printing objects of type Long, Calendar or Date. I think there is too much to list here, but a very few of the options available are

tY year displayed as 4 digits, eg "2005";

tA full name of day of the week, eg "Monday";

TA as above, but upper case: "MONDAY";

ta short name of day: "Mon";

tM minute within the hour, as 2 digits;

tm number of the month as 2 digits, counting January as number 1;

tT time formatted for the 24-hour clock as "%tH:%tM:%tS";

tD date formatted as "%tm/%td/%ty".

A bigger exercise

There are twelve shapes that can be made by joining five square s together by their edges to get a connected unit. It is possible to pack these shapes (the *pentominoes*) into a six by ten[50] rectangle in a number of ways. Here is one such packing, which will also serve to show you the shapes of all the pieces:

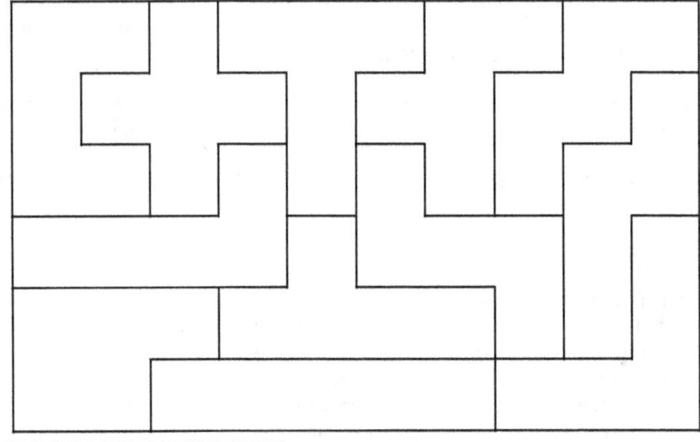

[50] also into a five by twelve or three by twenty.

The object of this exercise is to find other solutions to the pu zzle.

The suggested strategy is to represent the 10 by 6 board using 60 of the 64 bits in a long. You can them treat these as if they are arranged as a rectangular array, and then a single long value can represent a possible position of a piece. In this representation the twelve pieces can be described by the array:

```
final long [] rawPieces =
            { 0x000001f, 0x0100407, 0x000040f, 0x0300403,
              0x0401c01, 0x2008007, 0x0201c02, 0x0000c07,
        0x0301808, 0x0000c0e, 0x000100f, 0x0301802
};
```

where the values look pretty ugly but are at least all in quite a small table. A bulkier but perhaps cleaner way to set up the initial table of shapes would be to use a function such as:

```
long piece(String line1, String line2, String line3)
{ return (row(line1) << 2*boardWidth) | (row(line2) <<
             boardWidth) | row(line3);
}
long row(String line)
{  long r;
     for (int i=0; i<line.length(); i++)
     {  r <<= 1;
          if (line.charAt(i) == 'X') r |= 1;
     }
}
...
piece("X       ",
          "XXX",
          "X");
```

The init method for the applet should start by setting up a table first o f all the twelve pieces normalised so that they are down in one corner of the board, and then a larger table showing each piece in every location on the board that it could possibly be. Doing this will involve writing code that reflects and rotates pieces — not especially nice when using bits packed into a long — and which avoids setting up entries that are redundant because of symmetry. The code that is involved in getting this far is quite messy enough to keep you busy for a while.

The overall structure of the code that searches for solutions might then be

- search(i) looks for ways of placing piece
- i on the board. The array entry maps[i][j]
- is a bitmap showing the j-th place that
- piece i could bit, and the variable "board"
- shows which parts of the board have already
- been filled. There are 12 pieces, known as
- 0 to 11.

```
void search(int i, long board)
{  if (i == 12)
      {  // Here a solution has been found
            ... record it somehow ...
            return;
      }
      for (int trial=0; trial<maps[i].length; trial++)
      {  if ((maps[i][trial] & board) == 0)
            {  // no overlap with existing pieces
                      so put this in and next try to
                      fit in piece i+1.
                  search(i+1, board | maps[i][trial]);
            }
      }
}
```

The first challenge would be just to count the solutions, and s o the place in the above which is incomplete could be replaced by a single statement that incremented a variable. But since it is easy to use fillRect to draw filled-in rectangles in Java it would seen natural to try to draw some of the solutions and that would mean doing something distinctly harder.

The search function I have sketched tries the twelve pieces one after each other, and at each stage considers each piece at ever position on the board where it would still fit. A different search strategy would be to scan t he board at each stage and find the first vacant square. The program would then identi fy and try every piece that could be used to fill in that square. I believe that t his second search strategy is rather closer to the one most people would use than my original one was.

A curve to plot

Use Java to plot a picture of the following curve as t varies from 0 to 2p:

- = $\cos(t)(1 + \cos(40t))$
- = $\sin(t) + \cos(t)\sin(40t)$

Find a copy of *A Book of Curves*, E. H. Lockwood, Cambridge 1963, and in a similar style re-create variants on as many of the pictures as you can.

Reading hexadecimal numbers

We have seen various ways of decoding numeric input, eg Integer.parseInt and the whole set of joys associated with StreamTokenizer. You can note from the full documentation that there is a two-argument version of parseInt that allows you to specify what radix the input string was supposed to be in. You may also like to check details of the class smallScanner which has a method nextInt that can also accept an argument indicating what radix to read in.

Now imagine that these facilities did not exist, or that for some strange reason you could not use them. Implement your own functions that can be given strings as arguments and which will make it possible to convert the strings into int and long values, allowing for the possibility of octal or hexadecimal specifications.

Displaying floating point numbers

In versions of Java prior to 1.5/5.0 the functionality of printf was not available. This exercise is to re-create some of it thereby getting a chance to feel what work is involved in making worthwhile extensions to the existing libraries.

The method Double.toString allows you to generate a printable representation of a floating point number. However compared to the floa ting point layout flexibility available in many other languages it seems pathe tically simple-minded. A typical programming language will provide for three ways of printing floating point values:

F format: here numbers are written as illustrated in the following examples

```
-1.000
12345678900000000.0
0.000000005656
```

and even if the values are very large or very small their magnitude is indicated by having suitable numbers of leading or trailing zeros. It is typically possible to specify how many digits will be printed following the decimal point, and to indicate the width that the whole number will be padded to with either leading or trailing blanks.

E format: For very large or small numbers it may be convenient to use scientific notation. So with *E* format an explicit exponent will always be displayed:

```
-1.0e000
1.234568E018
5.656000e-009
```

Observe that there is always exactly one digit before the decimal point (sometimes a scaling option is provided to allow the user to specify a differ-ent number of digits before the point), and the exponent is always present and probably always displayed in a way where the largest possible exponent value could be fitted in. A “precision” specifier can indicate how many sig-nificant digits are to be shown, and the number will be padded w ith zeros or rounded to meet that requirement. Numbers close to 1.0 tend to look a bit ugly this way! Again it is useful to be able to place the number in a fixed-width field, either right or left-justified.

G format: Large numbers are best shown in *E* format while modest size ones do best in *F*. So *G* is a composite scheme that looks at the value of a num-ber and decides which of the other two formats would lead to the most compact representation, and it then uses that. It is roughly what Java's Double.toString method provides, but again we would really like op-tions to indicate precision and field width.

Implement functions which convert Java double values to strings in each of the above formats.

I might suggest that you start by using toString to do the basic conversion and then let your code restrict its worry to unpicking that string and re-formatting the characters. If you decide you want to do the numeric to string conversion from scratch you should be aware that preserving numeric accuracy is quite hard!

Write a test-suite that compares the strings your code generates with the ones that String.format produces. Then worry about NaNs, infinities, careful round-ing and the like!

Double as bit-patterns

Double.doubleToLongBits takes a double as an argument and returns a long. The long is the internal IEEE-format bit-pattern that represents the double The matching function longBitsToDouble accepts a long and manufactures a double in the same dubious sort of way. Investigate whether there is any double value x in Java so that

```
(double)Double.doubleToLongBits(x) == x
```

Continued fractions

Any positive number can be expanded as a *continued fraction* as in

$$x = x_0 + \cfrac{1}{x_1 + \cfrac{1}{x_2 + \ldots}}$$

where the values x_i are called *partial quotients* and are all positive integers. If the original number is rational the continued fraction terminates at some stage. Otherwise it goes on for ever, and can be viewed as providing an alternative to the usual decimal expansion of numbers. Instead of writing a value as say 1.414213562. . . the partial quotients would be listed [1, 2, 2, 2, . . .]. Gosh in fact for this number it looks as if the continued fraction is astonishingly regular!

The sequence of partial quotients in the expansion of a number are easy to compute - the first is just obtained by casting the number to an int. The rest can be obtained from the reciprocal of what you get by subtracting that value from the original number. Write code to do this and tabulate the first d ozen partial quotients you get in the expansions of the following numbers:

- $\sqrt{3}$
- $(\sqrt{5} + 1)/2$
- $\sqrt{7}$
- $e = 2.71828\ldots$
- π

4.8 Important features of the class libraries

The coverage thus far has shown the use of some small parts of the Java libraries, but has also missed a great deal out. In this course I will not have anything like enough time to describe everything that is available. However there are a few bits of functionality that either seem to be generally useful enough or sufficiently fun to be worth covering. The little bits of explanation given here are thus to be viewed as a sampler of what Java can do for you. If you can work through all these demonstrations and navigate the documentation of the classes that they introduce you should have got a reasonably broad idea of the system, and in looking up the documentation details while working on these cases you will as a side-effect be noticing what other classes are present. I will only give the most basic possible demonstrations of the things illustrated here. Full competent use of them can only come with serious work on rather larger bodies of code. I will also totally ignore several of the newer parts of the Java class libraries, or to be more precise, I will leave fuller details of some of these facilities and of the other ones to next year's "Concurrent Systems and Applications" course and/or your o wn private study.

4.8.1 File input and output

The character input and output shown so far has used the pre-defined "standard" streams System.in and System.out. Obviously in many real applications it is necessary to access named files.

In many programming languages there is a logical (and practical) distinction made between files that will contain text and those while will be used to hold binary information. Files processed as binary are thought of as sequences of 8-bit bytes, while ones containing text model sequences of characters. In Java this distinction has two main manifestations, one of which is somewhat frivolous but can matter on an every-day basis in the UK while the other is of wider importance but will not impinge on immediate coursework:

- Windows and some internet protocols use a pair of characters, carriage-return and line-feed, to mark the end of a line. Unix and Linux use a single character (newline). In text mode Java makes whatever adjustments are needed so that external files adhere to platform conventions , but your Java code sees just the character '\n'.

- In many parts of the world (and in particular in the Far East) text documents need to cope with alphabets that involve many thousands of symbols. Uni-code is designed to be able to cope with these, but there can be a variety of ways of encoding text as streams of bytes. When working in such an environment Java can be configures so it knows how to pack and u npack Unicode using various of the major encoding conventions. But obviously it will only even try to do this when it knows that the programmer wants data to be viewed as character-based rather than binary.

Java uses names typically based on the word Stream for binary access, and Reader and Writer for text. So when you read the documentation expect to find two broadly parallel sets of mechanisms, one for each style of access!

Java input and output can seem clumsy to start with because almost all of the functions involved are able to throw exceptions, and it is expected that Java code using them should be prepared to handle these. This is in fact *good* because experience with earlier languages indicates that most programmers do not find it easy or natural to put error-checks after simple I/O operations, even though logically almost any of them could fail. For instance writing a single character to a file could unexpectedly fail if the disc on which the file li ved became full[51], or it it was on a floppy disc and the disc was removed from the dri ve or had a scratch, or if there was a hardware glitch in a disc interface. Different but equally delicate issues arise with output that goes directly to a printer, across a network to

• remote file-system, or with input from a semi-reliable devi ce such as a bar-code scanner. The Java use of exceptions encourages all programmers to consider I/O failure right from the start.

There is one final complication about Java input and output th at ought to be mentioned up front. One use of Java is in applets to be embedded within web pages, and hence sometimes fetched from remote web-sites. It could be bad if code from an untrusted site could read and write all your files ! So Java introduces the idea of a security manager and can classify code as either trusted or untrusted. Untrusted code will not be permitted to access the local filin g system. The short form way around this is to make everything you do an application not an applet: security restrictions are then (by default) not imposed. If you do need to make applets that access disc or do other things that default controls lock out you need to impose security on an application then you will need to find out about the creation of custom Security Policies and signed Java code. I will not describe that here.

Java provides a rich and somewhat elaborate set of capabilities, but perhaps a good place to start will be simple reading of text files. The c lass FileReader does almost everything you are liable to need: here is a minimal demonstration that shows that you can use a method called read to read characters, and that it returns the integer -1 at end of file.

```
import java.io.*;

public class ReadDemo
{
public static void main(String [] args)
        throws IOException
{
    Reader r = new FileReader("filename"); int c;
    while ((c = r.read()) != -1)
    { System.out.printf(
            "Char code %x is \"%<c\"%n", c);
    }
    r.close();
}
}
```

* Or the user's quota expired.

There are a significant number of things about this small bit o f sample code that deserve further explanation, and by trying to be minimal the code is not really very good: an improved version is given soon.

Firstly note that FileReader is in the java.io package so we have an im-port statement to make use if it easy. Next observe that almost all input and output functions can raise exceptions, and this code just admits defeat and notes that its main method might therefor fail. I view it as bad style to do this and strongly believe that exceptions should be handled more locally.

Now FileReader is a subclass of Reader, which is the general class that reads from character streams. So I create a FileReader using a constructor that takes a file-name as its argument but store what I get as just a Reader . This helps stress to me and remind me that the rest of my code would be equally valid if using some other sort of Reader, such as one that gets its input from a pipe, from a string, from characters packed in an array, from a network connection, by running a character decoder on a stream of bytes or otherwise. The way I do things here supposes that the data in the file concerned is enc oded in the standard local character-set that Java has been set up for. For reading files imported from elsewhere in the world you have to do things a more complicated way!

The read method hands back either the numeric code for a character, or the value -1 to denote end-of-file. It perhaps seems odd that it re turns an int not a char, but doing so allows it to hand back -1 which does not stand for any normal character. You can of course case the int to a char any time you want to!

After having read the file you are expected to call the close method. If you fail to do this for an input file you may just leave some machine resources cluttered and unless you try to open and read very many files without clos ing any of them you will probably not feel any pain. However for output files i t may sometimes be that the last bit of your data is not actually sent to the file un til you do the close. You should get into the habit of ensuring that every file you op en does get closed.

A much improved version of the same code can be arrived at by handling the possible exceptions. You may note that FileNotFoundException is a sub-class of IOException which is why the throws clause above was sufficient, but which also allows us to see how the improved code is more precise. When you get an exception out of Java it can often be useful to print it, in that it is liable to carry some text that explains further what went wrong. I use finally to guarantee that the close method of the Reader will always be invoked.

```
import java.io.*;

public class BetterReadDemo
{
public static void main(String [] args)
```

```
{
        Reader r;
        try
        {  r = new FileReader("filename");
        }
        catch (FileNotFoundException e) {
        System.out.printf(e);
              return;
        }
        int c;
        try
        { while ((c = r.read()) != -1) {
              System.out.printf(
                          "Char code %x is \"%<c\"%n", c);
              }
        }
        catch (IOException e)
        {  System.out.printf("Reading failed (%s)%n", e);
              return;
        }
        finally
        {  r.close();
        }
}
}
```

Output to a file is somewhat similar, and if you only ever want t o write individual characters and simple strings then FileWriter will suffice. However you may like to be able to use println and printf when writing data to your file, and they come in a class called PrintWriter. Unlike the class FileWriter, PrintWriter hides all exceptions so you do not need to catch them, but you can check for error using the checkError method and you still need to ensure that close is called.

```
import java.io.*;

public class PrintDemo
{
public static void main(String [] args)
{
        try
        { PrintWriter w = new PrintWriter("filename"); try
```

```
            { w.printf("Hoorah%n"); assert
                !w.checkError();
            }
            finally
            {  w.close();
            }
        }
        catch (FileNotFoundException e)
        {  System.out.println("Sorry!");
        }
}
}
```

This time you must make w a PrintWriter and not just a Writer to gain access to printf and so on.

If errors arise on a PrintWriter the flag marking them persists so you do not need to use checkError after every single print statement - every so often and once when you have generated all that you want to end up in the fi le will suffice. Although I have used assert here I probably feel that error checking should be done always an that something along the lines of

```
if (w.checkError())
    throw new IOException("failure on PrintWriter");
```

might well be better policy.

The long-winded but more flexible way to access files is to star t by creating an instance of java.io.File. An object of this type can be created using either a constructor that takes a single String that names the file (as a complete path, if necessary), or with a two-argument constructor where one argument specifies the directory to look in and the other the file-name within tha t directory. A File object supports methods exists, canRead and canWrite and also one called isFile, which test for a "normal" file, ie one that is not a directory o r any of the exotic things that in Unix masquerade as sort-of-files. You c an pass a File rather than a string when opening a FileReader or FileWriter.

Other methods available via the File class include ones to check the length of a file [52], rename it, create new directories, list all the files in a dir ectory and delete files. You can also create a file by giving just a local na me (eg such as "java.tex") and call getAbsolutePath to obtain a fully-rooted file-path that identifies it. The exact result you get will clearly be system -dependent, and on one computer I tried that I got back

---

· The length reported is liable to count in bytes, and so for text files it can well be that the length reported differs from system to system.

"e:\UNIV\notes\java\java.tex"

while on another it was

"/home/acn1/javanotes/java.tex".

The fact that all these facilities are so conveniently supported may make Java one of the more useful programming languages for writing file - management util-ities. Once again if you look at Java code and compare it against other languages for very tiny tasks and where previously you would have missed out all error handling Java can look clumsy — but when you look at more reali stic and well-engineered examples it starts to feel much nicer.

Binary data access are useful for cases when your data really is raw data and not composed of characters. There classes called java.io.FileInputStream and (of course) FileOutputStream that take a File or a string as an argument and create streams. They of course throw exceptions if the fil es can not be opened as requested. Once a file has been opened you should in due cour se call the rele-vant close method to tidy up.

Earlier examples have shown an extra layer of Java constructor arranging to buffer input in the expectation that that may speed it up. I have done that here too.

Putting these together we might arrive at something like this to copy a file in binary mode:

```
String fromName = "source.file";
String toName = "destination.file";
File fromFile = new File(fromName),
     toFile = new File(toName);
if (!fromFile.exists() ||
      !fromFile.canRead() ||
      toFile.exists() ||
      !toFile.canWrite())
{ System.out.println("Can not copy"); return;
}
InputStream fromStream =
      new BufferedInputStream(
            new FileInputStream(fromFile));
try
{  OutputStream toStream =
            new BufferedOutputStream(
                  FileOutputStream(toFile));
      try
      {  for (;;)
            {  toStream.write(fromStream.read());
```

```
            }
        }
        catch (EOFException e)
        {} // Use exception to break out of for loop
        finally
        {  toStream.close();
        }
    }
    catch (IOException e)
    {  System.out.printf("IO error " + e);
    }
    finally
    {  fromStream.close();
    }
```

This code is in fact not yet complete! It needs yet more try blocks to guard against FileNotFoundException cases where the two streams are created. But it illus-trates how the EOFException can be used to stop processing at end of file, and demonstrates very clearly that in real file-processing appl ications most of what you write will be to do with setting everything up and arranging to handle excep-tions, while the central interesting bit of the code may be as short as just

```
for (;;)
{  toStream.write(fromStream.read());
}
```

Overall it may seem pretty grim, but in large programs the complication will still remain at the level of the dozen or so lines shown above, rather than growing out of control. It is also probable that the visible pain is because writing high qual-ity file-manipulation code is in fact nothing like as easy as e arlier programming languages have tried to make it out to be!

There is a potential down-side in Java being so very insistent that you catch all these errors, in that it can encourage a style of cop-out that just wraps all your code in

```
try
{  ...
}
catch (Exception e) {}
```

where the block is set up so it catches *all* sorts of Exception not just the very special ones that you know are liable to arise, and rather than doing anything it just ignores the error. This very much defeats the purpose Java is trying to achieve! If you are (quite reasonably!) in a rush some time at least go:

```
try
{ ...
}
catch (Exception e)
{ System.out.printf("Exception: %s%n", e);
     System.exit(1);
}
```

so that the exceptions you catch are reported and make your program stop.

The above example used BufferedInputStream which should not have any effect at all on what your program actually does, but may have an impact on performance when you work with big files. For binary data th ere are more interesting classes that you could use just as easily: ones to compress and and de-compress data, encryption and checksumming capabilities. For text data you can use LineNumberReader in place of BufferedReader and it will keep track of which line you are on in your input. See the classes FilterInputStream and FilterReader in the documentation for further details.

4.8.2 Big Integers

The Discrete Mathematics course had an extended section where it discussed highest common factors, modular arithmetic and eventually the RSA encryption scheme. To refine your understanding of all that you could qui te properly want to code it all up. To make any pretence at all of reasonable security this means that you need to do a lot of arithmetic on integers that are between 1024 and 1536 bits long. This sort of range of values is about what is required because there is a serious possibility that numbers smaller than that might be factorisable by the best current algorithms and fastest current computers. An implementation of RSA will also need to generate a couple of primes, each with around half that number of bits.

Java has thought of that and it provides a class java.math.BigInteger which does essentially everything you could need! And note that printf lets you print these big values easily.

In this class there are half a dozen constructors. The more obvious ones con-struct big integers from strings or byte arrays, and a valueOf method allows you to create a big integer from a long. The two interesting constructors create ran-dom big numbers. They both accept an argument that is an object from the class Random which actually gives them their randomness. One creates an arbitrary *n*-bit number while the other creates an *n*-bit number which is (almost certainly) prime. For the second of these it is possible to tune the degree of certainty that a prime has indeed been found by giving a "certainty" argument that tells the constructor how hard to work to check things. I might suggest that a value of 50 would be sufficient for all reasonable purposes.

I should provide a rather heavy health warning here. If you use the Java-provided Random class to help you create private keys or other values of cryptographic significance you will be throwing away almost all t he security that the RSA method could give you, since this random number generator comes too close to having a predictable behaviour. Specifically there is a ch ance that to arrange to get the same "random" values that you do it may suffice for so mebody to run a similar Java program having reset their computer so that their run appears to happen at the exact time of day that yours did. This may be hard but is nothing like as hard as factorising 1536-bit integers. If you ever wanted to use serious encryption you *must* instead use java.security.SecureRandom. Anybody really serious about security would think at length before trusting even the things in java.security: how is it possible to tell that they do what they are supposed to and that they do not include secret weaknesses? And even if they are honest it is astonishingly easy to lose all the security you thought you had by some appar-ently minor clumsiness in how you use your cryptographic primitives. A course on security later in the Tripos gives much more information about all of this!

Note that some of the functionality in the Java security and encryption pack-ages may be missing or limited unless your installation has provided some level of assertion that you are not a national of a country that the US Government does not like and that you are not a terrorist. But as is the way of any such attempt at blocking access to technology, there are easy to find drop-in replacements not hampered by (so many) export license issues. You might still be aware that good encryption is viewed by some as something with significant se curity implications and that it should not be given any opportunity to cross international borders until you at the very very least know what all the rules are! Java itself provides ways that those who satisfy the correct eligibility conditions can use the standard Java libraries and obtain unlimited security, via the installation of special "JCE policy files".

Once you have made suitable objects of class BigInteger the library provides you with methods to add, subtract, multiply and divide them, to even raise one big number to a huge power modulo another number (what a give-away about the expected use of this class!). The function that computes what the Discrete Mathematics notes called a Highest Common Factor is here known as a Great-est Common Divisor (gcd), but the change of name does not hide any change of behaviour[53].

· The javasecurity package provides easy to use functions for generating keys and com-puting message digests and digital signatures. There is a standard extension to Java that supplies encryption and further functionality: this part may be subject to export regulation and has to be fetched and installed as a separate item from the main SDK.

```
import java.math.*;
import java.util.*;
...
Random r = new Random(); // inadequate!
          use the SecureRandom class instead!!!
```

- Create two big primes p and q

```
    new BigInteger(768,          // length in bits
        50,    // only 1 in 2^50 prob of non-prime
        r);    // random number source
BigInteger q = new BigInteger(768, 50, r);
```

- form their product, n, which can be public BigInteger n

```
= p.multiply(q);
```

- compute phi = (p-1)*(q-1)

```
BigInteger bigOne = BigInteger.ONE; BigInteger pMinusOne =
p.subtract(bigOne); BigInteger qMinusOne =
q.subtract(bigOne); BigInteger phi =
pMinusOne.multiply(qMinusOne);
```

- select a random exponent whose HCF with phi
- is 1.

```
BigInteger e;
do
{  e = new BigInteger(1536, r);
} while (!phi.gcd(e).equals(bigOne)); // now (n, e)
is the public key
...
// Set up a message to encrypt
BigInteger msg =
    new BigInteger("12341234"); // silly message // Encrypt
with public key. One line of code! BigInteger k =
msg.modPow(e, n);
...
```

The code is clearly about as short as it possibly could be. Again let me warn you that cryptographically satisfactory random number generators are hard to come by, and that such issues as managing the secure distribution of public keys and keeping private ones truly private mean that security involves very much more than just these few lines of code. But Java is clearly making it easy to make a start on it.

How do you know that the Authorities and not bugging your computer while you run the above code? How do you know that no traces of the secret information remain anywhere when you have logged off or even powered down the computer? The Computer Lab's security group has a fine track-record of d emonstrating that even apparently safe computing habits leak information to a sufficiently skilful and ingenious snooper.

4.8.3 Collections

Java has an interface called Collection and a whole range of interesting classes derived form it. The general idea is that Collection covers ideas like “set”, “list” and “vector”. In some cases the elements in a collecti on can be ordered (in which case the objects included must all implement the Comparable interface[54]), but might not be. Collections may be implemented as linked lists or as vectors, but the library classes arrange that when a vector is used it will be enlarged as necessary so that the user does not have to specify a limit to the size of the collection too early. One sub-case of a Collection is a Map, which provides for general ways to organize various sorts of table or dictionary. I am not pro-viding any sample code using Collections in this little section since I believe that when you browse the documentation you will find them easy to cope with. However it may make sense for me to list more of the names of classes worth looking at: Collection, Collections, Set, HashSet, TreeSet, Vector, LinkedList.

The collection classes are keyed to the Java for statement to make it trivial to iterate over the values in a collection: as has been seen in various of the sample programs here.

Very typically when you create an instance of a Collection Class you will use the generics capability to indicate the type of the objects you will keep in it, eg

```
Vector<String> v = new Vector<String>();
```

and if you do so Java will know that the values you extract will be of the type indicated.

4.8.4 Simple use of Threads

A *thread* is a stream of computation that can go on in parallel with others. The term is used when the activities are part of a single program, and where there is no need for security barriers to protect one thread from the next. The more gen-eral term used when the extra overhead of protection is needed is *process*. Java is one of the first languages to make a big point of having threa ds supported as

---

* An especially interesting issue here is the way that Java can compare strings. To support the needs of different nationalities a class Collator is provided, and methods in it can order strings based on proper Locale-specific understandings of where accented or non-English l etters should go. Alphabetic ordering with international texts is a more complicated business that almost all of you would have imagined.

a standard facility. Many systems in the past have had threads, but usually in rather non-portable form. Almost any program that has to implement a complicated windowed user interface or which accesses remote computers[55] will need to use threads so that one high priority thread can ensure that the user always gets responses to requests, while several lower priority ones keep on with some bigger calculation. There are very many subtleties in any program that exhibits concur-rency. I will not describe these here, and in consequence I expect that people who try to make substantial use of threads based on just these notes will get themselves into deep water. There are two typical bad effects that can arise. In one the system just locks up as a chain of threads each wait for the others to complete some task. In the other two threads both attempt to update some data structure at around the same time and their activities interfere, leaving data in a corrupted state. The Java keyword synchronized is involved in some of the resolutions of these sorts of problem.

The example here is supposed to do not much more than to alert you to the possibility of writing multi-threaded Java programs, and to show how easy it is. I will start by defining a class that will encapsulate the beha viour I want in the rather silly thread that I will use here:

```
class Task extends Thread
{
      boolean resultShown;
      String result;
      int identification;
      Task(int i)
      { identification = i; resultShown
            = false;
      }
      public void run()
                  {  try { sleep(20+100*identification % 77); } catch
                                    (InterruptedException e) { return; }
            result = String.valueOf(identification);
      }
}
```

The two critical things are that my class extends Thread and that it implements run. The method run will be to a thread much what main is to a complete program. In this case I make my thread do something rather minimal. It goes to sleep for an amount of time that depends on the argument that was passed to its constructor, and it then sets one of its variables, result, to a string version of that value. When created my task also sets a flag that I will use later on to record whether I have picked up its result.

* Often a slow business.

To demonstrate use of threads I will create half a dozen instances of the above, and then wait around until each has finished its work. As I noti ce each task com-pleting I will pick up its result and display it. When I have done that I will set the resultShown flag so that I do not display any result twice. I could surely find a cleverer way of achieving that, but the solution I use he re is at least quite concise. Once all my threads have finished I will let my main pr ogram terminate. I let my top-level class inherit from Thread just because I want to use sleep in it so that while waiting for the sub-tasks to finish I am mostly idle.

```
public class Threads extends Thread
{
      static final int THREADCOUNT = 6;

      public static void main(String[] args)
      {
// Create and start six threads
            Task [] spawn = new Task [THREADCOUNT]; for (int i
            = 0; i<THREADCOUNT; i++)
            { spawn[i] = new Task(i);
                  spawn[i].start();
            }
            System.out.println("All running now"); int stillGoing
            = THREADCOUNT;
•   Scan looking for terminated threads while
            (stillGoing != 0)
            { for (int i=0; i<THREADCOUNT; i++) { if
                  (!spawn[i].isAlive() &&
                              !spawn[i].resultShown)
•   print result the first time I notice a thread dead {
                        System.out.println("Result from " +
                                    + " = " + spawn[i].result);
                              spawn[i].resultShown = true;
                              stillGoing–;
                        }
                  }
                  System.out.println("One scan done");
•   sleep for 7 milliseconds between scans to avoid waste try { sleep(7); }
                  catch (InterruptedException e) { break; }
            }
            System.out.println("All done");
      }
}
```

Observe that sleep can raise an exception if the sleeping task receives an interrupt from elsewhere, and I (have to) catch this and quit. The results I obtain follow, and you can see traces that show the main program scanning round look-ing for threads that have finished and also you can see that the different threads terminate in some curious order. Of course a more worthwhile example would put real computation into each of the threads and their termination would be based on how long that took rather than on the artificial sleeping I hav e used here!

```
java Threads
        All running     now
        One scan done
        One scan done
        One scan done
        Result from     0  = 0
        Result from     4  = 4
        One scan done
        Result from     1  = 1
        One scan done
        One scan done
        Result from     5  = 5
        One scan done
        Result from     2  = 2
        One scan done
        One scan done
        One scan done
        Result from     3  = 3
        One scan done
        All done
```

The reason my example is respectably simple and trouble-free is that the threads only communicate by receiving data when first created and by d elivering some-thing back when they have finished. Inter-process communica tion beyond that can be astonishingly hard to get right.

4.8.5 Network access

Java really hit the news as a language for animating your own web pages. One part of doing this is the set of graphical operations that it supports. Another less instantly visible but equally important thing is the ability to connect to remote computers and retrieve data from them. The set of rules that make up HTTP[56] are what defines the World Wide Web. Standard Java libraries prov ide various degrees of ability to connect using it. The small program shown here links through to a

---

* HyperText Transfer Protocol.

fixed location named as its fire command-line argument and dis plays the data found there. This data comes out as an HTML document with lots of tags that are enclosed in angle brackets.

```
// Read file from a possibly remote web server

import java.net.*;
import java.io.*;

public class Webget
{

public static void main(String [] args)
{
      URL target;
      try
      {  target = new URL(args[0]);
      }
      catch (MalformedURLException e)
      { return; } // Badly formed web-page address try
      { URLConnection link = target.openConnection(); link.connect();
            // connect to remote system
```

- Now just for fun I display size and type information
- about the document that is being fetched. Note that
- documents might be pictures or binary files as well
- as just text!

```
            System.out.println("size = " +
                  link.getContentLength());
            System.out.println("type = " +
                  link.getContentType());
```

- getInputStream() gives me a handle on the content, and
- I rather hope it is text. In that case I can get the
- characters that make it up from the InputStream. Reader in =

```
            new InputStreamReader(
                  link.getInputStream()); int c;
```

- Crude echo of text from the document to the screen.
- It will have lots of HTML encoding in it, I expect. while ((c = in.read())

```
            != -1)
                  System.out.print((char)c);
      }
```

- A handler is needed in case exceptions arise. catch

```
      (IOException e)
```

```
        { System.out.println("IO error on link"); }
• I am lazy here and do not close anything down.
}

}

// end of Webget.java
```

The data stored on the CL teaching support pages in mid February 1998 started off as follows, apart from the fact that I have split some of the lines to make the text fit neatly on the pages of these notes. It has of course cha nged by now! I keep this old material in the notes out of nostalgia.

```
<HTML>
<HEAD>
<TITLE>Comp.Sci. Teaching pages</TITLE>
</HEADER>
<BODY>

<H1> Computer Science teaching material on Thor</H1>

<P>
<UL>
<LI><A HREF="Java/java-index.html"> Some Information about Java
      </A> (on this server)
...
```

The main message here is that accessing a remote web-site is just about as trivial as reading from a local file.

4.8.6 Menus, scroll bars and dialog boxes

Back when Java 1.2 was released Sun finalised a whole set of win dows management code that they called Swing. This extended and in places replaced earlier windowing capabilities that were known as AWT. I believe that by now it is proper to use the Swing versions of things even in those cases where older AWT versions remain available. You can tell that you are doing that when you use a lot of class names that start with a capital “J”!

The code presented here is called MenuApp and is a pretty minimal demon-stration of menus! I will use this example to show how something can be both an application and an applet. The “application” bit of cours e defined a method called main, and this just sets up a window (frame) that can contain the applet stuff. There is a bit of mumbo jumbo to allow the application to stop properly when the window is closed. As usual I will show the inner bit of the code first – the fragment that actually does the work:

```
public static void main(String[] args)
{
      Menuapp window = new Menuapp();
      JFrame f = new JFrame("Menu Demonstration");
      f.addWindowListener(new WindowAdapter()
      {  public void windowClosing(WindowEvent e)
            {  System.exit(0);
            }
      });
      f.getContentPane().add(window, BorderLayout.CENTER);
      f.setSize(600, 400);
      f.setVisible(true);
}
```

I should point out the syntax

```
      new WindowAdapter()
      {  public void windowClosing(WindowEvent e)
            {  System.exit(0);
            }
      }
}
```

which extends the class WindowAdapter to produce a new (anonymous) class. In this new class it overrided the windowClosing method. It then creates an instance of the new anonymous class. This arrangement is known as an "Inner Class" and can be very handly when you need a small variant on some existing class and will use it just once so that giving it a name would be over-clumsy.

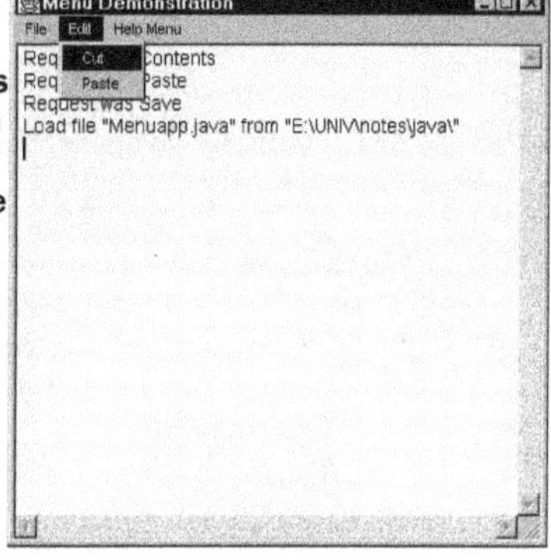

Menuapp running

The constructor for Menuapp will establish a menu bar at the top of itself, then makes menus on that bar, and places menu items on each menu. In much the way that mouse events were dealt with by registering a handler for them it is necessary to implement an

interface called ActionListener and
tell each menu to report via it. The report hands down an ActionEvent from which it is possible to extract the name of the menu item (and if need be which menu it was on) that was activated. I illustrate this by showing how to pop up a dialog box for selecting a file, although once I have the name of the file I just display that in the text area rather than actually opening it.

I put a scrollable editable window for the text. The version I use could in fact support multi-colour text in mixed fonts and with icons and other things inter-leaved with the words: finding out about that is an exercise fo r those of you who feel keen. You will also find that I have coded this using the "s wing" facilities (ie it will not compile on a simple un-extended installation of JDK 1.1.x), and the arrangements for selecting a file and for making the text wind ow scrollable relate to that. The inclusion of javax.swing classes gives access to the relevant bits of the class libraries. Furthermore the code can be run as either an applet or an application. So lots of things are being illustrated at once. You are not expected to be able to follow all of them at first, but maybe the code will be a useful model when sometime later you do need to use some of these facilities in anger. The complete code follows:

```
• Demonstration of Menus and a window created
• from an application rather than an applet.
//AC      Norman                                   1998-2000

import   java.awt.*;
import   java.awt.event.*;
import   javax.swing.*;

import   javax.swing.text.*;
public   class Menuapp extends JApplet
                              implements ActionListener
{

• This can be run as either an application or an applet! public static void
    main(String[] args)
    {
        Menuapp window = new Menuapp();
        JFrame f = new JFrame("Menu Demonstration");
        f.addWindowListener(new WindowAdapter()
        { public void windowClosing(WindowEvent e) {
            System.exit(0);
            }
        });
        f.getContentPane().add(window, BorderLayout.CENTER);
```

```
        f.setSize(600, 400);
        f.setVisible(true);
    }
```

- All real work happens because of this
- constructor. I create a JTextPane to hold
- input & output and make some menus.

```
    JTextPane text;
    Container cc;

    public Menuapp()
    {
            = getContentPane(); text =
        new JTextPane();
        text.setEditable(true);
        text.setFont(
            new Font("MonoSpaced", Font.BOLD, 24));
        JScrollPane scroll = new JScrollPane(text,
            JScrollPane.VERTICAL_SCROLLBAR_AS_NEEDED,
            JScrollPane.HORIZONTAL_SCROLLBAR_NEVER);
        cc.add(scroll);
```

- Menus hang off a menu bar and contain menu items JMenuBar

```
        bar;
        JMenu mFile, mEdit, mHelp; JMenuItem
        mNew, mOpen, mSave, mCut,
                mPaste, mContents;
```

- Create a menu bar first and add it to the Frame

```
        bar =    new JMenuBar();                setJMenuBar(bar);
// Create a menu and add it to the MenuBar
        mFile    = new JMenu("File");           bar.add(mFile);
// Create menu      items and add to menu
        mNew =  new JMenuItem("New");           mFile.add(mNew);
        mOpen  = new JMenuItem("Open");         mFile.add(mOpen);
        mSave  = new JMenuItem("Save");         mFile.add(mSave);

        mEdit   = new JMenu("Edit");            bar.add(mEdit);
        mCut =   new JMenuItem("Cut");          mEdit.add(mCut);
        mPaste  = new JMenuItem("Paste");mEdit.add(mPaste);

        mHelp = new JMenu("Help Menu");
```

```
        bar.add(mHelp);
        mContents = new JMenuItem("Contents");
        mHelp.add(mContents);
```

• Each menu has to be activated to be useful.

```
        mNew.addActionListener(this);
        mOpen.addActionListener(this);
        mSave.addActionListener(this);
        mCut.addActionListener(this);
        mPaste.addActionListener(this);
        mContents.addActionListener(this);
    }
```

• When a menu item is selected this gets called,
• and getActionCommand() retrieves the text from
• the menuItem. Here I clear the area when New
• is used, and do something with Open, but otherwise
• just display a message.

```
    public void actionPerformed(ActionEvent e)
    {
        String action = e.getActionCommand(); try
        { if (action.equals("New")) text.setText(""); else if
            (action.equals("Open")) openFile(); else
            { StyledDocument s =
                    text.getStyledDocument();
                s.insertString(s.getLength(),
                            "Request was " + action + "\n", null);
            }
        }
        catch (BadLocationException e1)
        {}
    }

    void openFile() throws BadLocationException
    { JFileChooser d = new JFileChooser("Open a file"); if
        (d.showOpenDialog(cc) ==
            JFileChooser.APPROVE_OPTION)
        { StyledDocument s = text.getStyledDocument();
            s.insertString(s.getLength(),
                "Load file \"" +
                d.getSelectedFile().getAbsolutePath() +
```

```
                        "\"\n", null);
            }
        }
}
```

// end of Menuapp.java

You should expect that extending the above example or writing your own code that sets up controllable visual effects will cause you to have to do rather a lot of reading of the class library documentation to plan which classes you will derive items from. Also when you have mastered the basics of GUI construction by hand you will very probably want to take advantage of one of the Java develop-ment environments that can set up frameworks for user-interfaces for you in really convenient ways.

4.8.7 Exercises

Replacement for "ls"

On Unix the command ls lists all the files in the current directory. With a command-line flag -R it also lists members of sub-directories. Investigate the Java File class and see how much of the behaviour of ls (or the DOS/Windows dir) you can re-create.

RSA

The code fragment above suggests how to create a public key and then how to use it to encrypt a message once that message has been reduced to a BigInteger of suitable size. Flesh this out with code that can use the private key to decrypt messages, and with some scheme that can read text from the standard input (or a file, maybe), split it up into chunks and represent each chunk as a BigInteger.

You might also want to investigate the Java Cryptographic Architecture and find out what is involved in creating cryptographic-grade ra ndom values. You should be made very aware that the ordinary Java random number generator does not pretend that the values it returns to you are suitable for use in security appli-cations.

Then do a literature search to discover just what you are permitted to do with an implementation of an idea that has been patented[57] and also what the Secu-

* The main RSA US patent expired on the 20th September 2000, but that does not necessar-ily mean that all associated techniques and uses are unprotected. Also note that there are other public key methods for both digital signatures and for encryption where the original patents have

rity Policies of various countries are about the use, import and export of strong encryption technology.

Note again that Java provides the specification of a security library that would do all this for you if it were not for the USA government's export restrictions, and if these restrictions do not apply to you you could use the Java strong security. There are international re-implementations of this library that can be fetched and used here. See for instance www.openjce.org. But also be aware that exporting code that includes strong encryption may be subject to government restriction.

Big Decimals

The class BigDecimal builds on BigInteger to provide for long precision decimal fractions. When a BigDecimal is created it will behave as if it has some specified number of digits to the right of its decimal point, b ut as arithmetic is carried out there can be any number of digits generated before the decimal point.

For any number z one can define a sequence of values x_i by $x_0 = 1$ and $x_{i+1} = (x_i + z/x_i)/2$. This sequence will converge to $\sqrt{z}$, and once it gets even reasonably close it homes in rapidly, roughly doubling the number of correct sig-nificant values at each step. For finding square roots of numbe rs between 0.5 and 2 (say) the starting value $x_0 = 1$ will be quite tolerable.

If one wanted the square root of a number larger than 2 or smaller than 0.5 it would make sense to augment the recurrence formula by use of the identity $\sqrt{4z} = 2\sqrt{z}$ to pre-normalise z.

Implement the method and use it to create a table of square roots of the integers from 1 to 10 all to 100 decimal places.

If you can perform high-precision arithmetic on floating poi nt numbers you should try the following calculation. I am going to use informal syntax with double constants written where you will need to use BigDecimals, and I will use the ordinary operators to work on values not calls to suitable methods in the BigDecimal class. I am also not going to tell you here either how many cycles of the loop you should expect the code to obey or what the values it prints out will look like! But I suggest that you work to (say) 1000 decimals and see what you get.

```
a = 1.0;
b = 1/sqrt(2.0);
u = 0.25;
x = 1.0;
pn = 4.0;
do
```

---

also expired, and so using these can also be of interest without patent worries about deployment.
Investigate "El Gamal".

```
{ p = pn; y = a;
        a = (a+b)/2.0; b =
        sqrt(y*b);
        u = u-x*(a-y)*(a-y);
        x = 2*x;
        pn = a*a/u;
        print(pn);
} while (pn < p);
```

When you have investigated this for yourself try looking for arithmetic-geometric mean (and the cross-references from there!) in Hakmem.

Mandelbrot set (again)

Adjust the Mandelbrot set program, as considered in an earlier exercise, so that at the start (maybe in an init method?) it allocates a 400 by 400 array of integers all initially set to 0. Change the paint method so that it just displays colours as recorded in this array, and have a separate thread that (a) computes values to go in the array and (b) uses repaint at the end of each of its resolution cycles to bring make sure that the screen is brought fully up to date then. The objective here is to arrange that each pixel is only calculated once and that thus the paint method is a lot quicker.

Further extension of this code would add mouse support so that (as a start) a mouse click would cause the display to re-centre at the selected point and start drawing again using half the previous range. Those of you who get that far are liable to be able to design more flexible and convenient user- driven controls than that, I expect!

Tickable exercise 7

Tick 5 was the largest single exercise. Tick 6 was a fairly easy example of getting an Applet working. This final exercise is intended to be a reas onably manageable one to end off the series of Java practicals.

The illustration of network code that I gave represents a minimal way of accessing a remote file.

1. Extend it so that it can be used as

   ```
   java Webget URL destination
   ```

   to fetch the contents of an arbitrary web document and store it on the local disc. If an explicit destination file is not specified your pro gram should display the document fetched on the screen;

- Investigate document types and encodings and try to arrange that text doc-uments are fetched as streams of characters while binary documents come across the net verbatim;
- *Optional:* Some files on the web are of type " zip", being compressed. Java provides a set of library functions for uncompressing such files. Use it so that when a zipped file is fetched the data that arrives locally is the decompressed form of it.
- *Very optional:* A javax.swing.JEditorPane can be set up so that it renders (a subset of) HTML for you. Using this perhaps you could go a significant way towards implementing your own light-weight web browser and you might only need a fairly modest amount of Java!

(End of tickable exercise)

Yet further network-related code

The parts of the Java libraries that can fetch material from remote ma-chines understand quite well that you will only occasionally be fetching raw text, and that fairly often the data to be accessed will be a picture or a sound. Investigate the documen-tation and sort out how to use these facilities. An image from a local student-run web site is shown here to illustrate the usefulness of these fa-cilities. Further parts of the network classes allow you to detect (to some extent) what sort of data is about to be fetched from a web location so that different sorts of data can each be handled in the most appropriate manner.

Figure 4.8: www.arthurnorman.org!

If you could write code that lo-cated words enclosed in angle brack-ets within text, and lay text out in a window in such a way that you could tell which word was the subject of a mouse click you might find y ourself half-way to writing your very own web browser!

A minimal text editor

The menu example already allows you to re-position the cursor and type in extra text. I have shown how to identify files to be loaded and saved. The TextArea class provides methods that would implement cut and paste. Put all these together to get a notepad-style editor.

More Fonts

The Unicode example showed that it is easy to select which font Java uses to paint characters. The class FontMetrics then provides methods that allow you to obtain very detailed measurements of both individual characters and rows of them. Using all this you can get rather fine control over visua l appearance. Using however many of few of these facilities you like create a Java applet that displays the word LATEX in something like the curious layout that the designers of that text-formatting program like to see.

Two flasks

This was a puzzle that I found in one of the huge anthologies of mathematical oddities:

> An apothecary has two spherical flasks, which between them ho ld ex-actly 9 measures of fluid. He explains this to his friend the ma thema-gician, and adds that the glass-blower who makes his flasks ca n make them perfectly spherical but will only make flasks whose diam eter is an exact rational number. The mathemagician looks unimpressed and says that the two flasks obviously have diameters 1 and 2, so th eir volume is proportional to $1^3 + 2^3 = 9$. Hmmm says the apothecary, that *would* have worked, but I already had a pair like that. This pair of flasks has exactly the same total capacity, still has linear d imensions that are exact fractions but the neither flask has diameter 1.
>
> Find a size that the smaller of his two flasks might have had.

This is clearly asking for positive solutions to $x^3 + y^3 = 9$ with the solution being a neat fraction. In an earlier exercise you were invited to write a class to handle fractions. Before continuing with this one you might like to ensure that you have a version of it that uses BigInteger just to be certain that overflow will not scupper you.

Here is an attack you can make on the problem. We are interested in solutions to $x^3 + y^3 = 9$ and know an initial solution $x = 1$, $y = 2$. Imagine the cubic equation drawn as a graph (I know it is an implicit equation, so for now I will be happy if you imagine that there is a graph and do not worry about actually drawing it!). The point (1,2) lies on the curve. Draw the tangent to the curve at (1,2). This straight line will have an equation of the form $lx + my + n = 0$ for some l, m and n which you can find after you have done a little differentiation. Now consider where the straight line meets the curve. If one eliminated y between the two equations the result is a cubic in x, but we know that $x = 1$ is one solution (because the curve and line meet there). In fact because the line is a tangent to the curve that is a double solution, and thus the cubic we had will necessarily have a factor $(x - 1)^2$. If you divide that out you get a *linear* equation that gives you the x co-ordinate of the other place where the tangent crosses the curve. Solve that and substitute into the line equation to find the corresponding value of y. The pair x, y were found by solving what were in the end only linear equations, and so the numbers must be at worst fractions. This has therefore given another rational point on the cubic curve. What you get there is not a solution to the problem as posed, since one of x and y will end up negative. But maybe if you take a tangent at the new point that will lead you to a third possibility and perhaps following this path you will eventually manage to find a solution that is both rational and where both c omponents are positive.

Write code to try this out, and produce the tidiest fractional solution to the original puzzle that you can, ie the one with smallest denominators.

A member of the audience checking a detailed point with the lecturer at the end of a session.

Figure 4.9: Odds and Ends follow: watch what the lecturer happens to cover.

Chapter 5

Designing and testing programs in Java

At this stage in the "Programming in Java" course I will start to concentrate more on the "programming" part than the "Java". This is on the basi s that you have now seen most of the Java syntax and a representative sampling of the libraries: now the biggest challenge is how to use the language with confiden ce and competence.

In parallel with this course you get other ones on *Software Engineering*. These present several major issues. One is that errors in software can have serious conse-quences, up to and including loss of life and the collapse of businesses. Another is that the construction of large computer-related products will involve teams of pro-grammers working to build and support software over many years, and this raises problems not apparent to an individual programmer working on a private project. A third is that formal methods can be used when defining an plan ning a project to build a stable base for it to grow on, and this can be a great help. The emphasis is on programming in the large, which is what the term "Software Engineering" is usually taken to have at its core. Overall the emphasis is on recognition of the full life-time costs associated with software and the management strategies that might keep these costs under control.

The remaining section of this Java course complements that perspective and looks at the job of one person or a rather small group, working on what may well be a software component or a medium sized program rather than on a mega-scale product. The intent of this part of the course is to collect together and emphasise some of the issues that lie behind the skill of programming. Good programmers will probably use many of the techniques mentioned here without being especially aware of what they are doing, but for everybody (even the most experienced) it can be very useful to bring these ideas out into the open. It seems clear to me that all computer science professionals should gain a solid grounding carrying out small projects before they actually embark on larger ones, even though a vision of what

•

will be needed in big projects help shape attitudes and habits.

It is at least a myth current in the Computer Laboratory that those who intend to become (mechanical) engineers have as an early part of their training an exer-cise where they fashion a simple cube of solid metal, and they are judged on the accuracy of their work. Such an activity can be part of bringing them into direct touch with the materials that they will later be working with in more elaborate contexts. It gets them to build experience with tools and techniques (including those of measurement and assessment). Programming in the small can serve simi-lar important purposes for those who will go on to develop large software systems: even when large projects introduce extra levels of complication and risk the design issues discussed here remain vital.

One of the major views I would like to bring to the art (or craft, or science, or engineering discipline, depending on how one likes to look at it) of programming is an awareness of the value of an idea described by George Orwell in his book "1984". This is *doublethink*, the ability to believe two contradictory ideas without becoming confused. Of course one of the original pillars of doublethink was the useful precept *Ignorance is Strength*, but collections of views specifically about the process of constructing programs. These notes will not be about the rest of the association of computers with surveillance, NewSpeak or other efficiency-enhancing ideas. The potentially conflicting views about pr ogramming that I want to push relate to the prospect of a project succeeding. Try to keep in your minds both the idea *Programming is incredibly difficult and this program will ne ver work correctly: I am going to have to spend utterly hopeless ages trying to coax it into passing even the most minimal test cases* and its optimistic other face, which claims cheerfully *In a couple of days I can crack the core of this problem, and then it will only take me another few to finish off all the detai ls. These days even young children can all write programs.* The concise way to express this particular piece of doublethink (and please remember that you really have to believe both part, for without the first you will make a total botch of every thing, while without the second you will be too paralysed ever to start actual coding), is

Writing programs is easy.

A rather closely related bit of doublethink alludes both to the joy of achieve-ment when a program appears to partially work and the simultaneous bitter way in which work with computers persistently fail. Computers show up our imperfec-tions and frailties, which range through unwillingness to read specifications via inability to think straight all the way to incompetence in mere mechanical typing skills. The short-hand for the pleasure that comes from discovering one of your own mistakes, and having spent many frustrating hours tracking down something that is essentially trivial comes out as

Writing programs is fun.

A further thing that will be curious about my presentation is that it does not present universal and provable absolute truths. It is much more in the style of collected good advice. Some of this is based on direct experience, other parts has emerged as an often-unstated collective view of those who work with computers. There are rather fewer books covering this subject than I might have expected. There is a very long reading list posted regularly on comp.software-eng, but most of it clearly assumes that by the time things get down to actually writing programs the reader will know from experience what to do. Despite the fact that it is more concerned with team-work rather than individual programming I want to direct you towards *the Mythical Man Month*[7], if only for the cover illustration of the La Brea Tar Pits[1] with the vision that programmers can become trapped just as

Figure 5.1: The La Brea tar pits.

the Ice Age mammoths and so on were. Brooks worked for IBM at a time that they were breaking ground with the ambitious nature of their operating systems. The analogous Microsoft experience is more up to date and can be found in *Writing*

[1]You may not be aware that the tar pits are in the middle of a thoroughly built-up part of Los Angeles, and when visiting them you can try to imagine some of the local school-children venturing too far and getting bogged down, thus luring their families, out for a week-end picnic, to a sticky doom.

•

Solid Code[18] which gives lots of advice that is clearly good way outside the context of porting Excel between Windows and the Macintosh. If you read the Solid Code book you will observe that it is concerned almost entirely with C, and its examples of horrors are often conditioned by that. You should therefore let it prompt you into thinking hard about where Java has made life safer than C and where it has introduced new and different potential pitfalls.

For looking at programming tasks that are fairly algorithmic in style the book by Dijkstra[10] is both challenging and a landmark. There are places where peo-ple have collected together some of the especially neat and clever **little** programs they have come across, and many of these indeed contain ideas or lessons that may be re-cyclable. Such examples have come to be referred to as " pearls"[4][5]. Once one has worked out what program needs to be written ideas (now so much in the mainstream that this book is perhaps now out of date) can be found in one of the big presentations by some of the early proponents of structured programming[19]. Stepping back and looking at the programming process with a view to estimating programmer productivity and the reliability of the end product, Halstead[14] in-troduced some interesting sorts of software metrics, which twenty years on are still not completely free of controversy. All these still leave me feeling that there is a gap between books that describe the specific detail of how to use one particular programming language, and those concerned with large scale software engineer-ing and project management. To date this gap has generally been filled by an ap-prentice system where trainee programmers are invited to work on progressively larger exercises and their output is graded and commented on by their superiors. Much like it is done here! With this course I can at least provide some back-ground thoughts that might help the apprentices start on their progression a little more smoothly.

When I started planning a course covering this material it was not quite ob-vious how much there was going to be for me to say that avoided recitations of the blindingly obvious and that was also reasonably generally applicable. As I started on the notes it became clear that there are actually a lot of points to be covered. To keep within the number of lectures that I have and to restrict these notes to a manageable bulk I am therefore restricting myself (mostly) to listing points for consideration and giving as concrete and explicit recommendations as I can: I am not including worked examples or lots of anecdotes that illustrate how badly things can go wrong when people set about tasks in wrong-minded ways. But perhaps I can suggest that as you read this document you imagine it expanded into a very much longer presentation with all that additional supporting material and with a few exercises at the end of each section. You can also think about all the points that I raise in the context of the various programming exercises that you are set or other practical work that you are involved with.

5.1 Different sorts of programming tasks

Java experience illustrates very clearly that there are several very different sorts of activity all of which are informally refereed to as "program ming". On style of use of Java — of great commercial importance — involves understa nding all of the libraries and stringing together uses of them to implement user interfaces and to move data around. In such cases the focus is entirely on exploiting the libraries, on human factors and on ensuring that the code's behaviour agrees with the man-ual or on-line documentation that its users will work from. At another extreme come tasks that involve the design of many new data-structures and algorithmic innovations in their use. Often in this second style of program there will also be significant concern over efficiency.

Given that there are different sorts of software it might be reasonable to start with a classification of possible sorts of program. There are three ways in which this may help with development:

- Different sorts of computer systems are not all equally easy to build. For instance industrial experience has shown repeatedly that the construction of (eg) an operating system is very much harder than building a (again eg) a compiler even when the initial specifications and the amount of code to be written seem very similar. Thinking about the category into which your par-ticular problem falls can help you to plan time-scales and predict possible areas of difficulty;

- The way you go about a project can depend critically on some very high level aspects of the task. A fuller list of possibilities is given below, but two extreme cases might be (a) a software component for inclusion in a safety-critical part of an aero-space application, where development budget and timescale are subservient to an over-riding requirement for reliability, and (b) a small program being written for fun as a first experim ent with a new programming language, where the program will be run just once and nothing of any real important hands on the results. It would be silly to carry forward either of the above two tasks using a mind-set tuned to the other: knowing where one is on the spectrum between can help make the selection of methodology and tools more rational;

- I will make a point in these notes that program development is not some-thing to be done in an isolated cell. It involves discussing ideas and progress with others and becoming aware of relevant prior art. Thinking about the broad area in which your work lies can help you focus on the resources worth investigating. Often some of these will not be at all specific to the immediate description of what you are suppose to achieve but will concerned with very general areas such as rapid prototyping, formal validation, real-time responsiveness, user interfaces or whatever.

I will give my list of possible project attributes. These are in general not mutually exclusive, and in all real cases one will find that th ese are not yes–no choices but more like items to be scored from 1 to 10. I would like to think of them as forming an initial survey that you should conduct before starting any detailed work on your program just to set it in context. When you find one or two of these scoring 9 or 10 out of 10 for relevance you know you have identified something important that ought to influence how you approach the work. If you find a project scores highly on *lots* of these items then you might consider trying to wriggle out of having to take responsibility for it, since there is a significant chance that it will be a disaster! The list here identifies pot ential issues, but does not discuss ways of resolving them: in many cases the project features identified here will just tell you which of the later sections in these notes are liable to be the more important ones for your particular piece of work. The wording in each of my descriptions will be intended to give some flavour of how *severe* instances of the issue being discussed can cause trouble, so keep cheerful because usually you will not be plunging in at the really deep end of the pool.

Ill-defined One of the most common and hardest situations to face up to is when a computer project is not clearly specified. I am going to take this case to include ones where there appears to be a detailed and precise specification document but on close inspection the requirements as written down boil down to "I don't know much about computer systems but I know wh at I like, so write me a program that I will like, please." Clearly the first thing to do in such a case is to schedule a sub-project that has the task of obtaining a clear and concise description of what is really required, and sometimes this will of itself be a substantial challenge;

Safety-critical It is presumably obvious that safety-critical applications need exceptional thought and effort put into their validation. But this need for reli-ability is far from an all-or-nothing one, in that the reputation of a software house (or indeed the grades obtained by a student) may depend on ensuring that systems run correctly at least most of the time, and that their failure modes appear to the user to be reasonable and soft. At the other extreme it is worth noting that in cases where robustness of code and reliability of results are not important at all (as can sometimes be the case, despite this seeming unreasonable) that fact can be exploited to give the whole project a much lighter structure and sometimes to make everything very much easier to achieve. A useful question to ask is "Does this program hav e to work correctly in *all* circumstances, or does it just need to work in *most* common cases, or indeed might it be sufficient to make it work in just *one* carefully chosen case?"

Large It is well established that as the size of a programming task increases the amount of work that goes into it grows much more rapidly than the number of lines of code (or whatever other simple measurement you like) does. At various levels of task size it becomes necessary to introduce project teams, extra layers of formal management and in general to move away from any pretence that any single individual will have a full understanding of the whole effort. If your task and the associated time-scales call for a team of 40 programmers and you try it on your own maybe you will have difficulty finishing it off! Estimating the exact size that a program wil l end up or just how long it will take to write is of course very hard, but identifying whether it can be done by one smart programmer in a month or if it is a big team project for five years is a much less difficult call to make.

Shifting sands If either project requirements or resources can change while soft-ware development is under way then this fact needs to be allowed for. Proba-ble only a tiny minority of real projects will be immune from this sort of dis-traction, since even for apparently well-specified tasks it is quite usual that experience with the working version of the program will lead to "wouldn't it be nice if . . . " ideas emerging even in the face of carefully discussed and thought out early design decisions that the options now requested would not be supportable. Remember that Shifting Sands easily turn into Tar Pits!

Figure 5.2: The museum frieze at La Brea.

Urgent When are you expected to get this piece of work done? How firm is the deadline? If time constraints (including the way that this project will com-pete with other things you are supposed to do) represents a real challenge it is best to notice that early on. Note that if, while doing final testing on your code, you find that it has a bug in it there may be no guarantee th at you can isolate or fix this to any pre-specified time-scale. This is be cause (at least for most people!) there is hardly any limit to the subtlety of bugs and the amount of time and re-work needed to remove them. If the delivery date for code is going to be rigidly enforced (as is the case with CST final year projects!) this fact may be important: even if there is plenty of the project as a whole a rigid deadline can make it suddenly become urgent at the last minute;

Unrealistic It is quite easy to write a project specification that sounds g ood, but is not grounded in the real world. A program that modelled the stock markets and thereby allowed you to predict how to manage your portfolio, or one to predict winning numbers in the national lottery, or one to play world-class chess. . . Now of course there are programs that play chess pretty well, and lots of people have made money out of the other two projects (in one case the statistics that one might apply is *much* easier than the other!), but the desirability of the finished program can astonishingly ofte n blind one to the difficulties that would arise in trying to achieve it. In some cases a project might be achievable in principle but is beyond either today's technology or this week's budget, while in other cases the idea being considered might not even realistic given unlimited budget and time-scales. There are of course places where near-unreasonable big ideas can have a very valuable part to play: in a research laboratory a vision of one of these (currently) unrealis-tic goals can provide direction to the various smaller and better contained projects that each take tiny steps towards the ideal. At present my favourite example of something like this is the idea of *nanotechnology* with armies of molecular-scale robots working together to build their own heirs and suc-cessors. The standard example of a real project that many (most?) realistic observers judged to be utterly infeasible was the "Star Wars " Strategic De-fence Initiative, but note that at that sort of level the political impact of even starting a project may be at least as important as delivery of a working product!

Multi-platform It is a luxury if a program only has to work on a single fixed com-puter system. Especially as projects become larger there is substantial extra effort required to keep them able to work smoothly on many different sys-tems. This problem can show up with simple issues such as word-lengths, byte-arrangements in memory and compiler eccentricities, but it gets much worse as one looks at windowed user interfaces, multi-media functions, net-work drivers and support for special extra plug-in hardware;

Long life-time The easiest sort of program gets written one afternoon and is thrown away the next day. It does not carry any serious long-term support concerns with it. However other programs (sometimes still initially written in little more than an afternoon) end up becoming part of your life and get themselves worked and re-worked every few years. In my case the program I have that has the longest history was written in around 1972 in Fortran, based on me having seen one of that year's Diploma dissertations and hav-ing (partly unreasonably) convinced myself I could do better. The code was developed on Titan, the then University main machine. I took it to the USA with me when I spent a year there and tried to remove the last few bugs and make it look nicer. When the University moved up to an IBM mainframe I ran it on that, and at a much later stage I translated it (semi automatically) into BBC basic and ran it (very slowly) on a BBC micro. By last year I had the code in C with significant parts of the middle of it totally re-written, but with still those last few bugs to find ways of working around. I f I had been able to predict when I started how long this would be of interest to me for maybe I would have tried harder to get it right first time! Note the radical changes in available hardware and sensible programming language over the lifetime of this program;

User interface For programs like modern word processors there is a real chance that almost all of the effort and a very large proportion of the code will go into supporting the fancy user interface, and trying to make it as helpful and intuitive as possible. Actually storing and editing the text could well be fairly straight forward. When the smoothness of a user interface is a serious priority for a project then the challenge of defining exactly what must happen is almost certainly severe too, and in significan t projects will involve putting test users in special usability laboratories where their eye-movement can be tracked by cameras and their key-strokes can be timed. The fact that an interface provides lots of windows and pull-down menus does not automatically make it easy to use;

Diverse users Many commercial applications need to satisfy multiple users with diverse needs as part of a single coherent system. This can extend to new computer systems that need to interwork seamlessly with multiple existing operational procedures, including existing computer packages. Some users may be nervous of the new technology, while others may find exc essive explanation an offensive waste of their time. The larger the number of in-terfaces needed and the wider the range of expectations the harder it will be to make a complete system deliver total satisfaction;

Speed critical Increasingly these days it makes sense to buy a faster computer if

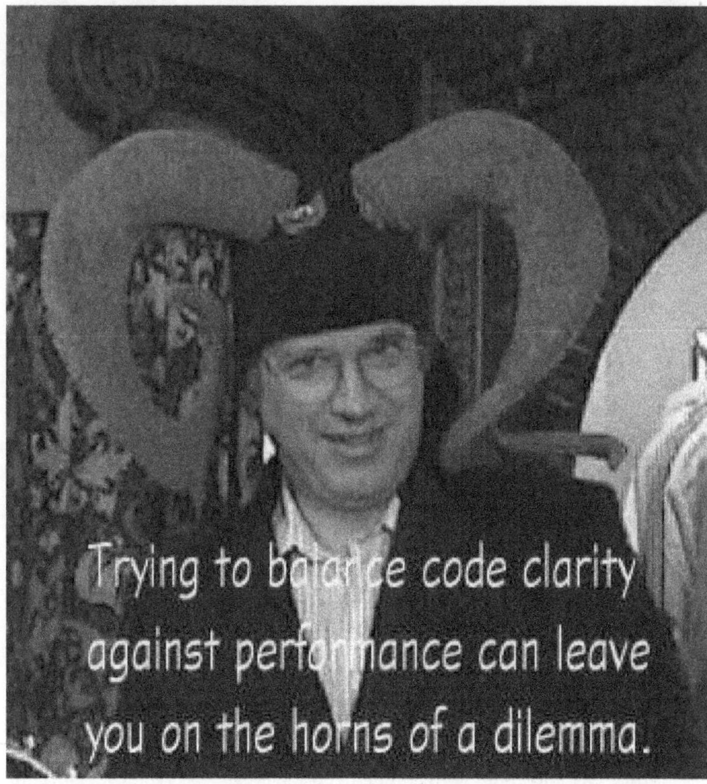

Figure 5.3: The search for speed can lead to eccentric-looking results.

some task seems to take a little longer than is comfortable. However there remain some areas where absolute performance is a serious issue and where getting the very best out of fixed hardware resources can give a competitive edge. The case most in my mind at present is that of (high security) encryp-tion, where the calculations needed are fairly demanding but where there is real interest in keeping some control over the extra hardware costs that user are expected to incur. If speed requirements lead to need for signifi-cant assembly code programming (or almost equivalently to the design of task-specific silicon) then the resource requirements of a p roject can jump dramatically. If in the other hand speed is of no importance at all for some task it may become possible to use a higher level programming system, simpler data structures and algorithms and generally save a huge amount of aggravation;

Real time Real-time responsiveness is characteristic of many control applications. It demands that certain external events be given a response within a pre-specified interval. At first this sounds like a variant o n tasks that are just speed-critical, but the fine granularity at which perfo rmance is spec-ified tends to influence the entire shape of software projects and rule out some otherwise sensible approaches. Some multi-media applications and video games will score highly in this category, as will engine management software for cars and flight control software for airports;

Memory critical A programming task can be made much harder if you are tight on memory. The very idea of being memory-limited can feel silly when we all know that it is easy to go out and buy another 64 Mbytes for (currently) of the order of £50[2]. But the computer in your cell-phone will have an amount of memory selected on the basis of a painful compromise between cost (measured in pennies), the power drain that the circuitry puts on the battery (and hence the expected battery life) and the set of features that can be supported. And the software developers are probably give the memory budget as a fixed quantity and invited to support as long a list of features as is at all possible within it;

Add-on A completely fresh piece of software is entitled to define its own file formats and conventions and can generally be designed and build without too much hindrance. But next year the extension to that original package is needed, or the new program is one that has to work gracefully with data from other people's programs. When building an add-on it is painfully often the case that the existing software base is not very well documented, and that the attempted new use of it reveals previously unknown bugs or limitations in the core system. Thus the effort that will need to be put into the second package may be much greater than would have been predicted based on experience from the first;

Embedded If the computer you are going to program is one in an electric egg-timer (or maybe a toy racing car, or an X-ray scanner) then testing may involve be a quite different experience from that you become used to when

[2]Last year these notes indicates 16 Mbytes for £50! I may have rounded prices up and down somewhat but still. . .

debugging ordinary applications that run on standard work-stations. In par-ticular it may become necessary to become something of an expert in the hardware and electronics and also in the application area of the system within which your code will be placed;

Tool-weak environment This is a follow-on from the "embedded" heading, in that it is perhaps easiest the envisage an electric pop-up toaster where any-thing that slowed down or enlarged the code being run would perturb system timing enough to burn the toast, and where the target hardware is not auto-matically equipped with printers and flashing lights that ca n be used to help sense what is going on inside its CPU. For some such cases it is possible to buy or build real-time emulators or to wire in extra probes into a debug-gable version of the hardware. There are other cases where either technol-ogy or budget mean that program development has to be done with a slow turn-around on testing and with only very limited ability to discover what happened when a bug surfaced. It is incredibly easy to simulate such a tool-weak environment for yourself by just avoiding the effort associated with becoming familiar with automated testing tools, debuggers and the like;

Novel One of the best and safest ways of knowing that a task is feasible is to observe that somebody else did it before, and their version was at least more or less satisfactory. The next best way is to observe that the new task is really rather similar to one that was carried out successfully in the past. This clearly leads to the obvious observation that if something is being attempted and there are no precedents to rely on then it becomes much harder to predict how well things will work out, and the chances of nasty surprises increases substantially.

There are two sort of program not listed above which deserve special mention. The first is the implementation of a known algorithm. This wil l usually end up as a package or a subroutine rather than a complete free-standing program, and there are plenty of algorithms that are complicated enough that programming them is a severe challenge. However the availability of a clear target and well specified direction will often make such programming tasks relatively tractable. It is how-ever important to distinguish between programming up a complete and known algorithm (easyish) from developing and then implementing a new one, and un-comfortably often things that we informally describe as algorithms are in fact just strategies, and lots of difficult and inventive fine detail ha s to be filled into make them realistic.

The second special sort of program is the little throw-away one, and the recog-nition that such programs can be lashed together really fast and without any fuss is important, since it can allow one to automate other parts of the program devel-opment task through strategic use of such bits of jiffy code.

5.2 Analysis and description of the objective

Sometimes a programming task starts with you being presented with a complete, precise and coherent explanation of exactly what has to be achieved. When this is couched in language so precise that there is not possible doubt about what is required you might like to ask why you are being asked to do anything, since almost all you need to do is to transcribe the specification in to the particular syntax of the (specified) programming language. Several of the Part IA tickable problems come fairly close to this pattern, and there the reason you are asked to do them is exactly so you get practical experience with the syntax of the given language and the practical details of presenting programs to the computer. But that hardly counts as serious programming!

Assuming that we are not in one of these artificial cases, it is necessary to think about what one should expect to find in a specification an d what does not belong there. It is useful to discuss the sorts of language used in specifications, and to consider who will end up taking prime responsibility for everything being correct.

A place to start is with the observation that a specification s hould describe what is wanted, rather than how the desired effect is to be achieved. This ideal can be followed up rather rapidly by the observation that it is often amazingly difficult to know what is really wanted, and usually quite a lot of important aspects of the full list of requirements will be left implicit or as items where you have to apply your own judgement. This is where it is useful to think back to the previous section and decide what style of project was liable to be intended and where the main pressure points are liable to be.

5.2.1 Important Questions

I have already given a check-list that should help work out what general class of problem you are facing. The next stage is to try to identify and concentrate on areas of uncertainty in your understanding of what has to be done. Furthermore initial effort ought to go into understanding aspects of the problem that are liable to shape the whole project: there is no point in agonising over cosmetic details until the big picture has become clear. Probably the best way of sorting this out is to imagine that some magic wand has been waved and it has conjured up a body of code and documentation that (if the fairy really was a good one!) probably does everything you need. However as a hard-headed and slightly cynical person

•

you need to check it first. Deciding what you are going to look f or to see if the submitted work actually satisfied the project's needs can le t you make explicit a lot of the previously slightly woolly expectations you might have. This viewpoint moves you from the initial statement "The program must achie ve X" a little closer to "I must end up convinced that the program achieves X and her e is the basis for how that conviction might be carried". Other things that mig ht (or indeed might not) reveal themselves at this stage are:

- Is user documentation needed, and if so how detailed is it expected to be? Is there any guess for how bulky the user manual will be?
- How formal should documentation of the inner workings of the code be?
- Was the implementation language to be used pre-specified, and if not what aspects of the problem or environment are relevant to the choice?
- Is the initial specification a water-tight one or does the i mplementer have to make detailed design decisions along the way?

With regard to choice of programming language note that evidence from stud-ies that have watched the behaviour of real programmers suggests that to a good first approximation it is possible to deliver the same number of lines of working documented code per week almost whatever language it is written in. A very striking consequence of this is that languages that are naturally concise and which provide built-in support for more of the high-level things you want to do can give major boosts to productivity.

The object of all this thought is to lead to a proper specificat ion of the task. Depending on circumstances this may take one of a number of possible forms:

5.2.2 Informal specifications

Documents written in English, however pedantically phrased and however voluminous, must be viewed as informal specifications. Those who have a lot of spare time might try reading the original description of the language C[16] where Ap-pendix A is called a reference manual and might be expected to form a useful basis for fresh implementations of the language. Superficially it looks pretty good, but it is only when you examine the careful (though still "inform al" in the current context) description in the official ANSI standard[22] that it becomes clear just how much is left unsaid in the first document. Note that ANSI C i s not the same language as that defined by Kernighan and Ritchie, and so the t wo documents just mentioned can not be compared quite directly, and also be aware that spotting and making clear places where specifications written in Engl ish are not precise is a great skill, and one that some people enjoy exercising more than others do! The description in section 5.18 is another rather more manageable example of an informal textual specification. When you get to it you might I ike to check to see what it tells you what to do about tabs and back-spaces, which are clearly charac-ters that have an effect on horizontal layout. What? It fails to mention them? Oh dear!

5.2.3 Formal descriptions

One response to the fact that almost all informal specificati ons are riddled with holes (not all of which will be important: for instance it might be taken as under-stood by all that messages that are printed so that they look like sentences should be properly spelt and punctuated) has been to look for ways of using formal de-scription languages. The ZED language (developed at Oxford[3], and sometimes written as just Z) is one such and has at times been taught in Software Engineer-ing courses here. The group concerned with the development of the language ML were keen to use formal mathematically-styled descriptive methods to define ex-actly what ML ought to do in all possible circumstances. Later on in the CST there are whole lecture courses on Specification and Verifica tion and so I am not going to give any examples here, but will content myself by observing that a good grounding in discrete mathematics is an absolute pre-requisite for anybody think-ing of working this way.

5.2.4 Executable specifications

One group of formal specification enthusiasts went off and de veloped ever more powerful mathematical notations to help them describe tasks. Another group ob-served that sometimes a careful description of what must be achieved looks a bit like a program in a super-compact super-high-level programming language. It may not look like a realistic program, in that it may omit lots of explana-tion about how objectives should be achieved and especially how they should be achieved reasonably efficiently. This leads to the idea of an *executable specifica-tion*, through building an implementation of the specification la nguage. This will permitted to run amazingly slowly, and its users will be encouraged to go all out for clarity and correctness. To give a small idea of what this might entail, consider the job of specifying a procedure to sort some data. The initial informal spec-ification might be that the output should be a re-ordering of t he input such that the values in the output be in non-descending order. An executable specification might consist of three components. The first would create a li st of all the different

[3]http://www.comlab.ox.ac.uk/oucl/prg.html

•

permutations of the input. The second would be a procedure to inspect a list and check to see if its elements were in non-descending order. The final part would compose these to generate all permutations then scan through them one at a time and return the first non-descending one found. This would not be a good practical sorting algorithm, but could provide a basis for very transparent demonstrations that the process shown did achieve the desired goal! It should be remembered that an executable specification needs to be treated as such, and n ot as a model for how the eventual implementation will work. A danger with the technique is that it is quite easy for accidental or unimportant consequences of how the specification is written to end up as part of the project requirements.

5.3 Ethical Considerations

Quite early on when considering a programming project you need to take explicit stack of any moral or ethical issues that it raises. Earlier in the year you have had more complete coverage of the problems of behaving professionally, so here I will just give a quick check-list of some of the things that might give cause for concern:

- Infringement of other people's intellectual property rights, be they patents, copyright or trade secrets. Some companies will at least try to prevent others from creating new programs that look too much like the original. When licensed software is being used the implications of the license agreement may become relevant;

- Responsibility to your employer or institution. It may be that certain sorts of work are contrary to local policy. For instance a company might not be willing to permit its staff to politically motivated virtual reality simulations using company resources, and this University has views about the commer-cial use of academic systems;

- A computing professional has a responsibility to give honest advice to their "customer" when asked about the reasonableness or feasibil ity of a project, and to avoid taking on work that they know they are not qualifie d to do;

- It can be proper to take a considered stance against the development of systems that are liable to have a seriously negative impact on society as a whole. I have known some people who consider this reason to avoid any involvement with military or defence-funded computing, while others will object to technology that seems especially liable to make tracking, surveil-lance or eavesdropping easier. Those of you with lurid imaginations can no doubt envisage plenty more applications of computers that might be seen as so undesirable that one should if necessary quit a job rather than work on them.

5.4 How much of the work has been done already?

The points that I have covered so far probably do not feel as if they really help you get started when faced with a hard-looking programming task, although I believe that working hard to make sure you really understand the specification you are faced with is in fact always a very valuable process. From now onwards I move closer to the concrete and visible parts of the programming task. The first question to ask here is "Do I actually have to do this or has it been done b efore?"

There are three notable cases where something has been done before but it is still necessary to do it again. Student exercises are one of these, and undue reliance on the efforts of your predecessors is gently discouraged. Sometimes a problem has been solved before, but a solution needs to be re-created without reference to the original version because the original is encumbered with awkward commer-cial[4] restrictions or is not locally available. The final cause for re-implementation is if the previous version of the program concerned was a failure and so much of a mess that any attempt to rely on it would start the new project off in wrong-minded directions.

Apart from these cases the best way to write any program at all is to adopt, adapt and improve as much existing technology as you can! This can range from making the very second program that you ever write a variation on that initial "Hello World" example you were given through to exploiting e xisting large soft-ware libraries. The material that can be reclaimed may be as minor as a bunch of initial comments saying who you (the author) are and including space to describe what the program does. It might just be some stylised "import " statements needed at the head of almost any program you write. If you need a tree structure in today's program do you have one written last week which gives you the data type defini-tion and some of the basic operations on trees? Have you been provided with a collection of nice neat sample programs (or do you have a book or CD ROM with some) that can help? Many programming languages are packaged with a fairly extensive collection of chunks of sample code.

Most programming languages come with standardised libraries that (almost al-ways) mean there is no need for you to write your own sorting procedure or code to convert floating point values into or out of textual form. In m any important areas

[4]Remember that if the restriction is in the form of a patent then no amount of re-implementation frees you from obligations to the patent-owner, and in other cases you may need to be able to give a very clear demonstration that your new version really has been created completely independently.

there will be separate libraries that contain much much more extensive collections of facilities. For instance numerical libraries (eg the one from NAG) are where you should look for code to solve sets of simultaneous equations or to maximise a messy function of several variables. When you need to implement a windowed interface with pull-down menus and all that sort of stuff again look to existing library code to cope with much of the low-level detail for you. Similarly for data compression, arbitrary precision integer arithmetic, image manipulation. . .

Observing that there is a lot of existing support around does not make the problem of program construction go away: knowing what existing code is available is not always easy, and understanding both how to use it and what constraints must be accepted if it is used can be quite a challenge. For instance with the NAG (numerical) library it may take beginners quite a while before they discover that E04ACF (say, and not one of the other half-dozen closely related routines) is the name of the function they need to call and before they understand exactly what arguments to pass to it.

As well as existing pre-written code (either in source or library form) that can help along with a new project there are also packages that write significant bodies of code for you, basing what they do one on either a compact descriptive input file or interaction with the user through some clever in terface. The well-established examples of this are the tools yacc and lex that provide a convenient and reliable way of creating parsers. Current users of Microsoft's Visual C++ system will be aware of the so-called "Wizards" that it provi des that help create code to implement the user interface you want, and there are other commercial program generators in this and a variety of business application areas. To use one of these you first have to know of its availability, and then le arn how to drive it: both of these may involve an investment of time, but with luck that will be re-paid with generous interest even on your first real use. In some cas es the correct use of a program generation tool is to accept its output uncritically, while on other occasions the proper view is to collect what it creates, study it and eventually adjust the generated code until you can take direct responsibility for subsequent support. Before deciding which to do you need to come to a judgement about the stability and reliability of the program generator and how often you will need to adjust your code by feeding fresh input in to the very start.

Another way in which existing code can be exploited is when new code is written so that it converts whatever input it accepts into the input format for some existing package, one that solves a sufficiently related pro blem that this makes some sense. For instance it is quite common to make an early implementation of a new programming language work by translating the new language into some existing one and then feeding the translated version into an existing compiler. For early versions of ML the existing language was Lisp, while for Modula 3 some compilers work by converting the Modula 3 source into C. Doing this may result in a complete compiler that is slower and bulkier than might otherwise be the case, but it can greatly reduce the effort in building it.

5.5 What skills and knowledge are available?

Figure 5.4: Nancy Silverton's bakery is in La Brea near the tar pits, and her book (*Bread from the La Brea Bakery*) is unutterably wonderful. I like her chocolate-cherry loaf. This photo is if the racks in her shop. Not much about Java I agree but baking good bread is at least as important to know about as computing.

A balance needs to be drawn between working through a programming project using only the techniques and tools that you already know and pushing it forward using valuable but unfamiliar new methods. Doing something new may slow you down substantially, but an unwillingness to accept that toll may lead to a very pedestrian style of code development using only a limited range of idioms. There is a real possibility that short-term expediency can be in conflict with longer term productivity. Examples where this may feel a strain include use of formal meth-ods, new programming languages and program generation tools. The main point to be got across here is that almost everything to do with computers changes every five years or so, and so all in the field need to invest some of the ir effort in con-tinual personal re-education so that their work does not look too much as if it has been chipped out using stone axes. The good news is that although detailed tech-nology changes the skills associated with working through a significant project should grow with experience, and the amount of existing code that an old hand will have to pillage may be quite large, and so there is a reasonable prospect for a long term future for those with skills in software design and construction. Re-member that all the books on Software Engineering tell us that the competence of

•

the people working on a project can make more difference to its success than any other single factor.

It is useful to have a conscious policy of collecting knowledge about what can be done and where to find the fine grubby details. For exampl e the standard textbook[9] contains detailed recipes for solving all sorts of basic tasks. Only rarely will any one of these be the whole of a program you need to write, but quite often a larger task will be able to exploit one or more of them. These and many of the other topics covered in the CST are there because there is at least a chance that they may occasionally be useful! It is much more important to know what can be done than how to do it, because the *how* can always be looked up when you need it.

5.6 Design of methods to achieve a goal

Perhaps the biggest single decision to be made when starting the detailed design of a program is where to begin. The concrete suggestions that I include here are to some extent caricatures; in reality few real projects will follow any of them totally but all should be recognisable as strategies. The crucial issue is that it will not be possible to design or write the whole of a program at once so it is necessary to split the work into phases or chunks.

5.6.1 Top-Down Design

In Top Down Design work on a problem starts by writing a "progr am" that is just one line long. Its text is:

```
{ solveMyProblem(); }
```

where of course the detailed punctuation may be selected to match the program-ming language being used. At this stage it is quite reasonable to be very informal about syntax. A next step will be to find some way of partitioni ng the whole task into components. Just how these components will be brought into existence is at present left in the air, however if we split things up in too unreasonable a way we will run into trouble later on. For many simple programs the second stage could look rather like:

```
/* My name, today's date, purpose of program */ import
Standard-libraries;
{
   /* declare variables here */
   data = readInData();
   results = calculate(data);
```

```
    displayResults(results);
}
```

The ideal is that the whole development of the program should take place in baby-sized steps like this. At almost every stage there will be a whole collection of worrying-looking procedures that remain undefined and no t yet thought about, such as Calculate above. It is critical not to worry too much about these, because each time a refinement is made although the number of t hese unresolved problems may multiply the expected difficulty of each will re duce. Well it had better, since all the ones that you introduce should be necessary steps towards the solution of your whole original task, and it makes sense to expect parts to be simpler than the whole.

After a rather few steps in the top-down development process one should ex-pect to have a fully syntactically correct main program that will not need any alterations later as the low level details of the procedures that it calls get sorted out. And each of the components that remain to be implemented should have a clearly understood purpose (for choice that should be written down) and each such component should be clearly separated from all the others. That is not to say that the component procedures might not call each other or rely on what they each can do, but the internal details of any one component should not matter to any other. This last point helps focus attention on interfaces. In my tiny example above the serious interfaces are represented by the variables data and results which pass information from one part of the design to the next. Working out ex-actly what must be captured in these interfaces would be generally need to be done fairly early on. After enough stages of elaboration the bits left over from top-down design are liable to end up small enough that you just code them up without need to worry: anything that is trivial you code up, anything that still looks murky you just apply one more expansion step to. With luck eventually the process ends.

There are two significant worries about top-down design. The se are "How do I know how to split the main task up?" and "But I can't test me code until everything is finished!". Both of these are proper concerns.

Splitting a big problem up involves finding a strategy for sol ving it. Even though this can be quite hard, it is almost always easier to invent a high-level idea for how to solve a problem than it is to work through all the details, and this is what top-down programming is all about. In many cases sketching on a piece of paper what you would do if you had to solve the problem by hand (rather than by computer) can help. Quite often the partition of a problem you make may end up leading your design into some uncomfortable dead end. In that case you need to look back and see which steps in your problem refinement rep resented places where you had real choice and which ones were pretty much inevitable. It is then necessary to go back to one of the stages where a choice was possible and to re-think things in the light of your new understanding. To make this process sensible

•

you should refuse to give up fleshing out one particular versi on of a top-down design until you are in a position to give a really clear explanation of why the route you have taken represents failure, because without this understanding you will not know how far back you need to go in the re-planning. As an example of what might go wrong, the code I sketched earlier here would end up being wrongly structured if user interaction was needed, and that interaction might be based on evaluation of partial results. To make that sort of interface possible it might be necessary to re-work the design as (say)

```
/* My name, today's date, purpose of program */ import
Standard-libraries;
{
    /* declare variables here */
    /* set empty data and results */
    while not finished do
    {
        extra = readInMoreData();
        if (endOfUserInput(extra)) finished = true;
        else
        {
            data = combine(data, extra);
            results = upDateResults(results, data);
            displaySomething(results);
        }
    }
    displayFinalResults(results);
}
```

which is clearly getting messier! And furthermore my earlier and shorter version looked generally valid for lots of tasks, while this one would need careful extra review depending on the exact for of user interaction required.

There is a huge amount to be said in favour of being able to test a program as it is built. Anybody who waits right to the end will have a dreadful mix of errors at all possible levels of abstraction to try to disentagle. At first sight it seems that top-down design precludes any early testing. This pessimism is not well founded. The main way out is to write *stubs* of code that fill in for all the parts of your program that have not yet been written. A stub is a short and simple piece of code that takes the place of something that will later on be much more messy. It does whatever is necessary to simulate some minimal behaviour that will make it possible to test the code around it. Sometimes a stub will just print a warning message and stop when it gets called! On other occasions one might make a stub print out its parameters and wait for human intervention: it then reads something back in, packages it up a bit and returns it as a result. The human assistant actually did all the clever work.

There are two other attitudes to take to top-down design. One of these is to limit it to **design** rather than implementation. Just use it to define a skeletal s hape for your code, and then make the coding and testing a separate activity. Obviously this only makes sense when you have enough confidence that you can be sure that the chunks left to be coded will in fact work out well. The final view is to think of top-down design as an ideal to be retrofitted to any project once it is complete. Even if the real work on a project went in fits and starts with lo ts of false trails and confusion, there is a very real chance that it can be rationalised afterwards and explained top-down. If that is done then it is almost certain that a clear framework has been built for anybody who needs to make future changes to the program.

5.6.2 Bottom-Up Implementation

Perhaps you are uncertain about exactly what your program is going to do or how it will solve its central problems. Perhaps you want to make sure that every line of code you ever write is documented, tested and validated to death before you move on from it and certainly before you start relying on it. Well these concerns lead you towards a bottom-up development strategy. The idea here is to identify a collection of smallish bits of functionality that will (almost) certainly be needed as part of your complete program, and to start by implementing these. This avoids having to thing about the hard stuff for a while. For instance a compiler-writer might start by writing code to read in lines of program and discard comments, or to build up a list of all the variable names seen. Somebody starting to write a word processor might begin with pattern-matching code ready for use in search-and-replace operations. In almost all large projects there are going to be quite a few fundamental units of code that are obviously going to be useful regardless of the high level structure you end up with.

The worry with bottom-up construction is that it does not correspond to having any overall vision of the final result. That makes it all to eas y to end up with a collection of ill-co-ordinated components that do not quite fit together and that do not really combine to solve the original problem. At the very least I would suggest

• serious bout of top-down design effort be done before any bottom-up work to try to put an overall framework into place. There is also a clear prospect that some of the units created during bottom-up work may end up not being necessary after all so the time spend on them was wasted.

An alternative way of thinking about bottom-up programming can soften the impact of these worries. It starts by viewing a programming language not just as a collection of fragments of syntax, but as a range of ways of structuring data and of performing operations upon it. The fact that some of these operations happen to be hard-wired into the language (as integer arithmetic usually is) while others exist as

•

collections of subroutines (floating point arithmetic on 30 00-digit numbers would normally be done that way) is of secondary importance. Considered this way each time you define a new data type or write a fresh procedure you ha ve extended and customised your programming language by giving it support for something new. Bottom-up programming can then be seen as gradually building layer upon layer of extra support into your language until it is rich in the operations most important in your problem area. Eventually one then hopes that the task that at first had seemed daunting becomes just half a dozen lines in the extended language. If some of the procedures built along the way do not happen to be used this time, they may well come in handy the next time you have to write a program in the same application area, so the work they consumed has not really been wasted after all. The language Lisp is notable for having sustained a culture based on this idea of language extension.

5.6.3 Data Centred Programming

Both top-down and bottom-up programming tend to focus on what your program looks like and the way in which it is structured into procedures. An alternative is to concentrate not on the actions performed by the code but on the way in which data is represented and the history of transformations that any bit of data will be subject to. These days this idea is often considered almost synonymous with an Object Oriented approach where the overall design of the class structure for a pro-gram is the most fundamental feature that it will have. Earlier (and pre-dating the widespread use of Object Oriented languages) convincing arguments for design based on the entities that a program must manipulate or model come from Jackson Structured Programming and Design[8]. More recently SSADM[3] has probably become one of the more widespread design and specification me thodologies for commercial projects.

5.6.4 Iterative Refinement

My final strategy for organising the design of a complete prog ram does not even expect to complete the job in one session. It starts by asking how the initial prob-lem can be restricted or simplified to make it easier to addres s. And perhaps it will spot how the most globally critical design decisions for the whole program could me made in two or three different ways, with it hard to tell in advance which would work out best in the end. The idea is then to start with code for a scruffy mock-up of a watered down version of the desired program using just one of these sets of design decisions. The time and effort needed to write a program grows much faster then linearly with the size of the program: the natural (but less obvi-ous) consequence of this is that writing a small program can be **much** quicker and easier than completing the full version. It may in some cases make sense even to write several competing first sketches of the code. When the fi rst sketch version is working it is possible to step back and evaluate it, to see if its overall shape is sound. When it has been adjusted until it is structurally correct, effort can go into adding in missing features and generally upgrading it until it eventually gets trans-formed into the beautiful butterfly that was really wanted. O f all the methods that I have described this is the one that comes closest to allowing for "experimental" programming. The discipline to adhere to is that experiments are worthy of that tag if the results from them can be evaluated and if something can thus be learned from them.

5.6.5 Which of the above is best?

The "best" technique for getting a program written will depe nd on its size as well as its nature. I think that puritanical adherence to any of the above would be unrea-sonable, and I also believe that inspiration and experience (and good taste) have important roles to play. However if pushed into an opinion I will vote for present-ing a design or a program (whether already finished or still un der construction) as if it were prepared top-down, with an emphasis on the early design of what information must be represented and where it must pass from one part of the code to another.

5.7 How do we know it will work?

Nobody should ever write a program unless they have good reason to believe that it ought to work. It is of course proper to recognise that it will not work, because typographic errors and all sorts of oversights will ensure that. But the code should have been written so that in slightly idealised world where these accidental imper-fections do not exist it would work perfectly. Blind and enthusiastic hope is not sufficient to make programs behave well, and so any proper des ign needs to have lurking behind it the seeds of a correctness proof. In easy-going times this can re-main untended as little comments that can just remind you of your thinking. When a program starts to get troublesome it can be worth growing these comments into short essays that explain what identities are being preserved intact across regions of code, why your loops are guaranteed to terminate and what assumptions about data are important, and why. In yet more demanding circumstances it can become necessary to conduct formal validation procedures for code.

The easiest advice to give here is that before you write even half a dozen lines of code you should write a short paragraph of comment that explains what the code is intended to achieve and why your method will work. The comment should usually not explain **how** it works (the code itself is all about "how"), but **why**. To try to show that I (at least sometimes!) follow this advice here is a short extract from one of my own[5] programs. . .

```
/*
 . Here is a short essay on the interaction between flags
 . and properties. It is written because the issue appears
 . to be delicate, especially in the face of a scheme that
 . I use to speed things up.
 . (a) If you use FLAG, REMFLAG and FLAGP with some
 .         indicator then that indicator is known as a flag.
 . (b) If you use PUT, REMPROP and GET with an indicator
 .         then what you have is a property.
 . (c) Providing the names of flags and properties are
 .         disjoint no difficulty whatever should arise.
 . (d) If you use PLIST to gain direct access to property
 .         lists then flags are visible as pairs (tag . t) and
 .         properties as (tag . value).
 . (e) Using RPLACx operations on the result of PLIST may
 .         cause system damage.  It is considered illegal.
 .         Also changes made that way may not be matched in
 .         any accelerating caches that I keep.
 . (f) After (FLAG '(id) 'tag) [when id did not previously
 .         have any flags or properties] a call (GET 'id 'tag)
 .         will return t.
 . (g) After (PUT 'id 'tag 'thing) a call (FLAGP 'id
 .         'tag) will return t whatever the value of "thing".
 .         A call (GET 'id 'tag) will return the saved value
 .         (which might be nil).  Thus FLAGP can be thought of
 .         as a function that tests if a given property is
 .         attached to a symbol.
 . (h) As a consequence of (g) REMPROP and REMFLAG are
 .         really the same operation.
 */


Lisp_Object get(Lisp_Object a, Lisp_Object b)
{
      Lisp_Object pl, prev, w, nil = C_nil; int n;
/*
```

[5] This happens to be written in C rather than Java, but since most of it is comment maybe that does not matter too much.

```
 .  In CSL mode plists are structured like association
 .  lists, and NOT as lists with alternate tags and values.
 .  There is also a bitmap that can provide a fast test for
 .  the presence of a property...
 */
    if (!symbolp(a))
    {
#ifdef RECORD_GET
        record_get(b, NO);
        errexit();
#endif
        return onevalue(nil);
    }
    ... etc etc
```

The exact details of what I am trying to do are not important here, but the evidence of mind-clearing so that there is a chance to get the code correct first time is. Note how little the comment before the procedure has to say about low-level implemen-tation details, but how much about specifications, assumpti ons and limitations.

I would note here that typing a program in is generally one of the least time-consuming parts of the whole programming process, and these days disc storage is pretty cheap, and thus various reasons which in earlier days may have discouraged layout and explanation in code no longer apply.

Before trying code and as a further check that it ought to work it can be useful to "walk through" the code. In other words to pretend to be a co mputer executing it and see if you follow the paths and achieve the results that you were supposed to. While doing this it can be valuable to think about which paths through the code are common and which are not, since when you get to testing it may be that the uncommon paths do not get exercised very much unless you take special steps to cause them to be activated.

The "correctness" that you will be looking for can be at sever al different lev-els. A *partially correct* program is one that can never give an incorrect answer. This sounds pretty good until you recognise that there is a chance that it may just get stuck in a loop and thereby never give any answer at all! It is amazingly often much easier to justify that a program is partially correct than to go the whole hog and show it is correct, ie that not only is it partially correct but that it will always terminate. Beyond even the requirements of correctness will be performance de-mands: in some cases a program will need not only to deliver the right answers but to meet some sort of resource budget. Especially if the performance target is specified as being for performance that is good "on the averag e" it can be dread-fully hard to prove, and usually the only proper way to start is by designing and justifying algorithms way before any mention of actual programming arises.

•

A final thing to check for is the possibility that your code can be derailed by unhelpful erroneous input. For instance significant securi ty holes in operating systems have in the past been consequences of trusted modules of code being too trusting of their input, and them getting caught out by (eg) input lines so long that internal buffers overflowed thereby corrupting adjacent da ta.

The proper mind-set to settle in to while designing and starting to implement code is pretty paranoid: you want the code to deliver either a correct result or a comprehensible diagnostic whenever anything imaginable goes wrong in either the data presented to it or its own internal workings. This last statement leads to a concrete suggestion: make sure that the code can test itself for sanity and correctness every so often and insert code that does just that. The assertions that you insert will form part of your argument for why the program is supposed to work, and can help you (later on) debug when it does not.

5.8 While you are writing the program

Please remember to get up and walk around, to stretch, drink plenty of water, sit up straight and all the other things mentioned at the Learning Day as relevant occupational health issues. My experience is that it is quite hard to do effective programming in 5 minute snippets, but that after a few hours constant work pro-ductivity decreases. A pernicious fact is that you may not notice this decrease at the time, in that the main way in which a programmer can become unproductive is by putting more bugs into a program. It is possible to keep churning out lines of code all through the night, but there is a real chance that the time you will spend afterwards trying to mend the last few of them will mean that the long session did not really justify itself.

In contrast to programming where long sessions can do real damage (because of the bugs that can be added by a tired programmer) I have sometimes found that long sessions have been the only way I can isolate bugs. Provided I can discipline myself not to try to correct anything but the very simplest bug while I am tired a long stretch can let me chase bugs in a painstakingly logical way, and this is sometimes necessary when intuitive bug-spotting fails.

Thus my general advice about the concrete programming task would be to schedule your time so you can work in bursts of around an hour per session, and that you should plan your work so that as much as possible of everything you do can be tested fairly enthusiastically while it is fresh in your mind. A natural corollary of this advice is that projects should always be started in plenty of time, and pushed forward consistently so that no last-minute panic can arise and force sub-optimal work habits.

5.9 Documenting a program or project

Student assessed exercises are expected to be handed in complete with a brief report describing what has been done. Larger undergraduate projects culminate in the submission of a dissertation, as do PhD studies. All commercial programming activities are liable to need two distinct layers of documentation: one for the user and one for the people who will support and modify the product in the future. All these facts serve to remind us that documentation is an intrinsic part of any program.

Two overall rules can guide the writing of good documentation. The first is to consider the intended audience, and think about what they need to know and how your document can be structured to help them find it. The se cond is to keep a degree of consistency and order to everything: documents with a coherent overall structure are both easier to update and to browse than sets of idiosyncratic jottings.

To help with the first of these, here are some potential styles of write-up that might be needed:

- Comments within the code to remind yourself or somebody who is already familiar with the program exactly what is going on at each point in it;
- An overview of the internal structure and organisation of the whole program so that somebody who does not already know it can start to find t heir way around;
- Documentation intended to show how reliable a program is, concentrating on discussions of ways in which the code has been built to be resilient in the face of unusual combinations of circumstance;
- A technical presentation of a program in a form suitable for publication in a journal or at a conference, where the audience will consist of people expert in the general field but not aware of exactly what your contrib ution is;
- An introductory user manual, intended to make the program usable even by the very very nervous;
- A user reference manual, documenting clearly and precisely all of the options and facilities that are available;
- On-line help for browsing by the user while they are trying to use the program;
- A description of the program suitable for presentation to the venture capi-talists who are considering investing in the next stage of its development.

It seems inevitable that the above list is not exhaustive, but my guess is that most programs could be presented in any one of the given ways, and the resulting document would be quite different in each case. It is not that one or the other of these styles is inherently better or more important than another, more that if you write the wrong version you will either not serve your reader well or you will find that you have had to put much more effort into the documentation than was really justified.

A special problem about documentation is that of when it should be written. For small projects at least it will almost always be produced only after the program has been (at least nearly) finished. This can be rationalised by claiming "how can I possibly document it before it exists?"

I will argue here for two ideals. The first is that documentati on ought to follow on from design and specification work, but precede detail ed programming. The second is that the text of the documentation should live closely linked to the developing source code. The reasoning behind the first of the se is that writing the text can really help to ensure that the specification of th e code has been fully thought through, and once it is done it provides an invaluable stable reference to keep the detailed programming on track. The second point recognises some sort of realism, and that all sorts of details of just what a program does will not be resolved until quite late in the implementation process. For instance the exact wording of messages that are printed will often not be decided until then, and it will certainly be hard to prepare sample transcripts from the use of the program ahead of its completion[6]. Thus when the documentation has been written early it will need completing when some of these final details get sett led and correcting when the code is corrected or extended. The most plausible way of making it feasible to keep code and description in step is to keep them together. The con-cept of Literate Programming[17] pursues this goal. A program is represented as a composite file that can be processed in (at least) two differ ent ways. One way "compiles" it to create typeset-quality human readable doc umentation, while the other leaves just statements in some quite ordinary programming language ready to be fed into a compiler. This goes beyond just having copious comments in the code in two ways. Firstly it expects that the generated documentation should be able to exploit the full range of modern typography and that it can include pic-tures or diagrams where relevant. It is supposed to end up as cleanly presented and readable as any fully free-standing document could ever be. Secondly Literate Programming recognises that the ordering and layout of the program that has to be compiled may not be the same as that in the ideal manual, and so the disentan-gling tool needs to be able to rearrange bits of text in a fairly flexible way so that description can simultaneously be thought of as close to the code it relates to and

[6] Even though these samples can be planned and sketched early.

to the section in the document where it belongs. This idea was initially developed as part of the project to implement the TEX typesetting program that is being used to prepare these lecture notes.

5.10 How do we know it does work?

Figure 5.5: Many people think that their work is over well before it actually is.

A conceptual difficulty that many people suffer from is a conf usion between whether a program should work and whether it does. A program should work if it has been designed so that there are clear and easily explained reasons why it can achieve what it should. Sometimes the term "easily expla ined" may conceal the mathematical proof of the correctness of an algorithm, but at least in theory it would be possible to talk anybody through the justification. As to programs that actually do work, well the reality seems to be that the only ones of these that you will ever see will be no more than around 100 lines long: empirically any program much longer than that will remain flawed even after extensive checking. Proper Oriental rugs will always have been woven with a deliberate mistake in them, in recognition of the fact that only Allah is perfect. Experience has shown very clearly indeed that in the case of writing programs we all have enough failings that there is no great need to insert extra errors — there will be plenty inserted however hard we try to avoid them. Thus (at least at the present state of the art) there is no such thing as a (non-trivial) program that works.

If, however, a program *should* work (in the above sense) then the residual errors in it will be ones that can be corrected without disturbing the concepts behind it or its overall structure. I would like to think of such problems as "little bugs". The fact that they are little does not mean that they mi ght not be important, in that missing commas or references to the wrong variable can cause aeroplanes to crash just as convincingly as can errors at a more conceptual level. But the big effort must have been to get to a first testable version of y our code with only little bugs left in it. What is then needed is a testing strategy to help locate as many of these as possible. Note of course that testing can only ever generate evidence for the presence of a bug: in general it can not prove absence. But careful and systematic testing is something we still need whenever there has been human involvement in the program construction process[7].

The following thoughts may help in planning a test regime:

- Even obvious errors in output can be hard to notice. Perhaps human society has been built up around a culture of interpreting slightly ambiguous input in the "sensible" way, and certainly we are all very used to se eing what we expect to see even when presented with something rather different. By the time you see this document I will have put some effort into checking its spelling, punctuation, grammar and general coherence, and I hope that you will not notice or be upset by the residual mistakes. But anybody who has tried serious proof-reading will be aware that blatant mistakes can emerge even when a document has been checked carefully several times;

- If you are checking your own code and especially if you know you can stop work once it is finished then you have a clear incentive **not** to notice mistakes. Even if a mistake you find is not going to cause you to have to spend time fixing it it does represent you having found yet ano ther instance of your own lack of attention, and so it may not be good for your ego;

[7] Some see this observation as a foundation for hope for the future

- It is very desirable to make a clear distinction between the job of testing a program to identify the presence of bugs and the separate activity of correct-ing things. It can be useful to take the time to try to spot as many mistakes as you can before changing anything at all;
- A program can contain many more bugs and oddities than your worst night-mares would lead you to believe!
- Testing strategies worked out as part of the initial design of a program are liable to be better than ones invented only once code has been completed;
- It can be useful to organise explicit test cases for extreme conditions that your program may face (eg sorting data where all the numbers to be sorted have the same value), and to collect test cases that cause each path through your code to be exercised. It is easy to have quite a large barrage of test cases but still have some major body of code unvisited.
- Regressions tests are a good thing. These are test cases that grow up during project development, and at each stage after any change is made all of them are re-run, and the output the produce is checked. When any error is de-tected a new item in the regression suite is prepared so that there can remain a definite verification that the error does not re-appear at so me future stage. Automating the application of regression tests is a very good thing, since otherwise laziness can too easily cause one to skip running them;

8. When you find one bug you may find that its nature gives you ide as for other funny cases to check. You should try to record your thoughts so that you do not forget this insight;

- Writing extra programs to help you test your main body of code is often a good investment in time. On especially interesting scheme is to generate pseudo-random test cases. I have done that while testing a polynomial fac-torising program and suffered randomly-generated tests of a C compiler I was involved with, and in each case the relentless random coverage of cases turned out to represent quite severe stress;
- You do not know how many bugs your code has in it, so do not know when to stop looking. One theoretical way to attack this worry would be to get some fresh known bugs injected into your code before testing, and then see what proportion of the bugs found were the seeded-in ones and which had been original. That may allow you to predict the total bug level remaining.

Having detected some bugs there are several possible things to do. One is to sit tight and hope that nobody else notices! Another is to document the deficiencies

•

at the end of your manual. The last is to try to correct some of them. The first two of these routes are more reasonable than might at first see m proper given that correcting bugs so very often introduces new ones.

In extreme cases it may be that the level of correctness that can be achieved by bug-hunting will be inadequate. Sometimes it may then be possible to attempt a formal proof of the correctness of your code. In all realistic circumstances this will involve using a large and complicated proof assistant program to help with all the very laborious details involved. Current belief is that it will be very unusual for bugs in the implementation of this tool to allow you to end up with a program that purports to be proved but which in fact still contains mistakes!

5.11 Is it efficient?

I have made this a separate section from the one on detecting the presence of errors because performance effects are only rarely the result of simple oversights. Let me start by stressing the distinction between a program that is expensive to run (eg the one that computes p to 20,000,000,000 decimal places) and ones that are inefficient (eg one that takes over half a second to comput e p correct to four places). The point being made is that unless you have a realistic idea of how long a task ought to take it is hard to know if your program is taking a reasonable amount of time. And similarly for memory requirements, disc I/O or any other important resource. Thus as always we are thrown back to design and specification time predictions as our only guideline, and sometimes even these will be based on little more than crude intuition.

If a program runs fast enough for reasonable purposes then there may be no benefit in making it more efficient however much scope for impr ovement there is. In such cases avoid temptation. It is also almost always by far best to concentrate on getting code correct first and only worry about performanc e afterwards, taking the view that a wrong result computed faster is still wrong, and correct results may be worth waiting for.

When collecting test cases for performance measurements it may be useful to think about whether speed is needed in every single case or just in most cases when the program is run. It can also be helpful to look at how costs are expected to (and do) grow as larger and larger test cases are attempted. For most programming tasks it will be possible to make a trade between the amount of time a program takes to run and the amount of memory it uses. Frequently this shows up in a decision as to whether some value should be stored away in case it is needed later or whether any later user should re-calculate it. Recognising this potential trade-off is part of performance engineering.

For probably the majority of expensive tasks there will be one single part of the entire program that is responsible for by far the largest amount of time spent. One would have expected that it would always be easy to predict ahead of time where that would be, but it is not! For instance when an early TITAN Fortran compiler was measured in an attempt to discover how it could be speeded up it was found that over half of its entire time was spent in a very short loop of instructions that were to do with discarding trailing blanks from the end of input lines. Once the programmers knew that it was easy to do something about it, but one suspects they were expecting to find a hot-spot in some more arcane part of the code. It is thus useful to see if the languages and system you use provide instrumentation that makes it easy to collect information to reveal which parts of your code are most critical. If there are no system tools to help you you may be able to add in time-recording statements to your code so it can collect its own break-down to show what is going on. Cunning optimisation of bits of code that hardly ever get used is probably a waste of effort.

Usually the best ways to gain speed involve re-thinking data structures to pro-vide cheap and direct support for the most common operations. This can some-times mean replacing a very simple structure by one that has huge amounts of al-gorithmic complexity (there are examples of such cases in the Part IB Complexity course and the Part II one on Advanced Algorithms). In almost all circumstances a structural improvement that gives a better big-O growth rate for some critical cost is what you should seek.

In a few cases the remaining constant factor improvement in speed may still be vital. In such cases it may be necessary to re-write fragments of your code in less portable ways (including the possibility of use of machine code) or do other things that tend to risk the reliability of your package. The total effort needed to complete a program can increase dramatically as the last few percent in absolute performance gets squeezed out.

5.12 Identifying errors

Section 5.7 was concerned with spotting the presence of errors. Here I want to talk about working out which part of your code was responsible for them. The sections are kept separate to help you to recognise this, and hence to allow you to separate noticing incorrect behaviour from spotting mistakes in your code. Of course if, while browsing code, you find a mistake you can work on from it t o see if it can ever cause the program to yield wrong results, and this study of code is one valid error-hunting activity. But even in quite proper programs it is possible to have errors that never cause the program to misbehave in any way that can be noticed. For instance the mistake might just have a small effect on the performance of some not too important subroutine, or it may be an illogicality that could only be triggered into causing real trouble by cases that some earlier line of code had filtered out.

You should also recognise that some visible bugs are not so much due to any single clear-cut error in a program but to an interaction between several parts of your code each of which is individually reasonable but which in combination fail. Most truly serious disasters caused by software failure arise because of compli-cated interactions between multiple "improbable" circums tances.

The first thing to try to locate the cause of an error is to start from the original test case that revealed it and to try to refine that down to give a minimal clear-cut demonstration of the bad behaviour. If this ends up small enough it may then be easy to trace through and work out what happened.

Pure thought and contemplation of your source code is then needed. Decide what Sherlock Holmes would have made of it! Run your compilers in whatever mode causes them to give as many warning messages as they are capable of, and see if any of those give valuable clues. Check out the assert facility and place copious assertions in your program that verify that all the high level expectations you have are satisfied.

If this fails the next thought is to arrange to get a view on the execution of your code as it makes its mistake. Even when clever language-specific debuggers are available it will often be either necessary or easiest to do this by extra print statements into your code so it can display a trace of its actions. There is a great delicacy here. The trace needs to be detailed enough to allow you to spot the first line in it where trouble has arisen, but concise enough to be manageable. My belief is that one should try to judge things so that the trace output from a failing test run is about two pages long.

There are those who believe that programs will end up with the best reliability if they start off written in as fragile way as possible. Code should always make as precise a test as possible, and should frequently include extra cross checks which, if failed, cause it to give up. The argument is that this way a larger number of latent faults will emerge in early testing, and the embedded assertions can point the programmer directly to the place where an expectation failed to be satisfied, which is at least a place to start working backwards from in a hunt for the actual bug.

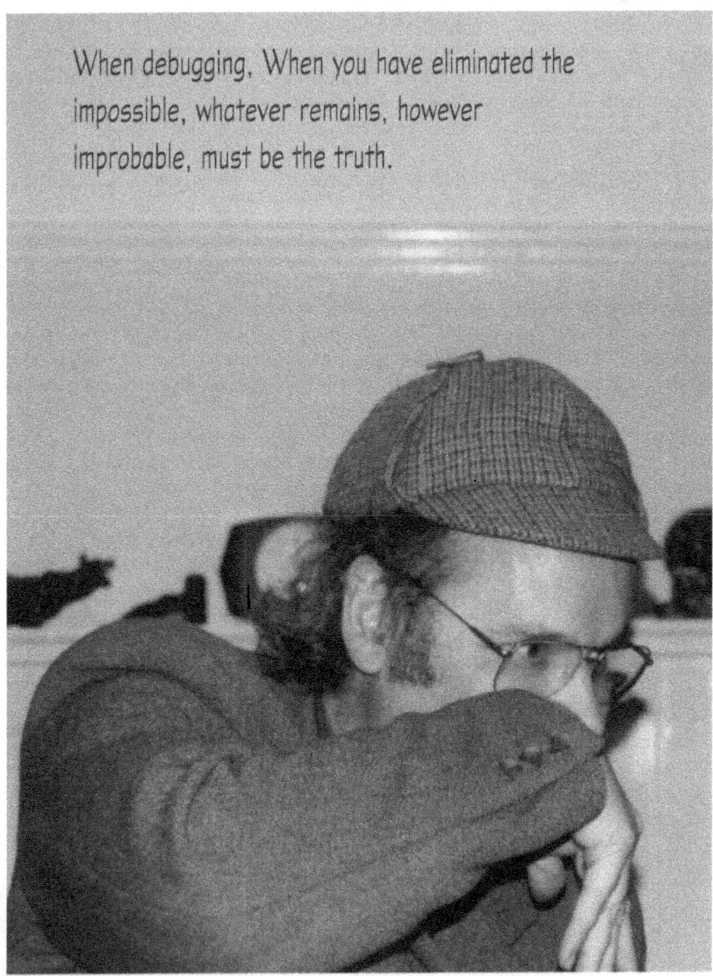

When debugging, When you have eliminated the
impossible, whatever remains, however
improbable, must be the truth.

Figure 5.6: Effective debugging calls for great skill.

•

With many sorts of bugs it can be possible to home in on the diffi culty by some sort of bisection search. Each test run should be designed to halve the range of code within which the error has been isolated.

Some horrible problems seem to vanish as soon as you enable any debugging features in your code or as soon as you insert extra print statements into it. These can be amazingly frustrating! They may represent your use of an unsafe language and code that writes beyond the limit of an array, or they could involve reliance on the unpredictable value of an un-initialised variable. Sometimes such problems turn out to be bugs in the compiler you are using, not in your own code. I believe that I have encountered trouble of some sort (often fairly minor, but trouble nev-ertheless) with every C compiler I have ever used, and I have absolute confidence that no other language has attained perfection in this regard. So sometimes trying your code on a different computer or with a different compiler will either give you a new diagnostic that provides the vital clue, or will behave differently thereby giving scope for debugging-by-comparison.

Getting into a panic and trying random changes to your code has no proper part to play either in locating or identifying bugs.

5.13 Corrections and other changes

With a number of bugs spotted and isolated the time comes to extirpate them. The ideal should be that when a bug is removed it should be removed totally and it should never ever be able to come back. Furthermore its friends and offspring should be given the same treatment at the same time, and of course no new mis-takes should be allowed to creep in while the changes are being made. This last is often taken for granted, but when concentrating on one particular bug it is all too easy to lose sight of the overall pattern of code and even introduce more new bugs than were being fixed in the first case. Regression testin g is at least one line of defence that one should have against this, but just taking the correction slowly and thinking through all its consequences what is mostly wanted. Small bugs (in the sense discussed earlier) that are purely local in scope give fewest problems. However sometimes testing reveals a chain of difficulties th at must eventually be recognised as a sign that the initial broad design of the program had been incor-rect, and that the proper correction strategy does not involve fixing the problems one at a time but calls for an almost fresh start on the whole project. I think that would be the proper policy for the program in section 5.18, and that is part of why the exercise there asks you to identify bugs but not to correct them.

Upgrading a program to add new features is at least as dangerous as correcting bugs, but in general any program that lasts for more than a year or so will end up with a whole raft of alterations having been made to it. These can very easily damage its structure and overall integrity, and the effect can be thought of as a form of *software rot* that causes old code to decay. Of course software rot would not arise if a program never needed correcting and never needed upgrading, but in that case the program was almost certainly not being used and was fossilised rather than rotting. Note that for elderly programs the person who makes correc-tions is never the original program author (even if they have the same name and birthday, the passage of time has rendered them different). This greatly increases the prospect of a would-be correction causing damage.

All but the most frivolous code should be kept under the control of some source management tool (perhaps rcs) that can provide an audit trail so that changes can be tracked. In some cases a discussion of a bug that has now been removed might properly remain as a comment in the main source code, but much more often a description of what was found to be wrong and what was changed to mend it belongs in a separate project log. After all if the bug really has been removed who has any interest in being reminded of the mistake that it represented?

Whenever a change is made to a program, be it a bug-fix or an upgr ade, there is a chance that some re-work will be needed in documentation, help files, sample logs and of course the comments. Once again the idea of literate programming comes to the fore in suggestion that all these can be kept together.

5.14 Portability of software

Most high level languages make enthusiastic claims that programs written in them will be portable from one brand of computer to another, just as most make claims that their compilers are "highly optimising". Java makes es pecially strong claims on this front, and its owners try rather hard to prevent anybody from diverging from a rigid standard. However even in this case there are differences between Java 1.0 and 1.1 (and no doubt 1.2) that may cause trouble to the unwary.

In reality achieving portability for even medium sized programs is not as easy as all that. To give a gross example of a problem not addressed at all by program-ming language or standard library design, a Macintosh comes as standard with a mouse with a single button, while most Unix X-windows systems have three-button mice. In one sense the difference is a frivolity, but at another it invites a quite substantial re-think of user interface design. At the user interface level a de-sign that makes good use of a screen with 640 by 480 pixels and 16 or 256 colours (as may be the best available on many slightly elderly computers) may look silly on a system with very much higher resolution and more colours.

For most programming languages you will find that implementa tions provided by different vendors do not quite match. Even with the most standardised lan-guages hardly any compiler supplier will manage to hold back from providing some private extra goodies that help distinguish them from their competitors. Such extras will often be things that it is very tempting to make use of. Around 1997-8 a good example of such a feature is "Active-X" which Microsof t is promoting. To use such a feature tends to lock you to one vendor or platform, while to ignore it means that you can not benefit from the advantages that it brin gs. By now you will know what my suggested response to conflicts like this will be . Yes, it is to make your decisions explicitly and consciously rather than by default, to make them in view of stated ideas about what the users of your code will need, and to include all the arguments you use to support your decision in your design portfolio.

There are frequently clever but non-portable tricks that can lead to big perfor-mance gains in code but at cost in portability. Sometimes the proper response to these is to have two versions of the program, one slow but very portable and the other that takes full advantage of every trick available on some platform that is especially important to you.

5.15 Team-work

Almost all of this course is about programming in the small, with a concentration on the challenges facing a lone programmer. It is still useful to think for a while how to handle the transition from this state into a large-team corporate mentality. One of the big emotional challenges in joining a team relates to the extent to which you end up "owning" the code you work on. It is very easy t o get into a state where you believe (perhaps realistically) that you are the only person who can properly do anything to the code you write. It is also easy to become rather defensive about your own work. A useful bit of jargon that refers to breaking out of these thought patterns is *ego-free programming*. In this ideal you step back and consider the whole project as the thing you are contributing to, not just the part that you are visibly involved in implementing. It may also be useful to recognise that code will end up with higher quality if understanding of it is shared between several people, and that bugs can be viewed as things to be found and overcome and never as personal flaws in the individual who happened to w rite that fragment of code.

When trying to design code or find a difficult bug it can be very v aluable to explain your thoughts to somebody else. It may be that they need not say much more than er and um, and maybe they hardly need to listen (but you probably need to believe that they are). By agreeing that you will listen to their problems at a later stage this may be a habit you can start right now with one or a group of your contemporaries.

Reading other people's code (with their permission, of course) and letting them read yours can also help you settle on a style or idiom that works well for you. It can also help get across the merits of code that is well laid out and where the comments are actually helpful to the reader.

If you get into a real group programming context, it may make sense to con-sider partitioning the work in terms of function, for instance system architect, programmer, test case collector, documentation expert,. . . rather than trying to dis-tribute the management effort and split the programming into lots of little mod-ules, but before you do anything too rash read some more books on software engi-neering so that once again you can make decisions in an informed and considered way.

5.16 Lessons learned

One of the oft-repeated observations about the demons of large-scale software construction is that *there is no silver bullet*. In other words we can not expect to find a single simple method that, as if by magic, washes away al l our difficulties. This situation also applies for tasks that are to be carried out by an individual programmer or a very small team. No single method gives a key that makes it possible to sit down and write perfect programs without effort. The closest I can come to an idea for something that is generally valuable is experience - experience on a wide range of programming projects in several different languages and with various different styles of project. This can allow you to spot features of a new task that have some commonalty with one seen before. This is, however, obviously no quick fix. The suggestions I have been putting forward here are to try to make your analysis of what you are trying to achieve as explicit in your mind as possible. The various sections in these notes provide headings that may help you organise your thoughts, and in general I have tried to cover topics in an order that might make sense in real applications. Of course all the details and conclusions will be specific to your problem, and nothing I can possibly say here c an show you how to track down your own very particular bug or confusion! I have to fall back on generalities. Keep thinking rather than trying random changes to your code. Try to work one step at a time. Accept that errors are a part of the human condition, and however careful you are your code will end up with them.

But always remember the two main slogans:

Programming is easy

and

Programming is fun.

•

5.17 Final Words

Do I follow my own advice? Hmmm I might have known you would ask that! Well most of what I have written about here is what I try to do, but I am not especially formal about any of it. I only really go overboard about design and making documentation precede implementation when starting some code that I expect to give me special difficulty. I have never got into the swing of literate programming, and suspect that I like the idea more than the reality. And I sometimes spend many more hours on a stretch at a keyboard than I maybe ought to. If this course and these notes help you think about the process of programming and allow you to make more conscious decisions about the style you will adopt then I guess I should be content. And if there is one very short way I would like to encapsulate the entire course, it would be the recommendation that you make all the decisions and thoughts you have about programming as open and explicit as possible.
Good luck!

5.18 Challenging exercises

Some of you may already consider yourselves to be seasoned programmers able to cope with even quite large and complicated tasks. In which case I do not you to feel this course is irrelevant, and so I provide here at the end of the notes some pro-gramming problems which I believe are hard enough to represent real challenges, even though the code that eventually has to be written will not be especially long. There is absolutely no expectation that anybody will actually complete any of these tasks, or even find good starting points. However these examples may help give you concrete cases to try out the analysis and design ideas I have discussed: identifying the key difficulties and working out how to parti tion the problems into manageable chunks. In some cases the hardest part of a proper plan would be the design of a good enough testing strategy. The tasks described here are all both reasonably compact and fairly precisely specified. I have fo ught most of these myself and found that producing solutions that were neat and convincing as well as correct involved thought as well as more coding skill. There are no prizes and no ticks, marks or other bean-counter's credit associated with attempting these tasks, but I would be jolly interested to see what any of you can come up with, provided it can be kept down to no more than around 4 sides of paper.

MULDIV

The requirement here is to produce a piece of code that accepts four integers and computes $(a * b + c)/d$ and also the remainder from the division. It should be assumed that the computer on which this code is to be run has 32-bit integers, and that integer arithmetic including shift and bitwise mask operations are available, but the difficulty in this exercise arises because $a * b$ will be up to 64-bits long and so it can not be computed directly. "Solutions" that use (eg) the direct 64-bit integer capabilities of a DEC Alpha workstation are not of interest!

It should be fairly simple to implement muldiv if efficiency where not an issue. To be specific this would amount to writing parts of a pa ckage that did double-length integer arithmetic. Here the additional expectation is that speed does matter, and so the best solution here will be one that makes the most effec-tive possible use of the 32-bit arithmetic that is available. Note also that code of this sort can unpleasantly easily harbour bugs, for instance due to some integer overflow of an intermediate result, that only show up in very r are circumstances, and that the pressure to achieve the best possible performance pushes towards code that comes very close to the limits of the underlying 32-bit arithmetic. Thought will be needed when some or all of the input values are negative. The desired be-haviour is one where the calculated quotient was rounded towards zero, whatever its sign.

Overlapping Triangles

A point in the $X - Y$ plane can be specified by giving its co-ordinates (x, y). A triangle can then be defined by giving three points. Given two triangles a number of possibilities arise: they may not overlap at all or they may meet in a point or a line segment, or they may overlap so that the area where they overlap forms a triangle, a quadrilateral, a pentagon or a hexagon. Write code that discovers which of these cases arises, returning co-ordinates that describe the overlap (if any).

A point to note here is that any naive attempt to calculate the point where two lines intersect can lead to attempts to divide by zero if the lines are parallel. Near-parallel lines can lead to division by very small numbers, possibly leading to subsequent numeric overflow. Such arithmetic oddities mu st not be allowed to arise in the calculations performed.

Matrix transposition

One way of representing an m by n matrix in a computer is to have a single vector of length mn and place the array element $a_{i,j}$ at offset $mi + j$ in the vector. Another would be to store the same element at offset $i + nj$. One of these representation means that items in the same row of the matrix live close together, the other that items in the same column are adjacent.

In some calculations it can make a significant difference to s peed which of these layouts is used. This is especially true for computers with virtual memory. Sometimes one part of a calculation would call for one layout, and a later part would prefer the other.

The task here is therefore to take integers *m* and *n* and a vector of length *mn*, and rearrange the values stored in the vector so that if they start off in one of as one representation of a matrix they end up as the other. Because the matrix should be assumed to be quite large you are not allowed to use any significant amount of temporary workspace (you can not just allocate a fresh vector of length *mn* and copy the data into it in the new order — you may assume you may us e extra space of around $m + n$ if that helps, but not dramatically more than that).

If the above explanation of the problem[8] feels out of touch with today's com-puter uses, note how the task relates to taking an *m* by *n* matrix representing a pic-ture and shuffling the entries to get the effect of rotating th e image by 90 degrees. Just that in the image processing case you may be working with data arranged in sub-word-sized bite-fields, say at 4 bits per pixel.

Sprouts

The following is a description of a game[9] to be played by two players using a piece of paper. The job of the project here is to read in a description of a position in the game and make a list of all the moves available to the next player. This would clearly be needed as part of any program that played the game against human opposition, but the work needed here does not have to consider any issues concerning the evaluation of positions or the identificatio n of good moves.

The game starts with some number of marks made on a piece of paper, each mark in the form of a capital `Y'. Observe that each junction has exactly three little edges jutting from it. A move is made by a player identifying two free edges and drawing a line between them. The line can snake around things that have been drawn before as much as the player making the move likes, but it must not cross any line that was drawn earlier. The player finishes the move b y drawing a dot somewhere along the new line and putting the stub of a new edge jutting out from it in one of the two possible directions. Or put a different but equivalent way, the player draws a new `Y' and joins two of its legs up to existing stubs with lines that do not cross any existing lines. The players make moves alternately and the first player unable to make a further legal move will be the loser.

---

[8] This is an almost standard classical problem and if you dig far enough back in the literature you will find explanations of a solution. If you thought to do t hat for yourself, well done!

[9] Due to John Conway

A variation on the game has the initial state of the game just dots (not `Y' shapes) and has each player draw a new dot on each edge they create, but still demands that no more that three edges radiate from each dot. The difference is that in one case a player can decide which side of a new line any future line must emerge from. I would be equally happy whichever version of the game was addressed by a program, provided the accompanying documentation makes it clear which has been implemented!

The challenge here clearly largely revolves around finding a way to describe the figures that get drawn. If you want to try sprouts out as a ga me between people before automating it, I suggest you start with five or six star ting points.

ML development environment

The task here is not to write a program, but just to sketch out the specification of one. Note clearly that an implementation of the task asked about here would be quite a lot of work and I do not want to provide any encouragement to you to attempt all that!

In the Michaelmas Term you were introduced to the language ML, and invited to prepare and test various pieces of test code using a version running under Mi-crosoft Windows. You probably used the regular Windows "not epad" as a little editor so you could change your code and then paste back corrected versions of it into the ML window. Recall that once you have defined a funct ion or value in ML that definition remains fixed for ever, and so if it is incorr ect you probably need to re-type not only it but everything you entered after it. All in all the ML environment you used was pretty crude (although I am proud of the greek letters in the output it generates), and it would become intolerable for use in medium or large-scale projects. Design a better environment, and append to your descrip-tion of it a commentary about which aspects of it represent just a generically nice programmer's work-bench and which are motivated by the special properties of ML.

An example from the literature

The following specification is given as a paragraph of reason ably readable English text, and there is then an associated program written in Java. This quite small chunk of code can give you experience of bug-hunting: please do not look up the original article in CACM[10] until you have spent some while working through the code checking how it works and finding some of the mistakes. In previous years when I have presented this material to our students they did almost as well as the professional programmers used in the original IBM study, but they still found only

· Communications of the ACM, vol 21, no 9, 1978.

•

a pathetically small proportion of the total number of known bugs! I am aware that the Java transcription of this program has changed its behaviour from the original PL/I version and the intermediate C one. I do not believe that the changes are a case of bugs evaporating in the face of Java, but some may be transcription errors I have made. But since the object of this exercise is that you locate bugs, whatever their source, this does not worry me much, and I present the example as it now stands, oddities and all.

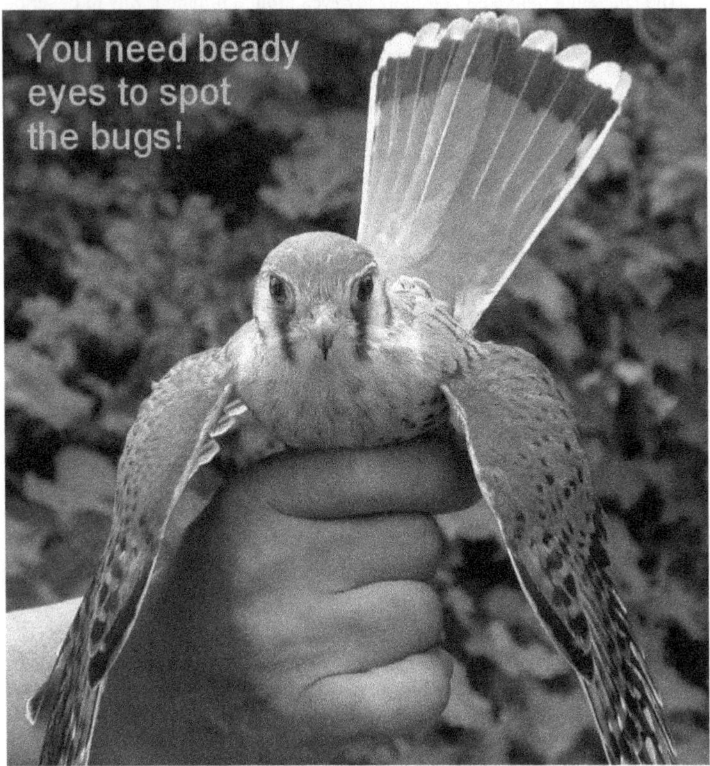

Figure 5.7: Picture courtesy Shamila Corless.

Formatting program for text input. Converted from the original PL/I version which is in a paper by Glen Myers, CACM vol 21 no 9, 1978

- This program compiles correctly: it is believed not to contain either syntax errors or abuses of the Java library.
- A specification is given below. You are to imagine that the code appended was produced by somebody who had been provided with the specification and asked to produce an implementation of the utility as described. But they are not a very good programmer!
- Your task is one of quality control - it is to check that the code as given is in agreement with the specification.
  If any bugs or mis-features are discovered they should be documented but it will be up to the original programmer to correct them. If there are bugs it is desirable that they all be found.
- For the purposes of this study, a bug or a mis-feature is some bad aspect of the code that could be visible to users of the binary version of the code. Ugly or inefficient code is deemed not to matter, but even small deviations from the letter of the specification and the things sensibly implicit in it do need detecting.
- Let me repeat point (a) again just to stress it - the code here has had its syntax carefully checked and uses the Java language and library in a legal straightforward way, so searching for bugs by checking fine details of the Java language specification is not expected to be productive.
  I have put in comments to gloss use of library functions to help those who do not have them all at their finger-tips. The code may be clumsy in places but I do not mind that!
  I have tried to keep layout of the code neat and consistent. There are few comments "because the original programmer who wrote the code delivered it in that state".

•

```
/*********************************************************************
* Specification * * ============= * * * * Given an input text consisting
of words separated by * * blanks or new-line characters, the program
formats it *
* into a line-by-line form such that (1) each output *
* line has a maximum of 30 characters, (2) a word in *
* the input text is placed on a single output line, and *
* (3) each output line is filled with as many words as *
* possible. *
* *
* The input text is a stream of characters, where the *
* characters are categorised as break or nonbreak *
* characters. A break character is a blank, a new-line *
* character (&), or an end of text character (/). *
* New-line characters have no special significance; *
* they are treated as blanks by the program. & and / *
* should not appear in the output. *
* *
* A word is defined as a nonempty sequence of non-break *
* characters. A break is a sequence of one or more *
* break characters. A break in the input is reduced to *
* a single blank or start of new line in the output. *
* *
* The input text is a single line entered from a *
* simple terminal with an fixed 80 character screen *
* width. When the program is invoked it waits for the *
* user to provide input. The user types the input line, *
* followed by a / (end of text) and a carriage return. *
* The program then formats the text and displays it on *
* the terminal. *
* *
* If the input text contains a word that is too long to *
* fit on a single output line, an error message is *
* typed and the program terminates. If the end-of-text *
* character is missing, an error message is issued and *
* the user is given a chance to type in a corrected *
* version of the input line. *
* *
* (end of specification) *
*********************************************************************/
```

```
import java.io.*;

public class Buggy
{

final static int LINESIZE = 31;

public static void main(String [] args)
{
        int k,
                bufpos,
                fill,
                maxpos = LINESIZE;
        char cw,
                blank = ' ',
                linefeed = '$',
                eotext = '/';
        boolean moreinput = true;
        char [] buffer = new char [LINESIZE];
        bufpos = 0;
        fill = 0;
        while (moreinput)
        {   cw = gchar();
                if (cw == blank || cw == linefeed || cw == eotext)
                {
                        if (cw == eotext) moreinput = false; if ((fill + 1 +
                        bufpos) <= maxpos)
                        {   pchar(blank);
                                fill = fill + 1;
                        }
                        else
                        {   pchar(linefeed);
                                fill = 0;
                        }
                        for (k = 0; k < bufpos; k++) pchar(buffer[k]);
                        fill = fill + bufpos;
                        bufpos = 0;
                }
                else if (bufpos == maxpos)
                { moreinput = false; System.out.println("Word to
                        long");
                }
```

•

```
            else
            {  bufpos = bufpos + 1;
                 buffer[bufpos-1] = cw;
            }
        }
        pchar(linefeed);
        return;
}
```

• I use B as a shorthand for the character ' '. final static char B = ' ';

final static int ILENGTH = 80;

- Make suitable array with initial contents Z
- then a load of blanks.

```
            static char [] buffer = {
               'Z',B,B,B,B,B,B,B,B,B,
                B,B,B,B,B,B,B,B,B,B,
                B,B,B,B,B,B,B,B,B,B,
                B,B,B,B,B,B,B,B,B,B,
                B,B,B,B,B,B,B,B,B,B,
                B,B,B,B,B,B,B,B,B,B,
                B,B,B,B,B,B,B,B,B,B,
                 B,B,B,B,B,B,B,B,B,B};
```

- bcount is defined here so that it keeps its values
- across several calls to gchar().

```
static int bcount = 1;

static char gchar()
{
       char [] inbuf = new char [ILENGTH];
       char eotext = '/';
       char c;
       if (buffer[0] == 'Z')
       {  getrecord(inbuf);
```

```
•indexOf returns the index of a position where the given
•character is present in a string, or -1 if it is not
•found.
                                    if (new String(inbuf).indexOf((int) eotext) == -1)
            {  System.out.println("No end of text mark");
                   buffer[1] = eotext;
            }
            else for (int j=0; j<ILENGTH; j++)
                   buffer[j] = inbuf[j];
      }
      •  = buffer[bcount-1];
      bcount = bcount + 1; return
      c;
}

•a static ouput buffer, again blank-filled. static char []
outline =
{ B,B,B,B,B,B,B,B,B,B,B,B,B,B,B,B,B,B,B,B,B,
   B,B,B,B,B,B,B,B,B,B,B
};

•i indicates which place in outline pchar should
•put the next character at.
static int i = 1;

static void pchar(char c)
{
      int linefeed = '$';
      if (c == linefeed)
      { System.out.println(outline); for (int j=0;
            j<LINESIZE; j++)
                  outline[j] = B;
            i = 1;
      }
      else
      { outline[i-1] = c; i = i + 1;
      }
}
```

•

• Get access to keyboard input. No tricks here! static BufferedReader in =

```
        new BufferedReader(
                new InputStreamReader(System.in), 1);

static void getrecord(char [] b)
{
        String s;
        try
        {   s = in.readLine();
        }
        catch (IOException e) { s = "
        ";
        }
        for (int i = 0; i < ILENGTH; i++)
        { if (i < s.length()) b[i] = s.charAt(i); else b[i] = ' ';
        }
}


}
/* End of file */
```

Chapter 6

How to create and destroy objects

1.1 Introduction

Java programming language, originated in Sun Microsystems and released back in 1995, is one of the most widely used pro-gramming languages in the world, according to TIOBE Programming Community Index. Java is a general-purpose programming language. It is attractive to software developers primarily due to its powerful library and runtime, simple syntax, rich set of sup-ported platforms (Write Once, Run Anywhere - WORA) and awesome community.

In this tutorial we are going to cover concepts, assuming that our readers already have some basic knowledge of the language. It is by no means a complete reference, rather a detailed guide to move your Java skills to the next level.

Along the course, there will be a lot of code snippets to look at. Where it makes sense, the same example will be presented using Java 7 syntax as well as Java 8 one.

1.2 Instance Construction

Java is object-oriented language and as such the creation of new class instances (objects) is, probably, the most important concept of it. Constructors are playing a central role in new class instance initialization and Java provides a couple of favors to define them.

1.2.1 Implicit (Generated) Constructor

Java allows to define a class without any constructors but it does not mean the class will not have any. For example, let us consider this class:

```
package com.javacodegeeks.advanced.construction;

public class NoConstructor {
}
```

This class has no constructor but Java compiler will generate one implicitly and the creation of new class instances will be possible using new keyword.

```
final NoConstructor noConstructorInstance = new NoConstructor();
```

1.2.2 Constructors without Arguments

The constructor without arguments (or no-arg constructor) is the simplest way to do Java compiler's job explicitly.

```
package com.javacodegeeks.advanced.construction;

    public class NoArgConstructor {
        public NoArgConstructor() {
            // Constructor body here
    }
}
```

This constructor will be called once new instance of the class is created using the new keyword.

```
final NoArgConstructor noArgConstructor = new NoArgConstructor();
```

1.2.3 Constructors with Arguments

The constructors with arguments are the most interesting and useful way to parameterize new class instances creation. The following example defines a constructor with two arguments.

```
package com.javacodegeeks.advanced.construction;

public class ConstructorWithArguments {
    public ConstructorWithArguments(final String arg1,final String arg2) { //
        Constructor body here

    }
}
```

In this case, when class instance is being created using the new keyword, both constructor arguments should be provided.

```
final ConstructorWithArguments constructorWithArguments =
    new ConstructorWithArguments( "arg1", "arg2" );
```

Interestingly, the constructors can call each other using the special this keyword. It is considered a good practice to chain constructors in such a way as it reduces code duplication and basically leads to having single initialization entry point. As an example, let us add another constructor with only one argument.

```
public ConstructorWithArguments(final String arg1) {
    this(arg1, null);
}
```

1.2.4 Initialization Blocks

Java has yet another way to provide initialization logic using initialization blocks. This feature is rarely used but it is better to know it exists.

```
package com.javacodegeeks.advanced.construction;

public class InitializationBlock {
    {
        // initialization code here
    }
}
```

In a certain way, the initialization block might be treated as anonymous no-arg constructor. The particular class may have multiple initialization blocks and they all will be called in the order they are defined in the code. For example:

```
package com.javacodegeeks.advanced.construction;

public class InitializationBlocks {
```

```
    {
        // initialization code here
    }

    {
        // initialization code here
    }
}
```

Initialization blocks do not replace the constructors and may be used along with them. But it is very important to mention that initialization blocks are always called before any constructor.

```
package com.javacodegeeks.advanced.construction;

public class InitializationBlockAndConstructor {
    {
        // initialization code here
    }

    public InitializationBlockAndConstructor() {
    }
}
```

1.2.5 Construction guarantee

Java provides certain initialization guarantees which developers may rely on. Uninitialized instance and class (static) variables are automatically initialized to their default values.

Table 1.1: datasheet

Type	Default Value
boolean	False
byte	0
short	0
int	0
long	0L
char	u0000
float	0.0f
double	0.0d
object reference	null

Let us confirm that using following class as a simple example:

```
package com.javacodegeeks.advanced.construction;

public class InitializationWithDefaults {
    private boolean booleanMember;
    private byte byteMember;
    private short shortMember;
```

```
private int intMember;
private long longMember;
private char charMember;
private float floatMember;
private double doubleMember;
private Object referenceMember;
```

```
    public InitializationWithDefaults() {
        System.out.println( "booleanMember = " + booleanMember );
        System.out.println( "byteMember = " + byteMember );
        System.out.println( "shortMember = " + shortMember );
        System.out.println( "intMember = " + intMember );
        System.out.println( "longMember = " + longMember );
        System.out.println( "charMember = " +
            Character.codePointAt( new char[] { charMember }, 0     ) );
        System.out.println( "floatMember = " + floatMember );
        System.out.println( "doubleMember = " + doubleMember );
        System.out.println( "referenceMember = " + referenceMember );
    }
}
```

Once instantiated using new keyword:

```
final InitializationWithDefaults initializationWithDefaults = new
    InitializationWithDefaults(),
```

The following output will be shown in the console:

```
booleanMember = false
byteMember = 0
shortMember = 0
intMember = 0
longMember = 0
charMember = 0
floatMember = 0.0
doubleMember = 0.0
referenceMember = null
```

1.2.6 Visibility

Constructors are subject to Java visibility rules and can have access control modifiers which determine if other classes may invoke a particular constructor.

Table 1.2: datasheet

Modifier	Package	Subclass	Everyone Else
public	accessible	accessible	accessible
protected	accessible	accessible	not accessible
<no modifier>	accessible	not accessible	not accessible
private	not accessible	not accessible	not accessible

1.2.7 Garbage collection

Java (and JVM in particular) uses automatic garbage collection. To put it simply, whenever new objects are created, the memory is automatically allocated for them. Consequently, whenever the objects are not referenced anymore, they are destroyed and their memory is reclaimed.

Java garbage collection is generational and is based on assumption that most objects die young (not referenced anymore shortly after their creation and as such can be destroyed safely). Most developers used to believe that objects creation in Java is slow and instantiation of the new objects should be avoided as much as possible. In fact, it does not hold true: the objects creation in Java is quite cheap and fast. What is expensive though is an unnecessary creation of long-lived objects which eventually may fill up old generation and cause stop-the-world garbage collection.

1.2.8 Finalizers

So far we have talked about constructors and objects initialization but have not actually mentioned anything about their counter-part: objects destruction. That is because Java uses garbage collection to manage objects lifecycle and it is the responsibility of garbage collector to destroy unnecessary objects and reclaim the memory.

However, there is one particular feature in Java called finalizers which resemble a bit the destructors but serves the different purpose of performing resources cleanup. Finalizers are considered to be a dangerous feature (which leads to numerous side-effects and performance issues). Generally, they are not necessary and should be avoided (except very rare cases mostly related to native objects). A much better alternative to finalizers is the introduced by Java 7 language construct called try-with-resources and AutoCloseable interface which allows to write clean code like this:

```
try ( final InputStream in = Files.newInputStream( path ) ) {
    // code here
}
```

1.3 Static initialization

So far we have looked through class instance construction and initialization. But Java also supports class-level initialization constructs called static initializers. There are very similar to the initialization blocks except for the additional static keyword. Please notice that static initialization is performed once per class-loader. For example:

```
package com.javacodegeeks.advanced.construction;

public class StaticInitializationBlock {
    static {
        // static initialization code here
    }
}
```

Similarly to initialization blocks, you may include any number of static initializer blocks in the class definition and they will be executed in the order in which they appear in the code. For example:

```
package com.javacodegeeks.advanced.construction;

public class StaticInitializationBlocks {
    static {
        // static initialization code here
    }

    static {
        // static initialization code here
    }
}
```

Because static initialization block can be triggered from multiple parallel threads (when the loading of the class happens in the first time), Java runtime guarantees that it will be executed only once and in thread-safe manner.

1.4 Construction Patterns

Over the years a couple of well-understood and widely applicable construction (or creation) patterns have emerged within Java community. We are going to cover the most famous of them: singleton, helpers, factory and dependency injection (also known as inversion of control).

1.4.1 Singleton

Singleton is one of the oldest and controversial patterns in software developer's community. Basically, the main idea of it is to ensure that only one single instance of the class could be created at any given time. Being so simple however, singleton raised a lot of the discussions about how to make it right and, in particular, thread-safe. Here is how a naive version of singleton class may look like:

```
package com.javacodegeeks.advanced.construction.patterns;

public class NaiveSingleton {
    private static NaiveSingleton instance;

    private NaiveSingleton() {
    }

    public static NaiveSingleton getInstance() {
        if( instance == null ) {
            instance = new NaiveSingleton();
        }

        return instance;
    }
}
```

At least one problem with this code is that it may create many instances of the class if called concurrently by multiple threads.
One of the ways to design singleton properly (but in non-lazy fashion) is using the static final property of the class.

```
final property of the class.
package com.javacodegeeks.advanced.construction.patterns;

public class EagerSingleton {
    private static final EagerSingleton instance = new EagerSingleton();

    private EagerSingleton() {
    }

    public static EagerSingleton getInstance() {
        return instance;
    }
}
```

If you do not want to waste your resources and would like your singletons to be lazily created when they are really needed, the explicit synchronization is required, potentially leading to lower concurrency in a multithreaded environments (more details about concurrency in Java will be discussing in part 9 of the tutorial, Concurrency best practices).

```
package com.javacodegeeks.advanced.construction.patterns;

public class LazySingleton {
    private static LazySingleton instance;

    private LazySingleton() {
```

```
    }

    public static synchronized LazySingleton getInstance() { if(
        instance == null ) {
            instance = new LazySingleton();
        }

        return instance;
    }
}
```

Nowadays, singletons are not considered to be a good choice in most cases, primarily because they are making a code very hard to test. The domination of dependency injection pattern (please see the Dependency Injection section below) also makes singletons unnecessary.

1.4.2 Utility/Helper Class

The utility or helper classes are quite popular pattern used by many Java developers. Basically, it represents the non-instantiable class (with constructor declared as private), optionally declared as final (more details about declaring classes as final will be provided in part 3 of the tutorial, How to design Classes and Interfaces) and contains static methods only. For example:

```
package com.javacodegeeks.advanced.construction.patterns;

public final class HelperClass {
    private HelperClass() {
    }

    public static void helperMethod1() {
        // Method body here
    }

    public static void helperMethod2() {
        // Method body here
    }
}
```

From seasoned software developer standpoint, such helpers often become containers for all kind of non-related methods which have not found other place to be put in but should be shared somehow and used by other classes. Such design decisions should be avoided in most cases: it is always possible to find another way to reuse the required functionality, keeping the code clean and concise.

1.4.3 Factory

Factory pattern is proven to be extremely useful technique in the hands of software developers. As such, it has several flavors in Java, ranging from factory method to abstract factory. The simplest example of factory pattern is a static method which returns new instance of a particular class (factory method). For example:

```
package com.javacodegeeks.advanced.construction.patterns;

public class Book {
    private Book( final String title) {
    }

    public static Book newBook( final String title ) { return
        new Book( title );
    }
}
```

The one may argue that it does not make a lot of sense to introduce the newBook factory method but using such a pattern often makes the code more readable. Another variance of factory pattern involves interfaces or abstract classes (abstract factory). For example, let us define a factory interface:

```
public interface BookFactory {
    Book newBook();
}
```

With couple of different implementations, depending on the library type:

```
public class Library implements BookFactory {
    @Override
    public Book newBook() {
        return new PaperBook();
    }
}

public class KindleLibrary implements BookFactory {
    @Override

    public Book newBook() {
        return new KindleBook();
    }
}
```

Now, the particular class of the Book is hidden behind BookFactory interface implementation, still providing the generic way to create books.

1.4.4 Dependency Injection

Dependency injection (also known as inversion of control) is considered as a good practice for class designers: if some class instance depends on the other class instances, those dependencies should be provided (injected) to it by means of constructors (or setters, strategies, etc.) but not created by the instance itself. Let us consider the following example:

```
package com.javacodegeeks.advanced.construction.patterns;

import java.text.DateFormat;
import java.util.Date;

public class Dependant {
    private final DateFormat format = DateFormat.getDateInstance();

    public String format( final Date date ) {
        return format.format( date );
    }
}
```

The class Dependant needs an instance of DateFormat and it just creates one by calling DateFormat.getDateInstanc e() at construction time. The better design would be to use constructor argument to do the same thing:

```
package com.javacodegeeks.advanced.construction.patterns;

import java.text.DateFormat;
import java.util.Date;

public class Dependant {
    private final DateFormat format;

    public Dependant( final DateFormat format ) {
```

```
        this.format = format;
    }

    public String format( final Date date ) {
        return format.format( date );
    }
}
```

In this case the class has all its dependencies provided from outside and it would be very easy to change date format and write test cases for it.

1.5 Download the Source Code

- **You may download the source code here:** com.javacodegeeks.advanced.java

1.6 What's next

In this part of the tutorial we have looked at classes and class instances construction and initialization techniques, along the way covering several widely used patterns. In the next part we are going to dissect the Object class and usage of its well-known methods: equals, hashCode, toString and clone.

Chapter 7

Using methods common to all objects

2.1 Introduction

From part 1 of the tutorial, How to create and destroy objects, we already know that Java is an object-oriented language (however, not a pure object-oriented one). On top of the Java class hierarchy sits the Object class and every single class in Java implicitly is inherited from it. As such, all classes inherit the set of methods declared in Object class, most importantly the following ones:

Table 2.1: datasheet

Method	Description
protected Object clone()	Creates and returns a copy of this object.
protected void finalize()	Called by the garbage collector on an object when garbage collection determines that there are no more references to the object. We have discussed finalizers in the part 1 of the tutorial, How to create and destroy objects.
boolean equals(Object obj)	Indicates whether some other object is "equal to" this one.
int hashCode()	Returns a hash code value for the object.
String toString()	Returns a string representation of the object.
void notify()	Wakes up a single thread that is waiting on this object's monitor. We are going to discuss this method in the part 9 of the tutorial, Concurrency best practices.
void notifyAll()	Wakes up all threads that are waiting on this object's monitor. We are going to discuss this method in the part 9 of the tutorial, Concurrency best practices.
void wait() void wait(long timeout) void wait(long timeout, int nanos)	Causes the current thread to wait until another thread invokes the notify() method or the notifyAll() method for this object. We are going to discuss these methods in the part 9 of the tutorial, Concurrency best

	practices.

In this part of the tutorial we are going to look at equals,hashCode,toString and clone methods, their usage and important constraints to keep in mind.

2.2 Methods equals and hashCode

By default, any two object references (or class instance references) in Java are equal only if they are referring to the same memory location (reference equality). But Java allows classes to define their own equality rules by overriding the equals() method of the Object class. It sounds like a powerful concept, however the correct equals() method implementation should conform to a set of rules and satisfy the following constraints:

- Reflexive. Object x must be equal to itself and equals(x) must return true.
- Symmetric. If equals(y) returns true then y.equals(x) must also return true.
- Transitive. If equals(y) returns true and y.equals(z) returns true, then x.equals(z) must also return true.
- Consistent. Multiple invocation of equals() method must result into the same value, unless any of the properties used for equality comparison are modified.
- Equals To Null. The result of equals(null) must be always false.

Unfortunately, the Java compiler is not able to enforce those constraints during the compilation process. However, not following these rules may cause very weird and hard to troubleshoot issues. The general advice is this: if you ever are going to write your own equals() method implementation, think twice if you really need it. Now, armed with all these rules, let us write a simple implementation of the equals() method for the Person class.

```
package com.javacodegeeks.advanced.objects;

public class Person {
    private final String firstName;
    private final String lastName;
    private final String email;

    public Person( final String firstName, final String lastName, final String email ) {
        this.firstName = firstName;

        this.lastName = lastName;
        this.email = email;
    }

    public String getEmail() {
        return email;
    }

    public String getFirstName() {
        return firstName;
    }

    public String getLastName() {
        return lastName;
    }

    • Step 0: Please add the @Override annotation, it will ensure that your
    • intention is to change the default implementation.
    @Override
    public boolean equals( Object obj ) {
```

- Step 1: Check if the 'obj' is null **if (obj == null) {**

```
    return false;
}
```

- Step 2: Check if the 'obj' is pointing to the this instance **if (this == obj) {**

```
    return true;
}
```

```
        • Step 3: Check classes equality. Note of caution here: please do not use the
        • 'instanceof' operator unless class is declared as final. It may cause
        • an issues within class hierarchies.
        if ( getClass() != obj.getClass() ) {
            return false;
        }

        • Step 4: Check individual fields equality final
        Person other = (Person) obj;
        if ( email == null ) {
            if ( other.email != null ) {
                return false;

            }
        } else if( !email.equals( other.email ) ) { return
            false;

        }

        if ( firstName == null ) {
            if ( other.firstName != null ) {
                return false;
            }
        } else if ( !firstName.equals( other.firstName ) ) { return
            false;

        }

        if ( lastName == null ) {
            if ( other.lastName != null ) {
                return false;
            }
        } else if ( !lastName.equals( other.lastName ) ) {
            return false;
        }

        return true;
    }
}
```

It is not by accident that this section also includes the hashCode() method in its title. The last, but not least, rule to remember: whenever you override equals() method, always override the hashCode() method as well. If for any two objects the equals() method returns true, then the hashCode() method on each of those two objects must return the same integer value (however the opposite statement is not as strict: if for any two objects the equals() method returns false, the hashCode() method on each of those two objects may or may not return the same integer value). Let us take a look on hashCode() method for the Person class.

```
• Please add the @Override annotation, it will ensure that your
• intention is to change the default implementation.
@Override
public int hashCode() {
    final int prime = 31;
```

```
        int result = 1;
        result = prime *    result + (    ( email ==    null ) ? 0 : email.hashCode() );
        result = prime *    result    + ( (  firstName == null ) ? 0 : firstName.hashCode() );
                                             lastNam
        result   = prime *  result    + ( (  e             == null ) ? 0 : lastName.hashCode() );
        return   result;
}
```

To protect yourself from surprises, whenever possible try to use final fields while implementing equals() and hashCod e(). It will guarantee that behavior of those methods will not be affected by the field changes (however, in real-world projects it is not always possible).

Finally, always make sure that the same fields are used within implementation of equals() and hashCode() methods. It will guarantee consistent behavior of both methods in case of any change affecting the fields in question.

2.3 Method toString

The toString() is arguably the most interesting method among the others and is being overridden more frequently. Its purpose is it to provide the string representation of the object (class instance). The properly written toString() method can greatly simplify debugging and troubleshooting of the issues in real-live systems.

The default toString() implementation is not very useful in most cases and just returns the full class name and object hash code, separated by @, f.e.:

```
com.javacodegeeks.advanced.objects.Person@6104e2ee
```

Let us try to improve the implementation and override the toString() method for our Person class example. Here is a one of the ways to make toString() more useful.

```
• Please add the @Override annotation, it will ensure that your
• intention is to change the default implementation.
@Override
public String toString() {
    return String.format( "%s[email=%s, first name=%s, last name=%s]",
        getClass().getSimpleName(), email, firstName, lastName );
}
```

Now, the toString() method provides the string version of the Person class instance with all its fields included. For example, while executing the code snippet below:

```
final Person person = new Person( "John", "Smith", "john.smith@domain.com" );
System.out.println( person.toString() );
```

The following output will be printed out in the console:

```
Person[email=john.smith@domain.com, first name=John, last name=Smith]
```

Unfortunately, the standard Java library has a limited support to simplify toString() method implementations, notably, the most useful methods are Objects.toString(), Arrays.toString() /Arrays.deepToString(). Let us take a look on the Office class and its possible toString() implementation.

```
package com.javacodegeeks.advanced.objects;

import java.util.Arrays;

public class Office {
    private Person[] persons;

    public Office( Person ... persons ) {
        this.persons = Arrays.copyOf( persons, persons.length );
    }

    @Override
```

```
    public String toString() {
        return String.format( "%s{persons=%s}",
            getClass().getSimpleName(), Arrays.toString( persons ) );
    }

    public Person[] getPersons() {
        return persons;
    }
}
```

The following output will be printed out in the console (as we can see the Person class instances are properly converted to string as well):

```
Office{persons=[Person[email=john.smith@domain.com, first name=John, last name=Smith]]}
```

The Java community has developed a couple of quite comprehensive libraries which help a lot to make toString() implemen-tations painless and easy. Among those are Google Guava's Objects.toStringHelper and Apache Commons Lang ToStringBuilder.

2.4 Method clone

If there is a method with a bad reputation in Java, it is definitely clone(). Its purpose is very clear - return the exact copy of the class instance it is being called on, however there are a couple of reasons why it is not as easy as it sounds.

First of all, in case you have decided to implement your own clone() method, there are a lot of conventions to follow as stated in Java documentation. Secondly, the method is declared protected in Object class so in order to make it visible, it should be overridden as public with return type of the overriding class itself. Thirdly, the overriding class should implement the Clo neable interface (which is just a marker or mixin interface with no methods defined) otherwise CloneNotSupportedException exception will be raised. And lastly, the implementation should call super.clone() first and then perform additional actions if needed. Let us see how it could be implemented for our sample Person class.

```
public class Person implements Cloneable {
    • Please add the @Override annotation, it will ensure that your
    • intention is to change the default implementation.
    @Override
    public Person clone() throws CloneNotSupportedException {
        return ( Person )super.clone();
    }
}
```

The implementation looks quite simple and straightforward, so what could go wrong here? Couple of things, actually. While the cloning of the class instance is being performed, no class constructor is being called. The consequence of such a behavior is that unintentional data sharing may come out. Let us consider the following example of the Office class, introduced in previous section:

```
package com.javacodegeeks.advanced.objects;

import java.util.Arrays;

public class Office implements Cloneable {
    private Person[] persons;

    public Office( Person ... persons ) {
        this.persons = Arrays.copyOf( persons, persons.length );
    }

    @Override
```

```
    public Office clone() throws CloneNotSupportedException {
        return ( Office )super.clone();
    }

    public Person[] getPersons() {
        return persons;
    }
}
```

In this implementation, all the clones of the Office class instance will share the same persons array, which is unlikely the desired behavior. A bit of work should be done in order to make the clone() implementation to do the right thing.

```
@Override
public Office clone() throws CloneNotSupportedException {
    final Office clone = ( Office )super.clone();
    clone.persons = persons.clone();
    return clone;
}
```

It looks better now but even this implementation is very fragile as making the persons field to be final will lead to the same data sharing issues (as final cannot be reassigned).

By and large, if you would like to make exact copies of your classes, probably it is better to avoid clone() and Cloneable and use much simpler alternatives (for example, copying constructor, quite familiar concept to developers with C++ background, or factory method, a useful construction pattern we have discussed in part 1 of the tutorial, How to create and destroy objects).

2.5 Method equals and == operator

There is an interesting relation between Java == operator and equals() method which causes a lot of issues and confusion. In most cases (except comparing primitive types), == operator performs referential equality: it returns true if both references point to the same object, and false otherwise. Let us take a look on a simple example which illustrates the differences:

```
final String str1 = new String( "bbb" );
System.out.println( "Using == operator: " + ( str1 == "bbb" ) );
System.out.println( "Using equals() method: " + str1.equals( "bbb" ) );
```

From the human being prospective, there are no differences between str1=="bbb" and str1.equals("bbb"): in both cases the result should be the same as str1 is just a reference to "bbb" string. But in Java it is not the case:

```
Using == operator: false
Using equals() method: true
```

Even if both strings look exactly the same, in this particular example they exist as two different string instances. As a rule of thumb, if you deal with object references, always use the equals() or Objects.equals() (see please next section Useful helper classes for more details) to compare for equality, unless you really have an intention to compare if object references are pointing to the same instance.

2.6 Useful helper classes

Since the release of Java 7, there is a couple of very useful helper classes included with the standard Java library. One of them is class Objects. In particular, the following three methods can greatly simplify your own equals() and hashCode() method implementations.

Table 2.2: datasheet

Method	Description
static boolean equals(Object a, Object	Returns true if the arguments are equal to each

b)	other and false otherwise.
static int hash(Object...values)	Generates a hash code for a sequence of input values.
static int hashCode(Object o)	Returns the hash code of a non-null argument and 0 for a null argument.

If we rewrite equals() and hashCode() method for our Person's class example using these helper methods, the amount of the code is going to be significantly smaller, plus the code becomes much more readable.

```
@Override
public boolean equals( Object obj ) {
    if ( obj == null ) {
        return false;
    }

      if ( this == obj ) {
         return true;
    }

    if ( getClass() != obj.getClass() ) {
        return false;
    }

    final PersonObjects other = (PersonObjects) obj; if(
    !Objects.equals( email, other.email ) ) {
        return false;
    } else if( !Objects.equals( firstName, other.firstName ) ) { return
        false;

    } else if( !Objects.equals( lastName, other.lastName ) ) { return
        false;

    }

    return true;
}

@Override
public int hashCode() {
    return Objects.hash( email, firstName, lastName );
}
```

2.7 Download the Source Code

- You may download the source code here: advanced-java-part-2

2.8 What's next

In this section we have covered the Object class which is the foundation of object-oriented programming in Java. We have seen how each class may override methods inherited from Object class and impose its own equality rules. In the next section we are going to switch our gears from coding and discuss how to properly design your classes and interfaces.

Chapter 8

How to design Classes and Interfaces

3.1 Introduction

Whatever programming language you are using (and Java is not an exception here), following good design principles is a key factor to write clean, understandable, testable code and deliver long-living, easy to maintain solutions. In this part of the tutorial we are going to discuss the foundational building blocks which the Java language provides and introduce a couple of design principles, aiming to help you to make better design decisions.

More precisely, we are going to discuss interfaces and interfaces with default methods (new feature of Java 8), abstract and final classes, immutable classes, inheritance, composition and revisit a bit the visibility (or accessibility) rules we have briefly touched in part 1 of the tutorial, How to create and destroy objects.

3.2 Interfaces

In object-oriented programming, the concept of interfaces forms the basics of contract-driven (or contract-based) development. In a nutshell, interfaces define the set of methods (contract) and every class which claims to support this particular interface must provide the implementation of those methods: a pretty simple, but powerful idea.

Many programming languages do have interfaces in one form or another, but Java particularly provides language support for that.

Let take a look on a simple interface definition in Java.

```
package com.javacodegeeks.advanced.design;

public interface SimpleInterface {
    void performAction();
}
```

In the code snippet above, the interface which we named SimpleInterface declares just one method with name perfo rmAction. The principal differences of interfaces in respect to classes is that interfaces outline what the contact is (declare methods), but do not provide their implementations.

However, interfaces in Java can be more complicated than that: they can include nested interfaces, classes, enumerations, an-notations (enumerations and annotations will be covered in details in part 5 of the tutorial, How and when to use Enums and Annotations) and constants. For example:

```
package com.javacodegeeks.advanced.design;

public interface InterfaceWithDefinitions {
    String CONSTANT = "CONSTANT";

    enum InnerEnum {
        E1, E2;
```

```
    }

    class InnerClass {
    }

    interface InnerInterface {
        void performInnerAction();
    }

    void performAction();
}
```

With this more complicated example, there are a couple of constraints which interfaces implicitly impose with respect to the nested constructs and method declarations, and Java compiler enforces that. First and foremost, even if it is not being said explicitly, every declaration in the interface is public (and can be only public, for more details about visibility and accessibility rules, please refer to section Visibility). As such, the following method declarations are equivalent:

```
public void performAction();
void performAction();
```

Worth to mention that every single method in the interface is implicitly declared as abstract and even these method declarations are equivalent:

```
public abstract void performAction();
public void performAction();
void performAction();
```

As for the constant field declarations, additionally to being public, they are implicitly static and final so the following declarations are also equivalent:

```
String CONSTANT = "CONSTANT";
public static final String CONSTANT = "CONSTANT";
```

And finally, the nested classes, interfaces or enumerations, additionally to being public, are implicitly declared as static.
For example, those class declarations are equivalent as well:

```
class InnerClass {
}

static class InnerClass {
}
```

Which style you are going to choose is a personal preference, however knowledge of those simple qualities of interfaces could save you from unnecessary typing.

3.3 Marker Interfaces

Marker interfaces are a special kind of interfaces which have no methods or other nested constructs defined. We have already seen one example of the marker interface in part 2 of the tutorial Using methods common to all objects, the interface Cloneable. Here is how it is defined in the Java library:

```
public interface Cloneable {
}
```

Marker interfaces are not contracts per se but somewhat useful technique to "attach" or "tie" some particular trait to the class. For example, with respect to Cloneable, the class is marked as being available for cloning however the way it should or could be done is not a part of the interface. Another very well-known and widely used example of marker interface is Serializable:

```
public interface Serializable {
}
```

This interface marks the class as being available for serialization and deserialization, and again, it does not specify the way it could or should be done.

The marker interfaces have their place in object-oriented design, although they do not satisfy the main purpose of interface to be a contract.

3.4 Functional interfaces, default and static methods

With the release of Java 8, interfaces have obtained new very interesting capabilities: static methods, default methods and automatic conversion from lambdas (functional interfaces).

In section Interfaces we have emphasized on the fact that interfaces in Java can only declare methods but are not allowed to provide their implementations. With default methods it is not true anymore: an interface can mark a method with the default keyword and provide the implementation for it. For example:

```
package com.javacodegeeks.advanced.design;

public interface InterfaceWithDefaultMethods {
    void performAction();

    default void performDefaulAction() {
        // Implementation here
    }
}
```

Being an instance level, defaults methods could be overridden by each interface implementer, but from now, interfaces may also include static methods, for example:

```
package com.javacodegeeks.advanced.design;

public interface InterfaceWithDefaultMethods {
    static void createAction() {
        // Implementation here
    }
}
```

One may say that providing an implementation in the interface defeats the whole purpose of contract-based development, but there are many reasons why these features were introduced into the Java language and no matter how useful or confusing they are, they are there for you to use.

The functional interfaces are a different story and they are proven to be very helpful add-on to the language. Basically, the functional interface is the interface with just a single abstract method declared in it. The Runnable interface from Java standard library is a good example of this concept:

```
@FunctionalInterface
public interface Runnable {
    void run();
}
```

The Java compiler treats functional interfaces differently and is able to convert the lambda function into the functional interface implementation where it makes sense. Let us take a look on following function definition:

```
public void runMe( final Runnable r ) {
    r.run();
}
```

To invoke this function in Java 7 and below, the implementation of the Runnable interface should be provided (for example using Anonymous classes), but in Java 8 it is enough to pass run() method implementation using lambda syntax:

```
runMe( () -> System.out.println( "Run!" ) );
```

Additionally, the @FunctionalInterface annotation (annotations will be covered in details in part 5 of the tutorial, How and when to use Enums and Annotations) hints the compiler to verify that the interface contains only one abstract method so any changes introduced to the interface in the future will not break this assumption.

3.5 Abstract classes

Another interesting concept supported by Java language is the notion of abstract classes. Abstract classes are somewhat similar to the interfaces in Java 7 and very close to interfaces with default methods in Java 8. By contrast to regular classes, abstract classes cannot be instantiated but could be subclassed (please refer to the section Inheritance for more details). More importantly, abstract classes may contain abstract methods: the special kind of methods without implementations, much like interfaces do. For example:

```
package com.javacodegeeks.advanced.design;

public abstract class SimpleAbstractClass {
    public void performAction() {
        // Implementation here
    }

    public abstract void performAnotherAction();
}
```

In this example, the class SimpleAbstractClass is declared as abstract and has one abstract method declaration as well. Abstract classes are very useful when most or even some part of implementation details could be shared by many subclasses. However, they still leave the door open and allow customizing the intrinsic behavior of each subclass by means of abstract methods.

One thing to mention, in contrast to interfaces which can contain only public declarations, abstract classes may use the full power of accessibility rules to control abstract methods visibility (please refer to the sections Visibility and Inheritance for more details).

3.6 Immutable classes

Immutability is becoming more and more important in the software development nowadays. The rise of multi-core systems has raised a lot of concerns related to data sharing and concurrency (in the part 9, Concurrency best practices, we are going to discuss in details those topics). But the one thing definitely emerged: less (or even absence of) mutable state leads to better scalability and simpler reasoning about the systems.

Unfortunately, the Java language does not provide strong support for class immutability. However using a combination of techniques it is possible to design classes which are immutable. First and foremost, all fields of the class should be final. It is a good start but does not guarantee immutability alone.

```
package com.javacodegeeks.advanced.design;

import java.util.Collection;

public class ImmutableClass {
    private final long id;
    private final String[] arrayOfStrings;
    private final Collection< String > collectionOfString;
}
```

Secondly, follow the proper initialization: if the field is the reference to a collection or an array, do not assign those fields directly from constructor arguments, make the copies instead. It will guarantee that state of the collection or array will not be changed from outside.

```
public ImmutableClass( final long id, final String[] arrayOfStrings, final
        Collection< String > collectionOfString) {
    this.id = id;
    this.arrayOfStrings = Arrays.copyOf( arrayOfStrings, arrayOfStrings.length );
    this.collectionOfString = new ArrayList<>( collectionOfString );
}
```

And lastly, provide the proper accessors (getters). For the collection, the immutable view should be exposed using Collecti ons.unmodifiableXxx wrappers.

```
public Collection<String> getCollectionOfString() {
    return Collections.unmodifiableCollection( collectionOfString );
}
```

With arrays, the only way to ensure true immutability is to provide a copy instead of returning reference to the array. That might not be acceptable from a practical standpoint as it hugely depends on array size and may put a lot of pressure on garbage collector.

```
public String[] getArrayOfStrings() {
    return Arrays.copyOf( arrayOfStrings, arrayOfStrings.length );
}
```

Even this small example gives a good idea that immutability is not a first class citizen in Java yet. Things can get really complicated if an immutable class has fields referencing another class instances. Those classes should also be immutable however there is no simple way to enforce that.

There are a couple of great Java source code analyzers like FindBugs) and PMD) which may help a lot by inspecting your code and pointing to the common Java programming flaws. Those tools are great friends of any Java developer.

3.7 Anonymous classes

In the pre-Java 8 era, anonymous classes were the only way to provide in-place class definitions and immediate instantiations. The purpose of the anonymous classes was to reduce boilerplate and provide a concise and easy way to represent classes as expressions. Let us take a look on the typical old-fashioned way to spawn new thread in Java:

```
package com.javacodegeeks.advanced.design;

public class AnonymousClass {
    public static void main( String[] args ) {
        new Thread(
            • Example of creating anonymous class which implements
            • Runnable interface
            new Runnable() {
                @Override
                public void run() {
                    // Implementation here
```

```
                }
            }
        ).start();
    }
}
```

In this example, the implementation of the Runnable interface is provided in place as anonymous class. Although there are some limitations associated with anonymous classes, the fundamental disadvantages of their usage are a quite verbose syntax constructs which Java imposes as a language. Even the simplest anonymous class which does nothing requires at least 5 lines of code to be written every time.

```
    new Runnable() {
        @Override
        public void run() {
        }
    }
```

Luckily, with Java 8, lambdas and functional interfaces all this boilerplate is about to gone away, finally making the Java code to look truly concise.

```
package com.javacodegeeks.advanced.design;

public class AnonymousClass {
    public static void main( String[] args ) {
        new Thread( () -> { /* Implementation here */ } ).start();
    }
}
```

3.8 Visibility

We have already talked a bit about Java visibility and accessibility rules in part 1 of the tutorial, How to design Classes and Interfaces. In this part we are going to get back to this subject again but in the context of subclassing.

Table 3.1: datasheet

Modifier	Package	Subclass	Everyone Else
public	accessible	accessible	Accessible
protected	accessible	accessible	not accessible
<no modifier>	accessible	not accessible	not accessible
private	not accessible	not accessible	not accessible

Different visibility levels allow or disallow the classes to see other classes or interfaces (for example, if they are in different packages or nested in one another) or subclasses to see and access methods, constructors and fields of their parents.

In next section, Inheritance, we are going to see that in action.

3.9 Inheritance

Inheritance is one of the key concepts of object-oriented programming, serving as a basis of building class relationships. Com-bined together with visibility and accessibility rules, inheritance allows designing extensible and maintainable class hierarchies.

Conceptually, inheritance in Java is implemented using subclassing and the extends keyword, followed by the parent class. The subclass inherits all of the public and protected members of its parent class. Additionally, a subclass inherits the package-private members of the parent class if both reside in the same package. Having said that, it is very important no matter what you are trying to design, to keep the minimal set of the methods which class exposes publicly or to its subclasses. For example, let us take a look on a class Parent and its subclass Child to demonstrate different visibility levels and their effect:

```
package com.javacodegeeks.advanced.design;

public class Parent {
    // Everyone can see it
    public static final String CONSTANT = "Constant";

    // No one can access it
```

```
    private String privateField;
    • Only subclasses can access it
    protected String protectedField;

    • No one can see it
    private class PrivateClass {
    }

    // Only visible to subclasses
    protected interface ProtectedInterface {
    }

    • Everyone can call it public
    void publicAction() {
    }

    • Only subclass can call it
    protected void protectedAction() {
    }

    • No one can call it
    private void privateAction() {
    }

    >>>        Only subclasses in the same package can
    call it void packageAction() {
    }
}
```

```
package com.javacodegeeks.advanced.design;

// Resides in the same package as parent class
public class Child extends Parent implements Parent.ProtectedInterface {
    @Override

    protected void protectedAction() {
        >>> Calls parent's method
        implementation super.protectedAction();
    }

    @Override
    void packageAction() {
        // Do nothing, no call to parent's method implementation
    }

    public void childAction() {
        this.protectedField = "value";
    }
}
```

Inheritance is a very large topic by itself, with a lot of subtle details specific to Java. However, there are a couple of easy to follow rules which could help a lot to keep your class hierarchies concise. In Java, every subclass may override any inherited method of its parent unless it was declared as final (please refer to the section Final classes and methods).

However, there is no special syntax or keyword to mark the method as being overridden which may cause a lot of confusion. That is why the @Override annotation has been introduced: whenever your intention is to override the inherited method, please always use the @Override annotation to indicate that.

Another dilemma Java developers are often facing in design is building class hierarchies (with concrete or abstract classes) versus interface implementations. It is strongly advised to prefer interfaces to classes or abstract classes whenever possible. Interfaces are much more lightweight, easier to test (using mocks) and maintain, plus they minimize the side effects of implementation changes. Many advanced programming techniques like creating class proxies in standard Java library heavily rely on interfaces.

3.10 Multiple Inheritance

In contrast to C++ and some other languages, Java does not support multiple inheritance: in Java every class has exactly one direct parent (with Object class being on top of the hierarchy as we have already known from part 2 of the tutorial, Using methods common to all objects). However, the class may implement multiple interfaces and as such, stacking interfaces is the only way to achieve (or mimic) multiple inheritance in Java.

```
package com.javacodegeeks.advanced.design;

public class MultipleInterfaces implements Runnable, AutoCloseable {
    @Override

    public void run() {
        // Some implementation here
    }

    @Override
    public void close() throws Exception {
        // Some implementation here
    }
}
```

Implementation of multiple interfaces is in fact quite powerful, but often the need to reuse an implementation leads to deep class hierarchies as a way to overcome the absence of multiple inheritance support in Java.

```
public class A implements Runnable {
    @Override
    public void run() {
        // Some implementation here
    }
}

>>>    Class B wants to inherit the implementation of run() method from class A.
public class B extends A implements AutoCloseable {
    @Override
    public void close() throws Exception {
            Some implementation here
    }
}

•  Class C wants to inherit the implementation of run() method from class A
•  and the implementation of close() method from class B.
public class C extends B implements Readable {
    @Override
    public int read(java.nio.CharBuffer cb) throws IOException { //
        Some implementation here
    }
}
```

And so on. . . The recent Java 8 release somewhat addressed the problem with the introduction of default methods. Because of default methods, interfaces actually have started to provide not only contract but also implementation. Consequently, the classes which implement those interfaces are automatically inheriting these implemented methods as well. For example:

```
package com.javacodegeeks.advanced.design;

public interface DefaultMethods extends Runnable, AutoCloseable {
    @Override

    default void run() {
        // Some implementation here
    }
```

```
    @Override
    default void close() throws Exception {
        // Some implementation here
    }
}
```

- Class C inherits the implementation of run() and close() methods from the
- DefaultMethods interface.

```
public class C implements DefaultMethods, Readable {
    @Override

    public int read(java.nio.CharBuffer cb) throws IOException { //
        Some implementation here
    }
}
```

Be aware that multiple inheritance is a powerful, but at the same time a dangerous tool to use. The well known "Diamond of Death" problem is often cited as the fundamental flaw of multiple inheritance implementations, so developers are urged to design class hierarchies very carefully. Unfortunately, the Java 8 interfaces with default methods are becoming the victims of those flaws as well.

```
interface A {
    default void performAction() {
    }
}

interface B extends A {
    @Override
    default void performAction() {
    }
}

interface C extends A {
    @Override
    default void performAction() {
    }
}
```

For example, the following code snippet fails to compile:

- E is not compilable unless it overrides performAction() as well

```
interface E extends B, C {
}
```

At this point it is fair to say that Java as a language always tried to escape the corner cases of object-oriented programming, but as the language evolves, some of those cases are started to pop up.

3.11 Inheritance and composition

Fortunately, inheritance is not the only way to design your classes. Another alternative, which many developers consider being better than inheritance, is composition. The idea is very simple: instead of building class hierarchies, the classes should be composed from other classes.

Let us take a look on this example:

```
public class Vehicle {
    private Engine engine;
    private Wheels[] wheels;
    // ...
}
```

The Vehicle class is composed out of engine and wheels (plus many other parts which are left aside for simplicity).
However, one may say that Vehicle class is also an engine and so could be designed using the inheritance.

```
public class Vehicle extends Engine {
    private Wheels[] wheels;
    // ...
}
```

Which design decision is right? The general guidelines are known as IS-A and HAS-A principles. IS-A is the inheritance relationship: the subclass also satisfies the parent class specification and a such IS-A variation of parent class. Consequently, HAS-A is the composition relationship: the class owns (or HAS-A) the objects which belong to it. In most cases, the HAS-A principle works better then IS-A for couple of reasons:

- The design is more flexible in a way it could be changed
- The model is more stable as changes are not propagating through class hierarchies
- The class and its composites are loosely coupled compared to inheritance which tightly couples parent and its subclasses
- The reasoning about class is simpler as all its dependencies are included in it, in one place

However, the inheritance has its own place, solves real design issues in different way and should not be neglected. Please keep those two alternatives in mind while designing your object-oriented models.

3.12 Encapsulation

The concept of encapsulation in object-oriented programming is all about hiding the implementation details (like state, internal methods, etc.) from the outside world. The benefits of encapsulation are maintainability and ease of change. The less intrinsic details classes expose, the more control the developers have over changing their internal implementation, without the fear to break the existing code (a real problem if you are developing a library or framework used by many people).

Encapsulation in Java is achieved using visibility and accessibility rules. It is considered a best practice in Java to never expose the fields directly, only by means of getters and setters (if the field is not declared as final). For example:

```
package com.javacodegeeks.advanced.design;

public class Encapsulation {
    private final String email;
    private String address;

    public Encapsulation( final String email ) {
        this.email = email;
    }

    public String getAddress() {
        return address;
    }

    public void setAddress(String address) {
        this.address = address;
    }

    public String getEmail() {
        return email;
    }
}
```

This example resembles what is being called JavaBeans in Java language: the regular Java classes written by following the set of conventions, one of those being allow the access to fields using getter and setter methods only.

As we already emphasized in the Inheritance section, please always try to keep the class public contract minimal, following the encapsulation principle. Whatever should not be public, should be private instead (or protected / package priv ate, depending on the problem you are solving). In long run it will pay off, giving you the freedom to evolve your design without introducing breaking changes (or at least minimize them).

3.13 Final classes and methods

In Java, there is a way to prevent the class to be subclassed by any other class: it should be declared as final.

```
package com.javacodegeeks.advanced.design;

public final class FinalClass {
}
```

The same final keyword in the method declaration prevents the method in question to be overridden in subclasses.

```
package com.javacodegeeks.advanced.design;

public class FinalMethod {
    public final void performAction() {
    }
}
```

There are no general rules to decide if class or method should be final or not. Final classes and methods limit the extensibility and it is very hard to think ahead if the class should or should not be subclassed, or method should or should not be overridden. This is particularly important to library developers as the design decisions like that could significantly limit the applicability of the library.

Java standard library has some examples of final classes, with most known being String class. On an early stage, the decision has been taken to proactively prevent any developer's attempts to come up with own, "better" string implementations.

3.14 Download the Source Code

This was a lesson on How to design Classes and Interfaces.

- You may download the source code here: advanced-java-part-3

3.15 What's next

In this part of the tutorial we have looked at object-oriented design concepts in Java. We also briefly walked through contract-based development, touched some functional concepts and saw how the language evolved over time. In next part of the tutorial we are going to meet generics and how they are changing the way we approach type-safe programming.

Chapter 9

Java Compiler API

13.1 Introduction

In this part of the tutorial we are going to take 10000 feet view of the Java Compiler API. This API provides programmatic access to the Java compiler itself and allows developers to compile Java classes from source files on the fly from application code.

More interestingly, we also are going to walk through the Java Compiler Tree API, which provides access to Java syntax parser functionality. By using this API, Java developers have the ability to directly plug into syntax parsing phase and post-analyze Java source code being compiled. It is a very powerful API which is heavily utilized by many static code analysis tools.

The Java Compiler API also supports annotation processing (for more details please refer to part 5 of the tutorial, How and when to use Enums and Annotations, more to come in part 14 of the tutorial, Annotation Processors) and is split between three different packages, shown below.

- javax.annotation.processing :Annotation processing.
- javax.lang.model : Language model used in annotation processing and Compiler Tree API (including Java language elements, types and utility classes).
- javax.tools : Java Compiler API itself.

On the other side, the Java Compiler Tree API is hosted under the com.sun.source package and, following Java standard library naming conventions, is considered to be non-standard (proprietary or internal). In general, these APIs are not very well documented or supported and could change any time. Moreover, they are tied to the particular JDK/JRE version and may limit the portability of the applications which use them.

13.2 Java Compiler API

Our exploration will start from the Java Compiler API, which is quite well documented and easy to use. The entry point into Java Compiler API is the ToolProvider class, which allows to obtain the Java compiler instance available in the system (the official documentation is a great starting point to get familiarized with the typical usage scenarios). For example:

```
final JavaCompiler compiler = ToolProvider.getSystemJavaCompiler();
for( final SourceVersion version: compiler.getSourceVersions() ) {
    System.out.println( version );
}
```

This small code snippet gets the Java compiler instances and prints out on the console a list of supported Java source versions.

For Java 7 compiler, the output looks like this:

```
RELEASE_3
RELEASE_4
RELEASE_5
RELEASE_6
RELEASE_7
```

It corresponds to more well-known Java version scheme: 1.3, 1.4, 5, 6 and 7. For Java 8 compiler, the list of supported versions looks a bit longer:

```
RELEASE_3
RELEASE_4
RELEASE_5
RELEASE_6
RELEASE_7
RELEASE_8
```

Once the instance of Java compiler is available, it could be used to perform different compilation tasks over the set of Java source files. But before that, the set of compilation units and diagnostics collector (to collect all encountered compilation errors) should be prepared. To experiment with, we are going to compile this simple Java class stored in SampleClass.java source file:

```
public class SampleClass {
    public static void main(String[] args) {
        System.out.println( "SampleClass has been compiled!" );
    }
}
```

Having this source file created, let us instantiate the diagnostics collector and configure the list of source files (which includes only SampleClass.java) to compile.

```
final DiagnosticCollector< JavaFileObject > diagnostics = new DiagnosticCollector<>(); final
StandardJavaFileManager manager = compiler.getStandardFileManager(
    diagnostics, null, null );

final File file = new File(
    CompilerExample.class.getResource("/SampleClass.java").toURI() );

final Iterable< ? extends JavaFileObject > sources =
    manager.getJavaFileObjectsFromFiles( Arrays.asList( file ) );
```

Once the preparation is done, the last step is basically to invoke Java compiler task, passing the diagnostics collector and list of source files to it, for example:

```
final CompilationTask task = compiler.getTask( null, manager, diagnostics,
    null, null, sources );
task.call();
```

That is, basically, it. After the compilation task finishes, the SampleClass.class should be available in the target/classes folder. We can run it to make sure compilation has been performed successfully:

```
java -cp target/classes SampleClass
```

The following output will be shown on the console, confirming that the source file has been properly compiled into byte code:

```
SampleClass has been compiled!
```

In case of any errors encountered during the compilation process, they will become available through the diagnostics collector (by default, any additional compiler output will be printed into System.err too). To illustrate that, let us try to compile the sample Java source file which by intention contains some errors (SampleClassWithErrors.java):

```
private class SampleClassWithErrors {
    public static void main(String[] args) {
        System.out.println( "SampleClass has been compiled!" );
    }
}
```

The compilation process should fail and error message (including line number and source file name) could be retrieved from diagnostics collector, for example:

```
for( final Diagnostic< ? extends JavaFileObject > diagnostic:
            diagnostics.getDiagnostics() ) {

        System.out.format("%s, line %d in %s",
            diagnostic.getMessage( null ),
            diagnostic.getLineNumber(),
            diagnostic.getSource().getName() );
}
```

Invoking the compilation task on the SampleClassWithErrors.java source file will print out on the console the following sample error description:

```
modifier private not allowed here, line 1 in SampleClassWithErrors.java
```

Last but not least, to properly finish up working with the Java Compiler API, please do not forget to close file manager:

```
manager.close();
```

Or even better, always use try-with-resources construct (which has been covered in part 8 of the tutorial, How and when to use Exceptions):

```
try( final StandardJavaFileManager manager =
        compiler.getStandardFileManager( diagnostics, null, null ) ) {
    // Implementation here
}
```

In a nutshell, those are typical usage scenarios of Java Compiler API. When dealing with more complicated examples, there is a couple of subtle but quite important details which could speed up the compilation process significantly. To read more about that please refer to the official documentation.

13.3 Annotation Processors

Fortunately, the compilation process is not limited to compilation only. Java Compiler supports annotation processors which could be thought as a compiler plugins. As the name suggests, annotation processors could perform addition processing (usually driven by annotations) over the code being compiled.

In the part 14 of the tutorial, Annotation Processors, we are going to have much more comprehensive coverage and examples of annotation processors. For the moment, please refer to official documentation to get more details.

13.4 Element Scanners

Sometimes it becomes necessary to perform shallow analysis across all language elements (classes, methods/constructors, fields, parameters, variables, . . .) during the compilation process. Specifically for that, the Java Compiler API provides the concept of element scanners. The element scanners are built around visitor pattern and basically require the implementation of the single scanner (and visitor). To simplify the implementation, a set of base classes is kindly provided.

The example we are going to develop is simple enough to show off the basic concepts of element scanners usage and is go-ing to count all classes, methods and fields across all compilation units. The basic scanner / visitor implementation extends ElementScanner7 class and overrides only the methods it is interested in:

```
public class CountClassesMethodsFieldsScanner extends ElementScanner7< Void, Void > {
    private int numberOfClasses;
    private int numberOfMethods;
    private int numberOfFields;

    public Void visitType( final TypeElement type, final Void p ) {
        ++numberOfClasses;

        return super.visitType( type, p );
    }

    public Void visitExecutable( final ExecutableElement executable, final Void p ) {
        ++numberOfMethods;

        return super.visitExecutable( executable, p );
    }

    public Void visitVariable( final VariableElement variable, final Void p ) { if (
        variable.getEnclosingElement().getKind() == ElementKind.CLASS ) {
            ++numberOfFields;
        }

        return super.visitVariable( variable, p );
    }
}
```

Quick note on the element scanners: the family of ElementScannerX classes corresponds to the particular Java version. For instance, ElementScanner8 corresponds to Java 8, ElementScanner7 corresponds to Java 7, ElementScanner6 corresponds to Java 6, and so forth. All those classes do have a family of visitXxx methods which include:

>>> visitPackage : Visits a package element.

>>> visitType : Visits a type element.

>>> visitVariable : Visits a variable element.

>>> visitExecutable : Visits an executable element.

>>> visitTypeParameter : Visits a type parameter element.

One of the ways to invoke the scanner (and visitors) during the compilation process is by using the annotation processor. Let us define one by extending AbstractProcessor class (please notice that annotation processors are also tight to particular Java version, in our case Java 7):

```
@SupportedSourceVersion( SourceVersion.RELEASE_7 )
@SupportedAnnotationTypes( "*" )
  public class CountElementsProcessor extends AbstractProcessor {
     private final CountClassesMethodsFieldsScanner scanner;

    public CountElementsProcessor( final CountClassesMethodsFieldsScanner scanner ) {
        this.scanner = scanner;
    }
```

```
public boolean process( final Set< ? extends TypeElement > types, final
        RoundEnvironment environment ) {

    if( !environment.processingOver() ) {
        for( final Element element: environment.getRootElements() ) {
            scanner.scan( element );
        }
    }

    return true;
```

```
    }
}
```

Basically, the annotation processor just delegates all the hard work to the scanner implementation we have defined before (in the part 14 of the tutorial, Annotation Processors, we are going to have much more comprehensive coverage and examples of annotation processors).

The SampleClassToParse.java file is the example which we are going to compile and count all classes, methods/con-structors and fields in:

```
public class SampleClassToParse {
    private String str;

    private static class InnerClass {
        private int number;

        public void method() {
            int i = 0;

            try {
                    Some      implementation
            here } catch( final Throwable ex ) {
                    Some implementation here
            }
        }
    }

    public static void main( String[] args ) {
        System.out.println( "SampleClassToParse has been compiled!" );
    }
}
```

The compilation procedure looks exactly like we have seen in the Java Compiler API section. The only difference is that compilation task should be configured with annotation processor instance(s). To illustrate that, let us take a look on the code snippet below:

```
final CountClassesMethodsFieldsScanner scanner = new CountClassesMethodsFieldsScanner();
final CountElementsProcessor processor = new CountElementsProcessor( scanner );

final CompilationTask task = compiler.getTask( null, manager, diagnostics, null,
    null, sources );

task.setProcessors( Arrays.asList( processor ) );
task.call();

System.out.format( "Classes %d, methods/constructors %d, fields %d",
    scanner.getNumberOfClasses(),
    scanner.getNumberOfMethods(),
    scanner.getNumberOfFields() );
```

Executing the compilation task against SampleClassToParse.java source file will output the following message in the console:

Classes 2, methods/constructors 4, fields 2

It makes sense: there are two classes declared, SampleClassToParse and InnerClass. SampleClassToParse class has default constructor (defined implicitly), method main and field str. In turn, InnerClass class also has defa ult constructor (defined implicitly), method method and field number.

This example is very naive but its goal is not to demonstrate something fancy but rather to introduce the foundational concepts (the part 14 of the tutorial, Annotation Processors, will include more complete examples).

13.5 Java Compiler Tree API

Element scanners are quite useful but the details they provide access to are quite limited. Once in a while it becomes necessary to parse Java source files into abstract syntax trees (or AST) and perform more deep analysis. Java Compiler Tree API is the tool we need to make it happen. Java Compiler Tree API works closely with Java Compiler API and uses javax.lang.model package.

The usage of Java Compiler Tree API is very similar to the element scanners from section Element Scanners and is built following the same patterns. Let us reuse the sample source file SampleClassToParse.java from Element Scanners section and count how many empty try/catch blocks are present across all compilation units. To do that, we have to define tree path scanner (and visitor), similarly to element scanner (and visitor) by extending TreePathScanner base class.

```
public class EmptyTryBlockScanner extends TreePathScanner< Object, Trees > {
    private int numberOfEmptyTryBlocks;

    @Override
    public Object visitTry(final TryTree tree, Trees trees) { if(
        tree.getBlock().getStatements().isEmpty() ){
            ++numberOfEmptyTryBlocks;
        }

        return super.visitTry( tree, trees );
    }

    public int getNumberOfEmptyTryBlocks() {
        return numberOfEmptyTryBlocks;
    }
}
```

The number of visitXxx methods is significantly richer (around 50 methods) comparing to element scanners and covers all Java language syntax constructs. As with element scanners, one of the ways to invoke tree path scanners is also by defining dedicate annotation processor, for example:

```
@SupportedSourceVersion( SourceVersion.RELEASE_7 )
@SupportedAnnotationTypes( "*" )
public class EmptyTryBlockProcessor extends AbstractProcessor {
    private final EmptyTryBlockScanner scanner;
    private Trees trees;

    public EmptyTryBlockProcessor( final EmptyTryBlockScanner scanner ) {
        this.scanner = scanner;
    }

    @Override
    public synchronized void init( final ProcessingEnvironment processingEnvironment ) {
        super.init( processingEnvironment );
        trees = Trees.instance( processingEnvironment );
    }

    public boolean process( final Set< ? extends TypeElement > types, final
            RoundEnvironment environment ) {

        if( !environment.processingOver() ) {
```

```
            for( final Element element: environment.getRootElements() ) {
                scanner.scan( trees.getPath( element ), trees );
            }
        }

        return true;
    }
}
```

The initialization procedure became a little bit more complex as we have to obtain the instance of Trees class and convert each element into tree path representation. At this moment, the compilation steps should look very familiar and be clear enough. To make it a little bit more interesting, let us run it against all source files we have experimenting with so far: SampleClassToP arse.java and SampleClass.java.

```
final EmptyTryBlockScanner scanner = new EmptyTryBlockScanner();
final EmptyTryBlockProcessor processor = new EmptyTryBlockProcessor( scanner );

final Iterable<? extends JavaFileObject> sources = manager.getJavaFileObjectsFromFiles(
    Arrays.asList(

        new File(CompilerExample.class.getResource("/SampleClassToParse.java").toURI()),
        new File(CompilerExample.class.getResource("/SampleClass.java").toURI())
    )
);

final CompilationTask task = compiler.getTask( null, manager, diagnostics, null,
    null, sources );

task.setProcessors( Arrays.asList( processor ) );
task.call();

System.out.format( "Empty try/catch blocks: %d", scanner.getNumberOfEmptyTryBlocks() );
```

Once run against multiple source files, the code snippet above is going to print the following output in the console:

```
Empty try/catch blocks: 1
```

The Java Compiler Tree API may look a little bit low-level and it certainly is. Plus, being an internal API, it does not have well-supported documentation available. However, it gives the full access to the abstract syntax trees and it is a life-saver when you need to perform deep source code analysis and post-processing.

13.6 Download

This was a lesson for the Java Compiler API, part 13 of Course. You can download the source code of the lesson here: advanced-java-part-13

13.7 What's next

In this part of the tutorial we have looked at programmatic access to Java Compiler API from within the Java applications. We also dug deeper, touched annotation processors and uncovered Java Compiler Tree API which provides the full access to abstract syntax trees of the Java source files being compiled (compilation units). In the next part of the tutorial we are going to continue in the same vein and take a closer look on annotation processors and their applicability.

Chapter 10

Programming in the Large II: Objects and Classes

Whereas a subroutine represents a single task, an object can encapsulate both data (in the form of instance variables) and a number of different tasks or "behaviors" related to that data (in the form of instance methods). Therefore objects provide another, more sophisticated type of structure that can be used to help manage the complexity of large programs.

This chapter covers the creation and use of objects in Java. Section 5.5 covers the central ideas of object-oriented programming: inheritance and polymorphism. However, in this text-book, we will generally use these ideas in a limited form, by creating independent classes and building on existing classes rather than by designing entire hierarchies of classes from scratch. Section 5.6 and Section 5.7 cover some of the many details of object oriented programming in Java. Although these details are used occasionally later in the book, you might want to skim through them now and return to them later when they are actually needed.

5.1 Objects, Instance Methods, and Instance Variables

Object-oriented programming (OOP) represents an attempt to make programs more closely model the way people think about and deal with the world. In the older styles of programming, a programmer who is faced with some problem must identify a computing task that needs to be performed in order to solve the problem. Programming then consists of finding a sequence of instructions that will accomplish that task. But at the heart of object-oriented programming, instead of tasks we find objects—entities that have behaviors, that hold information, and that can interact with one another. Programming consists of designing a set of objects that somehow model the problem at hand. Software objects in the program can represent real or abstract entities in the problem domain. This is supposed to make the design of the program more natural and hence easier to get right and easier to understand.

To some extent, OOP is just a change in point of view. We can think of an object in standard programming terms as nothing more than a set of variables together with some subroutines for manipulating those variables. In fact, it is possible to use object-oriented techniques in any programming language. However, there is a big difference between a language that makes OOP possible and one that actively supports it. An object-oriented programming language such as Java includes a number of features that make it very different from a standard language. In order to make effective use of those features, you have to "orient" your thinking correctly.

5.1.1 Objects, Classes, and Instances

Objects are closely related to classes. We have already been working with classes for several chapters, and we have seen that a class can contain variables and subroutines. If an object is also a collection of variables and subroutines, how do they differ from classes? And why does it require a different type of thinking to understand and use them effectively? In the one section where we worked with objects rather than classes, Section 3.8, it didn't seem to make much difference: We just left the word "static" out of the subroutine definitions!

I have said that classes "describe" objects, or more exactly that the non-static portions of classes describe objects. But it's probably not very clear what this means. The more usual terminology is to say that objects **belong to** classes, but this might not be much clearer. (There is a real shortage of English words to properly distinguish all the concepts involved. An object certainly doesn't "belong" to a class in the same way that a member variable "belongs" to a class.) From the point of view of programming, it is more exact to say that classes are used to create objects. A class is a kind of factory for constructing objects. The non-static parts of the class specify, or describe, what variables and subroutines the objects will contain. This is part of the explanation of how objects differ from classes: Objects are created and destroyed as the program runs, and there can be many objects with the same structure, if they are created using the same class.

Consider a simple class whose job is to group together a few static member variables. For example, the following class could be used to store information about the person who is using the program:

```
class UserData {
    static String name;
    static int age;
}
```

In a program that uses this class, there is only one copy of each of the variables UserData.name and UserData.age. There can only be one "user," since we only have memory space to store data about one user. The class, UserData, and the variables it contains exist as long as the program runs. Now, consider a similar class that includes non-static variables:

```
class PlayerData {
    String name;
    int age;
}
```

In this case, there is no such variable as PlayerData.name or PlayerData.age, since name and age are not static members of PlayerData. So, there is nothing much in the class at all— except the potential to create objects. But, it's a lot of potential, since it can be used to create any number of objects! Each object will have its **own** variables called name and age. There can be many "players" because we can make new objects to represent new players on demand. A program might use this class to store information about multiple players in a game. Each player has a name and an age. When a player joins the game, a new PlayerData object can be created to represent that player. If a player leaves the game, the

PlayerData object that represents that player can be destroyed. A system of objects in the program is being used to dynamically model what is happening in the game. You can't do this with "static" variables!

In Section 3.8, we worked with applets, which are objects. The reason they didn't seem to be any different from classes is because we were only working with one applet in each class that we looked at. But one class can be used to make many applets. Think of an applet that scrolls a message across a Web page. There could be several such applets on the same page, all created from the same class. If the scrolling message in the applet is stored in a non-static variable, then each applet will have its own variable, and each applet can show a different message. The situation is even clearer if you think about windows, which, like applets, are objects. As a program runs, many windows might be opened and closed, but all those windows can belong to the same class. Here again, we have a dynamic situation where multiple objects are created and destroyed as a program runs.

* * *

An object that belongs to a class is said to be an **instance** of that class. The variables that the object contains are called **instance variables**. The subroutines that the object contains are called **instance methods**. (Recall that in the context of object-oriented programming, **method** is a synonym for "subroutine". From now on, since we are doing object-oriented programming, I will prefer the term "method.") For example, if the PlayerData class, as defined above, is used to create an object, then that object is an instance of the PlayerData class, and name and age are instance variables in the object. It is important to remember that the class of an object determines the **types** of the instance variables; however, the actual data is contained inside the individual objects, not the class. Thus, each object has its own set of data.

An applet that scrolls a message across a Web page might include a subroutine named scroll(). Since the applet is an object, this subroutine is an instance method of the applet. The source code for the method is in the class that is used to create the applet. Still, it's better to think of the instance method as belonging to the object, not to the class. The non-static subroutines in the class merely specify the instance methods that every object created from the class will contain. The scroll() methods in two different applets do the same thing in the sense that they both scroll messages across the screen. But there is a real difference between the two scroll() methods. The messages that they scroll can be different. You might say that the method definition in the class specifies what type of behavior the objects will have, but the specific behavior can vary from object to object, depending on the values of their instance variables.

As you can see, the static and the non-static portions of a class are very different things and serve very different purposes. Many classes contain only static members, or only non-static. However, it is possible to mix static and non-static members in a single class, and we'll see a few examples later in this chapter where it is reasonable to do so. You should distiguish between the **source code** for the class, and the **class itself**. The source code determines both the class and the objects that are created from that class. The "static" definitions in the source code specify the things that are part of the class itself, whereas the non-static definitions in the source code specify things that will become part of every instance object that is created from the class. By the way, static member variables and static member subroutines in a class are sometimes called **class variables** and **class methods**, since they belong to the class itself, rather than to instances of that class.

5.1.2 Fundamentals of Objects

So far, I've been talking mostly in generalities, and I haven't given you much idea what you have to put in a program if you want to work with objects. Let's look at a specific example to see how it works. Consider this extremely simplified version of a Student class, which could be used to store information about students taking a course:

```
public class Student {

    public String name;   // Student's name.
    public double test1, test2, test3;          // Grades on three tests.

    public double getAverage() { // compute average test grade
        return (test1 + test2 + test3) / 3;
    }

} // end of class Student
```

None of the members of this class are declared to be static, so the class exists only for creating objects. This class definition says that any object that is an instance of the Student class will include instance variables named name, test1, test2, and test3, and it will include an instance method named getAverage(). The names and tests in different objects will generally have different values. When called for a particular student, the method getAverage() will compute an average using **that student's** test grades. Different students can have different averages. (Again, this is what it means to say that an instance method belongs to an individual object, not to the class.)

In Java, a class is a **type**, similar to the built-in types such as int and boolean. So, a class name can be used to specify the type of a variable in a declaration statement, the type of a formal parameter, or the return type of a function. For example, a program could define a variable named std of type Student with the statement

```
Student std;
```

However, declaring a variable does **not** create an object! This is an important point, which is related to this Very Important Fact:

In Java, no variable can ever hold an object.
A variable can only hold a reference to an object.

You should think of objects as floating around independently in the computer's memory. In fact, there is a special portion of memory called the **heap** where objects live. Instead of holding an object itself, a variable holds the information necessary to find the object in memory. This information is called a **reference** or **pointer** to the object. In effect, a reference to an object is the address of the memory location where the object is stored. When you use a variable of class type, the computer uses the reference in the variable to find the actual object.

In a program, objects are created using an operator called new, which creates an object and returns a reference to that object. For example, assuming that std is a variable of type Student, declared as above, the assignment statement

```
std = new Student();
```

would create a new object which is an instance of the class Student, and it would store a reference to that object in the variable std. The value of the variable is a reference to the object, not the object itself. It is not quite true, then, to say that the object is the "value of the variable std" (though sometimes it is hard to avoid using this terminology). It is certainly **not at all true** to say that the object is "stored in the variable std." The proper terminology is that "the variable std **refers to** the object," and I will try to stick to that terminology as much as possible.

So, suppose that the variable std refers to an object belonging to the class Student. That object has instance variables name, test1, test2, and test3. These instance variables can be referred to as std.name, std.test1, std.test2, and std.test3. This follows the usual naming convention that when B is part of A, then the full name of B is A.B. For example, a program might include the lines

```
System.out.println("Hello, "    + std.name +  ".   Your test grades are:");
System.out.println(std.test1);
System.out.println(std.test2);
System.out.println(std.test3);
```

This would output the name and test grades from the object to which std refers. Simi-larly, std can be used to call the getAverage() instance method in the object by saying std.getAverage(). To print out the student's average, you could say:

```
System.out.println( "Your average is "     + std.getAverage() );
```

More generally, you could use std.name any place where a variable of type String is legal. You can use it in expressions. You can assign a value to it. You can even use it to call subroutines from the String class. For example, std.name.length() is the number of characters in the student's name.

It is possible for a variable like std, whose type is given by a class, to refer to no object at all. We say in this case that std holds a **null reference**. The null reference is written in Java as "null". You can store a null reference in the variable std by saying

```
std = null;
```

and you could test whether the value of std is null by testing

```
if (std == null) . . .
```

If the value of a variable is null, then it is, of course, illegal to refer to instance variables or instance methods through that variable—since there is no object, and hence no instance variables to refer to. For example, if the value of the variable std is null, then it would be illegal to refer to std.test1. If your program attempts to use a null reference illegally like this, the result is an error called a **null pointer exception**.

Let's look at a sequence of statements that work with objects:

```
Student std, std1,          // Declare four variables of
          std2, std3;       //    type Student.
std = new Student();        // Create a new object belonging
                            //  to the class Student, and
                            //  store a reference to that
                            //  object in the variable std.
std1 = new Student();       // Create a second Student object
                            //  and store a reference to
                            //  it in the variable std1.
std2 = std1;                // Copy the reference value in std1
                            //  into the variable std2.
std3 = null;                // Store a null reference in the
                            //    variable std3.

std.name = "John Smith";  // Set values of some instance variables.
std1.name = "Mary Jones";
```

- (Other instance variables have default
- initial values of zero.)

After the computer executes these statements, the situation in the computer's memory looks like this:

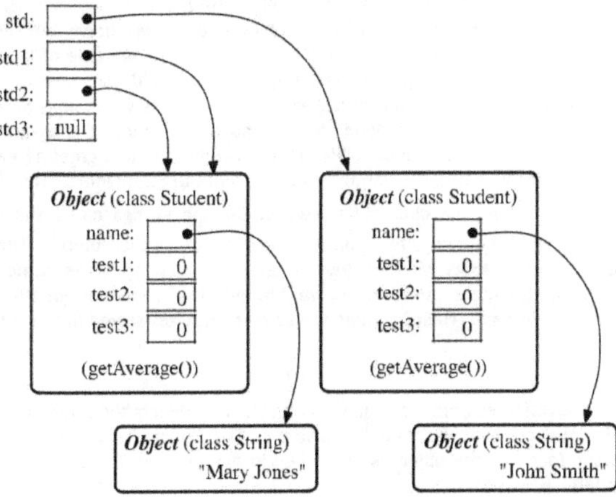

This picture shows variables as little boxes, labeled with the names of the variables. Objects are shown as boxes with round corners. When a variable contains a reference to an object, the value of that variable is shown as an arrow pointing to the object. The variable std3, with a value of null, doesn't point anywhere. The arrows from std1 and std2 both point to the same object. This illustrates a Very Important Point:

When one object variable is assigned to another, only a reference is copied. The object referred to is not copied.

When the assignment "std2 = std1;" was executed, no new object was created. Instead, std2 was set to refer to the very same object that std1 refers to. This has some consequences that might be surprising. For example, std1.name and std2.name are two different names for the same variable, namely the instance variable in the object that both std1 and std2 refer to. After the string "Mary Jones" is assigned to the variable std1.name, it is also true that the value of std2.name is "Mary Jones". There is a potential for a lot of confusion here, but you can help protect yourself from it if you keep telling yourself, "The object is not in the variable. The variable just holds a pointer to the object."

You can test objects for equality and inequality using the operators == and !=, but here again, the semantics are different from what you are used to. When you make a test "if (std1 == std2)", you are testing whether the values stored in std1 and std2 are the same. But the values are references to objects, not objects. So, you are testing whether std1 and std2 refer to the same object, that is, whether they point to the same location in memory. This is fine, if its what you want to do. But sometimes, what you want to check is whether the instance variables in the objects have the same values. To do that, you would need to ask whether "std1.test1 == std2.test1 && std1.test2 == std2.test2 && std1.test3 == std2.test3 && std1.name.equals(std2.name)".

I've remarked previously that Strings are objects, and I've shown the strings "Mary Jones" and "John Smith" as objects in the above illustration. A variable of type String can only hold a reference to a string, not the string itself. It could also hold the value null, meaning that it does not refer to any string at all. This explains why using the == operator to test strings for equality is not a good idea. Suppose that greeting is a variable of type String, and that the string it refers to is "Hello". Then would the test greeting == "Hello" be true? Well, maybe, maybe not. The variable greeting and the String literal "Hello" each refer to a string that contains the characters H-e-l-l-o. But the strings could still be different objects, that just happen to contain the same characters. The function greeting.equals("Hello") tests whether greeting and "Hello" contain the same characters, which is almost certainly the question you want to ask. The expression greeting == "Hello" tests whether greeting and "Hello" contain the same characters **stored in the same memory location.**

* * *

The fact that variables hold references to objects, not objects themselves, has a couple of other consequences that you should be aware of. They follow logically, if you just keep in mind the basic fact that the object is not stored in the variable. The object is somewhere else; the variable points to it.

Suppose that a variable that refers to an object is declared to be final. This means that the value stored in the variable can never be changed, once the variable has been initialized. The value stored in the variable is a reference to the object. So the variable will continue to refer to the same object as long as the variable exists. However, this does not prevent the data **in the object** from changing. The variable is final, not the object. It's perfectly legal to say

```
final Student stu = new Student();

stu.name = "John Doe";  // Change data in the object;
```

- The value stored in stu is not changed!
- It still refers to the same object.

Next, suppose that obj is a variable that refers to an object. Let's consider what happens when obj is passed as an actual parameter to a subroutine. The value of obj is assigned to a formal parameter in the subroutine, and the subroutine is executed. The subroutine has no power to change the value stored in the variable, obj. It only has a copy of that value. However, that value is a reference to an object. Since the subroutine has a reference to the object, it can change the data stored in the object. After the subroutine ends, obj still points to the same object, but the data stored **in the object** might have changed. Suppose x is a variable of type int and stu is a variable of type Student. Compare:

```
void dontChange(int z) {              void change(Student s) {
    z = 42;                                s.name = "Fred";
}                                     }
```

The lines: The lines:

```
x = 17;
dontChange(x);
System.out.println(x);
```

```
stu.name = "Jane";
change(stu);
System.out.println(stu.name);
```

output the value 17.

The value of x is not changed by the subroutine, which is equivalent to

```
z = x;
z = 42;
```

output the value "Fred".

The value of stu is not changed, but stu.name is. This is equivalent to

```
s = stu;
s.name = "Fred";
```

5.1.3 Getters and Setters

When writing new classes, it's a good idea to pay attention to the issue of access control. Recall that making a member of a class public makes it accessible from anywhere, including from other classes. On the other hand, a private member can only be used in the class where it is defined.

In the opinion of many programmers, almost all member variables should be declared private. This gives you complete control over what can be done with the variable. Even if the variable itself is private, you can allow other classes to find out what its value is by providing a public **accessor method** that returns the value of the variable. For example, if your class contains a private member variable, title, of type String, you can provide a method

```
public String getTitle() {
    return title;
}
```

that returns the value of title. By convention, the name of an accessor method for a variable is obtained by capitalizing the name of variable and adding "get" in front of the name. So, for the variable title, we get an accessor method named "get" + "Title", or getTitle(). Because of this naming convention, accessor methods are more often referred to as **getter methods**. A getter method provides "read access" to a variable.

You might also want to allow "write access" to a private variable. That is, you might want to make it possible for other classes to specify a new value for the variable. This is done with a **setter method** . (If you don't like simple, Anglo-Saxon words, you can use the fancier term **mutator method** .) The name of a setter method should consist of "set" followed by a capitalized copy of the variable's name, and it should have a parameter with the same type as the variable. A setter method for the variable title could be written

```
public void setTitle( String newTitle ) {
    title = newTitle;
}
```

It is actually very common to provide both a getter and a setter method for a private member variable. Since this allows other classes both to see and to change the value of the variable, you might wonder why not just make the variable public? The reason is that getters and setters are not restricted to simply reading and writing the variable's value. In fact, they can take any action at all. For example, a getter method might keep track of the number of times that the variable has been accessed:

```
public String getTitle() {
    titleAccessCount++;   // Increment member variable titleAccessCount.
    return title;
}
```

and a setter method might check that the value that is being assigned to the variable is legal:

```
public void setTitle( String newTitle ) {
    if ( newTitle == null )        // Don't allow null strings as titles!
        title = "(Untitled)";      // Use an appropriate default value instead.
    else
        title = newTitle;
}
```

Even if you can't think of any extra chores to do in a getter or setter method, you might change your mind in the future when you redesign and improve your class. If you've used a getter and setter from the beginning, you can make the modification to your class without affecting any of the classes that use your class. The private member variable is not part of the public interface of your class; only the public getter and setter methods are. If you **haven't** used get and set from the beginning, you'll have to contact everyone who uses your class and tell them, "Sorry guys, you'll have to track down every use that you've made of this variable and change your code to use my new get and set methods instead."

A couple of final notes: Some advanced aspects of Java rely on the naming convention for getter and setter methods, so it's a good idea to follow the convention rigorously. And though I've been talking about using getter and setter methods for a variable, you can define get and set methods even if there is no variable. A getter and/or setter method defines a **property** of the class, that might or might not correspond to a variable. For example, if a class includes a public void instance method with signature setValue(double), then the class has a "property" named value of type double, and it has this property whether or not the class has a member variable named value.

5.2 Constructors and Object Initialization

Object types in Java are very different from the primitive types. Simply declaring a variable whose type is given as a class does not automatically create an object of that class. Objects must be explicitly **constructed** . For the computer, the process of constructing an object means, first, finding some unused memory in the heap that can be used to hold the object and, second, filling in the object's instance variables. As a programmer, you don't care where in memory the object is stored, but you will usually want to exercise some control over what initial values are stored in a new object's instance variables. In many cases, you will also want to do more complicated initialization or bookkeeping every time an object is created.

5.2.1 Initializing Instance Variables

An instance variable can be assigned an initial value in its declaration, just like any other variable. For example, consider a class named PairOfDice. An object of this class will represent a pair of dice. It will contain two instance variables to represent the numbers showing on the dice and an instance method for rolling the dice:

```
public class PairOfDice {

    public int die1 = 3;      // Number showing on the first die.
    public int die2 = 4;      // Number showing on the second die.

    public void roll() {
```

- Roll the dice by setting each of the dice to be
- a random number between 1 and 6.

```
die1 = (int)(Math.random()*6) + 1;
```

```
        die2 = (int)(Math.random()*6) + 1;
    }

} // end class PairOfDice
```

The instance variables die1 and die2 are initialized to the values 3 and 4 respectively. These initializations are executed whenever a PairOfDice object is constructed. It's important to understand when and how this happens. There can be many PairOfDice objects. Each time one is created, it gets its own instance variables, and the assignments "die1 = 3" and "die2 = 4" are executed to fill in the values of those variables. To make this clearer, consider a variation of the PairOfDice class:

```
public class PairOfDice {

    public int die1 = (int)(Math.random()*6) + 1;
    public int die2 = (int)(Math.random()*6) + 1;

    public void roll() {
        die1 = (int)(Math.random()*6) + 1;
        die2 = (int)(Math.random()*6) + 1;
    }

} // end class PairOfDice
```

Here, the dice are initialized to random values, as if a new pair of dice were being thrown onto the gaming table. Since the initialization is executed for each new object, a set of random initial values will be computed for each new pair of dice. Different pairs of dice can have different initial values. For initialization of **static** member variables, of course, the situation is quite different. There is only one copy of a static variable, and initialization of that variable is executed just once, when the class is first loaded.

If you don't provide any initial value for an instance variable, a default initial value is pro-vided automatically. Instance variables of numerical type (int, double, etc.) are automatically initialized to zero if you provide no other values; boolean variables are initialized to false; and char variables, to the Unicode character with code number zero. An instance variable can also be a variable of object type. For such variables, the default initial value is null. (In particular, since Strings are objects, the default initial value for String variables is null.)

5.2.2 Constructors

Objects are created with the operator, new. For example, a program that wants to use a PairOfDice object could say:

```
PairOfDice dice;    // Declare a variable of type PairOfDice.

dice = new PairOfDice();    // Construct a new object and store a
                            • reference to it in the variable.
```

In this example, "new PairOfDice()" is an expression that allocates memory for the object, initializes the object's instance variables, and then returns a reference to the object. This reference is the value of the expression, and that value is stored by the assignment statement in the variable, dice, so that after the assignment statement is executed, dice refers to the newly created object. Part of this expression, "PairOfDice()", looks like a subroutine call, and that is no accident. It is, in fact, a call to a special type of subroutine called a **constructor** . This might puzzle you, since there is no such subroutine in the class definition. However, every class has at least one constructor. If the programmer doesn't write a constructor definition in a class, then the system will provide a **default constructor** for that class. This default constructor does nothing beyond the basics: allocate memory and initialize instance variables. If you want more than that to happen when an object is created, you can include one or more constructors in the class definition.

The definition of a constructor looks much like the definition of any other subroutine, with three exceptions. A constructor does not have any return type (not even void). The name of the constructor must be the same as the name of the class in which it is defined. The only modifiers that can be used on a constructor definition are the access modifiers public, private, and protected. (In particular, a constructor can't be declared static.)

However, a constructor does have a subroutine body of the usual form, a block of statements. There are no restrictions on what statements can be used. And it can have a list of formal parameters. In fact, the ability to include parameters is one of the main reasons for using constructors. The parameters can provide data to be used in the construction of the object. For example, a constructor for the PairOfDice class could provide the values that are initially showing on the dice. Here is what the class would look like in that case:

```
public class PairOfDice {

    public int die1;      // Number showing on the first die.
    public int die2;      // Number showing on the second die.

    public PairOfDice(int val1, int val2) {
            • Constructor. Creates a pair of dice that
            • are initially showing the values val1 and val2.
        die1 = val1; // Assign specified values
        die2 = val2;  //              to the instance variables.
    }

    public void roll() {
            • Roll the dice by setting each of the dice to be
            • a random number between 1 and 6.
        die1 = (int)(Math.random()*6) + 1;
        die2 = (int)(Math.random()*6) + 1;
    }

} // end class PairOfDice
```

The constructor is declared as "public PairOfDice(int val1, int val2) ...", with no return type and with the same name as the name of the class. This is how the Java com-piler recognizes a constructor. The constructor has two parameters, and values for these parameters must be provided when the constructor is called. For example, the expression "new PairOfDice(3,4)" would create a PairOfDice object in which the values of the instance variables die1 and die2 are initially 3 and 4. Of course, in a program, the value returned by the constructor should be used in some way, as in

```
PairOfDice dice;              // Declare a variable of type PairOfDice.

dice = new PairOfDice(1,1); // Let dice refer to a new PairOfDice
                        •     object that initially shows 1, 1.
```

Now that we've added a constructor to the PairOfDice class, we can no longer create an object by saying "new PairOfDice()"! The system provides a default constructor for a class

only if the class definition does not already include a constructor, so there is only one constructor in the class, and it requires two actual parameters. However, this is not a big problem, since we can add a second constructor to the class, one that has no parameters. In fact, you can have as many different constructors as you want, as long as their signatures are different, that is, as long as they have different numbers or types of formal parameters. In the PairOfDice class, we might have a constructor with no parameters which produces a pair of dice showing random numbers:

```
public class PairOfDice {

    public  int  die1;    // Number showing on the first die.
    public int die2;      // Number showing on the second die.

    public PairOfDice() {
            • Constructor. Rolls the dice, so that they initially
            • show some random values.
        roll();     // Call the roll() method to roll the dice.
    }

    public PairOfDice(int val1, int val2) {
            • Constructor. Creates a pair of dice that
            • are initially showing the values val1 and val2.
        die1 = val1; // Assign specified values
        die2 = val2;   //              to the instance variables.
    }

    public void roll() {
            • Roll the dice by setting each of the dice to be
            • a random number between 1 and 6.
        die1 = (int)(Math.random()*6) + 1;
        die2 = (int)(Math.random()*6) + 1;
    }

} // end class PairOfDice
```

Now we have the option of constructing a PairOfDice object either with "new PairOfDice()" or with "new PairOfDice(x,y)", where x and y are int-valued expressions.

This class, once it is written, can be used in any program that needs to work with one or more pairs of dice. None of those programs will ever have to use the obscure incantation "(int)(Math.random()*6)+1", because it's done inside the PairOfDice class. And the programmer, having once gotten the dice-rolling thing straight will never have to worry about it again. Here, for example, is a main program that uses the PairOfDice class to count how many times two pairs of dice are rolled before the two pairs come up showing the same value. This illustrates once again that you can create several instances of the same class:

```
public class RollTwoPairs {

    public static void main(String[] args) {

        PairOfDice firstDice;      // Refers to the first pair of dice.
        firstDice = new PairOfDice();

        PairOfDice secondDice; // Refers to the second pair of dice.
        secondDice = new PairOfDice();
                                        int countRolls;
```

```
                    // Counts how many times the two pairs of
                    // dice have been rolled.

int total1;         // Total showing on first pair of dice.
int total2;         // Total showing on second pair of dice.
```

```
        countRolls = 0;

        do {  // Roll the two pairs of dice until totals are the same.

            firstDice.roll(); // Roll the first pair of dice. total1 =
            firstDice.die1 + firstDice.die2; // Get total.
            System.out.println("First pair comes up " + total1);

            secondDice.roll(); // Roll the second pair of dice. total2 =
            secondDice.die1 + secondDice.die2; // Get total.
            System.out.println("Second pair comes up " + total2);

            countRolls++      // Count this roll.
            ;

            System.out.println();     // Blank line.

        } while (total1 != total2);

        System.out.println("It took " + countRolls
                             + " rolls until the totals were the same.");

    } // end main()

} // end class RollTwoPairs
```

* * *

Constructors are subroutines, but they are subroutines of a special type. They are certainly not instance methods, since they don't belong to objects. Since they are responsible for creating objects, they exist before any objects have been created. They are more like static member subroutines, but they are not and cannot be declared to be static. In fact, according to the Java language specification, they are technically not members of the class at all! In particular, constructors are **not** referred to as "methods."

Unlike other subroutines, a constructor can only be called using the new operator, in an expression that has the form

```
new class-name ( parameter-list )
```

where the **parameter-list** is possibly empty. I call this an expression because it computes and returns a value, namely a reference to the object that is constructed. Most often, you will store the returned reference in a variable, but it is also legal to use a constructor call in other ways, for example as a parameter in a subroutine call or as part of a more complex expression. Of course, if you don't save the reference in a variable, you won't have any way of referring to the object that was just created.

A constructor call is more complicated than an ordinary subroutine or function call. It is helpful to understand the exact steps that the computer goes through to execute a constructor call:

- First, the computer gets a block of unused memory in the heap, large enough to hold an object of the specified type.
- It initializes the instance variables of the object. If the declaration of an instance variable specifies an initial value, then that value is computed and stored in the instance variable. Otherwise, the default initial value is used.

- The actual parameters in the constructor, if any, are evaluated, and the values are assigned to the formal parameters of the constructor.

- The statements in the body of the constructor, if any, are executed.
- A reference to the object is returned as the value of the constructor call.

The end result of this is that you have a reference to a newly constructed object. You can use this reference to get at the instance variables in that object or to call its instance methods.

* * *

For another example, let's rewrite the Student class that was used in Section 1. I'll add a constructor, and I'll also take the opportunity to make the instance variable, name, private.

```
public class Student {

    private String name;                    // Student's name.
    public double test1, test2, test3;      // Grades on three tests.

    Student(String theName) {
        • Constructor for Student objects;
        • provides a name for the Student.
      name = theName;
    }

    public String getName() {
        • Getter method for reading the value of the private
        • instance variable, name.
      return name;
    }

    public double getAverage() {
        • Compute average test grade.
      return (test1 + test2 + test3) / 3;
    }

} // end of class Student
```

An object of type Student contains information about some particular student. The constructor in this class has a parameter of type String, which specifies the name of that student. Objects of type Student can be created with statements such as:

```
std = new Student("John Smith");
std1 = new Student("Mary Jones");
```

In the original version of this class, the value of name had to be assigned by a program after it created the object of type Student. There was no guarantee that the programmer would always remember to set the name properly. In the new version of the class, there is no way to create a Student object except by calling the constructor, and that constructor automatically sets the name. The programmer's life is made easier, and whole hordes of frustrating bugs are squashed before they even have a chance to be born.

Another type of guarantee is provided by the private modifier. Since the instance variable, name, is private, there is no way for any part of the program outside the Student class to get at the name directly. The program sets the value of name, indirectly, when it calls the constructor. I've provided a function, getName(), that can be used from outside the class to find out the name of the student. But I haven't provided any setter method or other way to change the name. Once a student object is created, it keeps the same name as long as it exists.

5.2.3 Garbage Collection

So far, this section has been about creating objects. What about destroying them? In Java, the destruction of objects takes place automatically.

An object exists in the heap, and it can be accessed only through variables that hold references to the object. What should be done with an object if there are no variables that refer to it? Such things can happen. Consider the following two statements (though in reality, you'd never do anything like this):

```
Student std = new Student("John Smith");
std = null;
```

In the first line, a reference to a newly created Student object is stored in the variable std. But in the next line, the value of std is changed, and the reference to the Student object is gone. In fact, there are now no references whatsoever to that object stored in any variable. So there is no way for the program ever to use the object again. It might as well not exist. In fact, the memory occupied by the object should be reclaimed to be used for another purpose.

Java uses a procedure called **garbage collection** to reclaim memory occupied by objects that are no longer accessible to a program. It is the responsibility of the system, not the programmer, to keep track of which objects are "garbage." In the above example, it was very easy to see that the Student object had become garbage. Usually, it's much harder. If an object has been used for a while, there might be several references to the object stored in several variables. The object doesn't become garbage until all those references have been dropped.

In many other programming languages, it's the programmer's responsibility to delete the garbage. Unfortunately, keeping track of memory usage is very error-prone, and many serious program bugs are caused by such errors. A programmer might accidently delete an object even though there are still references to that object. This is called a **dangling pointer error** , and it leads to problems when the program tries to access an object that is no longer there. Another type of error is a **memory leak** , where a programmer neglects to delete objects that are no longer in use. This can lead to filling memory with objects that are completely inaccessible, and the program might run out of memory even though, in fact, large amounts of memory are being wasted.

Because Java uses garbage collection, such errors are simply impossible. Garbage collection is an old idea and has been used in some programming languages since the 1960s. You might wonder why all languages don't use garbage collection. In the past, it was considered too slow and wasteful. However, research into garbage collection techniques combined with the incredible speed of modern computers have combined to make garbage collection feasible. Programmers should rejoice.

5.3 Programming with Objects

There are several ways in which object-oriented concepts can be applied to the process of designing and writing programs. The broadest of these is **object-oriented analysis and design** which applies an object-oriented methodology to the earliest stages of program devel-opment, during which the overall design of a program is created. Here, the idea is to identify things in the problem domain that can be modeled as objects. On another level, object-oriented programming encourages programmers to produce **generalized software components** that can be used in a wide variety of programming projects.

Of course, for the most part, you will experience "generalized software components" by using the standard classes that come along with Java. We begin this section by looking at some built-in classes that are used for creating objects. At the end of the section, we will get back to generalities.

5.3.1 Some Built-in Classes

Although the focus of object-oriented programming is generally on the design and implementa-tion of new classes, it's important not to forget that the designers of Java have already provided a large number of reusable classes. Some of these classes are meant to be extended to produce new classes, while others can be used directly to create useful objects. A true mastery of Java requires familiarity with a large number of built-in classes—something that takes a lot of time and experience to develop. In the next chapter, we will begin the study of Java's GUI classes, and you will encounter other built-in classes throughout the remainder of this book. But let's take a moment to look at a few built-in classes that you might find useful.

A string can be built up from smaller pieces using the + operator, but this is not very efficient. If str is a String and ch is a character, then executing the command "str = str + ch;" involves creating a whole new string that is a copy of str, with the value of ch appended onto the end. Copying the string takes some time. Building up a long string letter by letter would require a surprising amount of processing. The class StringBuffer makes it possible to be efficient about building up a long string from a number of smaller pieces. To do this, you must make an object belonging to the StringBuffer class. For example:

```
StringBuffer buffer = new StringBuffer();
```

(This statement both declares the variable buffer and initializes it to refer to a newly created StringBuffer object. Combining declaration with initialization was covered in Subsection 4.7.1 and works for objects just as it does for primitive types.)

Like a String, a StringBuffer contains a sequence of characters. However, it is possible to add new characters onto the end of a StringBuffer without making a copy of the data that it already contains. If x is a value of any type and buffer is the variable defined above, then the command buffer.append(x) will add x, converted into a string representation, onto the end of the data that was already in the buffer. This command actually modifies the buffer, rather than making a copy, and that can be done efficiently. A long string can be built up in a StringBuffer using a sequence of append() commands. When the string is complete, the function buffer.toString() will return a copy of the string in the buffer as an ordinary value of type String. The StringBuffer class is in the standard package java.lang, so you can use its simple name without importing it.

A number of useful classes are collected in the package java.util. For example, this package contains classes for working with collections of objects. We will study these collection classes in Chapter 10. Another class in this package, java.util.Date, is used to represent times. When a Date object is constructed without parameters, the result represents the current date and time, so an easy way to display this information is:

```
System.out.println( new Date() );
```

Of course, to use the Date class in this way, you must make it available by importing it with one of the statements "import java.util.Date;" or "import java.util.*;" at the beginning of your program. (See Subsection 4.5.3 for a discussion of packages and import.)

I will also mention the class java.util.Random. An object belonging to this class is a **source** of random numbers (or, more precisely pseudorandom numbers). The standard function

Math.random() uses one of these objects behind the scenes to generate its random numbers. An object of type Random can generate random integers, as well as random real numbers. If randGen is created with the command:

```
Random randGen = new Random();
```

and if N is a positive integer, then randGen.nextInt(N) generates a random integer in the range from 0 to N-1. For example, this makes it a little easier to roll a pair of dice. Instead of say-ing "die1 = (int)(6*Math.random())+1;", one can say "die1 = randGen.nextInt(6)+1;". (Since you also have to import the class java.util.Random and create the Random object, you might not agree that it is actually easier.) An object of type Random can also be used to generate so-called Gaussian distributed random real numbers.

The main point here, again, is that many problems have already been solved, and the solutions are available in Java's standard classes. If you are faced with a task that looks like it should be fairly common, it might be worth looking through a Java reference to see whether someone has already written a class that you can use.

5.3.2 Wrapper Classes and Autoboxing

We have already encountered the classes Double and Integer in Subsection 2.5.7. These classes contain the static methods Double.parseDouble and Integer.parseInteger that are used to convert strings to numerical values. We have also encountered the Character class in some examples, and static methods such as Character.isLetter, which can be used to test whether a given value of type char is a letter. There is a similar class for each of the other primitive types, Long, Short, Byte, Float, and Boolean. These classes are called **wrapper classes**. Although they contain useful static members, they have another use as well: They are used for creating objects that represent primitive type values.

Remember that the primitive types are not classes, and values of primitive type are not objects. However, sometimes it's useful to treat a primitive value as if it were an object. You can't do that literally, but you can "wrap" the primitive type value in an object belonging to one of the wrapper classes.

For example, an object of type Double contains a single instance variable, of type double. The object is a wrapper for the double value. For example, you can create an object that wraps the double value 6.0221415e23 with

```
Double d = new Double(6.0221415e23);
```

The value of d contains the same information as the value of type double, but it is an object. If you want to retrieve the double value that is wrapped in the object, you can call the function d.doubleValue(). Similarly, you can wrap an int in an object of type Integer, a boolean value in an object of type Boolean, and so on. (As an example of where this would be useful, the collection classes that will be studied in Chapter 10 can only hold objects. If you want to add a primitive type value to a collection, it has to be put into a wrapper object first.)

In Java 5.0, wrapper classes have become easier to use. Java 5.0 introduced automatic conversion between a primitive type and the corresponding wrapper class. For example, if you use a value of type int in a context that requires an object of type Integer, the int will automatically be wrapped in an Integer object. For example, you can say

```
Integer answer = 42;
```

and the computer will silently read this as if it were

Integer answer = new Integer(42);

This is called **autoboxing** . It works in the other direction, too. For example, if d refers to an object of type Double, you can use d in a numerical expression such as 2*d. The double value inside d is automatically **unboxed** and multiplied by 2. Autoboxing and unboxing also apply to subroutine calls. For example, you can pass an actual parameter of type int to a subroutine that has a formal parameter of type Integer. In fact, autoboxing and unboxing make it possible in many circumstances to ignore the difference between primitive types and objects.

* * *

The wrapper classes contain a few other things that deserve to be mentioned. Integer, for example, contains constants Integer.MIN VALUE and Integer.MAX VALUE, which are equal to the largest and smallest possible values of type int, that is, to -2147483648 and 2147483647 respectively. It's certainly easier to remember the names than the numerical values. There are similar named constants in Long, Short, and Byte. Double and Float also have constants named MIN VALUE and MAX VALUE. MAX VALUE still gives the largest number that can be represented in the given type, but MIN VALUE represents the smallest possible **positive** value. For type double, Double.MIN VALUE is 4.9 times 10^{-324}. Since double values have only a finite accuracy, they can't get arbitrarily close to zero. This is the closest they can get without actually being equal to zero.

The class Double deserves special mention, since doubles are so much more complicated than integers. The encoding of real numbers into values of type double has room for a few special val-ues that are not real numbers at all in the mathematical sense. These values are given by named constants in class Double: Double.POSITIVE INFINITY, Double.NEGATIVE INFINITY, and Double.NaN. The infinite values can occur as the values of certain mathematical expressions. For example, dividing a positive number by zero will give the result Double.POSITIVE INFINITY. (It's even more complicated than this, actually, because the double type includes a value called "negative zero", written -0.0. Dividing a positive number by negative zero gives Double.NEGATIVE INFINITY.) You also get Double.POSITIVE INFINITY whenever the mathe-matical value of an expression is greater than Double.MAX VALUE. For example, 1e200*1e200 is considered to be infinite. The value Double.NaN is even more interesting. "NaN" stands for **Not a Number** , and it represents an undefined value such as the square root of a negative number or the result of dividing zero by zero. Because of the existence of Double.NaN, no math-ematical operation on real numbers will ever throw an exception; it simply gives Double.NaN as the result.

You can test whether a value, x, of type double is infinite or undefined by calling the boolean-valued static functions Double.isInfinite(x) and Double.isNaN(x). (It's especially important to use Double.isNaN() to test for undefined values, because Double.NaN has re-ally weird behavior when used with relational operators such as ==. In fact, the values of

• == Double.NaN and x != Double.NaN are **both false**, no matter what the value of x, so you really can't use these expressions to test whether x is Double.NaN.)

5.3.3 The class "Object"

We have already seen that one of the major features of object-oriented programming is the ability to create subclasses of a class. The subclass inherits all the properties or behaviors of the class, but can modify and add to what it inherits. In Section 5.5, you'll learn how to create subclasses. What you don't know yet is that **every** class in Java (with just one exception) is a subclass of some other class. If you create a class and don't explicitly make it a subclass of some other class, then it automatically becomes a subclass of the special class named Object. (Object is the one class that is not a subclass of any other class.)

Class Object defines several instance methods that are inherited by every other class. These methods can be used with any object whatsoever. I will mention just one of them here. You will encounter more of them later in the book.

The instance method toString() in class Object returns a value of type String that is supposed to be a string representation of the object. You've already used this method implicitly, any time you've printed out an object or concatenated an object onto a string. When you use an object in a context that requires a string, the object is automatically converted to type String by calling its toString() method.

The version of toString that is defined in Object just returns the name of the class that the object belongs to, concatenated with a code number called the **hash code** of the object; this is not very useful. When you create a class, you can write a new toString() method for it, which will replace the inherited version. For example, we might add the following method to any of the PairOfDice classes from the previous section:

```
public String toString() {
        • Return a String representation of a pair of dice, where die1
        • and die2 are instance variables containing the numbers that are
        • showing on the two dice.
    if (die1 == die2)
        return "double " + die1;
    else
        return die1 + " and " + die2;
}
```

If dice refers to a PairOfDice object, then dice.toString() will return strings such as "3 and 6", "5 and 1", and "double 2", depending on the numbers showing on the dice. This method would be used automatically to convert dice to type String in a statement such as

```
System.out.println( "The dice came up " + dice );
```

so this statement might output, "The dice came up 5 and 1" or "The dice came up double 2".
You'll see another example of a toString() method in the next section.

5.3.4 Object-oriented Analysis and Design

Every programmer builds up a stock of techniques and expertise expressed as snippets of code that can be reused in new programs using the tried-and-true method of cut-and-paste: The old code is physically copied into the new program and then edited to customize it as necessary. The problem is that the editing is error-prone and time-consuming, and the whole enterprise is dependent on the programmer's ability to pull out that particular piece of code from last year's project that looks like it might be made to fit. (On the level of a corporation that wants to save money by not reinventing the wheel for each new project, just keeping track of all the old wheels becomes a major task.)

Well-designed classes are software components that can be reused without editing. A well-designed class is not carefully crafted to do a particular job in a particular program. Instead, it is crafted to model some particular type of object or a single coherent concept.

Since objects and concepts can recur in many problems, a well-designed class is likely to be reusable without modification in a variety of projects.

Furthermore, in an object-oriented programming language, it is possible to make **subclasses** of an existing class. This makes classes even more reusable. If a class needs to be customized, a subclass can be created, and additions or modifications can be made in the subclass without making any changes to the original class. This can be done even if the programmer doesn't have access to the source code of the class and doesn't know any details of its internal, hidden implementation.

* * *

The PairOfDice class in the previous section is already an example of a generalized software component, although one that could certainly be improved. The class represents a single, coherent concept, "a pair of dice." The instance variables hold the data relevant to the state of the dice, that is, the number showing on each of the dice. The instance method represents the behavior of a pair of dice, that is, the ability to be rolled. This class would be reusable in many different programming projects.

On the other hand, the Student class from the previous section is not very reusable. It seems to be crafted to represent students in a particular course where the grade will be based on three tests. If there are more tests or quizzes or papers, it's useless. If there are two people in the class who have the same name, we are in trouble (one reason why numerical student ID's are often used). Admittedly, it's much more difficult to develop a general-purpose student class than a general-purpose pair-of-dice class. But this particular Student class is good mostly as an example in a programming textbook.

* * *

A large programming project goes through a number of stages, starting with **specification** of the problem to be solved, followed by **analysis** of the problem and **design** of a program to solve it. Then comes **coding** , in which the program's design is expressed in some actual programming language. This is followed by **testing** and **debugging** of the program. After that comes a long period of **maintenance**, which means fixing any new problems that are found in the program and modifying it to adapt it to changing requirements. Together, these stages form what is called the **software life cycle**. (In the real world, the ideal of consecutive stages is seldom if ever achieved. During the analysis stage, it might turn out that the specifications are incomplete or inconsistent. A problem found during testing requires at least a brief return to the coding stage. If the problem is serious enough, it might even require a new design. Maintenance usually involves redoing some of the work from previous stages. . . .)

Large, complex programming projects are only likely to succeed if a careful, systematic approach is adopted during all stages of the software life cycle. The systematic approach to programming, using accepted principles of good design, is called **software engineering** . The software engineer tries to efficiently construct programs that verifiably meet their specifications and that are easy to modify if necessary. There is a wide range of "methodologies" that can be applied to help in the systematic design of programs. (Most of these methodologies seem to involve drawing little boxes to represent program components, with labeled arrows to represent relationships among the boxes.)

We have been discussing object orientation in programming languages, which is relevant to the coding stage of program development. But there are also object-oriented methodologies for analysis and design. The question in this stage of the software life cycle is, How can one discover or invent the overall structure of a program? As an example of a rather simple object-oriented approach to analysis and design, consider this advice: Write down a description of the problem. Underline all the nouns in that description. The nouns should be considered as candidates for becoming classes or objects in the program design. Similarly, underline all the verbs. These are candidates for methods. This is your starting point. Further analysis might uncover the need for more classes and methods, and it might reveal that subclassing can be used to take advantage of similarities among classes.

This is perhaps a bit simple-minded, but the idea is clear and the general approach can be effective: Analyze the problem to discover the concepts that are involved, and create classes to represent those concepts. The design should arise from the problem itself, and you should end up with a program whose structure reflects the structure of the problem in a natural way.

5.4 Programming Example: Card, Hand, Deck

In this section, we look at some specific examples of object-oriented design in a domain that is simple enough that we have a chance of coming up with something reasonably reusable. Consider card games that are played with a standard deck of playing cards (a so-called "poker" deck, since it is used in the game of poker).

5.4.1 Designing the classes

In a typical card game, each player gets a hand of cards. The deck is shuffled and cards are dealt one at a time from the deck and added to the players' hands. In some games, cards can be removed from a hand, and new cards can be added. The game is won or lost depending on the value (ace, 2, . . . , king) and suit (spades, diamonds, clubs, hearts) of the cards that a player receives. If we look for nouns in this description, there are several candidates for objects: game, player, hand, card, deck, value, and suit. Of these, the value and the suit of a card are simple values, and they will just be represented as instance variables in a Card object. In a complete program, the other five nouns might be represented by classes. But let's work on the ones that are most obviously reusable: card, hand, and deck.

If we look for verbs in the description of a card game, we see that we can shuffle a deck and deal a card from a deck. This gives use us two candidates for instance methods in a Deck class: shuffle() and dealCard(). Cards can be added to and removed from hands. This gives two candidates for instance methods in a Hand class: addCard() and removeCard(). Cards are relatively passive things, but we need to be able to determine their suits and values. We will discover more instance methods as we go along.

First, we'll design the deck class in detail. When a deck of cards is first created, it contains 52 cards in some standard order. The Deck class will need a constructor to create a new deck. The constructor needs no parameters because any new deck is the same as any other. There will be an instance method called shuffle() that will rearrange the 52 cards into a random order. The dealCard() instance method will get the next card from the deck. This will be a function with a return type of Card, since the caller needs to know what card is being dealt. It has no parameters—when you deal the next card from the deck, you don't provide any information to the deck; you just get the next card, whatever it is. What will happen if there are no more cards in the deck when its dealCard() method is called? It should probably be considered an error to try to deal a card from an empty deck, so the deck can throw an exception in that case. But this raises another question: How will the rest of the program know whether the deck is empty? Of course, the program could keep track of how many cards it has used. But the deck itself should know how many cards it has left, so the program should just be able to ask the deck object. We can make this possible by specifying another instance method, cardsLeft(), that returns the number of cards remaining in the deck. This leads to a full specification of all the subroutines in the Deck class:

Constructor and instance methods in class Deck:

public Deck()
// Constructor. Create an unshuffled deck of cards.

public void shuffle()
- Put all the used cards back into the deck,
- and shuffle it into a random order.

public int cardsLeft()
- As cards are dealt from the deck, the number of
- cards left decreases. This function returns the
- number of cards that are still left in the deck.

public Card dealCard()
- Deals one card from the deck and returns it.
- Throws an exception if no more cards are left.

This is everything you need to know in order to use the Deck class. Of course, it doesn't tell us how to write the class. This has been an exercise in design, not in programming. In fact, writing the class involves a programming technique, arrays, which will not be covered until Chapter 7. Nevertheless, you can look at the source code, **Deck.java**, if you want. Even though you won't understand the implementation, the Javadoc comments give you all the information that you need to understand the interface. With this information, you can use the class in your programs without understanding the implementation.

We can do a similar analysis for the Hand class. When a hand object is first created, it has no cards in it. An addCard() instance method will add a card to the hand. This method needs a parameter of type Card to specify which card is being added. For the removeCard() method, a parameter is needed to specify which card to remove. But should we specify the card itself ("Remove the ace of spades"), or should we specify the card by its position in the hand ("Remove the third card in the hand")? Actually, we don't have to decide, since we can allow for both options. We'll have two removeCard() instance methods, one with a parameter of type Card specifying the card to be removed and one with a parameter of type int specifying the position of the card in the hand. (Remember that you can have two methods in a class with the same name, provided they have different types of parameters.) Since a hand can contain a variable number of cards, it's convenient to be able to ask a hand object how many cards it contains. So, we need an instance method getCardCount() that returns the number of cards in the hand. When I play cards, I like to arrange the cards in my hand so that cards of the same value are next to each other. Since this is a generally useful thing to be able to do, we can provide instance methods for sorting the cards in the hand. Here is a full specification for a reusable Hand class:

Constructor and instance methods in class Hand:

public Hand() {
// Create a Hand object that is initially empty.

public void clear() {
// Discard all cards from the hand, making the hand empty.

public void addCard(Card c) {

- Add the card c to the hand. c should be non-null.
- If c is null, a NullPointerException is thrown.

public void removeCard(Card c) {
// If the specified card is in the hand, it is removed.

public void removeCard(int position) {
- Remove the card in the specified position from the
- hand. Cards are numbered counting from zero. If
- the specified position does not exist, then an
- exception is thrown.

public int getCardCount() {
// Return the number of cards in the hand.

public Card getCard(int position) {
- Get the card from the hand in given position, where
- positions are numbered starting from 0. If the
- specified position is not the position number of
- a card in the hand, an exception is thrown.

public void sortBySuit() {
- Sorts the cards in the hand so that cards of the same
- suit are grouped together, and within a suit the cards
- are sorted by value. Note that aces are considered
- to have the lowest value, 1.

public void sortByValue() {
- Sorts the cards in the hand so that cards are sorted into
- order of increasing value. Cards with the same value
- are sorted by suit. Note that aces are considered
- to have the lowest value.

Again, you don't yet know enough to implement this class. But given the source code, **Hand.java**, you can use the class in your own programming projects.

5.4.2 The Card Class

We **have** covered enough material to write a Card class. The class will have a constructor that specifies the value and suit of the card that is being created. There are four suits, which can be represented by the integers 0, 1, 2, and 3. It would be tough to remember which number represents which suit, so I've defined named constants in the Card class to represent the four possibilities. For example, Card.SPADES is a constant that represents the suit, spades. (These constants are declared to be public final static ints. It might be better to use an enumerated type, but for now we will stick to integer-valued constants. I'll return to the question of using enumerated types in this example at the end of the chapter.) The possible values of a card are the numbers 1, 2, . . . , 13, with 1 standing for an ace, 11 for a jack, 12 for a queen, and 13 for a king. Again, I've defined some named constants to represent the values of aces and face cards. (When you read the Card class, you'll see that I've also added support for Jokers.)

A Card object can be constructed knowing the value and the suit of the card. For example, we can call the constructor with statements such as:

```
card1 = new Card( Card.ACE, Card.SPADES );  // Construct ace of spades.
card2 = new Card( 10, Card.DIAMONDS );  // Construct 10 of diamonds.
```

```
card3 = new Card( v, s );        // This is OK, as long as v and s
                                 //                are integer expressions.
```

A Card object needs instance variables to represent its value and suit. I've made these private so that they cannot be changed from outside the class, and I've provided getter methods getSuit() and getValue() so that it will be possible to discover the suit and value from outside the class. The instance variables are initialized in the constructor, and are never changed after that. In fact, I've declared the instance variables suit and value to be final, since they are never changed after they are initialized. (An instance variable can be declared final provided it is either given an initial value in its declaration or is initialized in every constructor in the class.)

Finally, I've added a few convenience methods to the class to make it easier to print out cards in a human-readable form. For example, I want to be able to print out the suit of a card as the word "Diamonds", rather than as the meaningless code number 2, which is used in the class to represent diamonds. Since this is something that I'll probably have to do in many programs, it makes sense to include support for it in the class. So, I've provided instance methods getSuitAsString() and getValueAsString() to return string representations of the suit and value of a card. Finally, I've defined the instance method toString() to return a string with both the value and suit, such as "Queen of Hearts". Recall that this method will be used whenever a Card needs to be converted into a String, such as when the card is concatenated onto a string with the + operator. Thus, the statement

```
System.out.println( "Your card is the " + card );
```

is equivalent to

```
System.out.println( "Your card is the " + card.toString() );
```

If the card is the queen of hearts, either of these will print out "Your card is the Queen of Hearts".

Here is the complete Card class. It is general enough to be highly reusable, so the work that went into designing, writing, and testing it pays off handsomely in the long run.

```
/**
 • An object of type Card represents a playing card from a
 • standard Poker deck, including Jokers. The card has a suit, which
 • can be spades, hearts, diamonds, clubs, or joker. A spade, heart,
 • diamond, or club has one of the 13 values: ace, 2, 3, 4, 5, 6, 7,
 • 8, 9, 10, jack, queen, or king. Note that "ace" is considered to be
 • the smallest value. A joker can also have an associated value;
 • this value can be anything and can be used to keep track of several
 • different jokers.
 */
public class Card {

   public final static int SPADES = 0;
   public final static int HEARTS = 1;
   public final static int DIAMONDS = 2;
   public final static int CLUBS = 3; public
   final static int JOKER = 4;

   public final static int ACE = 1; public
   final static int JACK = 11; public final
static int QUEEN = 12; public
final static int KING = 13;

/**
```

- Codes for the 4 suits, plus Joker.

- Codes for the non-numeric cards.
- Cards 2 through 10 have their
- numerical values for their codes.

```
  • This card's suit, one of the constants SPADES, HEARTS, DIAMONDS,
  • CLUBS, or JOKER. The suit cannot be changed after the card is
  • constructed.
  */
private final int suit;

/**
  • The card's value. For a normal cards, this is one of the values
  • 1 through 13, with 1 representing ACE. For a JOKER, the value
  • can be anything. The value cannot be changed after the card
  • is constructed.
  */
private final int value;

/**
  • Creates a Joker, with 1 as the associated value. (Note that
  • "new Card()" is equivalent to "new Card(1,Card.JOKER)".)
  */
public Card() {
   suit = JOKER;
   value = 1;
}

/**
  • Creates a card with a specified suit and value.
  • @param theValue the value of the new card. For a regular card (non-joker),
  • the value must be in the range 1 through 13, with 1 representing an Ace.
  • You can use the constants Card.ACE, Card.JACK, Card.QUEEN, and Card.KING.
  • For a Joker, the value can be anything.
  • @param theSuit the suit of the new card. This must be one of the values
  • Card.SPADES, Card.HEARTS, Card.DIAMONDS, Card.CLUBS, or Card.JOKER.
  • @throws IllegalArgumentException if the parameter values are not in the
  • permissible ranges
  */
public Card(int theValue, int theSuit) {
   if (theSuit != SPADES && theSuit != HEARTS && theSuit != DIAMONDS
         && theSuit != CLUBS && theSuit != JOKER)
      throw new IllegalArgumentException("Illegal playing card suit"); if
   (theSuit != JOKER && (theValue < 1 || theValue > 13))
      throw new IllegalArgumentException("Illegal playing card value");
   value = theValue;
   suit = theSuit;
}

/**
  • Returns the suit of this card.
  • @returns the suit, which is one of the constants Card.SPADES,
  • Card.HEARTS, Card.DIAMONDS, Card.CLUBS, or Card.JOKER
  */
public int getSuit() {
```

return suit;
}

/**

- Returns the value of this card.
- @return the value, which is one the numbers 1 through 13, inclusive for

```
 • a regular card, and which can be any value for a Joker. */
public int getValue() {
    return value;
}

/**
 • Returns a String representation of the card's suit.
 • @return one of the strings "Spades", "Hearts", "Diamonds", "Clubs"
 • or "Joker".
 */
public String getSuitAsString() {
    switch ( suit ) {
    case SPADES:   return "Spades";
    case HEARTS:   return "Hearts";
    case DIAMONDS: return "Diamonds";
    case CLUBS:    return "Clubs";
    default:       return "Joker";
    }
}

/**
 • Returns a String representation of the card's value.
 • @return for a regular card, one of the strings "Ace", "2",
 • "3", ..., "10", "Jack", "Queen", or "King".  For a Joker, the
 • string is always a numerical.
 */
public String getValueAsString() {
    if (suit == JOKER)
        return "" + value;
    else {
        switch ( value ) {
        case 1:   return "Ace";
        case 2:   return "2";
        case 3:   return "3";
        case 4:   return "4";
        case 5:   return "5";
        case 6:   return "6";
        case 7:   return "7";
        case 8:   return "8";
        case 9:   return "9";
        case 10:  return "10";
        case 11:  return "Jack";
        case 12:  return "Queen";
        default:  return "King";
        }
    }
}

/**
 • Returns a string representation of this card, including both
```

- its suit and its value (except that for a Joker with value 1,
- the return value is just "Joker"). Sample return values
- are: "Queen of Hearts", "10 of Diamonds", "Ace of Spades",
- "Joker", "Joker #2"

```
    */
    public String toString() {
        if (suit == JOKER) {
            if (value == 1)
                return "Joker";
            else
                return "Joker #" + value;
        }
        else
            return getValueAsString() + " of " + getSuitAsString();
    }

} // end class Card
```

5.4.3 Example: A Simple Card Game

I will finish this section by presenting a complete program that uses the Card and Deck classes. The program lets the user play a very simple card game called HighLow. A deck of cards is shuffled, and one card is dealt from the deck and shown to the user. The user predicts whether the next card from the deck will be higher or lower than the current card. If the user predicts correctly, then the next card from the deck becomes the current card, and the user makes another prediction. This continues until the user makes an incorrect prediction. The number of correct predictions is the user's score.

My program has a subroutine that plays one game of HighLow. This subroutine has a return value that represents the user's score in the game. The main() routine lets the user play several games of HighLow. At the end, it reports the user's average score.

I won't go through the development of the algorithms used in this program, but I encourage you to read it carefully and make sure that you understand how it works. Note in particular that the subroutine that plays one game of HighLow returns the user's score in the game as its return value. This gets the score back to the main program, where it is needed. Here is the program:

```
/**
 • This program lets the user play HighLow, a simple card game
 • that is described in the output statements at the beginning of
 • the main() routine. After the user plays several games,
 • the user's average score is reported.
 */

public class HighLow {

    public static void main(String[] args) {

        System.out.println("This program lets you play the simple card game,");
        System.out.println("HighLow.   A card is dealt from a deck of cards.");
        System.out.println("You have to predict whether the next card will be");
        System.out.println("higher or lower.        Your score in the game is the");
        System.out.println("number of correct predictions you make before");
        System.out.println("you guess wrong.");
```

```
System.out.println();

int gamesPlayed = 0;        // Number of games user has played.
int sumOfScores = 0;        // The sum of all the scores from
```

```
                                  •         all the games played.
    double averageScore;       // Average score, computed by dividing
                                  •         sumOfScores by gamesPlayed.
    boolean playAgain;         // Record user's response when user is
                                  •     asked whether he wants to play
                                  •     another game.

    do {
        int scoreThisGame;          // Score for one game.
        scoreThisGame = play();     // Play the game and get the score.
        sumOfScores += scoreThisGame;
        gamesPlayed++;
        TextIO.put("Play again? ");
        playAgain = TextIO.getlnBoolean();
    } while (playAgain);

    averageScore = ((double)sumOfScores) / gamesPlayed;

    System.out.println();
    System.out.println("You played " + gamesPlayed + " games.");
    System.out.printf("Your average score was %1.3f.\n", averageScore);

} // end main()

/**
 • Lets the user play one game of HighLow, and returns the
 • user's score on that game. The score is the number of
 • correct guesses that the user makes.
 */
private static int play() {

    Deck deck = new Deck();  // Get a new deck of cards, and
                                  •     store a reference to it in
                                  •     the variable, deck.

    Card currentCard;   // The current card, which the user sees.

    Card nextCard;   // The next card in the deck.      The user tries
                         •      to predict whether this is higher or lower
                         •      than the current card.

    int correctGuesses ;     // The number of correct predictions the
                               •     user has made. At the end of the game,
                               •     this will be the user's score.

      char guess;    // The user's guess.   'H' if the user predicts that
                    •      the next card will be higher, 'L' if the user
                    •      predicts that it will be lower.

      deck.shuffle(); // Shuffle the deck into a random order before
                         •      starting the game.

    correctGuesses = 0;
```

```
currentCard = deck.dealCard();
TextIO.putln("The first card is the " + currentCard);

while (true) {      // Loop ends when user's prediction is wrong.

    /* Get the user's prediction, 'H' or 'L' (or 'h' or 'l'). */
```

```
TextIO.put("Will the next card be higher (H) or lower (L)? "); do {
      guess = TextIO.getInChar();
      guess = Character.toUpperCase(guess);
      if (guess != 'H' && guess != 'L')
          TextIO.put("Please respond with H or L: "); }
while (guess != 'H' && guess != 'L');

/* Get the next card and show it to the user. */

nextCard = deck.dealCard(); TextIO.putln("The
next card is " + nextCard);

/* Check the user's prediction. */

if (nextCard.getValue() == currentCard.getValue()) {
    TextIO.putln("The value is the same as the previous card.");
    TextIO.putln("You lose on ties. Sorry!");
    break;   // End the game.
}
else if (nextCard.getValue() > currentCard.getValue()) { if
    (guess == 'H') {
          TextIO.putln("Your prediction was correct.");
          correctGuesses++;
    }
    else {
          TextIO.putln("Your prediction was incorrect.");
          break; // End the game.
    }
}
else {    // nextCard is lower
    if (guess == 'L') {
          TextIO.putln("Your prediction was correct.");
          correctGuesses++;
    }
    else {
          TextIO.putln("Your prediction was incorrect.");
          break; // End the game.
    }
}

/* To set up for the next iteration of the loop, the nextCard
    becomes the currentCard, since the currentCard has to be the
    card that the user sees, and the nextCard will be
    set to the next card in the deck after the user makes his
    prediction. */

currentCard = nextCard;
TextIO.putln();
TextIO.putln("The card is " + currentCard);
```

```
}// end of while loop

TextIO.putln();
TextIO.putln("The game is over.");
TextIO.putln("You made " + correctGuesses
```

```
                                    + " correct predictions.");
        TextIO.putln();
        return correctGuesses;
    }// end play() }
// end class
```

5.5 Inheritance, Polymorphism, and Abstract Classes

A class represents a set of objects which share the same structure and behaviors. The class determines the structure of objects by specifying variables that are contained in each instance of the class, and it determines behavior by providing the instance methods that express the behavior of the objects. This is a powerful idea. However, something like this can be done in most programming languages. The central new idea in object-oriented programming—the idea that really distinguishes it from traditional programming—is to allow classes to express the similarities among objects that share **some**, but not all, of their structure and behavior. Such similarities can be expressed using **inheritance** and **polymorphism** .

5.5.1 Extending Existing Classes

The topics covered later in this section are relatively advanced aspects of object-oriented pro-gramming. Any programmer should know what is meant by subclass, inheritance, and polymor-phism. However, it will probably be a while before you actually do anything with inheritance except for extending classes that already exist. In the first part of this section, we look at how that is done.

In day-to-day programming, especially for programmers who are just beginning to work with objects, subclassing is used mainly in one situation: There is an existing class that can be adapted with a few changes or additions. This is much more common than designing groups of classes and subclasses from scratch. The existing class can be **extended** to make a subclass. The syntax for this is

```
public class   subclass-name extends existing-class-name   {
    .
    .   // Changes and additions.
.
}
```

As an example, suppose you want to write a program that plays the card game, Blackjack. You can use the Card, Hand, and Deck classes developed in Section 5.4. However, a hand in the game of Blackjack is a little different from a hand of cards in general, since it must be possible to compute the “value” of a Blackjack hand according to the rules of the game. The rules are as follows: The value of a hand is obtained by adding up the values of the cards in the hand. The value of a numeric card such as a three or a ten is its numerical value. The value of a Jack, Queen, or King is 10. The value of an Ace can be either 1 or 11. An Ace should be counted as 11 unless doing so would put the total value of the hand over 21. Note that this means that the second, third, or fourth Ace in the hand will always be counted as 1.

One way to handle this is to extend the existing Hand class by adding a method that computes the Blackjack value of the hand. Here's the definition of such a class:

```
public class BlackjackHand extends Hand {

    /**
     • Computes and returns the value of this hand in the game
     • of Blackjack.
     */
    public int getBlackjackValue() {

        int val;         // The value computed for the hand.
        boolean ace;     // This will be set to true if the
                         //    hand contains an ace.
        int cards;       // Number of cards in the hand.

        val = 0;
        ace = false;
        cards = getCardCount();

        for ( int i = 0;     i < cards;     i++ ) {
                // Add the value of the i-th card in the hand.
            Card card;      // The i-th card;
            int cardVal;    // The blackjack value of the i-th card.
            card = getCard(i);
            cardVal = card.getValue();     // The normal value, 1 to 13.
            if (cardVal > 10) {
                cardVal = 10;    // For a Jack, Queen, or King.
            }
            if (cardVal == 1) {
                ace = true;          // There is at least one ace.
            }
            val = val + cardVal;
        }

         • Now, val is the value of the hand, counting any ace as 1.
         • If there is an ace, and if changing its value from 1 to
         • 11 would leave the score less than or equal to 21,
         • then do so by adding the extra 10 points to val.

         if ( ace == true     && val + 10 <= 21 )
             val = val + 10;

         return val;

    } // end getBlackjackValue() }

// end class BlackjackHand
```

Since BlackjackHand is a subclass of Hand, an object of type BlackjackHand contains all the instance variables and instance methods defined in Hand, plus the new in-

stance method named getBlackjackValue(). For example, if bjh is a variable of type BlackjackHand, then the following are all legal: bjh.getCardCount(), bjh.removeCard(0), and bjh.getBlackjackValue(). The first two methods are defined in Hand, but are inherited by BlackjackHand.

Inherited variables and methods from the Hand class can also be used in the definition of BlackjackHand (except for any that are declared to be private, which prevents access even by subclasses). The statement "cards = getCardCount();" in the above definition of getBlackjackValue() calls the instance method getCardCount(), which was defined in Hand.

Extending existing classes is an easy way to build on previous work. We'll see that many standard classes have been written specifically to be used as the basis for making subclasses.

* * *

Access modifiers such as public and private are used to control access to members of a class. There is one more access modifier, **protected** , that comes into the picture when subclasses are taken into consideration. When protected is applied as an access modifier to a method or member variable in a class, that member can be used in subclasses—direcct or indirect—of the class in which it is defined, but it cannot be used in non-subclasses. (There is one exception: A protected member can also be accessed by any class in the same package as the class that contains the protected member. Recall that using no access modifier makes a member accessible to classes in the same package, and nowhere else. Using the protected modifier is strictly more liberal than using no modifier at all: It allows access from classes in the same package and from **subclasses** that are not in the same package.)

When you declare a method or member variable to be protected, you are saying that it is part of the implementation of the class, rather than part of the public interface of the class. However, you are allowing subclasses to use and modify that part of the implementation.

For example, consider a PairOfDice class that has instance variables die1 and die2 to represent the numbers appearing on the two dice. We could make those variables private to make it impossible to change their values from outside the class, while still allowing read access through getter methods. However, if we think it possible that PairOfDice will be used to create subclasses, we might want to make it possible for subclasses to change the numbers on the dice. For example, a GraphicalDice subclass that draws the dice might want to change the numbers at other times besides when the dice are rolled. In that case, we could make die1 and die2 protected, which would allow the subclass to change their values without making them public to the rest of the world. (An even better idea would be to define protected setter methods for the variables. A setter method could, for example, ensure that the value that is being assigned to the variable is in the legal range 1 through 6.)

5.5.2 Inheritance and Class Hierarchy

The term **inheritance** refers to the fact that one class can inherit part or all of its structure and behavior from another class. The class that does the inheriting is said to be a **subclass** of the class from which it inherits. If class B is a subclass of class A, we also say that class A is a **superclass** of class B. (Sometimes the terms **derived class** and **base class** are used instead of subclass and superclass; this is the common terminology in C++.) A subclass can add to the structure and behavior that it inherits. It can also replace or modify inherited behavior (though not inherited structure). The relationship between subclass and superclass is sometimes shown by a diagram in which the subclass is shown below, and connected to, its superclass, as shown here on the left.

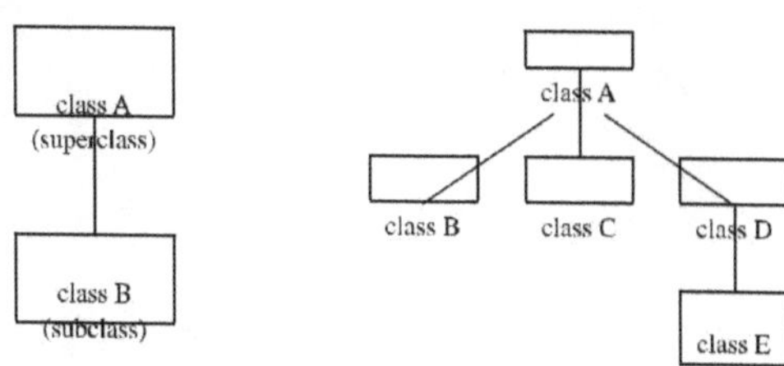

In Java, to create a class named "B" as a subclass of a class named "A", you would write

```
class B extends A {
   .
   // additions to, and modifications of,
   // stuff inherited from class A
   .
}
```

Several classes can be declared as subclasses of the same superclass. The subclasses, which might be referred to as "sibling classes," share some structures and behaviors—namely, the ones they inherit from their common superclass. The superclass expresses these shared structures and behaviors. In the diagram shown on the right, above, classes B, C, and D are sibling classes. Inheritance can also extend over several "generations" of classes. This is shown in the diagram, where class E is a subclass of class D which is itself a subclass of class A. In this case, class E is considered to be a subclass of class A, even though it is not a direct subclass. This whole set of classes forms a small **class hierarchy**.

5.5.3 Example: Vehicles

Let's look at an example. Suppose that a program has to deal with motor vehicles, including cars, trucks, and motorcycles. (This might be a program used by a Department of Motor Vehicles to keep track of registrations.) The program could use a class named Vehicle to represent all types of vehicles. Since cars, trucks, and motorcycles are types of vehicles, they would be represented by subclasses of the Vehicle class, as shown in this class hierarchy diagram:

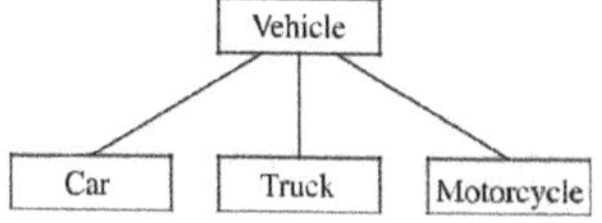

The Vehicle class would include instance variables such as registrationNumber and owner and instance methods such as transferOwnership(). These are variables and methods common to all vehicles. The three subclasses of Vehicle—Car, Truck, and Motorcycle—could

then be used to hold variables and methods specific to particular types of vehicles. The Car class might add an instance variable numberOfDoors, the Truck class might have numberOfAxles, and the Motorcycle class could have a boolean variable hasSidecar. (Well, it could in theory at least, even if it might give a chuckle to the people at the Department of Motor Vehicles.) The declarations of these classes in a Java program would look, in outline, like this (although in practice, they would probably be public classes, defined in separate files):

```
class Vehicle {
    int registrationNumber;
    Person owner;  // (Assuming that a Person class has been defined!)
    void transferOwnership(Person newOwner) {
        . . .
    }
    . . .
}

class Car extends Vehicle {
    int numberOfDoors;
    . . .
}

class Truck extends Vehicle {
    int numberOfAxles;
    . . .
}

class Motorcycle extends Vehicle {
    boolean hasSidecar;
    . . .
}
```

Suppose that myCar is a variable of type Car that has been declared and initialized with the statement

```
Car myCar = new Car();
```

Given this declaration, a program could refer to myCar.numberOfDoors, since numberOfDoors is an instance variable in the class Car. But since class Car extends class Vehicle, a car also has all the structure and behavior of a vehicle. This means that myCar.registrationNumber, myCar.owner, and myCar.transferOwnership() also exist.

Now, in the real world, cars, trucks, and motorcycles are in fact vehicles. The same is true in a program. That is, an object of type Car or Truck or Motorcycle is automatically an object of type Vehicle too. This brings us to the following Important Fact:

A variable that can hold a reference to an object of class A can also hold a reference to an object belonging to any subclass of A.

The practical effect of this in our example is that an object of type Car can be assigned to a variable of type Vehicle. That is, it would be legal to say

```
Vehicle myVehicle = myCar;
```

or even

```
Vehicle myVehicle = new Car();
```

After either of these statements, the variable myVehicle holds a reference to a Vehicle object that happens to be an instance of the subclass, Car. The object "remembers" that it is in fact a Car, and not **just** a Vehicle. Information about the actual class of an object is stored as part of that object. It is even possible to test whether a given object belongs to a given class, using the instanceof operator. The test:

```
if (myVehicle instanceof Car) ...
```

determines whether the object referred to by myVehicle is in fact a car.

On the other hand, the assignment statement

```
myCar = myVehicle;
```

would be illegal because myVehicle could potentially refer to other types of vehicles that are not cars. This is similar to a problem we saw previously in Subsection 2.5.6: The computer will not allow you to assign an int value to a variable of type short, because not every int is a short. Similarly, it will not allow you to assign a value of type Vehicle to a variable of type Car because not every vehicle is a car. As in the case of ints and shorts, the solution here is to use type-casting. If, for some reason, you happen to know that myVehicle does in fact refer to a Car, you can use the type cast (Car)myVehicle to tell the computer to treat myVehicle as if it were actually of type Car. So, you could say

```
myCar = (Car)myVehicle;
```

and you could even refer to ((Car)myVehicle).numberOfDoors. As an example of how this could be used in a program, suppose that you want to print out relevant data about a vehicle. You could say:

```
System.out.println("Vehicle Data:");
System.out.println("Registration number:    "
                                        • myVehicle.registrationNumber);
if (myVehicle instanceof Car) {
    System.out.println("Type of vehicle: Car"); Car
    c;
    c = (Car)myVehicle;
    System.out.println("Number of doors:  " + c.numberOfDoors);
}
else if (myVehicle instanceof Truck) {
    System.out.println("Type of vehicle: Truck");
    Truck t;
    t = (Truck)myVehicle;
    System.out.println("Number of axles:  " + t.numberOfAxles);
}
else if (myVehicle instanceof Motorcycle) {
    System.out.println("Type of vehicle: Motorcycle");
    Motorcycle m;
    m = (Motorcycle)myVehicle;
    System.out.println("Has a sidecar:" + m.hasSidecar);
}
```

Note that for object types, when the computer executes a program, it checks whether type-casts are valid. So, for example, if myVehicle refers to an object of type Truck, then the type cast (Car)myVehicle would be an error. When this happes, an exception of type ClassCastException is thrown.

5.5.4 Polymorphism

As another example, consider a program that deals with shapes drawn on the screen. Let's say that the shapes include rectangles, ovals, and roundrects of various colors. (A "roundrect" is just a rectangle with rounded corners.)

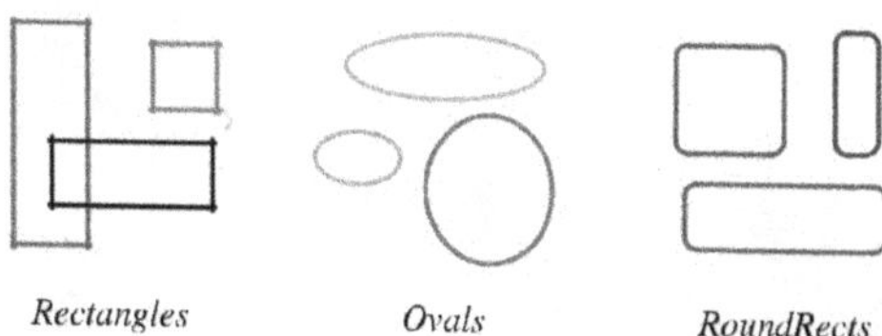

Three classes, Rectangle, Oval, and RoundRect, could be used to represent the three types of shapes. These three classes would have a common superclass, Shape, to represent features that all three shapes have in common. The Shape class could include instance variables to represent the color, position, and size of a shape, and it could include instance methods for changing the color, position, and size. Changing the color, for example, might involve changing the value of an instance variable, and then redrawing the shape in its new color:

```
class Shape {

    Color color;       // Color of the shape.    (Recall that class Color
                       • is defined in package java.awt. Assume
                       • that this class has been imported.)

    void setColor(Color newColor) {
          // Method to change the color of the shape.
       color = newColor; // change value of instance variable
       redraw(); // redraw shape, which will appear in new color
    }

    void redraw() {
              method for drawing the shape
       • ? ? // what commands should go here?
    }

      . . // more instance variables and methods } // end of
class Shape
```

Now, you might see a problem here with the method redraw(). The problem is that each different type of shape is drawn differently. The method setColor() can be called for any type of shape. How does the computer know which shape to draw when it executes the redraw()? Informally, we can answer the question like this: The computer executes redraw() by asking the shape to redraw **itself**. Every shape object knows what it has to do to redraw itself.

In practice, this means that each of the specific shape classes has its own redraw() method:

```
class Rectangle extends Shape {
   void redraw() {
      . . .      // commands for drawing a rectangle
```

```
    }
    . . . // possibly, more methods and variables
}
class Oval extends Shape {
    void redraw() {
        . . .    // commands for drawing an oval
    }
    . . . // possibly, more methods and variables
}
class RoundRect extends Shape {
    void redraw() {
        . . .    // commands for drawing a rounded rectangle
    }
    . . . // possibly, more methods and variables
}
```

If oneShape is a variable of type Shape, it could refer to an object of any of the types, Rectangle, Oval, or RoundRect. As a program executes, and the value of oneShape changes, it could even refer to objects of different types at different times! Whenever the statement

```
oneShape.redraw();
```

is executed, the redraw method that is actually called is the one appropriate for the type of object to which oneShape actually refers. There may be no way of telling, from looking at the text of the program, what shape this statement will draw, since it depends on the value that oneShape happens to have when the program is executed. Even more is true. Suppose the statement is in a loop and gets executed many times. If the value of oneShape changes as the loop is executed, it is possible that the very same statement "oneShape.redraw();" will call different methods and draw different shapes as it is executed over and over. We say that the redraw() method is **polymorphic**. A method is polymorphic if the action performed by the method depends on the actual type of the object to which the method is applied. Polymorphism is one of the major distinguishing features of object-oriented programming.

Perhaps this becomes more understandable if we change our terminology a bit: In object-oriented programming, calling a method is often referred to as sending a **message** to an object. The object responds to the message by executing the appropriate method. The statement "oneShape.redraw();" is a message to the object referred to by oneShape. Since that object knows what type of object it is, it knows how it should respond to the message. From this point of view, the computer always executes "oneShape.redraw();" in the same way: by sending a message. The response to the message depends, naturally, on who receives it. From this point of view, objects are active entities that send and receive messages, and polymorphism is a natural, even necessary, part of this view. Polymorphism just means that different objects can respond to the same message in different ways.

One of the most beautiful things about polymorphism is that it lets code that you write do things that you didn't even conceive of, at the time you wrote it. Suppose that I decide to add beveled rectangles to the types of shapes my program can deal with. A beveled rectangle has a triangle cut off each corner:

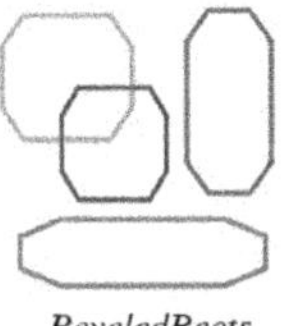

BeveledRects

To implement beveled rectangles, I can write a new subclass, BeveledRect, of class Shape and give it its own redraw() method. Automatically, code that I wrote previously—such as the statement oneShape.redraw()—can now suddenly start drawing beveled rectangles, even though the beveled rectangle class didn't exist when I wrote the statement!

In the statement "oneShape.redraw();", the redraw message is sent to the object oneShape. Look back at the method from the Shape class for changing the color of a shape:

```
void setColor(Color newColor) {
    color = newColor; // change value of instance variable
    redraw(); // redraw shape, which will appear in new color
}
```

A redraw message is sent here, but which object is it sent to? Well, the setColor method is itself a message that was sent to some object. The answer is that the redraw message is sent to that same object, the one that received the setColor message. If that object is a rectangle, then it is the redraw() method from the Rectangle class that is executed. If the object is an oval, then it is the redraw() method from the Oval class. This is what you should expect, but it means that the "redraw();" statement in the setColor() method does **not** necessarily call the redraw() method in the Shape class! The redraw() method that is executed could be in any subclass of Shape.

Again, this is not a real surprise if you think about it in the right way. Remember that an instance method is always contained in an object. The class only contains the source code for the method. When a Rectangle object is created, it contains a redraw() method. The source code for that method is in the Rectangle class. The object also contains a setColor() method. Since the Rectangle class does not define a setColor() method, the **source code** for the rectangle's setColor() method comes from the superclass, Shape, but the **method itself** is in the object of type Rectangle. Even though the source codes for the two methods are in different classes, the methods themselves are part of the same object. When the rectangle's setColor() method is executed and calls redraw(), the redraw() method that is executed is the one in the same object.

5.5.5 Abstract Classes

Whenever a Rectangle, Oval, or RoundRect object has to draw itself, it is the redraw() method in the appropriate class that is executed. This leaves open the question, What does the redraw() method in the Shape class do? How should it be defined?

The answer may be surprising: We should leave it blank! The fact is that the class Shape represents the abstract idea of a shape, and there is no way to draw such a thing. Only particular, concrete shapes like rectangles and ovals can be drawn. So, why should there even be a redraw() method in the Shape class? Well, it has to be there, or it would be illegal to call it in the setColor() method of the Shape class, and it would be illegal to write "oneShape.redraw();", where oneShape is a variable of type Shape. The compiler would complain that oneShape is a variable of type Shape and there's no redraw() method in the Shape class.

Nevertheless the version of redraw() in the Shape class itself will never actually be called. In fact, if you think about it, there can never be any reason to construct an actual object of type Shape! You can have **variables** of type Shape, but the objects they refer to will always belong to one of the subclasses of Shape. We say that Shape is an **abstract class**. An abstract class is one that is not used to construct objects, but only as a basis for making subclasses. An abstract class exists **only** to express the common properties of all its subclasses. A class that is not abstract is said to be **concrete**. You can create objects belonging to a concrete class, but not to an abstract class. A variable whose type is given by an abstract class can only refer to objects that belong to concrete subclasses of the abstract class.

Similarly, we say that the redraw() method in class Shape is an **abstract method** , since it is never meant to be called. In fact, there is nothing for it to do—any actual redrawing is done by redraw() methods in the subclasses of Shape. The redraw() method in Shape has to be there. But it is there only to tell the computer that all Shapes understand the redraw message. As an abstract method, it exists merely to specify the common interface of all the actual, concrete versions of redraw() in the subclasses of Shape. There is no reason for the abstract redraw() in class Shape to contain any code at all.

Shape and its redraw() method are semantically abstract. You can also tell the computer, syntactically, that they are abstract by adding the modifier "abstract" to their definitions. For an abstract method, the block of code that gives the implementation of an ordinary method is replaced by a semicolon. An implementation must be provided for the abstract method in any concrete subclass of the abstract class. Here's what the Shape class would look like as an abstract class:

```
public abstract class Shape {

    Color color;        // color of shape.

    void setColor(Color newColor) {
            // method to change the color of the shape
        color = newColor; // change value of instance variable
        redraw(); // redraw shape, which will appear in new color
    }

    abstract void redraw();
            • abstract method—must be defined in
            • concrete subclasses

      . . // more instance variables and methods } // end of

class Shape
```

Once you have declared the class to be abstract, it becomes illegal to try to create actual objects of type Shape, and the computer will report a syntax error if you try to do so.

* * *

Recall from Subsection 5.3.3 that a class that is not explicitly declared to be a subclass of some other class is automatically made a subclass of the standard class Object. That is, a class declaration with no "extends" part such as

```
public class myClass { . . .
```

is exactly equivalent to

```
public class myClass extends Object { . . .
```

This means that class Object is at the top of a huge class hierarchy that includes every other class. (Semantially, Object is an abstract class, in fact the most abstract class of all. Curiously, however, it is not declared to be abstract syntactially, which means that you can create objects of type Object. What you would do with them, however, I have no idea.)

Since every class is a subclass of Object, a variable of type Object can refer to any object whatsoever, of any type. Java has several standard data structures that are designed to hold Object s, but since every object is an instance of class Object, these data structures can actually hold any object whatsoever. One example is the "ArrayList" data structure, which is defined by the class ArrayList in the package java.util. (ArrayList is discussed more fully in Section 7.3.) An ArrayList is simply a list of Object s. This class is very convenient, because an ArrayList can hold any number of objects, and it will grow, when necessary, as objects are added to it. Since the items in the list are of type Object, the list can actually hold objects of any type.

A program that wants to keep track of various Shapes that have been drawn on the screen can store those shapes in an ArrayList. Suppose that the ArrayList is named listOfShapes. A shape, oneShape, can be added to the end of the list by calling the instance method "listOfShapes.add(oneShape);". The shape can be removed from the list with the instance method "listOfShapes.remove(oneShape);". The number of shapes in the list is given by the function "listOfShapes.size()". And it is possible to retrieve the i-th object from the list with the function call "listOfShapes.get(i)". (Items in the list are numbered from 0 to listOfShapes.size() - 1.) However, note that this method returns an Object, not a Shape. (Of course, the people who wrote the ArrayList class didn't even know about Shapes, so the method they wrote could hardly have a return type of Shape!) Since you know that the items in the list are, in fact, Shapes and not just Object s, you can type-cast the Object returned by listOfShapes.get(i) to be a value of type Shape:

```
oneShape = (Shape)listOfShapes.get(i);
```

Let's say, for example, that you want to redraw all the shapes in the list. You could do this with a simple for loop, which is lovely example of object-oriented programming and of polymorphism:

```
for (int i = 0; i < listOfShapes.size(); i++) {
    Shape s; // i-th element of the list, considered as a Shape s =
    (Shape)listOfShapes.get(i);
     s.redraw();      // What is drawn here depends on what type of shape s is!
}
```

* * *

The sample source code file **ShapeDraw.java** uses an abstract Shape class and an ArrayList to hold a list of shapes. The file defines an applet in which the user can add various shapes to a drawing area. Once a shape is in the drawing area, the user can use the mouse to drag it around.

You might want to look at this file, even though you won't be able to understand all of it at this time. Even the definitions of the shape classes are somewhat different from those that I have described in this section. (For example, the draw() method has a parameter of type Graphics. This parameter is required because of the way Java handles all drawing.) I'll return to this example in later chapters when you know more about GUI programming. However, it would still be worthwhile to look at the definition of the Shape class and its subclasses in the source code. You might also check how an ArrayList is used to hold the list of shapes.

In the applet the only time when the actual class of a shape is used is when that shape is added to the screen. Once the shape has been created, it is manipulated entirely as an abstract shape. The routine that implements dragging, for example, works only with variables of type Shape. As the Shape is being dragged, the dragging routine just calls the Shape's draw method each time the shape has to be drawn, so it doesn't have to know how to draw the shape or even what type of shape it is. The object is responsible for drawing itself. If I wanted to add a new type of shape to the program, I would define a new subclass of Shape, add another button to the applet, and program the button to add the correct type of shape to the screen. No other changes in the programming would be necessary.

If you want to try out the applet, you can find it at the end of the on-line version of this section.

5.6 this and super

Although the basic ideas of object-oriented programming are reasonably simple and clear, they are subtle, and they take time to get used to. And unfortunately, beyond the basic ideas there are a lot of details. This section and the next cover more of those annoying details. You should not necessarily master everything in these two sections the first time through, but you should read it to be aware of what is possible. For the most part, when I need to use this material later in the text, I will explain it again briefly, or I will refer you back to it. In this section, we'll look at two variables, this and super, that are automatically defined in any instance method.

5.6.1 The Special Variable this

A static member of a class has a simple name, which can only be used inside the class defi-nition. For use outside the class, it has a full name of the form **class-name** . **simple-name** . For example, "System.out" is a static member variable with simple name "out" in the class "System". It's always legal to use the full name of a static member, even within the class where it's defined. Sometimes it's even necessary, as when the simple name of a static member variable is hidden by a local variable of the same name.

Instance variables and instance methods also have simple names. The simple name of such an instance member can be used in instance methods in the class where the instance member is defined. Instance members also have full names, but remember that instance variables and methods are actually contained in objects, not classes. The full name of an instance member has to contain a reference to the object that contains the instance member. To get at an instance variable or method from outside the class definition, you need a variable that refers to the object. Then the full name is of the form **variable-name** . **simple-name** . But suppose you are writing the definition of an instance method in some class. How can you get a reference to the object that contains that instance method? You might need such a reference, for example, if you want to use the full name of an instance variable, because the simple name of the instance variable is hidden by a local variable or parameter.

Java provides a special, predefined variable named "this" that you can use for such purposes. The variable, this, is used in the source code of an instance method to refer to the object that contains the method. This intent of the name, this, is to refer to "this object," the one right here that this very method is in. If x is an instance variable in the same object, then this.x can be used as a full name for that variable. If otherMethod() is an instance method in the same object, then this.otherMethod() could be used to call that method. Whenever the computer executes an instance method, it automatically sets the variable, this, to refer to the object that contains the method.

One common use of this is in constructors. For example:

```
public class Student {

    private String name;    // Name of the student.

    public Student(String name) {
        • Constructor. Create a student with specified name.
        this.name = name;
    }
        .
        • // More variables and methods.
•
}
```

In the constructor, the instance variable called name is hidden by a formal parameter. However, the instance variable can still be referred to by its full name, this.name. In the assignment statement, the value of the formal parameter, name, is assigned to the instance variable, this.name. This is considered to be acceptable style: There is no need to dream up cute new names for formal parameters that are just used to initialize instance variables. You can use the same name for the parameter as for the instance variable.

There are other uses for this. Sometimes, when you are writing an instance method, you need to pass the object that contains the method to a subroutine, as an actual parameter. In that case, you can use this as the actual parameter. For example, if you wanted to print out a string representation of the object, you could say "System.out.println(this);". Or you could assign the value of this to another variable in an assignment statement. In fact, you can do anything with this that you could do with any other variable, except change its value.

5.6.2 The Special Variable super

Java also defines another special variable, named "super", for use in the definitions of instance methods. The variable super is for use in a subclass. Like this, super refers to the object that contains the method. But it's forgetful. It forgets that the object belongs to the class you are writing, and it remembers only that it belongs to the superclass of that class. The point is that the class can contain additions and modifications to the superclass. super doesn't know about any of those additions and modifications; it can only be used to refer to methods and variables in the superclass.

Let's say that the class that you are writing contains an instance method named doSomething(). Consider the subroutine call statement super.doSomething(). Now, super doesn't know anything about the doSomething() method in the subclass. It only knows about things in the superclass, so it tries to execute a method named doSomething() from the superclass. If there is none—if the doSomething() method was an addition rather than a modification—you'll get a syntax error.

The reason super exists is so you can get access to things in the superclass that are **hidden** by things in the subclass. For example, super.x always refers to an instance variable named x in the superclass. This can be useful for the following reason: If a class contains an instance variable with the same name as an instance variable in its superclass, then an object of that class will actually contain two variables with the same name: one defined as part of the class itself and one defined as part of the superclass. The variable in the subclass does not **replace** the variable of the same name in the superclass; it merely **hides** it. The variable from the superclass can still be accessed, using super.

When you write a method in a subclass that has the same signature as a method in its superclass, the method from the superclass is hidden in the same way. We say that the method in the subclass **overrides** the method from the superclass. Again, however, super can be used to access the method from the superclass.

The major use of super is to override a method with a new method that **extends** the behavior of the inherited method, instead of **replacing** that behavior entirely. The new method can use super to call the method from the superclass, and then it can add additional code to provide additional behavior. As an example, suppose you have a PairOfDice class that includes a roll() method. Suppose that you want a subclass, GraphicalDice, to represent a pair of dice drawn on the computer screen. The roll() method in the GraphicalDice class should do everything that the roll() method in the PairOfDice class does. We can express this with a call to super.roll(), which calls the method in the superclass. But in addition to that, the roll() method for a GraphicalDice object has to redraw the dice to show the new values. The GraphicalDice class might look something like this:

```
public class GraphicalDice extends PairOfDice {

    public void roll() {
            // Roll the   dice, and redraw   them.
        super.roll();     // Call the roll   method from PairOfDice.
        redraw();         // Call a method   to draw the dice.
    }
        .
        . // More stuff, including definition of redraw().
        .
}
```

Note that this allows you to extend the behavior of the roll() method even if you don't know how the method is implemented in the superclass!

Here is a more complete example. The applet at the end of Section 4.7 in the on-line version of this book shows a disturbance that moves around in a mosaic of little squares. As it moves, each square it visits become a brighter shade of red. The result looks interesting, but I think it would be prettier if the pattern were symmetric. A symmetric version of the applet is shown at the bottom of the Section 5.7 (in the on-line version). The symmetric applet can be programmed as an easy extension of the original applet.

In the symmetric version, each time a square is brightened, the squares that can be obtained from that one by horizontal and vertical reflection through the center of the mosaic are also brightened. This picture might make the symmetry idea clearer:

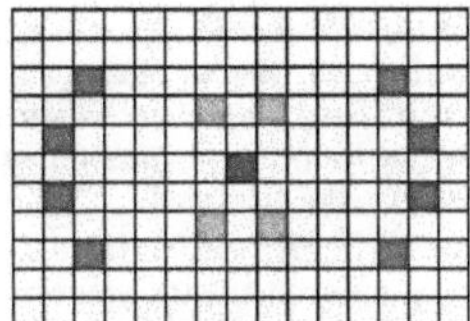

The four red squares in the picture, for example, form a set of such symmetrically placed squares, as do the purple squares and the green squares. (The blue square is at the center of the mosaic, so reflecting it doesn't produce any other squares; it's its own reflection.)

The original applet is defined by the class RandomBrighten. In that class, the actual task of brightening a square is done by a method called brighten(). If row and col are the row and column numbers of a square, then "brighten(row,col);" increases the brightness of that square. All we need is a subclass of RandomBrighten with a modified brighten() routine. Instead of just brightening one square, the modified routine will also brighten the horizontal and vertical reflections of that square. But how will it brighten each of the four individual squares? By calling the brighten() method from the original class. It can do this by calling super.brighten().

There is still the problem of computing the row and column numbers of the horizontal and vertical reflections. To do this, you need to know the number of rows and the number of columns. The RandomBrighten class has instance variables named ROWS and COLUMNS to represent these quantities. Using these variables, it's possible to come up with formulas for the reflections, as shown in the definition of the brighten() method below.

Here's the complete definition of the new class:

```
public class SymmetricBrighten extends RandomBrighten {
   void brighten(int row, int col) {
         • Brighten the specified square and its horizontal
         • and vertical reflections. This overrides the brighten
         • method from the RandomBrighten class, which just
         • brightens one square.
      super.brighten(row, col); super.brighten(ROWS - 1 -
      row, col); super.brighten(row, COLUMNS - 1 - col);
      super.brighten(ROWS - 1 - row, COLUMNS - 1 - col);
   }
} // end class SymmetricBrighten
```

This is the entire source code for the applet!

5.6.3 Constructors in Subclasses

Constructors are not inherited. That is, if you extend an existing class to make a subclass, the constructors in the superclass do not become part of the subclass. If you want constructors in the subclass, you have to define new ones from scratch. If you don't define any constructors in the subclass, then the computer will make up a default constructor, with no parameters, for you.

This could be a problem, if there is a constructor in the superclass that does a lot of necessary work. It looks like you might have to repeat all that work in the subclass! This could be a **real** problem if you don't have the source code to the superclass, and don't know how it works, or if the constructor in the superclass initializes private member variables that you don't even have access to in the subclass!

Obviously, there has to be some fix for this, and there is. It involves the special variable, super. As the very first statement in a constructor, you can use super to call a constructor from the superclass. The notation for this is a bit ugly and misleading, and it can only be used in this one particular circumstance: It looks like you are calling super as a subroutine (even though super is not a subroutine and you can't call constructors the same way you call other subroutines anyway). As an example, assume that the PairOfDice class has a constructor that takes two integers as parameters. Consider a subclass:

```
public class GraphicalDice extends PairOfDice {

    public GraphicalDice() {      // Constructor for this class.

        super(3,4);    // Call the constructor from the
                       •   PairOfDice class, with parameters 3, 4.

        initializeGraphics();     // Do some initialization specific //
                                  to the GraphicalDice class.

    }
        .
        • // More constructors, methods, variables...
•
}
```

The statement "super(3,4);" calls the constructor from the superclass. This call must be the first line of the constructor in the subclass. Note that if you don't explicitly call a constructor from the superclass in this way, then the default constructor from the superclass, the one with no parameters, will be called automatically.

This might seem rather technical, but unfortunately it is sometimes necessary. By the way, you can use the special variable this in exactly the same way to call another constructor in the same class. This can be useful since it can save you from repeating the same code in several constructors.

5.7 Interfaces, Nested Classes, and Other Details

THIS SECTION simply pulls together a few more miscellaneous features of object oriented programming in Java. Read it now, or just look through it and refer back to it later when you need this material. (You will need to know about the first topic, interfaces, almost as soon as we begin GUI programming.)

5.7.1 Interfaces

Some object-oriented programming languages, such as C++, allow a class to extend two or more superclasses. This is called **multiple inheritance**. In the illustration below, for example, class E is shown as having both class A and class B as direct superclasses, while class F has three direct superclasses.

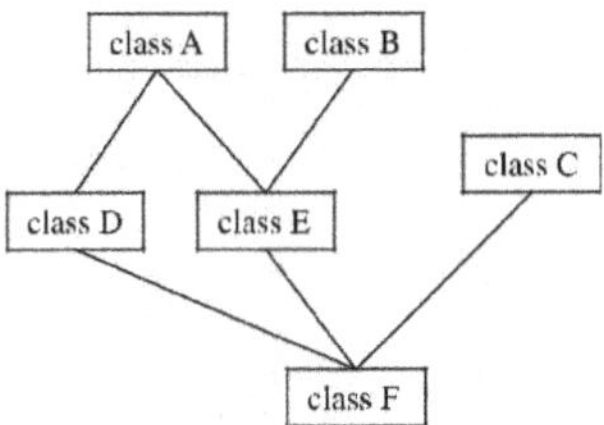

Multiple inheritance (NOT allowed in Java)

Such multiple inheritance is **not** allowed in Java. The designers of Java wanted to keep the language reasonably simple, and felt that the benefits of multiple inheritance were not worth the cost in increased complexity. However, Java does have a feature that can be used to accomplish many of the same goals as multiple inheritance: **Interfaces**.

We've encountered the term "interface" before, in connection with black boxes in general and subroutines in particular. The interface of a subroutine consists of the name of the subroutine, its return type, and the number and types of its parameters. This is the information you need to know if you want to call the subroutine. A subroutine also has an implementation: the block of code which defines it and which is executed when the subroutine is called.

In Java, interface is a reserved word with an additional, technical meaning. An "interface" in this sense consists of a set of instance method interfaces, without any associated implementations. (Actually, a Java interface can contain other things as well, but we won't discuss them here.) A class can **implement** an interface by providing an implemen-tation for each of the methods specified by the interface. Here is an example of a very simple Java interface:

```
public interface Drawable {
    public void draw(Graphics g);
}
```

This looks much like a class definition, except that the implementation of the draw() method is omitted. A class that implements the interface Drawable must provide an implementation for this method. Of course, the class can also include other methods and variables. For example,

```
public class Line implements Drawable {
    public void draw(Graphics g) {
        . . . // do something—presumably, draw a line
    }
    . . . // other methods and variables
}
```

Note that to implement an interface, a class must do more than simply provide an implementa-tion for each method in the interface; it must also **state** that it implements the interface, using the reserved word implements as in this example: "public class Line

Implements Drawable". Any class that implements the Drawable interface defines a draw() instance method. Any ob-ject created from such a class includes a draw() method. We say that an **object** implements an interface if it belongs to a class that implements the interface. For example, any object of type Line implements the Drawable interface.

While a class can **extend** only one other class, it can **implement** any number of interfaces. In fact, a class can both extend one other class and implement one or more interfaces. So, we can have things like

```
class FilledCircle extends Circle
                        implements Drawable, Fillable {
    . . .
}
```

The point of all this is that, although interfaces are not classes, they are something very similar. An interface is very much like an abstract class, that is, a class that can never be used for constructing objects, but can be used as a basis for making subclasses. The subroutines in an interface are abstract methods, which must be implemented in any concrete class that implements the interface. And as with abstract classes, even though you can't construct an object from an interface, you can declare a variable whose type is given by the interface. For example, if Drawable is an interface, and if Line and FilledCircle are classes that implement Drawable, then you could say:

```
Drawable figure; // Declare a variable of type Drawable.    It can
                 •     refer to any object that implements the
                 •     Drawable interface.

figure = new Line(); // figure now refers to an object of class Line
figure.draw(g); // calls draw() method from class Line

figure = new FilledCircle();        // Now, figure refers to an object
                                    •    of class FilledCircle.
figure.draw(g);       // calls draw() method from class FilledCircle
```

A variable of type Drawable can refer to any object of any class that implements the Drawable interface. A statement like figure.draw(g), above, is legal because figure is of type Drawable, and **any** Drawable object has a draw() method. So, whatever object figure refers to, that object must have a draw() method.

Note that a **type** is something that can be used to declare variables. A type can also be used to specify the type of a parameter in a subroutine, or the return type of a function. In Java, a type can be either a class, an interface, or one of the eight built-in primitive types. These are the only possibilities. Of these, however, only classes can be used to construct new objects.

You are not likely to need to write your own interfaces until you get to the point of writing fairly complex programs. However, there are a few interfaces that are used in important ways in Java's standard packages. You'll learn about some of these standard interfaces in the next few chapters.

5.7.2 Nested Classes

A class seems like it should be a pretty important thing. A class is a high-level building block of a program, representing a potentially complex idea and its associated data and behaviors. I've always felt a bit silly writing tiny little classes that exist only to group a few scraps of data together. However, such trivial classes are often useful and even essential.

Fortunately, in Java, I can ease the embarrassment, because one class can be nested inside another class. My trivial little class doesn't have to stand on its own. It becomes part of a larger more respectable class. This is particularly useful when you want to create a little class specifically to support the work of a larger class. And, more seriously, there are other good reasons for nesting the definition of one class inside another class.

In Java, a **nested class** is any class whose definition is inside the definition of another class. Nested classes can be either **named** or **anonymous**. I will come back to the topic of anonymous classes later in this section. A named nested class, like most other things that occur in classes, can be either static or non-static.

The definition of a static nested class looks just like the definition of any other class, except that it is nested inside another class and it has the modifier static as part of its declaration. A static nested class is part of the static structure of the containing class. It can be used inside that class to create objects in the usual way. If it has not been declared private, then it can also be used outside the containing class, but when it is used outside the class, its name must indicate its membership in the containing class. This is similar to other static components of a class: A static nested class is part of the class itself in the same way that static member variables are parts of the class itself.

For example, suppose a class named WireFrameModel represents a set of lines in three-dimensional space. (Such models are used to represent three-dimensional objects in graphics programs.) Suppose that the WireFrameModel class contains a static nested class, Line, that represents a single line. Then, outside of the class WireFrameModel, the Line class would be referred to as WireFrameModel.Line. Of course, this just follows the normal naming convention for static members of a class. The definition of the WireFrameModel class with its nested Line class would look, in outline, like this:

```
public class WireFrameModel {

   . . . // other members of the WireFrameModel class

   static public class Line {
               Represents a line from the point (x1,y1,z1)
               to the point (x2,y2,z2) in 3-dimensional space.
      double x1, y1, z1;
      double x2, y2, z2; }
   // end class Line

     . . // other members of the WireFrameModel class

} // end WireFrameModel
```

Inside the WireFrameModel class, a Line object would be created with the constructor "new Line()". Outside the class, "new WireFrameModel.Line()" would be used.

A static nested class has full access to the static members of the containing class, even to the private members. Similarly, the containing class has full access to the members of the nested class. This can be another motivation for declaring a nested class, since it lets you give one class access to the private members of another class without making those members generally available to other classes.

When you compile the above class definition, two class files will be created. Even though the definition of Line is nested inside WireFrameModel, the compiled Line class is stored in a separate file. The name of the class file for Line will be WireFrameModel$Line.class.

* * *

Non-static nested classes are referred to as **inner classes**. Inner classes are not, in practice, very different from static nested classes, but a non-static nested class is actually associated with an object rather than to the class in which it is nested. This can take some getting used to.

Any non-static member of a class is not really part of the class itself (although its source code is contained in the class definition). This is true for inner classes, just as it is for any other non-static part of a class. The non-static members of a class specify what will be contained in objects that are created from that class. The same is true—at least logically—for inner classes. It's as if each object that belongs to the containing class has its **own copy** of the nested class. This copy has access to all the instance methods and instance variables of the object, even to those that are declared private. The two copies of the inner class in two different objects differ because the instance variables and methods they refer to are in different objects. In fact, the rule for deciding whether a nested class should be static or non-static is simple: If the nested class needs to use any instance variable or instance method from the containing class, make the nested class non-static. Otherwise, it might as well be static.

From outside the containing class, a non-static nested class has to be referred to using a name of the form **variableName . NestedClassName** , where **variableName** is a variable that refers to the object that contains the class. This is actually rather rare, however. A non-static nested class is generally used only inside the class in which it is nested, and there it can be referred to by its simple name.

In order to create an object that belongs to an inner class, you must first have an object that belongs to the containing class. (When working inside the class, the object "this" is used implicitly.) The inner class object is permanently associated with the containing class object, and it has complete access to the members of the containing class object. Looking at an example will help, and will hopefully convince you that inner classes are really very natural. Consider a class that represents poker games. This class might include a nested class to represent the players of the game. This structure of the PokerGame class could be:

```
public class PokerGame {  // Represents a game of poker.

    private class Player {     // Represents one of the players in this game.
       .
       .
       .
    } // end class Player

    private Deck deck;         // A deck of cards for playing the game.
    private int pot;           // The amount of money that has been bet.

    .
    .
    .

} // end class PokerGame
```

If game is a variable of type PokerGame, then, conceptually, game contains its own copy of the Player class. In an an instance method of a PokerGame object, a new Player object would be created by saying “new Player()”, just as for any other class. (A Player object could be created outside the PokerGame class with an expression such as “game.new Player()”. Again, however, this is very rare.) The Player object will have access to the deck and pot instance variables in the PokerGame object. Each PokerGame object has its own deck and pot and Players. Players of that poker game use the deck and pot for that game; players of another poker game use the other game’s deck and pot. That’s the effect of making the Player class non-static. This is the most natural way for players to behave. A Player object represents a player of one particular poker game. If Player were a **static** nested class, on the other hand, it would represent the general idea of a poker player, independent of a particular poker game.

5.7.3 Anonymous Inner Classes

In some cases, you might find yourself writing an inner class and then using that class in just a single line of your program. Is it worth creating such a class? Indeed, it can be, but for cases like this you have the option of using an **anonymous inner class**. An anonymous class is created with a variation of the new operator that has the form

```
new     superclass-or-interface ( parameter-list ) {
        methods-and-variables
      }
```

This constructor defines a new class, without giving it a name, and it simultaneously creates an object that belongs to that class. This form of the new operator can be used in any statement where a regular "new" could be used. The intention of this expression is to create: "a new object belonging to a class that is the same as **superclass-or-interface** but with these **methods-and-variables** added." The effect is to create a uniquely customized object, just at the point in the program where you need it. Note that it is possible to base an anonymous class on an interface, rather than a class. In this case, the anonymous class must implement the interface by defining all the methods that are declared in the interface. If an interface is used as a base, the **parameter-list** must be empty. Otherwise, it can contain parameters for a constructor in the **superclass** .

Anonymous classes are often used for handling events in graphical user interfaces, and we will encounter them several times in the chapters on GUI programming. For now, we will look at one not-very-plausible example. Consider the Drawable interface, which is defined earlier in this section. Suppose that we want a Drawable object that draws a filled, red, 100-pixel square. Rather than defining a new, separate class and then using that class to create the object, we can use an anonymous class to create the object in one statement:

```
Drawable redSquare = new Drawable() {
        void draw(Graphics g) {
           g.setColor(Color.red);
           g.fillRect(10,10,100,100);
        }
};
```

The semicolon at the end of this statement is not part of the class definition. It's the semicolon that is required at the end of every declaration statement.

When a Java class is compiled, each anonymous nested class will produce a separate class file. If the name of the main class is MainClass, for example, then the names of the class files for the anonymous nested classes will be MainClass$1.class, MainClass$2.class, MainClass$3.class, and so on.

5.7.4 Mixing Static and Non-static

Classes, as I've said, have two very distinct purposes. A class can be used to group together a set of static member variables and static member subroutines. Or it can be used as a factory for making objects. The non-static variables and subroutines in the class definition specify the instance variables and methods of the objects. In most cases, a class performs one or the other of these roles, not both.

Sometimes, however, static and non-static members are mixed in a single class. In this case, the class plays a dual role. Sometimes, these roles are completely separate. It is also possible for the static and non-static parts of a class to interact. This happens when instance methods use static member variables or call static member subroutines. An instance method belongs to an object, not to the class itself, and there can be many objects with their own versions of the instance method. But there is only one copy of a static member variable. So, effectively, we have many objects sharing that one variable.

Suppose, for example, that we want to write a PairOfDice class that uses the Random class mentioned in Section 5.3 for rolling the dice. To do this, a PairOfDice object needs access to an object of type Random. But there is no need for each PairOfDice object to have a separate Random object. (In fact, it would not even be a good idea: Because of the way random number generators work, a program should, in general, use only one source of random numbers.) A nice solution is to have a single Random variable as a static member of the PairOfDice class, so that it can be shared by all PairOfDice objects. For example:

```
import java.util.Random;

public class PairOfDice {

    private static Random randGen = new Random();

    public int die1;      // Number showing on the first die.
    public int die2;      // Number showing on the second die.

    public PairOfDice() {
            • Constructor. Creates a pair of dice that
            • initially shows random values.
        roll();
    }

    public void roll() {
            • Roll the dice by setting each of the dice to be
            • a random number between 1 and 6.
        die1 = randGen.nextInt(6) + 1;
        die2 = randGen.nextInt(6) + 1;
    }

} // end class PairOfDice
```

As another example, let's rewrite the Student class that was used in Section 5.2. I've added an ID for each student and a static member called nextUniqueID. Although there is an ID variable in each student object, there is only one nextUniqueID variable.

```
public class Student {

    private String name;   // Student's name.
    private int ID;    // Unique ID number for this student.
    public double test1, test2, test3;        // Grades on three tests.

    private static int nextUniqueID = 0;
            // keep track of next available unique ID number
```

```
Student(String theName) {
    // Constructor for Student objects; provides a name for the Student,
```

```
        • and assigns the student a unique ID number.
      name = theName;
      nextUniqueID++;
      ID = nextUniqueID;
   }
   public String getName() {
        • Accessor method for reading value of private
        • instance variable, name.
      return name;
   }
   public int getID() {
        • Accessor method for reading value of ID.
      return ID;
   }
   public double getAverage() {
        • Compute average test grade.
      return (test1 + test2 + test3) / 3;
   }
} // end of class Student
```

The initialization "nextUniqueID = 0" is done only once, when the class is first loaded. Whenever a Student object is constructed and the constructor says "nextUniqueID++;", it's always the same static member variable that is being incremented. When the very first Student object is created, nextUniqueID becomes 1. When the second object is created, nextUniqueID becomes 2. After the third object, it becomes 3. And so on. The constructor stores the new value of nextUniqueID in the ID variable of the object that is being created. Of course, ID is an instance variable, so every object has its own individual ID variable. The class is constructed so that each student will automatically get a different value for its ID variable. Furthermore, the ID variable is private, so there is no way for this variable to be tampered with after the object has been created. You are guaranteed, just by the way the class is designed, that every student object will have its own permanent, unique identification number. Which is kind of cool if you think about it.

5.7.5 Static Import

The import directive makes it possible to refer to a class such as java.awt.Color using its simple name, Color. All you have to do is say import java.awt.Color or import java.awt.*. But you still have to use compound names to refer to static member variables such as System.out and to static methods such as Math.sqrt.

Java 5.0 introduced a new form of the import directive that can be used to import static members of a class in the same way that the ordinary import directive imports classes from a package. The new form of the directive is called a **static import** , and it has syntax

```
import static    package-name . class-name . static-member-name ;
```

to import one static member name from a class, or

```
import static    package-name . class-name .*;
```

to import all the public static members from a class. For example, if you preface a class definition with

to import all the public static members from a class. For example, if you preface a class definition with

```
import static java.lang.System.out;
```

then you can use the simple name out instead of the compound name System.out. This means you can use out.println instead of System.out.println. If you are going to work extensively with the Math class, you can preface your class definition with

```
import static java.lang.Math.*;
```

This would allow you to say sqrt instead of Math.sqrt, log instead of Math.log, PI instead of Math.PI, and so on.

Note that the static import directive requires a **package-name** , even for classes in the standard package java.lang. One consequence of this is that you can't do a static import from a class in the default package. In particular, it is not possible to do a static import from my TextIO class—if you wanted to do that, you would have to move TextIO into a package.

5.7.6 Enums as Classes

Enumerated types were introduced in Subsection 2.3.3. Now that we have covered more material on classes and objects, we can revisit the topic (although still not covering enumerated types in their full complexity).

Enumerated types are actually classes, and each enumerated type constant is a public, final, static member variable in that class (even though they are not declared with these modifiers). The value of the variable is an object belonging to the enumerated type class. There is one such object for each enumerated type constant, and these are the only objects of the class that can ever be created. It is really these objects that represent the possible values of the enumerated type. The enumerated type constants are actually variables that refer to these objects.

When an enumerated type is defined inside another class, it is a nested class inside the enclosing class. In fact, it is a static nested class, whether you declare it to be static or not. But it can also be declared as a non-nested class, in a file of its own. For example, we could define the following enumerated type in a file named Suit.java:

```
public enum Suit {

    SPADES, HEARTS, DIAMONDS, CLUBS

}
```

This enumerated type represents the four possible suits for a playing card, and it could have been used in the example **Card.java** from Subsection 5.4.2.

Furthermore, in addition to its list of values, an enumerated type can contain some of the other things that a regular class can contain, including methods and additional member variables. Just add a semicolon (;) at the end of the list of values, and then add definitions of the methods and variables in the usual way. For example, we might make an enumerated type to represent the possible values of a playing card. It might be useful to have a method that returns the corresponding value in the game of Blackjack. As another example, suppose that when we print out one of the values, we'd like to see something different from the default string representation (the identifier that names the constant). In that case, we can override the toString() method in the class to print out a different string representation. This would gives something like:

public enum CardValue {

```
ACE, TWO, THREE, FOUR, FIVE, SIX, SEVEN, EIGHT,
      NINE, TEN, JACK, QUEEN, KING;

/**
 • Return the value of this CardValue in the game of Blackjack.
 • Note that the value returned for an ace is 1.
 */
public int blackJackValue() {
   if (this == JACK || this == QUEEN || this == KING)
      return 10;
   else
      return 1 + ordinal();
}

/**
 • Return a String representation of this CardValue, using numbers
 • for the numerical cards and names for the ace and face cards.
 */
public String toString() {
   switch (this) {          // "this" is one of the enumerated type values
   case ACE:                // ordinal number of ACE
      return "Ace";
   case JACK:               // ordinal number of JACK
      return "Jack";
   case QUEEN:              // ordinal number of QUEEN
      return "Queen";
   case KING:               // ordinal number of KING
      return "King";
   default:                 // it's a numeric card value
      int numericValue = 1 + ordinal();
      return "" + numericValue;
}

} // end CardValue
```

The methods blackjackValue() and toString() are instance methods in CardValue. Since CardValue.JACK is an object belonging to that class, you can call CardValue.JACK.blackjackValue(). Suppose that cardVal is declared to be a variable of type CardValue, so that it can refer to any of the values in the enumerated type. We can call cardVal.blackjackValue() to find the Blackjack value of the CardValue object to which cardVal refers, and System.out.println(cardVal) will implicitly call the method cardVal.toString() to obtain the print representation of that CardValue. (One other thing to keep in mind is that since CardValue is a class, the value of cardVal can be null, which means it does not refer to any object.)

Remember that ACE, TWO, . . . , KING are the only possible objects of type CardValue, so in an instance method in that class, this will refer to one of those values. Recall that the instance method ordinal() is defined in any enumerated type and gives the position of the enumerated type value in the list of possible values, with counting starting from zero.

(If you find it annoying to use the class name as part of the name of every enumerated type constant, you can use static import to make the simple names of the constants directly available—but only if you put the enumerated type into a package. For example, if the enu-merated type CardValue is defined in a package named cardgames, then you could place

```
import static cardgames.CardValue.*;
```

at the beginning of a source code file. This would allow you, for example, to use the name JACK in that file instead of CardValue.JACK.)

for

- In all versions of the PairOfDice class in Section 5.2, the instance variables die1 and die2 are declared to be public. They really should be private, so that they are protected from being changed from outside the class. Write another version of the PairOfDice class in which the instance variables die1 and die2 are private. Your class will need "getter" methods that can be used to find out the values of die1 and die2. (The idea is to protect their values from being changed from outside the class, but still to allow the values to be read.) Include other improvements in the class, if you can think of any. Test your class with a short program that counts how many times a pair of dice is rolled, before the total of the two dice is equal to two.

- A common programming task is computing statistics of a set of numbers. (A statistic is a number that summarizes some property of a set of data.) Common statistics include the mean (also known as the average) and the standard deviation (which tells how spread out the data are from the mean). I have written a little class called StatCalc that can be used to compute these statistics, as well as the sum of the items in the dataset and the number of items in the dataset. You can read the source code for this class in the file **StatCalc.java**. If calc is a variable of type StatCalc, then the following methods are defined:

    calc.enter(item); where item is a number, adds the item to the dataset.

    calc.getCount() is a function that returns the number of items that have been added to the dataset.

    calc.getSum() is a function that returns the sum of all the items that have been added to the dataset.

    calc.getMean() is a function that returns the average of all the items.

    calc.getStandardDeviation() is a function that returns the standard deviation of the items.

Typically, all the data are added one after the other by calling the enter() method over and over, as the data become available. After all the data have been entered, any of the other methods can be called to get statistical information about the data. The methods getMean() and getStandardDeviation() should only be called if the number of items is greater than zero.

Modify the current source code, **StatCalc.java**, to add instance methods getMax() and getMin(). The getMax() method should return the largest of all the items that have been added to the dataset, and getMin() should return the smallest. You will need to add two new instance variables to keep track of the largest and smallest items that have been seen so far.

Test your new class by using it in a program to compute statistics for a set of non-zero numbers entered by the user. Start by creating an object of type StatCalc :

```
StatCalc  calc;     // Object to be used to process the data.
calc = new StatCalc();
```

Read numbers from the user and add them to the dataset. Use 0 as a sentinel value (that is, stop reading numbers when the user enters 0). After all the user's non-zero numbers have been entered, print out each of the six statistics that are available from calc.

- This problem uses the PairOfDice class from Exercise 5.1 and the StatCalc class from Exercise 5.2.

  The program in Exercise 4.4 performs the experiment of counting how many times a pair of dice is rolled before a given total comes up. It repeats this experiment 10000 times and then reports the average number of rolls. It does this whole process for each possible total (2, 3, . . . , 12).

  Redo that exercise. But instead of just reporting the average number of rolls, you should also report the standard deviation and the maximum number of rolls. Use a PairOfDice object to represent the dice. Use a StatCalc object to compute the statistics. (You'll need a new StatCalc object for each possible total, 2, 3, . . . , 12. You can use a new pair of dice if you want, but it's not necessary.)

- The BlackjackHand class from Subsection 5.5.1 is an extension of the Hand class from Sec-tion 5.4. The instance methods in the Hand class are discussed in that section. In addition to those methods, BlackjackHand includes an instance method, getBlackjackValue(), that returns the value of the hand for the game of Blackjack. For this exercise, you will also need the Deck and Card classes from Section 5.4.

  A Blackjack hand typically contains from two to six cards. Write a program to test the BlackjackHand class. You should create a BlackjackHand object and a Deck object. Pick a random number between 2 and 6. Deal that many cards from the deck and add them to the hand. Print out all the cards in the hand, and then print out the value computed for the hand by getBlackjackValue(). Repeat this as long as the user wants to continue.

  In addition to **TextIO.java**, your program will depend on **Card.java, Deck.java, Hand.java**, and **BlackjackHand.java**.

- Write a program that lets the user play Blackjack. The game will be a simplified version of Blackjack as it is played in a casino. The computer will act as the dealer. As in the previous exercise, your program will need the classes defined in **Card.java, Deck.java, Hand.java**, and **BlackjackHand.java**. (This is the longest and most complex program that has come up so far in the .)

  You should first write a subroutine in which the user plays one game. The subroutine should return a boolean value to indicate whether the user wins the game or not. Return true if the user wins, false if the dealer wins. The program needs an object of class Deck and two objects of type BlackjackHand, one for the dealer and one for the user. The general object in Blackjack is to get a hand of cards whose value is as close to 21 as possible, without going over. The game goes like this.

  > First, two cards are dealt into each player's hand. If the dealer's hand has a value of 21 at this point, then the dealer wins. Otherwise, if the user has 21, then the user wins. (This is called a "Blackjack".) Note that the dealer wins on a tie, so if both players have Blackjack, then the dealer wins.
  >
  > Now, if the game has not ended, the user gets a chance to add some cards to her hand. In this phase, the user sees her own cards and sees **one** of the dealer's two cards. (In a casino, the dealer deals himself one card face up and one card face

down. All the user's cards are dealt face up.) The user makes a decision whether to "Hit",

which means to add another card to her hand, or to "Stand", which means to stop taking cards.

- If the user Hits, there is a possibility that the user will go over 21. In that case, the game is over and the user loses. If not, then the process continues. The user gets to decide again whether to Hit or Stand.
- If the user Stands, the game will end, but first the dealer gets a chance to draw cards. The dealer only follows rules, without any choice. The rule is that as long as the value of the dealer's hand is less than or equal to 16, the dealer Hits (that is, takes another card). The user should see all the dealer's cards at this point. Now, the winner can be determined: If the dealer has gone over 21, the user wins. Otherwise, if the dealer's total is greater than or equal to the user's total, then the dealer wins. Otherwise, the user wins.

Two notes on programming: At any point in the subroutine, as soon as you know who the winner is, you can say "return true;" or "return false;" to end the subroutine and return to the main program. To avoid having an overabundance of variables in your subroutine, remember that a function call such as userHand.getBlackjackValue() can be used anywhere that a number could be used, including in an output statement or in the condition of an if statement.

Write a main program that lets the user play several games of Blackjack. To make things interesting, give the user 100 dollars, and let the user make bets on the game. If the user loses, subtract the bet from the user's money. If the user wins, add an amount equal to the bet to the user's money. End the program when the user wants to quit or when she runs out of money.

An applet version of this program can be found in the on-line version of this exercise. You might want to try it out before you work on the program.

- Subsection 5.7.6 discusses the possibility of representing the suits and values of playing cards as enumerated types. Rewrite the Card class from Subsection 5.4.2 to use these enumerated types. Test your class with a program that prints out the 52 possible playing cards. Suggestions: You can modify the source code file **Card.java**, but you should leave out support for Jokers. In your main program, use nested for loops to generated cards of all possible suits and values; the for loops will be "for-each" loops of the type discussed in Subsection 3.4.4. It would be nice to add a toString() method to the Suit class from Subsection 5.7.6, so that a suit prints out as "Spades" or "Hearts" instead of "SPADES" or "HEARTS".

Quiz on

- Object-oriented programming uses **classes** and **objects**. What are classes and what are objects? What is the relationship between classes and objects?

- Explain carefully what **null** means in Java, and why this special value is necessary.

- What is a **constructor?** What is the purpose of a constructor in a class?

- Suppose that Kumquat is the name of a class and that fruit is a variable of type Kumquat. What is the meaning of the statement "fruit = new Kumquat();"? That is, what does the computer do when it executes this statement? (Try to give a complete answer. The computer does several things.)

- What is meant by the terms **instance variable** and **instance method** ?

- Explain what is meant by the terms **subclass** and **superclass.**

- Modify the following class so that the two instance variables are private and there is a getter method and a setter method for each instance variable:

```
public class Player {
    String name;
    int score;
}
```

- Explain why the class Player that is defined in the previous question has an instance method named toString(), even though no definition of this method appears in the definition of the class.

- Explain the term **polymorphism.**

- Java uses "garbage collection" for memory management. Explain what is meant here by garbage collection. What is the alternative to garbage collection?

- For this problem, you should write a very simple but complete class. The class represents a counter that counts 0, 1, 2, 3, 4, ... The name of the class should be Counter. It has one private instance variable representing the value of the counter. It has two instance methods: increment() adds one to the counter value, and getValue() returns the current counter value. Write a complete definition for the class, Counter.

- This problem uses the Counter class from the previous question. The following program segment is meant to simulate tossing a coin 100 times. It should use two Counter objects, headCount and tailCount, to count the number of heads and the number of tails. Fill in the blanks so that it will do so:

```
Counter headCount, tailCount;
tailCount = new Counter();
headCount = new Counter();
for ( int flip = 0;  flip < 100;                flip++ ) {
    if (Math.random() < 0.5)              // There's a 50/50 chance that this is true.
            _______________   ;  // Count a "head".
    else
            _______________   ;  // Count a "tail".
}
System.out.println("There were " +            _____________ + " heads.");
System.out.println("There were " +            _____________ + " tails.");
```

Chapter 11

Introduction to GUI Programming

Computer users today expect to interact with their computers using a graphical user interface (GUI). Java can be used to write GUI programs ranging from simple applets which run on a Web page to sophisticated stand-alone applications.

GUI programs differ from traditional "straight-through" programs that you have encountered in the first few chapters of this book. One big difference is that GUI programs are **event-driven** . That is, user actions such as clicking on a button or pressing a key on the keyboard generate events, and the program must respond to these events as they occur. Event-driven programming builds on all the skills you have learned in the first five chapters of this text. You need to be able to write the subroutines that respond to events. Inside these subrou-tines, you are doing the kind of programming-in-the-small that was covered in Chapter 2 and Chapter 3.

And of course, objects are everywhere in GUI programming. Events are objects. Colors and fonts are objects. GUI components such as buttons and menus are objects. Events are handled by instance methods contained in objects. In Java, GUI programming is object-oriented programming.

This chapter covers the basics of GUI programming. The discussion will continue in Chap-ter 12 with more details and with more advanced techniques.

6.1 The Basic GUI Application

There are two basic types of GUI program in Java: **stand-alone applications** and **applets**. An applet is a program that runs in a rectangular area on a Web page. Applets are generally small programs, meant to do fairly simple things, although there is nothing to stop them from being very complex. Applets were responsible for a lot of the initial excitement about Java when it was introduced, since they could do things that could not otherwise be done on Web pages. However, there are now easier ways to do many of the more basic things that can be done with applets, and they are no longer the main focus of interest in Java. Nevertheless, there are still some things that can be done best with applets, and they are still fairly common on the Web. We will look at applets in the next section.

A stand-alone application is a program that runs on its own, without depending on a Web browser. You've been writing stand-alone applications all along. Any class that has a main() routine defines a stand-alone application; running the program just means executing this main() routine. However, the programs that you've seen up till now have been "command-line" programs, where the user and computer interact by typing things back and forth to each other. A GUI program offers a much richer type of user interface, where the user uses a mouse and keyboard to interact with GUI components such as windows, menus, buttons, check boxes, text input boxes, scroll bars, and so on. The main routine of a GUI program creates one or more such components and displays them on the computer screen. Very often, that's all it does. Once a GUI component has been created, it follows its **own** programming—programming that tells it how to draw itself on the screen and how to respond to events such as being clicked on by the user.

A GUI program doesn't have to be immensely complex. We can, for example, write a very simple GUI "Hello World" program that says "Hello" to the user, but does it by opening a window where the the greeting is displayed:

```
import javax.swing.JOptionPane;

public class HelloWorldGUI1 {

    public static void main(String[] args) {
        JOptionPane.showMessageDialog( null, "Hello World!" );
    }

}
```

When this program is run, a window appears on the screen that contains the message "Hello World!". The window also contains an "OK" button for the user to click after reading the message. When the user clicks this button, the window closes and the program ends. By the way, this program can be placed in a file named **HelloWorldGUI1.java**, compiled, and run just like any other Java program.

Now, this program is already doing some pretty fancy stuff. It creates a window, it draws the contents of that window, and it handles the event that is generated when the user clicks the button. The reason the program was so easy to write is that all the work is done by showMessageDialog(), a static method in the built-in class JOptionPane. (Note that the source code "imports" the class javax.swing.JOptionPane to make it possible to refer to the JOptionPane class using its simple name. See Subsection 4.5.3 for information about importing classes from Java's standard packages.)

If you want to display a message to the user in a GUI program, this is a good way to do it: Just use a standard class that already knows how to do the work! And in fact, JOptionPane is regularly used for just this purpose (but as part of a larger program, usually). Of course, if you want to do anything serious in a GUI program, there is a lot more to learn. To give you an idea of the types of things that are involved, we'll look at a short GUI program that does the same things as the previous program—open a window containing a message and an OK button, and respond to a click on the button by ending the program—but does it all by hand instead of by using the built-in JOptionPane class. Mind you, this is **not** a good way to write the program, but it will illustrate some important aspects of GUI programming in Java.

Here is the source code for the program. You are not expected to understand it yet. I will explain how it works below, but it will take the rest of the chapter before you will really understand completely. In this section, you will just get a brief overview of GUI programming.

```
import java.awt.*;
```

```
import java.awt.event.*;
import javax.swing.*;

public class HelloWorldGUI2 {

    private static class HelloWorldDisplay extends JPanel {
```

```
        public void paintComponent(Graphics g) {
            super.paintComponent(g);
            g.drawString( "Hello World!", 20, 30 );
        }
    }

    private static class ButtonHandler implements ActionListener {
        public void actionPerformed(ActionEvent e) {
            System.exit(0);
        }
    }

    public static void main(String[] args) {

        HelloWorldDisplay displayPanel = new HelloWorldDisplay();
        JButton okButton = new JButton("OK");
        ButtonHandler listener = new ButtonHandler();
        okButton.addActionListener(listener);

        JPanel content = new JPanel();
        content.setLayout(new BorderLayout());
        content.add(displayPanel, BorderLayout.CENTER);
        content.add(okButton, BorderLayout.SOUTH);

        JFrame window = new JFrame("GUI Test");
        window.setContentPane(content);
        window.setSize(250,100);
        window.setLocation(100,100);
        window.setVisible(true);

    }
}
```

6.1.1 JFrame and JPanel

In a Java GUI program, each GUI component in the interface is represented by an object in the program. One of the most fundamental types of component is the **window** . Windows have many behaviors. They can be opened and closed. They can be resized. They have "titles" that are displayed in the title bar above the window. And most important, they can contain other GUI components such as buttons and menus.

Java, of course, has a built-in class to represent windows. There are actually several different types of window, but the most common type is represented by the JFrame class (which is included in the package javax.swing). A JFrame is an independent window that can, for example, act as the main window of an application. One of the most important things to understand is that a JFrame object comes with many of the behaviors of windows already programmed in. In particular, it comes with the basic properties shared by all windows, such as a titlebar and the ability to be opened and closed. Since a JFrame comes with these behaviors, you don't have to program them yourself ! This is, of course, one of the central ideas of object-oriented programming. What a JFrame doesn't come with, of course, is **content** , the stuff that is contained in the window. If you don't add any other content to a JFrame, it will just display a large blank area. You can add content either by creating a JFrame object and then adding the content to it or by creating a subclass of JFrame and adding the content in the constructor of that subclass.

The main program above declares a variable, window, of type JFrame and sets it to refer to a new window object with the statement:

```
JFrame window = new JFrame("GUI Test");
```

The parameter in the constructor, “GUI Test”, specifies the title that will be displayed in the titlebar of the window. This line creates the window object, but the window itself is not yet visible on the screen. Before making the window visible, some of its properties are set with these statements:

```
window.setContentPane(content);
window.setSize(250,100);
window.setLocation(100,100);
```

The first line here sets the content of the window. (The content itself was created earlier in the main program.) The second line says that the window will be 250 pixels wide and 100 pixels high. The third line says that the upper left corner of the window will be 100 pixels over from the left edge of the screen and 100 pixels down from the top. Once all this has been set up, the window is actually made visible on the screen with the command:

```
window.setVisible(true);
```

It might look as if the program ends at that point, and, in fact, the main() routine does end. However, the the window is still on the screen and the program as a whole does not end until the user clicks the OK button.

* * *

The content that is displayed in a JFrame is called its **content pane.** (In addition to its content pane, a JFrame can also have a menu bar, which is a separate thing that I will talk about later.) A basic JFrame already has a blank content pane; you can either add things to that pane or you can replace the basic content pane entirely. In my sample program, the line window.setContentPane(content) replaces the original blank content pane with a different component. (Remember that a “component” is just a visual element of a graphical user interface). In this case, the new content is a component of type JPanel.

JPanel is another of the fundamental classes in Swing. The basic JPanel is, again, just a blank rectangle. There are two ways to make a useful JPanel : The first is to **add other components** to the panel; the second is to **draw something** in the panel. Both of these techniques are illustrated in the sample program. In fact, you will find two JPanel s in the program: content, which is used to contain other components, and displayPanel, which is used as a drawing surface.

Let's look more closely at displayPanel. This variable is of type HelloWorldDisplay, which is a nested static class inside the HelloWorldGUI2 class. (Nested classes were introduced in Subsection 5.7.2.) This class defines just one instance method, paintComponent(), which overrides a method of the same name in the JPanel class:

```
private static class HelloWorldDisplay extends JPanel {
    public void paintComponent(Graphics g) {
        super.paintComponent(g);
        g.drawString( "Hello World!", 20, 30 );
    }
}
```

The paintComponent() method is called by the system when a component needs to be painted on the screen. In the JPanel class, the paintComponent method simply fills the panel with the

panel's background color. The paintComponent() method in HelloWorldDisplay begins by call-ing super.paintComponent(g). This calls the version of paintComponent() that is defined in the superclass, JPanel ; that is, it fills the panel with the background color. (See Subsection 5.6.2 for a discussion of the special variable super.) Then it calls g.drawString() to paint the string "Hello World!" onto the panel. The net result is that whenever a HelloWorldDisplay is shown on the screen, it displays the string "Hello World!".

We will often use JPanel s in this way, as drawing surfaces. Usually, when we do this, we will define a nested class that is a subclass of JPanel and we will write a paintComponent method in that class to draw the desired content in the panel.

6.1.2 Components and Layout

Another way of using a JPanel is as a **container** to hold other components. Java has many classes that define GUI components. Before these components can appear on the screen, they must be **added** to a container. In this program, the variable named content refers to a JPanel that is used as a container, and two other components are added to that container. This is done in the statements:

```
content.add(displayPanel, BorderLayout.CENTER);
content.add(okButton, BorderLayout.SOUTH);
```

Here, content refers to an object of type JPanel ; later in the program, this panel becomes the content pane of the window. The first component that is added to content is displayPanel which, as discussed above, displays the message, "Hello World!". The second is okButton which represents the button that the user clicks to close the window. The variable okButton is of type JButton, the Java class that represents push buttons.

The "BorderLayout" stuff in these statements has to do with how the two components are arranged in the container. When components are added to a container, there has to be some way of deciding how those components are arranged inside the container. This is called "laying out" the components in the container, and the most common technique for laying out components is to use a **layout manager** . A layout manager is an object that implements some policy for how to arrange the components in a container; different types of layout manager implement different policies. One type of layout manager is defined by the BorderLayout class. In the program, the statement

```
content.setLayout(new BorderLayout());
```

creates a new BorderLayout object and tells the content panel to use the new object as its layout manager. Essentially, this line determines how components that are added to the content panel will be arranged inside the panel. We will cover layout managers in much more detail later, but for now all you need to know is that adding okButton in the BorderLayout.SOUTH position puts the button at the bottom of the panel, and putting displayPanel in the BorderLayout.CENTER position makes it fill any space that is not taken up by the button.

This example shows a general technique for setting up a GUI: Create a container and assign a layout manager to it, create components and add them to the container, and use the container as the content pane of a window or applet. A container is itself a component, so it is possible that some of the components that are added to the top-level container are themselves containers, with their own layout managers and components. This makes it possible to build up complex user interfaces in a hierarchical fashion, with containers inside containers inside containers. . .

6.1.3 Events and Listeners

The structure of containers and components sets up the physical appearance of a GUI, but it doesn't say anything about how the GUI **behaves**. That is, what can the user do to the GUI and how will it respond? GUIs are largely **event-driven** ; that is, the program waits for events that are generated by the user's actions (or by some other cause). When an event occurs, the program responds by executing an **event-handling method** . In order to program the behavior of a GUI, you have to write event-handling methods to respond to the events that you are interested in.

The most common technique for handling events in Java is to use **event listeners**. A listener is an object that includes one or more event-handling methods. When an event is detected by another object, such as a button or menu, the listener object is notified and it responds by running the appropriate event-handling method. An event is detected or generated by an object. Another object, the listener, has the responsibility of responding to the event. The event itself is actually represented by a third object, which carries information about the type of event, when it occurred, and so on. This division of responsibilities makes it easier to organize large programs.

As an example, consider the OK button in the sample program. When the user clicks the button, an event is generated. This event is represented by an object belonging to the class ActionEvent. The event that is generated is associated with the button; we say that the button is the **source** of the event. The listener object in this case is an object belonging to the class ButtonHandler, which is defined as a nested class inside HelloWorldGUI2 :

```
private static class ButtonHandler implements ActionListener {
    public void actionPerformed(ActionEvent e) {
        System.exit(0);
    }
}
```

This class implements the ActionListener interface—a requirement for listener objects that handle events from buttons. (Interfaces were introduced in Subsection 5.7.1.) The event-handling method is named actionPerformed, as specified by the ActionListener interface. This method contains the code that is executed when the user clicks the button; in this case, the code is a call to System.exit(), which will terminate the program.

There is one more ingredient that is necessary to get the event from the button to the listener object: The listener object must **register** itself with the button as an event listener. This is done with the statement:

```
okButton.addActionListener(listener);
```

This statement tells okButton that when the user clicks the button, the ActionEvent that is generated should be sent to listener. Without this statement, the button has no way of knowing that some other object would like to listen for events from the button.

This example shows a general technique for programming the behavior of a GUI: Write classes that include event-handling methods. Create objects that belong to these classes and register them as listeners with the objects that will actually detect or generate the events. When an event occurs, the listener is notified, and the code that you wrote in one of its event-handling methods is executed. At first, this might seem like a very roundabout and complicated way to get things done, but as you gain experience with it, you will find that it is very flexible and that it goes together very well with object oriented programming. (We will return to events and listeners in much more detail in Section 6.3 and later sections, and I do not expect you to completely understand them at this time.)

6.2 Applets and HTML

Although stand-alone applications are probably more important than applets at this point in the history of Java, applets are still widely used. They can do things on Web pages that can't easily be done with other technologies. It is easy to distribute applets to users: The user just has to open a Web page, and the applet is there, with no special installation required (although the user must have an appropriate version of Java installed on their computer). And of course, applets are fun; now that the Web has become such a common part of life, it's nice to be able to see your work running on a web page.

The good news is that writing applets is not much different from writing stand-alone appli-cations. The structure of an applet is essentially the same as the structure of the JFrames that were introduced in the previous section, and events are handled in the same way in both types of program. So, most of what you learn about applications applies to applets, and **vice versa**.

Of course, one difference is that an applet is dependent on a Web page, so to use applets effectively, you have to learn at least a little about creating Web pages. Web pages are written using a language called **HTML** (HyperText Markup Language). In Subsection 6.2.3, below, you'll learn how to use HTML to create Web pages that display applets.

6.2.1 JApplet

The JApplet class (in package javax.swing) can be used as a basis for writing applets in the same way that JFrame is used for writing stand-alone applications. The basic JApplet class represents a blank rectangular area. Since an applet is not a stand-alone application, this area must appear on a Web page, or in some other environment that knows how to display an applet. Like a JFrame, a JApplet contains a content pane (and can contain a menu bar). You can add content to an applet either by adding content to its content pane or by replacing the content pane with another component. In my examples, I will generally create a JPanel and use it as a replacement for the applet's content pane.

To create an applet, you will write a subclass of JApplet. The JApplet class defines several instance methods that are unique to applets. These methods are called by the applet's environ-ment at certain points during the applet's "life cycle." In the JApplet class itself, these methods do nothing; you can override these methods in a subclass. The most important of these special applet methods is

```
public void init()
```

An applet's init() method is called when the applet is created. You can use the init() method as a place where you can set up the physical structure of the applet and the event handling that will determine its behavior. (You can also do some initialization in the constructor for your class, but there are certain aspects of the applet's environment that are set up after its constructor is called but before the init() method is called, so there are a few operations that will work in the init() method but will not work in the constructor.) The other applet life-cycle methods are start(), stop(), and destroy(). I will not use these methods for the time being and will not discuss them here except to mention that destroy() is called at the end of

the applet's lifetime and can be used as a place to do any necessary cleanup, such as closing any windows that were opened by the applet.

With this in mind, we can look at our first example of a JApplet. It is, of course, an applet that says "Hello World!". To make it a little more interesting, I have added a button that changes the text of the message, and a state variable, currentMessage, that holds the text of the current message. This example is very similar to the stand-alone application **HelloWorldGUI2** from the previous section. It uses an event-handling class to respond when the user clicks the button, a panel to display the message, and another panel that serves as a container for the message panel and the button. The second panel becomes the content pane of the applet. Here is the source code for the applet; again, you are not expected to understand all the details at this time:

```
import java.awt.*;
import java.awt.event.*;
import javax.swing.*;

/**
 • A simple applet that can display the messages "Hello World"
 • and "Goodbye World". The applet contains a button, and it
 • switches from one message to the other when the button is
 • clicked.
 */
public class HelloWorldApplet extends JApplet {

    private String currentMessage = "Hello World!"; // Currently displayed message.
    private MessageDisplay displayPanel;    // The panel where the message is displayed.

    private class MessageDisplay extends JPanel { // Defines the display panel. public
        void paintComponent(Graphics g) {
            super.paintComponent(g);
            g.drawString(currentMessage, 20, 30);
        }
    }

    private class ButtonHandler implements ActionListener { // The event listener.
        public void actionPerformed(ActionEvent e) {
            if (currentMessage.equals("Hello World!"))
                currentMessage = "Goodbye World!";
            else
                currentMessage = "Hello World!";
            displayPanel.repaint(); // Paint display panel with new message.
        }
    }

    /**
     • The applet's init() method creates the button and display panel and
     • adds them to the applet, and it sets up a listener to respond to
     • clicks on the button.
     */
    public void init() {

        displayPanel = new MessageDisplay();
```

```
JButton changeMessageButton = new JButton("Change
Message"); ButtonHandler listener = new ButtonHandler();
changeMessageButton.addActionListener(listener);

JPanel content = new JPanel();
content.setLayout(new BorderLayout());
```

```
        content.add(displayPanel, BorderLayout.CENTER);
        content.add(changeMessageButton,
        BorderLayout.SOUTH);
        setContentPane(content);
    }
}
```

You should compare this class with **HelloWorldGUI2.java** from the previous section. One subtle difference that you will notice is that the member variables and nested classes in this example are non-static. Remember that an applet is an object. A single class can be used to make several applets, and each of those applets will need its own copy of the applet data, so the member variables in which the data is stored must be non-static instance variables. Since the variables are non-static, the two nested classes, which use those variables, must also be non-static. (Static nested classes cannot access non-static member variables in the containing class; see Subsection 5.7.2.) Remember the basic rule for deciding whether to make a nested class static: If it needs access to any instance variable or instance method in the containing class, the nested class must be non-static; otherwise, it can be declared to be static.

6.2.2 Reusing Your JPanels

Both applets and frames can be programmed in the same way: Design a JPanel, and use it to replace the default content pane in the applet or frame. This makes it very easy to write two versions of a program, one which runs as an applet and one which runs as a frame. The idea is to create a subclass of JPanel that represents the content pane for your program; all the hard programming work is done in this panel class. An object of this class can then be used as the content pane either in a frame or in an applet. Only a very simple main() program is needed to show your panel in a frame, and only a very simple applet class is needed to show your panel in an applet, so it's easy to make both versions.

As an example, we can rewrite HelloWorldApplet by writing a subclass of JPanel. That class can then be reused to make a frame in a standalone application. This class is very similar to HelloWorldApplet, but now the initialization is done in a constructor instead of in an init() method:

```
import java.awt.*;
import java.awt.event.*;
import javax.swing.*;

public class HelloWorldPanel extends JPanel {

    private String currentMessage = "Hello World!"; // Currently displayed message.
    private MessageDisplay displayPanel;    // The panel where the message is displayed.

    private class MessageDisplay extends JPanel { // Defines the display panel. public
        void paintComponent(Graphics g) {
            super.paintComponent(g);
            g.drawString(currentMessage, 20, 30);
        }
```

```
}

private class ButtonHandler implements ActionListener { // The event listener.
    public void actionPerformed(ActionEvent e) {
        if (currentMessage.equals("Hello World!"))
            currentMessage = "Goodbye World!";
```

```
            else
                currentMessage = "Hello World!";
            displayPanel.repaint(); // Paint display panel with new message.
        }
    }
    /**
     • The constructor creates the components that will be contained inside this
     • panel, and then adds those components to this panel.
     */
    public HelloWorldPanel() {

        displayPanel = new MessageDisplay();   // Create the display subpanel.

        JButton changeMessageButton = new JButton("Change Message"); // The
        button. ButtonHandler listener = new ButtonHandler();
        changeMessageButton.addActionListener(listener);

        setLayout(new BorderLayout());    // Set the layout manager for this panel.
        add(displayPanel, BorderLayout.CENTER);   // Add the display panel.
        add(changeMessageButton, BorderLayout.SOUTH);   // Add the button.

    }

}
```

Once this class exists, it can be used in an applet. The applet class only has to create an object of type HelloWorldPanel and use that object as its content pane:

```
import javax.swing.JApplet;

public class HelloWorldApplet2 extends JApplet {
    public void init() {
        HelloWorldPanel content = new HelloWorldPanel();
        setContentPane(content);
    }
}
```

Similarly, its easy to make a frame that uses an object of type HelloWorldPanel as its content pane:

```
import javax.swing.JFrame;

public class HelloWorldGUI3 {

    public static void main(String[] args) {
        JFrame window = new JFrame("GUI Test");
        HelloWorldPanel content = new HelloWorldPanel();
        window.setContentPane(content);
        window.setSize(250,100);
        window.setLocation(100,100);
        window.setDefaultCloseOperation( JFrame.EXIT_ON CLOSE );
        window.setVisible(true);
    }
```

```
}
```

One new feature of this example is the line

```
window.setDefaultCloseOperation( JFrame.EXIT_ON_CLOSE );
```

This says that when the user closes the window by clicking the close box in the title bar of the window, the program should be terminated. This is necessary because no other way is provided to end the program. Without this line, the default close operation of the window would simply hide the window when the user clicks the close box, leaving the program running. This brings up one of the difficulties of reusing the same panel class both in an applet and in a frame: There are some things that a stand-alone application can do that an applet can't do. Terminating the program is one of those things. If an applet calls System.exit(), it has no effect except to generate an error.

Nevertheless, in spite of occasional minor difficulties, many of the GUI examples in this book will be written as subclasses of JPanel that can be used either in an applet or in a frame.

6.2.3 Basic HTML

Before you can actually use an applet that you have written, you need to create a Web page on which to place the applet. Such pages are themselves written in a language called **HTML** (HyperText Markup Language). An HTML document describes the contents of a page. A Web browser interprets the HTML code to determine what to display on the page. The HTML code doesn't look much like the resulting page that appears in the browser. The HTML document does contain all the text that appears on the page, but that text is "marked up" with commands that determine the structure and appearance of the text and determine what will appear on the page in addition to the text.

HTML has become a rather complicated language. In this section, I will cover just the most basic aspects of the language. You can easily find more information on the Web, if you want to learn more. Although there are many Web-authoring programs that make it possible to create Web pages without ever looking at the underlying HTML code, it is possible to write an HTML page using an ordinary text editor, typing in all the mark-up commands by hand, and it is worthwhile to learn how to create at least simple pages in this way.

There is a strict syntax for HTML documents (although in practice Web browsers will do their best to display a page even if it does not follow the syntax strictly). Leaving out optional features, an HTML document has the form:

```
<html>
<head>
<title> document-title </title>
</head>
<body>
 document-content
</body>
</html>
```

The **document-title** is text that will appear in the title bar of the Web browser window when the page is displayed. The **document-content** is what is displayed on the page itself. The rest of this section describes some of the things that can go into the **document-content** section of an HTML document

* * *

The mark-up commands used by HTML are called **tags**. Examples include <html> and <title> in the document outline given above. An HTML tag takes the form

< tag-name   optional-modifiers >

where the **tag-name** is a word that specifies the command, and the **optional-modifiers** , if present, are used to provide additional information for the command (much like parameters in subroutines). A modifier takes the form

modifier-name = value

Usually, the **value** is enclosed in quotes, and it must be if it is more than one word long or if it contains certain special characters. There are a few modifiers which have no value, in which case only the name of the modifier is present. HTML is case insensitive, which means that you can use upper case and lower case letters interchangeably in tags and modifiers. (However, lower case is generally used because XHTML, a successor language to HTML, requires lower case.)

A simple example of a tag is <hr>, which draws a line—also called a "horizontal rule"—across the page. The hr tag can take several possible modifiers such as width and align. For example, a horizontal line that extends halfway across the page could be generated with the tag:

```
<hr  width="50%">
```

The width here is specified as 50% of the available space, meaning a line that extends halfway across the page. The width could also be given as a fixed number of pixels.

Many tags require matching closing tags, which take the form

</ tag-name >

For example, the <html> tag at the beginning of an HTML document must be matched by a closing </html> tag at the end of the document. As another example, the tag <pre> must always have a matching closing tag </pre> later in the document. An opening/closing tag pair applies to everything that comes between the opening tag and the closing tag. The <pre> tag tells a Web browser to display everything between the <pre> and the </pre> just as it is formatted in the original HTML source code, including all the spaces and carriage returns. (But tags between <pre> and </pre> are still interpreted by the browser.) "Pre" stands for preformatted text. All of the sample programs in the on-line version of this book are formatted using the <pre> command.

It is important for you to understand that when you don't use <pre>, the computer will completely ignore the formatting of the text in the HTML source code. The only thing it pays attention to is the tags. Five blank lines in the source code have no more effect than one blank line or even a single blank space. Outside of <pre>, if you want to force a new line on the Web page, you can use the tag <br>, which stands for "break". For example, I might give my address as:

```
David Eck<br>
Department of Mathematics and Computer Science<br>
Hobart and William Smith Colleges<br>
Geneva, NY 14456<br>
```

If you want extra vertical space in your web page, you can use several
's in a row.

Similarly, you need a tag to indicate how the text should be broken up into paragraphs. This is done with the <p> tag, which should be placed at the beginning of every paragraph. The <p> tag has a matching </p>, which should be placed at the end of each paragraph. The closing </p> is technically optional, but it is considered good form to use it. If you want all the lines of the paragraph to be shoved over to the right, you can use <p align=right> instead of

<p>. (This is mostly useful when used with one short line, or when used with <br> to make several short lines.) You can also use <p align=center> for centered lines.

By the way, if tags like <p> and <hr> have special meanings in HTML, you might wonder how one can get them to appear literally on a web page. To get certain special characters to appear on the page, you have to use an **entity name** in the HTML source code. The entity name for < is <, and the entity name for > is >. Entity names begin with & and end with a semicolon. The character & is itself a special character whose entity name is &. There are also entity names for nonstandard characters such as an accented "e", which has the entity name é.

There are several useful tags that change the appearance of text. For example, to get italic text, enclose the text between <i> and </i>. For example,

```
<i>Introduction to Programming using Java</i>
```

in an HTML document gives **Introduction to Programming using Java** in italics when the document is displayed as a Web page. Similarly, the tags <b>, <u>, and <tt> can be used for **bold**, underlined, and typewriter-style ("monospace") text.

A headline, with very large text, can be made by placing the the text between <h1> and </h1>. Headlines with smaller text can be made using <h2> or <h3> instead of <h1>. Note that these headline tags stand on their own; they are not used inside paragraphs. You can add the modifier align=center to center the headline, and you can include break tags (<br>) in a headline to break it up into multiple lines. For example, the following HTML code will produce a medium-sized, centered, two-line headline:

```
<h2 align=center>Chapter 6:<br>Introduction to GUI Programming</h2>
```

* * *

The most distinctive feature of HTML is that documents can contain **links** to other documents. The user can follow links from page to page and in the process visit pages from all over the Internet.

The <a> tag is used to create a link. The text between the <a> and its matching </a> appears on the page as the text of the link; the user can follow the link by clicking on this text. The <a> tag uses the modifier href to say which document the link should connect to. The value for href must be a **URL** (Uniform Resource Locator). A URL is a coded set of instructions for finding a document on the Internet. For example, the URL for my own "home page" is

```
http://math.hws.edu/eck/
```

To make a link to this page, I would use the HTML source code

```
<a href="http://math.hws.edu/eck/">David's Home Page</a>
```

The best place to find URLs is on existing Web pages. Web browsers display the URL for the page you are currently viewing, and they can display the URL of a link if you point to the link with the mouse.

If you are writing an HTML document and you want to make a link to another document that is in the same directory, you can use a **relative URL**. The relative URL consists of just the name of the file. For example, to create a link to a file named "s1.html" in the same directory as the HTML document that you are writing, you could use

```
<a href="s1.html">Section 1</a>
```

There are also relative URLs for linking to files that are in other directories. Using relative URLs is a good idea, since if you use them, you can move a whole collection of files without changing any of the links between them (as long as you don't change the relative locations of the files).

When you type a URL into a Web browser, you can omit the "http://" at the beginning of the URL. However, in an <a> tag in an HTML document, the "http://" can only be omitted if the URL is a relative URL. For a normal URL, it is required.

* * *

You can add images to a Web page with the <img> tag. (This is a tag that has no matching closing tag.) The actual image must be stored in a separate file from the HTML document. The <img> tag has a required modifier, named src, to specify the URL of the image file. For most browsers, the image should be in one of the formats PNG (with a file name ending in ".png"), JPEG (with a file name ending in ".jpeg" or ".jpg"), or GIF (with a file name ending in ".gif"). Usually, the image is stored in the same place as the HTML document, and a relative URL—that is, just the name of the image file—is used to specify the image file.

The <img> tag also has several optional modifiers. It's a good idea to always include the height and width modifiers, which specify the size of the image in pixels. Some browsers handle images better if they know in advance how big they are. The align modifier can be used to affect the placement of the image: "align=right" will shove the image to the right edge of the page, and the text on the page will flow around the image; "align=left" works similarly. (Unfortunately, "align=center" doesn't have the meaning you would expect. Browsers treat images as if they are just big characters. Images can occur inside paragraphs, links, and headings, for example. Alignment values of center, top, and bottom are used to specify how the image should line up with other characters in a line of text: Should the baseline of the text be at the center, the top, or the bottom of the image? Alignment values of right and left were added to HTML later, but they are the most useful values. If you want an image centered on the page, put it inside a <p align=center> tag.)

For example, here is HTML code that will place an image from a file named figure1.png on the page.

```
<img src="figure1.png" align=right height=150 width=100>
```

The image is 100 pixels wide and 150 pixels high, and it will appear on the right edge of the page.

6.2.4 Applets on Web Pages

The main point of this whole discussion of HTML is to learn how to use applets on the Web. The <applet> tag can be used to add a Java applet to a Web page. This tag must have a matching </applet>. A required modifier named code gives the name of the compiled class file that contains the applet class. The modifiers height and width are required to specify the size of the applet, in pixels. If you want the applet to be centered on the page, you can put the applet in a paragraph with center alignment So, an applet tag to display an applet named HelloWorldApplet centered on a Web page would look like this:

```
<p align=center>
<applet code="HelloWorldApplet.class" height=100 width=250>
```

```
</applet>
</p>
```

This assumes that the file HelloWorldApplet.class is located in the same directory with the HTML document. If this is not the case, you can use another modifier, codebase, to give the URL of the directory that contains the class file. The value of code itself is always just a class, not a URL.

If the applet uses other classes in addition to the applet class itself, then those class files must be in the same directory as the applet class (always assuming that your classes are all in the "default package"; see Subsection 2.6.4). If an applet requires more than one or two class files, it's a good idea to collect all the class files into a single jar file. Jar files are "archive files" which hold a number of smaller files. If your class files are in a jar archive, then you have to specify the name of the jar file in an archive modifier in the <applet> tag, as in

```
<applet code="HelloWorldApplet.class" archive="HelloWorld.jar" height=50...
```

I will have more to say about creating and using jar files at the end of this chapter.

Applets can use **applet parameters** to customize their behavior. Applet parameters are specified by using <param> tags, which can only occur between an <applet> tag and the closing </applet>. The param tag has required modifiers named name and value, and it takes the form

```
<param name=" param-name "  value=" param-value ">
```

The parameters are available to the applet when it runs. method getParameter() to check for parameters specified in method has the following interface:

An applet can use the predefined param tags. The getParameter()

```
String getParameter(String paramName)
```

The parameter paramName corresponds to the **param-name** in a param tag. If the specified paramName actually occurs in one of the param tags, then getParameter(paramName) returns the associated **param-value** . If the specified paramName does not occur in any param tag, then getParameter(paramName) returns the value null. Parameter names are case-sensitive, so you cannot use "size" in the param tag and ask for "Size" in getParameter. The getParameter() method is often called in the applet's init() method. It will not work correctly in the applet's constructor, since it depends on information about the applet's environment that is not available when the constructor is called.

Here is an example of an applet tag with several params:

```
<applet code="ShowMessage.class" width=200
   height=50> <param name="message"
   value="Goodbye World!"> <param name="font"
   value="Serif">
   <param name="size" value="36">
</applet>
```

The ShowMessage applet would presumably read these parameters in its init() method, which could go something like this:

```
String message;  // Instance variable: message to be displayed.
String fontName; // Instance variable: font to use for display.
int fontSize;        // Instance variable: size of the display font.
```

```
public void init() {
    String value;
    value = getParameter("message"); // Get message param, if any.
    if (value == null)
```

```
        message = "Hello World!"; // Default value, if no param is present.
    else
        message = value; // Value from PARAM tag.
    value = getParameter("font");
    if (value == null)
        fontName = "SansSerif"; // Default value, if no param is present.
    else
        fontName = value;
    value = getParameter("size");
    try {
        fontSize = Integer.parseInt(value);        // Convert string to number.
    }
    catch (NumberFormatException e) {
        fontSize = 20; // Default value, if no param is present, or if
    }                       //    the parameter value is not a legal integer.
     .
     .
     .
```

Elsewhere in the applet, the instance variables message, fontName, and fontSize would be used to determine the message displayed by the applet and the appearance of that message. Note that the value returned by getParameter() is always a String. If the param represents a numerical value, the string must be converted into a number, as is done here for the size parameter.

6.3 Graphics and Painting

Everthing you see on a computer screen has to be drawn there, even the text. The Java API includes a range of classes and methods that are devoted to drawing. In this section, I'll look at some of the most basic of these.

The physical structure of a GUI is built of components. The term **component** refers to a visual element in a GUI, including buttons, menus, text-input boxes, scroll bars, check boxes, and so on. In Java, GUI components are represented by objects belonging to subclasses of the class java.awt.Component. Most components in the Swing GUI—although not top-level com-ponents like JApplet and JFrame—belong to subclasses of the class javax.swing.JComponent, which is itself a subclass of java.awt.Component. Every component is responsible for drawing itself. If you want to use a standard component, you only have to add it to your applet or frame. You don't have to worry about painting it on the screen. That will happen automatically, since it already knows how to draw itself.

Sometimes, however, you do want to draw on a component. You will have to do this whenever you want to display something that is not included among the standard, pre-defined component classes. When you want to do this, you have to define your own component class and provide a method in that class for drawing the component. I will always use a subclass of JPanel when I need a drawing surface of this kind, as I did for the MessageDisplay class in the example **HelloWorldApplet.java** in the previous section. A JPanel, like any JComponent, draws its content in the method

```
public void paintComponent(Graphics g)
```

To create a drawing surface, you should define a subclass of JPanel and provide a custom paintComponent() method. Create an object belonging to this class and use it in your applet

or frame. When the time comes for your component to be drawn on the screen, the system will call its paintComponent() to do the drawing. That is, the code that you put into the paintComponent() method will be executed whenever the panel needs to be drawn on the screen; by writing this method, you determine the picture that will be displayed in the panel.

Note that the paintComponent() method has a parameter of type Graphics. The Graphics object will be provided by the system when it calls your method. You need this object to do the actual drawing. To do any drawing at all in Java, you need a **graphics context** . A graphics context is an object belonging to the class java.awt.Graphics. Instance methods are provided in this class for drawing shapes, text, and images. Any given Graphics object can draw to only one location. In this chapter, that location will always be a GUI component belonging to some subclass of JPanel. The Graphics class is an abstract class, which means that it is impossible to create a graphics context directly, with a constructor. There are actually two ways to get a graphics context for drawing on a component: First of all, of course, when the paintComponent() method of a component is called by the system, the parameter to that method is a graphics context for drawing on the component. Second, every component has an instance method called getGraphics(). This method is a function that returns a graphics context that can be used for drawing on the component outside its paintComponent() method. The official line is that you should **not** do this, and I will avoid it for the most part. But I have found it convenient to use getGraphics() in a few cases.

The paintComponent() method in the JPanel class simply fills the panel with the panel's background color. When defining a subclass of JPanel for use as a drawing surface, you will almost always want to fill the panel with the background color before drawing other content onto the panel (although it is not necessary to do this if the drawing commands in the method cover the background of the component completely.) This is traditionally done with a call to super.paintComponent(g), so most paintComponent() methods that you write will have the form:

```
public void paintComponent(g) {
    super.paintComponent(g);
    . . . // Draw the content of the component.
}
```

* * *

Most components do, in fact, do all drawing operations in their paintComponent() methods. What happens if, in the middle of some other method, you realize that the content of the component needs to be changed? You should **not** call paintComponent() directly to make the change; this method is meant to be called only by the system. Instead, you have to inform the system that the component needs to be redrawn, and let the system do its job by calling paintComponent(). You do this by calling the component's repaint() method. The method

```
public void repaint();
```

is defined in the Component class, and so can be used with any component. You should call repaint() to inform the system that the component needs to be redrawn. The repaint() method returns immediately, without doing any painting itself. The system will call the com-ponent's paintComponent() method **later**, as soon as it gets a chance to do so, after processing other pending events if there are any.

Note that the system can also call paintComponent() for other reasons. It is called when the component first appears on the screen. It will also be called if the component is resized or if it is covered up by another window and then uncovered. The system does not save a copy of the component's contents when it is covered. When it is uncovered, the component is responsible for redrawing itself. (As you will see, some of our early examples will not be able to do this correctly.)

This means that, to work properly, the paintComponent() method must be smart enough to correctly redraw the component at any time. To make this possible, a program should store data about the state of the component in its instance variables. These variables should contain all the information necessary to redraw the component completely. The paintComponent() method should use the data in these variables to decide what to draw. When the program wants to change the content of the component, it should not simply draw the new content. It should change the values of the relevant variables and call repaint(). When the system calls paintComponent(), that method will use the new values of the variables and will draw the component with the desired modifications. This might seem a roundabout way of doing things. Why not just draw the modifications directly? There are at least two reasons. First of all, it really does turn out to be easier to get things right if all drawing is done in one method. Second, even if you did make modifications directly, you would still have to make the paintComponent() method aware of them in some way so that it will be able to **redraw** the component correctly on demand.

You will see how all this works in practice as we work through examples in the rest of this chapter. For now, we will spend the rest of this section looking at how to get some actual drawing done.

6.3.1 Coordinates

The screen of a computer is a grid of little squares called **pixels**. The color of each pixel can be set individually, and drawing on the screen just means setting the colors of individual pixels.

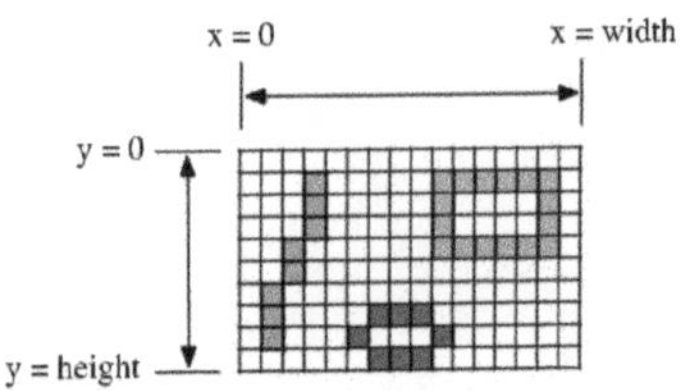

A graphics context draws in a rectangle made up of pixels. A position in the rectangle is specified by a pair of integer coordinates, (x,y). The upper left corner has coordinates (0,0). The x coordinate increases from left to right, and the y coordinate increases from top to bottom. The illustration shows a 16-by-10 pixel component (with very large pixels). A small line, rectangle, and oval are shown as they would be drawn by coloring individual pixels. (Note that, properly speaking, the coordinates don't belong to the pixels but to the grid lines between them.)

For any component, you can find out the size of the rectangle that it occupies by calling the instance methods getWidth() and getHeight(), which return the number of pixels in the horizontal and vertical directions, respectively. In general, it's not a good idea to assume that you know the size of a component, since the size is often set by a layout manager and can even change if the component is in a window and that window is resized by the user. This means that it's good form to check the size of a component before doing any drawing on that component. For example, you can use a paintComponent() method that looks like:

```
public void paintComponent(Graphics g) {
    super.paintComponent(g);
    int width =   getWidth();     // Find out the width of this component.
    int height = getHeight();     // Find out its height.
    . . .      // Draw the content of the component.
}
```

Of course, your drawing commands will have to take the size into account. That is, they will have to use (x,y) coordinates that are calculated based on the actual height and width of the component.

6.3.2 Colors

You will probably want to use some color when you draw. Java is designed to work with the **RGB color system** . An RGB color is specified by three numbers that give the level of red, green, and blue, respectively, in the color. A color in Java is an object of the class, java.awt.Color. You can construct a new color by specifying its red, blue, and green components. For example,

```
Color myColor = new Color(r,g,b);
```

There are two constructors that you can call in this way. In the one that I almost al-ways use, r, g, and b are integers in the range 0 to 255. In the other, they are num-bers of type float in the range 0.0F to 1.0F. (Recall that a literal of type float is written with an "F" to distinguish it from a double number.) Often, you can avoid constructing new colors altogether, since the Color class defines several named constants representing com-mon colors: Color.WHITE, Color.BLACK, Color.RED, Color.GREEN, Color.BLUE, Color.CYAN, Color.MAGENTA, Color.YELLOW, Color.PINK, Color.ORANGE, Color.LIGHT GRAY, Color.GRAY, and Color.DARK_GRAY. (There are older, alternative names for these constants that use lower case rather than upper case constants, such as Color.red instead of Color.RED, but the upper case versions are preferred because they follow the convention that constant names should be upper case.)

An alternative to RGB is the **HSB color system** . In the HSB system, a color is specified by three numbers called the **hue**, the **saturation**, and the **brightness**. The hue is the basic color, ranging from red through orange through all the other colors of the rainbow. The brightness is pretty much what it sounds like. A fully saturated color is a pure color tone. Decreasing the saturation is like mixing white or gray paint into the pure color. In Java, the hue, saturation and brightness are always specified by values of type float in the range from 0.0F to 1.0F. The Color class has a static member function named getHSBColor for creating HSB colors. To create the color with HSB values given by h, s, and b, you can say:

```
Color myColor = Color.getHSBColor(h,s,b);
```

For example, to make a color with a random hue that is as bright and as saturated as possible, you could use:

```
Color randomColor = Color.getHSBColor( (float)Math.random(), 1.0F, 1.0F );
```

The type cast is necessary because the value returned by Math.random() is of type double, and Color.getHSBColor() requires values of type float. (By the way, you might ask why RGB colors are created using a constructor while HSB colors are created using a static member function. The problem is that we would need two different constructors, both of them with three parameters of type float. Unfortunately, this is impossible. You can have two constructors only if the number of parameters or the parameter types differ.)

The RGB system and the HSB system are just different ways of describing the same set of colors. It is possible to translate between one system and the other. The best way to understand the color systems is to experiment with them. In the on-line version of this section, you will find an applet that you can use to experiment with RGB and HSB colors.

One of the properties of a Graphics object is the current drawing color, which is used for all drawing of shapes and text. If g is a graphics context, you can change the current drawing color for g using the method g.setColor(c), where c is a Color. For example, if you want to draw in green, you would just say g.setColor(Color.GREEN) before doing the drawing. The graphics context continues to use the color until you explicitly change it with another setColor() command. If you want to know what the current drawing color is, you can call the function g.getColor(), which returns an object of type Color. This can be useful if you want to change to another drawing color temporarily and then restore the previous drawing color.

Every component has an associated **foreground color** and **background color** . Generally, the component is filled with the background color before anything else is drawn (although some components are "transparent," meaning that the background color is ignored). When a new graphics context is created for a component, the current drawing color is set to the foreground color. Note that the foreground color and background color are properties of the component, not of a graphics context.

The foreground and background colors can be set by instance methods setForeground(c) and setBackground(c), which are defined in the Component class and therefore are available for use with any component. This can be useful even for standard components, if you want them to use colors that are different from the defaults.

6.3.3 Fonts

A **font** represents a particular size and style of text. The same character will appear different in different fonts. In Java, a font is characterized by a font name, a style, and a size. The available font names are system dependent, but you can always use the following four strings as font names: "Serif", "SansSerif", "Monospaced", and "Dialog". (A "serif" is a little decoration on a character, such as a short horizontal line at the bottom of the letter i. "SansSerif" means "without serifs." "Monospaced" means that all the characters in the font have the same width. The "Dialog" font is the one that is typically used in dialog boxes.)

The style of a font is specified using named constants that are defined in the Font class. You can specify the style as one of the four values:

- Font.PLAIN,
- Font.ITALIC,
- Font.BOLD, or
- Font.BOLD + Font.ITALIC.

The size of a font is an integer. Size typically ranges from about 10 to 36, although larger sizes can also be used. The size of a font is usually about equal to the height of the largest characters in the font, in pixels, but this is not an exact rule. The size of the default font is 12.

Java uses the class named java.awt.Font for representing fonts. You can construct a new font by specifying its font name, style, and size in a constructor:

```
Font plainFont = new Font("Serif", Font.PLAIN, 12); Font
bigBoldFont = new Font("SansSerif", Font.BOLD, 24);
```

Every graphics context has a current font, which is used for drawing text. You can change the current font with the setFont() method. For example, if g is a graphics context and bigBoldFont is a font, then the command g.setFont(bigBoldFont) will set the current font of g to bigBoldFont. The new font will be used for any text that is drawn **after** the setFont() command is given. You can find out the current font of g by calling the method g.getFont(), which returns an object of type Font.

Every component has an associated font. It can be set with the instance method setFont(font), which is defined in the Component class. When a graphics context is cre-ated for drawing on a component, the graphic context's current font is set equal to the font of the component.

6.3.4 Shapes

The Graphics class includes a large number of instance methods for drawing various shapes, such as lines, rectangles, and ovals. The shapes are specified using the (x,y) coordinate system described above. They are drawn in the current drawing color of the graphics context. The current drawing color is set to the foreground color of the component when the graphics context is created, but it can be changed at any time using the setColor() method.

Here is a list of some of the most important drawing methods. With all these commands, any drawing that is done outside the boundaries of the component is ignored. Note that all these methods are in the Graphics class, so they all must be called through an object of type Graphics.

- drawString(String str, int x, int y) — Draws the text given by the string str. The string is drawn using the current color and font of the graphics context. x specifies the position of the left end of the string. y is the y-coordinate of the baseline of the string. The baseline is a horizontal line on which the characters rest. Some parts of the characters, such as the tail on a y or g, extend below the baseline.
- drawLine(int x1, int y1, int x2, int y2) — Draws a line from the point (x1,y1) to the point (x2,y2). The line is drawn as if with a pen that hangs one pixel to the right and one pixel down from the (x,y) point where the pen is located. For example, if g refers to an object of type Graphics, then the command g.drawLine(x,y,x,y), which corresponds to putting the pen down at a point, colors the single pixel with upper left corner at the point (x,y).
- drawRect(int x, int y, int width, int height) — Draws the outline of a rectangle. The upper left corner is at (x,y), and the width and height of the rectangle are as specified. If width equals height, then the rectangle is a square. If the width or the height is negative, then nothing is drawn. The rectangle is drawn with the same pen that is used for drawLine(). This means that the actual width of the rectangle as drawn is width+1, and similarly for the height. There is an extra pixel along the right edge and the bottom edge. For example, if you want to draw a rectangle around the edges of the component, you can say "g.drawRect(0, 0, getWidth()-1, getHeight()-1);", where g is a graphics context for the component. If you use "g.drawRect(0, 0, getWidth(),

getHeight());", then the right and bottom edges of the rectangle will be drawn **outside** the component.

- drawOval(int x, int y, int width, int height) — Draws the outline of an oval. The oval is one that just fits inside the rectangle specified by x, y, width, and height. If width equals height, the oval is a circle.
- drawRoundRect(int x, int y, int width, int height, int xdiam, int ydiam) — Draws the outline of a rectangle with rounded corners. The basic rectangle is specified by x, y, width, and height, but the corners are rounded. The degree of rounding is given by xdiam and ydiam. The corners are arcs of an ellipse with horizontal diameter xdiam and vertical diameter ydiam. A typical value for xdiam and ydiam is 16, but the value used should really depend on how big the rectangle is.
- draw3DRect(int x, int y, int width, int height, boolean raised) — Draws the outline of a rectangle that is supposed to have a three-dimensional effect, as if it is raised from the screen or pushed into the screen. The basic rectangle is specified by x, y, width, and height. The raised parameter tells whether the rectangle seems to be raised from the screen or pushed into it. The 3D effect is achieved by using brighter and darker versions of the drawing color for different edges of the rectangle. The documentation recommends setting the drawing color equal to the background color before using this method. The effect won't work well for some colors.
- drawArc(int x, int y, int width, int height, int startAngle, int arcAngle) — Draws part of the oval that just fits inside the rectangle specified by x, y, width, and height. The part drawn is an arc that extends arcAngle degrees from a starting angle at startAngle degrees. Angles are measured with 0 degrees at the 3 o'clock position (the positive direction of the horizontal axis). Positive angles are measured counterclockwise from zero, and negative angles are measured clockwise. To get an arc of a circle, make sure that width is equal to height.
- fillRect(int x, int y, int width, int height) — Draws a filled-in rectangle. This fills in the interior of the rectangle that would be drawn by drawRect(x,y,width,height). The extra pixel along the bottom and right edges is not included. The width and height parameters give the exact width and height of the rectangle. For example, if you wanted to fill in the entire component, you could say "g.fillRect(0, 0, getWidth(), getHeight());"
- fillOval(int x, int y, int width, int height) — Draws a filled-in oval.
- fillRoundRect(int x, int y, int width, int height, int xdiam, int ydiam) — Draws a filled-in rounded rectangle.
- fill3DRect(int x, int y, int width, int height, boolean raised) — Draws a filled-in three-dimensional rectangle.
- fillArc(int x, int y, int width, int height, int startAngle, int arcAngle) — Draw a filled-in arc. This looks like a wedge of pie, whose crust is the arc that would be drawn by the drawArc method.

6.3.5 Graphics2D

All drawing in Java is done through an object of type Graphics. The Graphics class provides basic commands for such things as drawing shapes and text and for selecting a drawing color.

These commands are adequate in many cases, but they fall far short of what's needed in a serious computer graphics program. Java has another class, Graphics2D, that provides a larger set of drawing operations. Graphics2D is a sub-class of Graphics, so all the methods from the Graphics class are also available in a Graphics2D.

The paintComponent() method of a JComponent gives you a graphics context of type Graphics that you can use for drawing on the component. In fact, the graphics context actually belongs to the sub-class Graphics2D (in Java version 1.2 and later), and can be type-cast to gain access to the advanced Graphics2D drawing methods:

```
public void paintComponent(Graphics g) {
    super.paintComponent(g);
    Graphics2D g2;
    g2 = (Graphics2D)g;
     .
     • // Draw on the component using g2.
•
}
```

Drawing in Graphics2D is based on shapes, which are objects that implement an interface named Shape. Shape classes include Line2D, Rectangle2D, Ellipse2D, Arc2D, and CubicCurve2D, among others; all these classes are defined in the package java.awt.geom. CubicCurve2D can be used to draw Bezier Curves, which are used in many graphics programs. Graphics2D has methods draw(Shape) and fill(Shape) for drawing the outline of a shape and for filling its interior. Advanced capabilities include: lines that are more than one pixel thick, dotted and dashed lines, filling a shape with a texture (this is, with a repeated image), filling a shape with a gradient, and drawing translucent objects that will blend with their background.

In the Graphics class, coordinates are specified as integers and are based on pixels. The shapes that are used with Graphics2D use real numbers for coordinates, and they are not neces-sarily bound to pixels. In fact, you can change the coordinate system and use any coordinates that are convenient to your application. In computer graphics terms, you can apply a "transfor-mation" to the coordinate system. The transformation can be any combination of translation, scaling, and rotation.

I mention Graphics2D here for completeness. I will not use any of the advanced capabilities of Graphics2D in this chapter, but I will cover a few of them in Section 12.2.

6.3.6 An Example

Let's use some of the material covered in this section to write a subclass of JPanel for use as a drawing surface. The panel can then be used in either an applet or a frame, as discussed in Subsection 6.2.2. All the drawing will be done in the paintComponent() method of the panel class. The panel will draw multiple copies of a message on a black background. Each copy of the message is in a random color. Five different fonts are used, with different sizes and styles. The message can be specified in the constructor; if the default constructor is used, the message is the string “Java!”. The panel works OK no matter what its size. Here is what the panel looks like:

There is one problem with the way this class works. When the panel's paintComponent() method is called, it chooses random colors, fonts, and locations for the messages. The informa-tion about which colors, fonts, and locations are used is not stored anywhere. The next time paintComponent() is called, it will make different random choices and will draw a different picture. For this particular applet, the problem only really appears when the panel is **partially** covered and then uncovered (and even then the problem does not show up in all environments). It is possible that only the part that was covered will be redrawn, and in the part that's not redrawn, the old picture will remain. The user might see partial messages, cut off by the di-viding line between the new picture and the old. A better approach would be to compute the contents of the picture elsewhere, outside the paintComponent() method. Information about the picture should be stored in instance variables, and the paintComponent() method should use that information to draw the picture. If paintComponent() is called twice, it should draw the same picture twice, unless the data has changed in the meantime. Unfortunately, to store the data for the picture in this applet, we would need to use either arrays, which will not be covered until Chapter 7, or off-screen images, which will not be covered until Chapter 12. Other examples in this chapter will suffer from the same problem.

The source for the panel class is shown below. I use an instance variable called message to hold the message that the panel will display. There are five instance variables of type Font that represent different sizes and styles of text. These variables are initialized in the constructor and are used in the paintComponent() method.

The paintComponent() method for the panel simply draws 25 copies of the message. For each copy, it chooses one of the five fonts at random, and it calls g.setFont() to select that font for drawing the text. It creates a random HSB color and uses g.setColor() to select that color for drawing. It then chooses random (x,y) coordinates for the location of the message. The x coordinate gives the horizontal position of the left end of the string. The formula used for the x coordinate, "-50 + (int)(Math.random() * (width+40))" gives a random integer in the range from -50 to width-10. This makes it possible for the string to extend beyond the left edge or the right edge of the panel. Similarly, the formula for y allows the string to extend beyond the top and bottom of the applet.

Here is the complete source code for the RandomStringsPanel

```
import java.awt.Color;
import java.awt.Font;
import java.awt.Graphics;
```

```
import javax.swing.JPanel;

/**
 • This panel displays 25 copies of a message. The color and
 • position of each message is selected at random. The font
```

```
 • of each message is randomly chosen from among five possible
 • fonts. The messages are displayed on a black background.
 • <p>Note: The style of drawing used here is bad, because every
 • time the paintComponent() method is called, new random values are
 • used. This means that a different picture will be drawn each
 • time. This is particularly bad if only part of the panel
 • needs to be redrawn, since then the panel will contain
 • cut-off pieces of messages.
 • <p>This panel is meant to be used as the content pane in
 • either an applet or a frame.
 */
public class RandomStringsPanel extends JPanel {

   private String message;   // The message to be displayed.   This can be set in
                             • the constructor. If no value is provided in the
                             • constructor, then the string "Java!" is used.

   private Font font1, font2, font3, font4, font5;        // The five fonts.

   /**
    • Default constructor creates a panel that displays the message "Java!".

    */
   public RandomStringsPanel() {
      this(null);     // Call the other constructor, with parameter null.
   }

   /**
    • Constructor creates a panel to display 25 copies of a specified message.
    • @param messageString The message to be displayed. If this is null,
    • then the default message "Java!" is displayed.
    */
   public RandomStringsPanel(String messageString) {

      message = messageString;
      if (message == null)
          message = "Java!";

      font1 = new Font("Serif", Font.BOLD, 14);
      font2 = new Font("SansSerif", Font.BOLD + Font.ITALIC, 24);
      font3 = new Font("Monospaced", Font.PLAIN, 30); font4 = new
      Font("Dialog", Font.PLAIN, 36);
      font5 = new Font("Serif", Font.ITALIC, 48);

      setBackground(Color.BLACK);

   }

   /**
    • The paintComponent method is responsible for drawing the content of the panel.
    • It draws 25 copies of the message string, using a random color, font, and
    • position for each string.
    */
```

```
public void paintComponent(Graphics g) {

    super.paintComponent(g);  // Call the paintComponent method from the
```

- superclass, JPanel. This simply fills the
- entire panel with the background color, black.

```
int width = getWidth();
int height = getHeight();

for (int i = 0; i < 25; i++) {

   • Draw one string. First, set the font to be one of the five
   • available fonts, at random.

   int fontNum = (int)(5*Math.random()) + 1;
   switch (fontNum) {
      case 1:
         g.setFont(font1);
         break;
      case 2:
         g.setFont(font2);
         break;
      case 3:
         g.setFont(font3);
         break;
      case 4:
         g.setFont(font4);
         break;
      case 5:
         g.setFont(font5);
         break;
   } // end switch

   // Set the color to a bright, saturated color, with random hue.

   float hue = (float)Math.random();
   g.setColor( Color.getHSBColor(hue, 1.0F, 1.0F) );

   // Select the position of the string, at random.

   int x,y;
   • = -50 + (int)(Math.random()*(width+40)); y
   = (int)(Math.random()*(height+20));

      Draw the message.

   g.drawString(message,x,y);

} // end for

} // end paintComponent()

} // end class RandomStringsPanel
```

This class defines a panel, which is not something that can stand on its own. To see it on the screen, we have to use it in an applet or a frame. Here is a simple applet class that uses a RandomStringsPanel as its content pane:

```
import javax.swing.JApplet;
```

/**

- A RandomStringsApplet displays 25 copies of a string, using random colors,
- fonts, and positions for the copies. The message can be specified as the
- value of an applet param with name "message." If no param with name
- "message" is present, then the default message "Java!" is displayed.

```
    • The actual content of the applet is an object of type RandomStringsPanel. */
public class RandomStringsApplet extends JApplet {

    public void init() {
        String message = getParameter("message");
        RandomStringsPanel content = new
        RandomStringsPanel(message); setContentPane(content);
    }

}
```

Note that the message to be displayed in the applet can be set using an applet parameter when the applet is added to an HTML document. Using applets on Web pages was discussed in Sub-section 6.2.4. Remember that to use the applet on a Web page, you must include both the panel class file, RandomStringsPanel.class, and the applet class file, RandomStringsApplet.class, in the same directory as the HTML document (or, alternatively, bundle the two class files into a jar file, and put the jar file in the document directory).

Instead of writing an applet, of course, we could use the panel in the window of a stand-alone application. You can find the source code for a main program that does this in the file **RandomStringsApp.java**.

6.4 Mouse Events

Events are central to programming for a graphical user interface. A GUI program doesn't have a main() routine that outlines what will happen when the program is run, in a step-by-step process from beginning to end. Instead, the program must be prepared to respond to various kinds of events that can happen at unpredictable times and in an order that the program doesn't control. The most basic kinds of events are generated by the mouse and keyboard. The user can press any key on the keyboard, move the mouse, or press a button on the mouse. The user can do any of these things at any time, and the computer has to respond appropriately.

In Java, events are represented by objects. When an event occurs, the system collects all the information relevant to the event and constructs an object to contain that information. Different types of events are represented by objects belonging to different classes. For example, when the user presses one of the buttons on a mouse, an object belonging to a class called MouseEvent is constructed. The object contains information such as the source of the event (that is, the component on which the user clicked), the (x,y) coordinates of the point in the component where the click occurred, and which button on the mouse was pressed. When the user presses a key on the keyboard, a KeyEvent is created. After the event object is constructed, it is passed as a parameter to a designated subroutine. By writing that subroutine, the programmer says what should happen when the event occurs.

As a Java programmer, you get a fairly high-level view of events. There is a lot of processing that goes on between the time that the user presses a key or moves the mouse and the time that a subroutine in your program is called to respond to the event. Fortunately, you don't need to know much about that processing. But you should understand this much: Even though your GUI program doesn't have a main() routine, there is a sort of main routine running somewhere that executes a loop of the form

```
while the program is still running:
```

Wait for the next event to occur
Call a subroutine to handle the event

This loop is called an **event loop**. Every GUI program has an event loop. In Java, you don't have to write the loop. It's part of "the system." If you write a GUI program in some other language, you might have to provide a main routine that runs an event loop.

In this section, we'll look at handling mouse events in Java, and we'll cover the framework for handling events in general. The next section will cover keyboard-related events and timer events. Java also has other types of events, which are produced by GUI components. These will be introduced in Section 6.6.

6.4.1 Event Handling

For an event to have any effect, a program must detect the event and react to it. In order to detect an event, the program must "listen" for it. Listening for events is something that is done by an object called an **event listener** . An event listener object must contain instance methods for handling the events for which it listens. For example, if an object is to serve as a listener for events of type MouseEvent, then it must contain the following method (among several others):

```
public void mousePressed(MouseEvent evt) { . . . }
```

The body of the method defines how the object responds when it is notified that a mouse button has been pressed. The parameter, evt, contains information about the event. This information can be used by the listener object to determine its response.

The methods that are required in a mouse event listener are specified in an interface named MouseListener. To be used as a listener for mouse events, an object must implement this MouseListener interface. Java interfaces were covered in Subsection 5.7.1. (To review briefly: An interface in Java is just a list of instance methods. A class can "implement" an interface by doing two things. First, the class must be declared to implement the interface, as in "class MyListener implements MouseListener" or "class MyApplet extends JApplet implements MouseListener". Second, the class must include a definition for each instance method specified in the interface. An interface can be used as the type for a variable or formal parameter. We say that an object implements the MouseListener interface if it belongs to a class that implements the MouseListener interface. Note that it is not enough for the object to include the specified methods. It must also belong to a class that is specifically declared to implement the interface.)

Many events in Java are associated with GUI components. For example, when the user presses a button on the mouse, the associated component is the one that the user clicked on. Before a listener object can "hear" events associated with a given component, the listener object must be registered with the component. If a MouseListener object, mListener, needs to hear mouse events associated with a Component object, comp, the listener must be **registered** with the component by calling "comp.addMouseListener(mListener);". The addMouseListener() method is an instance method in class Component, and so can be used with any GUI component object. In our first few examples, we will listen for events on a JPanel that is being used as a drawing surface.

The event classes, such as MouseEvent, and the listener interfaces, such as MouseListener, are defined in the package java.awt.event. This means that if you want to work with events, you should either include the line "import java.awt.event.*;" at the beginning of your source code file or import the individual classes and interfaces.

Admittedly, there is a large number of details to tend to when you want to use events. To summarize, you must

- Put the import specification "import java.awt.event.*;" (or individual imports) at the beginning of your source code;
- Declare that some class implements the appropriate listener interface, such as MouseLis-tener ;
- Provide definitions in that class for the subroutines from the interface;
- Register the listener object with the component that will generate the events by calling a method such as addMouseListener() in the component.

Any object can act as an event listener, provided that it implements the appropriate interface. A component can listen for the events that it itself generates. A panel can listen for events from components that are contained in the panel. A special class can be created just for the purpose of defining a listening object. Many people consider it to be good form to use anonymous inner classes to define listening objects (see Subsection 5.7.3). You will see all of these patterns in examples in this textbook.

6.4.2 MouseEvent and MouseListener

The MouseListener interface specifies five different instance methods:

```
public void mousePressed(MouseEvent evt);
public void mouseReleased(MouseEvent evt);
public void mouseClicked(MouseEvent evt);
public void mouseEntered(MouseEvent evt);
public void mouseExited(MouseEvent evt);
```

The mousePressed method is called as soon as the user presses down on one of the mouse buttons, and mouseReleased is called when the user releases a button. These are the two methods that are most commonly used, but any mouse listener object must define all five methods; you can leave the body of a method empty if you don't want to define a response. The mouseClicked method is called if the user presses a mouse button and then releases it quickly, without moving the mouse. (When the user does this, all three routines—mousePressed, mouseReleased, and mouseClicked—will be called in that order.) In most cases, you should define mousePressed instead of mouseClicked. The mouseEntered and mouseExited methods are called when the mouse cursor enters or leaves the component. For example, if you want the component to change appearance whenever the user moves the mouse over the component, you could define these two methods.

As an example, we will look at a small addition to the RandomStringsPanel example from the previous section. In the new version, the panel will repaint itself when the user clicks on it. In order for this to happen, a mouse listener should listen for mouse events on the panel, and when the listener detects a mousePressed event, it should respond by calling the repaint() method of the panel.

For the new version of the program, we need an object that implements the MouseListener interface. One way to create the object is to define a separate class, such as:

```
import java.awt.Component;
import java.awt.event.*;

/**
 • An object of type RepaintOnClick is a MouseListener that
```

- will respond to a mousePressed event by calling the repaint()
- method of the source of the event. That is, a RepaintOnClick

```
• object can be added as a mouse listener to any Component;
• when the user clicks that component, the component will be
• repainted.
*/
public class RepaintOnClick implements MouseListener {

   public void mousePressed(MouseEvent evt) {
      Component source =
      (Component)evt.getSource();
      source.repaint();     // Call repaint() on the Component that was clicked.
   }

   public void mouseClicked(MouseEvent evt) { }
   public void mouseReleased(MouseEvent evt) { }
   public void mouseEntered(MouseEvent evt) { }
   public void mouseExited(MouseEvent evt) { }

}
```

This class does three of the four things that we need to do in order to handle mouse events: First, it imports java.awt.event.* for easy access to event-related classes. Second, it is declared that the class "implements MouseListener". And third, it provides definitions for the five methods that are specified in the MouseListener interface. (Note that four of the five event-handling methods have empty defintions. We really only want to define a response to mousePressed events, but in order to implement the MouseListener interface, a class **must** define all five methods.)

We must do one more thing to set up the event handling for this example: We must register an event-handling object as a listener with the component that will generate the events. In this case, the mouse events that we are interested in will be generated by an object of type RandomStringsPanel. If panel is a variable that refers to the panel object, we can create a mouse listener object and register it with the panel with the statements:

```
RepaintOnClick listener = new RepaintOnClick();    // Create MouseListener object.
panel.addMouseListener(listener);    // Register MouseListener with the panel.
```

Once this is done, the listener object will be notified of mouse events on the panel. When a mousePressed event occurs, the mousePressed() method in the listener will be called. The code in this method calls the repaint() method in the component that is the source of the event, that is, in the panel. The result is that the RandomStringsPanel is repainted with its strings in new random colors, fonts, and positions.

Although we have written the RepaintOnClick class for use with our RandomStringsPanel example, the event-handling class contains no reference at all to the RandomStringsPanel class. How can this be? The mousePressed() method in class RepaintOnClick looks at the source of the event, and calls its repaint() method. If we have registered the RepaintOnClick object as a listener on a RandomStringsPanel, then it is that panel that is repainted. But the listener object could be used with any type of component, and it would work in the same way.

Similarly, the RandomStringsPanel class contains no reference to the RepaintOnClick class— in fact, RandomStringsPanel was written before we even knew anything about mouse events! The panel will send mouse events to any object that has registered with it as a mouse listener. It does not need to know anything about that object except that it is capable of receiving mouse events.

The relationship between an object that generates an event and an object that responds to that event is rather loose. The relationship is set up by registering one object to listen for events from the other object. This is something that can potentially be done from outside both objects. Each object can be developed independently, with no knowledge of the internal operation of the other object. This is the essence of **modular design**: Build a complex system out of modules that interact only in straightforward, easy to understand ways. Then each module is a separate design problem that can be tackled independently.

To make this clearer, consider the application version of the ClickableRandomStrings program. I have included RepaintOnClick as a nested class, although it could just as easily be a separate class. The main point is that this program uses the same RandomStringsPanel class that was used in the original program, which did not respond to mouse clicks. The mouse handling has been "bolted on" to an existing class, without having to make any changes at all to that class:

```
import java.awt.Component;
import java.awt.event.MouseEvent;
import java.awt.event.MouseListener;
import javax.swing.JFrame;

/**
 • Displays a window that shows 25 copies of the string "Java!" in
 • random colors, fonts, and positions. The content of the window
 • is an object of type RandomStringsPanel. When the user clicks
 • the window, the content of the window is repainted, with the
 • strings in newly selected random colors, fonts, and positions. */
public class ClickableRandomStringsApp {

    public static void main(String[] args) {
        JFrame window = new JFrame("Random Strings");
        RandomStringsPanel content = new RandomStringsPanel();
        content.addMouseListener( new RepaintOnClick() );    // Register mouse listener.
        window.setContentPane(content);
        window.setDefaultCloseOperation(JFrame.EXIT ON CLOSE);
        window.setLocation(100,75);
        window.setSize(300,240);
        window.setVisible(true);
    }

    private static class RepaintOnClick implements MouseListener {

        public void mousePressed(MouseEvent evt) {
            Component source =
            (Component)evt.getSource(); source.repaint();
        }

        public void mouseClicked(MouseEvent evt) { }
        public void mouseReleased(MouseEvent evt) { }
        public void mouseEntered(MouseEvent evt) { }
        public void mouseExited(MouseEvent evt) { }
```

```
    }
}
```

6.4.3 Mouse Coordinates

Often, when a mouse event occurs, you want to know the location of the mouse cursor. This information is available from the MouseEvent parameter to the event-handling method, which contains instance methods that return information about the event. If evt is the parame-ter, then you can find out the coordinates of the mouse cursor by calling evt.getX() and evt.getY(). These methods return integers which give the x and y coordinates where the mouse cursor was positioned at the time when the event occurred. The coordinates are ex-pressed in the coordinate system of the component that generated the event, where the top left corner of the component is (0,0).

The user can hold down certain **modifier keys** while using the mouse. The possible mod-ifier keys include: the Shift key, the Control key, the ALT key (called the Option key on the Macintosh), and the Meta key (called the Command or Apple key on the Macintosh). You might want to respond to a mouse event differently when the user is holding down a modi-fier key. The boolean-valued instance methods evt.isShiftDown(), evt.isControlDown(), evt.isAltDown(), and evt.isMetaDown() can be called to test whether the modifier keys are pressed.

You might also want to have different responses depending on whether the user presses the left mouse button, the middle mouse button, or the right mouse button. Now, not every mouse has a middle button and a right button, so Java handles the information in a peculiar way. It treats pressing the right button as equivalent to holding down the Meta key while pressing the left mouse button. That is, if the right button is pressed, then the instance method evt.isMetaDown() will return true (even if the Meta key is not pressed). Similarly, pressing the middle mouse button is equivalent to holding down the ALT key. In practice, what this really means is that pressing the right mouse button under Windows is equivalent to holding down the Command key while pressing the mouse button on Macintosh. A program tests for either of these by calling evt.isMetaDown().

As an example, consider a JPanel that does the following: Clicking on the panel with the left mouse button will place a red rectangle on the panel at the point where the mouse was clicked. Clicking with the right mouse button (or holding down the Command key while clicking on a Macintosh) will place a blue oval on the applet. Holding down the Shift key while clicking will clear the panel by removing all the shapes that have been placed.

There are several ways to write this example. I could write a separate class to handle mouse events, as I did in the previous example. However, in this case, I decided to let the panel respond to mouse events itself. Any object can be a mouse listener, as long as it imple-ments the MouseListener interface. In this case, the panel class implements the MouseListener interface, so any object belonging to that class can act as a mouse listener. The constructor for the panel class registers the panel with **itself** as a mouse listener. It does this with the statement "addMouseListener(this)". Since this command is in a method in the panel class, the addMouseListener() method in the panel object is being called, and a listener is being registered with that panel. The parameter "this" also refers to the panel object, so it is the same panel object that is listening for events. Thus, the panel object plays a dual role here. (If you find this too confusing, remember that you can always write a separate class to define the listening object.)

The source code for the panel class is shown below. You should check how the instance methods in the MouseEvent object are used. You can also check for the Four Steps of Event Handling ("import java.awt.event.*", "implements MouseListener", definitions for the event-handling methods, and "addMouseListener"):

```
import java.awt.*;
import java.awt.event.*;
import javax.swing.*;

/**
 • A simple demonstration of MouseEvents. Shapes are drawn
 • on a black background when the user clicks the panel If
 • the user Shift-clicks, the applet is cleared. If the user
 • right-clicks the applet, a blue oval is drawn. Otherwise,
 • when the user clicks, a red rectangle is drawn. The contents of
 • the panel are not persistent. For example, they might disappear
 • if the panel is covered and uncovered.
 */
public class SimpleStamperPanel extends JPanel implements MouseListener {

    /**
     • This constructor simply sets the background color of the panel to be black
     • and sets the panel to listen for mouse events on itself.
     */
    public SimpleStamperPanel() {
        setBackground(Color.BLACK);
        addMouseListener(this);
    }

    /**
     •  Since this panel has been set to listen for mouse events on itself,
     •  this method will be called when the user clicks the mouse on the panel.
     •  This method is part of the MouseListener interface.
     */
    public void mousePressed(MouseEvent evt) {

        if ( evt.isShiftDown() ) {
                •  The user was holding down the Shift key. Just repaint the panel.
                •  Since this class does not define a paintComponent() method, the
                •  method from the superclass, JPanel, is called. That method simply
                •  fills the panel with its background color, which is black. The
                •  effect is to clear the panel.
            repaint();
            return;
        }

        int x = evt.getX();        // x-coordinate where user clicked.
        int y = evt.getY();        // y-coordinate where user clicked.

        Graphics g = getGraphics();    // Graphics context for drawing directly.
                                       // NOTE: This is considered to be bad style!

        if ( evt.isMetaDown() ) {
                •  User right-clicked at the point (x,y). Draw a blue oval centered
                •  at the point (x,y). (A black outline around the oval will make it
```

- more distinct when ovals and rects overlap.)

g.setColor(Color.BLUE); // Blue interior. g.fillOval(x - 30, y - 15, 60, 30); g.setColor(Color.BLACK); // Black outline. g.drawOval(x - 30, y - 15, 60, 30);

}

```
else {
        • User left-clicked (or middle-clicked) at (x,y).
        • Draw a red rectangle centered at (x,y).
    g.setColor(Color.RED); //           Red interior.
    g.fillRect( x - 30, y - 15,         60, 30  );
    g.setColor(Color.BLACK); //         Black outline.
    g.drawRect( x - 30, y - 15,         60, 30  );
}

g.dispose();    // We are finished with the graphics context, so dispose of it.

} // end mousePressed();
```

- The next four empty routines are required by the MouseListener interface.
- Since they don't do anything in this class, so their definitions are empty.

```
public void mouseEntered(MouseEvent evt) { }
public void mouseExited(MouseEvent evt) { }
public void mouseClicked(MouseEvent evt) { }
public void mouseReleased(MouseEvent evt) { }

} // end class SimpleStamperPanel
```

Note, by the way, that this class violates the rule that all drawing should be done in a paintComponent() method. The rectangles and ovals are drawn directly in the mousePressed() routine. To make this possible, I need to obtain a graphics context by saying "g = getGraphics()". After using g for drawing, I call g.dispose() to inform the operating system that I will no longer be using g for drawing. It is a good idea to do this to free the system resources that are used by the graphics context. I do not advise doing this type of direct drawing if it can be avoided, but you can see that it does work in this case, and at this point we really have no other way to write this example.

6.4.4 MouseMotionListeners and Dragging

Whenever the mouse is moved, it generates events. The operating system of the computer detects these events and uses them to move the mouse cursor on the screen. It is also possible for a program to listen for these "mouse motion" events and respond to them. The most common reason to do so is to implement **dragging** . Dragging occurs when the user moves the mouse while holding down a mouse button.

The methods for responding to mouse motion events are defined in an interface named MouseMotionListener. This interface specifies two event-handling methods:

```
public void mouseDragged(MouseEvent evt);
public void mouseMoved(MouseEvent evt);
```

The mouseDragged method is called if the mouse is moved while a button on the mouse is pressed. If the mouse is moved while no mouse button is down, then mouseMoved is called instead. The parameter, evt, is an object of type MouseEvent. It contains the x and y coordi-nates of the mouse's location. As long as the user continues to move the mouse, one of these methods will be called over and over. (So many events are generated that it would be inefficient for a program to hear them all, if it doesn't want to do anything in response. This is why the mouse motion event-handlers are defined in a separate interface from the other mouse events: You can listen for the mouse events defined in MouseListener without automatically hearing all mouse motion events as well.)

If you want your program to respond to mouse motion events, you must create an object that implements the MouseMotionListener interface, and you must register that object to listen for events. The registration is done by calling a component's addMouseMotionListener method. The object will then listen for mouseDragged and mouseMoved events associated with that component. In most cases, the listener object will also implement the MouseListener interface so that it can respond to the other mouse events as well.

To get a better idea of how mouse events work, you should try the SimpleTrackMouseApplet in the on-line version of this section. The applet is programmed to respond to any of the seven different kinds of mouse events by displaying the coordinates of the mouse, the type of event, and a list of the modifier keys that are down (Shift, Control, Meta, and Alt). You can experiment with the applet to see what happens when you use the mouse on the applet. (Alternatively, you could run the stand-alone application version of the program, **SimpleTrackMouse.java**.)

The source code for the applet can be found in **SimpleTrackMousePanel.java**, which defines the panel that is used as the content pane of the applet, and in **SimpleTrackMouseApplet.java**, which defines the applet class. The panel class includes a nested class, MouseHandler, that defines the mouse-handling object. I encourage you to read the source code. You should now be familiar with all the techniques that it uses.

It is interesting to look at what a program needs to do in order to respond to dragging op-erations. In general, the response involves three methods: mousePressed(), mouseDragged(), and mouseReleased(). The dragging gesture starts when the user presses a mouse button, it continues while the mouse is dragged, and it ends when the user releases the button. This means that the programming for the response to one dragging gesture must be spread out over the three methods! Furthermore, the mouseDragged() method can be called many times as the mouse moves. To keep track of what is going on between one method call and the next, you need to set up some instance variables. In many applications, for example, in order to process a mouseDragged event, you need to remember the previous coordinates of the mouse. You can store this information in two instance variables prevX and prevY of type int. It can also be useful to save the starting coordinates, where the mousePressed event occurred, in instance variables. I also suggest having a boolean variable, dragging, which is set to true while a dragging gesture is being processed. This is necessary because not every mousePressed event starts a dragging operation to which you want to respond. The mouseDragged and mouseReleased methods can use the value of dragging to check whether a drag operation is actually in progress. You might need other instance variables as well, but in general outline, a class that handles mouse dragging looks like this:

```
import java.awt.event.*;

public class MouseDragHandler implements MouseListener, MouseMotionListener {

   private int startX, startY; // Point where mouse is pressed.
   private int prevX, prevY;        // Most recently processed mouse coords.
   private boolean dragging;      // Set to true when dragging is in process.
   . . . // other instance variables for use in dragging

   public void mousePressed(MouseEvent evt) {
      if ( we-want-to-start-dragging ) {
```

```
dragging = true;
startX = evt.getX();        // Remember starting position.
startY = evt.getY();
prevX = startX;             // Remember most recent coords.
prevY = startY;
```

```
            .
            . // Other processing.
.
        }
    }

    public void mouseDragged(MouseEvent evt) {
        if ( dragging == false )       // First, check if we are
            return;                    //    processing a dragging gesture.
        int x = evt.getX(); // Current position of Mouse.
        int y = evt.getY();
          .
          . // Process a mouse movement from (prevX, prevY) to (x,y).
          .
        prevX = x;   // Remember the current position for the next call.
        prevY = y;
    }

    public void mouseReleased(MouseEvent evt) {
        if ( dragging == false )       // First, check if we are
            return;                    //    processing a dragging gesture.
        dragging = false;    // We are done dragging.
          .
          . // Other processing and clean-up.
.
    }
}
```

As an example, let's look at a typical use of dragging: allowing the user to sketch a curve by dragging the mouse. This example also shows many other features of graphics and mouse pro-cessing. In the program, you can draw a curve by dragging the mouse on a large white drawing area, and you can select a color for drawing by clicking on one of several colored rectangles to the right of the drawing area. The complete source code can be found in **SimplePaint.java**, which can be run as a stand-alone application, and you can find an applet version in the on-line version of this section. Here is a picture of the program:

I will discuss a few aspects of the source code here, but I encourage you to read it carefully in its entirety. There are lots of informative comments in the source code. (The source code uses one unusual technique: It defines a subclass of JApplet, but it also includes a main() routine. The main() routine has nothing to do with the class's use as an applet, but it makes it possible to run the class as a stand-alone application. When this is done, the application opens a window that shows the same panel that would be shown in the applet version. This example thus shows how to write a single file that can be used either as a stand-alone application or as an applet.)

The panel class for this example is designed to work for any reasonable size, that is, unless the panel is too small. This means that coordinates are computed in terms of the actual width and height of the panel. (The width and height are obtained by calling getWidth() and getHeight().) This makes things quite a bit harder than they would be if we assumed some particular fixed size for the panel. Let's look at some of these computations in detail. For example, the large white drawing area extends from y = 3 to y = height - 3 vertically and from x = 3 to x = width - 56 horizontally. These numbers are needed in order to interpret the meaning of a mouse click. They take into account a gray border around the panel and the color palette along the right edge of the panel. The border is 3 pixels wide. The colored rectangles are 50 pixels wide. Together with the 3-pixel border around the panel and a 3-pixel divider between the drawing area and the colored rectangles, this adds up to put the right edge of the drawing area 56 pixels from the right edge of the panel.

A white square labeled "CLEAR" occupies a 50-by-50 pixel region beneath the colored rect-angles on the right edge of the panel. Allowing for this square, we can figure out how much vertical space is available for the seven colored rectangles, and then divide that space by 7 to get the vertical space available for each rectangle. This quantity is represented by a variable, colorSpace. Out of this space, 3 pixels are used as spacing between the rectangles, so the height of each rectangle is colorSpace - 3. The top of the N-th rectangle is located (N*colorSpace

• 3) pixels down from the top of the panel, assuming that we count the rectangles starting with zero. This is because there are N rectangles above the N-th rectangle, each of which uses colorSpace pixels. The extra 3 is for the border at the top of the panel. After all that, we can write down the command for drawing the N-th rectangle:

```
g.fillRect(width - 53, N*colorSpace + 3, 50, colorSpace - 3);
```

That was not easy! But it shows the kind of careful thinking and precision graphics that are sometimes necessary to get good results.

The mouse in this panel is used to do three different things: Select a color, clear the drawing, and draw a curve. Only the third of these involves dragging, so not every mouse click will start a dragging operation. The mousePressed routine has to look at the (x,y) coordinates where the mouse was clicked and decide how to respond. If the user clicked on the CLEAR rectangle, the drawing area is cleared by calling repaint(). If the user clicked somewhere in the strip of colored rectangles, the selected color is changed. This involves computing which color the user clicked on, which is done by dividing the y coordinate by colorSpace. Finally, if the user clicked on the drawing area, a drag operation is initiated. A boolean variable, dragging, is set to true so that the mouseDragged and mouseReleased methods will know that a curve is being drawn. The code for this follows the general form given above. The actual drawing of the curve is done in the mouseDragged method, which draws a line from the previous location of the mouse to its current location. Some effort is required to make sure that the line does not extend beyond the white drawing area of the panel. This is not automatic, since as far as the computer is concerned, the border and the color bar are part of the drawing surface. If the user drags the mouse outside the drawing area while drawing a line, the mouseDragged routine changes the x and y coordinates to make them lie within the drawing area.

6.4.5 Anonymous Event Handlers

As I mentioned above, it is a fairly common practice to use anonymous nested classes to define listener objects. As discussed in Subsection 5.7.3, a special form of the new operator is used to create an object that belongs to an anonymous class. For example, a mouse listener object can be created with an expression of the form:

```
new MouseListener() {
    public void mousePressed(MouseEvent evt) { . . . }
    public void mouseReleased(MouseEvent evt) { . . . }
    public void mouseClicked(MouseEvent evt) { . . . }
    public void mouseEntered(MouseEvent evt) { . . . }
    public void mouseExited(MouseEvent evt) { . . . }
}
```

This is all just one long expression that both defines an un-named class and creates an object that belongs to that class. To use the object as a mouse listener, it should be passed as the parameter to some component's addMouseListener() method in a command of the form:

```
component.addMouseListener( new MouseListener() { public
      void mousePressed(MouseEvent evt) { . . . } public void
      mouseReleased(MouseEvent evt) { . . . } public void
      mouseClicked(MouseEvent evt) { . . . } public void
      mouseEntered(MouseEvent evt) { . . . } public void
      mouseExited(MouseEvent evt) { . . . }
   } );
```

Now, in a typical application, most of the method definitions in this class will be empty. A class that implements an interface must provide definitions for all the methods in that interface, even if the definitions are empty. To avoid the tedium of writing empty method definitions in cases like this, Java provides **adapter classes**. An adapter class implements a listener interface by providing empty definitions for all the methods in the interface. An adapter class is useful only as a basis for making subclasses. In the subclass, you can define just those methods that you actually want to use. For the remaining methods, the empty definitions that are provided by the adapter class will be used. The adapter class for the MouseListener interface is named MouseAdapter. For example, if you want a mouse listener that only responds to mouse-pressed events, you can use a command of the form:

```
component.addMouseListener( new MouseAdapter() {
      public void mousePressed(MouseEvent evt) { . . . }
   } );
```

To see how this works in a real example, let's write another version of the ClickableRandomStringsApp application from Subsection 6.4.2. This version uses an anony-mous class based on MouseAdapter to handle mouse events:

```
import java.awt.Component;
```

```
import java.awt.event.MouseEvent;
import java.awt.event.MouseListener;
import javax.swing.JFrame;

public class ClickableRandomStringsApp {
```

```
public static void main(String[] args) {
    JFrame window = new JFrame("Random Strings");
    RandomStringsPanel content = new RandomStringsPanel();

    content.addMouseListener( new MouseAdapter() {
            • Register a mouse listener that is defined by an anonymous subclass
            • of MouseAdapter. This replaces the RepaintOnClick class that was
            • used in the original version.
        public void mousePressed(MouseEvent evt) {
            Component source =
            (Component)evt.getSource(); source.repaint();
        }
    } );

    window.setContentPane(content);
    window.setDefaultCloseOperation(JFrame.EXIT ON CLOSE);
    window.setLocation(100,75);
    window.setSize(300,240);
    window.setVisible(true);
}

}
```

Anonymous inner classes can be used for other purposes besides event handling. For ex-ample, suppose that you want to define a subclass of JPanel to represent a drawing surface. The subclass will only be used once. It will redefine the paintComponent() method, but will make no other changes to JPanel. It might make sense to define the subclass as an anony-mous nested class. As an example, I present **HelloWorldGUI4.java**. This version is a variation of **HelloWorldGUI2.java** that uses anonymous nested classes where the original program uses ordinary, named nested classes:

```
import java.awt.*;
import java.awt.event.*;
import javax.swing.*;

/**
  • A simple GUI program that creates and opens a JFrame containing
  • the message "Hello World" and an "OK" button. When the user clicks
  • the OK button, the program ends. This version uses anonymous
  • classes to define the message display panel and the action listener
  • object. Compare to HelloWorldGUI2, which uses nested classes.
  */
public class HelloWorldGUI4 {

    /**
      • The main program creates a window containing a HelloWorldDisplay
      • and a button that will end the program when the user clicks it. */
    public static void main(String[] args) {

        JPanel displayPanel = new JPanel() {
```

- An anonymous subclass of JPanel that displays "Hello World!".

```
public void paintComponent(Graphics g) {
    super.paintComponent(g);
    g.drawString( "Hello World!", 20, 30 );
}
```

```
        };

        JButton okButton = new JButton("OK");

        okButton.addActionListener( new ActionListener() {
                   An anonymous class that defines the listener object.
           public void actionPerformed(ActionEvent e) {
              System.exit(0);
           }
        });

        JPanel content = new JPanel();
        content.setLayout(new BorderLayout());
        content.add(displayPanel, BorderLayout.CENTER);
        content.add(okButton, BorderLayout.SOUTH);

        JFrame window = new JFrame("GUI Test");
        window.setContentPane(content);
        window.setSize(250,100);
        window.setLocation(100,100);
        window.setVisible(true);

    }
}
```

6.5 Timer and Keyboard Events

Not every event is generated by an action on the part of the user. Events can also be generated by objects as part of their regular programming, and these events can be monitored by other objects so that they can take appropriate actions when the events occur. One example of this is the class javax.swing.Timer. A Timer generates events at regular intervals. These events can be used to drive an animation or to perform some other task at regular intervals. We will begin this section with a look at timer events and animation. We will then look at another type of basic user-generated event: the KeyEvent s that are generated when the user types on the keyboard. The example at the end of the section uses both a timer and keyboard events to implement a simple game.

6.5.1 Timers and Animation

An object belonging to the class javax.swing.Timer exists only to generate events. A Timer, by default, generates a sequence of events with a fixed delay between each event and the next. (It is also possible to set a Timer to emit a single event after a specified time delay; in that case, the timer is being used as an "alarm.") Each event belongs to the class ActionEvent. An object that is to listen for the events must implement the interface ActionListener, which defines just one method:

```
public void actionPerformed(ActionEvent evt)
```

To use a Timer, you must create an object that implements the ActionListener interface. That is, the object must belong to a class that is declared to "implement ActionListener", and that class must define the actionPerformed method. Then, if the object is set to listen for events from the timer, the code in the listener's actionPerformed method will be executed every time the timer generates an event.

Since there is no point to having a timer without having a listener to respond to its events, the action listener for a timer is specified as a parameter in the timer's constructor. The time delay between timer events is also specified in the constructor. If timer is a variable of type Timer, then the statement

```
timer = new Timer( millisDelay, listener );
```

creates a timer with a delay of millisDelay milliseconds between events (where 1000 milliseconds equal one second). Events from the timer are sent to the listener. (millisDelay must be of type int, and listener must be of type ActionListener.) Note that a timer is not guaranteed to deliver events at precisely regular intervals. If the computer is busy with some other task, an event might be delayed or even dropped altogether.

A timer does not automatically start generating events when the timer object is created. The start() method in the timer must be called to tell the timer to start generating events. The timer's stop() method can be used to turn the stream of events off—it can be restarted by calling start() again.

* * *

One application of timers is computer animation. A computer animation is just a sequence of still images, presented to the user one after the other. If the time between images is short, and if the change from one image to another is not too great, then the user perceives continuous motion. The easiest way to do animation in Java is to use a Timer to drive the animation. Each time the timer generates an event, the next frame of the animation is computed and drawn on the screen—the code that implements this goes in the actionPerformed method of an object that listens for events from the timer.

Our first example of using a timer is not exactly an animation, but it does display a new image for each timer event. The program shows randomly generated images that vaguely resemble works of abstract art. In fact, the program draws a new random image every time its paintComponent() method is called, and the response to a timer event is simply to call repaint(), which in turn triggers a call to paintComponent. The work of the program is done in a subclass of JPanel, which starts like this:

```
import java.awt.*;
import java.awt.event.*;
import javax.swing.*;

public class RandomArtPanel extends JPanel {

   /**
    • A RepaintAction object calls the repaint method of this panel each
    • time its actionPerformed() method is called. An object of this
    • type is used as an action listener for a Timer that generates an
    • ActionEvent every four seconds. The result is that the panel is
    • redrawn every four seconds.
    */
   private class RepaintAction implements ActionListener {
      public void actionPerformed(ActionEvent evt) {
         repaint();    // Call the repaint() method in the panel class.
      }
```

```
}
```

```
/**
 • The constructor creates a timer with a delay time of four seconds
 • (4000 milliseconds), and with a RepaintAction object as its
 • ActionListener. It also starts the timer running.
 */
public RandomArtPanel() {
   RepaintAction action = new RepaintAction();
   Timer timer = new Timer(4000, action);
   timer.start();
}

/**
 • The paintComponent() method fills the panel with a random shade of
 • gray and then draws one of three types of random "art". The type
 • of art to be drawn is chosen at random.
 */
public void paintComponent(Graphics g) {
      .
      •   // The rest of the class is omitted
•
```

You can find the full source code for this class in the file **RandomArtPanel.java**; An application version of the program is **RandomArt.java**, while the applet version is **RandomArtApplet.java**. You can see the applet version in the on-line version of this section.

Later in this section, we will use a timer to drive the animation in a simple computer game.

6.5.2 Keyboard Events

In Java, user actions become events in a program. These events are associated with GUI components. When the user presses a button on the mouse, the event that is generated is associated with the component that contains the mouse cursor. What about keyboard events? When the user presses a key, what component is associated with the key event that is generated?

A GUI uses the idea of **input focus** to determine the component associated with keyboard events. At any given time, exactly one interface element on the screen has the input focus, and that is where all keyboard events are directed. If the interface element happens to be a Java component, then the information about the keyboard event becomes a Java object of type KeyEvent, and it is delivered to any listener objects that are listening for KeyEvents associated with that component. The necessity of managing input focus adds an extra twist to working with keyboard events.

It's a good idea to give the user some visual feedback about which component has the input focus. For example, if the component is the typing area of a word-processor, the feedback is usually in the form of a blinking text cursor. Another common visual clue is to draw a brightly colored border around the edge of a component when it has the input focus, as I do in the examples given later in this section.

A component that wants to have the input focus can call the method requestFocus(), which is defined in the Component class. Calling this method does not absolutely guarantee that the component will actually get the input focus. Several components might request the focus; only one will get it. This method should only be used in certain circumstances in any case, since it can be a rude surprise to the user to have the focus suddenly pulled away from a component that the user is working with. In a typical user interface, the user can choose to give the focus to a component by clicking on that component with the mouse. And pressing the tab key will often move the focus from one component to another.

Some components do not automatically request the input focus when the user clicks on them. To solve this problem, a program has to register a mouse listener with the component to detect user clicks. In response to a user click, the mousePressed() method should call requestFocus() for the component. This is true, in particular, for the components that are used as drawing surfaces in the examples in this chapter. These components are defined as subclasses of JPanel, and JPanel objects do not receive the input focus automatically. If you want to be able to use the keyboard to interact with a JPanel named drawingSurface, you have to register a listener to listen for mouse events on the drawingSurface and call drawingSurface.requestFocus() in the mousePressed() method of the listener object.

As our first example of processing key events, we look at a simple program in which the user moves a square up, down, left, and right by pressing arrow keys. When the user hits the 'R', 'G', 'B', or 'K' key, the color of the square is set to red, green, blue, or black, respectively. Of course, none of these key events are delivered to the program unless it has the input focus. The panel in the program changes its appearance when it has the input focus: When it does, a cyan-colored border is drawn around the panel; when it does not, a gray-colored border is drawn. Also, the panel displays a different message in each case. If the panel does not have the input focus, the user can give the input focus to the panel by clicking on it. The complete source code for this example can be found in the file **KeyboardAndFocusDemo.java.** I will discuss some aspects of it below. After reading this section, you should be able to understand the source code in its entirety. Here is what the program looks like in its focussed state:

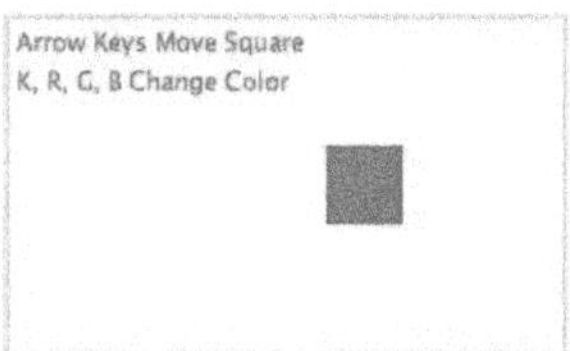

In Java, keyboard event objects belong to a class called KeyEvent. An object that needs to listen for KeyEvent s must implement the interface named KeyListener. Furthermore, the object must be registered with a component by calling the component's addKeyListener() method. The registration is done with the command "component.addKeyListener(listener);" where listener is the object that is to listen for key events, and component is the object that will generate the key events (when it has the input focus). It is possible for component and listener to be the same object. All this is, of course, directly analogous to what you learned about mouse events in the previous section. The KeyListener interface defines the following methods, which must be included in any class that implements KeyListener :

```
public void keyPressed(KeyEvent evt);
public void keyReleased(KeyEvent evt);
public void keyTyped(KeyEvent evt);
```

Java makes a careful distinction between **the keys that you press** and **the characters that you type**. There are lots of keys on a keyboard: letter keys, number keys, modifier keys such as Control and Shift, arrow keys, page up and page down keys, keypad keys, function keys. In many cases, pressing a key does not type a character. On the other hand, typing a character sometimes involves pressing several keys. For example, to type an uppercase 'A', you have to press the Shift key and then press the A key before releasing the Shift key. On my Macintosh computer, I can type an accented e, by holding down the Option key, pressing the E key, releasing the Option key, and pressing E again. Only one character was typed, but I had to perform three key-presses and I had to release a key at the right time. In Java, there are three types of KeyEvent. The types correspond to pressing a key, releasing a key, and typing a character. The keyPressed method is called when the user presses a key, the keyReleased method is called when the user releases a key, and the keyTyped method is called when the user types a character. Note that one user action, such as pressing the E key, can be responsible for two events, a keyPressed event and a keyTyped event. Typing an upper case 'A' can generate two keyPressed, two keyReleased, and one keyTyped event.

Usually, it is better to think in terms of two separate streams of events, one consisting of keyPressed and keyReleased events and the other consisting of keyTyped events. For some applications, you want to monitor the first stream; for other applications, you want to monitor the second one. Of course, the information in the keyTyped stream could be extracted from the keyPressed/keyReleased stream, but it would be difficult (and also system-dependent to some extent). Some user actions, such as pressing the Shift key, can only be detected as keyPressed events. I have a solitaire game on my computer that hilites every card that can be moved, when I hold down the Shift key. You could do something like that in Java by hiliting the cards when the Shift key is pressed and removing the hilite when the Shift key is released.

There is one more complication. Usually, when you hold down a key on the keyboard, that key will **auto-repeat** . This means that it will generate multiple keyPressed events, as long as it is held down. It can also generate multiple keyTyped events. For the most part, this will not affect your programming, but you should not expect every keyPressed event to have a corresponding keyReleased event.

Every key on the keyboard has an integer code number. (Actually, this is only true for keys that Java knows about. Many keyboards have extra keys that can't be used with Java.) When the keyPressed or keyReleased method is called, the parameter, evt, contains the code of the key that was pressed or released. The code can be obtained by calling the function evt.getKeyCode(). Rather than asking you to memorize a table of code numbers, Java provides a named constant for each key. These constants are defined in the KeyEvent class. For example the constant for the shift key is KeyEvent.VK_SHIFT. If you want to test whether the key that the user pressed is the Shift key, you could say "if (evt.getKeyCode()

• KeyEvent.VK SHIFT)". The key codes for the four arrow keys are KeyEvent.VK LEFT, KeyEvent.VK_RIGHT, KeyEvent.VK_UP, and KeyEvent.VK_DOWN. Other keys have similar codes. (The "VK" stands for "Virtual Keyboard". In reality, different keyboards use different key codes, but Java translates the actual codes from the keyboard into its own "virtual" codes. Your program only sees these virtual key codes, so it will work with various keyboards on various platforms without modification.)

In the case of a keyTyped event, you want to know which character was typed. This information can be obtained from the parameter, evt, in the keyTyped method by calling the function evt.getKeyChar(). This function returns a value of type char representing the character that was typed.

In the KeyboardAndFocusDemo program, I use the keyPressed routine to respond when the user presses one of the arrow keys. The applet includes instance variables, squareLeft and squareTop, that give the position of the upper left corner of the movable square. When the user presses one of the arrow keys, the keyPressed routine modifies the appropriate instance variable and calls repaint() to redraw the panel with the square in its new position. Note that the values of squareLeft and squareTop are restricted so that the square never moves outside the white area of the panel:

```
/**
 • This is called each time the user presses a key while the panel has
 • the input focus. If the key pressed was one of the arrow keys,
 • the square is moved (except that it is not allowed to move off the
 • edge of the panel, allowing for a 3-pixel border).
*/
public void keyPressed(KeyEvent evt) {

    int key = evt.getKeyCode();     // keyboard code for the pressed key

    if (key == KeyEvent.VK LEFT) { // move the square left
        squareLeft -= 8;

        if (squareLeft < 3)
            squareLeft = 3;
        repaint();
    }
    else if (key == KeyEvent.VK RIGHT) { // move the square right
        squareLeft += 8;

        if (squareLeft > getWidth() - 3 - SQUARE SIZE)
            squareLeft = getWidth() - 3 - SQUARE SIZE;
        repaint();
    }
    else if (key == KeyEvent.VK UP) { // move the squre up
        squareTop -= 8;

        if (squareTop < 3)
            squareTop = 3;
        repaint();
    }
    else if (key == KeyEvent.VK DOWN) { // move the square down
        squareTop += 8;

        if (squareTop > getHeight() - 3 - SQUARE SIZE)
            squareTop = getHeight() - 3 - SQUARE SIZE;
        repaint();
    }

} // end keyPressed()
```

Color changes—which happen when the user types the characters 'R', 'G', 'B', and 'K', or the lower case equivalents—are handled in the keyTyped method. I won't include it here, since it is so similar to the keyPressed method. Finally, to complete the KeyListener interface, the keyReleased method must be defined. In the sample program, the body of this method is empty since the applet does nothing in response to keyReleased events.

6.5.3 Focus Events

If a component is to change its appearance when it has the input focus, it needs some way to know when it has the focus. In Java, objects are notified about changes of input focus by events of type FocusEvent. An object that wants to be notified of changes in focus can implement the FocusListener interface. This interface declares two methods:

```
public void focusGained(FocusEvent evt);
public void focusLost(FocusEvent evt);
```

Furthermore, the addFocusListener() method must be used to set up a listener for the focus events. When a component gets the input focus, it calls the focusGained() method of any object that has been registered with that component as a FocusListener. When it loses the focus, it calls the listener's focusLost() method. Sometimes, it is the component itself that listens for focus events.

In the sample KeyboardAndFocusDemo program, the response to a focus event is simply to redraw the panel. The paintComponent() method checks whether the panel has the input focus by calling the boolean-valued function hasFocus(), which is defined in the Component class, and it draws a different picture depending on whether or not the panel has the input focus. The net result is that the appearance of the panel changes when the panel gains or loses focus. The methods from the FocusListener interface are defined simply as:

```
public void focusGained(FocusEvent evt) {
        // The panel now has the input focus.
    repaint();    // will redraw with a new message and a cyan border
}

public void focusLost(FocusEvent evt) {
       // The panel has now lost the input focus.
    repaint();    // will redraw with a new message and a gray border
}
```

The other aspect of handling focus is to make sure that the panel gets the focus when the user clicks on it. To do this, the panel implements the MouseListener interface and listens for mouse events on itself. It defines a mousePressed routine that asks that the input focus be given to the panel:

```
public void mousePressed(MouseEvent evt) {
    requestFocus();
}
```

The other four methods of the mouseListener interface are defined to be empty. Note that the panel implements three different listener interfaces, KeyListener, FocusListener, and MouseLis-tener, and the constructor in the panel class registers itself to listen for all three types of events with the statements:

```
addKeyListener(this);
addFocusListener(this);
addMouseListener(this);
```

There are, of course, other ways to organize this example. It would be possible, for example, to use a nested class to define the listening object. Or anonymous classes could be used to define separate listening objects for each type of event. In my next example, I will take the latter approach.

6.5.4 State Machines

The information stored in an object's instance variables is said to represent the **state** of that object. When one of the object's methods is called, the action taken by the object can depend on its state. (Or, in the terminology we have been using, the definition of the method can look at the instance variables to decide what to do.) Furthermore, the state can change. (That is, the definition of the method can assign new values to the instance variables.) In computer science, there is the idea of a **state machine**, which is just something that has a state and can change state in response to events or inputs. The response of a state machine to an event or input depends on what state it's in. An object is a kind of state machine. Sometimes, this point of view can be very useful in designing classes.

The state machine point of view can be especially useful in the type of event-oriented programming that is required by graphical user interfaces. When designing a GUI program, you can ask yourself: What information about state do I need to keep track of ? What events can change the state of the program? How will my response to a given event depend on the current state? Should the appearance of the GUI be changed to reflect a change in state? How should the paintComponent() method take the state into account? All this is an alternative to the top-down, step-wise-refinement style of program design, which does not apply to the overall design of an event-oriented program.

In the KeyboardAndFocusDemo program, shown above, the state of the program is recorded in the instance variables squareColor, squareLeft, and squareTop. These state variables are used in the paintComponent() method to decide how to draw the panel. They are changed in the two key-event-handling methods.

In the rest of this section, we'll look at another example, where the state plays an even bigger role. In this example, the user plays a simple arcade-style game by pressing the arrow keys. The main panel of the program is defined in the souce code file **SubKillerPanel.java**. An applet that uses this panel can be found in **SubKillerApplet.java**, while the stand-alone application version is **SubKiller.java**. You can try out the applet in the on-line version of this section. Here is what it looks like:

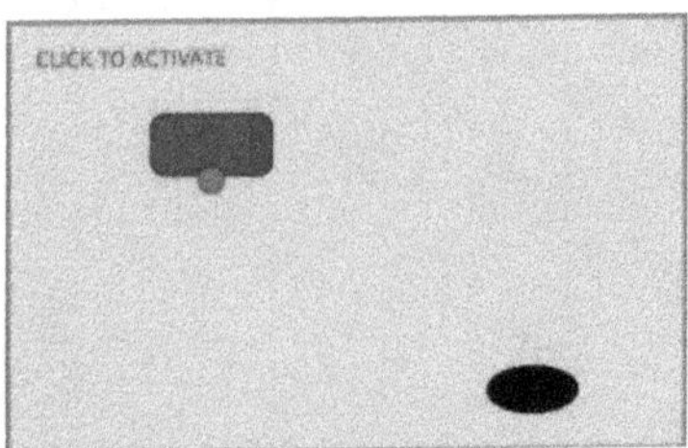

You have to click on the panel to give it the input focus. The program shows a black "submarine" near the bottom of the panel. When the panel has the input focus, this submarine moves back and forth erratically near the bottom. Near the top, there is a blue "boat". You can move this boat back and forth by pressing the left and right arrow keys. Attached to the boat is a red "bomb" (or "depth charge"). You can drop the bomb by hitting the down arrow key. The objective is to blow up the submarine by hitting it with the bomb. If the bomb falls off the bottom of the screen, you get a new one. If the submarine explodes, a new sub is created and you get a new bomb. Try it! Make sure to hit the sub at least once, so you can see the explosion.

Let's think about how this program can be programmed. First of all, since we are doing object-oriented programming, I decided to represent the boat, the depth charge, and the sub-marine as objects. Each of these objects is defined by a separate nested class inside the main panel class, and each object has its own state which is represented by the instance variables in the corresponding class. I use variables boat, bomb, and sub in the panel class to refer to the boat, bomb, and submarine objects.

Now, what constitutes the "state" of the program? That is, what things change from time to time and affect the appearance or behavior of the program? Of course, the state includes the positions of the boat, submarine, and bomb, so I need variables to store the positions. Anything else, possibly less obvious? Well, sometimes the bomb is falling, and sometimes it's not. That is a difference in state. Since there are two possibilities, I represent this aspect of the state with a boolean variable in the bomb object, bomb.isFalling. Sometimes the submarine is moving left and sometimes it is moving right. The difference is represented by another boolean variable, sub.isMovingLeft. Sometimes, the sub is exploding. This is also part of the state, and it is represented by a boolean variable, sub.isExploding. However, the explosions require a little more thought. An explosion is something that takes place over a series of frames. While an explosion is in progress, the sub looks different in each frame, as the size of the explosion increases. Also, I need to know when the explosion is over so that I can go back to moving and drawing the sub as usual. So, I use an integer variable, sub.explosionFrameNumber to record how many frames have been drawn since the explosion started; the value of this variable is used only when an explosion is in progress.

How and when do the values of these state variables change? Some of them seem to change on their own: For example, as the sub moves left and right, the state variables the that specify its position are changing. Of course, these variables are changing because of an animation, and that animation is driven by a timer. Each time an event is generated by the timer, some of the state variables have to change to get ready for the next frame of the animation. The changes are made by the action listener that listens for events from the timer. The boat, bomb, and sub objects each contain an updateForNextFrame() method that updates the state variables of the object to get ready for the next frame of the animation. The action listener for the timer calls these methods with the statements

```
boat.updateForNewFrame();
bomb.updateForNewFrame();
sub.updateForNewFrame();
```

The action listener also calls repaint(), so that the panel will be redrawn to reflect its new state. There are several state variables that change in these update methods, in addition to the position of the sub: If the bomb is falling, then its y-coordinate increases from one frame to the next. If the bomb hits the sub, then the isExploding variable of the sub changes to true, and the isFalling variable of the bomb becomes false. The isFalling variable also becomes false when the bomb falls off the bottom of the screen. If the sub is exploding, then its explosionFrameNumber increases from one frame to the next, and when it reaches a certain value, the explosion ends and isExploding is reset to false. At random times, the sub switches between moving to the left and moving to the right. Its direction of motion is recorded in the the sub's isMovingLeft variable. The sub's updateForNewFrame() method includes the lines

```
if ( Math.random() < 0.04 )
    isMovingLeft = ! isMovingLeft;
```

There is a 1 in 25 chance that Math.random() will be less than 0.04, so the statement "isMovingLeft = ! isMovingLeft" is executed in one in every twenty-five frames, on the average. The effect of this statement is to reverse the value of isMovingLeft, from false to true or from true to false. That is, the direction of motion of the sub is reversed.

In addtion to changes in state that take place from one frame to the next, a few state variables change when the user presses certain keys. In the program, this is checked in a method that responds to user keystrokes. If the user presses the left or right arrow key, the position of the boat is changed. If the user presses the down arrow key, the bomb changes from not-falling to falling. This is coded in the keyPressed()method of a KeyListener that is registered to listen for key events on the panel; that method reads as follows:

```
public void keyPressed(KeyEvent   evt) {
  int code = evt.getKeyCode();      // which key was pressed.
   if (code == KeyEvent.VK _LEFT) {
        • Move the boat left. (If this moves the boat out of the frame, its
        • position will be adjusted in the boat.updateForNewFrame() method.)
      boat.centerX -= 15;
  }
  else if (code == KeyEvent.VK RIGHT) {
        • Move the boat right. (If this moves boat out of the frame, its
        • position will be adjusted in the boat.updateForNewFrame() method.)
      boat.centerX += 15;
  }
  else if (code == KeyEvent.VK DOWN) {
         • Start the bomb falling, it is is not already falling. if (
      bomb.isFalling == false )
          bomb.isFalling = true;
  }
}
```

Note that it's not necessary to call repaint() when the state changes, since this panel shows an animation that is constantly being redrawn anyway. Any changes in the state will become visible to the user as soon as the next frame is drawn. At some point in the program, I have to make sure that the user does not move the boat off the screen. I could have done this in keyPressed(), but I choose to check for this in another routine, in the boat object.

I encourage you to read the source code in **SubKillerPanel.java**. Although a few points are tricky, you should with some effort be able to read and understand the entire program. Try to understand the program in terms of state machines. Note how the state of each of the three objects in the program changes in response to events from the timer and from the user.

You should also note that the program uses four listeners, to respond to action events from the timer, key events from the user, focus events, and mouse events. (The mouse is used only to request the input focus when the user clicks the panel.) The timer runs only when the panel has the input focus; this is programmed by having the focus listener start the timer when the panel gains the input focus and stop the timer when the panel loses the input focus. All four listeners are created in the constructor of the SubKillerPanel class using anonymous inner classes. (See Subsection 6.4.5.)

While it's not at all sophisticated as arcade games go, the SubKiller game does use some interesting programming. And it nicely illustrates how to apply state-machine thinking in event-oriented programming.

6.6 Basic Components

In preceding sections, you've seen how to use a graphics context to draw on the screen and how to handle mouse events and keyboard events. In one sense, that's all there is to GUI programming. If you're willing to program all the drawing and handle all the mouse and keyboard events, you have nothing more to learn. However, you would either be doing a lot more work than you need to do, or you would be limiting yourself to very simple user interfaces. A typical user interface uses standard GUI components such as buttons, scroll bars, text-input boxes, and menus. These components have already been written for you, so you don't have to duplicate the work involved in developing them. They know how to draw themselves, and they can handle the details of processing the mouse and keyboard events that concern them.

Consider one of the simplest user interface components, a push button. The button has a border, and it displays some text. This text can be changed. Sometimes the button is disabled, so that clicking on it doesn't have any effect. When it is disabled, its appearance changes. When the user clicks on the push button, the button changes appearance while the mouse button is pressed and changes back when the mouse button is released. In fact, it's more complicated than that. If the user moves the mouse outside the push button before releasing the mouse button, the button changes to its regular appearance. To implement this, it is necessary to respond to mouse exit or mouse drag events. Furthermore, on many platforms, a button can receive the input focus. The button changes appearance when it has the focus. If the button has the focus and the user presses the space bar, the button is triggered. This means that the button must respond to keyboard and focus events as well.

Fortunately, you don't have to program **any** of this, provided you use an object belonging to the standard class javax.swing.JButton. A JButton object draws itself and processes mouse, keyboard, and focus events on its own. You only hear from the Button when the user triggers it by clicking on it or pressing the space bar while the button has the input focus. When this happens, the JButton object creates an event object belonging to the class java.awt.event.ActionEvent. The event object is sent to any registered listeners to tell them that the button has been pushed. Your program gets only the information it needs—the fact that a button was pushed.

* * *

The standard components that are defined as part of the Swing graphical user interface API are defined by subclasses of the class JComponent, which is itself a subclass of Component. (Note that this includes the JPanel class that we have already been working with extensively.) Many useful methods are defined in the Component and JComponent classes and so can be used with any Swing component. We begin by looking at a few of these methods. Suppose that comp is a variable that refers to some JComponent. Then the following methods can be used:

- comp.getWidth() and comp.getHeight() are functions that give the current size of the component, in pixels. One warning: When a component is first created, its size is zero. The size will be set later, probably by a layout manager. A common mistake is to check the size of a component before that size has been set, such as in a constructor.
- comp.setEnabled(true) and comp.setEnabled(false) can be used to enable and disable the component. When a component is disabled, its appearance might change, and the user cannot do anything with it. There is a boolean-valued function, comp.isEnabled() that you can call to discover whether the component is enabled.
- comp.setVisible(true) and comp.setVisible(false) can be called to hide or show the component.

- comp.setFont(font) sets the font that is used for text displayed on the component. See Subsection 6.3.3 for a discussion of fonts.
- comp.setBackground(color) and comp.setForeground(color) set the background and foreground colors for the component. See Subsection 6.3.2.

- comp.setOpaque(true) tells the component that the area occupied by the component should be filled with the component's background color before the content of the component is painted. By default, only JLabels are non-opaque. A non-opaque, or "transparent", component ignores its background color and simply paints its content over the content of its container. This usually means that it inherits the background color from its container.
- comp.setToolTipText(string) sets the specified string as a "tool tip" for the component. The tool tip is displayed if the mouse cursor is in the component and the mouse is not moved for a few seconds. The tool tip should give some information about the meaning of the component or how to use it.
- comp.setPreferredSize(size) sets the size at which the component should be displayed, if possible. The parameter is of type java.awt.Dimension, where an object of type Di-mension has two public integer-valued instance variables, width and height. A call to this method usually looks something like "setPreferredSize(new Dimension(100,50))". The preferred size is used as a hint by layout managers, but will not be respected in all cases. Standard components generally compute a correct preferred size automatically, but it can be useful to set it in some cases. For example, if you use a JPanel as a drawing surface, it might be a good idea to set a preferred size for it.

Note that using any component is a multi-step process. The component object must be created with a constructor. It must be added to a container. In many cases, a listener must be registered to respond to events from the component. And in some cases, a reference to the component must be saved in an instance variable so that the component can be manipulated by the program after it has been created. In this section, we will look at a few of the basic standard components that are available in Swing. In the next section we will consider the problem of laying out components in containers.

6.6.1 JButton

An object of class JButton is a push button that the user can click to trigger some action. You've already seen buttons used in Section 6.1 and Section 6.2, but we consider them in much more detail here. To use any component effectively, there are several aspects of the corresponding class that you should be familiar with. For JButton, as an example, I list these aspects explicitely:

- **Constructors**: The JButton class has a constructor that takes a string as a parameter. This string becomes the text displayed on the button. For example: stopGoButton = new JButton("Go"). This creates a button object that will display the text, "Go" (but remember that the button must still be added to a container before it can appear on the screen).
- **Events**: When the user clicks on a button, the button generates an event of type Action-Event. This event is sent to any listener that has been registered with the button as an ActionListener.
- **Listeners**: An object that wants to handle events generated by buttons must implement the ActionListener interface. This interface defines just one method, "public void actionPerformed(ActionEvent evt)", which is called to notify the object of an action event.

- **Registration of Listeners**: In order to actually receive notification of an event from a button, an ActionListener must be registered with the button. This is done with the button's addActionListener() method. For example: stopGoButton.addActionListener(buttonHandler);
- **Event methods**: When actionPerformed(evt) is called by the button, the parameter, evt, contains information about the event. This information can be retrieved by calling methods in the ActionEvent class. In particular, evt.getActionCommand() returns a String giving the command associated with the button. By default, this command is the text that is displayed on the button, but it is possible to set it to some other string. The method evt.getSource() returns a reference to the Object that produced the event, that is, to the JButton that was pressed. The return value is of type Object, not JButton, because other types of components can also produce ActionEvent s.
- **Component methods**: Several useful methods are defined in the JButton class. For example, stopGoButton.setText("Stop") changes the text displayed on the button to "Stop". And stopGoButton.setActionCommand("sgb") changes the action command associated to this button for action events.

Of course, JButtons also have all the general Component methods, such as setEnabled() and setFont(). The setEnabled() and setText() methods of a button are particularly useful for giving the user information about what is going on in the program. A disabled button is better than a button that gives an obnoxious error message such as "Sorry, you can't click on me now!"

6.6.2 JLabel

JLabel is certainly the simplest type of component. An object of type JLabel exists just to display a line of text. The text cannot be edited by the user, although it can be changed by your program. The constructor for a JLabel specifies the text to be displayed:

```
JLabel message = new JLabel("Hello World!");
```

There is another constructor that specifies where in the label the text is located, if there is extra space. The possible alignments are given by the constants JLabel.LEFT, JLabel.CENTER, and JLabel.RIGHT. For example,

```
JLabel message = new JLabel("Hello World!", JLabel.CENTER);
```

creates a label whose text is centered in the available space. You can change the text displayed in a label by calling the label's setText() method:

```
message.setText("Goodby World!");
```

Since the JLabel class is a subclass of JComponent, you can use methods such as setForeground() with labels. If you want the background color to have any effect, you should call setOpaque(true) on the label, since otherwise the JLabel might not fill in its background. For example:

```
JLabel message = new JLabel("Hello World!", JLabel.CENTER);
message.setForeground(Color.RED); // Display red text...
message.setBackground(Color.BLACK); //      on a black background...
message.setFont(new Font("Serif",Font.BOLD,18)); // in a big bold font.
message.setOpaque(true); // Make sure background is filled in.
```

6.6.3 JCheckBox

A JCheckBox is a component that has two states: selected or unselected. The user can change the state of a check box by clicking on it. The state of a checkbox is represented by a boolean value that is true if the box is selected and false if the box is unselected. A checkbox has a label, which is specified when the box is constructed:

```
JCheckBox showTime = new JCheckBox("Show Current Time");
```

Usually, it's the user who sets the state of a JCheckBox, but you can also set the state in your program. The current state of a checkbox is set using its setSelected(boolean) method. For example, if you want the checkbox showTime to be checked, you would say "showTime.setSelected(true)". To uncheck the box, say "showTime.setSelected(false)". You can determine the current state of a checkbox by calling its isSelected() method, which returns a boolean value.

In many cases, you don't need to worry about events from checkboxes. Your program can just check the state whenever it needs to know it by calling the isSelected() method. However, a checkbox does generate an event when its state is changed by the user, and you can detect this event and respond to it if you want something to happen at the moment the state changes. When the state of a checkbox is changed by the user, it generates an event of type ActionEvent. If you want something to happen when the user changes the state, you must register an ActionListener with the checkbox by calling its addActionListener() method. (Note that if you change the state by calling the setSelected() method, no ActionEvent is generated. However, there is another method in the JCheckBox class, doClick(), which simulates a user click on the checkbox and does generate an ActionEvent.)

When handling an ActionEvent, you can call evt.getSource() in the actionPerformed() method to find out which object generated the event. (Of course, if you are only listening for events from one component, you don't even have to do this.) The returned value is of type Object, but you can type-cast it to another type if you want. Once you know the object that generated the event, you can ask the object to tell you its current state. For example, if you know that the event had to come from one of two checkboxes, cb1 or cb2, then your actionPerformed() method might look like this:

```
public void actionPerformed(ActionEvent evt) {
    Object source = evt.getSource();
    if (source == cb1) {
        boolean newState = cb1.isSelected();
        ... // respond to the change of state
    }
    else if (source == cb2) {
        boolean newState = cb2.isSelected();
        ... // respond to the change of state
    }
}
```

Alternatively, you can use evt.getActionCommand() to retrieve the action command asso-ciated with the source. For a JCheckBox, the action command is, by default, the label of the checkbox.

6.6.4 JTextField and JTextArea

The JTextField and JTextArea classes represent components that contain text that can be edited by the user. A JTextField holds a single line of text, while a JTextArea can hold multiple lines. It is also possible to set a JTextField or JTextArea to be read-only so that the user can read the text that it contains but cannot edit the text. Both classes are subclasses of an abstract class, JTextComponent, which defines their common properties.

JTextField and JTextArea have many methods in common. The instance method setText(), which takes a parameter of type String, can be used to change the text that is displayed in an input component. The contents of the component can be retrieved by calling its getText() instance method, which returns a value of type String. If you want to stop the user from modifying the text, you can call setEditable(false). Call the same method with a parameter of true to make the input component user-editable again.

The user can only type into a text component when it has the input focus. The user can give the input focus to a text component by clicking it with the mouse, but sometimes it is useful to give the input focus to a text field programmatically. You can do this by calling its requestFocus() method. For example, when I discover an error in the user's input, I usually call requestFocus() on the text field that contains the error. This helps the user see where the error occurred and lets the user start typing the correction immediately.

By default, there is no space between the text in a text component and the edge of the component, which usually doesn't look very good. You can use the setMargin() method of the component to add some blank space between the edge of the component and the text. This method takes a parameter of type java.awt.Insets which contains four integer instance variables that specify the margins on the top, left, bottom, and right edge of the component. For example,

```
textComponent.setMargin( new Insets(5,5,5,5) );
```

adds a five-pixel margin between the text in textComponent and each edge of the component.

* * *

The JTextField class has a constructor

```
public JTextField(int columns)
```

where columns is an integer that specifies the number of characters that should be visible in the text field. This is used to determine the preferred width of the text field. (Because characters can be of different sizes and because the preferred width is not always respected, the actual number of characters visible in the text field might not be equal to columns.) You don't have to specify the number of columns; for example, you might use the text field in a context where it will expand to fill whatever space is available. In that case, you can use the constructor JTextField(), with no parameters. You can also use the following constructors, which specify the initial contents of the text field:

```
public JTextField(String contents);
public JTextField(String contents, int columns);
```

The constructors for a JTextArea are

```
public JTextArea()
public JTextArea(int rows, int columns)
public JTextArea(String contents)
```

public JTextArea(String contents, int rows, int columns)

The parameter rows specifies how many lines of text should be visible in the text area. This determines the preferred height of the text area, just as columns determines the preferred width. However, the text area can actually contain any number of lines; the text area can be scrolled to reveal lines that are not currently visible. It is common to use a JTextArea as the CENTER component of a BorderLayout. In that case, it is less useful to specify the number of lines and columns, since the TextArea will expand to fill all the space available in the center area of the container.

The JTextArea class adds a few useful methods to those inherited from JTextComponent. For example, the instance method append(moreText), where moreText is of type String, adds the specified text at the end of the current content of the text area. (When using append() or setText() to add text to a JTextArea, line breaks can be inserted in the text by using the newline character, '\n'.) And setLineWrap(wrap), where wrap is of type boolean, tells what should happen when a line of text is too long to be displayed in the text area. If wrap is true, then any line that is too long will be "wrapped" onto the next line; if wrap is false, the line will simply extend outside the text area, and the user will have to scroll the text area horizontally to see the entire line. The default value of wrap is false.

Since it might be necessary to scroll a text area to see all the text that it contains, you might expect a text area to come with scroll bars. Unfortunately, this does not happen automatically. To get scroll bars for a text area, you have to put the JTextArea inside another component, called a JScrollPane. This can be done as follows:

```
JTextArea inputArea = new JTextArea();
JScrollPane scroller = new JScrollPane( inputArea );
```

The scroll pane provides scroll bars that can be used to scroll the text in the text area. The scroll bars will appear only when needed, that is when the size of the text exceeds the size of the text area. Note that when you want to put the text area into a container, you should add the scroll pane, not the text area itself, to the container.

* * *

When the user is typing in a JTextField and presses return, an ActionEvent is generated. If you want to respond to such events, you can register an ActionListener with the text field, using the text field's addActionListener() method. (Since a JTextArea can contain multiple lines of text, pressing return in a text area does not generate an event; is simply begins a new line of text.)

JTextField has a subclass, JPasswordField, which is identical except that it does not reveal the text that it contains. The characters in a JPasswordField are all displayed as asterisks (or some other fixed character). A password field is, obviously, designed to let the user enter a password without showing that password on the screen.

Text components are actually quite complex, and I have covered only their most basic properties here. I will return to the topic of text components in Subsection 12.4.4.

6.6.5 JComboBox

The JComboBox class provides a way to let the user select one option from a list of options. The options are presented as a kind of pop-up menu, and only the currently selected option is visible on the screen.

When a JComboBox object is first constructed, it initially contains no items. An item is added to the bottom of the menu by calling the combo box's instance method, addItem(str), where str is the string that will be displayed in the menu.

For example, the following code will create an object of type JComboBox that contains the options Red, Blue, Green, and Black:

```
JComboBox colorChoice = new JComboBox();
colorChoice.addItem("Red");
colorChoice.addItem("Blue");
colorChoice.addItem("Green");
colorChoice.addItem("Black");
```

You can call the getSelectedIndex() method of a JComboBox to find out which item is currently selected. This method returns an integer that gives the position of the selected item in the list, where the items are numbered starting from zero. Alternatively, you can call getSelectedItem() to get the selected item itself. (This method returns a value of type Object, since a JComboBox can actually hold other types of objects besides strings.) You can change the selection by calling the method setSelectedIndex(n), where n is an integer giving the position of the item that you want to select.

The most common way to use a JComboBox is to call its getSelectedIndex() method when you have a need to know which item is currently selected. However, like other components that we have seen, JComboBox components generate ActionEvent s when the user selects an item. You can register an ActionListener with the JComboBox if you want to respond to such events as they occur.

JComboBoxes have a nifty feature, which is probably not all that useful in practice. You can make a JComboBox "editable" by calling its method setEditable(true). If you do this, the user can edit the selection by clicking on the JComboBox and typing. This allows the user to make a selection that is not in the pre-configured list that you provide. (The "Combo" in the name "JComboBox" refers to the fact that it's a kind of combination of menu and text-input box.) If the user has edited the selection in this way, then the getSelectedIndex() method will return the value -1, and getSelectedItem() will return the string that the user typed. An ActionEvent is triggered if the user presses return while typing in the JComboBox.

6.6.6 JSlider

A JSlider provides a way for the user to select an integer value from a range of possible values. The user does this by dragging a "knob" along a bar. A slider can, optionally, be decorated with tick marks and with labels. This picture shows three sliders with different decorations and with different ranges of values:

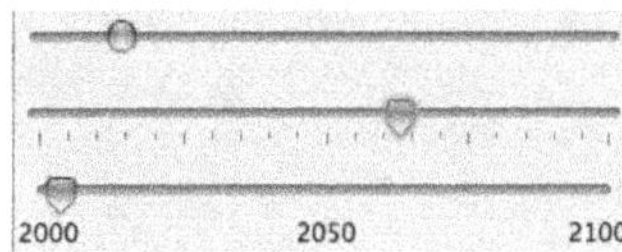

Here, the second slider is decorated with ticks, and the third one is decorated with labels. It's possible for a single slider to have both types of decorations.

The most commonly used constructor for JSliders specifies the start and end of the range of values for the slider and its initial value when it first appears on the screen:

public JSlider(int minimum, int maximum, int value)

If the parameters are omitted, the values 0, 100, and 50 are used. By default, a slider is horizon-tal, but you can make it vertical by calling its method setOrientation(JSlider.VERTICAL). The current value of a JSlider can be read at any time with its getValue() method, which returns a value of type int. If you want to change the value, you can do so with the method setValue(n), which takes a parameter of type int.

If you want to respond immediately when the user changes the value of a slider, you can register a listener with the slider. JSliders, unlike other components we have seen, do not generate ActionEvents. Instead, they generate events of type ChangeEvent. ChangeEvent and related classes are defined in the package javax.swing.event rather than java.awt.event, so if you want to use ChangeEvents, you should import javax.swing.event.* at the beginning of your program. You must also define some object to implement the ChangeListener interface, and you must register the change listener with the slider by calling its addChangeListener() method. A ChangeListener must provide a definition for the method:

```
public void stateChanged(ChangeEvent evt)
```

This method will be called whenever the value of the slider changes. (Note that it will also be called when you change the value with the setValue() method, as well as when the user changes the value.) In the stateChanged() method, you can call evt.getSource() to find out which object generated the event.

Using tick marks on a slider is a two-step process: Specify the interval between the tick marks, and tell the slider that the tick marks should be displayed. There are actually two types of tick marks, "major" tick marks and "minor" tick marks. You can have one or the other or both. Major tick marks are a bit longer than minor tick marks. The method setMinorTickSpacing(i) indicates that there should be a minor tick mark every i units along the slider. The parameter is an integer. (The spacing is in terms of values on the slider, not pixels.) For the major tick marks, there is a similar command, setMajorTickSpacing(i). Calling these methods is not enough to make the tick marks appear. You also have to call setPaintTicks(true). For example, the second slider in the above picture was created and configured using the commands:

```
slider2 = new JSlider();        // (Uses default min, max, and value.)
slider2.addChangeListener(this);
slider2.setMajorTickSpacing(25);
slider2.setMinorTickSpacing(5);
slider2.setPaintTicks(true);
```

Labels on a slider are handled similarly. You have to specify the labels and tell the slider to paint them. Specifying labels is a tricky business, but the JSlider class has a method to simplify it. You can create a set of labels and add them to a slider named sldr with the command:

```
sldr.setLabelTable( sldr.createStandardLabels(i) );
```

where i is an integer giving the spacing between the labels. To arrange for the labels to be displayed, call setPaintLabels(true). For example, the third slider in the above picture was created and configured with the commands:

```
slider3 = new JSlider(2000,2100,2006);
```

```
slider3.addChangeListener(this);
slider3.setLabelTable( slider3.createStandardLabels(50) );
slider3.setPaintLabels(true);
```

6.7 Basic Layout

Components are the fundamental building blocks of a graphical user interface. But you have to do more with components besides create them. Another aspect of GUI programming is **laying out** components on the screen, that is, deciding where they are drawn and how big they are. You have probably noticed that computing coordinates can be a difficult problem, especially if you don't assume a fixed size for the drawing area. Java has a solution for this, as well.

Components are the visible objects that make up a GUI. Some components are **containers**, which can hold other components. Containers in Java are objects that belong to some subclass of java.awt.Container. The content pane of a JApplet or JFrame is an example of a container. The standard class JPanel, which we have mostly used as a drawing surface up till now, is another example of a container.

Because a JPanel object is a container, it can hold other components. Because a JPanel is itself a component, you can add a JPanel to another JPanel. This makes complex nesting of components possible. JPanels can be used to organize complicated user interfaces, as shown in this illustration:

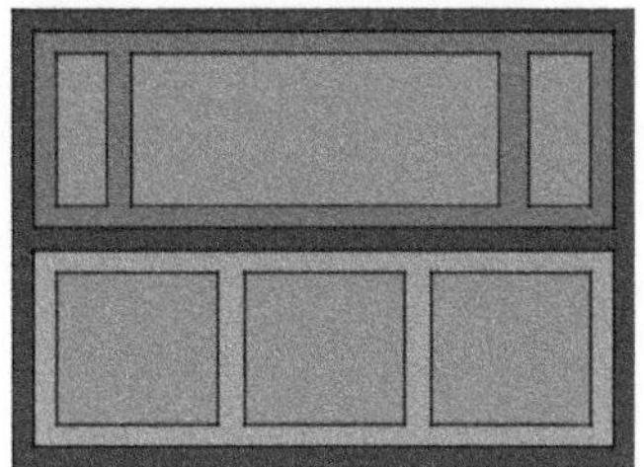

Three panels, shown in color, containing six other components, shown in gray.

The components in a container must be "laid out," which means setting their sizes and positions. It's possible to program the layout yourself, but ordinarily layout is done by a **layout manager** . A layout manager is an object associated with a container that implements some policy for laying out the components in that container. Different types of layout manager implement different policies. In this section, we will cover the three most common types of layout manager, and then we will look at several programming examples that use components and layout.

Every container has an instance method, setLayout(), that takes a parameter of type LayoutManager and that is used to specify the layout manager that will be responsible for laying out any components that are added to the container. Components are added to a container by calling an instance method named add() in the container object. There are actually several versions of the add() method, with different parameter lists. Different versions of add() are appropriate for different layout managers, as we will see below.

6.7.1 Basic Layout Managers

Java has a variety of standard layout managers that can be used as parameters in the setLayout() method. They are defined by classes in the package java.awt. Here, we will look at just three of these layout manager classes: FlowLayout, BorderLayout, and GridLayout.

A FlowLayout simply lines up components in a row across the container. The size of each component is equal to that component's "preferred size." After laying out as many items as will fit in a row across the container, the layout manager will move on to the next row. The default layout for a JPanel is a FlowLayout ; that is, a JPanel uses a FlowLayout unless you specify a different layout manager by calling the panel's setLayout() method.

The components in a given row can be either left-aligned, right-aligned, or centered within that row, and there can be horizontal and vertical gaps between components. If the default constructor, "new FlowLayout()", is used, then the components on each row will be centered and both the horizontal and the vertical gaps will be five pixels. The constructor

```
public FlowLayout(int align, int hgap, int vgap)
```

can be used to specify alternative alignment and gaps. The possible values of align are FlowLayout.LEFT, FlowLayout.RIGHT, and FlowLayout.CENTER.

Suppose that cntr is a container object that is using a FlowLayout as its layout manager. Then, a component, comp, can be added to the container with the statement

```
cntr.add(comp);
```

The FlowLayout will line up all the components that have been added to the container in this way. They will be lined up in the order in which they were added. For example, this picture shows five buttons in a panel that uses a FlowLayout :

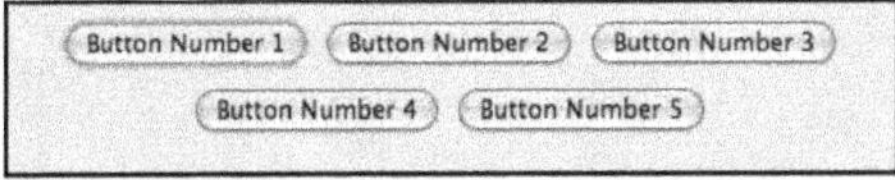

Note that since the five buttons will not fit in a single row across the panel, they are arranged in two rows. In each row, the buttons are grouped together and are centered in the row. The buttons were added to the panel using the statements:

```
panel.add(button1);
panel.add(button2);
panel.add(button3);
panel.add(button4);
panel.add(button5);
```

When a container uses a layout manager, the layout manager is ordinarily responsible for computing the preferred size of the container (although a different preferred size could be set by calling the container's setPreferredSize method). A FlowLayout prefers to put its components in a single row, so the preferred width is the total of the preferred widths of all the components, plus the horizontal gaps between the components. The preferred height is the maximum preferred height of all the components.

* * *

A BorderLayout layout manager is designed to display one large, central component, with up to four smaller components arranged along the edges of the central component. If a container, cntr, is using a BorderLayout, then a component, comp, should be added to the container using a statement of the form

```
cntr.add( comp, borderLayoutPosition );
```

where borderLayoutPosition specifies what position the component should occupy in the layout and is given as one of the constants BorderLayout.CENTER, BorderLayout.NORTH, BorderLayout.SOUTH, BorderLayout.EAST, or BorderLayout.WEST. The meaning of the five positions is shown in this diagram:

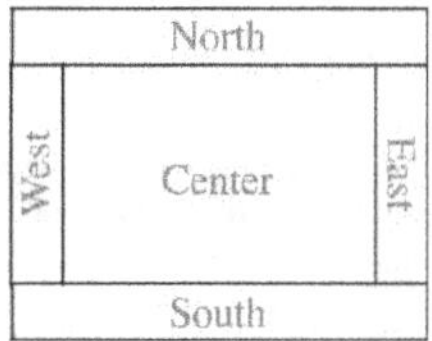

Note that a border layout can contain fewer than five compompontnts, so that not all five of the possible positions need to be filled.

A BorderLayout selects the sizes of its components as follows: The NORTH and SOUTH com-ponents (if present) are shown at their preferred heights, but their width is set equal to the full width of the container. The EAST and WEST components are shown at their preferred widths, but their height is set to the height of the container, minus the space occupied by the NORTH and SOUTH components. Finally, the CENTER component takes up any remaining space; the preferred size of the CENTER component is completely ignored. You should make sure that the components that you put into a BorderLayout are suitable for the positions that they will occupy. A horizontal slider or text field, for example, would work well in the NORTH or SOUTH position, but wouldn't make much sense in the EAST or WEST position.

The default constructor, new BorderLayout(), leaves no space between components. If you would like to leave some space, you can specify horizontal and vertical gaps in the constructor of the BorderLayout object. For example, if you say

```
panel.setLayout(new BorderLayout(5,7));
```

then the layout manager will insert horizontal gaps of 5 pixels between components and vertical gaps of 7 pixels between components. The background color of the container will show through in these gaps. The default layout for the original content pane that comes with a JFrame or JApplet is a BorderLayout with no horizontal or vertical gap.

* * *

Finally, we consider the GridLayout layout manager. A grid layout lays out components in a grid of equal sized rectangles. This illustration shows how the components would be arranged in a grid layout with 3 rows and 2 columns:

#1	#2
#3	#4
#5	#6

If a container uses a GridLayout, the appropriate add method for the container takes a single parameter of type Component (for example: cntr.add(comp)). Components are added to the grid in the order shown; that is, each row is filled from left to right before going on the next row.

The constructor for a GridLayout takes the form "new GridLayout(R,C)", where R is the number of rows and C is the number of columns. If you want to leave horizontal gaps of H pixels between columns and vertical gaps of V pixels between rows, use "new GridLayout(R,C,H,V)" instead.

When you use a GridLayout, it's probably good form to add just enough components to fill the grid. However, this is not required. In fact, as long as you specify a non-zero value for the number of rows, then the number of columns is essentially ignored. The system will use just as many columns as are necessary to hold all the components that you add to the container. If you want to depend on this behavior, you should probably specify zero as the number of columns. You can also specify the number of rows as zero. In that case, you must give a non-zero number of columns. The system will use the specified number of columns, with just as many rows as necessary to hold the components that are added to the container.

Horizontal grids, with a single row, and vertical grids, with a single column, are very com-mon. For example, suppose that button1, button2, and button3 are buttons and that you'd like to display them in a horizontal row in a panel. If you use a horizontal grid for the panel, then the buttons will completely fill that panel and will all be the same size. The panel can be created as follows:

JPanel buttonBar = new JPanel();

buttonBar.setLayout(new GridLayout(1,3));

- (Note: The "3" here is pretty much ignored, and
- you could also say "new GridLayout(1,0)".
- To leave gaps between the buttons, you could use
- "new GridLayout(1,0,5,5)".)

buttonBar.add(button1);

buttonBar.add(button2);

buttonBar.add(button3);

You might find this button bar to be more attractive than the one that uses the default FlowLay-out layout manager.

6.7.2 Borders

We have seen how to leave gaps between the components in a container, but what if you would like to leave a border around the outside of the container? This problem is not handled by layout managers. Instead, borders in Swing are represented by objects. A Border object can be added to any JComponent, not just to containers. Borders can be more than just empty space. The class javax.swing.BorderFactory contains a large number of static methods for creating border objects. For example, the function

BorderFactory.createLineBorder(Color.BLACK)

returns an object that represents a one-pixel wide black line around the outside of a component. If comp is a JComponent, a border can be added to comp using its setBorder() method. For example:

comp.setBorder(BorderFactory.createLineBorder(Color.BLACK));

When a border has been set for a JComponent, the border is drawn automatically, without any further effort on the part of the programmer. The border is drawn along the edges of the component, just inside its boundary. The layout manager of a JPanel or other container will take the space occupied by the border into account. The components that are added to the container will be displayed in the area inside the border. I don't recommend using a border on a JPanel that is being used as a drawing surface. However, if you do this, you should take the border into account. If you draw in the area occupied by the border, that part of your drawing will be covered by the border.

Here are some of the static methods that can be used to create borders:

- BorderFactory.createEmptyBorder(top,left,bottom,right) — leaves an empty bor-der around the edges of a component. Nothing is drawn in this space, so the background color of the component will appear in the area occupied by the border. The parameters are integers that give the width of the border along the top, left, bottom, and right edges of the component. This is actually very useful when used on a JPanel that contains other components. It puts some space between the components and the edge of the panel. It can also be useful on a JLabel, which otherwise would not have any space between the text and the edge of the label.
- BorderFactory.createLineBorder(color,thickness) — draws a line around all four edges of a component. The first parameter is of type Color and specifies the color of the line. The second parameter is an integer that specifies the thickness of the border. If the second parameter is omitted, a line of thickness 1 is drawn.
- BorderFactory.createMatteBorder(top,left,bottom,right,color) — is similar to createLineBorder, except that you can specify individual thicknesses for the top, left, bottom, and right edges of the component.
- BorderFactory.createEtchedBorder() — creates a border that looks like a groove etched around the boundary of the component. The effect is achieved using lighter and darker shades of the component's background color, and it does not work well with every background color.
- BorderFactory.createLoweredBevelBorder()—gives a component a three-dimensional effect that makes it look like it is lowered into the computer screen. As with an Etched-Border, this only works well for certain background colors.
- BorderFactory.createRaisedBevelBorder()—similar to a LoweredBevelBorder, but the component looks like it is raised above the computer screen.
- BorderFactory.createTitledBorder(title)—creates a border with a title. The title is a String, which is displayed in the upper left corner of the border.

There are many other methods in the BorderFactory class, most of them providing variations of the basic border styles given here. The following illustration shows six

components with six different border styles. The text in each component is the command that created the border for that component:

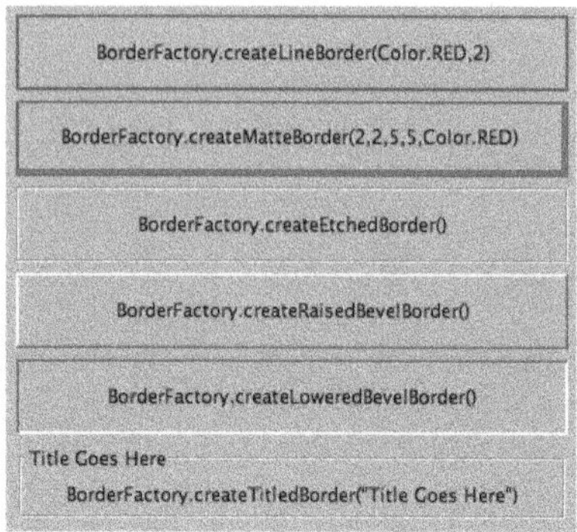

(The source code for the applet that produced this picture can be found in **BorderDemo.java**.)

6.7.3 SliderAndComboBoxDemo

Now that we have looked at components and layouts, it's time to put them together into some complete programs. We start with a simple demo that uses a JLabel, a JComboBox, and a couple of JSlider s, all laid out in a GridLayout, as shown in this picture:

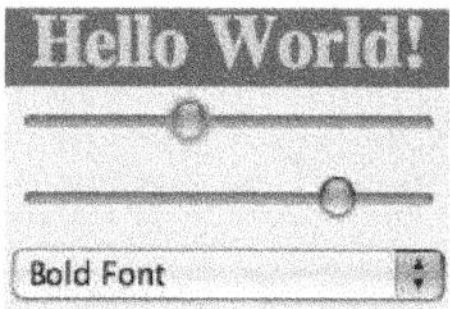

The sliders in this applet control the foreground and background color of the label, and the combo box controls its font style. Writing this program is a matter of creating the components, laying them out, and programming listeners to respond to events from the sliders and combo box. In my program, I define a subclass of JPanel which will be used for the applet's content pane. This class implements ChangeListener and ActionListener, so the panel itself can act as the listener for change events from the sliders and action events from the combo box. In the constructor, the four components are created and configured, a GridLayout is installed as the layout manager for the panel, and the components are added to the panel:

```
/* Create the sliders, and set up this panel to listen for
   ChangeEvents that are generated by the sliders. */

bgColorSlider = new JSlider(0,255,100);
bgColorSlider.addChangeListener(this);
```

```
fgColorSlider = new JSlider(0,255,200);
fgColorSlider.addChangeListener(this);
```

```
/* Create the combo box, and add four items to it, listing
   different font styles. Set up the panel to listen for
   ActionEvents from the combo box. */

fontStyleSelect = new JComboBox();
fontStyleSelect.addItem("Plain Font");
fontStyleSelect.addItem("Italic Font");
fontStyleSelect.addItem("Bold Font");
fontStyleSelect.addItem("Bold Italic Font");
fontStyleSelect.setSelectedIndex(2);
fontStyleSelect.addActionListener(this);

/* Create the display label, with properties to match the values
   of the sliders and the setting of the combo box. */

displayLabel = new JLabel("Hello World!", JLabel.CENTER);
displayLabel.setOpaque(true); displayLabel.setBackground(
new Color(100,100,100) ); displayLabel.setForeground( new
Color(255, 200, 200) ); displayLabel.setFont( new
Font("Serif", Font.BOLD, 30) );

/* Set the layout for the panel, and add the four components.
   Use a GridLayout with 4 rows and 1 column. */

setLayout(new GridLayout(4,1));
add(displayLabel);
add(bgColorSlider);
add(fgColorSlider);
add(fontStyleSelect);
```

The class also defines the methods required by the ActionListener and ChangeListener inter-faces. The actionPerformed() method is called when the user selects an item in the combo box. This method changes the font in the JLable, where the font depends on which item is currently selected in the combo box, fontStyleSelect:

```
public void actionPerformed(ActionEvent evt) {
   switch ( fontStyleSelect.getSelectedIndex() ) {
   case 0:
      displayLabel.setFont( new Font("Serif", Font.PLAIN, 30) );
      break;
   case 1:
      displayLabel.setFont( new Font("Serif", Font.ITALIC, 30) );
      break;
   case 2:
      displayLabel.setFont( new Font("Serif", Font.BOLD, 30) );
      break;
   case 3:
      displayLabel.setFont( new Font("Serif", Font.BOLD + Font.ITALIC, 30) );
      break;
```

```
        }
    }
```

And the stateChanged() method, which is called when the user manipulates one of the sliders, uses the value on the slider to compute a new foreground or background color for the label. The method checks evt.getSource() to determine which slider was changed:

```
public void stateChanged(ChangeEvent evt) {
        if (evt.getSource() == bgColorSlider) {
          int bgVal = bgColorSlider.getValue();
        displayLabel.setBackground( new Color(bgVal,bgVal,bgVal) );
          • NOTE: The background color is a shade of gray,
          •           determined by the setting on the slider.
  }
  else {
      int fgVal = fgColorSlider.getValue(); displayLabel.setForeground(
      new Color( 255, fgVal, fgVal) );
          • Note: The foreground color ranges from pure red to pure
          •           white as the slider value increases from 0 to 255.
  }
}
```

(The complete source code is in the file **SliderAndComboBoxDemo.java**.)

6.7.4 A Simple Calculator

As our next example, we look briefly at an example that uses nested subpanels to build a more complex user interface. The program has two JTextField s where the user can enter two numbers, four JButtons that the user can click to add, subtract, multiply, or divide the two numbers, and a JLabel that displays the result of the operation:

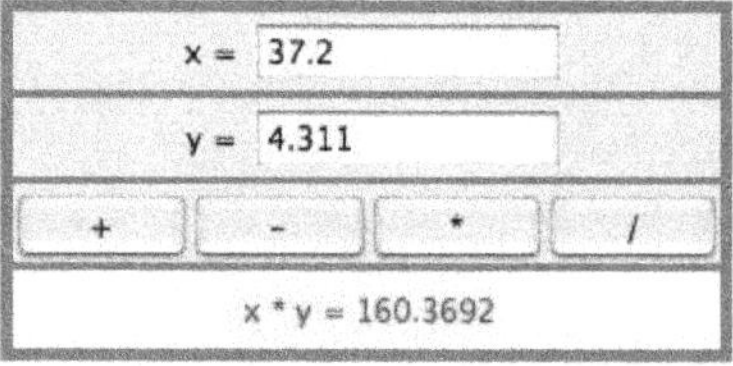

Like the previous example, this example uses a main panel with a GridLayout that has four rows and one column. In this case, the layout is created with the statement:

```
setLayout(new GridLayout(4,1,3,3));
```

which allows a 3-pixel gap between the rows where the gray background color of the panel is visible. The gray border around the edges of the panel is added with the statement

```
setBorder( BorderFactory.createEmptyBorder(5,5,5,5) );
```

The first row of the grid layout actually contains two components, a JLabel displaying the text "x =" and a JTextField. A grid layout can only only have one component in each position. In this case, that component is a JPanel, a subpanel that is nested inside the main panel. This subpanel in turn contains the label and text field. This can be programmed as follows:

```
xInput = new JTextField("0", 10); // Create a text field sized to hold 10 chars. JPanel
xPanel = new JPanel(); // Create the subpanel. xPanel.add( new JLabel(" x = ")); //
```

Add a label to the subpanel. xPanel.add(xInput); // Add the text field to the subpanel mainPanel.add(xPanel); // Add the subpanel to the main panel.

The subpanel uses the default FlowLayout layout manager, so the label and text field are simply placed next to each other in the subpanel at their preferred size, and are centered in the subpanel.

Similarly, the third row of the grid layout is a subpanel that contains four buttons. In this case, the subpanel uses a GridLayout with one row and four columns, so that the buttons are all the same size and completely fill the subpanel.

One other point of interest in this example is the actionPerformed() method that responds when the user clicks one of the buttons. This method must retrieve the user's numbers from the text field, perform the appropriate arithmetic operation on them (depending on which button was clicked), and set the text of the label to represent the result. However, the contents of the text fields can only be retrieved as strings, and these strings must be converted into numbers. If the conversion fails, the label is set to display an error message:

```
public void actionPerformed(ActionEvent evt) {

    double x, y;     // The numbers from the input boxes.

    try {
        String xStr = xInput.getText();
        x = Double.parseDouble(xStr);
    }
    catch (NumberFormatException e) {
            • The string xStr is not a legal number.
        answer.setText("Illegal data for x.");
        xInput.requestFocus();
        return;
    }

    try {
        String yStr = yInput.getText();
        y = Double.parseDouble(yStr);
    }
    catch (NumberFormatException e) {
            • The string yStr is not a legal number.
        answer.setText("Illegal data for y.");
        yInput.requestFocus();
        return;
    }

    /* Perfrom the operation based on the action command from the
      button. The action command is the text displayed on the button.
      Note that division by zero produces an error message. */

    String op = evt.getActionCommand();
    if (op.equals("+"))
        answer.setText( "x + y = " + (x+y) );
    else if (op.equals("-"))
        answer.setText( "x - y = " + (x-y) );
    else if (op.equals("*"))
        answer.setText( "x * y = " + (x*y) );
```

```
else if (op.equals("/")) {
    if (y == 0)
        answer.setText("Can't divide by zero!");
    else
        answer.setText( "x / y = " + (x/y) );
```

```
    }
  }// end actionPerformed()
```

(The complete source code for this example can be found in **SimpleCalc.java**.)

6.7.5 Using a null Layout

As mentioned above, it is possible to do without a layout manager altogether. For out next example, we'll look at a panel that does not use a layout manager. If you set the layout manager of a container to be null, by calling container.setLayout(null), then you assume complete responsibility for positioning and sizing the components in that container.

If comp is any component, then the statement

```
comp.setBounds(x, y, width, height);
```

puts the top left corner of the component at the point (x,y), measured in the coordinate system of the container that contains the component, and it sets the width and height of the component to the specified values. You should only set the bounds of a component if the container that contains it has a null layout manager. In a container that has a non-null layout manager, the layout manager is responsible for setting the bounds, and you should not interfere with its job.

Assuming that you have set the layout manager to null, you can call the setBounds() method any time you like. (You can even make a component that moves or changes size while the user is watching.) If you are writing a panel that has a known, fixed size, then you can set the bounds of each component in the panel's constructor. Note that you must also add the components to the panel, using the panel's add(component) instance method; otherwise, the component will not appear on the screen.

Our example contains four components: two buttons, a label, and a panel that displays a checkerboard pattern:

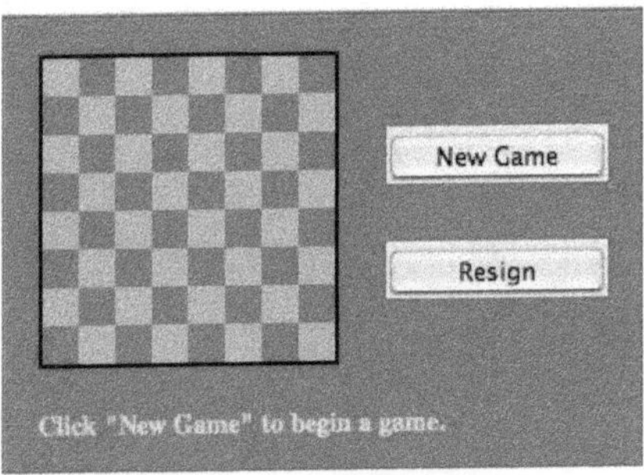

This is just an example of using a null layout; it doesn't do anything, except that clicking the buttons changes the text of the label. (We will use this example in Section 7.5 as a starting point for a checkers game.)

For its content pane, this example uses a main panel that is defined by a class named NullLayoutPanel. The four components are created and added to the panel in the constructor of the NullLayoutPanel class. Then the setBounds() method of each component is called to set the size and position of the component:

```
public NullLayoutPanel() {

   setLayout(null);    // I will do the layout myself!

   setBackground(new Color(0,150,0));  // A dark green background.

   setBorder( BorderFactory.createEtchedBorder() );

   setPreferredSize( new Dimension(350,240) );
        // I assume that the size of the panel is, in fact, 350-by-240.

   /* Create the components and add them to the content pane. If you
    don't add them to the a container, they won't appear, even if you set
    their bounds! */


   board = new Checkerboard();
       • (Checkerborad is a subclass of JPanel, defined elsewhere.)
   add(board);

   newGameButton = new JButton("New Game");
   newGameButton.addActionListener(this);
   add(newGameButton);

   resignButton = new JButton("Resign");
   resignButton.addActionListener(this);
   add(resignButton);

   message = new JLabel("Click \"New Game\" to begin a game.");
   message.setForeground( new Color(100,255,100) ); // Light green.
   message.setFont(new Font("Serif", Font.BOLD, 14)); add(message);

   /* Set the position and size of each component by calling its
    setBounds() method. */

   board.setBounds(20,20,164,164);
   newGameButton.setBounds(210, 60, 120, 30);
   resignButton.setBounds(210, 120, 120, 30);
   message.setBounds(20, 200, 330, 30);

} // end constructor
```

It's reasonably easy, in this case, to get an attractive layout. It's much more difficult to do your own layout if you want to allow for changes of size. In that case, you have to respond to changes in the container's size by recomputing the sizes and positions of all the components that it contains. If you want to respond to changes in a container's size, you can register an appropriate listener with the container. Any component generates an event of type ComponentEvent when its size changes (and also when it is moved, hidden, or shown). You can register a ComponentListener with the container and respond to size change events by recomputing the sizes and positions of all the components in the container. Consult a Java reference for more information about ComponentEvents.

However, my real advice is that if you want to allow for changes in the container's size, try to find a layout manager to do the work for you.

(The complete source code for this example is in **NullLayoutDemo.java**.)

6.7.6 A Little Card Game

For a final example, let's look at something a little more interesting as a program. The example is a simple card game in which you look at a playing card and try to predict whether the next card will be higher or lower in value. (Aces have the lowest value in this game.) You've seen a text-oriented version of the same game in Subsection 5.4.3. Section 5.4 also introduced Deck, Hand, and Card classes that are used in the game program. In this GUI version of the game, you click on a button to make your prediction. If you predict wrong, you lose. If you make three correct predictions, you win. After completing one game, you can click the "New Game" button to start a new game. Here is what the game looks like:

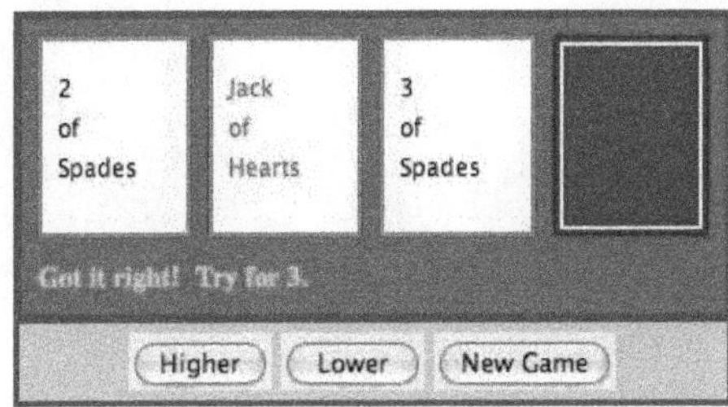

The complete source code for this example is in the file **HighLowGUI.java**. You can try out the game in the on-line version of this section, or by running the program as a stand-alone application.

The overall structure of the main panel in this example should be clear: It has three buttons in a subpanel at the bottom of the main panel and a large drawing surface that displays the cards and a message. The main panel uses a BorderLayout. The drawing surface occupies the CENTER position of the border layout. The subpanel that contains the buttons occupies the SOUTH position of the border layout, and the other three positions of the layout are empty.

The drawing surface is defined by a nested class named CardPanel, which is a subclass of JPanel. I have chosen to let the drawing surface object do most of the work of the game: It listens for events from the three buttons and responds by taking the appropriate actions. The main panel is defined by HighLowGUI itself, which is another subclass of JPanel. The constructor of the HighLowGUI class creates all the other components, sets up event handling, and lays out the components:

```
public HighLowGUI() {     // The constructor.

   setBackground( new Color(130,50,40) );

   setLayout( new BorderLayout(3,3) );         BorderLayout with 3-pixel gaps.

   CardPanel board = new                       • Where the cards are drawn.
   CardPanel(); add(board,
   BorderLayout.CENTER);
```

```
JPanel buttonPanel = new JPanel(); // The subpanel that holds the buttons.
buttonPanel.setBackground( new Color(220,200,180) ); add(buttonPanel,
BorderLayout.SOUTH);

JButton higher = new JButton( "Higher" );
```

```
        higher.addActionListener(board);         // The CardPanel listens for events.
        buttonPanel.add(higher);

        JButton lower = new JButton( "Lower" );
        lower.addActionListener(board);
        buttonPanel.add(lower);

        JButton newGame = new JButton( "New Game" );
        newGame.addActionListener(board);
        buttonPanel.add(newGame);

        setBorder(BorderFactory.createLineBorder( new Color(130,50,40), 3) );

    } // end constructor
```

The programming of the drawing surface class, CardPanel, is a nice example of thinking in terms of a state machine. (See Subsection 6.5.4.) It is important to think in terms of the states that the game can be in, how the state can change, and how the response to events can depend on the state. The approach that produced the original, text-oriented game in Subsection 5.4.3 is not appropriate here. Trying to think about the game in terms of a process that goes step-by-step from beginning to end is more likely to confuse you than to help you.

The state of the game includes the cards and the message. The cards are stored in an object of type Hand. The message is a String. These values are stored in instance variables. There is also another, less obvious aspect of the state: Sometimes a game is in progress, and the user is supposed to make a prediction about the next card. Sometimes we are between games, and the user is supposed to click the "New Game" button. It's a good idea to keep track of this basic difference in state. The CardPanel class uses a boolean instance variable named gameInProgress for this purpose.

The state of the game can change whenever the user clicks on a button. The CardPanel class implements the ActionListener interface and defines an actionPerformed() method to respond to the user's clicks. This method simply calls one of three other methods, doHigher(), doLower(), or newGame(), depending on which button was pressed. It's in these three event-handling methods that the action of the game takes place.

We don't want to let the user start a new game if a game is currently in progress. That would be cheating. So, the response in the newGame() method is different depending on whether the state variable gameInProgress is true or false. If a game is in progress, the message instance variable should be set to show an error message. If a game is not in progress, then all the state variables should be set to appropriate values for the beginning of a new game. In any case, the board must be repainted so that the user can see that the state has changed. The complete newGame() method is as follows:

```
    /**
     * Called by the CardPanel constructor, and called by actionPerformed() if
     * the user clicks the "New Game" button.  Start a new game.
     */
    void doNewGame() {
        if (gameInProgress) {
                // If the current game is not over, it is an error to try
                // to start a new game.
```

```
    message = "You still have to finish this game!";
    repaint();
    return;
}
```

```
        deck = new Deck();    // Create the deck and hand to use for this game.
        hand = new
        Hand();
        deck.shuffle();
        hand.addCard( deck.dealCard() );    // Deal the first card into the hand.
        message = "Is the next card higher or lower?";
        gameInProgress = true;
        repaint();
    } // end doNewGame()
```

The doHigher() and doLower() methods are almost identical to each other (and could probably have been combined into one method with a parameter, if I were more clever). Let's look at the doHigher() routine. This is called when the user clicks the "Higher" button. This only makes sense if a game is in progress, so the first thing doHigher() should do is check the value of the state variable gameInProgress. If the value is false, then doHigher() should just set up an error message. If a game is in progress, a new card should be added to the hand and the user's prediction should be tested. The user might win or lose at this time. If so, the value of the state variable gameInProgress must be set to false because the game is over. In any case, the board is repainted to show the new state. Here is the doHigher() method:

```
    /**
     • Called by actionPerformmed() when user clicks "Higher" button.
     • Check the user's prediction.  Game ends if user guessed
     • wrong or if the user has made three correct predictions.
     */
    void doHigher() {
        if (gameInProgress == false) {
                •  If the game has ended, it was an error to click "Higher",
                •  So set up an error message and abort processing.
            message = "Click \"New Game\" to start a new game!";
            repaint();
            return;
        }
        hand.addCard( deck.dealCard() );                    // Deal a card to the hand.
        int cardCt = hand.getCardCount();
        Card thisCard = hand.getCard( cardCt -        1   );         // Card just dealt.
        Card prevCard = hand.getCard( cardCt -        2   );       // The previous card.
        if ( thisCard.getValue() < prevCard.getValue() ) {
            gameInProgress = false;
            message = "Too bad! You lose.";
        }
        else if ( thisCard.getValue() == prevCard.getValue() ) {
            gameInProgress = false;
            message = "Too bad!  You lose on ties.";
        }
        else if ( cardCt == 4) {
```

```
        gameInProgress = false;
        message = "You win!  You made three correct guesses.";
    }
    else {
        message = "Got it right!      Try for " + cardCt + ".";
    }
    repaint();
} // end doHigher()
```

The paintComponent() method of the CardPanel class uses the values in the state variables to decide what to show. It displays the string stored in the message variable. It draws each of the cards in the hand. There is one little tricky bit: If a game is in progress, it draws an extra face-down card, which is not in the hand, to represent the next card in the deck. Drawing the cards requires some care and computation. I wrote a method, "void drawCard(Graphics g, Card card, int x, int y)", which draws a card with its upper left corner at the point (x,y). The paintComponent() routine decides where to draw each card and calls this routine to do the drawing. You can check out all the details in the source code, **HighLowGUI.java.**

* * *

One further note on the programming of this example: The source code defines HighLowGUI as a subclass of JPanel. The class contains a main() routine so that it can be run as a stand-alone application; the main() routine simply opens a window that uses a panel of type HighLowGUI as its content pane. In addition, I decided to write an applet version of the program as a static nested class named Applet inside the HighLowGUI class. Since this is a nested class, its full name is HighLowGUI.Applet and the class file that is produced when the source code is compiled is named HighLowGUI$Applet.class. This class is used for the applet version of the program in the on-line version of the book. The <applet> tag lists the class file for the applet as code="HighLowGUI$Applet.class". This is admittedly an unusual way to organize the program, and it is probably more natural to have the panel, applet, and stand-alone program defined in separate classes. However, writing the program in this way does show the flexibility of Java classes. (Nested classes were discussed in Subsection 5.7.2.)

6.8 Menus and Dialogs

We have already encountered many of the basic aspects of GUI programming, but professional programs use many additional features. We will cover some of the advanced features of Java GUI programming in Chapter 12, but in this section we look briefly at a few more basic features that are essential for writing GUI programs. I will discuss these features in the context of a "MosaicDraw" program that is shown in this picture:

As the user clicks-and-drags the mouse in the large drawing area of this program, it leaves a trail of little colored squares. There is some random variation in the color of the squares. (This is meant to make the picture look a little more like a real mosaic, which is a picture made out of small colored stones in which there would be some natural color variation.) There is a menu bar above the drawing area. The "Control" menu contains commands for filling and clearing the drawing area, along with a few options that affect the appearance of the picture. The "Color" menu lets the user select the color that will be used when the user draws. The "Tools" menu affects the behavior of the mouse. Using the default "Draw" tool, the mouse leaves a trail of single squares. Using the "Draw 3x3" tool, the mouse leaves a swath of colored squares that is three squares wide. There are also "Erase" tools, which let the user set squares back to their default black color.

The drawing area of the program is a panel that belongs to the MosaicPanel class, a subclass of JPanel that is defined in **MosaicPanel.java**. MosaicPanel is a highly reusable class for repre-senting mosaics of colored rectangles. It does not directly support drawing on the mosaic, but it does support setting the color of each individual square. The MosaicDraw program installs a mouse listener on the panel; the mouse listener responds to mousePressed and mouseDragged events on the panel by setting the color of the square that contains the mouse. This is a nice example of applying a listener to an object to do something that was not programmed into the object itself.

Most of the programming for MosaicDraw can be found in **MosaicDrawController.java**. (It could have gone into the MosaicPanel class, if I had not decided to use that pre-existing class in unmodified form.) It is the MosaicDrawController class that creates a MosaicPanel object and adds a mouse listener to it. It also creates the menu bar that is shown at the top of the program and implements all the commands in the menu bar. It has an instance method getMosaicPanel() that returns a reference to the mosaic panel that it has created, and it has another instance method getMenuBar() that returns a menu bar for the program. These methods are used to obtain the panel and menu bar so that they can be added to an applet or a frame.

To get a working program, an object of type JApplet or JFrame is needed. The files **MosaicDrawApplet.java** and **MosaicDrawFrame.java** define the applet and frame versions of the program. These are rather simple classes; they simply create a MosaicDrawController object and use its mosaic panel and menu bar. I urge you to study these files, along with **MosaicDraw-Controller.java**. I will not be discussing all aspects of the code here, but you should be able to understand it all after reading this section. As for **MosaicPanel.java**, it uses some techniques that you would not understand at this point, but I encourage you to at least read the comments in this file to learn about the API for mosaic panels.

6.8.1 Menus and Menubars

MosaicDraw is the first example that we have seen that uses a menu bar. Fortunately, menus are very easy to use in Java. The items in a menu are represented by the class JMenuItem (this class and other menu-related classes are in package javax.swing). Menu items are used in almost exactly the same way as buttons. In fact, JMenuItem and JButton are both subclasses of a class, AbstractButton, that defines their common behavior. In particular, a JMenuItem is created using a constructor that specifies the text of the menu item, such as:

```
JMenuItem fillCommand = new JMenuItem("Fill");
```

You can add an ActionListener to a JMenuItem by calling the menu item's addActionListener()

method. The actionPerformed() method of the action listener is called when the user selects the item from the menu. You can change the text of the item by calling its setText(String) method, and you can enable it and disable it using the setEnabled(boolean) method. All this works in exactly the same way as for a JButton.

The main difference between a menu item and a button, of course, is that a menu item is meant to appear in a menu rather than in a panel. A menu in Java is represented by the class JMenu. A JMenu has a name, which is specified in the constructor, and it has an add(JMenuItem) method that can be used to add a JMenuItem to the menu. So, the "Tools" menu in the MosaicDraw program could be created as follows, where listener is a variable of type ActionListener:

```
JMenu toolsMenu = new                    // Create a menu with name "Tools"
JMenu("Tools");

JMenuItem drawCommand = new                        // Create a menu item.
JMenuItem("Draw");                                 // Add listener to menu item.
drawCommand.addActionListener(listener);           // Add menu item to menu.
toolsMenu.add(drawCommand);

JMenuItem eraseCommand = new JMenuItem("Erase"); // Create a menu item.
eraseCommand.addActionListener(listener);          // Add listener to menu item.
toolsMenu.add(eraseCommand);                       // Add menu item to menu.
    .
    .  // Create and add other menu items.
    .
```

Once a menu has been created, it must be added to a menu bar. A menu bar is represented by the class JMenuBar. A menu bar is just a container for menus. It does not have a name, and its constructor does not have any parameters. It has an add(JMenu) method that can be used to add menus to the menu bar. For example, the MosaicDraw program uses three menus, controlMenu, colorMenu, and toolsMenu. We could create a menu bar and add the menus to it with the statements:

```
JMenuBar menuBar = new JMenuBar();
menuBar.add(controlMenu);
menuBar.add(colorMenu);
menuBar.add(toolsMenu);
```

The final step in using menus is to use the menu bar in a JApplet or JFrame. We have already seen that an applet or frame has a "content pane." The menu bar is another component of the applet or frame, not contained inside the content pane. Both the JApplet and the JFrame classes include an instance method setMenuBar(JMenuBar) that can be used to set the menu bar. (There can only be one, so this is a "set" method rather than an "add" method.) In the MosaicDraw program, the menu bar is created by a MosaicDrawController object and can be obtained by calling that object's getMenuBar() method. Here is the basic code that is used (in somewhat modified form) to set up the interface both in the applet and in the frame version of the program:

```
MosaicDrawController controller = new MosaicDrawController();
```

```
MoasicPanel content = controller.getMosaicPanel();
setContentPane( content );    // Use panel from controller as content pane.

JMenuBar menuBar = controller.getMenuBar();
setJMenuBar( menuBar );    // Use the menu bar from the controller.
```

Using menus always follows the same general pattern: Create a menu bar. Create menus and add them to the menu bar. Create menu items and add them to the menus (and set up listening to handle action events from the menu items). Use the menu bar in a JApplet or JFrame by calling the setJMenuBar() method of the applet or frame.

* * *

There are other kinds of menu items, defined by subclasses of JMenuItem, that can be added to menus. One of these is JCheckBoxMenuItem, which represents menu items that can be in one of two states, selected or not selected. A JCheckBoxMenuItem has the same functionality and is used in the same way as a JCheckBox (see Subsection 6.6.3). Three JCheckBoxMenuItems are used in the "Control" menu of the MosaicDraw program. One can be used to turn the random color variation of the squares on and off. Another turns a symmetry feature on and off; when symmetry is turned on, the user's drawing is reflected horizontally and vertically to produce a symmetric pattern. And the third check box menu item shows and hides the "grouting" in the mosaic; the grouting is the gray lines that are drawn around each of the little squares in the mosaic. The menu item that corresponds to the "Use Randomness" option in the "Control" menu could be set up with the statements:

```
JMenuItem useRandomnessToggle = new JCheckBoxMenuItem("Use
Randomness"); useRandomnessToggle.addActionListener(listener); // Set
up a listener.
useRandomnessToggle.setSelected(true); // Randomness is initially turned on.
controlMenu.add(useRandomnessToggle);// Add the menu item to the menu.
```

The "Use Randomness" JCheckBoxMenuItem corresponds to a boolean-valued instance vari-able named useRandomness in the MosaicDrawController class. This variable is part of the state of the controller object. Its value is tested whenever the user draws one of the squares, to decide whether or not to add a random variation to the color of the square. When the user selects the "Use Randomness" command from the menu, the state of the JCheckBoxMenuItem is re-versed, from selected to not-selected or from not-selected to selected. The ActionListener for the menu item checks whether the menu item is selected or not, and it changes the value of useRandomness to match. Note that selecting the menu command does not have any immediate effect on the picture that is shown in the window. It just changes the state of the program so that future drawing operations on the part of the user will have a different effect. The "Use Symmetry" option in the "Control" menu works in much the same way. The "Show Grouting" option is a little different. Selecting the "Show Grouting" option does have an immediate effect: The picture is redrawn with or without the grouting, depending on the state of the menu item.

My program uses a single ActionListener to respond to all of the menu items in all the menus. This is not a particularly good design, but it is easy to implement for a small program like this one. The actionPerformed() method of the listener object uses the statement

```
String command = evt.getActionCommand();
```

to get the action command of the source of the event; this will be the text of the menu item. The listener tests the value of command to determine which menu item was selected by the user. If the menu item is a JCheckBoxMenuItem, the listener must check the state of the menu item. Then menu item is the source of the event that is being processed. The listener can get its hands on the menu item object by calling evt.getSource(). Since the return value of getSource() is Object, the the return value must be type-cast to the correct type. Here, for example, is the code that handles the "Use Randomness" command:

```
if (command.equals("Use Randomness")) {
        // Set the value of useRandomness depending on the menu item's state.
```

```
        JCheckBoxMenuItem toggle =
        (JCheckBoxMenuItem)evt.getSource(); useRandomness =
        toggle.isSelected();
    }
```

* * *

In addition to menu items, a menu can contain lines that separate the menu items into groups. In the MosaicDraw program, the "Control" menu contains a separator. A JMenu has an instance method addSeparator() that can be used to add a separator to the menu. For example, the separator in the "Control" menu was created with the statement:

```
controlMenu.addSeparator();
```

A menu can also contain a submenu. The name of the submenu appears as an item in the main menu. When the user moves the mouse over the submenu name, the submenu pops up. (There is no example of this in the MosaicDraw program.) It is very easy to do this in Java: You can add one JMenu to another JMenu using a statement such as mainMenu.add(submenu).

6.8.2 Dialogs

One of the commands in the "Color" menu of the MosaicDraw program is "Custom Color. . . ". When the user selects this command, a new window appears where the user can select a color. This window is an example of a **dialog** or **dialog box** . A dialog is a type of window that is generally used for short, single purpose interactions with the user. For example, a dialog box can be used to display a message to the user, to ask the user a question, to let the user select a file to be opened, or to let the user select a color. In Swing, a dialog box is represented by an object belonging to the class JDialog or to a subclass.

The JDialog class is very similar to JFrame and is used in much the same way. Like a frame, a dialog box is a separate window. Unlike a frame, however, a dialog is not completely independent. Every dialog is associated with a frame (or another dialog), which is called its **parent window** . The dialog box is dependent on its parent. For example, if the parent is closed, the dialog box will also be closed. It is possible to create a dialog box without specifying a parent, but in that case a an invisible frame is created by the system to serve as the parent.

Dialog boxes can be either **modal** or **modeless**. When a modal dialog is created, its parent frame is blocked. That is, the user will not be able to interact with the parent until the dialog box is closed. Modeless dialog boxes do not block their parents in the same way, so they seem a lot more like independent windows. In practice, modal dialog boxes are easier to use and are much more common than modeless dialogs. All the examples we will look at are modal.

Aside from having a parent, a JDialog can be created and used in the same way as a JFrame. However, I will not give any examples here of using JDialog directly. Swing has many convenient methods for creating many common types of dialog boxes. For example, the color choice dialog that appears when the user selects the "Custom Color" command in the MosaicDraw program belongs to the class JColorChooser, which is a subclass of JDialog. The JColorChooser class has a static method static method that makes color choice dialogs very easy to use:

```
Color JColorChooser.showDialog(Component parentComp,
                               String title, Color initialColor)
```

When you call this method, a dialog box appears that allows the user to select a color. The first parameter specifies the parent of the dialog; the parent window of the dialog will be the window (if any) that contains parentComp; this parameter can be null and it can itself be a frame or dialog object. The second parameter is a string that appears in the title bar of the dialog box. And the third parameter, initialColor, specifies the color that is selected when the color choice dialog first appears. The dialog has a sophisticated interface that allows the user to change the selected color. When the user presses an "OK" button, the dialog box closes and the selected color is returned as the value of the method. The user can also click a "Cancel" button or close the dialog box in some other way; in that case, null is returned as the value of the method. By using this predefined color chooser dialog, you can write one line of code that will let the user select an arbitrary color. Swing also has a JFileChooser class that makes it almost as easy to show a dialog box that lets the user select a file to be opened or saved.

The JOptionPane class includes a variety of methods for making simple dialog boxes that are variations on three basic types: a "message" dialog, a "confirm" dialog, and an "input" dialog. (The variations allow you to provide a title for the dialog box, to specify the icon that appears in the dialog, and to add other components to the dialog box. I will only cover the most basic forms here.) The on-line version of this section includes an applet that demonstrates JOptionPane as well as JColorChooser.

A message dialog simply displays a message string to the user. The user (hopefully) reads the message and dismisses the dialog by clicking the "OK" button. A message dialog can be shown by calling the static method:

```
void JOptionPane.showMessageDialog(Component parentComp, String message)
```

The message can be more than one line long. Lines in the message should be separated by newline characters, \n. New lines will not be inserted automatically, even if the message is very long.

An input dialog displays a question or request and lets the user type in a string as a response.

You can show an input dialog by calling:

```
String JOptionPane.showInputDialog(Component parentComp, String question)
```

Again, the question can include newline characters. The dialog box will contain an input box, an "OK" button, and a "Cancel" button. If the user clicks "Cancel", or closes the dialog box in some other way, then the return value of the method is null. If the user clicks "OK", then the return value is the string that was entered by the user. Note that the return value can be an empty string (which is not the same as a null value), if the user clicks "OK" without typing anything in the input box. If you want to use an input dialog to get a numerical value from the user, you will have to convert the return value into a number; see Subsection 3.7.2.

Finally, a confirm dialog presents a question and three response buttons: "Yes", "No", and "Cancel". A confirm dialog can be shown by calling:

```
int JOptionPane.showConfirmDialog(Component parentComp, String question)
```

The return value tells you the user's response. It is one of the following constants:

- JOptionPane.YES_OPTION — the user clicked the "Yes" button
- JOptionPane.NO_OPTION — the user clicked the "No" button
- JOptionPane.CANCEL_OPTION — the user clicked the "Cancel" button
- JOptionPane.CLOSE_OPTION — the dialog was closed in some other way.

By the way, it is possible to omit the Cancel button from a confirm dialog by calling one of the other methods in the JOptionPane class. Just call:

```
JOptionPane.showConfirmDialog(
                    parent, question, title, JOptionPane.YES_NO_OPTION )
```

The final parameter is a constant which specifies that only a "Yes" button and a "No" button should be used. The third parameter is a string that will be displayed as the title of the dialog box window.

If you would like to see how dialogs are created and used in the sample applet, you can find the source code in the file **SimpleDialogDemo.java**.

6.8.3 Fine Points of Frames

In previous sections, whenever I used a frame, I created a JFrame object in a main() routine and installed a panel as the content pane of that frame. This works fine, but a more object-oriented approach is to define a subclass of JFrame and to set up the contents of the frame in the constructor of that class. This is what I did in the case of the MosaicDraw program. MosaicDrawFrame is defined as a subclass of JFrame. The definition of this class is very short, but it illustrates several new features of frames that I want to discuss:

```
public class MosaicDrawFrame extends JFrame {

    public static void main(String[] args) { JFrame window = new
        MosaicDrawFrame();
        window.setDefaultCloseOperation(JFrame.EXIT_ON
        CLOSE); window.setVisible(true);
    }

    public MosaicDrawFrame() {
        super("Mosaic Draw");
        MosaicDrawController controller = new MosaicDrawController();
        setContentPane( controller.getMosaicPanel() ); setJMenuBar(
        controller.getMenuBar() ); pack();
        Dimension screensize = Toolkit.getDefaultToolkit().getScreenSize();
        setLocation( (screensize.width - getWidth())/2,
                                  (screensize.height - getHeight())/2 );
    }

}
```

The constructor in this class begins with the statement super("Mosaic Draw"), which calls the constructor in the superclass, JFrame. The parameter specifies a title that will appear in the title bar of the window. The next three lines of the constructor set up the contents of the window; a MosaicDrawController is created, and the content pane and menu bar of the window are obtained from the controller. The next line is something new. If window is a variable of type JFrame (or JDialog), then the statement window.pack() will resize the window so that its size matches the preferred size of its contents. (In this case, of course, "pack()" is equivalent to "this.pack()"; that is, it refers to the window that is being created by the constructor.) The pack() method is usually the best way to set the size of a window. Note that it will only work correctly if every component in the window has a correct preferred size. This is only a problem in two cases: when a panel is used as a drawing surface and when a panel is used as a container with a null layout manager. In both these cases there is no way for the system to determine the correct preferred size automatically, and you should set a preferred size by hand. For example:

```
panel.setPreferredSize( new Dimension(400, 250) );
```

The last two lines in the constructor position the window so that it is exactly centered on the screen. The line

Dimension screensize = Toolkit.getDefaultToolkit().getScreenSize();

determines the size of the screen. The size of the screen is screensize.width pixels in the hor-izontal direction and screensize.height pixels in the vertical direction. The setLocation() method of the frame sets the position of the upper left corner of the frame on the screen. The expression "screensize.width - getWidth()" is the amount of horizontal space left on the screen after subtracting the width of the window. This is divided by 2 so that half of the empty space will be to the left of the window, leaving the other half of the space to the right of the window. Similarly, half of the extra vertical space is above the window, and half is below.

Note that the constructor has created the window and set its size and position, but that at the end of the constructor, the window is not yet visible on the screen. (More exactly, the constructor has created the window **object**, but the visual representation of that object on the screen has not yet been created.) To show the window on the screen, it will be necessary to call its instance method, window.setVisible(true).

In addition to the constructor, the MosaicDrawFrame class includes a main() routine. This makes it possible to run MosaicDrawFrame as a stand-alone application. (The main() routine, as a static method, has nothing to do with the function of a MosaicDrawFrame object, and it could (and perhaps should) be in a separate class.) The main() routine creates a MosaicDrawFrame and makes it visible on the screen. It also calls

window.setDefaultCloseOperation(JFrame.EXIT ON CLOSE);

which means that the program will end when the user closes the window. Note that this is not done in the constructor because doing it there would make MosaicDrawFrame less flexible. It would be possible, for example, to write a program that lets the user open multiple MosaicDraw windows. In that case, we don't want to end the program just because the user has closed **one** of the windows. Furthermore, it is possible for an applet to create a frame, which will open as a separate window on the screen. An applet is not allowed to "terminate the program" (and it's not even clear what that should mean in the case of an applet), and attempting to do so will produce an exception. There are other possible values for the default close operation of a window:

- JFrame.DO NOTHING ON CLOSE — the user's attempts to close the window by clicking its close box will be ignored.
- JFrame.HIDE ON CLOSE — when the user clicks its close box, the window will be hidden just as if window.setVisible(false) were called. The window can be made visible again by calling window.setVisible(true). This is the value that is used if you do not specify another value by calling setDefaultCloseOperation.
- JFrame.DISPOSE ON CLOSE — the window is closed and any operating system resources used by the window are released. It is not possible to make the window visible again. (This is the proper way to permanently get rid of a window without ending the program. You can accomplish the same thing by calling the instance method window.dispose().)

I've written an applet version of the MosaicDraw program that appears on a Web page as a single button. When the user clicks the button, the applet opens a MosaicDrawFrame.

In this case, the applet sets the default close operation of the window to JFrame.DISPOSE ON CLOSE. You can try the applet in the on-line version of this section.

The file **MosaicDrawLauncherApplet.java** contains the source code for the applet. One interesting point in the applet is that the text of the button changes depending on whether a window is open or not. If there is no window, the text reads "Launch MosaicDraw". When the window is open, it changes to "Close MosaicDraw", and clicking the button will close the window. The change is implemented by attaching a WindowListener to the window. The listener responds to WindowEvent s that are generated when the window opens and closes. Although I will not discuss window events further here, you can look at the source code for an example of how they can be used.

6.8.4 Creating Jar Files

As the final topic for this chapter, we look again at jar files. Recall that a jar file is a "java archive" that can contain a number of class files. When creating a program that uses more than one class, it's usually a good idea to place all the classes that are required by the program into a jar file, since then a user will only need that one file to run the program. Subsection 6.2.4 discusses how a jar file can be used for an applet. Jar files can also be used for stand-alone applications. In fact, it is possible to make a so-called **executable jar file**. A user can run an executable jar file in much the same way as any other application, usually by double-clicking the icon of the jar file. (The user's computer must have a correct version of Java installed, and the computer must be configured correctly for this to work. The configuration is usually done automatically when Java is installed, at least on Windows and Mac OS.)

The question, then, is how to create a jar file. The answer depends on what programming environment you are using. The two basic types of programming environment—command line and IDE—were discussed in Section 2.6. Any IDE (Integrated Programming Environment) for Java should have a command for creating jar files. In the Eclipse IDE, for example, it's done as follows: In the Package Explorer pane, select the programming project (or just all the individual source code files that you need). Right-click on the selection, and choose "Export" from the menu that pops up. In the window that appears, select "JAR file" and click "Next". In the window that appears next, enter a name for the jar file in the box labeled "JAR file". (Click the "Browse" button next to this box to select the file name using a file dialog box.) The name of the file should end with ".jar". If you are creating a regular jar file, not an executable one, you can hit "Finish" at this point, and the jar file will be created. You could do this, for example, if the jar file contains an applet but no main program. To create an executable file, hit the "Next" button **twice** to get to the "Jar Manifest Specification" screen. At the bottom of this screen is an input box labeled "Main class". You have to enter the name of the class that contains the main() routine that will be run when the jar file is executed. If you hit the "Browse" button next to the "Main class" box, you can select the class from a list of classes that contain main() routines. Once you've selected the main class, you can click the "Finish" button to create the executable jar file.

It is also possible to create jar files on the command line. The Java Development Kit includes a command-line program named jar that can be used to create jar files. If all your classes are in the default package (like the examples in this book), then the jar command is easy to use. To create a non-executable jar file on the command line, change to the directory that contains the class files that you want to include in the jar. Then give the command

```
jar cf JarFileName.jar *.class
```

where JarFileName can be any name that you want to use for the jar file. The "*" in "*.class" is a wildcard that makes *.class match every class file in the current directory. This means that all the class files in the directory will be included in the jar file. If you want to include only certain class files, you can name them individually, separated by spaces. (Things get more complicated if your classes are not in the default package. In that case, the class files must be in subdirectories of the directory in which you issue the jar file. See Subsection 2.6.4.)

Making an executable jar file on the command line is a little more complicated. There has to be some way of specifying which class contains the main() routine. This is done by creating a **manifest file**. The manifest file can be a plain text file containing a single line of the form

```
Main-Class: ClassName
```

where ClassName should be replaced by the name of the class that contains the main() routine. For example, if the main() routine is in the class MosaicDrawFrame, then the manifest file should read "Main-Class: MosaicDrawFrame". You can give the manifest file any name you like. Put it in the same directory where you will issue the jar command, and use a command of the form

```
jar cmf ManifestFileName JarFileName.jar *.class
```

to create the jar file. (The jar command is capable of performing a variety of different opera-tions. The first parameter to the command, such as "cf" or "cmf", tells it which operation to perform.)

By the way, if you have successfully created an executable jar file, you can run it on the command line using the command "java -jar". For example:

```
java -jar JarFileName.jar
```

- In the SimpleStamperPanel example from Subsection 6.4.2, a rectangle or oval is drawn on the panel when the user clicks the mouse, except that when the user shift-clicks, the panel is cleared instead. Modify this class so that the modified version will continue to draw figures as the user drags the mouse. That is, the mouse will leave a trail of figures as the user drags the mouse. However, if the user shift-clicks, the panel should simply be cleared and no figures should be drawn even if the user drags the mouse after shift-clicking. Use your panel either in an applet or in a stand-alone application (or both). Here is a picture of my solution:

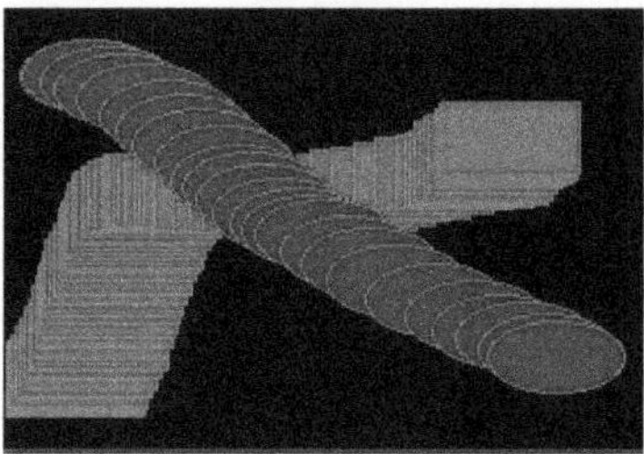

  The source code for the original panel class is **SimpleStamperPanel.java**. An applet that uses this class can be found in **SimpleStamperApplet.java**, and a main program that uses the panel in a frame is in **SimpleStamper.java**. See the discussion of dragging in Subsection 6.4.4. (Note that in the original version, I drew a black outline around each shape. In the modified version, I decided that it would look better to draw a gray outline instead.)

- Write a panel that shows a small red square and a small blue square. The user should be able to drag either square with the mouse. (You'll need an instance variable to remember which square the user is dragging.) The user can drag the square off the applet if she wants; if she does this, it's gone. Use your panel in either an applet or a stand-alone application.

- Write a panel that shows a pair of dice. When the user clicks on the panel, the dice should be rolled (that is, the dice should be assigned newly computed random values). Each die should be drawn as a square showing from 1 to 6 dots. Since you have to draw two dice, its a good idea to write a subroutine, "void drawDie(Graphics g, int val, int x, int y)", to draw a die at the specified (x,y) coordinates. The second parameter, val, specifies the value that is showing on the die. Assume that the size of the panel is 100 by 100 pixels. Also write an applet that uses your panel as its content pane. Here is a picture of the applet:

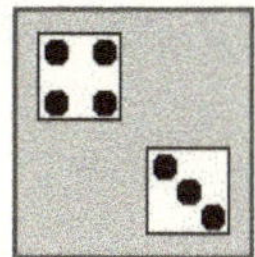

- In Exercise 6.3, you wrote a pair-of-dice panel where the dice are rolled when the user clicks on the panel Now make a pair-of-dice program in which the user rolls the dice by clicking a button. The button should appear under the panel that shows the dice. Also make the following change: When the dice are rolled, instead of just showing the new value, show a short animation during which the values on the dice are changed in every frame. The animation is supposed to make the dice look more like they are actually rolling. Write your program as a stand-alone application.

- In Exercise 3.6, you drew a checkerboard. For this exercise, write a checkerboard applet where the user can select a square by clicking on it. Hilite the selected square by drawing a colored border around it. When the applet is first created, no square is selected. When the user clicks on a square that is not currently selected, it becomes selected. If the user clicks the square that is selected, it becomes unselected. Assume that the size of the applet is exactly 160 by 160 pixels, so that each square on the checkerboard is 20 by 20 pixels.

- For this exercise, you should modify the SubKiller game from Subsection 6.5.4. You can start with the existing source code, from the file **SubKillerPanel.java**. Modify the game so it keeps track of the number of hits and misses and displays these quantities. That is, every time the depth charge blows up the sub, the number of hits goes up by one. Every time the depth charge falls off the bottom of the screen without hitting the sub, the number of misses goes up by one. There is room at the top of the panel to display these numbers. To do this exercise, you only have to add a half-dozen lines to the source code. But you have to figure out what they are and where to add them. To do this, you'll have to read the source code closely enough to understand how it works.

- Exercise 5.2 involved a class, **StatCalc.java**, that could compute some statistics of a set of numbers. Write a program that uses the StatCalc class to compute and display statistics of numbers entered by the user. The panel will have an instance variable of type StatCalc that does the computations. The panel should include a JTextField where the user enters a number. It should have four labels that display four statistics for the numbers that have been entered: the number of numbers, the sum, the mean, and the standard deviation. Every time the user enters a new number, the statistics displayed on the labels should change. The user enters a number by typing it into the JTextField and pressing return. There should be a "Clear" button that clears out all the data. This means creating a new StatCalc object and resetting the displays on the labels. My panel also has an "Enter" button that does the same thing as pressing the return key in the JTextField. (Recall that a JTextField generates an ActionEvent when the user presses return, so your panel should register itself to listen for ActionEvents from the JTextField.) Write your program as a stand-alone application. Here is a picture of my solution to this problem:

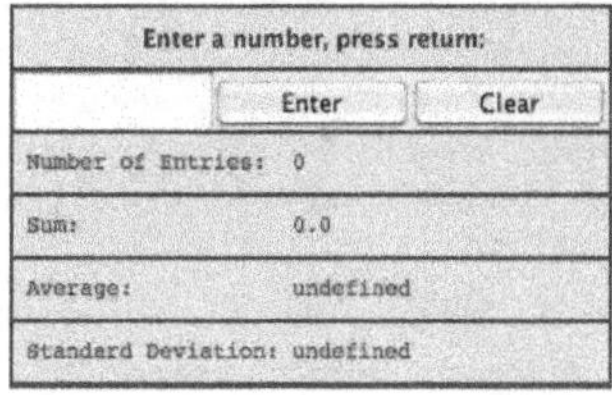

- Write a panel with a JTextArea where the user can enter some text. The panel should have a button. When the user clicks on the button, the panel should count the number of lines in the user's input, the number of words in the user's input, and the number of characters in the user's input. This information should be displayed on three labels in the panel. Recall that if textInput is a JTextArea, then you can get the contents of the JTextArea by calling the function textInput.getText(). This function returns a String containing all the text from the text area. The number of characters is just the length of this String. Lines in the String are separated by the new line character, '\n', so the number of lines is just the number of new line characters in the String, plus one. Words are a little harder to count. Exercise 3.4 has some advice about finding the words in a String. Essentially, you want to count the number of characters that are first characters in words. Don't forget to put your JTextArea in a JScrollPane, and add the scroll pane to the container, not the text area. Scrollbars should appear when the user types more text than will fit in the available area. Here is a picture of my solution:

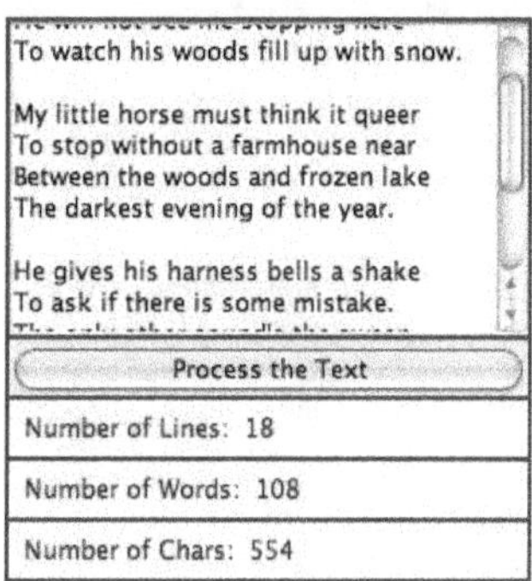

- Write a Blackjack program that lets the user play a game of Blackjack, with the computer as the dealer. The applet should draw the user's cards and the dealer's cards, just as was done for the graphical HighLow card game in Subsection 6.7.6. You can use the source code for that game, **HighLowGUI.java**, for some ideas about how to write your Blackjack game. The structures of the HighLow panel and the Blackjack panel are very similar. You will certainly want to use the drawCard() method from the HighLow program.

You can find a description of the game of Blackjack in Exercise 5.5. Add the following rule to that description: If a player takes five cards without going over 21, that player wins immediately. This rule is used in some casinos. For your program, it means that you only have to allow room for five cards. You should assume that the panel is just wide enough to show five cards, and that it is tall enough show the user's hand and the dealer's hand.

Note that the design of a GUI Blackjack game is very different from the design of the text-oriented program that you wrote for Exercise 5.5. The user should play the game by clicking on "Hit" and "Stand" buttons. There should be a "New Game" button that can be used to start another game after one game ends. You have to decide what happens when each of these buttons is pressed. You don't have much chance of getting this right unless you think in terms of the states that the game can be in and how the state can change.

Your program will need the classes defined in **Card.java**, **Hand.java**, **Deck.java**, and **BlackjackHand.java**.

- In the Blackjack game from Exercise 6.9, the user can click on the "Hit", "Stand", and "NewGame" buttons even when it doesn't make sense to do so. It would be better if the buttons were disabled at the appropriate times. The "New Game" button should be dis-abled when there is a game in progress. The "Hit" and "Stand" buttons should be disabled when there is not a game in progress. The instance variable gameInProgress tells whether or not a game is in progress, so you just have to make sure that the buttons are properly enabled and disabled whenever this variable changes value. I strongly advise writing a sub-routine that can be called whenever it is necessary to set the value of the gameInProgress variable. Then the subroutine can take responsibility for enabling and disabling the but-tons. Recall that if bttn is a variable of type JButton, then bttn.setEnabled(false) disables the button and bttn.setEnabled(true) enables the button.

As a second (and more difficult) improvement, make it possible for the user to place bets on the Blackjack game. When the applet starts, give the user $100. Add a JTextField to the strip of controls along the bottom of the applet. The user can enter the bet in this JTextField. When the game begins, check the amount of the bet. You should do this when the game begins, not when it ends, because several errors can occur: The contents of the JTextField might not be a legal number. The bet that the user places might be more money than the user has, or it might be <= 0. You should detect these errors and show an error message instead of starting the game. The user's bet should be an integral number of dollars.

It would be a good idea to make the JTextField uneditable while the game is in progress. If betInput is the JTextField, you can make it editable and uneditable by the user with the commands betInput.setEditable(true) and betInput.setEditable(false).

In the paintComponent() method, you should include commands to display the amount of money that the user has left.

There is one other thing to think about: Ideally, the applet should not start a new game when it is first created. The user should have a chance to set a bet amount before the game starts. So, in the constructor for the drawing surface class, you should not call doNewGame(). You might want to display a message such as "Welcome to Blackjack" before the first game starts.

Here is a picture of my program:

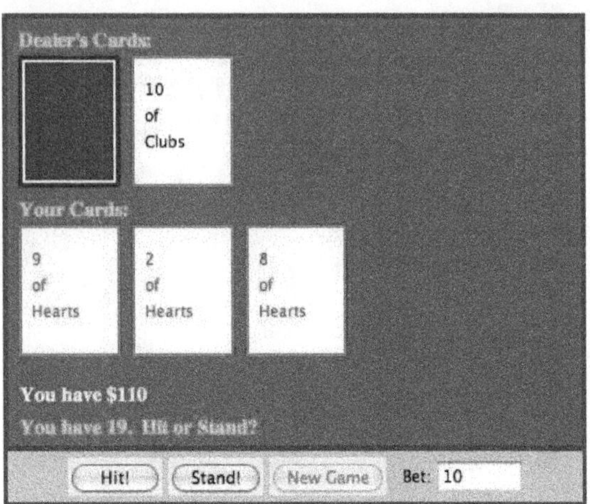
Dealer's Cards:
10
of
Clubs
Your Cards:
9
of
Hearts
2
of
Hearts
8
of
Hearts
You have $110
You have 19. Hit or Stand?
Hit!
Stand!
New Game
Bet:
10

Quiz on Chapter 6

- Programs written for a graphical user interface have to deal with "events." Explain what is meant by the term **event.** Give at least two different examples of events, and discuss how a program might respond to those events.
- Explain carefully what the repaint() method does.
- What is HTML?
- Java has a standard class called JPanel. Discuss **two** ways in which JPanels can be used.
- Draw the picture that will be produced by the following paintComponent() method:

```
public static void paintComponent(Graphics g) {
    super.paintComponent(g);
    for (int i=10; i <= 210; i = i + 50)
       for (int j = 10; j <= 210; j = j + 50)
          g.drawLine(i,10,j,60);
}
```

- Suppose you would like a panel that displays a green square inside a red circle, as illus-trated. Write a paintComponent() method for the panel class that will draw the image.

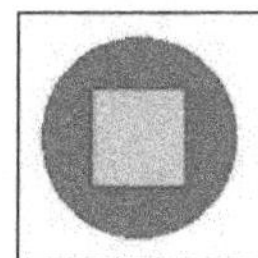

- Java has a standard class called MouseEvent. What is the purpose of this class? What does an object of type MouseEvent do?
- One of the main classes in Swing is the JComponent class. What is meant by a component? What are some examples?
- What is the function of a LayoutManager in Java?
- What type of layout manager is being used for each of the three panels in the following illustration from Section 6.7?

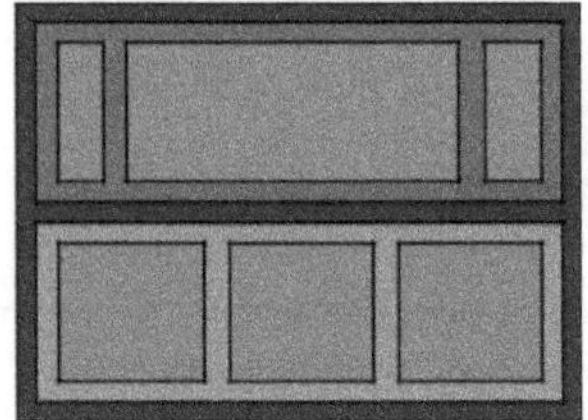

- Explain how Timers are used to do animation.
- What is a JCheckBox and how is it used?

Chapter 12

Arrays

Computers get a lot of their power from working with **data structures**. A data structure is an organized collection of related data. An object is a data structure, but this type of data structure—consisting of a fairly small number of named instance variables—is just the beginning. In many cases, programmers build complicated data structures by hand, by linking objects together. We'll look at these custom-built data structures in Chapter 9. But there is one type of data structure that is so important and so basic that it is built into every programming language: the array.

An **array** is a data structure consisting of a numbered list of items, where all the items are of the same type. In Java, the items in an array are always numbered from zero up to some maximum value, which is set when the array is created. For example, an array might contain 100 integers, numbered from zero to 99. The items in an array can belong to one of Java's primitive types. They can also be references to objects, so that you could, for example, make an array containing all the buttons in a GUI program.

This chapter discusses how arrays are created and used in Java. It also covers the standard class java.util.ArrayList. An object of type ArrayList is very similar to an array of Objects, but it can grow to hold any number of items.

7.1 Creating and Using Arrays

When a number of data items are chunked together into a unit, the result is a **data structure**. Data structures can be very complex, but in many applications, the appropriate data structure consists simply of a sequence of data items. Data structures of this simple variety can be either **arrays** or **records**.

The term "record" is not used in Java. A record is essentially the same as a Java object that has instance variables only, but no instance methods. Some other languages, which do not support objects in general, nevertheless do support records. The C programming language, for example, is not object-oriented, but it has records, which in C go by the name "struct." The data items in a record—in Java, an object's instance variables—are called the **fields** of the record. Each item is referred to using a **field name**. In Java, field names are just the names of the instance variables. The distinguishing characteristics of a record are that the data items in the record are referred to by name and that different fields in a record are allowed to be of different types. For example, if the class Person is defined as:

```
class Person {
    String name;
```

```
        int id number;
        Date birthday;
        int age;
    }
```

then an object of class Person could be considered to be a record with four fields. The field names are name, id number, birthday, and age. Note that the fields are of various types: String, int, and Date.

Because records are just a special type of object, I will not discuss them further.

7.1.1 Arrays

Like a record, an array is a sequence of items. However, where items in a record are referred to by **name**, the items in an array are numbered, and individual items are referred to by their **position number**. Furthermore, all the items in an array must be of the same type. The definition of an array is: a numbered sequence of items, which are all of the same type. The number of items in an array is called the **length** of the array. The position number of an item in an array is called the **index** of that item. The type of the individual items in an array is called the **base type** of the array.

The base type of an array can be any Java type, that is, one of the primitive types, or a class name, or an interface name. If the base type of an array is int, it is referred to as an "array of ints." An array with base type String is referred to as an "array of Strings." However, an array is not, properly speaking, a list of integers or strings or other **values**. It is better thought of as a list of **variables** of type int, or of type String, or of some other type. As always, there is some potential for confusion between the two uses of a variable: as a name for a memory location and as a name for the value stored in that memory location. Each position in an array acts as a variable. Each position can hold a value of a specified type (the base type of the array). The value can be changed at any time. Values are stored **in** an array. The array **is** the container, not the values.

The items in an array—really, the individual variables that make up the array—are more often referred to as the **elements** of the array. In Java, the elements in an array are always numbered starting from zero. That is, the index of the first element in the array is zero. If the length of the array is N, then the index of the last element in the array is N-1. Once an array has been created, its length cannot be changed.

Java arrays are **objects**. This has several consequences. Arrays are created using a form of the new operator. No variable can ever **hold** an array; a variable can only **refer** to an array. Any variable that can refer to an array can also hold the value null, meaning that it doesn't at the moment refer to anything. Like any object, an array belongs to a class, which like all classes is a subclass of the class Object. The elements of the array are, essentially, instance variables in the array object, except that they are referred to by number rather than by name.

Nevertheless, even though arrays are objects, there are differences between arrays and other kinds of objects, and there are a number of special language features in Java for creating and using arrays.

7.1.2 Using Arrays

Suppose that A is a variable that refers to an array. Then the element at index k in A is referred to as A[k]. The first element is A[0], the second is A[1], and so forth. “A[k]” is really a variable, and it can be used just like any other variable. You can assign values to it, you can use it in expressions, and you can pass it as a parameter to a subroutine. All of this will be discussed in more detail below. For now, just keep in mind the syntax

array-variable [integer-expression]

for referring to an element of an array.

Although every array, as an object, belongs to some class, array classes never have to be defined. Once a type exists, the corresponding array class exists automatically. If the name of the type is BaseType, then the name of the associated array class is BaseType[ ]. That is to say, an object belonging to the class BaseType[ ] is an array of items, where each item is a variable of type BaseType. The brackets, "[]", are meant to recall the syntax for referring to the individual items in the array. "BaseType[ ]" is read as "array of BaseType" or "BaseType array." It might be worth mentioning here that if ClassA is a subclass of ClassB, then the class ClassA[ ] is automatically a subclass of ClassB[ ].

The base type of an array can be any legal Java type. From the primitive type int, the array type int[ ] is derived. Each element in an array of type int[ ] is a variable of type int, which holds a value of type int. From a class named Shape, the array type Shape[ ] is derived. Each item in an array of type Shape[ ] is a variable of type Shape, which holds a value of type Shape. This value can be either null or a reference to an object belonging to the class Shape. (This includes objects belonging to subclasses of Shape.)

* * *

Let's try to get a little more concrete about all this, using arrays of integers as our first example. Since int[ ] is a class, it can be used to declare variables. For example,

```
int[] list;
```

creates a variable named list of type int[ ]. This variable is **capable** of referring to an array of ints, but initially its value is null (if list is a member variable in a class) or undefined (if list is a local variable in a method). The new operator is used to create a new array object, which can then be assigned to list. The syntax for using new with arrays is different from the syntax you learned previously. As an example,

```
list = new int[5];
```

creates an array of five integers. More generally, the constructor "new BaseType[N]" is used to create an array belonging to the class BaseType[ ]. The value N in brackets specifies the length of the array, that is, the number of elements that it contains. Note that the array "knows" how long it is. The length of the array is an instance variable in the array object. In fact, the length of an array, list, can be referred to as list.length. (However, you are not allowed to change the value of list.length, so it's really a "final" instance variable, that is, one whose value cannot be changed after it has been initialized.)

The situation produced by the statement "list = new int[5];" can be pictured like this:

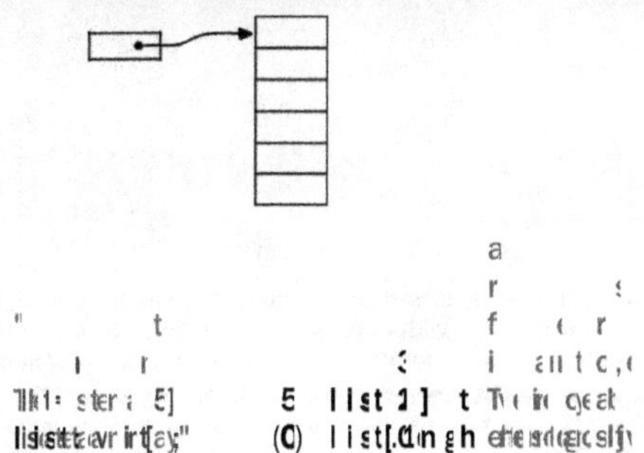

Note that the newly created array of integers is automatically filled with zeros. In Java, a newly created array is **always** filled with a known, default value: zero for numbers, false for boolean, the character with Unicode number zero for char, and null for objects.

The elements in the array, list, are referred to as list[0], list[1], list[2], list[3], and list[4]. (Note again that the index for the last item is one less than list.length.) However, array references can be much more general than this. The brackets in an array reference can contain any expression whose value is an integer. For example if indx is a variable of type int, then list[indx] and list[2*indx+7] are syntactically correct references to elements of the array list. Thus, the following loop would print all the integers in the array, list, to standard output:

```
for (int i = 0; i < list.length; i++) {
    System.out.println( list[i] );
}
```

The first time through the loop, i is 0, and list[i] refers to list[0]. So, it is the value stored in the variable list[0] that is printed. The second time through the loop, i is 1, and the value stored in list[1] is printed. The loop ends after printing the value of list[4], when i becomes equal to 5 and the continuation condition "i < list.length" is no longer true. This is a typical example of using a loop to process an array. I'll discuss more examples of array processing throughout this chapter.

Every use of a variable in a program specifies a memory location. Think for a moment about what the computer does when it encounters a reference to an array element, list[k], while it is executing a program. The computer must determine which memory location is being referred to. To the computer, list[k] means something like this: "Get the pointer that is stored in the variable, list. Follow this pointer to find an array object. Get the value of k. Go to the k-th position in the array, and that's the memory location you want." There are two things that can go wrong here. Suppose that the value of list is null. If that is the case, then list doesn't even refer to an array. The attempt to refer to an element of an array that doesn't exist is an error that will cause an exception of type NullPointerException to be thrown. The second possible error occurs if list does refer to an array, but the value of k is outside the legal range of indices for that array. This will happen if k < 0 or if k >= list.length. This is called an "array index out of bounds" error. When an error of this type occurs, an exception of type ArrayIndexOutOfBoundsException is thrown. When you use arrays in a program, you should be mindful that both types of errors are possible. However, array index out of bounds errors are by far the most common error when working with arrays.

7.1.3 Array Initialization

For an array variable, just as for any variable, you can declare the variable and initialize it in a single step. For example,

```
int[] list = new int[5];
```

If list is a local variable in a subroutine, then this is exactly equivalent to the two statements:

```
int[] list;
list = new int[5];
```

(If list is an instance variable, then of course you can't simply replace "int[] list = new int[5];" with "int[] list; list = new int[5];" since the assignment statement "list = new int[5];" is only legal inside a subroutine.)

The new array is filled with the default value appropriate for the base type of the array—zero for int and null for class types, for example. However, Java also provides a way to initialize an array variable with a new array filled with a specified list of values. In a declaration statement that creates a new array, this is done with an **array initializer** . For example,

```
int[] list = { 1, 4, 9, 16, 25, 36, 49 };
```

creates a new array containing the seven values 1, 4, 9, 16, 25, 36, and 49, and sets list to refer to that new array. The value of list[0] will be 1, the value of list[1] will be 4, and so forth. The length of list is seven, since seven values are provided in the initializer.

An array initializer takes the form of a list of values, separated by commas and enclosed between braces. The length of the array does not have to be specified, because it is implicit in the list of values. The items in an array initializer don't have to be constants. They can be variables or arbitrary expressions, provided that their values are of the appropriate type. For example, the following declaration creates an array of eight Colors. Some of the colors are given by expressions of the form "new Color(r,g,b)" instead of by constants:

```
Color[] palette = {
                Color.BLACK,
                Color.RED,
                Color.PINK,
                new Color(0,180,0),   // dark green
                Color.GREEN,
                Color.BLUE,
                new Color(180,180,255), // light blue
                Color.WHITE
            };
```

A list initializer of this form can be used **only** in a declaration statement, to give an initial value to a newly declared array variable. It cannot be used in an assignment statement to assign a value to a variable that has been previously declared. However, there is another, similar notation for creating a new array that can be used in an assignment statement or passed as a parameter to a subroutine. The notation uses another form of the new operator to both create and initialize a new array object at the same time. (The rather odd syntax is similar to the syntax for anonymous classes, which were discussed in Subsection 5.7.3.) For example to assign a new value to an array variable, list, that was declared previously, you could use:

```
list = new int[] { 1, 8, 27, 64, 125, 216, 343 };
```

The general syntax for this form of the new operator is

```
new base-type  [ ] {    list-of-values    }
```

This is actually an whose value is a reference to a newly created array object. expression means that it This any context where an object of type **base-type** [] is can be used in For example, expected. is a method that takes an array of Strings as a if makeButtons could say: parameter, you

```
makeButtons( new String[] { "Stop", "Go", "Next", "Previous" } );
```

Being able to create and use an array "in place" in this way can be very convenient, in the same way that anonymous nested classes are convenient.

By the way, it is perfectly legal to use the "new BaseType[] { ... }" syntax instead of the array initializer syntax in the declaration of an array variable. For example, instead of saying:

```
int[] primes = { 2, 3, 5, 7, 11, 13, 17, 19 };
```

you can say, equivalently,

```
int[] primes = new int[] { 2, 3, 5, 7, 11, 17, 19 };
```

In fact, rather than use a special notation that works only in the context of declaration state-ments, I prefer to use the second form.

* * *

One final note: For historical reasons, an array declaration such as

```
int[] list;
```

can also be written as

```
int list[];
```

which is a syntax used in the languages C and C++. However, this alternative syntax does not really make much sense in the context of Java, and it is probably best avoided. After all, the intent is to declare a variable of a certain type, and the name of that type is "int[ ]". It makes sense to follow the " **type-name variable-name** ;" syntax for such declarations.

7.2 Programming With Arrays

Arrays are the most basic and the most important type of data structure, and tech-niques for processing arrays are among the most important programming techniques you can learn. Two fundamental array processing techniques—searching and sorting—will be covered in Section 7.4. This section introduces some of the basic ideas of array processing in general.

7.2.1 Arrays and for Loops

In many cases, processing an array means applying the same operation to each item in the array. This is commonly done with a for loop. A loop for processing all the elements of an array A has the form:

```
• do any necessary initialization for
(int i = 0; i < A.length; i++) {
    . . . // process A[i]
}
```

Suppose, for example, that A is an array of type double[ ]. Suppose that the goal is to add up all the numbers in the array. An informal algorithm for doing this would be:

```
Start with 0;
Add A[0];    (process the first item in A)
Add A[1];    (process the second item in A)
   .
   .
   .
Add A[ A.length - 1 ];    (process the last item in A)
```

Putting the obvious repetition into a loop and giving a name to the sum, this becomes:

```
double sum;  // The sum of the numbers in A.
sum = 0;     // Start with 0.
for (int i = 0; i < A.length; i++)
    sum += A[i];  // add A[i] to the sum, for
                  •     i = 0, 1, ..., A.length - 1
```

Note that the continuation condition, "i < A.length", implies that the last value of i that is actually processed is A.length-1, which is the index of the final item in the array. It's important to use "<" here, not "<=", since "<=" would give an array index out of bounds error. There is no element at position A.length in A.

Eventually, you should just about be able to write loops similar to this one in your sleep. I will give a few more simple examples. Here is a loop that will count the number of items in the array A which are less than zero:

```
int count;   // For counting the items.
count = 0;   // Start with 0 items counted.
for (int i = 0; i < A.length; i++) {
    if (A[i] < 0.0)      // if this item is less than zero...
        count++;         //       ...then count it
}
• At this point, the value of count is the number
• of items that have passed the test of being < 0
```

Replace the test "A[i] < 0.0", if you want to count the number of items in an array that satisfy some other property. Here is a variation on the same theme. Suppose you want to count the number of times that an item in the array A is equal to the item that follows it. The item that follows A[i] in the array is A[i+1], so the test in this case is "if (A[i] == A[i+1])". But there is a catch: This test cannot be applied when A[i] is the last item in the array, since then there is no such item as A[i+1]. The result of trying to apply the test in this case would be an ArrayIndexOutOfBoundsException. This just means that we have to stop one item short of the final item:

```
int count = 0;
for (int i = 0; i < A.length - 1; i++) {
    if (A[i] == A[i+1])
        count++;
}
```

Another typical problem is to find the largest number in A. The strategy is to go through the array, keeping track of the largest number found so far. We'll store the largest number found so far in a variable called max. As we look through the array, whenever we find a number larger than the current value of max, we change the value of max to that larger value. After the whole array has been processed, max is the largest item in the array overall. The only question is, what should the original value of max be? One possibility is to start with max equal to A[0], and then to look through the rest of the array, starting from A[1], for larger items:

```
double max = A[0];
for (int i = 1; i < A.length; i++) {
    if (A[i] > max)
        max = A[i];
```

```
}
// at this point, max is the largest item in A
```

(There is one subtle problem here. It's possible in Java for an array to have length zero. In that case, A[0] doesn't exist, and the reference to A[0] in the first line gives an array index out of bounds error. However, zero-length arrays are normally something that you want to avoid in real problems. Anyway, what would it mean to ask for the largest item in an array that contains no items at all?)

As a final example of basic array operations, consider the problem of copying an array. To make a copy of our sample array A, it is **not** sufficient to say

```
double[] B = A;
```

since this does not create a new array object. All it does is declare a new array variable and make it refer to the same object to which A refers. (So that, for example, a change to A[i] will automatically change B[i] as well.) To make a new array that is a copy of A, it is necessary to make a new array object and to copy each of the individual items from A into the new array:

```
double[] B = new double[A.length]; // Make a new array object, //
                                        the same size as A.
for (int i = 0; i < A.length; i++)
   B[i] = A[i];        // Copy each item from A to B.
```

Copying values from one array to another is such a common operation that Java has a predefined subroutine to do it. The subroutine, System.arraycopy(), is a static member subroutine in the standard System class. Its declaration has the form

```
public static void arraycopy(Object sourceArray, int sourceStartIndex,
          Object destArray, int destStartIndex, int count)
```

where sourceArray and destArray can be arrays with any base type. Values are copied from sourceArray to destArray. The count tells how many elements to copy. Values are taken from sourceArray starting at position sourceStartIndex and are stored in destArray starting at position destStartIndex. For example, to make a copy of the array, A, using this subroutine, you would say:

```
double B = new double[A.length];
System.arraycopy( A, 0, B, 0, A.length );
```

7.2.2 Arrays and for-each Loops

Java 5.0 introduced a new form of the for loop, the "for-each loop" that was introduced in Subsection 3.4.4. The for-each loop is meant specifically for processing all the values in a data structure. When used to process an array, a for-each loop can be used to perform the same operation on each value that is stored in the array. If anArray is an array of type BaseType[ ], then a for-each loop for anArray has the form:

```
for ( BaseType item : anArray ) {
     .
     • // process the item
•
}
```

In this loop, item is the loop control variable. It is being declared as a variable of type BaseType, where BaseType is the base type of the array. (In a for-each loop, the loop control variable **must** be declared in the loop.) When this loop is executed, each value from the array is assigned to item in turn and the body of the loop is executed for each value. Thus, the above loop is exactly equivalent to:

```
for ( int index = 0; index < anArray.length; index++ ) {
    BaseType item;
    item = anArray[index];    // Get one of the values from the array
      .
      • // process the item

}
```

For example, if A is an array of type int[ ], then we could print all the values from A with the for-each loop:

```
for ( int item : A )
    System.out.println( item );
```

and we could add up all the positive integers in A with:

```
int sum = 0; // This will be the sum of all the positive numbers in A for ( int
item : A ) {
    if (item > 0)
        sum = sum + item;
}
```

The for-each loop is not always appropriate. For example, there is no simple way to use it to process the items in just a part of an array. However, it does make it a little easier to process all the values in an array, since it eliminates any need to use array indices.

It's important to note that a for-each loop processes the **values** in the array, not the **elements** (where an element means the actual memory location that is part of the array). For example, consider the following incorrect attempt to fill an array of integers with 17's:

```
int[] intList = new int[10];
for ( int item : intList ) {        // INCORRECT! DOES NOT MODIFY THE ARRAY!
    item = 17;
}
```

The assignment statement item = 17 assigns the value 17 to the loop control variable, item. However, this has nothing to do with the array. When the body of the loop is executed, the value from one of the elements of the array is copied into item. The statement item = 17 replaces that copied value but has no effect on the array element from which it was copied; the value in the array is not changed.

7.2.3 Array Types in Subroutines

Any array type, such as double[ ], is a full-fledged Java type, so it can be used in all the ways that any other Java type can be used. In particular, it can be used as the type of a formal parameter in a subroutine. It can even be the return type of a function. For example, it might be useful to have a function that makes a copy of an array of double:

```
/**
 • Create a new array of doubles that is a copy of a given array.
 • @param source the array that is to be copied; the value can be null
 • @return a copy of source; if source is null, then the return value is also null
 */
```

```
public static double[] copy( double[] source ) { if (
    source == null )
```

```
            return null;
        double[]  cpy;  // A copy of the source array.
        cpy = new double[source.length];
        System.arraycopy( source, 0, cpy, 0, source.length );
        return cpy;
    }
```

The main() routine of a program has a parameter of type String[ ]. You've seen this used since all the way back in Section 2.1, but I haven't really been able to explain it until now. The parameter to the main() routine is an array of String s. When the system calls the main() routine, the strings in this array are the **command-line arguments** from the command that was used to run the program. When using a command-line interface, the user types a command to tell the system to execute a program. The user can include extra input in this command, beyond the name of the program. This extra input becomes the command-line arguments. For example, if the name of the class that contains the main() routine is myProg, then the user can type "java myProg" to execute the program. In this case, there are no command-line arguments. But if the user types the command

```
java myProg one two three
```

then the command-line arguments are the strings "one", "two", and "three". The system puts these strings into an array of String s and passes that array as a parameter to the main() routine. Here, for example, is a short program that simply prints out any command line arguments entered by the user:

```
public class CLDemo {

    public static void main(String[] args) {
        System.out.println("You entered " + args.length
                                   + " command-line arguments");
        if (args.length > 0) {
            System.out.println("They were:");
            for (int i = 0; i < args.length; i++)
                System.out.println("      " + args[i]);
        }
    } // end main()

} // end class CLDemo
```

Note that the parameter, args, is never null when main() is called by the system, but it might be an array of length zero.

In practice, command-line arguments are often the names of files to be processed by the program. I will give some examples of this in Chapter 11, when I discuss file processing.

7.2.4 Random Access

So far, all my examples of array processing have used **sequential access**. That is, the elements of the array were processed one after the other in the sequence in which they occur in the array. But one of the big advantages of arrays is that they allow **random access**. That is, every element of the array is equally accessible at any given time.

As an example, let's look at a well-known problem called the birthday problem: Suppose that there are N people in a room. What's the chance that there are two people in the room who have the same birthday? (That is, they were born on the same day in the same month, but not necessarily in the same year.) Most people severely underestimate the probability. We will actually look at a different version of the question: Suppose you choose people at random and check their birthdays. How many people will you check before you find one who has the same birthday as someone you've already checked? Of course, the answer in a particular case depends on random factors, but we can simulate the experiment with a computer program and run the program several times to get an idea of how many people need to be checked on average.

To simulate the experiment, we need to keep track of each birthday that we find. There are 365 different possible birthdays. (We'll ignore leap years.) For each possible birthday, we need to keep track of whether or not we have already found a person who has that birthday. The answer to this question is a boolean value, true or false. To hold the data for all 365 possible birthdays, we can use an array of 365 boolean values:

```
boolean[] used;
used = new boolean[365];
```

The days of the year are numbered from 0 to 364. The value of used[i] is true if someone has been selected whose birthday is day number i. Initially, all the values in the array, used, are false. When we select someone whose birthday is day number i, we first check whether used[i] is true. If so, then this is the second person with that birthday. We are done. If used[i] is false, we set used[i] to be true to record the fact that we've encountered someone with that birthday, and we go on to the next person. Here is a subroutine that carries out the simulated experiment (of course, in the subroutine, there are no simulated people, only simulated birthdays):

```
/**
 • Simulate choosing people at random and checking the day of the year they
 • were born on. If the birthday is the same as one that was seen previously,
 • stop, and output the number of people who were checked.
 */
private static void birthdayProblem() {

   boolean[] used;  // For recording the possible birthdays
                    •       that have been seen so far. A value
                    •       of true in used[i] means that a person
                    •       whose birthday is the i-th day of the
                    •       year has been found.

   int count;       // The number of people who have been checked.

   used = new boolean[365]; // Initially, all entries are false.

   count = 0;

   while (true) {
         • Select a birthday at random, from 0 to 364.
         • If the birthday has already been used, quit.
         • Otherwise, record the birthday as used.
      int birthday;    // The selected birthday.
      birthday = (int)(Math.random()*365);
      count++;
      if ( used[birthday] )       // This day was found before; It's a duplicate.
```

```
            break;
        used[birthday] = true;
    }

    System.out.println("A duplicate birthday was found after "
```

```
+ count + " tries.");
} // end birthdayProblem()
```

This subroutine makes essential use of the fact that every element in a newly created array of boolean is set to be false. If we wanted to reuse the same array in a second simulation, we would have to reset all the elements in it to be false with a for loop:

```
for (int i = 0; i < 365; i++)
    used[i] = false;
```

The program that uses this subroutine is **BirthdayProblemDemo.java**. An applet version of the program can be found in the online version of this section.

7.2.5 Arrays of Objects

One of the examples in Subsection 6.4.2 was an applet that shows multiple copies of a message in random positions, colors, and fonts. When the user clicks on the applet, the positions, colors, and fonts are changed to new random values. Like several other examples from that chapter, the applet had a flaw: It didn't have any way of storing the data that would be necessary to redraw itself. Arrays provide us with one possible solution to this problem. We can write a new version of the RandomStrings applet that uses an array to store the position, font, and color of each string. When the content pane of the applet is painted, this information is used to draw the strings, so the applet will paint itself correctly whenever it has to be redrawn. When the user clicks on the applet, the array is filled with new random values and the applet is repainted using the new data. So, the only time that the picture will change is in response to a mouse click.

In this applet, the number of copies of the message is given by a named constant, MESSAGE COUNT. One way to store the position, color, and font of MESSAGE COUNT strings would be to use four arrays:

```
int[] x = new int[MESSAGE COUNT];
int[] y = new int[MESSAGE COUNT];
Color[] color = new Color[MESSAGE_COUNT];
Font[] font = new Font[MESSAGE COUNT];
```

These arrays would be filled with random values. In the paintComponent() method, the i-th copy of the string would be drawn at the point (x[i],y[i]). Its color would be given by color[i]. And it would be drawn in the font font[i]. This would be accomplished by the paintComponent() method

```
public void paintComponent(Graphics g) {
    super.paintComponent(); // (Fill with background color.) for
    (int i = 0; i < MESSAGE COUNT; i++) {
        g.setColor( color[i] );
        g.setFont( font[i] );
        g.drawString( message, x[i], y[i] );
    }
}
```

This approach is said to use **parallel arrays.** The data for a given copy of the message is spread out across several arrays. If you think of the arrays as laid out in parallel columns—

array x in the first column, array y in the second, array color in the third, and array font in the fourth—then the data for the i-th string can be found along the the i-th row. There is nothing wrong with using parallel arrays in this simple example, but it does go against the object-oriented philosophy of keeping related data in one object. If we follow this rule, then we don't have to **imagine** the relationship among the data, because all the data for one copy of the message is physically in one place. So, when I wrote the applet, I made a simple class to represent all the data that is needed for one copy of the message:

```
/**
 * An object of this type holds the position, color, and font
 * of one copy of the string.
 */
private static class StringData {
    int x, y;         // The coordinates of the left end of baseline of string.
    Color color;      // The color in which the string is drawn.
    Font font;        // The font that is used to draw the string.
}
```

(This class is actually defined as a static nested class in the main applet class.) To store the data for multiple copies of the message, I use an array of type StringData[ ]. The array is declared as an instance variable, with the name stringData:

```
StringData[] stringData;
```

Of course, the value of stringData is null until an actual array is created and assigned to it. This is done in the init() method of the applet with the statement

```
stringData = new StringData[MESSAGE COUNT];
```

The base type of this array is StringData, which is a class. We say that stringData is an **array of objects**. This means that the elements of the array are variables of type StringData. Like any object variable, each element of the array can either be null or can hold a reference to an object. (Note that the term "array of objects" is a little misleading, since the objects are not in the array; the array can only contain references to objects). When the stringData array is first created, the value of each element in the array is null.

The data needed by the RandomStrings program will be stored in objects of type StringData, but no such objects exist yet. All we have so far is an array of variables that are capable of referring to such objects. I decided to create the StringData objects in the applet's init method. (It could be done in other places—just so long as we avoid trying to use an object that doesn't exist. This is important: Remember that a newly created array whose base type is an object type is always filled with null elements. There are **no** objects in the array until you put them there.) The objects are created with the for loop

```
for (int i = 0; i < MESSAGE COUNT; i++)
    stringData[i] = new StringData();
```

For the RandomStrings applet, the idea is to store data for the i-th copy of the message in the variables stringData[i].x, stringData[i].y, stringData[i].color, and stringData[i].font. Make sure that you understand the notation here: stringData[i] refers to an object. That object contains instance variables. The notation stringData[i].x tells the computer: "Find your way to the object that is referred to by stringData[i]. Then go to the instance variable named x in that object." Variable names can get even more com-plicated than this, so it is important to learn how to read them. Using the array, stringData, the paintComponent() method for the applet could be written

```
public void paintComponent(Graphics g) {
    super.paintComponent(g); // (Fill with background color.) for
    (int i = 0; i < MESSAGE COUNT; i++) {
        g.setColor( stringData[i].color );
        g.setFont( stringData[i].font );
        g.drawString( message, stringData[i].x, stringData[i].y );
    }
}
```

However, since the for loop is processing every value in the array, an alternative would be to use a for-each loop:

```
public void paintComponent(Graphics g) {
    super.paintComponent(g);
    for ( StringData data : stringData) {
            • Draw a copy of the message in the position, color,
            • and font stored in data.
        g.setColor( data.color );
        g.setFont( data.font );
        g.drawString( message, data.x, data.y );
    }
}
```

In the loop, the loop control variable, data, holds a copy of one of the values from the array. That value is a reference to an object of type StringData, which has instance variables named color, font, x, and y. Once again, the use of a for-each loop has eliminated the need to work with array indices.

There is still the matter of filling the array, data, with random values. If you are interested, you can look at the source code for the applet, **RandomStringsWithArray.Java**.

* * *

The RandomStrings applet uses one other array of objects. The font for a given copy of the message is chosen at random from a set of five possible fonts. In the original version of the applet, there were five variables of type Font to represent the fonts. The variables were named font1, font2, font3, font4, and font5. To select one of these fonts at random, a switch statement could be used:

```
Font                // One of the 5 fonts, chosen at random.
randomFont; int     // A random integer in the range 0 to 4.
rand;

rand = (int)(Math.random() * 5);
switch (rand) {
    case 0:
        randomFont = font1;
        break;
    case 1:
        randomFont = font2;
        break;
    case 2:
        randomFont = font3;
        break;
```

```
case 3:
    randomFont = font4;
    break;
case 4:
```

```
            randomFont = font5;
            break;
      }
```

In the new version of the applet, the five fonts are stored in an array, which is named fonts. This array is declared as an instance variable of type Font[ ]

```
Font[] fonts;
```

The array is created in the init() method of the applet, and each element of the array is set to refer to a new Font object:

```
fonts = new Font[5];   // Create the array to hold the five fonts.

fonts[0] = new Font("Serif", Font.BOLD, 14);
fonts[1] = new Font("SansSerif", Font.BOLD + Font.ITALIC, 24);
fonts[2] = new Font("Monospaced", Font.PLAIN, 20);
fonts[3] = new Font("Dialog", Font.PLAIN, 30);
fonts[4] = new Font("Serif", Font.ITALIC, 36);
```

This makes it much easier to select one of the fonts at random. It can be done with the statements

```
Font randomFont; // One of the 5 fonts, chosen at random.
int fontIndex;       // A random number in the range 0 to 4.
fontIndex = (int)(Math.random() * 5);
randomFont = fonts[ fontIndex ];
```

The switch statement has been replaced by a single line of code. In fact, the preceding four lines could be replaced by the single line:

```
Font randomFont = fonts[ (int)(Math.random() * 5) ];
```

This is a very typical application of arrays. Note that this example uses the random access property of arrays: We can pick an array index at random and go directly to the array element at that index.

Here is another example of the same sort of thing. Months are often stored as numbers 1, 2, 3, . . . , 12. Sometimes, however, these numbers have to be translated into the names January, February, . . . , December. The translation can be done with an array. The array can be declared and initialized as

```
static String[] monthName = { "January",   "February",  "March",
                              "April",     "May",       "June",
                              "July",      "August",    "September",
                              "October",   "November",  "December" };
```

If mnth is a variable that holds one of the integers 1 through 12, then monthName[mnth-1] is the name of the corresponding month. We need the "-1" because months are numbered starting from 1, while array elements are numbered starting from 0. Simple array indexing does the translation for us!

7.2.6 Variable Arity Methods

Arrays are used in the implementation of one of the new features in Java 5.0. Before version 5.0, every method in Java had a fixed arity. (The **arity** of a subroutine is defined as the number of parameters in a call to the method.) In a fixed arity method, the number of parameters must be the same in every call to the method. Java 5.0 introduced **variable arity methods.** In a variable arity method, different calls to the method can have different numbers of parameters. For example, the formatted output method System.out.printf, which was introduced in Sub-section 2.4.4, is a variable arity method. The first parameter of System.out.printf must be a String, but it can have any number of additional parameters, of any types.

Calling a variable arity method is no different from calling any other sort of method, but writing one requires some new syntax. As an example, consider a method that can compute the average of any number of values of type double. The definition of such a method could begin with:

```
public static double average( double...     numbers ) {
```

Here, the ... after the type name, double, indicates that any number of values of type double can be provided when the subroutine is called, so that for example average(1,2,3), average(3.14,2.17), average(0.375), and even average() are all legal calls to this method. Note that actual parameters of type int can be passed to average. The integers will, as usual, be automatically converted to real numbers.

When the method is called, the values of all the actual parameters that correspond to the variable arity parameter are placed into an array, and it is this array that is actually passed to the method. That is, in the body of a method, a variable arity parameter of type T actually looks like an ordinary parameter of type T[ ]. The length of the array tells you how many actual parameters were provided in the method call. In the average example, the body of the method would see an array named numbers of type double[ ]. The number of actual parameters in the method call would be numbers.length, and the values of the actual parameters would be numbers[0], numbers[1], and so on. A complete definition of the method would be:

```
public static double average( double... numbers ) {
    double sum;      // The sum of all the actual parameters.
    double average;  // The average of all the actual parameters.
    sum = 0;
    for (int i = 0; i < numbers.length; i++) {
        sum = sum + numbers[i];  // Add one of the actual parameters to the sum.
    }
    average = sum / numbers.length;
    return average;
}
```

Note that the "..." can be applied only to the **last** formal parameter in a method definition. Note also that it is possible to pass an actual array to the method, instead of a list of individual values. For example, if salesData is a variable of type double[ ], then it would be legal to call average(salesData), and this would compute the average of all the numbers in the array.

As another example, consider a method that can draw a polygon through any number of points. The points are given as values of type Point, where an object of type Point has two instance variables, x and y, of type int. In this case, the method has one ordinary parameter— the graphics context that will be used to draw the polygon—in addition to the variable arity parameter:

```
public static void drawPolygon(Graphics g, Point... points) {
```

```
if (points.length > 1) {         // (Need at least 2 points to draw anything.)
    for (int i = 0; i < points.length - 1; i++) {
        // Draw a line from i-th point to (i+1)-th point
        g.drawline( points[i].x, points[i].y, points[i+1].x, points[i+1].y );
    }
```

```
            // Now, draw a line back to the starting point.
            g.drawLine( points[points.length-1].x, points[points.length-1].y,
                                  points[0].x, points[0].y );
        }
    }
```

Because of automatic type conversion, a variable arity parameter of type "Object..." can take actual parameters of any type whatsoever. Even primitive type values are allowed, because of autoboxing. (A primitive type value belonging to a type such as int is converted to an object belonging to a "wrapper" class such as Integer. See Subsection 5.3.2.) For example, the method definition for System.out.printf could begin:

```
public void printf(String format, Object... values) {
```

This allows the printf method to output values of any type. Similarly, we could write a method that strings together the string representations of all its parameters into one long string:

```
public static String concat( Object... values ) { String
   str = ""; // Start with an empty string.
   for ( Object obj : values ) { // A "for each" loop for processing the values. if (obj ==
      null )

         str = str + "null";        // Represent null values by "null".
      else
         str = str + obj.toString();
   }
}
```

7.3 Dynamic Arrays and ArrayLists

The size of an array is fixed when it is created. In many cases, however, the number of data items that are actually stored in the array varies with time. Consider the following examples: An array that stores the lines of text in a word-processing program. An array that holds the list of computers that are currently downloading a page from a Web site. An array that contains the shapes that have been added to the screen by the user of a drawing program. Clearly, we need some way to deal with cases where the number of data items in an array is not fixed.

7.3.1 Partially Full Arrays

Consider an application where the number of items that we want to store in an array changes as the program runs. Since the size of the array can't actually be changed, a separate counter variable must be used to keep track of how many spaces in the array are in use. (Of course, every space in the array has to contain something; the question is, how many spaces contain useful or valid items?)

Consider, for example, a program that reads positive integers entered by the user and stores them for later processing. The program stops reading when the user inputs a number that is less than or equal to zero. The input numbers can be kept in an array, numbers, of type int[ ]. Let's say that no more than 100 numbers will be input. Then the size of the array can be fixed at 100. But the program must keep track of how many numbers have actually been read and stored in the array. For this, it can use an integer variable, numCount. Each time a number is stored in the array, numCount must be incremented by one. As a rather silly example, let's write a program that will read the numbers input by the user and then print them in reverse order. (This is, at least, a processing task that requires that the numbers be saved in an array. Remember that many types of processing, such as finding the sum or average or maximum of the numbers, can be done without saving the individual numbers.)

```
public class ReverseInputNumbers {

    public static void main(String[] args) {

        int[] numbers;      // An array for storing the input        values.
        int numCount;       // The number of numbers saved in         the array.
        int num;            // One of the numbers input by the user.

        numbers = new int[100];   // Space for 100 ints.
        numCount = 0;             // No numbers have been saved yet.

        TextIO.putln("Enter up to 100 positive integers; enter 0 to end.");

        while (true) {        // Get the numbers and put them in the array.
            TextIO.put("? ");
            num = TextIO.getlnInt();
            if (num <= 0)
                break;
            numbers[numCount] = num;
            numCount++;
        }

        TextIO.putln("\nYour numbers in reverse order are:\n");

        for (int i = numCount - 1; i >= 0; i--) {
             TextIO.putln( numbers[i] );
        }

    } // end main();

} // end class ReverseInputNumbers
```

It is especially important to note that the variable numCount plays a dual role. It is the number of items that have been entered into the array. But it is also the index of the next available spot in the array. For example, if 4 numbers have been stored in the array, they occupy locations number 0, 1, 2, and 3. The next available spot is location 4. When the time comes to print out the numbers in the array, the last occupied spot in the array is location numCount - 1, so the for loop prints out values starting from location numCount - 1 and going down to 0.

Let's look at another, more realistic example. Suppose that you write a game program, and that players can join the game and leave the game as it progresses. As a good object-oriented programmer, you probably have a class named Player to represent the individual players in the game. A list of all players who are currently in the game could be stored in an array, playerList, of type Player[ ]. Since the number of players can change, you will also need a variable, playerCt, to record the number of players currently in the game. Assuming that there will never be more than 10 players in the game, you could declare the variables as:

```
Player[] playerList = new Player[10];      // Up to 10 players.
int      playerCt = 0;   // At the start, there are no players.
```

After some players have joined the game, playerCt will be greater than 0, and the player objects representing the players will be stored in the array elements playerList[0], playerList[1], . . . , playerList[playerCt-1]. Note that the array element playerList[playerCt] is **not** in use. The procedure for adding a new player, newPlayer, to the game is simple:

```
playerList[playerCt] = newPlayer; // Put new player in next
                                  •      available spot.
playerCt++; // And increment playerCt to count the new player.
```

Deleting a player from the game is a little harder, since you don't want to leave a "hole" in the array. Suppose you want to delete the player at index k in playerList. If you are not worried about keeping the players in any particular order, then one way to do this is to move the player from the last occupied position in the array into position k and then to decrement the value of playerCt:

```
playerList[k] = playerList[playerCt - 1];
playerCt–;
```

The player previously in position k is no longer in the array. The player previously in position playerCt - 1 is now in the array twice. But it's only in the occupied or valid part of the array once, since playerCt has decreased by one. Remember that every element of the array has to hold some value, but only the values in positions 0 through playerCt - 1 will be looked at or processed in any way. (By the way, you should think about what happens if the player that is being deleted is in the last position in the list. The code does still work in this case. What exactly happens?)

Suppose that when deleting the player in position k, you'd like to keep the remaining players in the same order. (Maybe because they take turns in the order in which they are stored in the array.) To do this, all the players in positions k+1 and above must move down one position in the array. Player k+1 replaces player k, who is out of the game. Player k+2 fills the spot left open when player k+1 is moved. And so on. The code for this is

```
for (int i = k+1; i < playerCt; i++) {
    playerList[i-1] = playerList[i];
}
playerCt–;
```

* * *

It's worth emphasizing that the Player example deals with an array whose base type is a class. An item in the array is either null or is a reference to an object belonging to the class, Player. The Player objects themselves are not really stored in the array, only references to them. Note that because of the rules for assignment in Java, the objects can actually belong to subclasses of Player. Thus there could be different classes of players such as computer players, regular human players, players who are wizards, . . . , all represented by different subclasses of Player.

As another example, suppose that a class Shape represents the general idea of a shape drawn on a screen, and that it has subclasses to represent specific types of shapes such as lines, rectangles, rounded rectangles, ovals, filled-in ovals, and so forth. (Shape itself would be an abstract class, as discussed in Subsection 5.5.5.) Then an array of type Shape[ ] can hold references to objects belonging to the subclasses of Shape. For example, the situation created by the statements

```
Shape[] shapes = new Shape[100]; // Array to hold up to 100 shapes.
shapes[0] = new Rect();          // Put some objects in the array.
shapes[1] = new Line();
shapes[2] = new FilledOval();
```

```
int shapeCt = 3;     // Keep track of number of objects in array.
```

could be illustrated as:

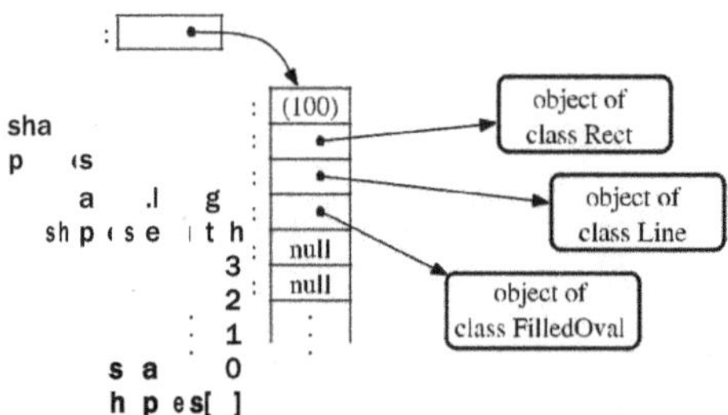

Such an array would be useful in a drawing program. The array could be used to hold a list of shapes to be displayed. If the Shape class includes a method, "void redraw(Graphics g)", for drawing the shape in a graphics context g, then all the shapes in the array could be redrawn with a simple for loop:

```
for (int i = 0; i < shapeCt; i++)
    shapes[i].redraw(g);
```

The statement "shapes[i].redraw(g);" calls the redraw() method belonging to the partic-ular shape at index i in the array. Each object knows how to redraw itself, so that repeated executions of the statement can produce a variety of different shapes on the screen. This is nice example both of polymorphism and of array processing.

7.3.2 Dynamic Arrays

In each of the above examples, an arbitrary limit was set on the number of items—100 ints, 10 Players, 100 Shapes. Since the size of an array is fixed, a given array can only hold a certain maximum number of items. In many cases, such an arbitrary limit is undesirable. Why should a program work for 100 data values, but not for 101? The obvious alternative of making an array that's so big that it will work in any practical case is not usually a good solution to the problem. It means that in most cases, a lot of computer memory will be wasted on unused space in the array. That memory might be better used for something else. And what if someone is using a computer that could handle as many data values as the user actually wants to process, but doesn't have enough memory to accommodate all the extra space that you've allocated for your huge array?

Clearly, it would be nice if we could increase the size of an array at will. This is not possible, but what **is** possible is almost as good. Remember that an array variable does not actually hold an array. It just holds a reference to an array object. We can't make the array bigger, but we can make a new, bigger array object and change the value of the array variable so that it refers to the bigger array. Of course, we also have to copy the contents of the old array into the new array. The array variable then refers to an array object that contains all the data of the old array, with room for additional data. The old array will be garbage collected, since it is no longer in use.

Let's look back at the game example, in which playerList is an array of type Player[ ] and playerCt is the number of spaces that have been used in the array. Suppose that we don't want to put a pre-set limit on the number of players. If a new player joins the game and the current array is full, we just make a new, bigger one. The same variable, playerList, will refer to the new array. Note that after this is done, playerList[0] will refer to a different memory location, but the value stored in playerList[0] will still be the same as it was before. Here is some code that will do this:

```
// Add a new player, even if the current array is full.

if (playerCt == playerList.length) {
        • Array is full. Make a new, bigger array,
        • copy the contents of the old array into it,
        • and set playerList to refer to the new array.
    int newSize = 2 * playerList.length; // Size of new array.
    Player[] temp = new Player[newSize]; // The new array.
    System.arraycopy(playerList, 0, temp, 0, playerList.length);
    playerList = temp; // Set playerList to refer to new array.
}

// At this point, we KNOW there is room in the array.

playerList[playerCt] = newPlayer; // Add the new player...
playerCt++;                       //     ...and count it.
```

If we are going to be doing things like this regularly, it would be nice to define a reusable class to handle the details. An array-like object that changes size to accommodate the amount of data that it actually contains is called a **dynamic array** . A dynamic array supports the same operations as an array: putting a value at a given position and getting the value that is stored at a given position. But there is no upper limit on the positions that can be used (except those imposed by the size of the computer's memory). In a dynamic array class, the put and get operations must be implemented as instance methods. Here, for example, is a class that implements a dynamic array of ints:

```
/**
  • An object of type DynamicArrayOfInt acts like an array of int
  • of unlimited size. The notation A.get(i) must be used instead
  • of A[i], and A.set(i,v) must be used instead of A[i] = v.
  */
public class DynamicArrayOfInt {

    private int[] data;      // An array to hold the data.

    /**
      • Constructor creates an array with an initial size of 1,
      • but the array size will be increased whenever a reference
      • is made to an array position that does not yet exist.
      */
    public DynamicArrayOfInt() {
        data = new int[1];
    }

    /**
      • Get the value from the specified position in the array.
      • Since all array elements are initialized to zero, when the
```

- specified position lies outside the actual physical size
- of the data array, a value of 0 is returned. Note that
- a negative value of position will still produce an
- ArrayIndexOutOfBoundsException.

```
 */
public int get(int position) {
   if (position >= data.length)
      return 0;
   else
      return data[position];
}

/**
 • Store the value in the specified position in the array.
 • The data array will increase in size to include this
 • position, if necessary.
 */
public void put(int position, int value) {
   if (position >= data.length) {
         • The specified position is outside the actual size of
         • the data array.  Double the size, or if that still does
         • not include the specified position, set the new size
         • to 2*position.
      int newSize = 2 * data.length;
      if (position >= newSize)
         newSize = 2 * position;
      int[] newData = new int[newSize];
      System.arraycopy(data, 0, newData, 0, data.length);
      data = newData;
         • The following line is for demonstration purposes only !!
      System.out.println("Size of dynamic array increased to " + newSize);
   }
   data[position] = value;
}

} // end class DynamicArrayOfInt
```

The data in a DynamicArrayOfInt object is actually stored in a regular array, but that array is discarded and replaced by a bigger array whenever necessary. If numbers is a variable of type DynamicArrayOfInt, then the command numbers.put(pos,val) stores the value val at position number pos in the dynamic array. The function numbers.get(pos) returns the value stored at position number pos.

The first example in this section used an array to store positive integers input by the user. We can rewrite that example to use a DynamicArrayOfInt. A reference to numbers[i] is replaced by numbers.get(i). The statement "numbers[numCount] = num;" is replaced by "numbers.put(numCount,num);". Here's the program:

```
public class ReverseWithDynamicArray {

   public static void main(String[] args) {

      DynamicArrayOfInt numbers; // To hold the input numbers.
      int numCount;  // The number of numbers stored in the array.
      int num;       // One of the numbers input by the user.

      numbers = new DynamicArrayOfInt();
```

numCount = 0;

TextIO.putln("Enter some positive integers; Enter 0 to end"); while (true) { // Get numbers and put them in the dynamic array.

```
            TextIO.put("? ");
            num = TextIO.getlnInt();
            if (num <= 0)
               break;
            numbers.put(numCount, num);// Store num in the dynamic array.
            numCount++;
        }

        TextIO.putln("\nYour numbers in reverse order are:\n");

        for (int i = numCount - 1; i >= 0; i--) {
            TextIO.putln( numbers.get(i) );        // Print the i-th number.
        }

    }// end main();

} // end class ReverseWithDynamicArray
```

7.3.3 ArrrayLists

The DynamicArrayOfInt class could be used in any situation where an array of int with no preset limit on the size is needed. However, if we want to store Shapes instead of ints, we would have to define a new class to do it. That class, probably named "DynamicArrayOfShape", would look exactly the same as the DynamicArrayOfInt class except that everywhere the type "int" appears, it would be replaced by the type "Shape". Similarly, we could define a DynamicArrayOfDouble class, a DynamicArrayOfPlayer class, and so on. But there is something a little silly about this, since all these classes are close to being identical. It would be nice to be able to write some kind of source code, once and for all, that could be used to generate any of these classes on demand, given the type of value that we want to store. This would be an example of **generic programming** . Some programming languages, including C++, have had support for generic programming for some time. With version 5.0, Java introduced true generic programming, but even before that it had something that was very similar: One can come close to generic programming in Java by working with data structures that contain elements of type Object. We will first consider the almost-generic programming that has been available in Java from the beginning, and then we will look at the change that was introduced in Java 5.0. A full discussion of generic programming will be given in Chapter 10.

In Java, every class is a subclass of the class named Object. This means that every object can be assigned to a variable of type Object. Any object can be put into an array of type Object[ ]. If we defined a DynamicArrayOfObject class, then we could store objects of any type. This is not true generic programming, and it doesn't apply to the primitive types such as int and double. But it does come close. In fact, there is no need for us to define a DynamicArrayOfObject class. Java already has a standard class named ArrayList that serves much the same purpose. The ArrayList class is in the package java.util, so if you want to use it in a program, you should put the directive "import java.util.ArrayList;" at the beginning of your source code file.

The ArrayList class differs from my DynamicArrayOfInt class in that an ArrayList object always has a definite size, and it is illegal to refer to a position in the ArrayList that lies outside its size. In this, an ArrayList is more like a regular array. However, the size of an ArrayList can be increased at will. The ArrayList class defines many instance methods. I'll describe some of the most useful. Suppose that list is a variable of type ArrayList. Then we have:

- list.size() — This function returns the current size of the ArrayList. The only valid positions in the list are numbers in the range 0 to list.size()-1. Note that the size can be zero. A call to the default constructor new ArrayList() creates an ArrayList of size zero.
- list.add(obj) — Adds an object onto the end of the list, increasing the size by 1. The parameter, obj, can refer to an object of any type, or it can be null.
- list.get(N) — This function returns the value stored at position N in the ArrayList. N must be an integer in the range 0 to list.size()-1. If N is outside this range, an error of type IndexOutOfBoundsException occurs. Calling this function is similar to referring to A[N] for an array, A, except that you can't use list.get(N) on the left side of an assignment statement.
- list.set(N, obj) — Assigns the object, obj, to position N in the ArrayList, replacing the item previously stored at position N. The integer N must be in the range from 0 to list.size()-1. A call to this function is equivalent to the command A[N] = obj for an array A.
- list.remove(obj) — If the specified object occurs somewhere in the ArrayList, it is removed from the list. Any items in the list that come after the removed item are moved down one position. The size of the ArrayList decreases by 1. If obj occurs more than once in the list, only the first copy is removed.
- list.remove(N) — For an integer, N, this removes the N-th item in the ArrayList. N must be in the range 0 to list.size()-1. Any items in the list that come after the removed item are moved down one position. The size of the ArrayList decreases by 1.
- list.indexOf(obj) — A function that searches for the object, obj, in the ArrayList. If the object is found in the list, then the position number where it is found is returned. If the object is not found, then -1 is returned.

For example, suppose again that players in a game are represented by objects of type Player. The players currently in the game could be stored in an ArrayList named players. This variable would be declared as

```
ArrayList players;
```

and initialized to refer to a new, empty ArrayList object with

```
players = new ArrayList();
```

If newPlayer is a variable that refers to a Player object, the new player would be added to the ArrayList and to the game by saying

```
players.add(newPlayer);
```

and if player number i leaves the game, it is only necessary to say

```
players.remove(i);
```

Or, if player is a variable that refers to the Player that is to be removed, you could say

```
players.remove(player);
```

All this works very nicely. The only slight difficulty arises when you use the function players.get(i) to get the value stored at position i in the ArrayList. The return type of this function is Object. In this case the object that is returned by the function is actually of type Player. In order to do anything useful with the returned value, it's usually necessary to type-cast it to type Player :

```
Player plr = (Player)players.get(i);
```

For example, if the Player class includes an instance method makeMove() that is called to allow a player to make a move in the game, then the code for letting every player make a move is

```
for (int i = 0;   i < players.size();      i++) {
    Player plr = (Player)players.get(i);
    plr.makeMove();
}
```

The two lines inside the for loop can be combined to a single line:

```
((Player)players.get(i)).makeMove();
```

This gets an item from the list, type-casts it, and then calls the makeMove() method on the resulting Player. The parentheses around "(Player)players.get(i)" are required because of Java's precedence rules. The parentheses force the type-cast to be performed before the makeMove() method is called.

For-each loops work for ArrayLists just as they do for arrays. But note that since the items in an ArrayList are only known to be Objects, the type of the loop control variable must be Object. For example, the for loop used above to let each Player make a move could be written as the for-each loop

```
for ( Object plrObj : players ) {
    Player plr = (Player)plrObj;
    plr.makeMove();
}
```

In the body of the loop, the value of the loop control variable, plrObj, is one of the objects from the list, players. This object must be type-cast to type Player before it can be used.

* * *

In Subsection 5.5.5, I discussed a program, ShapeDraw, that uses ArrayLists. Here is another version of the same idea, simplified to make it easier to see how ArrayList is being used. The program supports the following operations: Click the large white drawing area to add a colored rectangle. (The color of the rectangle is given by a "rainbow palette" along the bottom of the applet; click the palette to select a new color.) Drag rectangles using the right mouse button. Hold down the Alt key and click on a rectangle to delete it. Shift-click a rectangle to move it out in front of all the other rectangles. You can try an applet version of the program in the on-line version of this section.

Source code for the main panel for this program can be found in **SimpleDrawRects.java**. You should be able to follow the source code in its entirety. (You can also take a look at the file **RainbowPalette.java**, which defines the color palette shown at the bottom of the applet, if you like.) Here, I just want to look at the parts of the program that use an ArrayList.

The applet uses a variable named rects, of type ArrayList, to hold information about the rectangles that have been added to the drawing area. The objects that are stored in the list belong to a static nested class, ColoredRect, that is defined as

```
/**
  • An object of type ColoredRect holds the data for one colored rectangle. */
private static class ColoredRect {
    int x,y;               // Upper left corner of the rectangle.
    int width,height;      // Size of the rectangle.
    Color color;           // Color of the rectangle.
```

}

If g is a variable of type Graphics, then the following code draws all the rectangles that are stored in the list rects (with a black outline around each rectangle):

```
for (int i = 0; i < rects.size(); i++) { ColoredRect rect
    = (ColoredRect)rects.get(i); g.setColor( rect.color
    );
    g.fillRect( rect.x, rect.y, rect.width, rect.height);
    g.setColor( Color.BLACK );
    g.drawRect( rect.x, rect.y, rect.width - 1, rect.height - 1);
}
```

The i-th rectangle in the list is obtained by calling rects.get(i). Since this method returns a value of type Object, the return value must be typecast to its actual type, ColoredRect, to get access to the data that it contains.

To implement the mouse operations, it must be possible to find the rectangle, if any, that contains the point where the user clicked the mouse. To do this, I wrote the function

```
/**
 • Find the topmost rect that contains the point (x,y). Return null
 • if no rect contains that point. The rects in the ArrayList are
 • considered in reverse order so that if one lies on top of another,
 • the one on top is seen first and is returned.
 */
ColoredRect findRect(int x, int y) {

    for (int i = rects.size() - 1; i >= 0; i–) { ColoredRect
        rect = (ColoredRect)rects.get(i); if ( x >= rect.x
        && x < rect.x + rect.width
                    •   y >= rect.y && y < rect.y + rect.height )
        return rect; // (x,y) is inside this rect.
    }

    return null;     // No rect containing (x,y) was found.

}
```

The code for removing a ColoredRect, rect, from the drawing area is simply rects.remove(rect) (followed by a repaint()). Bringing a given rectangle out in front of all the other rectangles is just a little harder. Since the rectangles are drawn in the order in which they occur in the ArrayList, the rectangle that is in the last position in the list is in front of all the other rectangles on the screen. So we need to move the selected rectangle to the last position in the list. This can most easily be done in a slightly tricky way using built-in ArrayList operations: The rectangle is simply removed from its current position in the list and then adding back at the end of the list:

```
void bringToFront(ColoredRect rect) {
    if (rect != null) {
        rects.remove(rect); // Remove rect from the list.
        rects.add(rect);         // Add it back; it will be placed in the last position.
        repaint();
    }
}
```

This should be enough to give you the basic idea. You can look in the source code for more details.

7.3.4 Parameterized Types

The main difference between true generic programming and the ArrayList examples in the previous subsection is the use of the type Object as the basic type for objects that are stored in a list. This has at least two unfortunate consequences: First, it makes it necessary to use type-casting in almost every case when an element is retrieved from that list. Second, since any type of object can legally be added to the list, there is no way for the compiler to detect an attempt to add the wrong type of object to the list; the error will be detected only at run time when the object is retrieved from the list and the attempt to type-cast the object fails. Compare this to arrays. An array of type BaseType[ ] can **only** hold objects of type BaseType. An attempt to store an object of the wrong type in the array will be detected by the compiler, and there is no need to type-cast items that are retrieved from the array back to type BaseType.

To address this problem, Java 5.0 introduced **parameterized types**. ArrayList is an example: Instead of using the plain "ArrayList" type, it is possible to use ArrayList<BaseType>, where BaseType is any object type, that is, the name of a class or of an interface. (BaseType **cannot** be one of the primitive types.) ArrayList<BaseType> can be used to create lists that can hold only objects of type BaseType. For example,

```
ArrayList<ColoredRect> rects;
```

declares a variable named rects of type ArrayList<ColoredRect>, and

```
rects = new ArrayList<ColoredRect>();
```

sets rects to refer to a newly created list that can only hold objects belonging to the class ColoredRect (or to a subclass). The funny-looking name "ArrayList<ColoredRect>" is being used here in exactly the same way as an ordinary class name—don't let the "<ColoredRect>" confuse you; it's just part of the name of the type. When a statement such as rects.add(x); occurs in the program, the compiler can check whether x is in fact of type ColoredRect. If not, the compiler will report a syntax error. When an object is retrieve from the list, the compiler knows that the object must be of type ColoredRect, so no type-cast is necessary. You can say simply:

```
ColoredRect rect = rects.get(i)
```

You can even refer directly to an instance variable in the object, such as rects.get(i).color. This makes using ArrayList<ColoredRect> very similar to using ColoredRect[ ] with the added advantage that the list can grow to any size. Note that if a for-each loop is used to process the items in rects, the type of the loop control variable can be ColoredRect, and no type-cast is necessary. For example, when using ArrayList<ColoredRect> as the type for the list rects, the code for drawing all the rectangles in the list could be rewritten as:

```
for ( ColoredRect rect : rects ) {
    g.setColor( rect.color );
    g.fillRect( rect.x, rect.y, rect.width, rect.height);
    g.setColor( Color.BLACK );
    g.drawRect( rect.x, rect.y, rect.width - 1, rect.height - 1);
}
```

You can use ArrayList<ColoredRect> anyplace where you could use a normal type: to declare variables, as the type of a formal parameter in a subroutine, or as the return type of a subroutine. You can even create a subclass of ArrayList<ColoredRect>! (Nevertheless, technically speaking, ArrayList<ColoredRect> is not considered to be a separate class from ArrayList. An object of

a subroutine. You can even create a subclass of ArrayList<ColoredRect>! (Nevertheless, technically speaking, ArrayList<ColoredRect> is not considered to be a separate class from ArrayList. An object of type ArrayList<ColoredRect> actually belongs to the class ArrayList, but the compiler restricts the type of objects that can be added to the list.)

The only drawback to using parameterized types is that the base type cannot be a primitive type. For example, there is no such thing as "ArrayList<int>". However, this is not such a big drawback as it might seem at first, because of the "wrapper types" and "autoboxing" that were introduced in Subsection 5.3.2. A wrapper type such as Double or Integer can be used as a base type for a parameterized type. An object of type ArrayList<Double> can hold objects of type Double. Since each object of type Double holds a value of type double, it's almost like having a list of doubles. If numlist is declared to be of type ArrayList<Double> and if x is of type double, then the value of x can be added to the list by saying:

```
numlist.add( new Double(x) );
```

Furthermore, because of autoboxing, the compiler will automatically do double-to-Double and Double-to-double type conversions when necessary. This means that the compiler will treat "numlist.add(x)" as begin equivalent to "numlist.add(new Double(x))". So, behind the scenes, "numlist.add(x)" is actually adding an object to the list, but it looks a lot as if you are working with a list of doubles.

* * *

The sample program **SimplePaint2.java** demonstrates the use of parameterized types. In this program, the user can sketch curves in a drawing area by clicking and dragging with the mouse. The curves can be of any color, and the user can select the drawing color using a menu. The background color of the drawing area can also be selected using a menu. And there is a "Control" menu that contains several commands: An "Undo" command, which removes the most recently drawn curve from the screen, a "Clear" command that removes all the curves, and a "Use Symmetry" command that turns a symmetry feature on and off. Curves that are drawn by the user when the symmetry option is on are reflected horizontally and vertically to produce a symmetric pattern. You can try an applet version of the program in the on-line version of this section.

Unlike the original SimplePaint program in Subsection 6.4.4, this new version uses a data structure to store information about the picture that has been drawn by the user. This data is used in the paintComponent() method to redraw the picture whenever necessary. Thus, the picture doesn't disappear when, for example, the picture is covered and then uncovered. The data structure is implemented using ArrayLists.

The main data for a curve consists of a list of the points on the curve. This data can be stored in an object of type ArrayList<Point>, where java.awt.Point is one of Java's standard classes. (A Point object contains two public integer variables x and y that represent the coordinates of a point.) However, to redraw the curve, we also need to know its color, and we need to know whether the symmetry option should be applied to the curve. All the data that is needed to redraw the curve can be grouped into an object of type CurveData that is defined as

```
private static class CurveData {
    Color color;    // The color of the curve.
    boolean symmetric; // Are horizontal and vertical reflections also drawn?
    ArrayList<Point> points; // The points on the curve.
}
```

However, a picture can contain many curves, not just one, so to store all the data necessary to redraw the entire picture, we need a **list** of objects of type CurveData. For this list, we can use a variable curves declared as

```
ArrayList<CurveData> curves = new ArrayList<CurveData>();
```

Here we have a list of objects, where each object contains a list of points as part of its data! Let's look at a few examples of processing this data structure. When the user clicks the mouse on the drawing surface, it's the start of a new curve, and a new CurveData object must be created and added to the list of curves. The instance variables in the new CurveData object must also be initialized. Here is the code from the mousePressed() routine that does this:

```
currentCurve = new CurveData();          // Create a new CurveData object.

currentCurve.color = currentColor;       // The color of the curve is taken from an //
                                         instance variable that represents the //
                                         currently selected drawing color.

currentCurve.symmetric =                 // The "symmetric" property of the curve
useSymmetry;                             // is also copied from the current value //
                                         of an instance variable, useSymmetry.

currentCurve.points = new ArrayList<Point>();     // Create a new point list object.

currentCurve.points.add( new Point(evt.getX(), evt.getY()) );
```

- The point where the user pressed the mouse is the first point on
- the curve. A new Point object is created to hold the coordinates
- of that point and is added to the list of points for the curve.

```
curves.add(currentCurve);     // Add the CurveData object to the list of curves.
```

As the user drags the mouse, new points are added to currentCurve, and repaint() is called. When the picture is redrawn, the new point will be part of the picture.

The paintComponent() method has to use the data in curves to draw all the curves. The basic structure is a for-each loop that processes the data for each individual curve in turn. This has the form:

```
for ( CurveData curve : curves ) {
   .
   • // Draw the curve represented by the object, curve, of type CurveData.
•
}
```

In the body of this loop, curve.points is a variable of type ArrayList<Point> that holds the list of points on the curve. The i-th point on the curve can be obtained by calling the get() method of this list: curve.points.get(i). This returns a value of type Point which contains instance variables named x and y. We can refer directly to the x-coordinate of the i-th point as:

```
curve.points.get(i).x
```

This might seem rather complicated, but it's a nice example of a complex name that specifies a path to a desired piece of data: Go to the object, curve. Inside curve, go to points. Inside points, get the i-th item. And from that item, get the instance variable named x. Here is the complete definition of the paintCompontent() method:

```
public void paintComponent(Graphics g) {
```

```
super.paintComponent(g);
for ( CurveData curve : curves) {
    g.setColor(curve.color);
    for (int i = 1; i < curve.points.size(); i++) {
```

```
• Draw a line segment from point number i-1 to point number i.
int x1 = curve.points.get(i-1).x;
int y1 = curve.points.get(i-1).y; int
x2 = curve.points.get(i).x; int y2 =
curve.points.get(i).y;
g.drawLine(x1,y1,x2,y2);
if (curve.symmetric) {
        Also draw the horizontal and vertical reflections
        of the line segment.
    int w = getWidth();
    int h = getHeight();
    g.drawLine(w-x1,y1,w-x2,y2);
    g.drawLine(x1,h-y1,x2,h-y2);
    g.drawLine(w-x1,h-y1,w-x2,h-y2);
}
}
}
} // end paintComponent()
```

I encourage you to read the full source code, **SimplePaint2.java**. In addition to serving as an example of using parameterized types, it also serves an another example of creating and using menus.

7.3.5 Vectors

The ArrayList class was introduced in Java version 1.2, as one of a group of classes designed for working with collections of objects. We'll look at these "collection classes" in Chapter 10. Early versions of Java did not include ArrayList, but they did have a very similar class named java.util.Vector. You can still see Vectors used in older code and in many of Java's standard classes, so it's worth knowing about them. Using a Vector is similar to using an ArrayList, except that different names are used for some commonly used instance methods, and some instance methods in one class don't correspond to any instance method in the other class.

Like an ArrayList, a Vector is similar to an array of Objects that can grow to be as large as necessary. The default constructor, new Vector(), creates a vector with no elements. Suppose that vec is a Vector. Then we have:

- vec.size() — a function that returns the number of elements currently in the vector.
- vec.elementAt(N) — returns the N-th element of the vector, for an integer N. N must be in the range 0 to vec.size()-1. This is the same as get(N) for an ArrayList.
- vec.setElementAt(obj,N) — sets the N-th in element in the vector to be obj. N must be the range 0 to vec.size()-1. This is the same as set(N,obj) for an ArrayList.
- vec.addElement(obj) — adds the Object, obj, to the end of the vector. This is the same as the add() method of an ArrayList.
- vec.removeElement(obj) — removes obj from the vector, if it occurs. Only the first occurrence is removed. This is the same remove(obj) for an ArrayList. as

- vec.removeElementAt(N) — removes the N-th element, for an integer N. N must be in the range 0 to vec.size()-1. This is the same as remove(N) for an ArrayList.
- vec.setSize(N) — sets the size of the vector to N. If there were more than N elements in vec, the extra elements are removed. If there were fewer than N elements, extra spaces are filled with null. The ArrayList class, unfortunately, does not have a setSize() method.

The Vector class includes many more methods, but these are probably the most commonly used. Note that in Java 5.0, Vector can be used as a paramaterized type in exactly the same way as ArrayList. That is, if BaseType is any class or interface name, then Vector<BaseType> represents vectors that can hold only objects of type BaseType.

7.4 Searching and Sorting

Two array processing techniques that are particularly common are **searching** and **sort-ing** . Searching here refers to finding an item in the array that meets some specified criterion. Sorting refers to rearranging all the items in the array into increasing or decreasing order (where the meaning of increasing and decreasing can depend on the context).

Sorting and searching are often discussed, in a theoretical sort of way, using an array of numbers as an example. In practical situations, though, more interesting types of data are usually involved. For example, the array might be a mailing list, and each element of the array might be an object containing a name and address. Given the name of a person, you might want to look up that person's address. This is an example of searching, since you want to find the object in the array that contains the given name. It would also be useful to be able to sort the array according to various criteria. One example of sorting would be ordering the elements of the array so that the names are in alphabetical order. Another example would be to order the elements of the array according to zip code before printing a set of mailing labels. (This kind of sorting can get you a cheaper postage rate on a large mailing.)

This example can be generalized to a more abstract situation in which we have an array that contains objects, and we want to search or sort the array based on the value of one of the instance variables in that array. We can use some terminology here that originated in work with "databases," which are just large, organized collections of data. We refer to each of the objects in the array as a **record** . The instance variables in an object are then called **fields** of the record. In the mailing list example, each record would contain a name and address. The fields of the record might be the first name, last name, street address, state, city and zip code. For the purpose of searching or sorting, one of the fields is designated to be the **key** field. Searching then means finding a record in the array that has a specified value in its key field. Sorting means moving the records around in the array so that the key fields of the record are in increasing (or decreasing) order.

In this section, most of my examples follow the tradition of using arrays of numbers. But I'll also give a few examples using records and keys, to remind you of the more practical applications.

7.4.1 Searching

There is an obvious algorithm for searching for a particular item in an array: Look at each item in the array in turn, and check whether that item is the one you are looking for. If so, the search is finished. If you look at every item without finding the one you want, then you can be sure that the item is not in the array. It's easy to write a subroutine to implement this algorithm. Let's say the array that you want to search is an array of ints. Here is a method that will search the array for a specified integer. If the integer is found, the method returns the index of the location in the array where it is found. If the integer is not in the array, the method returns the value -1 as a signal that the integer could not be found:

/**

```
 • Searches the array A for the integer N. If N is not in the array,
 • then -1 is returned. If N is in the array, then return value is
 • the first integer i that satisfies A[i] == N.
 */
static int find(int[] A, int N) {

   for (int index = 0; index < A.length; index++) {
      if ( A[index] == N )
         return index;    // N has been found at this index!
   }

   • If we get this far, then N has not been found
   • anywhere in the array. Return a value of -1.

   return -1;

}
```

This method of searching an array by looking at each item in turn is called **linear search** . If nothing is known about the order of the items in the array, then there is really no better alternative algorithm. But if the elements in the array are known to be in increasing or decreas-ing order, then a much faster search algorithm can be used. An array in which the elements are in order is said to be **sorted** . Of course, it takes some work to sort an array, but if the array is to be searched many times, then the work done in sorting it can really pay off.

Binary search is a method for searching for a given item in a **sorted** array. Although the implementation is not trivial, the basic idea is simple: If you are searching for an item in a sorted list, then it is possible to eliminate half of the items in the list by inspecting a single item. For example, suppose that you are looking for the number 42 in a sorted array of 1000 integers. Let's assume that the array is sorted into increasing order. Suppose you check item number 500 in the array, and find that the item is 93. Since 42 is less than 93, and since the elements in the array are in increasing order, we can conclude that if 42 occurs in the array at all, then it must occur somewhere before location 500. All the locations numbered 500 or above contain values that are greater than or equal to 93. These locations can be eliminated as possible locations of the number 42.

The next obvious step is to check location 250. If the number at that location is, say, -21, then you can eliminate locations before 250 and limit further search to locations between 251 and 499. The next test will limit the search to about 125 locations, and the one after that to about 62. After just 10 steps, there is only one location left. This is a whole lot better than looking through every element in the array. If there were a million items, it would still take only 20 steps for binary search to search the array! (Mathematically, the number of steps is approximately equal to the logarithm, in the base 2, of the number of items in the array.)

In order to make binary search into a Java subroutine that searches an array A for an item N, we just have to keep track of the range of locations that could possibly contain N. At each step, as we eliminate possibilities, we reduce the size of this range. The basic operation is to look at the item in the middle of the range. If this item is greater than N, then the second half of the range can be eliminated. If it is less than N, then the first half of the range can be eliminated. If the number in the middle just happens to be N exactly, then the search is finished. If the size of the range decreases to zero, then the number N does

not occur in the array. Here is a subroutine that returns the location of N in a sorted array A. If N cannot be found in the array, then a value of -1 is returned instead:

```
/**
```

```
• Searches the array A for the integer N.
• Precondition: A must be sorted into increasing order.
• Postcondition: If N is in the array, then the return value, i,
•     satisfies A[i] == N.  If N is not in the array, then the
•     return value is -1.
*/
static int binarySearch(int[] A, int N) {

    int lowestPossibleLoc = 0;
    int highestPossibleLoc = A.length - 1;

    while (highestPossibleLoc >= lowestPossibleLoc) {
        int middle = (lowestPossibleLoc + highestPossibleLoc) / 2; if
        (A[middle] == N) {
                  • N has been found at this index!
            return middle;
        }
        else if (A[middle] > N) {
                  • eliminate locations >= middle
            highestPossibleLoc = middle - 1;
        }
        else {
                  • eliminate locations <= middle
            lowestPossibleLoc = middle + 1;
        }
    }

    • At this point, highestPossibleLoc < LowestPossibleLoc,
    • which means that N is known to be not in the array.  Return
    • a -1 to indicate that N could not be found in the array.

    return -1;

}
```

7.4.2 Association Lists

One particularly common application of searching is with **association lists**. The standard example of an association list is a dictionary. A dictionary associates definitions with words. Given a word, you can use the dictionary to look up its definition. We can think of the dictionary as being a list of **pairs** of the form (w,d), where w is a word and d is its definition. A general association list is a list of pairs (k,v), where k is some "key" value, and v is a value associated to that key. In general, we want to assume that no two pairs in the list have the same key. There are two basic operations on association lists: Given a key, k, find the value v associated with k, if any. And given a key, k, and a value v, add the pair (k,v) to the association list (replacing the pair, if any, that had the same key value). The two operations are usually called **get** and **put** .

Association lists are very widely used in computer science. For example, a compiler has to keep track of the location in memory associated with each variable. It can do this with an association list in which each key is a variable name and the associated value is the address of that variable in memory. Another example would be a mailing list, if we think of it as associating an address to each name on the list. As a related example, consider a phone directory that associates a phone number to each name. The items in the list could be objects belonging to the class:

```
class PhoneEntry {
    String name;
    String phoneNum;
}
```

The data for a phone directory consists of an array of type PhoneEntry[ ] and an integer variable to keep track of how many entries are actually stored in the directory. The technique of "dynamic arrays" (Subsection 7.3.2) can be used in order to avoid putting an arbitrary limit on the number of entries that the phone directory can hold. Using an ArrayList would be another possibility. A PhoneDirectory class should include instance methods that implement the "get" and "put" operations. Here is one possible simple definition of the class:

```
/**
 • A PhoneDirectory holds a list of names with a phone number for
 • each name.  It is possible to find the number associated with
 • a given name, and to specify the phone number for a given name.
 */
public class PhoneDirectory {

    /**
     • An object of type PhoneEntry holds one name/number
     pair. */
    private static class PhoneEntry {
        String name;      // The name.
        String number;    // The associated phone number.
    }

    private PhoneEntry[] data;      // Array that holds the name/number pairs.
    private int dataCount;          // The number of pairs stored in the array.

    /**
     • Constructor creates an initially empty directory. */
    public PhoneDirectory() {
        data = new PhoneEntry[1];
        dataCount = 0;
    }

    /**
     • Looks for a name/number pair with a given name.  If found, the index
     • of the pair in the data array is returned.  If no pair contains the
     • given name, then the return value is -1.
     */
    private int find( String name ) {
        for (int i = 0; i < dataCount; i++) {
            if (data[i].name.equals(name))
                return i;          // The name has been found in position i.
        }
```

```
    return -1;     // The name does not exist in the array.
}

/**
 * Finds the phone number, if any, for a given name.
```

```
  • @return The phone number associated with the name; if the name does
  •     not occur in the phone directory, then the return value is null.
  */
public String getNumber( String name ) {
   int position = find(name);
   if (position == -1)
      return null;      // There is no phone entry for the given name.
   else
      return data[position].number;
}

/**
  • Associates a given name with a given phone number.  If the name
  • already exists in the phone directory, then the new number replaces
  • the old one.  Otherwise, a new name/number pair is added.  The
  • name and number should both be non-null.  An IllegalArgumentException
  • is thrown if this is not the case.
  */
public void putNumber( String name, String number ) { if
   (name == null || number == null)
      throw new IllegalArgumentException("name and number cannot be null");
   int i = find(name);
   if (i >= 0) {
         • The name already exists, in position i in the array.
         • Just replace the old number at that position with the new.
      data[i].number = number;
   }
   else {
        • Add a new name/number pair to the array.  If the array is
        • already full, first create a new, larger array.
      if (dataCount == data.length) {
         PhoneEntry[] newData = new PhoneEntry[ 2*data.length ];
         System.arraycopy(newData,0,data,0,dataCount); data =
         newData;
      }
      PhoneEntry newEntry = new PhoneEntry();  // Create a new pair.
      newEntry.name = name;
      newEntry.number = number;
      data[dataCount] = newEntry;     // Add the new pair to the array.
      dataCount++;
   }
}

} // end class PhoneDirectory
```

The class defines a private instance method, find(), that uses linear search to find the position of a given name in the array of name/number pairs. The find() method is used both in the getNumber() method and in the putNumber() method. Note in particular that putNumber(name,number) has to check whether the name is in the phone directory. If so, it just changes the number in the existing entry; if not, it has to create a new phone entry and add it to the array.

This class could use a lot of improvement. For one thing, it would be nice to use binary search instead of simple linear search in the getNumber method. However, we could only do that if the list of PhoneEntries were sorted into alphabetical order according to name. In fact, it's really not all that hard to keep the list of entries in sorted order, as you'll see in the next subsection.

7.4.3 Insertion Sort

We've seen that there are good reasons for sorting arrays. There are many algorithms available for doing so. One of the easiest to understand is the **insertion sort** algorithm. This method is also applicable to the problem of **keeping** a list in sorted order as you add new items to the list. Let's consider that case first:

Suppose you have a sorted list and you want to add an item to that list. If you want to make sure that the modified list is still sorted, then the item must be inserted into the right location, with all the smaller items coming before it and all the bigger items after it. This will mean moving each of the bigger items up one space to make room for the new item.

```
/*
 • Precondition: itemsInArray is the number of items that are
 •     stored in A. These items must be in increasing order
 •     (A[0] <= A[1] <= ... <= A[itemsInArray-1]).
 •     The array size is at least one greater than itemsInArray.
 • Postcondition: The number of items has increased by one,
 •     newItem has been added to the array, and all the items
 •     in the array are still in increasing order.
 • Note: To complete the process of inserting an item in the
 •     array, the variable that counts the number of items
 •     in the array must be incremented, after calling this
 •     subroutine.
 */
static void insert(int[] A, int itemsInArray, int newItem) {

    int loc = itemsInArray - 1;      // Start at the end of the array.

    /* Move items bigger than newItem up one space;
       Stop when a smaller item is encountered or when the
       beginning of the array (loc == 0) is reached. */

    while (loc >= 0 && A[loc] > newItem) {
        A[loc + 1] = A[loc];       // Bump item from A[loc] up to loc+1.
        loc = loc - 1;             // Go on to next location.
    }

    A[loc + 1] = newItem;   // Put newItem in last vacated space.

}
```

Conceptually, this could be extended to a sorting method if we were to take all the items out of an unsorted array, and then insert them back into the array one-by-one, keeping the list in sorted order as we do so. Each insertion can be done using the insert routine given above. In the actual algorithm, we don't really take all the items from the array; we just remember what part of the array has been sorted:

```
static void insertionSort(int[] A) {
        // Sort the array A into increasing order.
```

```
int itemsSorted; // Number of items that have been sorted so far.
for (itemsSorted = 1; itemsSorted < A.length; itemsSorted++) {
```

```
        • Assume that items A[0], A[1], ... A[itemsSorted-1]
        • have already been sorted. Insert A[itemsSorted]
        • into the sorted part of the list.

      int temp = A[itemsSorted];    // The item to be inserted.
      int loc = itemsSorted - 1;    // Start at end of list.

      while (loc >= 0 && A[loc] > temp) {
         A[loc + 1] = A[loc]; // Bump item from A[loc] up to loc+1.
         loc = loc - 1;              // Go on to next location.
      }

      A[loc + 1] = temp; // Put temp in last vacated space.
   }
}
```

The following is an illustration of one stage in insertion sort. It shows what happens during one execution of the for loop in the above method, when itemsSorted is 5:

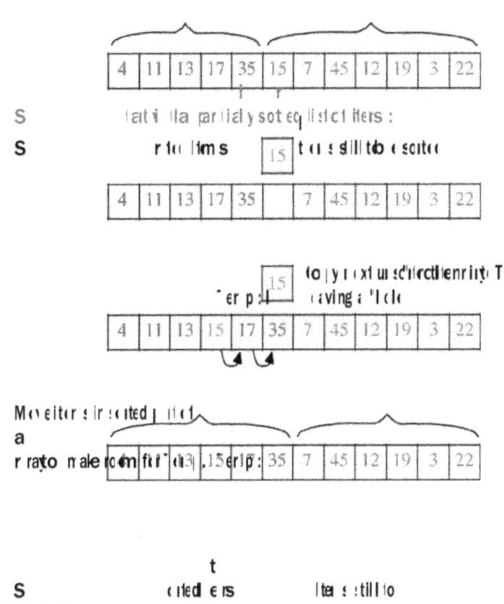

7.4.4 Selection Sort

Another typical sorting method uses the idea of finding the biggest item in the list and moving it to the end—which is where it belongs if the list is to be in increasing order. Once the biggest item is in its correct location, you can then apply the same idea to the remaining items. That is, find the next-biggest item, and move it into the next-to-last space, and so forth. This algorithm is called **selection sort** . It’s easy to write:

```
static void selectionSort(int[] A) {
        // Sort A into increasing order, using selection sort

    for (int lastPlace = A.length-1; lastPlace > 0; lastPlace–) {
            • Find the largest item among A[0], A[1], ...,
            • A[lastPlace], and move it into position lastPlace
            • by swapping it with the number that is currently
            • in position lastPlace.

        int maxLoc = 0;   // Location of largest item seen so far.

        for (int j = 1; j <= lastPlace; j++) {
            if (A[j] > A[maxLoc]) {
                    • Since A[j] is bigger than the maximum we've seen
                    • so far, j is the new location of the maximum value
                    • we've seen so far.
                maxLoc = j;
            }
        }

        int temp = A[maxLoc];   // Swap largest item with A[lastPlace].
        A[maxLoc] = A[lastPlace];
        A[lastPlace] = temp;

    }  // end of for loop

}
```

Insertion sort and selection sort are suitable for sorting fairly small arrays (up to a few hun-dred elements, say). There are more complicated sorting algorithms that are much faster than insertion sort and selection sort for large arrays. I'll discuss one such algorithm in Chapter 9.

* * *

A variation of selection sort is used in the Hand class that was introduced in Subsection 5.4.1. (By the way, you are finally in a position to fully understand the source code for both the Hand class and the Deck class from that section. See the source files **Deck.java** and **Hand.java**.)

In the Hand class, a hand of playing cards is represented by a Vector. This is older code, which used Vector instead of ArrayList, and I have chosen not to modify it so that you would see at least one example of using Vectors. See Subsection 7.3.5 for a discussion of Vectors.

The objects stored in the Vector are of type Card. A Card object contains instance methods getSuit() and getValue() that can be used to determine the suit and value of the card. In my sorting method, I actually create a new vector and move the cards one-by-one from the old vector to the new vector. The cards are selected from the old vector in increasing order. In the end, the new vector becomes the hand and the old vector is discarded. This is certainly not the most efficient procedure! But hands of cards are so small that the inefficiency is negligible. Here is the code for sorting cards by suit:

```
/**
 • Sorts the cards in the hand so that cards of the same suit are
```

```
 • grouped together, and within a suit the cards are sorted by value.
 • Note that aces are considered to have the lowest value, 1.
 */
public void sortBySuit() {
   Vector newHand = new Vector();
   while (hand.size() > 0) {
```

```
            int pos = 0;     // Position of minimal card found so far.
            Card c = (Card)hand.elementAt(0);    // The minimal card.
            for (int i = 1; i < hand.size(); i++) {
                Card c1 = (Card)hand.elementAt(i);
                if ( c1.getSuit() < c.getSuit() ||
                        (c1.getSuit() == c.getSuit() && c1.getValue() < c.getValue()) ) {
                    pos = i;
                    c = c1;
                }
            }
            hand.removeElementAt(pos);
            newHand.addElement(c);
        }
        hand = newHand;
    }
```

This example illustrates the fact that comparing items in a list is not usually as simple as using the operator "<". In this case, we consider one card to be less than another if the suit of the first card is less than the suit of the second, and also if the suits are the same and the value of the second card is less than the value of the first. The second part of this test ensures that cards with the same suit will end up sorted by value.

Sorting a list of Strings raises a similar problem: the "<" operator is not defined for strings. However, the String class does define a compareTo method. If str1 and str2 are of type String, then

```
str1.compareTo(str2)
```

returns an int that is 0 when str1 is equal to str2, is less than 0 when str1 preceeds str2, and is greater than 0 when str1 follows str2. The definition of "succeeds" and "follows" for strings uses what is called **lexicographic ordering** , which is based on the Unicode values of the characters in the strings. Lexicographic ordering is not the same as alphabetical ordering, even for strings that consist entirely of letters (because in lexicographic ordering, all the upper case letters come before all the lower case letters). However, for words consisting strictly of the 26 lower case letters in the English alphabet, lexicographic and alphabetic ordering are the same. Thus, if str1 and str2 are strings containing only letters from the English alphabet, then the test

```
str1.toLowerCase().compareTo(str2.toLowerCase()) < 0
```

is true if and only if str1 comes before str2 in alphabetical order.

7.4.5 Unsorting

I can't resist ending this section on sorting with a related problem that is much less common, but is a bit more fun. That is the problem of putting the elements of an array into a random order. The typical case of this problem is shuffling a deck of cards. A good algorithm for shuffling is similar to selection sort, except that instead of moving the biggest item to the end of the list, an item is selected at random and moved to the end of the list. Here is a subroutine to shuffle an array of ints:

```
/**
```

- Postcondition: The items in A have been rearranged into a random order. */
static void shuffle(int[] A) {

```
        for (int lastPlace = A.length-1; lastPlace > 0; lastPlace–) {
              • Choose a random location from among 0,1,...,lastPlace.
           int randLoc = (int)(Math.random()*(lastPlace+1));
              • Swap items in locations randLoc and lastPlace.
           int temp = A[randLoc];
           A[randLoc] = A[lastPlace];
           A[lastPlace] = temp;
        }
    }
```

7.5 Multi-dimensional Arrays

Any type can be used as the base type of an array. You can have an array of ints, an array of Strings, an array of Objects, and so on. In particular, since an array type is a first-class Java type, you can have an array of arrays. For example, an array of ints has type int[ ]. This means that there is automatically another type, int[ ][ ], which represents an "array of arrays of ints". Such an array is said to be a **two-dimensional array** . Of course once you have the type int[ ][ ], there is nothing to stop you from forming the type int[ ][ ][ ], which represents a **three-dimensional array** —and so on. There is no limit on the number of dimensions that an array type can have. However, arrays of dimension three or higher are fairly uncommon, and I concentrate here mainly on two-dimensional arrays. The type BaseType[ ][ ] is usually read "two-dimensional array of BaseType" or "BaseType array array".

7.5.1 Creating Two-dimensional Arrays

The declaration statement "int[][] A;" declares a variable named A of type int[ ][ ]. This variable can hold a reference to an object of type int[ ][ ]. The assignment statement "A = new int[3][4];" creates a new two-dimensional array object and sets A to point to the newly cre-ated object. As usual, the declaration and assignment could be combined in a single declaration statement "int[][] A = new int[3][4];". The newly created object is an array of arrays-of-ints. The notation int[3][4] indicates that there are 3 arrays-of-ints in the array A, and that there are 4 ints in each array-of-ints. However, trying to think in such terms can get a bit confusing—as you might have already noticed. So it is customary to think of a two-dimensional array of items as a rectangular **grid** or **matrix** of items. The notation "new int[3][4]" can then be taken to describe a grid of ints with 3 rows and 4 columns. The following picture might help:

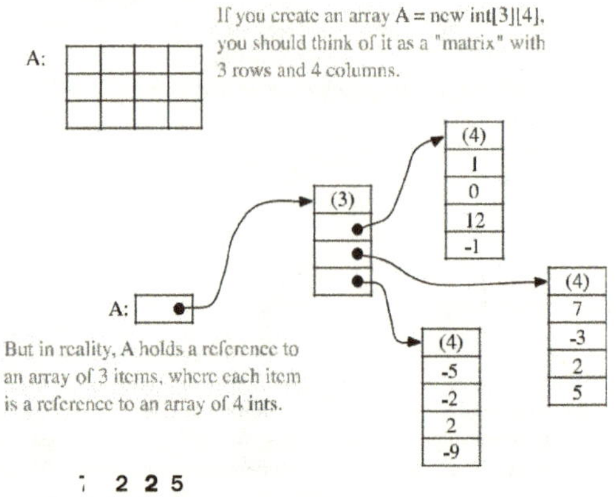

A:
If you create an array A = new int[3][4], you should think of it as a "matrix" with 3 rows and 4 columns.
(3)
(4)
1
0
12
-1
(4)
7
-3
2
5
A:
But in reality, A holds a reference to an array of 3 items, where each item is a reference to an array of 4 ints.
(4)
-5
-2
2
-9

7 2 2 5
5 03 1² 9:

For the most part, you can ignore the reality and keep the picture of a grid in mind. Sometimes, though, you will need to remember that each row in the grid is really an array in itself. These arrays can be referred to as A[0], A[1], and A[2]. Each row is in fact a value of type int[ ]. It could, for example, be passed to a subroutine that asks for a parameter of type int[ ].

The notation A[1] refers to one of the rows of the array A. Since A[1] is itself an array of ints, you can use another subscript to refer to one of the positions in that row. For example, A[1][3] refers to item number 3 in row number 1. Keep in mind, of course, that both rows and columns are numbered starting from zero. So, in the above example, A[1][3] is 5. More generally, A[i][j] refers to the grid position in row number i and column number j. The 12 items in A are named as follows:

```
A[0][0]   A[0][1]   A[0][2]   A[0][3]
A[1][0]   A[1][1]   A[1][2]   A[1][3]
A[2][0]   A[2][1]   A[2][2]   A[2][3]
```

A[i][j] is actually a variable of type int. You can assign integer values to it or use it in any other context where an integer variable is allowed.

It might be worth noting that A.length gives the number of rows of A. To get the number of columns in A, you have to ask how many ints there are in a row; this number would be given by A[0].length, or equivalently by A[1].length or A[2].length. (There is actually no rule that says that all the rows of an array must have the same length, and some advanced applications of arrays use varying-sized rows. But if you use the new operator to create an array in the manner described above, you'll always get an array with equal-sized rows.)

Three-dimensional arrays are treated similarly. For example, a three-dimensional array of ints could be created with the declaration statement "int[][][] B = new int[7][5][11];". It's possible to visualize the value of B as a solid 7-by-5-by-11 block of cells. Each cell holds an int and represents one position in the three-dimensional array. Individual positions in the array can be referred to with variable names of the form B[i][j][k]. Higher-dimensional arrays follow the same pattern, although for dimensions greater than three, there is no easy way to visualize the structure of the array.

It's possible to fill a multi-dimensional array with specified items at the time it is declared. Recall that when an ordinary one-dimensional array variable is declared, it can be assigned an "array initializer," which is just a list of values enclosed between braces, { and }. Array initializers can also be used when a multi-dimensional array is declared. An initializer for a two-dimensional array consists of a list of one-dimensional array initializers, one for each row in the two-dimensional array. For example, the array A shown in the picture above could be created with:

```
int[][]    A  =  {  {  1,  0, 12, -1 },
                     {  7, -3,  2,  5 },
                     { -5, -2,  2, -9 }
                 };
```

If no initializer is provided for an array, then when the array is created it is automatically filled with the appropriate value: zero for numbers, false for boolean, and null for objects.

7.5.2 Using Two-dimensional Arrays

Just as in the case of one-dimensional arrays, two-dimensional arrays are often processed using for statements. To process all the items in a two-dimensional array, you have to use one for statement nested inside another. If the array A is declared as

```
int[][]    A  =  new int[3][4];
```

then you could store a zero into each location in A with:

```
for (int row = 0;      row < 3;    row++) {
   for (int column = 0; column < 4; column++) {
      A[row][column] = 0;
   }
}
```

The first time the outer for loop executes (with row = 0), the inner for loop fills in the four values in the first row of A, namely A[0][0] = 0, A[0][1] = 0, A[0][2] = 0, and A[0][3]
• 0. The next execution of the outer for loop fills in the second row of A. And the third and final execution of the outer loop fills in the final row of A.

Similarly, you could add up all the items in A with:

```
int sum = 0;
for (int i = 0; i < 3; i++)
   for (int j = 0; j < 4; j++)
      sum = sum + A[i][j];
```

This could even be done with nested for-each loops. Keep in mind that the elements in A are objects of type int[ ], while the elements in each row of A are of type int:

```
int sum = 0;
for ( int[] row : A ) {           // For each row in A...
   for ( int item : row )         // For each item in that row...
      sum = sum + item;           // Add item to the sum.
```

}

To process a three-dimensional array, you would, of course, use triply nested for loops.

* * *

A two-dimensional array can be used whenever the data that is being represented can be arranged into rows and columns in a natural way. Often, the grid is built into the problem. For example, a chess board is a grid with 8 rows and 8 columns. If a class named ChessPiece is available to represent individual chess pieces, then the contents of a chess board could be represented by a two-dimensional array:

```
ChessPiece[][]  board  =  new ChessPiece[8][8];
```

Or consider the "mosaic" of colored rectangles used in an example in Subsection 4.6.2. The mosaic is implemented by a class named **MosaicCanvas.java**. The data about the color of each of the rectangles in the mosaic is stored in an instance variable named grid of type Color[ ][ ]. Each position in this grid is occupied by a value of type Color. There is one position in the grid for each colored rectangle in the mosaic. The actual two-dimensional array is created by the statement:

```
grid  =  new Color[ROWS][COLUMNS];
```

where ROWS is the number of rows of rectangles in the mosaic and COLUMNS is the number of columns. The value of the Color variable grid[i][j] is the color of the rectangle in row number i and column number j. When the color of that rectangle is changed to some color, c, the value stored in grid[i][j] is changed with a statement of the form "grid[i][j] = c;". When the mosaic is redrawn, the values stored in the two-dimensional array are used to decide what color to make each rectangle. Here is a simplified version of the code from the MosaicCanvas class that draws all the colored rectangles in the grid. You can see how it uses the array:

```
int rowHeight = getHeight() / ROWS;
int colWidth = getWidth() / COLUMNS;
for (int row = 0; row < ROWS; row++) {
    for (int col = 0; col < COLUMNS; col++) {
        g.setColor( grid[row][col] ); // Get color from array.
        g.fillRect( col*colWidth, row*rowHeight,
                                colWidth, rowHeight );
    }
}
```

Sometimes two-dimensional arrays are used in problems in which the grid is not so visually obvious. Consider a company that owns 25 stores. Suppose that the company has data about the profit earned at each store for each month in the year 2006. If the stores are numbered from 0 to 24, and if the twelve months from January '06 through December '06 are numbered from 0 to 11, then the profit data could be stored in an array, profit, constructed as follows:

```
double[][]  profit  =  new double[25][12];
```

profit[3][2] would be the amount of profit earned at store number 3 in March, and more generally, profit[storeNum][monthNum] would be the amount of profit earned in store number storeNum in month number monthNum. In this example, the one-dimensional array profit[storeNum] has a very useful meaning: It is just the profit data for one particular store for the whole year.

Let's assume that the profit array has already been filled with data. This data can be processed in a lot of interesting ways. For example, the total profit for the company—for the whole year from all its stores—can be calculated by adding up all the entries in the array:

```
double totalProfit;      // Company's total profit in 2006.

totalProfit = 0;
for (int store = 0; store < 25; store++) {
    for (int month = 0; month < 12; month++)
        totalProfit += profit[store][month];
}
```

Sometimes it is necessary to process a single row or a single column of an array, not the entire array. For example, to compute the total profit earned by the company in December, that is, in month number 11, you could use the loop:

```
double decemberProfit = 0.0;
for (storeNum = 0; storeNum < 25; storeNum++)
    decemberProfit += profit[storeNum][11];
```

Let's extend this idea to create a one-dimensional array that contains the total profit for each month of the year:

```
double[] monthlyProfit;    // Holds profit for each month.
monthlyProfit = new double[12];

for (int month = 0; month < 12; month++) {
    • compute the total profit from all stores in this month.
    monthlyProfit[month] = 0.0;
    for (int store = 0; store < 25; store++) {
                Add the profit from this store in this month
                into the total profit figure for the month.
        monthlyProfit[month] += profit[store][month];
    }
}
```

As a final example of processing the profit array, suppose that we wanted to know which store generated the most profit over the course of the year. To do this, we have to add up the monthly profits for each store. In array terms, this means that we want to find the sum of each row in the array. As we do this, we need to keep track of which row produces the largest total.

```
double maxProfit; //     Maximum profit earned by a store.
int bestStore;           // The number of the store with the
                         //    maximum profit.

double total = 0.0;         // Total profit for one store.

// First compute the       profit from store number 0.

for (int month = 0;      month < 12; month++)
    total += profit[0][month];

bestStore = 0;           // Start by assuming that the best
maxProfit = total;       // store is store number 0.
```

- Now, go through the other stores, and whenever we
- find one with a bigger profit than maxProfit, revise
- the assumptions about bestStore and maxProfit.

for (store = 1; store < 25; store++) {

- Compute this store's profit for the year.

total = 0.0;

```
for (month = 0; month < 12; month++)
      total += profit[store][month];
```

- Compare this store's profits with the highest
- profit we have seen among the preceding stores.

```
  if (total > maxProfit) {
    maxProfit = total;        // Best profit seen so far! //
    bestStore = store;        It came from this store.
}

}// end for
```

- At this point, maxProfit is the best profit of any
- of the 25 stores, and bestStore is a store that
- generated that profit. (Note that there could also be
- other stores that generated exactly the same profit.)

7.5.3 Example: Checkers

For the rest of this section, we'll look at a more substantial example. We look at a program that lets two users play checkers against each other. A player moves by clicking on the piece to be moved and then on the empty square to which it is to be moved. The squares that the current player can legally click are hilited. The square containing a piece that has been selected to be moved is surrounded by a white border. Other pieces that can legally be moved are surrounded by a cyan-colored border. If a piece has been selected, each empty square that it can legally move to is hilited with a green border. The game enforces the rule that if the current player can jump one of the opponent's pieces, then the player must jump. When a player's piece becomes a king, by reaching the opposite end of the board, a big white "K" is drawn on the piece. You can try an applet version of the program in the on-line version of this section. Here is what it looks like:

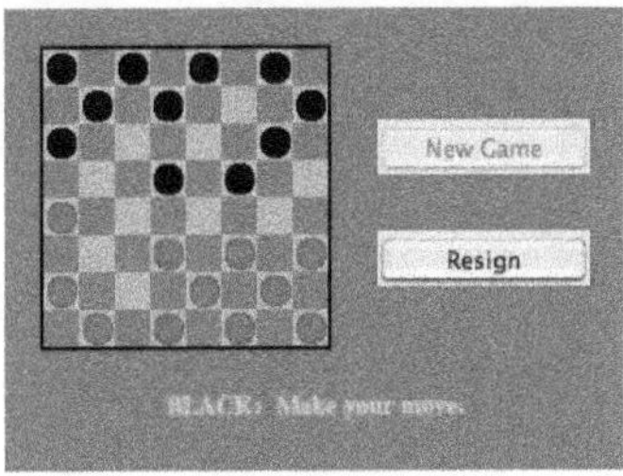

I will only cover a part of the programming of this applet. I encourage you to read the complete source code, **Checkers.java**. At over 750 lines, this is a more substantial example than anything you've seen before in this course, but it's an excellent example of state-based, event-driven programming.

The data about the pieces on the board are stored in a two-dimensional array. Because of the complexity of the program, I wanted to divide it into several classes. In addition to the main class, there are several nested classes. One of these classes is CheckersData, which handles the data for the board. It is mainly this class that I want to talk about.

The CheckersData class has an instance variable named board of type int[][]. The value of board is set to "new int[8][8]", an 8-by-8 grid of integers. The values stored in the grid are defined as constants representing the possible contents of a square on a checkerboard:

```
static final int
          EMPTY = 0,          // Value representing an empty square.
          RED = 1,            // A regular red piece.
          RED_KING = 2,       // A red king.
          BLACK = 3,          // A regular black piece.
          BLACK_KING = 4;     // A black king.
```

The constants RED and BLACK are also used in my program (or, perhaps, misused) to represent the two players in the game. When a game is started, the values in the variable, board, are set to represent the initial state of the board. The grid of values looks like

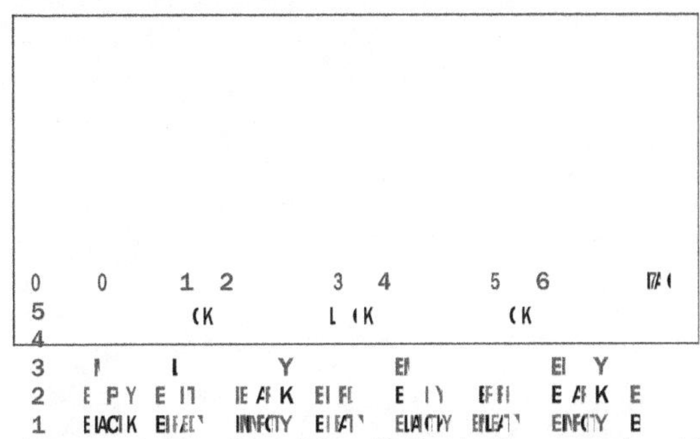

A black piece can only move "down" the grid. That is, the row number of the square it moves to must be greater than the row number of the square it comes from. A red piece can only move up the grid. Kings of either color, of course, can move in both directions.

One function of the CheckersData class is to take care of all the details of making moves on the board. An instance method named makeMove() is provided to do this. When a player moves a piece from one square to another, the values stored at two positions in the array are changed. But that's not all. If the move is a jump, then the piece that was jumped is removed from the board. (The method checks whether the move is a jump by checking if the square to which the piece is moving is two rows away from the square where it starts.) Furthermore, a RED piece that moves to row 0 or a BLACK piece that moves to row 7 becomes a king. This is good programming: the rest of the program doesn't have to worry about any of these details. It just calls this makeMove() method:

```
/**
 * Make the move from (fromRow,fromCol) to (toRow,toCol). It is
 * ASSUMED that this move is legal! If the move is a jump, the
 * jumped piece is removed from the board. If a piece moves
 * to the last row on the opponent's side of the board, the
```

```
 • piece becomes a king.
 */
void makeMove(int fromRow, int fromCol, int toRow, int toCol) {
```

```
board[toRow][toCol] = board[fromRow][fromCol]; // Move the piece.
board[fromRow][fromCol] = EMPTY;

if (fromRow - toRow == 2 || fromRow - toRow == -2) {
    • The move is a jump. Remove the jumped piece from the board.
  int jumpRow = (fromRow + toRow) / 2; // Row of the jumped piece. int
  jumpCol = (fromCol + toCol) / 2; // Column of the jumped piece.
  board[jumpRow][jumpCol] = EMPTY;
}

if (toRow == 0 && board[toRow][toCol] == RED)
  board[toRow][toCol] = RED_KING; // Red piece becomes a king.
if (toRow == 7 && board[toRow][toCol] == BLACK)
  board[toRow][toCol] = BLACK_KING; // Black piece becomes a king.

} // end makeMove()
```

An even more important function of the CheckersData class is to find legal moves on the board. In my program, a move in a Checkers game is represented by an object belonging to the following class:

```
/**
 • A CheckersMove object represents a move in the game of
 • Checkers. It holds the row and column of the piece that is
 • to be moved and the row and column of the square to which
 • it is to be moved. (This class makes no guarantee that
 • the move is legal.)
 */
private static class CheckersMove {

  int fromRow, fromCol;  // Position of piece to be moved.
  int toRow, toCol;      // Square it is to move to.
```

```
CheckersMove(int r1, int c1, int r2, int c2) {
      • Constructor. Set the values of the instance variables.
   fromRow = r1;
   fromCol = c1;
   toRow = r2;
   toCol = c2;
}
boolean isJump() {
      • Test whether this move is a jump. It is assumed that
      • the move is legal. In a jump, the piece moves two
      • rows. (In a regular move, it only moves one row.)
   return (fromRow - toRow == 2 || fromRow - toRow == -2);
}
} // end class CheckersMove.
```

The CheckersData class has an instance method which finds all the legal moves that are currently available for a specified player. This method is a function that returns an array of type CheckersMove[ ]. The array contains all the legal moves, represented as CheckersMove objects. The specification for this method reads


```
/**
 • Return an array containing all the legal CheckersMoves
 • for the specified player on the current board. If the player
 • has no legal moves, null is returned. The value of player
 • should be one of the constants RED or BLACK; if not, null
 • is returned. If the returned value is non-null, it consists
 • entirely of jump moves or entirely of regular moves, since
 • if the player can jump, only jumps are legal moves.
 */
CheckersMove[] getLegalMoves(int player)
```

A brief pseudocode algorithm for the method is

```
Start with an empty list of moves
Find any legal jumps and add them to the list if
there are no jumps:
    Find any other legal moves and add them to the list if
the list is empty:
    return null
else:
    return the list
```

Now, what is this “list”? We have to return the legal moves in an array. But since an array has a fixed size, we can't create the array until we know how many moves there are, and we don't know that until near the end of the method, after we've already made the list! A neat solution is to use an ArrayList instead of an array to hold the moves as we find them. In fact, I use an object defined by the parameterized type ArrayList<CheckersMove> so that the list is restricted to holding objects of type CheckersMove. As we add moves to the list, it will grow just as large as necessary. At the end of the method, we can create the array that we really want and copy the data into it:

```
Let "moves" be an empty
ArrayList<CheckerMove> Find any legal jumps
and add them to moves if moves.size() is 0:
   Find any other legal moves and add them to
moves if moves.size() is 0:
   return null
else:
   Let moveArray be an array of CheckersMoves of length moves.size()
   Copy the contents of moves into moveArray
   return moveArray
```

Now, how do we find the legal jumps or the legal moves? The information we need is in the board array, but it takes some work to extract it. We have to look through all the positions in the array and find the pieces that belong to the current player. For each piece, we have to check each square that it could conceivably move to, and check whether that would be a legal move. There are four squares to consider. For a jump, we want to look at squares that are two rows and two columns away from the piece. Thus, the line in the algorithm that says "Find any legal jumps and add them to moves" expands to:

```
For each row of the board:
   For each column of the board:
      if one of the player's pieces is at this location:
         if it is legal to jump to row + 2, column + 2
              add this move to moves
```

```
if it is legal to jump to row - 2, column + 2 add
     this move to moves
if it is legal to jump to row + 2, column - 2 add
     this move to moves
if it is legal to jump to row - 2, column - 2 add
     this move to moves
```

The line that says "Find any other legal moves and add them to moves" expands to some-thing similar, except that we have to look at the four squares that are one column and one row away from the piece. Testing whether a player can legally move from one given square to another given square is itself non-trivial. The square the player is moving to must actually be on the board, and it must be empty. Furthermore, regular red and black pieces can only move in one direction. I wrote the following utility method to check whether a player can make a given non-jump move:

```
/**
 • This is called by the getLegalMoves() method to determine
 • whether the player can legally move from (r1,c1) to (r2,c2).
 • It is ASSUMED that (r1,c1) contains one of the player's
 • pieces and that (r2,c2) is a neighboring square.
 */
private boolean canMove(int player, int r1, int c1, int r2, int c2) {

   if (r2 < 0 || r2 >= 8 || c2 < 0 || c2 >= 8) return
      false; // (r2,c2) is off the board.

   if (board[r2][c2] != EMPTY)
      return false;    // (r2,c2) already contains a piece.

   if (player == RED) {
      if (board[r1][c1] == RED && r2 > r1)
           return false;     // Regular red piece can only move down.
        return true;    // The move is legal.
   }
   else {
      if (board[r1][c1] == BLACK && r2 < r1)
           return false;     // Regular black piece can only move up.
        return true;    // The move is legal.
   }

} // end canMove()
```

This method is called by my getLegalMoves() method to check whether one of the possible moves that it has found is actually legal. I have a similar method that is called to check whether a jump is legal. In this case, I pass to the method the square containing the player's piece, the square that the player might move to, and the square between those two, which the player would be jumping over. The square that is being jumped must contain one of the opponent's pieces. This method has the specification:

```
/**
 • This is called by other methods to check whether
 • the player can legally jump from (r1,c1) to (r3,c3).
 • It is assumed that the player has a piece at (r1,c1), that
```

- (r3,c3) is a position that is 2 rows and 2 columns distant
- from (r1,c1) and that (r2,c2) is the square between (r1,c1)
- and (r3,c3).

```
*/
private boolean canJump(int player, int r1, int c1,
                                    int r2, int c2, int r3, int c3) { . . .
```

Given all this, you should be in a position to understand the complete getLegalMoves() method. It's a nice way to finish off this chapter, since it combines several topics that we've looked at: one-dimensional arrays, ArrayLists, and two-dimensional arrays:

```
CheckersMove[] getLegalMoves(int player) {

   if (player != RED && player != BLACK)
      return null;

   int playerKing;    // The constant for a King belonging to the player.
   if (player == RED)
      playerKing = RED_KING;
   else
      playerKing = BLACK KING;

  ArrayList<ChecherMove> moves = new ArrayList<CheckerMove>();
                     // Moves will be stored in this list.

   /* First, check for any possible jumps. Look at each square on the
      board. If that square contains one of the player's pieces, look at a
      possible jump in each of the four directions from that square. If
      there is a legal jump in that direction, put it in the moves ArrayList.
   */

   for (int row = 0; row < 8; row++) {
      for (int col = 0; col < 8; col++) {
                  if (board[row][col] == player || board[row][col] == playerKing) { if
                     (canJump(player, row, col, row+1, col+1, row+2, col+2))
                     moves.add(new CheckersMove(row, col, row+2, col+2));
                    if (canJump(player, row, col, row-1, col+1, row-2, col+2))
                    moves.add(new CheckersMove(row, col, row-2, col+2)); if
                     (canJump(player, row, col, row+1, col-1, row+2, col-2))
                    moves.add(new CheckersMove(row, col, row+2, col-2)); if
                     (canJump(player, row, col, row-1, col-1, row-2, col-2))
                     moves.add(new CheckersMove(row, col, row-2, col-2));
         }
      }
   }

   /* If any jump moves were found, then the user must jump, so we
      don't add any regular moves. However, if no jumps were found,
      check for any legal regular moves. Look at each square on
      the board. If that square contains one of the player's pieces, look
      at a possible move in each of the four directions from that square.
      If there is a legal move in that direction, put it in the moves
      ArrayList.
```

```
*/
if (moves.size() == 0) {
    for (int row = 0; row < 8; row++) {
        for (int col = 0; col < 8; col++) {
            if (board[row][col] == player || board[row][col] == playerKing) {
```

```
                    if (canMove(player,row,col,row+1,col+1))
                       moves.add(new
                       CheckersMove(row,col,row+1,col+1));
                    if (canMove(player,row,col,row-1,col+1))
                       moves.add(new CheckersMove(row,col,row-
                       1,col+1));
                    if (canMove(player,row,col,row+1,col-1))
                       moves.add(new CheckersMove(row,col,row+1,col-
                       1));
                    if (canMove(player,row,col,row-1,col-1)) moves.add(new
                       CheckersMove(row,col,row-1,col-1));
                 }
              }
           }
        }

        /* If no legal moves have been found, return null. Otherwise, create an
           array just big enough to hold all the legal moves, copy the legal moves
           from the ArrayList into the array, and return the array.
        */

        if (moves.size() == 0)
           return null;
        else {
           CheckersMove[] moveArray = new
           CheckersMove[moves.size()]; for (int i = 0; i < moves.size();
           i++)
              moveArray[i] = moves.get(i);
           return moveArray;
        }

     }  // end getLegalMoves
```

for Chapter 7

- An example in Subsection 7.2.4 tried to answer the question, How many random people do you have to select before you find a duplicate birthday? The source code for that program can be found in the file **BirthdayProblemDemo.java**. Here are some related questions:

  How many random people do you have to select before you find **three** people who share the same birthday? (That is, all three people were born on the same day in the same month, but not necessarily in the same year.)

  Suppose you choose 365 people at random. How many different birthdays will they have? (The number could theoretically be anywhere from 1 to 365).

  How many different people do you have to check before you've found at least one person with a birthday on each of the 365 days of the year?

  Write **three** programs to answer these questions. Each of your programs should sim-ulate choosing people at random and checking their birthdays. (In each case, ignore the possibility of leap years.)

- Write a program that will read a sequence of positive real numbers entered by the user and will print the same numbers in sorted order from smallest to largest. The user will input a zero to mark the end of the input. Assume that at most 100 positive numbers will be entered.

- A **polygon** is a geometric figure made up of a sequence of connected line segments. The points where the line segments meet are called the **vertices** of the polygon. The Graph-ics class includes commands for drawing and filling polygons. For these commands, the coordinates of the vertices of the polygon are stored in arrays. If g is a variable of type Graphics then

  g.drawPolygon(xCoords, yCoords, pointCt) will draw the outline of the polygon with vertices at the points (xCoords[0],yCoords[0]), (xCoords[1],yCoords[1]),
  . . . , (xCoords[pointCt-1],yCoords[pointCt-1]). The third parameter, pointCt, is an int that specifies the number of vertices of the polygon. Its value
  should be 3 or greater. The first two parameters are arrays of type int[]. Note that the polygon automatically includes a line from the last point, (xCoords[pointCt-1],yCoords[pointCt-1]), back to the starting point (xCoords[0],yCoords[0]).

  g.fillPolygon(xCoords, yCoords, pointCt) fills the interior of the polygon with the current drawing color. The parameters have the same meaning as in the drawPolygon() method. Note that it is OK for the sides of the polygon to cross each other, but the interior of a polygon with self-intersections might not be exactly what you expect.

  Write a panel class that lets the user draw polygons, and use your panel as the content pane in an applet (or standalone application). As the user clicks a sequence of points, count them and store their x- and y-coordinates in two arrays. These points will be the vertices of the polygon. Also, draw a line between each consecutive pair of points to give the user some visual feedback. When the user clicks near the starting point, draw the complete polygon. Draw it with a red interior and a black border. The user should then be able to start drawing a new polygon. When the user shift-clicks on the applet, clear it.

For this exercise, there is no need to store information about the contents of the applet. Do the drawing directly in the mouseDragged() routine, and use the getGraphics() method to get a Graphics object that you can use to draw the line. (Remember, though, that this is considered to be bad style.) You will not need a paintComponent() method, since the default action of filling the panel with its background color is good enough.

Here is a picture of my solution after the user has drawn a few polygons:

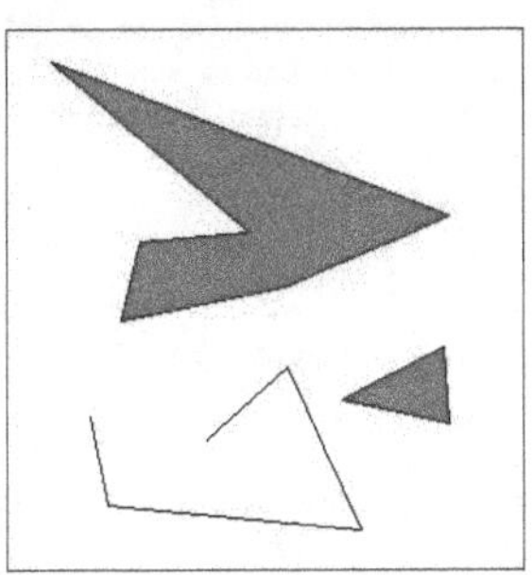

- For this problem, you will need to use an array of objects. The objects belong to the class MovingBall, which I have already written. You can find the source code for this class in the file **MovingBall.java**. A MovingBall represents a circle that has an associated color, radius, direction, and speed. It is restricted to moving in a rectangle in the (x,y) plane. It will "bounce back" when it hits one of the sides of this rectangle. A MovingBall does not actually move by itself. It's just a collection of data. You have to call instance methods to tell it to update its position and to draw itself. The constructor for the MovingBall class takes the form

  new MovingBall(xmin, xmax, ymin, ymax)

  where the parameters are integers that specify the limits on the x and y coordinates of the ball. In this exercise, you will want balls to bounce off the sides of the applet, so you will create them with the constructor call

new MovingBall(0, getWidth(), 0, getHeight())

The constructor creates a ball that initially is colored red, has a radius of 5 pixels, is located at the center of its range, has a random speed between 4 and 12, and is headed in a random direction. There is one **problem** here: You can't use this constructor until the width and height of the component are known. It would be OK to use it in the init() method of an applet, but not in the constructor of an applet or panel class. If you are using a panel class to display the ball, one slightly messy solution is to create the MovingBall objects in the panel's paintComponent() method the first time that method is called. You can be sure that the size of the panel has been determined before paintComponent() is called. This is what I did in my own solution to this exercise.

These are the methods that you will need for this exercise. There are also methods for setting various properties of the ball, such as

366

If ball is a variable of type MovingBall, then the following methods are available:

- ball.draw(g) — draw the ball in a graphics context. The parameter, g, must be of type Graphics. (The drawing color in g will be changed to the color of the ball.)
- ball.travel() — change the (x,y)-coordinates of the ball by an amount equal to its speed. The ball has a certain direction of motion, and the ball is moved in that direction. Ordinarily, you will call this once for each frame of an animation, so the speed is given in terms of "pixels per frame". Calling this routine does not move the ball on the screen. It just changes the values of some instance variables in the object. The next time the object's draw() method is called, the ball will be drawn in the new position.
- ball.headTowards(x,y) — change the direction of motion of the ball so that it is headed towards the point (x,y). This does not affect the speed.

ball.setColor(color) for changing the color and ball.setRadius(radius) for changing its size. See the source code for more information.

For this exercise, you should create an applet that shows an animation of balls bouncing around on a black background. Use a Timer to drive the animation. (See Subsection 6.5.1.) Use an array of type MovingBall[] to hold the data for the balls. In addition, your program should listen for mouse and mouse motion events. When the user presses the mouse or drags the mouse, call each of the ball's headTowards() methods to make the balls head towards the mouse's location. My solution uses 50 balls and a time delay of 50 milliseconds for the timer.

- The sample program **RandomArtPanel.java** from Subsection 6.5.1 shows a different ran-dom "artwork" every four seconds. There are three types of "art", one made from lines, one from circles, and one from filled squares. However, the program does not save the data for the picture that is shown on the screen. As a result, the picture cannot be redrawn when necessary. In fact, every time paintComponent() is called, a new picture is drawn.

  Write a new version of **RandomArtPanel.java** that saves the data needed to redraw its pictures. The paintComponent() method should simply use the data to draw the picture. New data should be recomputed only every four seconds, in response to an event from the timer that drives the program.

  To make this interesting, write a separate class for each of the three different types of art. Also write an abstract class to serve as the common base class for the three classes. Since all three types of art use a random gray background, the background color can be defined in their superclass. The superclass also contains a draw() method that draws the picture; this is an abstract method because its implementation depends on the particular type of art that is being drawn. The abstract class can be defined as:

```
private abstract class ArtData {
   Color backgroundColor;   // The background color for the art.
   ArtData() {   // Constructor sets background color to be a random gray.
      int x = (int)(256*Math.random());
      backgroundColor = new Color( x, x, x, );
```

```
    }
    abstract void draw(Graphics g);      // Draws
    this artwork.
}
```

Each of the three subclasses of ArtData must define its own draw() method. It must also define instance variables to hold the data necessary to draw the picture. I suggest that you should create random data for the picture in the constructor of the class, so that constructing the object will automatically create the data for a random artwork. (One problem with this is that you can't create the data until you know the size of the panel, so you can't create an artdata object in the constructor of the panel. One solution is to create an artdata object at the beginning of the paintComponent() method, if the object has not already been created.) In all three subclasses, you will need to use several arrays to store the data.

The file **RandomArtPanel.java** only defines a panel class. A main program that uses this panel can be found in **RandomArt.java**, and an applet that uses it can be found in **RandomArtApplet.java**.

- Write a program that will read a text file selected by the user, and will make an alphabetical list of all the different words in that file. All words should be converted to lower case, and duplicates should be eliminated from the list. The list should be written to an output file selected by the user. As discussed in Subsection 2.4.5, you can use TextIO to read and write files. Use a variable of type ArrayList<String> to store the words. (See Subsection 7.3.4.) It is not easy to separate a file into words as you are reading it. You can use the following method:

367

/**

- Read the next word from TextIO, if there is one. First, skip past
- any non-letters in

the input. If an end-of-file is encountered before

- a word is found, return null. Otherwise, read and return the word.

A word is defined as a sequence of letters. Also, a word can include

- an apostrophe if the apostrophe is surrounded by letters on each side.
- @return the next word from TextIO, or null if an end-of-file is
- encountered

*/
private static String readNextWord() {
char ch = TextIO.peek(); // Look at next character in input.
while (ch != TextIO.EOF && ! Character.isLetter(ch)) {

```
    TextIO.getAnyChar();    // Read the
    character.
    ch = TextIO.peek();     // Look at the
    next character.
}
if (ch ==
    TextIO.EO
    F) //
    Encounter
    ed end-of-
    file return
    null;
```

• At this point, we know the next character is a letter, so read a word.

```
String
word =
""; //
This will
be the
word
```

that is read.
while (true) {

word +=
TextIO.getAnyChar(); //
Append the letter onto
word. ch = TextIO.peek(); //
Look at next character.
if (ch == '\'') {

The next character is an apostrophe. Read it, and if the following character is a letter, add both the apostrophe and the letter onto the word and continue reading the word. If the character after the apostrophe

is not a letter, the word is done, so break out of the loop.

TextIO.getAnyChar(); // Read the apostrophe.
ch = TextIO.peek(); // Look at char that follows apostrophe.
if (Character.isLetter(ch)) {

```
                word += "\'" + TextIO.getAnyChar();
                ch = TextIO.peek();     // Look at next char.
            }
            else
                break;
        }
        if ( ! Character.isLetter(ch) ) {
```

- If the next character is not a letter, the word is
- finished, so break out of the loop.

```
            break;
        }
        // If we haven't broken out of the loop, next char is a letter.
    }
    return word;     // Return the word that has been read.
}
```

Note that this method will return null when the file has been entirely read. You can use this as a signal to stop processing the input file.

- The game of Go Moku (also known as Pente or Five Stones) is similar to Tic-Tac-Toe, except that it played on a much larger board and the object is to get five squares in a row rather than three. Players take turns placing pieces on a board. A piece can be placed in any empty square. The first player to get five pieces in a row—horizontally, vertically, or diagonally—wins. If all squares are filled before either player wins, then the game is a draw. Write a program that lets two players play Go Moku against each other.

Your program will be simpler than the Checkers program from Subsection 7.5.3. Play alternates strictly between the two players, and there is no need to hilite the legal moves. You will only need two classes, a short panel class to set up the interface and a Board class to draw the board and do all the work of the game. Nevertheless, you will probably want to look at the source code for the checkers program, **Checkers.java**, for ideas about the general outline of the program.

The hardest part of the program is checking whether the move that a player makes is a winning move. To do this, you have to look in each of the four possible directions from the square where the user has placed a piece. You have to count how many pieces that player has in a row in that direction. If the number is five or more in any direction, then that player wins. As a hint, here is part of the code from my applet. This code counts the number of pieces that the user has in a row in a specified direction. The direction is specified by two integers, dirX and dirY. The values of these variables are 0, 1, or -1, and at least one of them is non-zero. For example, to look in the horizontal direction, dirX is 1 and dirY is 0.

```
int ct = 1;       // Number of pieces in a row belonging to the player.

int r, c;         // A row and column to be examined

r = row + dirX;     // Look at square in specified direction.
c = col + dirY;
while ( r >= 0 && r < 13 && c >= 0 && c < 13
                                   && board[r][c] == player ) {
```

- Square is on the board, and it
- contains one of the players's pieces.

```
    ct++;
```

```
    r += dirX;     // Go on to next square in this direction.
    c += dirY;
}
r = row - dirX;      // Now, look in the opposite direction.
c = col - dirY;
while ( r >= 0 && r < 13 && c >= 0 && c < 13
                                            && board[r][c] == player ) {
    ct++;
    r -= dirX;       // Go on to next square in this direction.
    c -= dirY;
}
```

www.ingramcontent.com/pod-product-compliance
Lightning Source LLC
Chambersburg PA
CBHW031216050326
40689CB00009B/1356

* 9 7 8 1 0 8 5 9 5 6 6 3 5 *